Learn to Program
with Java JDK 15.0™

John Smiley

Smiley Publishing
Philadelphia

Smiley Publishing

PO Box 2062

Riverton, NJ 08077-2062

U.S.A.

smileypublishing@johnsmiley.com

Learn to Program with Java JDK 15.0™

ISBN: 978-1-61274-084-3

Other books by John Smiley:

Learn to Program with C#

Learn to Program with C++

Learn to Program with Java

Learn to Program with Java 2014 Edition

Learn to Program with Java SE6

Learn to Program with JavaScript

Learn to Program with VB.Net 2002/2003

Learn to Program with VB.Net 2005 Express

Learn to Program with VB.Net 2008 Express

Learn to Program with Visual Basic 6

Learn to Program with Visual Basic 6 Examples

Learn to Program am with Visual Basic 6 Objects

Learn to Program with Visual Basic 6 Databases

Learn to Program with Visual Baisc 2010 Express

Learn to Program with Visual C# 2005 Express

Learn to Program with Visual C# 2008 Express

Learn to Program with Visual C# 2010 Express

My Climb To The Top (of the Bell Atlantic Tower)

The Complete Book of Stair Climbing 2012 Edition

This book is dedicated to my wife Linda

About the Author

John Smiley, a Microsoft Certified Professional (MCP) and Microsoft Certified Solutions Developer (MCSD) in Visual Basic, has been programming and teaching for more than 20 years. He is the President of John Smiley and Associates, a computer consulting firm serving clients both large and small in the Philadelphia Metropolitan area. John is an adjunct professor of Computer Science at Penn State University, Philadelphia University, and Holy Family College, and also teaches in a variety of Internet venues including SmartPlanet and ElementK.

On the writing front, John is the author of the immensely popular **Learn to Program with Visual Basic 6**, along with Learn to Program with Visual Basic Examples, Learn to Program Databases with Visual Basic 6, Learn to Program Objects with Visual Basic 6, Learn to Program with Java, Learn to Program with VB.Net 2002/2003, Learn to Program with VB.Net 2005 Express, Learn to Program with C#, Learn to Program with C++ and Learn to Program with JavaScript..

Feel free to visit John's Web Site at

http://www.johnsmiley.com

or contact him via email at johnsmiley@johnsmiley.com. He religiously answers all of his emails, although not necessarily instantaneously!

Contents

Acknowledgments

I want to thank first and foremost my wife Linda for her love and support, and putting up with my harangues about "having to write an hour today."

Many thanks to my friend Lynda Dehring, one of my students and reader of previous books, who patiently read through the many drafts of this book and found errors and offered suggestions on how to make it better. It wouldn't be nearly as good as it is without her!

Thanks to my son Kevin for his technical assistance with this book---he's one of the best programmers on the planet!

Many thanks to a number of people who kept asking how I was making out with the book, particularly Fred Forshee and Rich Blitz. Knowing someone was waiting for the book to be finished helped me continue writing it.

Thanks also go to the thousands of students I've taught over the years for your tireless dedication to learning the art and science of Computer Programming. Your great questions and demanding persistence in getting the most out of your learning experience truly inspired me, and has contributed greatly to my books. Many of you dragged yourself to class after a long hard day of work, or woke up early on your Saturday day off to learn Visual Basic and the other programming languages I have taught. You have my greatest respect and admiration.

I also want to thank the many readers of my many books who have taken the time to write or email me about the books. Most of the time, the correspondence is incredibly glowing---I truly appreciate hearing from each of you, and I want you to know that I read and respond to each email I receive.

I want to thank all the members of my family for their continued belief in and support of me over the years, in particular my mother, who always prayed for the success of my books. She is no longer with us here, but I see her light every morning when I jog in the dark, and I'm sure she is now with my father, surely together flipping through the pages of this book now.

It's been over forty years since I last saw my father---and his role in the writing of this and my others books can never be understated. He and my mother were a great inspiration and role model for me.

I know that the God who made us all will someday permit us to be together again.

Organizations/Conventions Used in the Book

Each chapter of the book follows in a session in a make-believe college classroom. Read along and learn the material with the rest of the students.

Every chapter has example programs and practical exercises for you to complete. I encourage you to follow along with the example programs---and by all means complete the exercises in the book as well. If typing is not your strong suit, you can download both the completed examples and exercises via this link

http://www.johnsmiley.com/main/mybooks.htm

Care to take a quiz to test your knowledge? Follow this link and you can take a series of multiple choice quizzes drawn from the book

http://www.johnsmiley.com/tester/login.asp

Finally, if the book isn't enough for you to get going with Java, consider joining me in an Internet-based Java class. My introductory classes are held several times throughout the year---and I'll be teaching these classes for as long as I'm sojourning in this dimension. For more information, follow this link...

http://www.johnsmiley.com/main/training.htm

Chapter 1---Where Do I Begin?

"Where do I begin?" is a question I am frequently asked by my students, and this seems like a good question to tackle right at the beginning of this book. In this first chapter, we'll look at the development process of an actual working program through the eyes and ears of my university programming class and you will also be introduced to our 'class project'. By the end of the book, we'll have taken a real-life application through from the concept all the way to the finished product!

> NOTE: Occasionally, my students get disillusioned when they hear that we won't be diving straight in and coding our application. However, when I remind them that programming is much the same as writing a report (or in other words, it is a two stage process of planning and then producing) they tend to settle down.

> NOTE: For directions on finding, downloading, and installing Java to your PC, follow this link to my website. The directions are right on the front page :)

http://www.johnsmiley.com

Where Do We Begin

As part of answering the question, "Where do we begin?" this chapter looks at the Systems Development Life Cycle, which is a methodology that has been developed to ensure that systems are developed in a methodical, logical and step-by-step approach. We'll be looking at the Systems Development Life Cycle in quite a bit of detail, since the majority of this book will be spent in developing a real-world application. In this chapter we'll meet with a prospective client and conduct a preliminary interview with him. From that interview (and a subsequent one!) we'll develop a Requirements Statement, which provides details as to what the program should do. This Requirements Statement will form the basis of the application that we will develop throughout the rest of the book

> NOTE: From this point on, you will follow me as I lead a group of my university students in an actual class on Java. If I do my job right, you will be a part of the class, learning along with them as we complete a 14-week course about programming in Java.

Many books on computer programming have the reader, perhaps as early as the first chapter, code a program which 'cutely' displays a message box that says 'Hello World'. Then the author will point to the fact that within the first few minutes of reading their book, the reader has already written a working program. I'm not so naive as to believe that writing such a program makes you a programmer. Therefore, we'll opt for a slower approach. Simple programs, although great for the ego, are not the programs that are found in the real world. Real-world programs are written to meet someone's needs. These needs are frequently complex and difficult to verbalize. In this book, you and I will embark on a journey together that will see us complete the prototyping stage of a real-world project. I believe that this is the best way to learn programming.

In my university classes, I don't usually introduce the class project until several weeks into the semester. When I finally do introduce the class project, I give the students in my class a Requirements Statement. Since the class project is to develop a Java application, with an event-driven paradigm (look that one up in the dictionary), I never tell my students exactly *how* the application should look, or how to program it. I tell them only what is required. In other words, I complete the hard part for them - gathering the user requirements.

Programming the Easy Way

When I first began to teach programming, some of my students would tell me that they just didn't know where to start when they first began to work on their programming assignments. They would start to program the application, then stop. Some of them would find themselves re-writing their code and re-designing their application several times. Then they would change it again. Face to face I could usually clear things up for them by giving them a gentle nudge or hint in the right direction. However, their work would show a definite lack of direction. Why the problem? They lacked a plan.

As soon as I realized this, I began to teach them more than just programming. I began to teach them the Systems Development Life Cycle (SDLC), the methodology I mentioned earlier. You see, people need blueprints or maps.

They need something tangible, usually in writing, before they can begin a project. Just about all of my students agree that having a blueprint of some kind makes the development process that much easier.

Sometimes I'll meet former students of mine at the university, and I'll ask them how their other programming classes are coming along. Occasionally, they'll tell me that they're working on a great real-world assignment of some kind, but they just don't know where to begin. At that point, I'll remind them of what I told them in class - that they should begin with the design of the user interface, observe the default behavior of the design and then add code to fill in the gaps. That's not the problem, they tell me. The problem is that they don't know how to gather the user requirements for the system. They don't really know what the system should do.

Often the real problem is that the client isn't prepared to give the programmers a detailed enough Requirements Statement. In class the professor distributes a well-defined Requirements Statement but in the real world, programmers need to develop this themselves. Unfortunately, they may not know how to sit down with the prospective user of their system to determine what is required to satisfy the user's needs.

That skill, to listen to the user and determine their needs, is something that I now teach to some extent in all of my computer classes - whether they are programming courses, courses on Systems Analysis and Design, or Database Management.

Planning a Program is Like Planning a House

A friend of mine is a general contractor and home-builder. His job is similar to that of a programmer or system designer. He recently built an addition to a customer's house. He wouldn't think of beginning that work without first meeting with the owner of the house to determine their needs. He couldn't possibly presume to know what the owner wants or needs. The builder's role, in meeting with the owner, is largely to listen and then to advise.

My friend the home builder tells me that certain home owners may want a design that is architecturally unsound - either because their ideas and design are unsafe and would violate accepted building code regulations, or because they would violate local zoning regulations for their neighborhood. In some cases, he tells me, owners ask for features that he is certain they will later regret - and probably hold him responsible for. His role as an advisor demands that he inform the homeowner of these problems.

As soon as my friend believes that he understands what the owner wants, then he prepares a set of blueprints to be reviewed by the homeowner. Frequently the owner, after seeing his own vision on paper, will decide to change something, such as the location of a window or the size of a closet. The concrete characteristics of the blueprints make an agreement between the builder and owner easier to arrive at. The same can be said of a concrete plan for the writing of a program or the development of a system.

The big advantage of developing a plan on paper is that, while the project is still on paper, it's relatively painless to change it. Once the house has been assembled and bolted together, it becomes much more of a problem to change something.

The same is true of a computer program. Although it's not physically nailed or bolted together, once a programmer has started to write a program, changing it becomes very labor-intensive. It's much easier to change the design of a system prior to writing the first line of code.

In the world of software development, you would be surprised how many programmers begin work on an application without really having listened to the user. I know some programmers who get a call from a user, take some quick notes over the phone, and deliver an application without ever having met them! It could be that the user's requirements sound similar to something the programmer wrote last year, so the developer feels that will be good enough for the new client.

Other developers go a step further, and may actually meet with the client to discuss the user's needs. Nevertheless, sometimes the developer may not be a good listener, or just as likely, the user may communicate their needs poorly. The result may be that the user receives a program that doesn't come close to doing what they wanted it to do.

In this course, we'll develop a prototype for a real-world application called the Grades Calculation Project, and then take it through to the complete product. As we progress through the course together, we will work through one possible solution, but I want you to know that in Java programming, the number of solutions are almost infinite. As I tell my students all the time, there are many ways to paint a picture. One of the things I love about teaching Java is that I have never received the same solution to a project twice. Everyone brings his or her own unique qualities to the project.

I want you to feel free to take the Grades Calculation Project and make your solution different from mine. In fact, I encourage it, but you should stick close to the Requirements Statement that we are going to develop in this chapter.

We Receive a Call from our 'client'

During my Fall Semester Visual Basic class, I had been lucky enough to be contacted by a client, Joe Bullina, owner of the Bullina China Shop, who needed a fairly high tech computer program written to produce price quotation for the customers in his shop, and I had used the development of his program as the class project for my Visual Basic course.

Java, by its very nature, is a bit more difficult to learn than Visual Basic, and although I knew I could ask the students in my Java class to write the same program in Java, I also knew that incorporating every feature found in the Visual Basic version of the China Shop program would be difficult to 'squeeze' into a one semester Java course. Furthermore, I also knew that many of those same Visual Basic students would be present in the Java class, and most likely they would be in the mood for a fresh 'challenge'--not a rehash of the China Shop program.

And so I was glad when one Monday morning, about a week before meeting with my Java class for the first time, I received a phone call from Frank Olley, a fellow professor at the University, and Dean of the English Department. Frank and I knew each other well--in fact, at one time he had been a teacher of mine. Frank was wondering if I could write a program that he could use to calculate student grades.

I asked Frank if he had considered using a spreadsheet program like Excel to do the calculations---his requirement sounded like a fine application for that.

He told me he had considered Excel, but he ultimately wanted the program to be able to prompt the user for the correct grade "pieces" necessary to calculate the student's final grade—something he didn't know how to do in Excel.

Frank and I agreed to meet on Tuesday afternoon in his office.

We Meet with Our Client

I arrived at Frank Olley's office around 2 p.m. on a sunny Tuesday afternoon. Entering the Liberal Arts building, a large brick building, brought back pleasant memories of my college years. I hadn't been in the Liberal Arts building since I graduated some years back--the Computer Science building was now my haunt.

I found Frank's office, and was greeted by his secretary, Rita Toughill.

"Hi, I'm John Smiley, I'm here to meet Frank Olley."

"Just a minute Mr. Smiley, Mr. Olley is expecting you."

A few moments later, Frank came out of his office.

"Sorry to keep you waiting, John" Frank said, warmly extending his hand. "I was on the phone with Robin Aronstam and David Burton--I believe you know who they are."

Indeed I did---Robin Aronstam was the chairman of the Mathematics Department and David Burton was the chairman of the Science Department.

"I hope you don't mind if Robin and David attend our meeting," Frank continued, "I think they may want to 'piggyback' some requirements of their own on top of mine.

"Piggyback?" I asked.

"That's right, John," Frank replied. "I saw them both in the Faculty dining room today at lunch, and I mentioned to them that you were coming over to discuss writing a program to calculate student grades---they were wondering if you could include their requirements in the program also."

"I don't see why not," I said. Just then Robin and David arrived. During the course of the next twenty minutes or so the three of them laid out for me their unique requirements. There was a commonality in that each one required a program that could calculate the final grade for a student in their own department---English, Math and Science. On the other hand, each had their own requirements.

NOTE: This project, though 'real world' has been simplified a bit for learning purposes.

"The English Department," Frank Olley explained, "calculates the Final grade for a student taking an English course as 25% of their Midterm grade, 25% of their Final Examination grade, 30% for a semester long Research paper, and--because we expect our students to be able to speak in public and make oral presentations---20% for a half hour long Class presentation."

"The Science Department is similar," David chimed in, "except that we don't require a Class presentation. We calculate the grade for a student taking a Science course as 40% of their Midterm grade, 40% of their Final Examination grade, and 20% for a semester long Research paper."

Robin then explained that for a student taking a Math course, only a Midterm and Final Examination grade entered into the equation. "Each counts 50% toward their final grade," she said.

"Those requirements don't seem terribly complicated," I assured them. "Do you have any details in your mind as to what you want the program to look like?"

"Not really," Frank said. "I guess we were really hoping that you could take care of those details. Don't get us wrong. We know what we want the program to do, that is, calculate a student's grade. Beyond that, our biggest requirement is that the program be simple to use."

"Can you think of anything else?" I asked.

"Eventually, we'd like to have the program be accessible from the Web" David added . He hesitated for a moment and then added hopefully. "What do you think? The program doesn't sound too difficult, does it?"

Famous last words, I thought to myself. "No David, it doesn't," I said, "I could probably write this program in an hour or so...."

Robin noticed that my voice had trailed off.

"What's wrong?" she asked.

"Nothing's wrong," I said, "I was just thinking.."

I explained to Frank, Robin and David that on Saturday I would be meeting with my 'Introduction to Programming with Java ' Spring Semester class for the first time. I then went on to explain to them that in my Fall Semester Visual Basic course, the class and I had developed a real-world application for a client in West Chester.

"Perhaps," I said, "this time around, we could have them work on your requirements as their class project."

Frank looked excited and nervous at the same time. "How would that work?" he asked.

"Well," I said, "each semester I give my Java programming students a project to work on. Java is a bit more complicated than Visual Basic, so although I was tempted to have them work on the same project as my fall semester Visual Basic students, I really thought that might be too much for a first Java class. However, your project sounds ideal, and I think it will excite them. It's better than anything I could ever dream up, because it's real, with a real 'client'--you--- expecting real results. And your requirements, though they seem simple enough from a user point of view, have a few 'quirks' that will make it pretty challenging from a Java programming perspective."

I looked at the group for a reaction. I saw a look of unease on David's face.

"I can take these requirements," I continued, "distribute them to my students on Saturday, and over the course of the semester, they can write the program for you. By the end of the semester, you'll have your program, and they'll have some real experience under their belts. Unless of course, you're in a huge hurry..."

"No," Frank said, "as long as they finish the program by the end of the Spring semester, we can use the program to calculate the grades in each of our departments. Of course, I'm guessing that the program your students write won't be as sophisticated as one that you would write. After all, your students are just beginners."

"Not at all, Frank" I said. "I'll be working with them every step of the way. You can expect a top-notch program, and I have no doubt that we can finish it on time for you to use in May."

I must have said the magic words; at this Frank smiled, extended his hand and said, "That sounds like a deal to me."

"There's just one more thing Frank," I said sheepishly.

"What's that John?" he asked.

"Would it be possible to 'pay' my students something for the development of the program?", I asked. "It doesn't have to be much---but paying them will permit them to legitimately cite this experience as paid professional experience."

"I'm sure there's something in the English Department budget to pay them," Frank said smiling. "How about the Math and Science departments?"

"That shouldn't be a problem," Robin said. "You mentioned that your Fall Semester Visual Basic class wrote a program for a local business. How much did you charge him?"

"He paid us $450," I said. "I was able to give each one of my students."

"Sounds like a bargain to me," David said, "I'm sure each of our departments will be able to kick in $150 for your students work---sounds like a great idea to me."

As I prepared to leave, I warned the group that what we had done this afternoon merely represented the first step, the tip of the iceberg, so to speak, in a six step process known as the Systems Development Life Cycle (SDLC). The first phase, the Preliminary Investigation, had begun and ended with our initial interview. Five phases of the SDLC remained.

As I walked to the door, Frank and I mutually agreed that I would deliver to him, in a week or so, a Requirements Statement drawn from the notes taken at today's meeting. I warned the group that when they read the Requirements Statement that I would send to them, the possibility existed that they would find some things that I had misinterpreted, and perhaps some things that they would be sure they had mentioned that wouldn't appear at all. I told him that the Requirements Statement would act as a starting point for their project. Until I received a confirmation from them confirming the Requirements, neither my student team nor I would proceed with the development of the program.

As I walked out the door of Frank's office, we all exchanged warm 'good byes'. Frank, David and Robin were all genuinely likable people, and I hoped this experience would be a rewarding one for them and the students in my class. I left Frank, Robin and David discussing an upcoming Freshman Social, and I headed off to teach a late afternoon class at the university.

The Systems Development Life Cycle (SDLC)

During my walk to my late afternoon class, I gave a lot of thought to Frank's program. The more I thought about it, the more I believed that having my students write the program was a great idea, and I was sure they would think so too. Working on a real-world application would be a great practical assignment for them. Even more so than something I made up, this project would give each of them a chance to become deeply involved in the various aspects of the SDLC. For instance:

- someone in the class would need to work on the user requirements

- someone else would be involved in a detailed analysis of the Grading program

- everyone would be involved in coding the program

- some students would work on installing the software

- some students would be involved in training and implementation

Four days later, on Saturday morning, I met my 'Introductory Programming with Java' class for the first time. For the last few semesters, my university has been using both Visual Basic and Java as our introductory programming language. Probably nothing is as easy as Visual Basic to learn—and probably nothing is a flexible and platform independent as Java.

As is my custom during my first class, I took roll, and asked each of the students to write a brief biography about themselves on a sheet of paper. Doing this gives me a chance to get to know my new students, without the pressure of them having to open themselves up to a room full of strangers, although many of them will become good friends during the course of the class.

As I read the class list, I only called out their first names as I like to personalize the class as much as possible. Usually, I have some duplicated first names, but this semester, there were none.

"Valerie, Peter, Linda, Steve, Katherine Rose."

"If you don't mind, just call me Rose," she said.

"Rhonda, Joe, John."

"Jack, if you don't mind."

"Barbara, Kathy, Dave, Ward, Blaine, Kate, Mary, Chuck, Lou, Bob."

That made eighteen students.

After giving them a few minutes to write their biography, I collected them, and I began reading them over. A few students had some programming experience (some from my Visual Basic class), others using languages that were a bit dated. A number were looking to get into the exciting world of computer programming, either because they had an opportunity at work, or believed one would open up shortly. A couple of them were looking to get into the work force after years away from it. One of the students, Chuck, was just fifteen, a local high school student. Another student, Lou, was permanently disabled, and although he didn't look ill, he wrote that his disability would probably end up restricting him to a wheelchair in a year or so..

My classroom is about 40 feet by 20 feet and there are three rows of tables containing PCs. Each student has their own PC, and at the front of the classroom I have my own PC, cabled to a projector that enables me to display the contents of my video display on a huge screen.

My first lecture usually involves bringing the class up to a common level so that they feel comfortable with both the terminology and methodology of using a PC-based environment. This time, however, instead of waiting a few weeks before introducing the class project, I could hardly wait to tell them. In the first few minutes of class, I introduced the students to the Grades Calculation Project. Just about everyone in the class seemed genuinely excited at the prospect of developing a real-world application. They were even more excited after I offered to 'split the profits' with them. For most of the class, this was their first programming course---and at its conclusion, they would all be paid as professionals, with a legitimate project to add to their resumes.

"You mean this course isn't going to be the usual 'read the textbook, and code the examples' course," Ward said.

"Exactly," I said, "we'll be developing a real world application, and getting paid for it!"

"How will we know what to do?" Rose asked nervously.

I explained that in today's class, we'd actually develop a Requirements Statement.

"A Requirements Statement," I said, "is just an agreement between the contractor (in this case us) and the customer (in this case Frank, Robin and David) that specifies in detail exactly what work will be performed, when it will be completed, and how much it will cost."

I continued by explaining that at this point, all we had were my notes from my initial interview with Frank, Robin and David. For the most part, this was just a quick sketch of the program. While we might very well have produced a quick sketch of the user interface in the following hour or so, we still did not know how to write a single line of code in Java. There was still much to learn! Furthermore, while we could probably pretty easily come up with a sketch of what the program would look like, we still needed to concern ourselves with the processing rules (e.g., the calculated grades of the various student types) which Frank, Robin and David had given to me during our meeting.

> TIP: Processing rules are known either as Business Rules or Work Rules.

"Can you give us an example of a business rule?" Peter asked.

"Sure Peter," I answered. "A good example would be a web-based ticket purchasing Web site, where customers are typically restricted from ordering large quantities of tickets. The Web site might have a business rule that prohibits the same customer from purchasing more than 4 tickets to the same event."

"That very thing happened to me just last week," Valerie said. "I tried to purchase an entire row of tickets to the upcoming Elton John concert, but the Web site restricted me to just 4."

I pointed out that I had agreed to drop off the Requirements Statement to Frank Olley sometime before we met for class next Saturday. I told my class that there was the possibility that the Requirements Statement would have some mistakes in it, and even some missing items. Frank might very well see something on the Requirements Statement that would cause him to think of something else he wants to the program to do. I cautioned them not to be too hasty at this point in the project. There was still a lot of planning left to do!

"Such hastiness," I said, "is exactly why the Systems Development Life Cycle was developed."

> TIP: The SDLC was developed because many systems projects were developed which did not satisfy user requirements and the projects that did satisfy user requirements were being developed over budget or over time.

I saw some puzzled looks. I explained that the Systems Development Life Cycle (SDLC) is a methodology that was developed to ensure that systems are developed in a methodical, logical and step-by-step approach. There are six steps, known as phases, in the Systems Development Life Cycle:

Different companies may have different 'versions' of the SDLC. The point is that just about everyone who does program development can benefit from one form or other of a structured development process such as this one.

- The Preliminary Investigation Phase

- The Analysis Phase

- The Design Phase

- The Development Phase

- The Implementation Phase

- The Maintenance Phase

I continued by explaining that out of each phase of the SDLC, a tangible product, or deliverable, is produced. This deliverable may consist of a Requirements Statement, or it may be a letter informing the customer that the project cannot be completed within their time and financial constraints. An important component of the SDLC is that at each phase in the SDLC, a conscious decision is made to continue development of the project, or to drop it. In the past, projects developed without the guidance of the SDLC were continued well after 'common sense' dictated that it made no sense to proceed further.

"Many people say that the SDLC is just common sense," I said. "Let's examine the elements of the SDLC here. You can then judge for yourself."

Phase 1: The Preliminary Investigation

I told my class of my meeting with Frank, Robin and David, which essentially constituted the Preliminary Investigation Phase of the SDLC.

"This first phase of the SDLC," I said, "may begin with a phone call from a customer, a memorandum from a Vice President to the director of Systems Development, or a letter from a customer to discuss a perceived problem or deficiency, or to express a requirement for something new in an existing system. In the case of the Grades Calculation program, it was a desire on the part of Frank Olley to develop a 'program' to calculate grades of English students in his department---of course, you already know how it's quickly grown beyond that to include the Math and Science departments."

I continued by explaining that the purpose of the Preliminary Investigation is not to develop a system, but to verify that a problem or deficiency really exists, or to pass judgment on the new requirement. The duration of the preliminary investigation is typically very short, usually not more than a day or two for a big project, and in the instance of the Grades Calculation Project, about an hour.

The end result, or deliverable, from the Preliminary Investigation phase is either a willingness to proceed further, or the decision to 'call it quits'. What influences the decision to abandon a potential project at this point? There are three factors, typically called constraints, which result in a go or no-go decision.

- Technical. The project can't be completed with the technology currently in existence. This constraint is typified by Leonardo Da Vinci's inability to build a helicopter even though he is credited with designing one in the 16th century. Technological constraints made the construction of the helicopter impossible.

- Time. The project can be completed, but not in time to satisfy the user's requirements. This is a frequent reason for the abandonment of the project after the Preliminary Investigation phase.

- Budgetary. The project can be completed, and completed on time to satisfy the user's requirements, but the cost is prohibitive.

"In the case of the Grades Calculation Project," I told my students, "Frank and I never came close to dropping the project. This is a project that all of us really wanted to pursue. And paying us something to do the programming is just icing on the cake!"

Needless to say, the students and I formally decided to take on the project, and proceed with the second phase of the SDLC.

Phase 2: Analysis Phase

The second phase of the SDLC, the Analysis phase, is sometimes called the Data Gathering phase.

> **NOTE: In this phase we study the problem, deficiency or new requirement in detail. Depending upon the size of the project being undertaken, this phase could be as short as the Preliminary Investigation, or it could take months.**

I explained that what this meant for my class was potentially another trip to the Liberal Arts building to meet with Frank, Robin and David to gather more detailed requirements, or to seek clarification of information gathered during the Preliminary Investigation.

> **WARNING: As a developer, you might be inclined to believe that you know everything you need to know about the project from your preliminary investigation. However, you would be surprised to find out how much additional information you can glean if you spend just a little more time with the user.**

You might be inclined to skip portions of what the SDLC calls for, but it forces you to follow a standardized methodology for developing programs and systems. As we'll see shortly, skipping parts of the SDLC can be a big mistake, whereas adhering to it ensures that you give the project the greatest chance for success.

I told them that while some developers would make the case that we have gathered enough information in Phase 1 of the SDLC to begin programming, the SDLC dictates that Phase 2 should be completed before actual writing of the program begins.

"The biggest mistake we could make at this point would be to begin coding the program. Why is that? As we'll see shortly, we need to gather more information about the business from the 'owner'---in this case Frank, Robin and David. There are still some questions that have to be asked."

In discussing the SDLC with the class, I discovered that one of my students, Linda Schwartzer, had some Systems Analysis experience. Linda offered to contact Frank Olley, to set up an appointment to spend part of the day with the person who currently calculates the grades for the English department. This meeting would fulfill the data-gathering component of the Analysis Phase. In the short time I had spent with Linda, I sensed a great communicative ability about her, and so I felt very comfortable with Linda tackling the Analysis phase of the SDLC.

Typically, our first class meeting is abbreviated, and since we were basically frozen in time until we could complete Phase 2 of the SDLC, I dismissed the class for the day. Prior to Linda's meeting with Frank Olley, I emailed the following to him:

Hi Frank,

I want to thank you for taking the time to meet with me last Tuesday afternoon. As I discussed with you at that time, it is my desire to work with you in developing a program that can calculate student grades for the English, Math and Science departments.

The program will be developed as part of my Introduction to Java computer class at the university. As such, your costs will be $450, payable upon final delivery of the program. In return, you agree to allow me to use your contract to provide my students with a valuable learning experience in developing a real-world application.

Sometime during the coming week, one of my students, Linda Schwartzer, will be contacting you to arrange to spend time meeting with the person who currently calculate grades in the English department. Although you may not see the necessity in this additional meeting, it will satisfy the next phase of the Systems Development Life Cycle I discussed with you at our meeting. Adhering strictly to the SDLC will result in the best possible program we can develop for you.

I'd like to take this opportunity to highlight the major points we discussed last week. We will develop a PC-based program, for you, with an eye toward web enabling it also. Here are the major functions that the developed program will perform:

1. This program will provide the user with a user-friendly interface for calculating a student's grade.

2. The user will be requested to designate the type of student--English, Math or Science---for which they wish to calculate a grade.

3. If the user indicates they wish to calculate the grade for an English student, the interface will prompt them for a Midterm examination grade, a Final examination grade, a Research Paper grade, and a Presentation grade. The final

grade will be calculated as 25% of the Midterm examination grade, 25% of the Final examination grade, 30% of the Research Paper grade, and 20% of the Presentation grade.

4. If the user indicates they wish to calculate the grade for a Science student, the interface will prompt them for a Midterm examination grade, a Final examination grade, and a Research Paper grade. The final grade will be calculated as 40% of the Midterm examination grade, 40% of the Final examination grade, and 20% of the Research Paper grade.

5. If the user indicates they wish to calculate the grade for a Math student, the interface will prompt them for a Midterm examination grade, and a Final examination grade. The final grade will be calculated as 50% of the Midterm examination grade and 50% of the Final examination grade.

6. Once calculated, the grade will be displayed on the interface.

I think I've covered everything that we discussed last Tuesday. If I have missed anything, please let Linda know when she arrives in your office.

Regards,

John Smiley

This email, in essence, will become the Requirements Statement that we will formally develop shortly. The next day I received the following fax from Frank Olley:

Dear John

I reviewed your email, and everything looks fine.

One thing we forgot to mention last Tuesday is that the numeric grades need to be converted to 'letter' grades for report card purposes. Complicating matters is that the letter grade equivalents of all the departments are different. Here is a table explaining the breakdown.

DEPT	ENGLISH	MATH	SCIENCE
A	93 OR GREATER	90 OR GREATER	90 OR GREATER
B	85 TO 93	83 TO 90	80 TO 90
C	78 TO 85	76 TO 83	70 TO 80
D	70 TO 78	65 TO 76	60 TO 70
F	LESS THAN 70	LESS THAN 65	LESS THAN 60

Regards,

Frank Olley

Complicate the program? Sure, a bit. I was sure Linda would more than likely find other surprises as well. This new 'requirement' was about par for the course. I checked my notes, and Frank was correct---he never mentioned it. Of course, a good developer can anticipate requirements such as these. I just missed it.

Linda called me on Monday morning to tell me that she had arranged to meet with Frank Olley on Thursday morning. That Thursday evening Linda called to tell me that her observations of the English, Math and Science Department's current operations had gone well. Contrary to what I expected, she saw nothing in her observations of their day-to-day operation that contradicted the notes that I took during my preliminary investigation.

However, Linda reported that nothing out of the usual occurred. She did tell me that from her observations, it was obvious that the program would pay for itself in no time. All three departments had work-study students performing the calculations manually---and making lots of mistakes.

That Saturday, I again met with our class. After ensuring that I hadn't lost anyone in the intervening week (yes, everyone came back), we began to discuss the third phase of the SDLC---the Design phase.

Phase 3: Design Phase

"Phase 3 of the SDLC is the Design phase," I said.

I explained that design in the SDLC encompasses many different elements. Here is a list of the different components that are 'designed' in this phase:

- Input

- Output

- Processing

- File

"Typically," I said, "too little time is spent on the design phase. Programmers love to start programming." I continued by saying that you can hardly blame them, writing a program is exciting, and everyone wants to jump and in and start writing code right away. Unfortunately, jumping immediately into coding is a huge mistake.

"After all," I said, "you wouldn't start building a house without a blueprint, would you? You simply cannot and should not start programming without a good solid design."

NOTE: Even though at this point the class knew very little about Java, they were already familiar with computer applications of one kind or other--either Microsoft Windows program, Macintosh programs, Linux programs or Web based programs (a knowledge of one of these is a requirement for the course). Designing and developing the 'look' of an application program is really independent of the tool that you'll use to program it.

I should point out here that my role in the Design Phase was to act as a guide for my students. Frank Olley had told us what he wanted the program to do. Like any 'client', he described his program requirements in functional terms that he understood.

My students were already familiar with computer applications, but at this point in our course, they were not Java experts. However, knowing how to use a program was not sufficient for them to know how Frank Olley's requirements translated into the terms of a Java program. Ultimately, it was my job to help them translate those requirements into Java terms.

I pointed out that critics of the SDLC agree that it can take months to complete a house, and making a mistake in the building of a house can be devastating; writing a Java program, on the other hand, can be accomplished in a matter of hours, if not minutes. If there's a mistake, it can be corrected quickly.

Critics of the SDLC further argue that time constraints and deadlines can make taking the 'extra' time necessary to properly complete the Design Phase a luxury that many programmers can't afford.

"I answer that criticism in this way," I said, citing a familiar phrase that you have probably heard before. "It seems there is never time to do something right the first time, but there's always time to do it over."

The exceptional (and foolish) programmer can begin coding without a good design. Programmers who do so may find themselves going back to modify pieces of code they've already written as they move through the project. They may discover a technique halfway through the project that they wish they had incorporated in the beginning, and then go back and change code. Worse yet, they may find themselves with a program that 'runs' but doesn't really work, with the result that they must go back and start virtually from the beginning.

"With a good design," I said, "the likelihood of this nightmare happening will be reduced dramatically. The end result is a program that will behave in the way it was intended, and generally with a shorter overall program development time."

Armed with our notes from the Preliminary Investigation, Linda's notes from the Detailed Analysis, and Frank Olley's emails, my students and I began the Design Phase of the SDLC in earnest. By the end of the design phase, we hoped to have a formal Requirements Statement for the program, and perhaps even a rough sketch of what the user interface will look like.

I reminded everyone that the Requirements Statement would form the basis of our agreement with Frank, Robin and David. For some developers, the Requirements Statement becomes the formal contract to which both they and the customer agree, and sign.

Linda began the design phase by giving the class a summary of the three or four hours she spent in the English, Math and Science departments. Linda said that she felt comfortable in stating that nothing she had observed that day contradicted the view expressed in my notes, and in my email to Frank Olley.

Not everyone in the class had had the benefit of seeing my notes or the email, so I distributed to the class copies of my notes, my email to Frank Olley, and his reply email to me. I gave everyone a few minutes to review and digest the material.

We began to discuss the program requirements. I could see there was some hesitation as to where to begin, so I began the process with a question. "Let's begin by making a statement as to what we are trying to accomplish here," I said.

"We need to write a program to display the calculate final grade for a student in either the English, Math or Science departments," Dave said.

"Excellent," I said. Dave had hit the nail squarely on the head. The primary purpose of the program was to calculate a student's grade. To be sure, there would be more to the program than that, but from Frank Olley's point of view, all he needed the program to do was to display a student's grade.

"To clarify," Kate said, "we should probably state the student's 'letter grade' as opposed to the student's numeric grade."

"Good clarification Kate," I said, "Frank did add that in his email didn't he."

Frequently, new programmers are unable to come to grips as to where they should begin in the Design Phase. I suggested to my class that most programs are designed by first determining the output of the program. The reasoning behind starting with the output is that if you know what the output of the program should be, you can determine the input needed to produce that output pretty easily. Once you know both the output from, and the input to the program, you can then determine what processing or calculations that need to be performed to convert that input to output.

Output Design

I told my students that we were fortunate, in that the class's first project was one where the output requirements could be stated so simply: a grade calculation.

"Where will the grade calculation go?" I asked.

"To a printer?" Jack suggested. "On the computer screen," Rose countered.

"I agree with Rose," I said, "probably to the computer screen."

Some of the students seemed perplexed by my answer.

Probably?" Dave asked.

I explained that Frank Olley and I had never formally agreed where the grade calculation would be displayed. The issue had never really come up.

"Let's be sure," I said, "to explicitly specify a display of the grade calculation in the Requirements Statement. Speaking of which…would anyone care to volunteer to begin to write up the specifications for it?"

Dave volunteered to begin writing our Requirements Statement, so he started up Microsoft Word and started typing away.

Rhonda made a suggestion for the color and font size for the program's calculated grade display, but Peter said that it was probably a bit premature to be talking about colors and font sizes at this point in our design. I agreed, and told them that I never include that amount of detail on a Requirements Statement.

"Is there any other output from the program?" I asked and several moments went by.

"I'd like to suggest that we display the date and time on the computer screen," Valerie suggested.

"Good idea," Mary said.

However, Linda disagreed, arguing that the display of the date and time was unnecessary considering the fact that the PC's at the university were all running Windows---and displayed the current time on the Windows TaskBar anyway.

"We could display the current date and time," I said, "but I'm inclined to agree with Linda---all of the PC's at the University that will run our program are Microsoft Windows based---and capable of displaying a date and time on their own. And while it's true that the beauty of the Java programs we will learn how to write in this class are that they can run on virtually any operating system---I can't think of any environment in which the user can't be aware of the current date and time if they so desire."

The majority of the class agreed.

"Getting back to the display of the grade," Peter said, "do you think it would be a good idea to display the calculated numeric grade as well as the letter grade?"

"Yes, I think that's a great idea," Kathy added.

Taking a moment to summarize, I said, "I agree also. So we now have two output requirements---a grade calculation, where we display both the calculated numeric grade for the student, and the corresponding letter grade. I can't think of anything else from an output point of view, can you?"

"What about the individual components that make up the grade?" Rhonda asked. "Should we display those?"

"I think you'll see in a few moments Rhonda," I replied, "that the individual components that comprise the student's grade will be displayed in a 'window'."

"When you say window do you mean Microsoft Windows?" Joe asked.

"Not necessarily," I replied. "The term 'window' is a generic Java term. Using Java, we can write programs for virtually any operating system for which there is a Java compiler. In this class, we'll be using the Java compiler that has been developed to produce programs that can run in Microsoft Windows. But if we were using Linux-based computers we could write the same program using the Linux-based Java compiler, and we could produce windows in that program as well. In fact, later on in the course, we'll produce something called an 'applet,' which is a Java program that can run within a web page, and we'll see that the same program we write can run within a web browser as well."

I waited to see if there were any questions--but there were none.

"I think we now have enough information to proceed to our next step," I said. "Does anyone know what that is?"

Barbara suggested that since we seemed to have the output requirements identified, we should move onto a discussion of processing.

"As I explained earlier, it will be easier for us if we discuss input into the program prior to discussing processing," I said. "It's just about impossible to determine processing requirements if we don't know our input requirements."

Input Design

"So does anyone have any suggestions as to what input requirements we need?" I asked the class.

Dave quickly rattled off several input requirements: a Midterm grade, a Final Examination grade, a Research Paper grade, and a Presentation grade.

"Excellent," I said. "of course, those requirements will vary depending upon the type of student that is being calculated."

"Is that another piece of Input?" Mary suggested, "the type of student whose grade is being calculated."

"Excellent observation Mary," I said. "Only for an English student will all four grades be required. A Science student's final grade is comprised of three component pieces---Midterm Final Examination and Research Paper, and a Math student's final grade is comprised of only two pieces---the Midterm and Final Examination grades."

"Anything else?" I asked.

"How will the input be entered into the program?" Kathy asked. "How will the user of the program let the program know what type of student they are entering?"

Designating the type of Student

Several students suggested that the user of the program could designate the type of student by entering the type using the computer's keyboard.

"My motto is to have the user do as little typing as possible," I said. "If we ask the user of the program to use the keyboard to enter the type of student into the program, we're going to have to insist that each user of the program type it consistently---that's something we can't count on. For instance, one user may type 'Math', another may type 'Mathematics', and still a third may type 'Calculus'.

"I see what you mean," Rhonda said. "But what's our alternative?"

I could see that some of the students were perplexed considering the alternatives to entering the type of student via the PC's keyboard---but you must remember that a number of them had come from the DOS world, and were accustomed to writing programs where there was a great deal of typing required of the user.

I explained that typically in a 'widows' based program, when there are a finite number of choices, it's best to display a list of choices for the user to choose from. Although Java is capable of producing programs for operating systems besides Microsoft Windows, the class and I agreed that we would use our common knowledge of Microsoft Windows as a basis of our discussion for our Java program that would be 'windows' oriented.

"Does anyone know of anything they've seen in Microsoft Windows that displays a list of alternatives for the user to choose from?" I asked. Mary said she recalled seeing a list of Font names and Font sizes to choose from on the Microsoft Word toolbar:

"That's a list of choices," she said.

"Excellent, Mary," I said.

I said this list was actually a Windows ListBox object---and Java was capable of producing a similar 'object'. Such a ListBox would be a good choice to use to display the available 'student types' in our program--alternatively, we could also use something known as a Radio Button to present the choices for student type to the user.

"Can anyone find an example of a Radio Button in Word?" I asked.

Ward said that he recalled seeing boxes on the Options submenu of the Tools menu that permitted him to specify 'settings' for saving documents in Word. I asked all of the students to take a look at this menu, and sure enough, there were several boxes, which the user can click with their mouse to select settings for saving documents in Word:

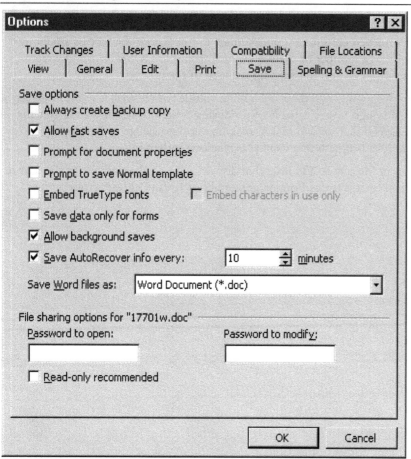

"Aren't those Check Boxes?" Dave asked. "I thought Radio Buttons were 'circles'?"

"You're right Dave," I answered, "these are Check Boxes--another type of interface object that is similar to a Radio Button. A Check Box is an object that can either be selected or not selected. Check Boxes enable the user to make a selection by clicking on the box with their mouse. The user can then de-select it by clicking on the Check Box again with their mouse."

"Why can't we use Check Boxes in our program?" Bob asked. "Can't we have one each to represent the English, Math and Science student?"

"We could use a Check Box to represent Student Types," I said, "but dong so presents a problem. As you'll see in a moment, only one Radio Button in a group of Radio Buttons can be selected at one time--and that's the behavior we want here. After all, a student can't be both an English student and a Math student at the same time. If the user of the program designates the student for whom they are calculating the grade to be an English student, we don't want the user to be able to select any other student type. Unfortunately, with a Check Box object, more than one Check Box can be selected at the same time."

"So with a Check Box object, more than one Student Type can be selected at the same time?" Rhonda asked. "We certainly don't want that."

"That's exactly right Rhonda," I said. "Check Boxes are fine for certain types of applications where more than one selection is permissible."

"Such as?" Chuck asked.

"For instance," I said, "if we were to write a program that asked the user to select their favorite sports---we could use Check Boxes to represent Baseball, Basketball, Football and Hockey. And a Check Box would be fine here--since it's perfectly reasonable for someone to have more than one favorite sport, and that's the way we phrased the question. But suppose we asked the user to specify their one and only, their absolute favorite sport---in this case a Radio Button would be the object to use to represent their four choices--since by it's very nature it prevents more than one selection from being made."

"You've used the term object several times?" Valerie said, "It's my understanding that Java is an object-oriented programming language. Is that right?"

"That's right Valerie," I said. "In Java, you'll see that when we designate a Radio Button to represent an item that the user can select, we're actually creating an instance of a Radio Button object from an already existing Radio Button template--called a class. This class has built in behavior--and in the case of a Radio Button object, it's that built in behavior that prevents more than one from being selected at the same time. We'll discuss Radio Button objects--as well as the other types of Java objects---later on in the course."

"Can we see an example of a Radio Button object?" Joe asked.

"Sure thing," I said, "Check out the Print submenu of Word." I displayed it on the classroom project at the same time.

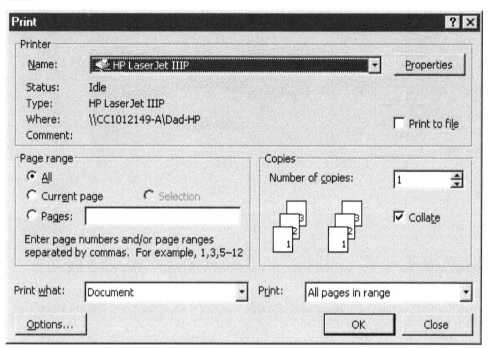

"Now take a look at the Page Range frame," I said. "For those of you not familiar with the term, a Frame is a section of a window---and as you can see, there are three Radio Buttons in the Page Range Frame. You'll notice that only one Radio Button within a Frame can be selected at one time."

"Sounds like a great object to use to represent the Student Type," Dave said.

"I agree," Peter said. "No typing required."

Just about everyone in the class---one student thought a Listbox was a better choice---agreed that using Radio Buttons to represent the Student Type was a good idea, so Dave added this to the Requirements Statement.

Designating the component grades

"OK," Ward said, "now that we had identified the Student Type, what happens--how do we get the user to enter the value for the component grades---Midterm examination, Final Examination, Research Paper and Presentation. We can't do that using any of the objects we've explorer so far, can we?"

"That's right Ward," I said, "we do need a way to permit the user to enter the component grades that make up the student's final grade. Does anyone see anything in Word that fits that bill?"

"How about the box next to the 'Pages' Radio Button in the Print Sub menu," Lou asked. "I just checked--and it permits the user to type something into it."

"That's excellent Lou," I agreed. "In Windows, that box is called a Text Box---Java calls them TextFields. Regardless of what you call them, they are ideal for our application, since they permit the user to make an entry into them."

"Will we have four of them?" Rose asked. "One for each of the component grades?"

"Yes we will," I said. "Later on, you'll see that we can selectively hide some of the TextFields that are not appropriate for the Student Type the user selects."

"So you're saying if the user selects a Math Student Type, only two TextFields will be visible?" Valerie asked.

"That's right," I said, "and if the user selects a Science Student Type, three TextFields will be visible."

"This sounds like it's all going to be a lot of fun," Rhonda said, "I just wish I could envision what the interface will look like. Do we have to wait until we write the program to see what the interface will actually look like."

"Good question Rhonda," I said. "No we don't have to wait that long--there's no rule that says we can't sketch the User Interface using pencil and paper well before that."

The First Interface Design

As it turned out, during the course of our discussions, Barbara had been sketching a preliminary interface design. Upon hearing my remarks about sketching the interface, she offered to show the class what she had sketched so far, and I displayed it on the classroom projector.

```
 ┌──────────────────────────────────────────────┐
 │                                                │
 │   ○  English Student     Midterm:     [      ] │
 │                                                │
 │   ○  Math Student        Final:       [      ] │
 │                                                │
 │   ○  Science Student     Research Paper: [   ] │
 │                                                │
 │                          Class Presentation: [ ]│
 │                                                │
 │          ┌──────────────────┐                  │
 │          │  Calculate Grade  │                 │
 │          └──────────────────┘                  │
 │                                                │
 └──────────────────────────────────────────────┘
```

"That looks great Barbara," Rhonda said, "seeing the interface design on paper really makes this easier for me to envision."

"I agree Rhonda," I said, "and you'll find that having a 'blueprint' like this will make programming the interface much easier later on."

I then asked Barbara if she would mind explaining the interface design to the rest of the class.

"Based on my experience with Windows," she said, "I figured that the program would have a windows look and feel, although from what I've read of Java, I know that's not necessarily the case."

"Good point, Barbara," I said, directing my comments to the rest of the class. "Java can produce programs with a windows look and feel, but it can also produce what are known as console programs."

"Console programs," Ward said. "Those sound like old-time DOS programs."

"That's one way of looking at it," I said. "But remember, Java can produce programs for just about every operating system. The windows look and feel of Microsoft Windows, Linux, and Macintosh operating systems are pretty interfaces designed to make things easier for the user. Java was designed to work at a much lower level than the user interface. As a result, Java can produce programs that don't necessarily have a windows look and feel, and these are called console programs."

"Will we be writing console programs in this class?" Kate asked.

"Yes, we will," I said. "In fact, that's the type of program we'll start working with. We'll actually write the grade calculation as a console program. We'll test it and prove it that way and then add the windows-like user interface to the program towards the end of the class."

I apologized to Barbara for interrupting her discussion of the interface and asked her to continue.

"Based on our discussion of Radio Buttons," she said, "I drew a Radio Button for each of the three Student types we have---English, Math and Science--each with an appropriate label. Pictured in the sketch is a TextField for each of the four component grades, again appropriately labeled. As we discussed earlier, however, all four of the TextFields will not necessarily be visible---which of the four is visible will depend upon the Radio Button that the user selects."

"That's great Barbara," I said. "I noticed you also included a button captioned 'Calculate Grades.'"

"I thought it made sense," Barbara said, "to include a button that, when clicked, would trigger the calculation and display of the student's final grade."

"Do you have any ideas as to how and where we'll display the student's final grade?" Dave asked.

"I hadn't gotten that far," Barbara said, "I guess we could display the grade on the interface itself---or perhaps display a message. Can Java display a message box?"

"Yes Barbara," I said, "Java is capable of displaying a message box."

"A message box can be quite an attention getter," Dave said. "I've seen some users entirely miss the display of information on the interface itself. Plus, with a message box, won't that continue to display until the user clicks on an OK button or something like that?"

"That's right Dave," I said, "a message box remains until the user clicks on an OK button."

"I vote for the message box," Rhonda said.

That seemed to be the majority opinion of the class---a message box it would be, although I emphasized that during the class, they could deviate from this design if they wished--by displaying the calculation in a Java Label or TextField or TexstArea object if they chose.

NOTE: We'll learn more about Java Labels and TextField and TextArea objects in Chapter 13

"What happens after the student's final grade is displayed in a message box?" Chuck asked. "I mean, should we automatically clear the TextFields to work on the next student."

"I was thinking the same thing," Kate said. "I suppose we could automatically clear the TextFields in preparation for the next student---but perhaps it would be better to have another button captioned 'Reset' which would unselect the Student type Radio Button currently selected, make all four TextFields visible, and at the same time clear them?"

"I like that idea a lot," Barbara said. So did everyone else, and so I asked Barbara to add a Reset button to the sketch. She did, and I then displayed the modified sketch of the user interface on the classroom projector.

I asked everyone to take a good, careful look at the interface.

"Remember what I told you earlier," I said, "now's the time to uncover anything that isn't quite right---changing the design on paper is a lot easier than changing the code after we've written it."

"I don't want to appear picky," Mary said, "but the sketch doesn't include a title bar for the window. Plus I presume that Java windows have a Control Menu icon, plus the standard Minimize, Maximize, and Close buttons?"

"Mary's right," Barbara answered, "I didn't include any of those elements in the sketch. Should we be that detailed here?"

"It can't hurt," I said. "It's one less thing to forget when it comes time to actually write our code."

"I think I understand what the Minimize, Maximize and Close buttons are," Rhonda said, "those are the buttons on the right side of a window's Title bar--but what's a Control Menu Icon?"

"The Control Menu Icon," I said, "is the Icon on the left hand side of a window's Title bar--if you click on it, a submenu with menu items for Restore, Move, Size, Minimize, Maximize and Close will appear. We should probably include the Control Menu Icon on our sketch as well."

"What about menus," Steve asked. "Should we develop a menu for the Grades Calculation project?"

"That's a good question Steve," I said. "Creating menus in Java is a bit of an advanced topic--and something we cover here at the university in our Advanced Java class. For our purposes, this application doesn't 'cry out' for a menu since it's basically a program that performs a single function. In fact, the only thing I could think to add to any menu that we would develop would be a File | Exit menu item, but the user can perform that function simply by clicking the Close button on the title Bar."

I noticed that Barbara had finished making the last changes to our interface on her sketch, and I took it from her and displayed it on the classroom projector.

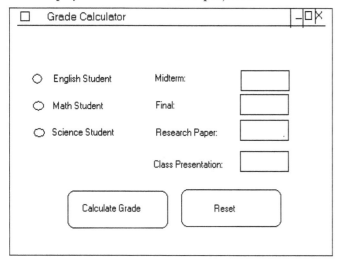

"That really is beginning to shape up," Ward said. "Did we forget anything?"

"I can't think of anything," I said, "but the great thing about doing the design on paper first is that if you do forget anything, it's a matter of making some changes to a sheet of paper--not to your program code."

"I have a question," Rhonda asked. "Are the captions that appear in the window objects themselves---or do they belong to the Radio Buttons and TextFields."

"That's an excellent question, Rhonda," I said. "The captions next to the radio buttons 'belong' to the RadioButton-we'll see much later in the class that when we 'create' a RadioButton, we specify its caption at that time. The captions next to the TextFields are another story, however. These captions don't really 'belong' to the TextFields and will need to be created by using the Java label object."

I waited to see if there were any questions, but there were none.

The Requirements Statement

We had been working pretty intensely, and in my opinion making some excellent progress, and so I suggested that we take a break. Before adjourning, I asked Dave, the student who was developing the Requirements Statement, to let us see what he had developed so far. I made copies of his work, and after break, handed these out to the rest of the class for discussion. Here is the copy of the Requirements Statement I gave to everyone.

REQUIREMENTS STATEMENT

Grades Calculation Program

GENERAL DESCRIPTION

The program will consist of an Interface on which there will be:

3 Radio Buttons, representing the three types of students for which grades can be calculated.

4 TextFields, appropriately labeled Midterm, Final, Research Paper, and Class Presentation, into which the user will enter the component grades necessary to calculate the student's final grade.

A button, captioned 'Calculate grade, which when clicked will display the student's Final numeric grade and letter grade in a message box.

A button, captioned 'Reset', which when clicked will clear the contents of the four TextFields.

OUTPUT FROM THE SYSTEM

The student's final numeric grade and letter grade in a message box

INPUT TO THE SYSTEM

The user will specify the following

The type of student whose grade is to be calculated

If an English student, the Midterm, Final examination, Research Paper and Class Presentation grades will be entered in the appropriate TextField.

If a Math student, the Midterm and Final examination grades will be entered in the appropriate TextField.

If a Science student, the Midterm, Final examination and Research Paper grades will be entered in the appropriate TextField.

BUSINESS RULES

An English student's grade is calculated as 25% of the Midterm grade, 25% of the Final examination grade, 30% of the Research Paper grade and 20% of the Class Presentation grade.

A Math student's grade is calculated as 50% of the Midterm grade and 50% of the Final examination grade.

A Science student's grade is calculated as 40% of the Midterm grade, 40% of the Final examination grade, and 20% of the Research paper grade.

Each department has unique letter grade equivalents for the student's calculated final numeric average. Here is a table of the letter grade equivalents:

DEPARTMENT	ENGLISH	MATH	SCIENCE
A	93 OR GREATER	90 OR GREATER	90 OR GREATER
B	85 TO 93	83 TO 90	80 TO 90
C	78 TO 85	76 TO 83	70 TO 80
D	70 TO 78	65 TO 76	60 TO 70
F	LESS THAN 70	LESS THAN 65	LESS THAN 60

I explained to the class that the Requirements Statement could easily form the basis of a contract between the customer and the developer of the program. The Requirements Statement should list all of the major details of the program. You should take care not to paint yourself into any unnecessary programming corners by including any 'window dressing'. These can just get you into trouble later.

For instance, notice here that we didn't specify precisely where, on the interface, we would display the various Java objects. Suppose, for instance, we had specified that both buttons are side by side at the bottom of the interface---but then decide later than we want to align them vertically instead. Theoretically, deviating from the Requirements Statement could be construed as a violation of contractual terms.

I asked for comments on the Requirements Statement and everyone seemed to think that it was just fine. However, several students turned their attention to the sketch of the user interface, and indicated that they believed there were still some problems with it.

Blaine suggested that our sketch didn't have identifying captions--specifically, he thought that we should have an identifying caption for the column of Radio Buttons and for the column of TextFields.

"That's not a bad idea Blaine," I said, and I asked Barbara if she would mind modifying her sketch.

"We can insert add two Java label objects to provide identifying captions. Anything else?"

No one had anything else, and with that, we proclaimed the user interface designed---always subject to change of course at a later time if needed. I displayed the final sketch of the interface on the classroom projector. Barbara quickly made the changes to the sketch.

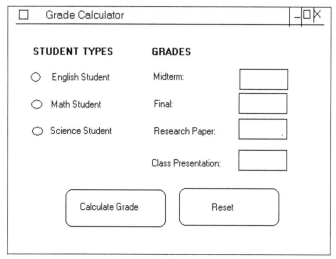

Neither one of these changes were detailed enough to warrant mentioning them on the Requirements Statement, so Dave needed to make no changes to the Requirements Statement. Everyone agreed that the interface had come along quite nicely, but as they say, 'the proof is in the pudding.' It's only the customer's opinion that counts---and we'd have to see how Frank, Robin and David felt about it. With no more comments or suggestions on the user interface or the Requirements Statement, we set about completing the Design Phase of the SDLC by looking at Processing.

Processing Design

"Processing is the conversion of inputs to outputs, the conversion of Data to Information," I said. "At this point in the Design phase of the SDLC, we should have now identified all of the output from the program---a calculation of the student's grade---and all of the input necessary to produce that output--the component pieces of the grade."

I explained that just as a good novel will typically have several subplots; a Java program is no exception. It contains several processing 'subplots' as well.

We have the main 'plot', that is the calculation of the student's grade, but we also have 'subplots' such as:

- Determining the type of student whose grade is being entered

- Selectively hiding and displaying the appropriate TextFields

- Ensuring that valid data---numbers between 0 and 100---are entered into the TextFields.

- Making the appropriate calculation.

- Displaying the calculated grade.

It's important to note that in Processing Design, we don't actually write the program. That's done later. In Processing Design, we specify the processes that need to be performed to convert input into output.

Looking at Processing in Detail

"Let's look at a simple example which isn't part of the Grades Calculation Project," I said, "that most of you are probably familiar with, the calculation of your paycheck."

I continued by saying that if you want to calculate your net pay, you need to perform several steps. Here are the steps or functions necessary to calculate your net pay:

1. Calculate gross pay

2. Calculate tax deductions

3. Calculate net pay

> **NOTE:** Programming is done in the next phase of the SDLC, the Development Phase. Specifying how processing is to occur is not as important in this phase as specifying what is to occur. For instance, this sequence identifies the 'what' of processing, not the how. The 'how' is a part of the Development phase.

These functions can be broken down even further. For instance, the calculation of your gross pay will vary depending upon whether you are a salaried employee or an hourly employee. If you are an hourly employee, your gross pay is equal to your hourly pay rate multiplied by the number of hours worked in the pay period. The specification of these functions is exactly what the designer must detail in the Processing Design phase of the SDLC.

When it comes to processing design, documenting the processing rules is crucial because translating processing rules into a narrative form can sometimes result in confusion or misinterpretation. Over the years, systems designers have used various 'tools' to aid them in documenting the design of their systems.

Some designers have used tools called flowcharts. Flowcharts use symbols to graphically document the system's processing rules. Here are the net pay processing rules we discussed earlier depicted using a flowchart. (My apologies to any accountants reading this; these calculations have been simplified for illustration purposes.)

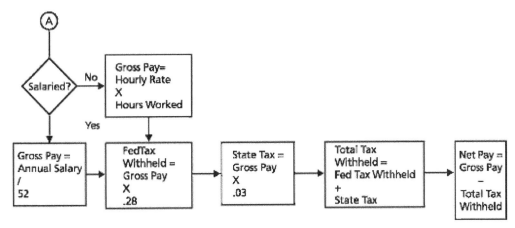

Other designers favor pseudo-code. Pseudo-code is an English-like language that describes in non-graphical form how a program should execute. Here are the same net pay processing rules depicted using pseudo-code:

Assumption: Pay is calculated on a weekly basis (52 pay periods per year).

Assumption: Salaried employee pay is Annual Salary divided by 52.

Assumption: Hourly employee pay is Hourly Rate multiplied by hours worked.

1. If employee is salaried, then go to Step 4

2. Employee is hourly, then calculate gross pay equal to hourly wage rate multiplied by hours worked in pay period

3. Go to Step 5

4. Employee is salaried, so calculate Gross Pay equal to Annual Salary divided by 52

5. Calculate Federal Tax withheld equal to Gross Pay multiplied by 0.28

6. Calculate State Tax withheld equal to Gross pay multiplied by 0.03

7. Calculate Total Tax withheld equal to Federal Tax withheld + State Tax withheld

8. Calculate Net Pay equal to Gross Pay less Total Tax withheld

> **NOTE:** Both of these techniques found favor in the era of the Procedural Program.
>
> A **Procedural Program** is one that executes from top to bottom virtually without interruption. A procedural program ordains to the user exactly how they will interact with your program. For instance, in the Grades Calculation Project, the user will select a type of student, and then enter values for component grade pieces such as the Midterm or Final Examination grade.

I frequently find students who have a strong programming background writing procedural programs. Procedural Programming (using languages like Basic, Fortran and COBOL) is like taking a ride on a tour bus, where all of the destination stops are pre-determined, and pre-ordered.

Windows programs are Event-Driven programs. Event-Driven programs (using languages such as Visual Basic, C++ and Java) don't force the user to behave in a certain way, but rather react to the user.

An event-driven program does not attempt to 'dictate' to the user what they should do in the program, and when they should do it. Instead an event-driven program presents the user with a visual interface that permits them to interact with the program. This is more like choosing the rides at a carnival.

Once entry has been gained, the rides they go on and the order in which they ride them is entirely up to the user. An event-driven program must be able to work and respond to any eventuality.

"In my classes," I said, "I don't require the use of either flowcharting or pseudo-code. All that I ask from you is that you give careful thought to the processing that is necessary to solve the problem before beginning to code in Java."

I could see some happy faces and I continued by saying that invariably, this means working out a solution on a piece of paper prior to coding it. Some students are more 'visual' than others, and they prefer to design their solution in graphical terms. Others are less 'visual' and their solutions look very much like the pseudo-code we saw earlier. The point is, without some written plan, the programming process can go awry.

I cited this example. Several years ago, I was teaching a class on another language called COBOL, and I gave my students the following programming problem:

Write a program to calculate the net wage of a laborer who works 40 hours at a pay rate of $5 per hour. Income tax at the rate of 20% of the gross pay will be deducted. What is the net pay?

The correct answer is $160. Forty hours multiplied by $5 per hour results in a gross pay of $200. The income tax deduction is 20% of $200, which is $40. $200 less the $40 income tax deduction results in a net pay of $160.

A number of students calculated the net pay as $240. Instead of deducting the income tax deduction of $40 from the gross pay, they added it instead. When I questioned the methodology behind their incorrect answer, most of them told me they thought the problem had been so simple, that they hadn't bothered to work out the solution on a piece of paper ahead of time. They just started coding. Had they taken the time to work out the solution on paper first, they would have known what the answer should be and they wouldn't have submitted a program to me that calculated the results incorrectly.

"This is what I'm suggesting to you," I said. "Take the time to work out the solution on paper. You'll be happy that you did."

Back to the Grades Calculation Program

We continued by discussing processing design. I reminded my students that, in general, design is an iterative process. It's rare that the designer or programmer hits the nail perfectly on the head the first time. It's very possible that after going through processing design, you will discover that you are missing some crucial piece of input necessary to produce a piece of output. In this case, you would need to look at your input processing again. For instance, with the Grades Calculation program, we could have forgotten to ask the user to specify the type of student whose grade they wished to calculate--such an omission would have catastrophic consequences.

As a starting point in our processing discussion, we agreed to begin with our primary goal: To calculate a student's grade. We had already determined that in order to calculate a grade, we needed to know the type of student, and once we knew that, the individual grade components that made up the final grade.

We started with a hypothetical user entering a hypothetical student's information.

"Can anyone tell me," I asked "what the final grade for an English student would be if he or she scored an 88 on their midterm examination, a 90 on their final examination, an 85 on their Research paper, and a 75 on their Class presentation? Plus, can you tell me how you arrive at the result?"

"If I were solving this problem using pencil and paper," Ward said, "I would take the score for the student's midterm grade-88--and multiply it by .2, giving me a result of 22 which I would then set aside. I would then take the score for the final examination--90---and multiply it by .2, giving me a result of 22.5, which I would then set aside. I would then take the score for the student's Research paper---85---and multiply it by .3, giving me a result of 25.5, which I would then set aside. I would then take the score for the Class Presentation---75---and multiply it by .2, giving me a result of 15, which I would then set aside. Finally, I would take the four 'set aside; results---22, 22.5 25.5 and 15, and add them together to arrive at a sum of 85--which, if we refer to the Requirements Statement, equates to the letter 'B' for an English student."

"That's excellent Ward," I said. "

"I think we've got a problem here," Chuck said. "I went through the same process Ward just did--but I come up with a letter grade of 'C'."

Sure enough, we did have a problem. In looking over the Requirements Statement, it indicated that for an English Student, the numeric grade of 85 equated to both the letter 'B' and the letter 'C'.

"How did that happen?" Kate asked.

"Those are the numbers that Frank Olley supplied in his email," I said, "unfortunately, I missed catching this. Right now we have a little problem---but I happen to know that Frank is in his office today---hopefully he can give us a quick solution to the problem."

I pulled out my cell phone (ah, the conveniences of modern living!) and gave Frank a quick call. Fortunately, he was still in his office. I explained that in his email to me outlining the numeric grade-letter equivalents, he had used the phrase '78 to 85' to describe the letter grade of 'C' for an English student---and then the phrase '85 to 93' to describe the letter grade of 'B'--what happens if the student scores a final numeric grade of '85' right on the nose.

I had to explain the problem once more for Frank--and then he apologized and explained that a numeric grade of '85' was the starting point for a 'B'---anything less than '85' was a C. I asked him if the same applied to the other categories--since we also had overlapping there. He said that it did, and based on our discussion, the class and I re-worked that table from the Requirements Statement to look like this…

DEPARTMENT	ENGLISH	MATH	SCIENCE
A	>= 93	>= 90	>= 90
B	< 93 AND >= 85	< 90 AND >= 83	< 90 AND >= 80
C	< 85 AND >= 78	< 83 AND >= 76	< 80 AND >= 70
D	< 78 AND >= 70	< 76 AND >= 65	< 70 AND >= 60
F	< 70	< 65	< 60

"That's better," I said, admiring my work.

"Maybe for you," Rhonda responded, "but this reminds me of Algebra, and I think the table is a lot more difficult to read this way. Do we really have to express the rules for the letter grade computations this way? Those less than and greater than symbols always confused me."

"In the long run, we'll be better off," I said, "the way we've phrased the rules for forming the letter grades isn't much different from the Java code we'll write. Plus, these are expressed in certain terms--unlike the previous version of the table which can the overlapping values."

"Have we missed anything with the grade calculation?" I asked.

"Suppose," I added, "the user selects a student type of 'English' and enters value for a Midterm, a Final examination, and a Research paper--but fails to enter a value for the Class presentation--what should the program do?"

Everyone agreed that we needed to display some sort of error message if we didn't have all of the 'ingredients' necessary to arrive at a valid grade calculation. An error message is another form of output.

"I think we've already agreed on this," I said, "but how and when should the grade calculation take place?" I asked.

Mary suggested that we could trigger the grade calculation when the last component piece of the grade was entered.

"I think that would look pretty 'spiffy'," she said, "if we displayed an English student's grade right after the Class Presentation grade was entered into the TextField--can we do that?"

"We can do that Mary," I said, "but you've got to be careful about anticipating the order in which the user of our program will interact with the objects in the window. Aren't you pre-supposing that the user will enter values into the various TextFields from top to bottom?"

Mary admitted that she was. I agreed. "You've got to be careful not to try to anticipate the order in which you think the user will interact with the objects in your pogrom," I said. "Midterm grade, Final Examination grade, Research Paper and Class Presentation---that's probably the order that you would make your selections. But that's not going to be the case with every user."

I explained that expecting users to perform actions in a particular order sounded very much like procedural programming. Like a trip to the Automated Teller Machine:

- insert card
- enter PIN number
- select withdrawal or deposit
- specify an amount
- deposit your cash or take your cash
- take your receipt
- take your card

I explained that Procedural Programming is something we want to avoid. Procedural programming often gives the user the feeling that they are being pushed or rushed---that they aren't really in control. When we write Windows programs, it's a great idea to give the user the impression that they are in control.

"That's why I suggested earlier the use of a button captioned 'Calculate Grade' to allow the user to tell the program when they are ready for a grade calculation," I said. "This way they won't get the impression that the program is waiting for them to do something."

The students thought about this for a moment, and agreed with the concept. We confirmed that we would place a button on the form captioned 'Calculate Grade'---and we further agreed that we would not perform a grade calculation until the user clicked on that button.

Now it seemed as though we were gaining momentum. As I mentioned earlier, during the course of processing design, we may uncover 'holes' in the input or output design---such as the 'overlapping' grade. That had been the case here. While it's certain that we would have eventually noticed these holes when we were coding the program, fixing these flaws while you are still in the design phase of the SDLC is much easier and cheaper than fixing them in the midst of programming the application.

In large projects particularly, portions of the project may be given to different programmers or even different teams of programmers for coding. It could be some time before flaws in the design are uncovered, in some cases weeks or even months. The longer it takes to discover these flaws, the more likely it is that some coding will have to be scrapped and re-done. A well thought out design phase can eliminate many problems down the line.

We'd plugged the hole in the grade calculation processing---now it remained to be seen if there were any other processing design issues.

"What about ending the program?" Steve asked. "Do we need to write code for that?"

I explained that we would need to write a few lines of Java code to end the program--but that there was no need to formally state that in the Requirements statement. After a few moments of silence, it seemed that we were finished with the Design phase of the SDLC. Here is the **Final Requirements Statement** that the class approved:

<u>**REQUIREMENTS STATEMENT**</u>

Grades Calculation Program

GENERAL DESCRIPTION

The program will consist of an Interface on which there will be:

3 Radio Buttons, representing the three types of students for which grades can be calculated.

4 TextFields, appropriately labeled Midterm, Final, Research Paper, and Class Presentation, into which the user will enter the component grades necessary to calculate the student's final grade.

A button, captioned 'Calculate grade, which when clicked will display the student's Final numeric grade and letter grade in a message box.

A button, captioned 'Reset', which when clicked will clear the contents of the four TextFields.

OUTPUT FROM THE SYSTEM

The student's final numeric grade and letter grade in a message box

INPUT TO THE SYSTEM

The customer will specify:

The type of student whose grade is to be calculated

If an English student, the Midterm, Final examination, Research Paper and Class Presentation grades will be entered in the appropriate TextField.

If a Math student, the Midterm and Final examination grades will be entered in the appropriate TextField.

If a Science student, the Midterm, Final examination and Research Paper grades will be entered in the appropriate TextField.

BUSINESS RULES

An English student's grade is calculated as 25% of the Midterm grade, 25% of the Final examination grade, 30% of the Research Paper grade and 20% of the Class Presentation grade.

A Math student's grade is calculated as 50% of the Midterm grade and 50% of the Final examination grade.

A Science student's grade is calculated as 40% of the Midterm grade, 40% of the Final examination grade, and 20% of the Research paper grade.

Each department has unique letter grade equivalents for the student's calculated final numeric average. Here is a table of the letter grade equivalents:

DEPARTMENT	ENGLISH	MATH	SCIENCE
A	>= 93	>= 90	>= 90
B	< 93 AND >= 85	< 90 AND >= 83	< 90 AND >= 80
C	< 85 AND >= 78	< 83 AND >= 76	< 80 AND >= 70
D	< 78 AND >= 70	< 76 AND >= 65	< 70 AND >= 60
F	< 70	< 65	< 60

I polled the class to see if everyone agreed with the Requirements Statement, and then revealed that we were now done with the Design Phase of the SDLC. I once again reminded everyone that the Design Phase of the SDLC tends to be an iterative process, and that we might find ourselves back here at some point. We then moved on to a discussion of the fourth phase of the SDLC--the Development Phase.

Phase 4: Development Phase

I told my class that we wouldn't spend a great deal of time discussing the Development Phase here since the rest of the course would be spent in developing the Grades Calculation Project, in which they would play an active role!

"The Development phase is," I said, "in many ways the most exciting time of the SDLC. During this phase, computer hardware is purchased, if necessary, and the software is developed. Yes, that means we actually start coding the program during the Development phase, and in this class, we'll be using Java as our development tool."

I explained that during the Development Phase, we'd constantly examine and re-examine the Requirements Statement to ensure that we were following it to the letter, and I encourage all of them to do the same. I explained that any deviations (and there may be a surprise or two down the road) would have to be approved either by the project leader (me) or by our clients--Frank, Robin and David.

I also explained that our Development Phase would be split into two sections. First, we would develop a Java Console Program that would perform the grade calculations that our final windows version would---with the difference being that the Console program wouldn't have a windows user interface.

"The Console program will allow us to prove that the logic behind the scenes of our program works," I said. "Once we've proven that, we'll spend the last few weeks of the class building the User Interface, and incorporating our already written logic into that version."

Everyone in the class seemed anxious to begin, but they promised me they would remain patient while I discussed the final two phases of the SDLC.

Phase 5: Implementation Phase

The Implementation Phase is the phase in the SDLC when the project reaches fruition. I explained to my students that after the Development phase of the SDLC is complete, we begin to actually implement the system. In a typical project, what this means is that any hardware that has been purchased will be delivered and installed in the client's location.

In the instance of our clients," I said, "they already have the equipment. So instead, during the Implementation phase, the Java program that we write will be loaded onto their PC's."

Not surprisingly, everyone in the class agreed that they wanted to be there for that exciting day.

Barbara raised the issue of program testing. During the Implementation phase, both hardware and software is tested. We agreed that students in the class would perform most of the testing of the program, as we agreed that it would be unreasonable and unfair to expect our clients to test the software that we had developed in a 'live' situation. Naturally, our goal was that when the software was installed in the English, Math and Science departments, that the program should be bug (problem) free.

On the other hand, I cautioned them, almost invariably, the user will uncover problems that the developer has been unable to generate. I told them we would discuss handling these types of problems in more detail in our class on error handling.

"I've heard the term 'debugging used among the programmers at work," Valerie said. 'Is that something we'll be doing?"

"Most definitely Valerie," I said. "Debugging is a process in which we run the program, thoroughly test it, and systematically eliminate all of the errors that we can uncover. We'll be doing this prior to delivering the program to Frank, Robin and David."

I then explained that during the Implementation phase, we would also be training the users of the program-most likely work study students in the English, Math and Science departments---but perhaps Frank, Robin and David as well. Again, everyone in the class wanted to participate in user training. One of my students noted that she thought that there needed to be two levels of training performed:

Several students thought that it would be a good idea to have a student observing the users of the program during its first week of operation, in order to assist users in the operation of the system, and to ease any 'computer' anxiety that the users might be suffering. I thought this was a great idea, and also pointed out these observations would provide valuable feedback on the operation of the program from the most important people in the loop, the end users.

In fact, the mention of the word 'feedback' led quite naturally into a discussion of the final phase of the SDLC--- Audit (sometimes called Feedback) and Maintenance.

Phase 6: Audit and Maintenance Phase

Phase 6 of the SDLC is the Audit and Maintenance Phase. In this phase, someone, usually the client, but sometimes a third party such as an auditor, studies the implemented system to ensure that it actually fulfills the details of the

Requirements Statement. The bottom line is that the system should have solved the problem or deficiency, or satisfied the desire that was identified in Phase 1 of the SDLC - the preliminary investigation.

More than a few programs and systems have been fully developed that, for one reason or another simply never met the original requirements. The Maintenance portion of this phase deals with any changes that need to be made to the system.

Changes are sometimes the result of the system not completely fulfilling its original requirements, but it could also be the result of customer satisfaction. Sometimes the customer is so happy with what they have got that they want more. Changes can also be forced upon the system because of governmental regulations, such as changing tax laws, while at other times changes come about due to alterations in the business rules of the customer.

As I mentioned in the previous section, we intended to have one or more members of the class in the English, Math and Science departments during the first week of system operation. That opportunity for the user to provide direct feedback to a member of the development team would more than satisfy the Audit portion of Phase 6.

In the future, we hoped that Frank, Robin and David would be so happy with the program that we had written for them, that he would think of even more challenging requirements to request of the class.

Where To From Here?

It had been a long and productive session for everyone. I told my students that in our next meeting we would start to discuss how a computer works, and we would actually begin to work with Java.

Ward asked me how the progression of the project would work, that is, would we finish the project during our last class meeting, or would we be working on it a little bit each week? I said that I thought it was important that we develop the program incrementally. Each week we meet, we would attempt to finish some portion of the project. Developing the project in steps like this would hold everyone's interest, and give us a chance to catch any problems well before the last week of class.

Summary

The aim of this chapter was to tackle the question "Where do I begin?" We saw that the design of an application is best done systematically, with a definite plan of action. That way, you know that everything has been taken into account.

A good place to begin is with a Requirements Statement, which is a list of what the program has to be able to do. Usually, you get the information for this from whoever is asking you to write the program. It's a good idea to keep in continuous contact with this person, so that any changes they want can be tackled before it becomes too much of a problem.

A good systematic approach is embodied in the systems development life cycle (SDLC), which consists of six phases:

· The Preliminary Investigation: Considering the technical, time, and budgetary constraints and deciding on the viability of continuing development of the application.

The Analysis Phase: Gathering the information needed to continue.

The Design Phase: Creating a blueprint of the program's appearance and program structure without actually starting any programming.

The Development Phase: Creating the application, including all interface and code.

The Implementation Phase: Using and testing the program.

The Maintenance Phase: Making refinements to the product to eliminate any problems or to cover new needs that have developed.

Using the SDLC method can make any problems you encounter in your design more obvious, making it easier for you to tackle them at a more favorable point in your design, rather than changing existing code.

Chapter 2--- Getting Comfortable With Java

In this chapter, we'll follow my computer class as they take their first look at the Java environment. The purpose of this chapter is to give you an overview of how to create a Java program using Windows Notepad, how to compile it, and how to run it. Throughout this chapter, as the class and I entered various commands into our PCs, I displayed the results of what we entered on the classroom projector that shows the contents of my video display. These results are shown throughout this chapter where appropriate.

Getting Comfortable with Java

I began our second class by getting straight to the point.

"In today's class," I said, "we're going to concentrate on writing our first Java program. Let's do that now."

I then started Windows Notepad.

"Are you going to write this program using Notepad?" Ward asked. "Doesn't Java have an Integrated Development Environment—an IDE—like Visual Basic?"

"That's a loaded question," I said. "As you may know, you can download the Java Developer's Kit—also called the JDK—for free from the Sun Microsystems web site. There is an IDE of sorts that you can also download from the Sun site, but the JDK itself doesn't come with an IDE. There are third-party IDEs available from many vendors, but most Java students learn by writing their code using an editor like Windows Notepad and using a command prompt for the Windows Run button to compile and run their programs."

"Are you talking about the MS-DOS prompt?" Rhonda asked with a worried look on her face. "I know next to nothing about DOS."

"Don't worry, Rhonda," I said. "Once you have the Java Developer's Kit downloaded and installed, compiling and executing your programs isn't difficult. I'll be showing you how to do that today, and you'll have some exercises of your own to complete later on in the class for reinforcement."

> NOTE: The Java Developer's Kit can be downloaded from Sun Microsystems web site at http://java.sun.com

I waited to see if I was about to lose any of my students. No one got up in a panic to leave the classroom (you think I'm kidding, but I've seen it happen!), so I continued.

Writing Our First Java program

"Creating a Java program is a three step process," I said, and told the students that the steps were as follows.

1. Create the source file (although not required, it's a good idea to name your source file with a filename extension of .java)

2. Use the Java compiler to create a Bytecode file with a filename extension of .class

3. Run the program using the Java Interpreter.

Create the Source File with a file name extension of .java

"First, we use a text editor—Notepad is easiest one to use in the Microsoft Windows environment— to create what is known as a source file. The source file is just an ordinary text file containing Java code. We then save the Java source file to the hard drive of our PC, giving it virtually any name of our choice. However, by convention, the name of a Java source file should end with a period, followed by the letters java; this is called its filename extension. For instance, shortly, we'll create a Java source file whose name is ILoveJava.java where the period followed by the word 'java' is the filename extension."

> TIP: Although not required, it's a good idea for your Java source file to end with the filename extension .java.

I paused to see if I had lost anyone. "Once we use a text editor to create a source file," I continued, "we use a Java compiler to convert or *compile* that source file into what is called a **Bytecode** file.

"Is a Bytecode file like a compiled executable file, the kind we created last semester in our Visual Basic class that had a filename extension of .exe?" Dave asked.

"Not quite, Dave," I said. "An .exe file is unique to a specific operating system. For instance, an .exe file compiled and generated for a Microsoft Windows PC will not run in a web browser, neither will it run on a Linux PC or a Macintosh. On the other hand, a compiled Java source file—in other words, a Bytecode file—can run on virtually any computer, provided that computer has a Java Interpreter."

"Also known as the Java Virtual Machine," Dave added.

NOTE: The Java Interpreter is also known as the Java Virtual Machine, or JVM for short

"That's right, Dave," I agreed.

"So are you saying that each operating system has its own unique Java Virtual Machine?" Kate asked.

"Exactly, Kate," I said. "Each operating system and also most web browsers. For instance, when you go to the Sun Microsystems web site to download the Java Developer's Kit, you select the JDK to download based on your PC's operating system. However, once you create a Java source file and use your Java compiler to create the Bytecode file, that Bytecode file can then be run, without modification, on another PC. This feature is known in the Java community as 'write once, run anywhere' and, as you can imagine, this capability makes Java a very popular choice for development."

"I'm afraid I don't quite understand what you are talking about," Rhonda said. "Write once, run anywhere?"

"Let me try to clarify, Rhonda," I said. "For instance, the China Shop program we wrote last semester in our Visual Basic class can run only on a Microsoft Windows PC—it won't run on a PC running Linux or the Macintosh operating system because Visual Basic can only produce an executable program to run on a PC with the Windows operating system."

"And it's the fact that the Java compiler produces a Bytecode file and *not* an executable file that produces this transportability, is that right?" Barbara asked.

"That's the reason," I answered. "Once the Bytecode file is generated, it's up to the Java Interpreter—the JVM—found on the PC to interpret and execute the instructions in it. In many cases, that JVM is part of a web browser."

"So the Java Virtual Machine is actually an interpreter?" Joe asked. "I remember reading somewhere that interpreted programs are much slower than programs compiled into an .exe file. Is that true?"

"It's true that running an interpreted program is slower than running an .exe file," I replied. "But the key word here is how much slower. In modern software development, the major issue is more often transportability, not speed. The knowledge that a Java program you write can run on literally hundreds of different platforms negates the slight disadvantage of speed in a Java program. Besides, it is possible to compile a Java program into native code—that is, an .exe—but it's something that you would want to consider very carefully before doing. Unless you're developing a program where speed of execution is absolutely critical—such as a program to target and destroy an asteroid about to hit the earth—interpreted Bytecode files will be perfectly fine. And if that's the kind of program you need to write, you wouldn't be using Java to write the program anyway—you would probably write it in C or even machine-code itself."

Again I paused to see if there were any questions before continuing. "Using Notepad to write our first Java program is a snap," I said. "Let's write a Java program that will display the message, 'I love Java!'"

I then entered the following code into Notepad:

```
/**
   This program displays "I Love Java!" to the standard output.
*/
class ILoveJava {
    public static void main(String[] args) {
        System.out.println("I Love Java!");
    }
}
```

"Before I discuss this code," I said, "let's save this source file first by selecting File-Save As from Notepad's Menu Bar...

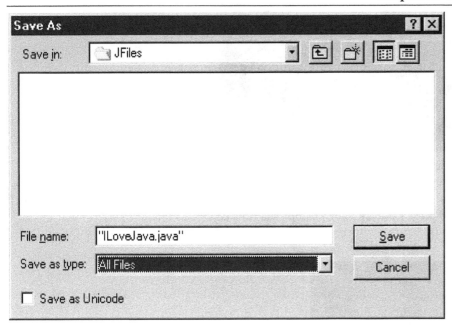

"I like to save all of my files in a folder called JFiles," I said, "which is why I'm specifying JFiles in the Save In drop-down list box. Notice how I have sandwiched the name of my Java source file within quotation marks, ensuring that the filename extension ends in .java. I also need to specify **All Files** in the Save As Type drop-down list box. After clicking the Save button, you should notice that Notepad reflects the new filename."

```
/**
   This program displays "I Love Java!" to the standard output.
*/
class ILoveJava {
    public static void main(String[] args) {
        System.out.println("I Love Java!");
    }
}
```

"Now that we have a good Java source file," I said, "our second step is to compile this source file into a Bytecode file. To do that, we need to bring up an MS-DOS command prompt. The command prompt can appear in a number of different places. For instance, it can be a shortcut on the desktop, or it can appear in the Control Panel. If you can't find it, you can just click the Windows Start menu, choose Run, enter **command.com (or cmd for the latest Windows versions)**, and click the OK button. If you are running Windows 10 (as I am) press the Windows Button + R to open up the Run window and enter cmd.

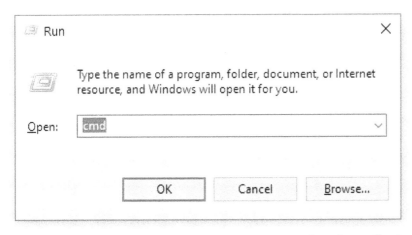

"This will launch the command prompt application. When the application launches, it should look like this."

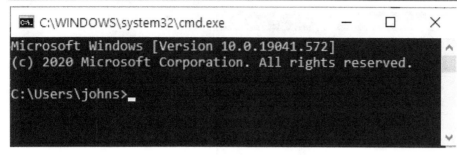

"The prompt shows you the current directory, which is usually Windows for Windows 95/98 or WINNT for Windows NT or Windows 2000 or Windows XP for Windows XP versions. To compile our source code file, we need to change the current directory to the folder where our Java source code file is located. To do that, enter CD C:\JFiles at the command prompt and press ENTER. The prompt will now change to this."

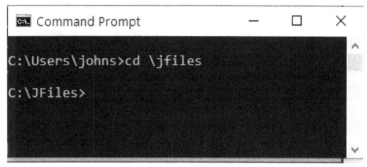

"At this point, we can confirm the location of our Java source file by entering DIR at the command prompt and pressing ENTER."

   NOTE: The Java source file is circled in red and it is indeed in the correct location.

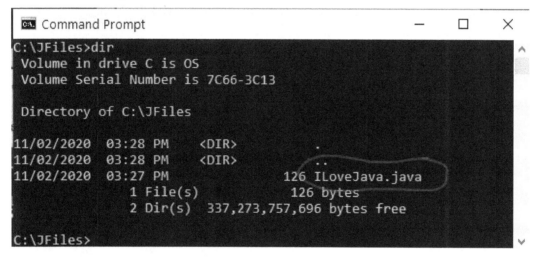

Compile the Java Source File into a Bytecode File

"Now we can compile our source file into a Bytecode file," I said. "To do that, we enter the following instructions at the command prompt and press ENTER:"

javac IloveJava.java

The following then appeared on the classroom projector:

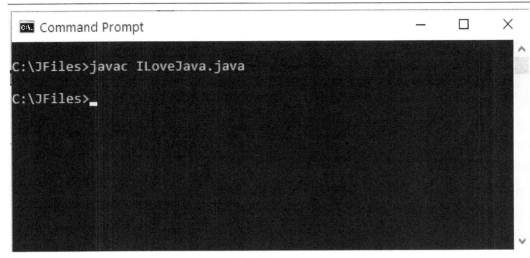

"Nothing seems to have happened," Linda said.

"If you receive *no* error messages," I replied, "that's good. Any problems with the Java source file would manifest themselves in the form of error messages here. We can confirm that our Java source file has been compiled into a Bytecode file by executing the DIR statement we executed earlier."

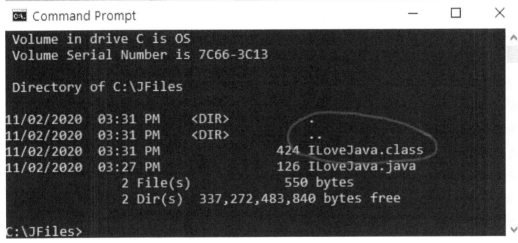

"Notice that our source file has been compiled into a Bytecode file, one ending with the extension .class."

Common Compiler Errors

"I've been following along with you," Rhonda said, "but when I tried to compile my source file, I didn't have much luck. I received an error message, something about an invalid option."

Oops: Invalid Option or Argument

"Compiling a Java source file can be pretty easy, Rhonda," I said, "but there are three types of errors that are pretty common, especially when you first start out writing Java programs. The first occurs if you forget to include the .java extension as part of your command prompt when you compile the source file, like this:"

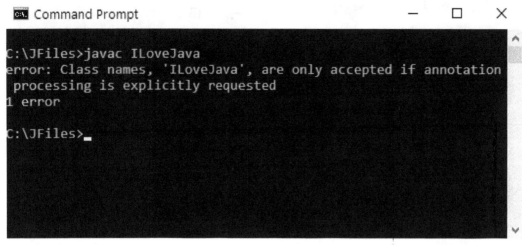

"That's exactly what I did," Rhonda admitted. "I didn't realize I needed to specify the .java filename extension when compiling the source file."

Oops: NoClassDefFoundError

"A second common error," I said, "is to refer to the name of the Java source file with a name that is different from the class name within the Java source file itself. This error will not manifest itself until you try to run your Java program. For instance, if I were to name my source file Smiley.java, with an internal class name of ILoveJava, the program would compile fine, but when I tried to run it, this error message would result:"

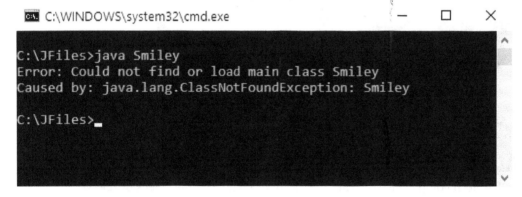

Oops: Can't Find the Compiler

"A third common type of error," I said, "occurs if something is wrong with your Java setup and Windows cannot find the Java compiler necessary to compile your source file into a Bytecode file. In that case, you'll receive this error message when you attempt to compile your source file."

I then intentionally caused the error message that would be displayed if Windows cannot find the Java compiler:

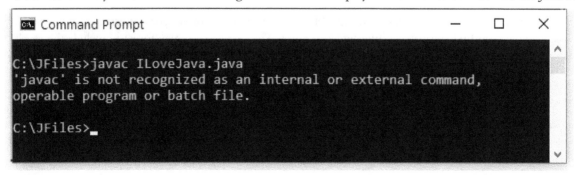

"If you receive this error message, it means that either the Java Developer's Kit has not been properly installed on your PC, or Windows cannot find the Java compiler. In both cases, reinstalling the Java Developer's Kit will usually take care of the problem."

Run the Java Program

"Now that we have a Java Bytecode file—the .class file—" I said, "we can run the program by firing up the Java Interpreter—the Java Virtual Machine—by executing this statement at the command prompt:"

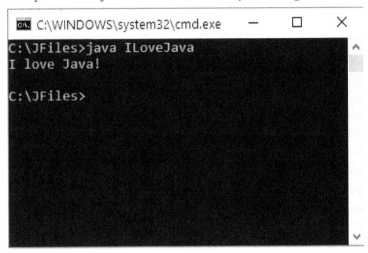

"Be careful to maintain the rules for case sensitivity that we discussed earlier," I said.

"Java is the name of the Java Interpreter, is that correct?" Kathy asked.

"That's right, Kathy," I said. "The name of the Java compiler is javac, the program that compiles the source file into a Bytecode file, and Java is the name of the Java Interpreter, the program that interprets and executes the Bytecode file."

> NOTE: A Java source file must end with the extension .java. and a Java Bytecode file must end with the extension .class.

"Are you going to explain this code?" Rose asked.

You bet, " I answered. I suggested that since we had been working for a while, it would be a great time to take a break.

Elements of a Java program

Fifteen minutes later, I debated with myself as to whether I should begin my discussion of the code with a full-fledged entry into object-oriented programming, something that can be confusing to beginner students but is something that Java excels at. My other option was to simply explain what the code was doing and then relate it to object-oriented programming. I decided to begin with a simple discussion of the code, so I displayed it on the classroom

```
/**
This program displays "I love Java!" to the standard output.
*/
class ILoveJava {
  public static void main(String[] args) {
    System.out.println("I love Java!");
  }
}
```

Program Comments

"These first three lines of code," I said, "are program comments. Program comments are explanatory statements that you can include in the Java code that you write. All programming languages allow for some form of comments. The trick is how to tell Java that the statement you are entering is a comment and not a Java command. In Java, there are three ways to specify that the code that follows is a comment."

"Is that what the asterisks indicate?" Mary asked. "They remind me of the comments from C."

"That's right, Mary," I said. "These three lines of code do look like comments in the C language." I pointed to the following lines that were displayed on the classroom projector:

```
/*
   This program displays "I love Java!" to the standard output.
*/
```

"You can also use this form, which is a little different from C."

```
/**
   This program displays "I love Java!" to the standard output.
*/
```

"Both of these comment forms," I said, "are used when your comment spans more than one line; this is known as a block comment. In either case, anything within the two delimiters is considered a comment. There's also this form of comment." I input the following:

```
//This program written by John Smiley
```

"The compiler ignores everything from the // to the end of the line."

"Can a comment only appear on a line by itself," Dave asked, "or can it follow a Java statement?"

I answered, "You can place a comment after a Java statement. Just follow the Java statement with the characters //, like this…"

```
System.out.println("I love Java!");   //Displays an output message
```

"Is there a standard format for comments?" Rose asked. "Should they always appear at the top of the code, or can they appear anywhere?"

"I wouldn't say there's a real standard," I said. "Some programmers include a comment at the top of their code, indicating the author of the program, the date the program was written, and anything else they or someone reading it later might find useful. Some programmers never comment their code. Myself, I use comments whenever I write code that I needed to look up in a help file or a reference manual. I figure that if I needed to look it up, a comment explaining the code will be helpful the next time I or someone else views the code. Some programmers really make their comments elaborate by using asterisks surrounding the comments, something that is known as a 'flower box,' like this." I input the following:

```
/**********************************************************************
* Programmer: John Smiley
* Date Written: November 9, 2020
* This program displays "I love Java!" to the standard output.
**********************************************************************
/
```

"I know you said earlier that we would be doing exercises of our own for practice," Kathy said. "Will we be coding comments in the exercises that we do?"

"I've already noticed," I said, "that some of you are not the fastest typists in the world, so our exercises will not explicitly include comments---I'll leave the comments up to you to insert as you complete the exercises."

"Getting back to the intricacies of a comment," Rhonda said, "are you saying that the first three lines of code in our Java program really don't mean anything? Does Java just ignore them?"

"Exactly right," I answered. "As far as Java is concerned, those first three lines of code are meaningless. When the Java compiler evaluates these lines of code, it doesn't translate them into Bytecode. As a result, when the Java Interpreter runs the Bytecode file, these lines of code are effectively ignored."

No one had any other questions about comments.

The Class: The Essence of a Java Program

"Let's take a look at the next line of code following the comments," I said. "It seems simple enough, but it may be the most important line of code in a Java program."

```
class ILoveJava {
```

"Java," I began, "is an object-oriented language, and we'll learn more about exactly what that means and its significance as our course proceeds. For now, you need to understand that the basic building block of any object-oriented language is something called a class. A class is a template or a blueprint for an object."

"When you say object," Steve asked, "are you talking about tangible items that we can see or touch?"

"That's one way of looking at it, Steve," I said. "In object-oriented programming environments such as Java, it is frequently easier to solve problems when you think of the pieces you are working with as actual real-world objects instead of some abstract algorithm to solve. For instance, in the program we're developing for the English, Math, and Science Departments, eventually we'll build a Java program consisting of a Student object. We'll define that object in terms of the Student class, and we'll describe the Student object with characteristics, such as a name and final grade. We'll also bestow upon it certain types of behaviors, such as Calculate, which, when executed by our program, will result in the final grade being calculated. Later on in the course you'll learn that attributes are defined in terms of something in the programming world we call a variable, and methods are implemented using something we call functions."

"You said that a class is a template for an object," Dave said. "How do we go from a blueprint to an actual object?"

"Once we create the template for an object via the class," I said, "we create an instance of that object when we run our program. It's at that time that we give values to those attributes and trigger the object's built-in behavior by executing its methods. By the way, this will come in handy later—together, a class's attributes and methods are collectively referred to as its *members*."

> NOTE: When you <u>instantiate</u> a class, you create an <u>instance</u> of its object

"Is all of that—the blueprint for the object, its attributes and methods—is all of that going on in that single line of code?" Joe asked. "Where are the attributes and methods being defined?"

"Joe, this is just about the simplest program we could write," I said. "This particular class has no attributes and just one method called **main()**. This first line of code is where we give the name to the class. As you can see, the keyword Class begins the definition for the class ILoveJava."

```
class ILoveJava {
```

"Following the name of the class comes a left curly bracket—this begins the actual class definition, and the class definition ends when Java finds the corresponding right curly bracket."

The main() Method

"As I mentioned, this class has no attributes, and it has just a single method called **main().**"

```
public static void main(String[] args) {
```

I hesitated as I debated the merits of taking this single line of code apart. I had done so in previous Java courses I taught, and the discussion dragged and dragged. After my other classes ended, my students had told me that in the beginning of a Java class, it's best to keep things moving. Dissecting this single line of code frequently involved many minutes of discussion, so I decided against it.

"When you write a Java program," I said, "the Java Virtual Machine looks for a method called **main()**. This line of code fulfills that requirement and should *always* look like this. We'll talk about writing methods of our own later on in the course, but for now, take my word for it that this line of code is one you must have in each Java program you write."

"I have a question," Dave said, "about the first line of code. I've seen some of the programmers at work write Java code where the square brackets follow the word 'args'"

"They must be programmers with a C background," I said. "Java prefers the square brackets to follow the word String, but allows the square brackets to follow 'args' because so many programmers familiar with C are used to that notation in that language

> NOTE: Java prefers the square brackets to follow the word String, but allows the square brackets to follow 'args' because so many programmers familiar with C are used to that notation in that language

"Those lines of code between the curly braces of the **main()** method," Kate asked, "is that the actual program?"

"That's right, Kate. Everything between the curly left bracket and the curly right bracket here represents the instructions in the **main()** method," I said as I displayed the one and only line of code in the **main()** method on the classroom projector:

```
System.out.println("I love Java!");
```

"This line of code," I continued, "when executed, results in the phrase 'I love Java' being displayed in a console window. Ordinarily, there would be more than just a single Java instruction in the **main()** method. The **main()** method is a section of code where the major instructions of a Java program are placed. Quite frequently, within the **main()** method, we instantiate objects from classes that have been compiled in other source files. For instance, in our Grade Calculation Project, we'll define a Student class in a source file, then compile it and be able to instantiate it from a second source file."

I could see some puzzled faces, so I drew this illustration on the class projector:

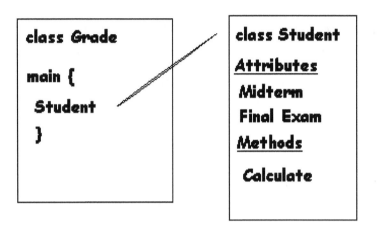

"No entry point means that the source file does not contain a **main()** method," I said. "Later on in the course, you'll learn that you can write programs that have functions or methods of your own, but for now, take my word for it that this line of code is one you must have in each Java program you write."

"Those lines of code between the curly braces of the **main()** method," Kate asked, "is that the actual program?"

"That's right, Kate. Everything between the curly left bracket and the curly right bracket here represents the instructions in the **main()** method," I said as I displayed the one and only line of code in the **main()** method on the classroom projector:

```
System.out.println("I love Java!");
```

"This line of code," I continued, "when executed, results in the phrase 'I love Java!' being displayed in a console window. Ordinarily, there would be more than just a single Java instruction in the **main()** method. The **main()** method is typically where the major instructions of a Java program are placed. Quite frequently, within the **main()** method, we instantiate objects from other classes that have been compiled from other source files. For instance, in our Grade Calculation Project, we'll define a Student class in a source file, then compile it and be able to instantiate it from a second source file."

I could see some puzzled faces, so I drew this illustration on the class projector:

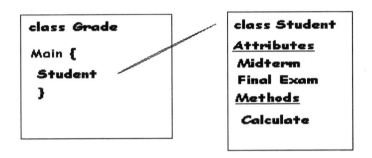

"Most likely," I said, "we'll create a Student class and compile it into a Bytecode file called Student. We'll then create our main class—perhaps we'll call it Grade—and within the **main()** method of that class, instantiate a Student object."

"So if I understand you correctly," Dave said, "we'll be working with more than one class?"

"That's right, Dave," I said. "In Java, everything is a class and an object—they are the building blocks of our programs. It's not unusual for a Java program to work with dozens of classes and objects—that's fundamental to the language. In a workplace environment, you might have a team of several programmers, each creating classes that form pieces of the larger puzzle. Although everyone in this course will create all of the classes and objects for the Grade Calculation Project, because Java is object-oriented, we could assign the creating of the classes that will make up our project to different teams of students that could each work fairly independently to arrive at the solution to their piece of the puzzle."

"I think I understand," Rhonda said, "but I do have a question. Are all of the objects with which we'll work in our Java program objects that we create classes for ourselves?"

"That's a great question, Rhonda," I answered. "Java has a bunch of already-built classes from which we can instantiate objects. That's one of the reasons the Java language is so powerful. Suppose tonight, when you open your front door at home, your doorknob were to break. Imagine the dilemma you would face if you couldn't just drive down to your local hardware store and pick up a replacement doorknob. Many of the parts in a home are made from readily available components that can be used to customize a home. The same is true of Java. Java classes and objects are like the objects you see in a home. Using them is just a matter of knowing what they are, where to find them, how to install them, and how to work with their attributes and methods."

"Are there any of these built-in objects in the sample program you wrote?" Barbara asked.

"Yes there are," I said. "In fact, this line of code makes use of the Java System object."

System.out.println("I love Java!");

"The use of the dot following the word 'System' is called object dot notation and, according to the rules, what follows is either another object, an attribute, or a method. In this case, 'out' is a special Java object that represents what is known as the standard output—usually, but not always, the PC's monitor or, as we'll call it in this class, the console—and **println()** is a method which prints a line of text to the console. Notice the semicolon at the end of the line—Java statements must be terminated with a semicolon. Finally, these last two lines of code complete our work."

```
    }

}
```

NOTE: All Java statements must end with a semicolon (;)

"Notice that we have two right curly braces," I said.

"Why is that?" Blaine asked. "I figured we needed a right curly bracket to mark the end of the **main()** method, but why do need the second one?"

"The second right curly brace marks the end of the class," I said. I then displayed this illustration on the classroom projector:

```
/*
  This program displays "I love Java!" to the standard
output.
  */
class ILoveJava {
    public static void main(String [] args ) {          Beginning of class
        System.out.println("I love Java!");             Start of main
    }                                                    End of main
}                                                        End of class
```

"Do we need to do anything special to use the System object?" Mary asked. "Didn't you say we had to instantiate objects before we could work with attributes and methods?"

"That's right, Mary," I replied. "Ordinarily, to work with an object, you must first instantiate it, but the System object is different. To use its attributes and methods, you just start working with it the way we did here."

"Is there a list of these built-in objects anywhere?" Blaine asked.

"Yes, there is," I answered. "When you install your Java Developer's Kit, documentation should be installed on your PC, and you should be able to find it within the program group that the Java setup program creates. The Java Developer's Kit comes with a load of information, and if you search for information on the Java 2 platform packages, you'll find information on the built-in objects I've been talking about. But you don't need to concern yourself with that too much in this class. I'll be pointing out and giving you directions on the objects that you'll need to use."

"Can we get back to the code you wrote?" Ward asked. "How important is indentation? And you mentioned that Java is case sensitive—I guess my question is how case sensitive is it?"

"The answer to your second question," I answered, "is that you need to be very careful about the spelling of class names in Java. For instance, this line of code,"

System.out.println("I love Java!");

"is not the same as this line,"

system.out.println("I love Java!");

"Spelling 'System' in lowercase will cause Java to be **unable** to find the System class," I said, "resulting in a compiler error. In the same way, spelling 'out' as O-u-t or spelling 'println' as P-r-i-n-t-l-n will result in the same error. I tell my students that if they receive a compiler error indicating that it can't find a class, attribute, or method, check the spelling of those names immediately—they must match exactly the way they are specified in the Java Help files."

"As for your first question, indentation and blank lines in code are ignored by the Java compiler," I said. "For instance, I know it's a far-fetched example, but we could have written this entire program as a single line of code."

"Then why do we indent at all?" Blaine asked.

"It's important for readability," I said. "That is, you want other programmers to be able to read your code as easily as possible, and indenting the way we did here can make it easier for someone who understands the language to more easily pick out where a class definition begins and ends and the methods within a class."

"What is white space?" Kate asked. "Some of the Java programmers at work refer to this from time to time."

"White space refers to space between Java statements and blank lines in the code," I answered. "You can use white space, once again, to make your code more readable. For instance, this code,"

System.out.println("I love Java!");

"using white space could look like this,"

```
System.out.println          ("I love Java!")              ;
```

"and still function in the same way. The thing to remember is that you don't want to go to one extreme or another with this. While it's possible to write a Java program on a single line, it would be very difficult to read it. And while you can insert lots of white space in your program, most programmers like the condensed nature of their program code, so you won't see a lot of blank lines and spaces in their code."

"Will we be learning about inheritance, encapsulation, polymorphism, and some of those other object-oriented terms I've heard about?" Bob asked.

"We will," I said, "but not in today's class. We'll save those for a few weeks down the line."

"Is there a continuation character in Java like there is in Visual Basic?" Rose asked. "In Visual Basic, if we want to split up a long line of code into two pieces, we needed to use an underscore. Does Java have something similar?"

"Because of the white space nature of Java code," I answered, "if you want to split up a single line of code into two or more lines, you just hit the ENTER key. Java doesn't care. For instance, this line of code,"

```
System.out.println("I love Java!");
```

"can be broken up into two lines of code, like this:"

```
System.out.println
   ("I love Java!");
```

"The only place that you can't split the line is within the middle of a quoted string—the code between the quotation marks that is displayed on the console. For instance, this code would result in a syntax error."

```
System.out.println("I love
   Java!");
```

I waited to see if there were any other questions, but no one seemed to have any.

"What I'd like to do now," I said, "is to give you a chance to write, compile, and run a Java program of your own with my assistance. As we'll do during the remainder of the course, I have a series of exercises for you to complete that will lead you through that process."

I then distributed this exercise for the class to complete.

Exercise 2-1 Coding your first Java program---Grades.java

In this exercise you'll write your first Java program--which will form the basis of our class project. Remember, in Java, everything is based on classes, so your program will actually consist of a class definition that contains a single method called **main()**.

By the way, if **typing** these exercises bores you, feel free to follow this link to find the completed solutions for all of the exercises in the book. Just click on the Java book, then follow the link entitled exercises ☺

http://www.johnsmiley.com/main/books.htm

1. Using Windows Explorer, create a folder on your hard drive called \JFiles\Grades. This will be the home of our class project, the Grades Calculation Project.
2. Use the editor of your choice (if you are using Windows, use Notepad) and enter the following code. Be extremely careful of the capitalization..

```
class Grades {
  public static void main(String[] args) {
    System.out.println("It's not much, but it's a start!");
  }
}
```

3. Save your source file as **'Grades.java'** in the \JFiles\Grades folder (select File-Save As from Notepad's Menu Bar). Be sure to save your source file with the file name extension 'java'.

Discussion

Aside from some people in the class who didn't seem very familiar with Notepad, this exercise seemed to go pretty smoothly. In just a few moments, everyone in the class had completed coding their first Java program--the Grades program. This source file, although very simplistic, would eventually form the basis of the program we would give to Frank, Robin and Dave.

"Is this the program we'll be using to calculate grades for the English, Math and Science departments?" Mary asked. "It looks like all this does is display a message to the Console."

"That's right, Mary," I said. "Perhaps you've heard the expression that the journey of a thousand miles begins with the first step? This is the first step: the creation of the Grades class. From here, everything else will be built. And even though displaying this message isn't part of the user requirements, I want the program to do something when you compile and run it, just to prove to you that there is some activity going on in there."

There were no questions about the actual coding of the class—it was almost identical to the sample we had been working on. Next, I distributed a second exercise for the class to complete.

Exercise 2-2 Compiling Grades.java

In this exercise, you'll compile the source file you created in Exercise 2-1, Grades.java, into a Bytecode file called Grades.class.

1. Bring up the MS-DOS command prompt application. You can do this in a number of ways—one easy way is to select Start | Run and enter command.com (or cmd) in the Open box. If you are using Windows 10 (as I am), Press the Windows key + R to open the "Run" box.

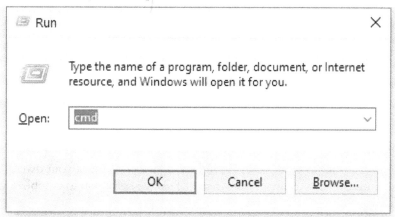

2. At the command prompt, change to the directory (folder) containing your Grades.java source file by entering CD C:\JFiles\GRADES and pressing the ENTER key (pressing the ENTER key is necessary for all of the command prompt steps).

NOTE: If you saved your source file to another drive, substitute that drive letter for 'C'

3. Confirm the existence and location of your Java source file: at the command prompt, enter DIR and press ENTER. You should see an entry for Grades.java similar to this screenshot:

```
C:\JFiles\GRADES>dir
 Volume in drive C is OS
 Volume Serial Number is 7C66-3C13

 Directory of C:\JFiles\GRADES

11/09/2020  10:00 AM    <DIR>          .
11/09/2020  10:00 AM    <DIR>          ..
11/09/2020  10:05 AM               155 Grades.java
               1 File(s)            155 bytes
               2 Dir(s)  341,593,481,216 bytes free

C:\JFiles\GRADES>
```

If you don't see your source file, something went wrong in Exercise 2-1 and you will need to verify your work there before proceeding.

4. Compile your Grades.java file by entering javac Grades.java at the command prompt and press ENTER. The absence of any error messages will indicate that your source file has been compiled into a Bytecode file.

5. Confirm the existence of your Java Bytecode file: at the command prompt, enter DIR and press ENTER. You should see an entry for Grades.class, as in this screenshot:

```
C:\WINDOWS\system32\cmd.exe                    —    □    ×

C:\JFiles\GRADES>dir
 Volume in drive C is OS
 Volume Serial Number is 7C66-3C13

 Directory of C:\JFiles\GRADES

11/09/2020  10:07 AM    <DIR>          .
11/09/2020  10:07 AM    <DIR>          ..
11/09/2020  10:07 AM               438 Grades.class
11/09/2020  10:05 AM               155 Grades.java
               2 File(s)            593 bytes
               2 Dir(s)  341,592,424,448 bytes free

C:\JFiles\GRADES>
```

Discussion

As smoothly and easily as the first exercise went, this one was the opposite: over half of the students in the class had problems of one form or other compiling their first Java program. The typical errors were the ones I had warned everyone about just a few minutes earlier, but warning students about problems is different from having them experience them on their own. Experience is the greatest teacher, so I gave everyone a lot of time to try to complete the exercise on their own.

"I just can't get this thing to compile," Rhonda complained. "This exercise seemed simple enough. I can't believe I'm having so much trouble with it."

I took a quick walk to Rhonda's workstation. In her command prompt window, was this message:

```
Select C:\WINDOWS\system32\cmd.exe            —    □    ×

C:\JFiles\GRADES>java Grades.java
Error: Could not find or load main class Grades.java
Caused by: java.lang.ClassNotFoundException: Grades.java

C:\JFiles\GRADES>
```

"That one's easy, Rhonda," I said. "Although most beginners wouldn't notice this: you're trying to compile your Java source file using by executing 'java' not 'javac'---in other words, you're not using the Java compiler, you're using the Java Interpreter. A lot of beginners at first believe the name of the compiler is the same as the Java filename extension. Just change your command from this…"

java Grades.java

"…to this."

javac Grades.java

"And see what happens."

Sure enough, as soon as she did this, her source file was compiled into a Bytecode file, and a big smile appeared on her face.

Next up was Ward. This is the error message his PC was displaying:

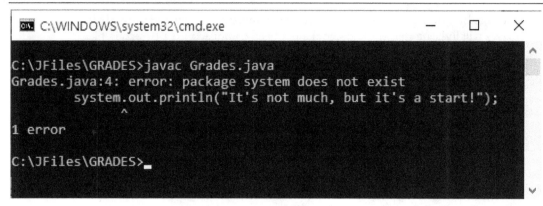

Dave, who had already successfully compiled his source file already, knew immediately what the problem was.

"I see the problem," Dave said.

"Well, don't just stand there, Dave," Ward said, smiling. "What is it?"

"You spelled 'System' with a lowercase s," Dave said. "The Java System class begins with an uppercase S. The same thing happened to me."

Dave was right, and I took the opportunity to call out to the rest of the class that attention to case sensitivity would be crucial during the course. Ward made the change to his source file, and then compiled it, and he too was soon happy as his program compiled successfully.

On the way back to my PC at the front of the classroom, I passed Kate's PC and saw her staring at this error message:

```
C:\WINDOWS\system32\cmd.exe                           —    □    ✕

C:\JFiles\GRADES>javac Grades.java
Grades.java:4: error: ';' expected
        System.out.println("It's not much, but it's a start!")
                                                              ^
1 error

C:\JFiles\GRADES>
```

"Need help?" I asked her.

"I've been trying to fix this for the last ten minutes," she said. "This isn't as easy as it first seems is it??"

"Java requires a lot more attention to detail," I said. "Actually, this is a fairly common error. Remember, in Java, statements need to end with a semicolon. You need to add one following the parenthesis."

Kate smiled, then added the semicolon and recompiled her program successfully. Everyone else in the class who had been having problems managed to fix them on their own. For the most part, they were the errors I noted here or variations thereof. I did spot something in Steve's source file that had not prevented the program from compiling but which might cause a problem down the road.

"What's that?" he asked, when I told him he had a potential problem.

"Look at your source file," I said. "It may not seem like much, but you spelled the class name 'Grades' in lowercase. Everyone else in the class has spelled it as 'Grades.' In the next exercise, when you try to run the program Grades, it will fail unless you spell it in lowercase."

"Is that a big deal?' Linda asked. "Couldn't he just run the program by executing grades in lowercase?"

"Yes, he could," I answered, "but later on in the course you'll see that in some cases it's necessary for the name of your class to match the exact name of the file in which it is saved. In this case, since the word 'public' does not precede the class name, there's a way around it, but it's a good idea to get into the habit of following Java naming conventions by naming your classes with the first letter capitalized."

Ward took me up on my suggestion and changed his source file, then recompiled his program. At this point, everyone had a compiled Bytecode file, and they were anxiously looking forward to running their program. I then distributed this exercise for them to complete.

Exercise 2-3 Executing (Running) Grades.java

In this exercise, you'll run the program you created in Exercise 2-2, Grades.class.

1. Bring up the MS-DOS command prompt application.
2. At the command prompt, change to the directory (folder) containing your Grades.java source file.
3. At the command prompt, run your program by entering **java Grades** and pressing ENTER. You should see the following displayed in your command prompt window:

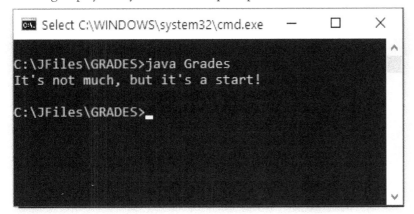

Discussion

As dejected as some members of the class had been while completing the previous exercise, this one produced just the opposite effect: just about everyone's program ran on their first attempt. The only one who had a problem was Peter, who had apparently missed my discussion with Ward concerning naming conventions and had named his class 'grades' and then tried to execute Grades. His problem was relatively easy to fix: either execute 'grades'; or change the name of the class to Grades, recompile, and then run Grades. He chose to be in conformance with the rest of the class and the Java community in general, which capitalizes the first letter of a class name. After he changed the source file and recompiled the program, his program worked fine.

"I know we haven't done all that much," Rhonda said, "but I feel pretty good about what we've done so far. My programming friends all told me how difficult Java was but so far, so good."

"Java can be difficult," I said, "but as you know, here at the university, we have a reputation for doing a pretty good job with beginners. One step at a time, I always say. The next logical step in next week's class will be to give you a Java code overview to show you what the language can do."

It had been a very productive class: everyone now had the beginnings of the Grades Calculation program in place. It had also been a pretty long class. I glanced up at the clock on the wall and realized our class was over, so I dismissed class for the day.

Summary

In this chapter, you were exposed to the nitty gritty of the Java environment. You saw that writing a program in Java is pretty basic. You use an editor (in our case, Notepad) to create a Java source file, compile the program from a command prompt using the Java compiler javac, and then run the program from that same command prompt using the Interpreter Java.

In the next chapter, you'll see the basic building blocks of any computer program: sequence structures, selection structures, and loops.

Chapter 3---Data

In a computer program, data is extremely important. As we saw in Chapter 1, data is brought in or 'input' into a computer program in order to be processed into meaningful output. In this chapter, we'll discuss the concept of data in a computer program. You'll learn about program variables, the different types of Java Data Types, and the many operations that can be performed on that data.

Computer Data

"Data can be a very complex topic," I said to the class at our third meeting, "but it's an extremely important one. Failure to understand data can lead to problems with your programs down the line. What you learn today may seem very theoretical to you, but it will be vital for your future-programming career. Even if you don't see an immediate application for it, look at the information you receive today as something that you can tuck into your programming back pocket for future use."

Variables

"In the Java programs that we write," I said, "the data with which we work will come from three places: the user, in the form of selections that they make, usually from objects that we place on a window; external sources, such as a disk file or a database; or sometimes internal sources in the form of variables."

"Variables?" Rhonda asked.

I explained that variables are placeholders in the computer's memory where we can temporarily store information. Values—numbers and characters, for example—are stored in variables while the program is running. As their name implies, the values of the variables can change at any time.

"I'm a little confused as to why we would create a variable in the first place," Barbara said. "Isn't all of the data that we need—especially in the program we're writing in this class—entered by the user? Why do we need to store anything temporarily?"

"That's a good question, Barbara," I said. "And to a great degree, you're right. Most of the data that computer programs need is entered by the user, or comes from a disk file or database. However, there may be times when your program will need to create and use a variable to store the answer to a question that you have asked of the user, or the result of a calculation, or as we will see a little later on in today's class, to keep track of a counter, which is a variable that counts something."

"You said that variables enable us to store information temporarily," Kate said. "I assume that means until our program ends? A variable can't last beyond the running of a program, can it?"

"For the most part that's true, Kate," I said. "In most other programming languages, variables are born when the program in which they appear starts to execute and die when that program ends. But Java is a little different. Java has a special type of variable called a Class variable, which, we'll see a little later, lives as long as any object that has been created from the class template is running. We'll take a closer look at the Class variable, as well as the other two, Local and Instance variables, later on in today's class."

Our first variable: The Local Variable

I asked everyone to consider a hypothetical program that I hoped would illustrate the need for variables in a program.

"Let's write a Java program," I said, "to take two numbers and display their sum in the console. Later on in the course (next week, in fact), you'll learn that there are ways for the user to communicate with our running program, but for now, the best we can do is to declare two numeric variables, assign values to them, and then display their sum in the console. I should warn you that most of what you will see in this program you haven't learned yet—but you will today."

I then displayed this program on the classroom projector:

```
class Example3_1 {
  public static void main(String[] args) {
    int number1;
    int number2;
```

```
   number1 = 12;
   number2 = 23;
   System.out.println(number1 + number2);
 }
}
```

Note: Java variable names are case sensitive. A variable declared with the name number is considered to be different than a variable declared with the name Number. Be careful!

I saved the program as Example3_1.java, compiled it, and ran it for the class. The following screen was displayed on the classroom projector:

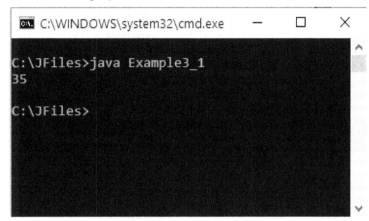

"Let me explain what's going on here," I said. "We saw this line of code last week. It's the first line of code in a Java program, the Class statement. Since this is our first example program in Week 3 of the course, I've named the class Example3_1." I went back to the program and pointed to the line of code that indicated the class name:

```
class Example3_1 {
```

"This line of code we also saw last week," I said, "It's the first line of the **main()** method. Every Java class that runs directly using the Java Interpreter must have a public method named **main()**."

```
public static void main(String[] args) {
```

"What exactly do you mean by that?" Kate asked. "Are you implying there are some classes that won't be executed using the Java Interpreter?"

"That's right, Kate," I answered. "Remember, everything in Java is an object. Last week we created our first piece of the class project puzzle, the Grades class. Grades will be executed using the Java Interpreter, but as the course progresses, we'll also create other classes, such as Student, EnglishStudent, MathStudent, and ScienceStudent, each of which will have their objects instantiated by the Grades class."

"In other words," Dave said, "they won't be executed directly using the Java command-line statement?"

"Exactly, Dave," I said. "In a Java application, there may be a series of classes created, but only one class— sometimes called the main class—will be executed directly by the Java Interpreter. Others, such as the ones I cited here, will have objects instantiated from them within that main class. Those other classes—sometimes called support classes— do not need to have a **main()** method."

I waited to see if anyone had any other questions before continuing.

Declaring a Variable

"This next line of code," I said, "declares an Integer type variable called number1. We'll be discussing exactly what an Integer is in just a few moments."

```
int number1;
```

"In a similar way, this next line of code declares an Integer type variable called number2."

```
int number2;
```

Assigning a Value to a Variable

"Now that we've announced to Java that we wish to have two Integer variables in our program called number1 and number2, these next two lines of code assign values to those variables."

```
number1 = 12;
number2 = 23;
```

"Because both of these variables are declared within a method—the **main()** method—they are called Local variables. That means that the variables and the values they contain can only be seen or accessed by code within the **main()** method. In fact, this next line of code is doing exactly that—accessing the values of the variables number1 and number2, adding them together, and displaying the result in the console using the **println()** method of the System object we saw last week."

```
System.out.println(number1 + number2); } }
```

"What's going on inside those parentheses?" Rhonda asked. "Last week when we used this method, we had 'I love Java!' inside the parentheses within quotation marks."

"In this case, Rhonda," I answered, "we are telling Java to take the value of the variables number1 and number2, add them together, and display them in the console."

"That makes sense," Blaine said. "Although I must confess, I'm still not totally clear on this concept of a variable."

> Note: In Java, variable names must start with either a letter, an underscore, or a dollar sign.

"I like to compare a variable," I said, "to a post office box. When you rent a post office box, you are assigned a box number. When mail for your box arrives, the postal clerk places your mail in your box according to the number you've been assigned. If you need to retrieve your mail, you can use your key to access it because you know the number of your box. Variables in Java are very similar. When you declare a variable, you use this syntax:"

```
int number1;
```

"which tells Java that you wish to declare an Integer type variable with the name number1. This is similar to going to the post office and renting a box. The great thing about Java—and other programs as well—is that you can give the variable an easy-to-remember name that you can recognize later. You don't need to work with a hard-to-remember post office box number. Thereafter, whenever you need to interact with the variable, you use its easy-to-remember name, as we did when we assigned a value to number1 using the Java assignment statement."

```
number1 = 12;
```

"We also did this when we used the variable's name in the **println()** method."

```
System.out.println(number1 + number2);
```

"Do you need to assign a value to a variable after you've declared it?" Chuck asked. "In other words, do you have to initialize it?"

"Excellent question," I said. "For local variables, you must assign a value to local variable prior to referring to it somewhere within your program or you will generate a syntax error when you compile your program. For instance, you couldn't display the value of number1 using the **println()** method unless you had first assigned it a value. Instance variables, as we'll see later, do not have to be initialized, although to improve program readability, it's a good idea."

> Note: Assigning an initial value to a variable is called Initialization

"If Instance variables don't have to be initialized, what values will they have?" Dave asked.

"That depends on the data type of the variable," I said. "We'll learn what these are shortly, but Byte, Short, Int, and Long data types are initialized to 0. Float and Double data types are initialized to 0.0. The Char data type and nonprimitive data types are initialized to something called the Null character. Boolean data types are initialized to the value False."

Declaration and Assignment Combined

"I think some languages permit you to combine the declaration and assignment of a value to a variable," Dave said, "Can you do that in Java?"

"Yes you can combine them Dave," I answered. "Here's the same program using that technique..."

```
class Example3_2 {
  public static void main(String[] args) {
    int number1 = 12;
    int number = 23;
    System.out.println(number1 + number2);
  }
}
```

"…in a language such as Java that tends to be 'wordy'," I said, "programmers frequently look for ways to streamline their code---this is one way to do it…"

```
int number1 = 12;
```

"One more thing I'd like to show you," I said, "is how to make our output in the console a little more user friendly." I displayed this code on the classroom projector:

```
class Example3_3 {
  public static void main(String[] args) {
    int number1 = 12;
    int number2 = 23;
    System.out.print("The answer is ");
    System.out.println(number1 + number2);
  }
}
```

Then I compiled the program and executed it. The following screenshot was displayed on the classroom projector:

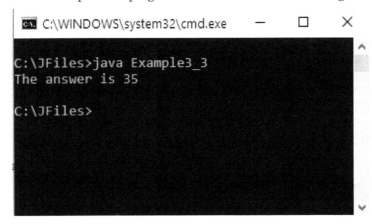

"This line of code," I said,

```
System.out.print("The answer is ");
```

"uses the **print()** method of the System object to display the phrase 'The answer is' in the console.

Notice that this time we execute the **print()** method, not the **println()** method."

"Why is that?" Rhonda asked. "What's the difference between **print()** and **println()**?"

"Observe that the number 35—the result of the addition of the values of the variables number1 and number2—is displayed on the same line as the phrase 'The answer is.' That's the difference: **println()** tells Java to send the output in the console and then to issue a carriage return and line feed to move the current print position to the beginning of the next line; **print()** tells Java to send the output in the console but to leave the current print position exactly where it is. That's why the number 35 is displayed following the space and the word 'is' when we execute this line of code,"

```
System.out.println(number1 + number2);
```

"Can we see what would happen if you used **println()** on both lines of code?" Rose asked.

"Sure thing, Rose." I said and made that change. This is what was displayed:

```
class Example3_4 {
  public static void main(String[] args) {
    int number1 = 12;
    int number2 = 23;
```

```
    System.out.println("The answer is ");
    System.out.println(number1 + number2);
  }
}
```

Then I compiled the program and executed it. The following screenshot was displayed on the classroom projector:

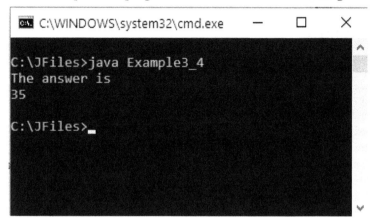

"See the difference?" I asked. "Because we executed the **println()** method to display 'The answer is,' the number 35 was forced to the next line when we displayed it on the console."

"Is it possible to declare more than one variable on the same line of code?" Steve asked.

"Yes you can, Steve," I said. "In fact, you can declare and initialize more than one variable on the same line of code, provided they are all the same data type, like this."

```
int number1 = 12, number2 = 23;
```

"What are the rules for naming a variable?" Jack asked.

"Variables should begin with a lowercase letter," I said, "and can be of any length. But remember this: Variables with long names make coding more difficult, as invariably you'll need to refer to it again somewhere in your code. Make your variable names short but meaningful—you should also avoid single-character variable names such as x, unless it's what the Java documentation refers to as a 'throwaway variable.'"

"Where is this Java documentation that you refer to?" Mary asked.

"You can find it on the Internet at this link," I said, as I displayed it on the classroom projector:

http://java.sun.com/javase/reference/api.jsp

"There you'll find information on naming classes, variables, and constants—something we'll be examining shortly."

I waited to see if there were any other questions before proceeding.

"Bearing in mind," I said, "that Java programmers like to cut down on the number of lines of code that they write, if you wish, you can streamline this code a little bit by using this syntax:"

```
class Example3_5 {
  public static void main(String[] args) {
    int number1 = 12;
    int number2 = 23;
    System.out.println("The answer is " + (number1 + number2));
  }
}
```

I then compiled the program and executed it. The following screenshot was displayed on the classroom projector:

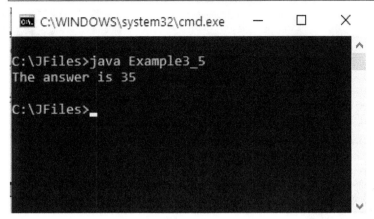

"As you can see, we achieved the same results," I said, "by using something known as 'concatenation.' Concatenation means to join, and in Java, you use the concatenation operator, the + sign, to join a string. In this example, we joined the phrase 'The answer is' to the result of the addition of the values of number1 and number2."

"I've worked in some languages," Dave said, "where concatenating a number such as 35 to a string would have caused the program to bomb, but that didn't happen here."

"What is Dave saying?" Mary asked.

"Dave is pointing out that the number 35 is not a string," I said. "We'll discuss data types in more detail later on in the class, but Dave is right: in some other languages, concatenating a number to a string of characters would cause the program to bomb. Java is doing us a favor here.

If any part of the concatenation operation is a string, then all elements of the operation are treated as if they are strings."

"I don't find the concept as confusing as the number of parentheses," Kate said. "How do you know how many and where to put them?"

"I admit, that can be confusing, Kate," I answered. "One quick rule of thumb is that you must always have an even number of parentheses, and you must have the same number of left parentheses as right parentheses. Aside from that, here are some other hints. The argument to the **println()** method must be contained with parentheses, and because I wanted to concatenate the result of the addition operation of number1 and number2 to the end of the string, I placed that addition operation within parentheses also."

```
System.out.println("The answer is " + (number1 + number2));
```

"If I hadn't done that and had instead written the code like this," I entered the following code and displayed it on the classroom projector:

```
class Example3_6 {
  public static void main(String[] args) {
    int number1 = 12;
    int number2 = 23;
    System.out.println("The answer is " + number1 + number2);
  }
}
```

"we would have gotten and entirely different result."

I then compiled the program and executed it. The following screenshot was displayed on the classroom projector:

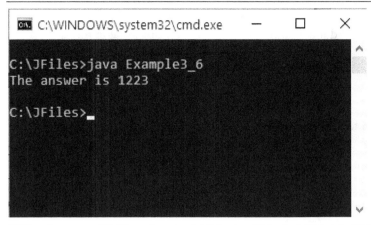

"What happened?" Rhonda asked. "12 plus 23 isn't 1,223, it's 35!"

"What happened here," I said, "is that we wound up concatenating the string 12 to the end of the string 'The answer is ' and then concatenating the string '23' to the end of that concatenated string--like this…"

"All of which proves that a number and a String are two different animals!" Ward said. "So are you saying placing parentheses around the addition operation caused the addition to be performed first--and that sum--35--was then concatenated to the string 'The answer is '?"

"Exactly right Ward," I said.

I waited to see if there were any questions about variables.

"You mentioned that there are two other types of variables that we can declare in Java," Barbara said. "Will you be showing us those today?"

"I'll mention the other two types, Instance variables and Class variables, when we start to get deeper into creating our own classes and objects. For today, we'll only be discussing Local variables, which are variables declared and used in a method."

A Quick Look at Instance and Static Variables

"I know this may be premature," Mary said, "but even if you want to postpone a discussion of them for a later time, can we see what the declaration of an Instance and Static variable looks like?"

"That's probably a good idea," I agreed, after thinking about it for a minute. "Instance variables are variables declared outside of a method, and Class variables look just like Instance variables except they are declared with the keyword Static, like this." I entered the following code and displayed it on the classroom projector:

```
class Example3_7 {
  int number3 = 44; // instance variable
  static int number4 = 55; // class variable
  public static void main(String[] args) {
    int number1 = 12;
    int number2 = 23;
    System.out.println("The answer is " + (number1 + number2));
  }
}
```

"So *number3* is an Instance variable because it appears above the **main()** method?" Rhonda said.

"Not so much that it's above the **main()** method, Rhonda," I answered, "but because it appears outside *any* method."

"And preceding the variable declaration of number4 with the keyword Static is what makes it a Static variable?" Ward asked.

"Exactly," I said. "The declaration of these other variable types isn't difficult; it's understanding how they affect the behavior of our program that's harder to understand. And that's something we'll learn more about in the upcoming weeks."

Variable Scope and Lifetime

"I think I understand what a variable is and what it's used for," Rhonda said. "But what do the programmers I work with mean when they talk about variable scope and lifetime?"

"Scope and lifetime?" Chuck asked, adding emphasis to Rhonda's question.

"Scope," I said, "refers to what parts of your Java program can **see** the variable you've declared. As I've mentioned, some Java programs that we write will consist of more than one class in which one class, called the Startup class—the one containing a **main()** method—creates or instantiates objects from the other support classes. Scope is a term that describes whether a variable declared in **Class1** can be seen in **Class2**."

"So what's the answer?" Ward asked.

"I suspect," Dave chimed in, "that all Local variables can be seen only in the method in which they are declared?"

"That's right, Dave," I said. "Local variables have what is known as Local scope. If you want to be able to access variables declared in other classes, you have two choices: Instance variables or Class variables." We'll be talking about those in the coming weeks."

"I'm a little confused," Rhonda said. "Is local scope a good thing or a bad thing?"

"The rule of thumb," I said, "is to declare your variable with as narrow a scope as possible. Provided its value does not need to be accessible to code in other methods, local scope is a good thing. On the other hand, if you need to have the value of that variable accessible from another method in your class, then that's—"

"A bad thing!" Rhonda answered, finishing my sentence, and obviously understanding what I was getting at. "OK, I think I'm beginning to understand. Declaring variables requires a bit more thought than I believed."

"If you wanted to make the value of that variable visible to other methods in your class," Steve said, "that's when you would declare it as an Instance variable."

"What about lifetime?" Lou asked.

"Lifetime refers to how **long** a variable, once declared, lives," I said. "Again, as was the case with Scope, your choice will depend upon the type of variable that you declare. Local variables exist for as long as the method is executing: as soon as the method ends, the variable---and its value---goes away. Instance variables, as we'll see a few weeks from now, exist for as long as the object, created from the class, exists. And Class variables are the most interesting of all: these variables exist as long as any object created from their template or blueprint exists. We'll learn more about these in a future class."

"Can I ask a question that I'm not entirely sure is on-topic?" Barbara asked. "You keep talking about objects—and I know I'll become more comfortable with these as time goes by—but where exactly do these objects exist?"

"Objects exist in the computer's memory," I said. "I know the name sounds intimidating, but we'll see, when we start creating more robust objects of our own, that objects consist of data and procedures called functions or methods to operate on that data. When objects are created from a class, they are set up in the computer's memory with space made available for their data and for these methods. As long as a program maintains a reference to the object—that is, the program is using the object in some way by executing its code or referring to its data—the computer's Operating System maintains a reference to it. When no programs are referring to the object any longer (it's possible for more than one program to refer to the same object), the operating system decides it is no longer being referenced and uses the space it occupied in memory for something else. Does that help?"

> **NOTE: A reference is a pointer to an object in the computer's memory**

"That's a little better," Barbara answered, "but, like a lot of things, your answer has generated more questions in my mind. But I'll hold off on those for a while."

I didn't dissuade her. Java is highly object oriented, and when it comes to objects, everyone (beginners and experienced programmers alike) needs some time to acquire a comfort level. My experience teaching Java indicated that time and practice would eventually give my students this comfort level.

Constants

"So far," I said, "we've spent most of this class looking at program variables, which are placeholders in memory given an easy-to-remember name that contain a value. Now it's time to take a look at constants."

"Constant?" Linda asked. "That sounds like it should be the opposite of a variable."

"You're right, Linda," I said. "That's exactly how it sounds, but the constant is very much like a variable. A Java constant, like a variable, is a placeholder in the computer's memory that's given an easy-to-remember name that holds a value. Unlike a variable, however, once you assign it a value, its value can never be changed."

"How are constants declared?" Peter asked.

"You declare constants in a manner similar to a variable," I answered. "In Java, you use the keyword **final** to designate a constant, like this." I entered the following code and displayed it on the classroom projector:

```
class Example3_8 {
   public static void main(String[] args) {
      int number1 = 12;
      final int BOOSTER = 100;
      System.out.println("The answer is " + (number1 + BOOSTER));
   }
}
```

I then compiled the program and executed it. The following screenshot was displayed on the classroom projector:

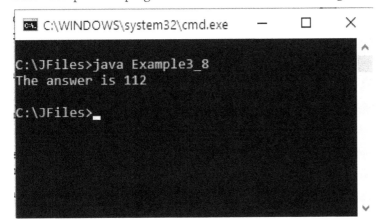

"It's this line of code that tells Java that BOOSTER is a constant," I said.

```
final int BOOSTER = 100;
```

"In Java, as in many other languages" I continued, "by convention, constants are named using all capital letters. Once we've declared and initialized the constant, we can use it in our code in the same way we would a variable. In this case, we take the value of the constant BOOSTER, add it to the value of the variable number1, and display the result in the console."

"What's the purpose of a constant?" Steve asked. "That is, when should you use one?"

I thought for a moment. "One good rule of thumb is this: whenever you find yourself declaring a variable and assigning it a value that never changes, it should probably be a constant. Also, if you use numeric literals in your code—a numeric literal is just a number—consider using a constant instead. It can save you some headaches down the road."

"I was going to ask," Kate said, "why you didn't simply take the number 100 and add it to the value of the variable number1 instead? Is it more efficient to use a constant?"

"Using a constant makes your program more readable and easier to modify," I answered.

"Can you give us an example to illustrate why?" Linda asked.

"Sure thing, Linda," I replied. "Let's say you are writing a program to calculate payroll. Let's assume that there's a State Income tax rate equal to 1 percent of an employee's gross pay. Somewhere in your program, you are going to need to multiply the gross pay amount by 0.01, and in Java, that would look something like this."

```
GrossPayAmount * .01
```

"where GrossPayAmount is a variable in which you've stored the employee's gross pay. Now, further suppose you perform this same calculation in several different places in your program, each time multiplying the value of the GrossPayAmount variable pay by the number 0.01. Now let me ask this question: What happens to your program if the State Income tax rate changes from 1 percent to 2 percent?"

"Obviously," Dave said, "we would have to change the number we've been using from 0.01 to 0.02."

"That's right Dave," I agreed, "and because we have that number hard-coded in several places in our program, we would need to go through each and every line of code in our program looking for the value 0.01 and then change it to 0.02."

"How can a constant help here?" Steve asked.

"Instead of using the number 0.01 in our calculations a number of times," I answered, "we could instead declare a constant called STATETAXRATE, assign it the value of 0.01, and then use the constant in all of our calculations instead, like this...."

```
GrossPayAmount * STATETAXRATE
```

"I see now," Rhonda said. "So if the state tax rate changes, since we used the name of the constant, not the number 0.01 in our calculation, we only need to change the declaration statement for the constant to reflect the new value."

"That's perfect, Rhonda, " I said.

"Can we see that constant declaration?" Barbara asked. I displayed the declaration on the classroom projector:

```
final double STATETAXRATE = .01
```

"As I mentioned before," I said, "by convention, constants are named using all capital letters.

This makes it pretty easy to identify constants in your code."

"I see what you mean," Dave said, "about a constant being very similar to a variable. In fact, they don't seem very different at all. I guess the primary difference is that a constant, once assigned a value, can never be changed."

"Why did you declare the constant STATETAXRATE as a double?" Kate asked. "Wouldn't a float data type be a better choice?"

"Good question, Kate," I said. "As you'll see in just a few minutes, the float data type is not a good choice for very small numbers—in fact, the Java compiler would flag that line of code as an error if we tried to assign a number that small to a float data type."

"I have a question," Rhonda said. "In your example of the state tax rate, couldn't you have declared a variable, assigned it a value and then used that variable in all of your calculations?"

"You've raised an interesting point," I said. "In fact, that's what a lot of programmers do, which is why I suggested that if you declare a variable, assign it a value, and the value of the variable never changes, it should have been declared a constant instead. But you should bear in mind that there are two big benefits to using constants. First, and perhaps most importantly, it's possible to declare a constant as a Class constant—that is, to declare it outside of any particular method by using the Static keyword. In Java, when you declare a variable or a constant at the class level, only one copy of the value is stored in the computer's memory, no matter how many instances of your class might be running at one time. You may not realize why this can be a 'good thing' right now, but it can help solve troublesome programming problems—more on that in a few weeks.

"Does that happen all that often?" Ward asked. "How many instances of the program we are writing for the English, Math, and Science Departments will be running simultaneously?"

"In the case of our class project, Ward," I answered, "you're probably right. But don't forget, after this class, you may go on to do more advanced Java programming, perhaps even writing programs for the Internet. How many people do you think access your favorite web site simultaneously? I bet you my salary for this course that most likely when you connect to that web site, a Java object of some kind is being created from a class template somewhere."

"And your point is that if that class uses a Class constant, there's only one constant loaded in the web server's memory, is that right?" Dave asked.

"Exactly, Dave," I said, "and the same would apply to a Class variable."

"You said there are two big benefits to using constants in our program," Barbara asked.

"What's the second?"

"Secondly," I continued, "the value of a constant can't be accidentally changed once it's been declared. This can prevent disastrous results in a program. The bottom line is: if you declare a variable, assign it a value, and there is no chance that the value of that variable will ever change, what you have there is a constant, and you should declare it as such."

I realized that we had been working pretty intensely for some time and, since there were no more questions, I suggested that we take a break.

Java Data Types

Resuming after a 15-minute break, I said, "Let's take a closer look at the available data types in Java. An understanding of the Java data types and their characteristics is essential. We saw earlier that in order to declare a variable or a constant, we need to designate its data type. In our simple examples this morning, we used Int for an Integer data type. Now it's time to learn what the others are."

"How many data types are there in Java?" Rose asked.

"There are eight basic data types," I said, "that are known as primitive data types. In addition to its eight primitive data types, as I've mentioned, Java also allows you to work with objects using reference data types."

"What type of objects?" Rhonda asked.

"Objects," I said, "such as the System object we've used to output in the console and also objects that we'll create from classes that we build. In order to work with an object, we first need to declare a variable of that object's class name. For instance, as we progress in working with our class project, we'll eventually create a class called Student. You'll see that in order to create an instance of a Student object, we will first need to declare a variable of type Student. We'll discuss how to do that in just a few weeks."

I could see some confusion on my students' faces, but they seemed to trust me enough to wait for a fuller explanation until then.

> **NOTE: A reference data type is one whose value is actually an address in your computer's memory that points to an object**

"The choice of a data type for your variable," I said, "can be crucial to the proper operation of your program. Each Java data type has unique memory requirements, along with capabilities and operations that you can perform on them. Declaring a data type that is not appropriate for the data you wish to store in it is a common beginner's error and can result in a range of problems, from your program not compiling to it compiling and running but giving incorrect results."

I then displayed this list of the 8 Java primitive data types on the classroom projector:

Data Type	Storage Size	Value Range
byte	8 bits	−128 to 127
Short	16 bits	−32,768 to 32,767
Int	32 bits	−2,147,483,648 to 2,147,483,647
Long	64 bits	-9.2×10^{15} to 9.2×10^{15}
Float	32 bits	-3.4×10^{-45} to 3.4×10^{38}
Double	64 bits	-1.8×10^{308} to 1.8×10^{308}
Char	16 bits	0 to 65,535
Boolean	1 bit	False or True

"The first six data types displayed in the table," I said, "are numeric data types. Of the final two, Char is a character data type, and Boolean is a special data type with only two possible values: True or False. As you can see, each data type has different storage requirements in the computer's memory and different range values. For the next half-hour or so we'll discuss all of these data types in detail. Let's start with the data types that are used to store numbers."

Numeric Data Types

I began to discuss the Java Numeric data types. "You should declare your variable as one of the Java Numeric data types," I said, "when you know you will be using that variable to store a number which will later be used in a mathematical calculation."

"Like we did when we declared number1 and number2 variables of the Int data type?" Blaine asked.

"That's right Blaine," I said. "In Java, there are two categories of numeric data types: Integers, which are whole numbers, such as 1 or 2, and Floating Point numbers, which are numbers with a fractional part, such as 1.2 or 2.4."

"What about a telephone number or a social security number?" Ward asked. "Those both contain numbers but are usually written with dashes in them. Should we use a numeric data type to store these?"

"A String data type is a better choice for those two," I said. "Although both of the examples you cite contain numbers, neither one of them is likely to be used in a mathematical calculation."

"I don't see a String data type in the list of data types you displayed," Linda said. "Did you forget to include in your table?"

"Good question, Linda," I said. "The String data type is technically not a primitive data type. The String data type is actually an object—but don't worry, we'll be discussing the String data type later on in today's class. Here are some general recommendations on the numeric data types:"

- Choose Byte, Short, Int, and Long data types to store whole numbers (called Integers) such as 23, 45, and 34470.

- Choose Float or Double data types to store numbers with fractions such as 3.1416, 23.12, 45.22, or 357644.67. In Java, the Float data type is not as precise as the Double. Therefore, if accuracy is important, select the Double data type.

- Select a data type appropriate for the values you wish to store in the variable. If the data type has a range much larger than you will need, you will waste valuable computer memory. If the data type has a range smaller than the value you attempt to store in it, your program may bomb.

"What do you mean when you say the program will bomb?" Rhonda asked.

"That's a term that means the program will come to an abnormal termination," I said. "For instance, look at this code in which I've declared a Byte data type variable, and I am attempting to assign a value to it beyond the range for a byte data type." I displayed the following code:

```
class Example3_9 {
  public static void main(String[] args) {
    byte number1 = 1234;        //byte upper range is 127
    System.out.println("The value of number1 is " + number1));
  }
}
```

I then compiled the program but received this error message during the compile:

```
C:\WINDOWS\system32\cmd.exe                    —    □    ✕

C:\JFiles>javac Example3_9.java
Example3_9.java:5: error: incompatible types: possible lossy conve
rsion from int to byte
        byte number1 = 1234;                    //byte upper range is 127
                       ^
1 error

C:\JFiles>
```

"In this case," I said, "the program would not compile successfully because Java recognized that the value we were assigning to the variable would exceed its upper range. However, this program would have compiled successfully if, instead of assigning a numeric literal to the variable, we were assigning a value we read from an external source such as a data file or a web page."

"In which case, the program would then bomb when we ran it, is that right?" Joe asked.

"Absolutely correct," I said. "This example illustrates how important it is to pick the appropriate data type for our variables."

Byte

"So what kind of variables are candidates to be Byte data types?" Bob asked.

"The Byte data type can hold only whole, positive numbers; it can't be used to store a number with a fractional part. The size of the number that you can store in a Byte data type is not very large—from –128 to 127. Only use the Byte data type if you are certain that the number you will store in it is within that range—otherwise you will generate an error."

"Can you give us an example of a real world example for a Byte data type?" Kate asked.

"How about a variable to store Fahrenheit temperature readings in Minneapolis? I suggested. "It gets pretty cold in Minneapolis, so we need a data type capable of storing negative numbers. And I know for a fact that the upper range of 127 is more than enough for the summertime in Minneapolis."

Short

"Next in line," I said, "in terms of storage capacity, is the Short data type, also known as the Short Integer. Like the Byte data type, the Short data type can store only a whole number. Its storage range is much larger than the Byte data type: –32,768 to 32,767."

Int

"Next up is the Int data type," I said, "which stands for Integer. Int is a larger version of the Short data type. Like all the numeric data types we've discussed so far, the Int data type can store only whole numbers. Its storage range is pretty large: –2,147,483,648 to 2,147,483,647."

"What happens if you try to store a number with a fractional part in a variable declared as an int?" Dave asked.

"You'll get the same type of compiler error we saw when we tried to store a value too large for the Byte data type," I said. "When Java can recognize that you're going to get yourself in trouble, it won't even allow you to compile the program."

"Can you give us some examples of when we would want to use the various data types?" Rose asked.

"Sure thing, Rose," I said. "As I mentioned, we could use the Byte data type to store the temperatures in Minneapolis. We could also use the Byte data type to store the number of students in this class. Because it's a lot colder at the North Pole, the Byte data type won't do, so we would need to use a Short data type to store the temperature at the North Pole. Finally, we could use the Int data type to store the number of people in the United States, but it wouldn't suffice to store the number of people in the world. That would require the Long data type, which we're about to examine."

"Would it hurt to declare all of our numeric variables as an Int?" Linda asked.

"Declaring a variable larger than it needs to be is a waste of storage," I said. "As you can see from our table, the Int data type requires 32 bits or 4 bytes of storage. That may not seem like a big deal, but if you know that the values you'll be storing in a variable require the storage capacity of a Short data type, which requires only 16 bits or 2 bytes of storage, you should declare the variable as a Short. This type of attention to detail can make your program run faster, reduce its runtime memory requirements, and will be something that a prospective employer will be looking for when examining any sample code you write or bring to a job interview."

Long

"Next up is the Long data type," I said, "which is the largest version of the Integer data types. Like all the numeric data types we've discussed so far, the Long data type can store whole numbers only. Its storage range is huge: –9.2 × 1015 to 9.2 × 1015."

"What kind of number is that?" Peter asked.

"Unless you're fresh from a Math class," I said, "you may have trouble reading that range, since it's expressed in a format known as scientific or exponential notation, which is a special notation used to represent very large numbers. The positive range for this number is read as '9.2 multiplied by 10 raised to the 15th power.' That's a pretty large number, and if we were to write out the range in normal notation, it would look like this:"

–9,200,000,000,000,000 to 9,200,000,000,000,000

"Notice," I continued, "that there are 15 numbers that follow the leading 9—that's the significance of the characters 1015. Trying to write out the range for the Float data type is a great deal more difficult, since each end of the range has 38 zeros in it. And for the Double data type, each range has 308 zeroes in it. Quite honestly, we wouldn't have room on a piece of paper to write that number—that's why larger numbers like this are represented with exponential or scientific notation to represent the number."

"I'm sold," Kate said laughing. "I guess any way you look at it, those are huge numbers. I'm not likely to think of a number that requires those values."

"I know that the range for a Long data type is large," Valerie said, "but I'm sure there are numbers in common, ordinary life, such as the number of stars in the sky, for instance, that even the Long data type can't handle. What do we do then?"

"That's when we need to use either the Float or Double data type," I said.

Float

"The difference between the Float and Double data types and the Integer data types that we've examined is that both the Float and Double can store values that mathematicians call real numbers, which are numbers with fractional parts. You may also hear the Single and Double data types referred to as Floating-Point data types."

I explained that variables declared as Float data types require 32 bits or 4 bytes of computer memory to hold them. Values for the Float data type can range from -3.4×10^{38} to 3.4×10^{38}. If you need to store a value with a fractional part in a variable, you'll need to use one of these two data types. It's significant to note that the Float data type is not nearly as precise as the Double. In fact, if you try to assign a very small number to a Float data type, the Java compiler will flag that line of code as an error. For very small or very large numbers, choose the Double data type instead."

Double

"Just as the Long data type is really a bigger version of the Int data type," I said, "the Double data type is a bigger version of the float."

I explained that variables declared as Double data types require 64 bits or 8 bytes of computer memory. Values for the Double can range from 5.0×10^{-324} to 1.7×10^{308}.

"If you take the upper limit for the Float data type," I said, "and add about 263 zeros to it, that will give a good idea for the upper limit of the Double!"

I doubted there was anyone in the class who could think of a value that would exceed the range for the double data type.

Nonnumeric Data Types

"We've discussed six data types of the eight primitive data types that Java has to offer," I said. "We'll finish our discussion of data types by looking at the special Boolean data type, followed by two character type data types: the Char data type and the String data type."

Boolean

"Boolean data types," I said, "can have only two possible values: True or False." I displayed this code on the classroom projector:

```
class Example3_10 {
  public static void main(String[] args) {
    boolean married = true;
    boolean retired = false;
    System.out.println("The value of married is " + married);
    System.out.println("The value of retired is " + retired);
  }
}
```

I then compiled the program and executed it. The following screenshot was displayed on the classroom projector:

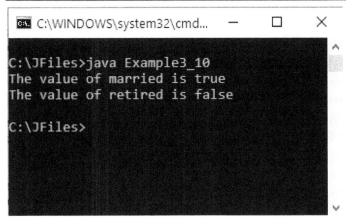

I explained that I had declared two Boolean variables, one called married and the other retired, and then assigned the values True and False to the respective variables.

"What we've done here," I said, "is to declare two Boolean variables: one to represent someone's marital status and the other to represent their retirement status. The Boolean variable is ideal to use when the value of the variable can only be a True-False or a Yes-No outcome. Notice how the assignment of true or false to a Boolean variable is made without enclosing it within quotation marks or apostrophes, something that beginning students sometime do."

Char

"The Char data type is used to store a single character," I continued. "Java documentation indicates that the storage requirement for this data type is 16 bits or 2 bytes and that the value range is 0 to 65,535."

"I thought this was a Character data type," Kate said. "Why is the value range expressed in numbers?"

"We're not talking about storing numbers per se here," I said. "We're talking about storing numbers that equate to a character, like the letter C or any of the characters you see on the keyboard."

"Why do we need a data type so large to store a single character?" Ward asked. "As I recall, ASCII code is used to represent characters—and the ASCII values range from 0 to 255."

"That's true, Ward," I said. "Many languages use the ASCII code to represent characters, but ASCII is an older coding scheme," I said. "Since Java is such a new programming language, it uses the new Unicode standard, which is capable of displaying character sets from every language and alphabet in existence. As a result, the Char data type requires an extra byte of storage, which is why its range of values is so high."

"Would an assignment to a Char data type be the same as the assignment of a number?" Linda asked.

"Assigning values to a Char data type is different than assigning values to a numeric or Boolean variable," I said. "Let me show you." I entered the following code on the classroom projector:

```
class Example3_11 {
public static void main(String[] args) {
    char character1 = 'a';
    System.out.println("The value of character1 is " + character1);
  }
}
```

"Assignments to a Char data type are done by enclosing the character within apostrophes, not quotation marks."

"Can you assign more than one character to a Char data type?" Mary asked.

"No, you can't, Mary," I said. "The Char data type is limited to storing a single character. If you try to assign more than one character to a Char data type, you'll generate an error when you compile your program."

The String Object

"Suppose you need to store more than one character in a variable then?" Blaine asked.

"If you need to store more than one character in a variable," I said, "you'll need to declare a String data type instead. Strictly speaking, a String is not a primitive data type. In Java, a String is an object, but a String variable is declared just like any other data type. However, the assignment of characters to a String variable is slightly different from the Char data type. Let me show you." I entered the following code:

```
class Example3_12 {
  public static void main(String[] args) {
    String string1 = "John Smiley";
    System.out.println("The value of string1 is " + string1);
  }
}
```

"Assignments to a String data type are done by enclosing the character within quotation marks, not apostrophes as we used with the Char data type."

"I just realized," Rhonda said, "that when we assign values to a numeric variable, we don't use apostrophes or quotation marks."

"That's right, Rhonda," I said. I pointed out some different lines of code on the classroom projector. "Numeric literals—numbers—are not sandwiched in any way:"

```
int number1 = 12;
```

"Char variables are assigned using apostrophes like this:"

```
char character1 = 'a';
```

"And String variables are assigned using quotation marks like this:"

```
String String1 = "John Smiley";
```

"Is it important that the word 'String' be spelled that way?" Jack asked. "I noticed that when you declared the other data types, they were all in lowercase. I tried to spell 'String' in lowercase and my program wouldn't compile—I got an error message, something about resolving a symbol."

"That's a good question, Jack." I said. "You're right. When we declared the Java primitive data types, we designated the type in lowercase, such as int and byte. Primitive data types are declared using lowercase. However, the data type String is different—String is the name of a Java object, and since Java is case sensitive, the object name must be spelled exactly the way the class is, which is 'String.' That's why when you spelled 'String' in lowercase, the compiler told you it couldn't resolve the symbol. In other words, it was trying to tell you that there is no class spelled 'string.'"

"Java sure is picky, isn't it?" Lou said.

"When it comes to class names—actually any names at all—Java is very much case sensitive," I said. "In the same way, if you declare a variable as number1 but then refer to it elsewhere in your code as Number1, you'll get that same unresolved symbol error."

No one had any other questions about Java data types, and so, after a quick break, we moved onto a discussion of data operations.

Operations on Data

"Since you now all know something about Java's data types," I said after the break, "now's the time to learn how to perform operations on that data. Let's start with arithmetic operations."

Arithmetic Operations

I explained that arithmetic operations are performed on data stored in numeric variables or numeric constants.

"You can't perform arithmetic operations on any other kind of data," I said. "If you try, you'll either get a compiler error or a runtime error. Let's look at the various arithmetic operations available in Java."

I paused a moment before continuing.

"Before I begin," I said, "it's important to note that most operations are performed on operands. Operands appear on either side of an operator, and when the statement is executed, some result is generated. You have several choices as to what to do with this result. You can choose to ignore it or discard it. You can assign it to a variable, or you can use it in an expression of some kind, as we did earlier today when we displayed the result of an addition operation in the console by using it with the **println()** method. Here's a list of the Java arithmetic operators:"

Operator	Meaning	Example
+	Addition	11 + 22
−	Subtraction	22 − 11

*	Multiplication	5 * 6	
/	Division	21 / 3	
%	Modulus	12 % 2	
++	Adds 1 to the value of a variable	x++	
--	Subtracts 1 from the value of a variable	x--	

The Addition Operator (+)

"The addition operation (+) adds two operands," I said, as I displayed this example of the addition operation on the classroom projector:

```
number3 = number1 + number2;
```

"In this example, we're taking the result of the addition of the variables number1 and number2 and assigning that value to the variable number3. Notice that I didn't say that the addition operation adds two numbers—that's not necessarily the case, as it wasn't here. In Java, an expression can be a number, a variable, a constant, or any expression that results in a number. Ultimately, as long as Java can evaluate the expression as a number, the addition operation will work."

"What do you mean when you say evaluate?" Kate asked.

"When Java evaluates an expression," I replied, "it examines the expression, substituting actual values for any variables or constants that it finds."

I took a moment to emphasize that Java performs operations on only one pair of operands at one time. "That means that even a complex expression like this will be done one step at a time:"

```
number4 = number1 + number2 + number3;
```

"We'll learn more about complex expressions like this later," I promised.

"What's an operand, again?" Ward asked.

"An operand is something to the left or right of the operator symbol," I said. "No matter how many operators appear in an expression, Java performs an operation on just two operands at a time."

"That's a little surprising to me," Rhonda said. "Are you saying that no matter how fast my PC is, it still performs arithmetic the way I was taught in school, one step at a time?"

"That's right, Rhonda," I said. "One operation at a time—at the speed of light!" I then displayed this program from Example3_5 to my students once more:

```
class Example3_5 {
  public static void main(String[] args) {
    int number1 = 12;
    int number2 = 23;
    System.out.println("The answer is " + (number1 + number2));
  }
}
```

"Remember this one?" I asked. "Here we're taking the result of the addition operation of number1 and number2 and using it as an expression with the **println()** method of the System object. The parentheses around the addition operation ensures that it is executed first, prior to its concatenation to the string 'The answer is '."

"In this example," Linda said, "you first assigned values to variables and then performed the addition operation on the value of the variables. Is it possible to perform the addition on numeric literals?"

"Yes you can," I said, as I displayed this code:

```
class Example3_13 {
  public static void main(String[] args) {
    System.out.println("The answer is " + (12 + 23));
  }
}
```

I compiled and ran the program and, once again, the number 35 was displayed in the console.

"What are the numeric literals that Linda was talking about?" Rhonda asked. "Are those the numbers in the **println()** method?"

"Exactly, Rhonda," I replied. "Those are the numeric literals." I waited to see if there were any other questions before moving onto the subtraction operator.

The Subtraction Operator (-)

"As you may have guessed," I said, "the subtraction operator (-) works by subtracting one operand from another and returning a result. More precisely, it subtracts the operand on the **right** side of the subtraction operator from the operand on the **left**. Look at this example:"

```java
class Example3_14 {
  public static void main(String[] args) {
    int number1 = 44;
    int number2 = 33;
    int result = 0;
    result = number1 - number2;
    System.out.println("The answer is " + result);
  }
}
```

I then compiled the program and executed it. The following screenshot was displayed on the classroom projector:

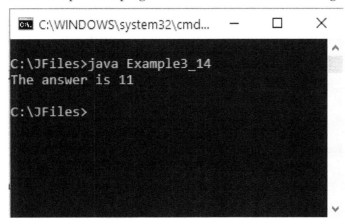

"As you can see," I said, "number2 was subtracted from number1, and the result was then—"

"You switched things up a bit here," Ward interrupted.

"What do you mean?" I answered.

"You declared an extra variable called *result*," he answered.

"That's right," I said. "I wanted to show you how you can assign the result of the subtraction operation to another variable. In this case, I called that variable *result*, but we could call it anything we want."

The Multiplication Operator (*)

"The multiplication operator (*) multiplies two operands," I said.

"Now this is a little different than what I used in school," Mary said. "In school, we used the letter X to denote multiplication."

"I did as well," I said, "but the computer uses the asterisk instead—except for the operator, everything works as you would expect." I displayed the following code on the classroom projector:

```java
class Example3_15 {
  public static void main(String[] args) {
    int number1 = 4;
    int number2 = 3;
    int result = 0;
    result = number1 * number2;
    System.out.println("The answer is " + result);
  }
}
```

I then compiled the program and executed it. The following screenshot was displayed on the classroom projector:

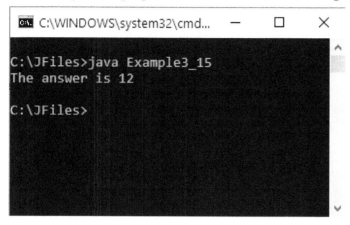

The Division Operator (/)

"The division operator (/) works by dividing one operand from another and returning a result. In actuality, it divides the operand on the left side of the division operator by the operand on the right. Division can be a little tricky in Java because you must be conscious that the result may be something other than an integer—that has implications if you decide to assign the result to a variable that you have declared as an Integer. Look at this example:"

```java
class Example3_16 {
  public static void main(String[] args) {
    int number1 = 5;
    int number2 = 2;
    int result = 0;
    result = number1 / number2;
    System.out.println("The answer is " + result);
  }
}
```

I then compiled the program and executed it. The following screenshot was displayed on the classroom projector:

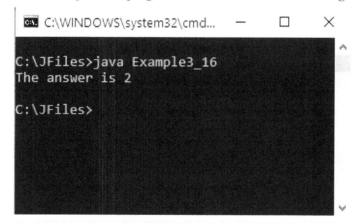

Don't Forget: If typing these examples and exercises isn't something you want to do, feel free to follow this link to find and download the completed solutions for all of the examples and exercises in the book. Just click on the Java book, then follow the link entitled exercises ☺

http://www.johnsmiley.com/main/books.htm

"Wait a minute," Linda said. "That answer's not correct—it should be 2.5. It looks like we got an integer result."

"That's exactly the problem I was alluding to a moment ago," I answered. "Because we assigned the result of the subtraction operation to an Integer variable, Java truncated, not rounded, our result. If this program had been one of the many pieces of a critical application, like the computer program that keeps the International Space Station aloft, we would have a serious problem."

"What can we do to fix this?" Ward asked.

"Let's change the data type for our *result* variable and see if that helps," I answered. I changed the code as follows:

```java
class Example3_17 {
  public static void main(String[] args) {
    int number1 = 5;
    int number2 = 2;
    float result = 0;
    result = number1 / number2;
    System.out.println("The answer is " + result);
  }
}
```

I then compiled the program and executed it. The following screenshot was displayed on the classroom projector:

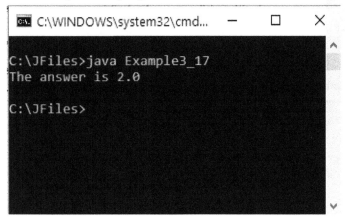

"The answer's still wrong." Rose said. "Although this time we have a fraction, it looks like Java lost the remainder."

"You're right, Rose," I said. "The answer should be 2.5, and this time around the answer displayed was 2.0. The problem here is that Java has rules for dealing with divergent data types. One of these rules is that when Java divides one integer by another, the result will always be an integer, but because we assigned that integer result to a Float variable, the displayed answer had a decimal point."

"Should we have declared number1 and number2 as float types?" Kate asked.

"You hit the nail on the head, Kate," I said. "In order to calculate a result that is a Float data type, the two operands in the division operator need to be float data types also. Like this." I showed them this code:

```java
class Example3_18 {
  public static void main(String[] args) {
    float number1 = 5;
    float number2 = 2;
    float result = 0;
    result = number1 / number2;
    System.out.println("The answer is " + result);
  }
}
```

I then compiled the program and executed it. The following screenshot was displayed on the classroom projector:

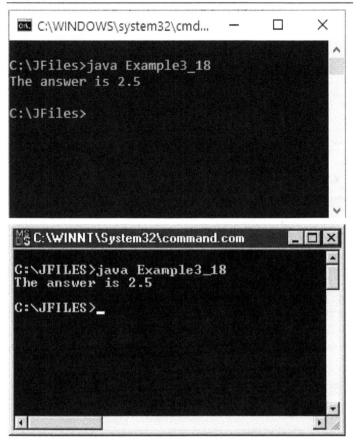

"That's better," Steve said. "Do we need to be this careful in Java? In Visual Basic, it seemed that a lot of this was taken care of for us."

"You're right, Steve," I replied. "In some languages, particularly Visual Basic, you hardly need to concern yourself with the data types you are dealing with when performing operations. Java is different. If you're not careful, what your program does versus what you intend it to do may be vastly different. Most languages expect the programmer to be aware of the types of data they are working with and to be careful when working with that data."

The Modulus Operator (%)

I continued. "A few moments ago, Rose mentioned the remainder that we lost when we performed division with two integer operands. The Modulus operation—sometimes called the Remainder Operation—deals with remainders. In fact, you can think of the Modulus operation as the reverse: the result of the Modulus operation is the remainder of a division operation. For instance, 5 divided by 2 is 2, with a remainder of 1. It's that simple, really."

"What's the symbol for the Modulus operation?" Ward asked.

"It's the percent (%) sign," I said. "Let me give you an example of the Modulus operation:"

```
class Example3_19 {
  public static void main(String[] args) {
    int number1 = 5;
    int number2 = 2;
    int result = 0;
    result = number1 % number2;
    System.out.println("The answer is " + result);
  }
}
```

I then compiled the program and executed it. The following screenshot was displayed on the classroom projector:

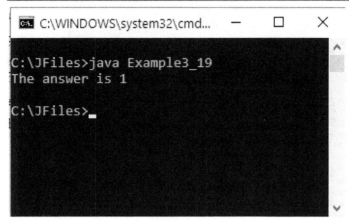

"As you can see," I said, "the Modulus operation has resulted in the remainder of 1 being displayed in the console."

"I think I'm OK with the mechanics of the Modulus operation," Rhonda said. "I just can't understand **why** you would ever want to use it. Can you give us an example?"

"The usefulness of the Modulus operation," I said, "is not as obvious as some of the other arithmetic operators. One of the more useful characteristics of a Modulus operation is that if the result of the Modulus operation is zero, you know that the first expression is **evenly divisible** by the second expression. Even better, if you perform the Modulus operation of operand1 by 2, and the result is 0, that means that operand1 was an **even** number. If the result is 1, operand1 was **odd**."

I gave everyone a chance to think about this for a moment.

"So if you *mod* a number by 2, there are only two possible results, 0 and 1?" Ward asked.

"That's right, Ward," I said. "Let me show you." I displayed the following:

```java
class Example3_20 {
  public static void main(String[] args) {
    int oddnumber1 = 3;
    int evennumber1 = 4;
    int oddnumber2 = 5;
    int evennumber2 = 6;
    int result = 0;
    result = oddnumber1 % 2;
    System.out.println("The answer is " + result);
    result = evennumber1 % 2;
    System.out.println("The answer is " + result);
    result = oddnumber2 % 2;
    System.out.println("The answer is " + result);
    result = evennumber1 % 2;
    System.out.println("The answer is " + result);
  }
}
```

"What I'm doing here," I pointed out, "is declaring four variables and assigning two of them even numbers and two of them odd. Using the Modulus operator, we can determine if the number is even or odd by its result. A result of 1 from the Modulus operation indicates an odd number and a result of 0 from the Modulus operation indicates an even number."

I then compiled the program and executed it. The following screenshot was displayed on the classroom projector:

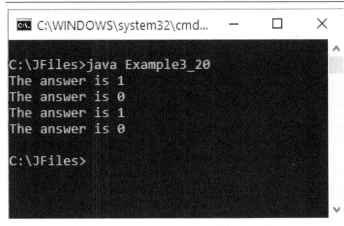

"As you can see," I said, "the result of the Modulus operation is either a 0 or a 1; 0 indicates an even number and 1 indicates an odd number."

"It can't be that easy," Ward said. "I think I had a programming assignment like this to do in a class I took several years ago, and as I recall, it was quite a bear to solve—the Modulus operator. I'll need to remember that one."

"Could we have used an If statement here to make this code a bit more elegant?" Dave asked.

"We could have, Dave," I said, "except we won't be talking about the If statement until next week. Remind me about it then and we'll use the Modulus operator along with an If statement."

I glanced at the clock on the wall, and knew it was just about time for a break.

"We have two more operators to discuss before break," I said, "the increment operator and the decrement operator."

The Increment Operator (++)

"One of the most common operations performed on a variable," I said, "is to increment it--that is to add 1 to its value. One way to do that is to use this code…"

```java
class Example3_21 {
  public static void main(String[] args) {
    int number1 = 5;
    number1 = number1 + 1;
    System.out.println("The answer is " + number1);
  }
}
```

I then compiled the program and executed it. The following screenshot was displayed on the classroom projector:

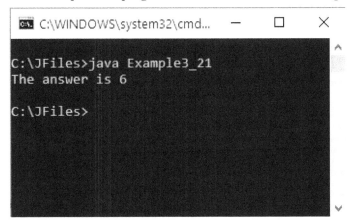

"How is that assignment statement read," Rhonda asked, "it's confusing me a little bit."

"The expression to the right of the equal sign is performed first," I said. "Read it this way---take the current value of the variable number1--which is 5---add 1 to it, giving a result of 6--and then assign that value to the variable number1. As a result, number1 has been incremented by 1."

"So that's how that's done," Blaine said. "But what about this Increment operator you mentioned?"

"The Increment operator is a shortcut method," I said. "Take a look at this..."

I then modified the code to look like this...

```
class Example3_22 {
  public static void main(String[] args) {
    int number1 = 5;
    number1++;
    System.out.println("The answer is " + number1);
  }
}
```

"In Java," I said, "the increment operator is two plus signs (++), which tells Java to take the current value of the variable and add 1 to it."

I then compiled the program and executed it. The following screenshot was displayed on the classroom projector:

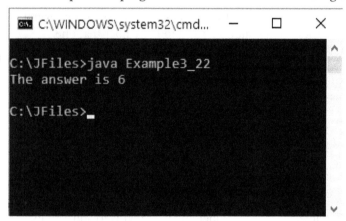

"The increment operator produces the same results," I said, "but saves us a few keystrokes and probably results in fewer mistakes by programmers overall. The increment operator is often used on variables that are used to count things. You'll see this when you learn about loops in a few weeks time."

The Decrement Operator (--)

"What about the Decrement Operator?" Dave asked, "is that the opposite of the Increment Operator. Does it subtract one from the value of the variable."

"You're psychic Dave," I said, "that is exactly what it does. In Java, the decrement operator is two hyphens (--). Take a look at this code..."

```
class Example3_23 {
  public static void main(String[] args) {
    int number1 = 5;
    number1--;
    System.out.println("The answer is " + number1);
  }
}
```

I then compiled the program and executed it. The following screenshot was displayed on the classroom projector:

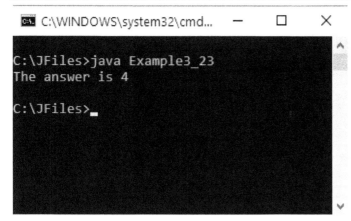

"As you can see," I said, "*number1* was initialized with a value of 5. We subtracted 1 from it using the decrement operator, giving us a result of 4. Again, this is just a shortcut to using this method."

number1 = number1 - 1;

No one seemed to have any problems with either the increment or decrement operators, so I called for a break.

> NOTE: Both the Increment and Decrement operators described here have been shown in what is known as Postfix notation, where the operators are to the 'right' of the variable. Both operators have another option, called Prefix Notation, where the operand is written to the left of the operator, like this...
>
> ++x
>
> --y

Both notations work identically in simple expressions, but in complex expressions, where many operations are being performed, the differences can be subtle, and difficult for a beginner to the language to fully understand.

Order of Operations

"I mentioned earlier," I said, as we resumed after break, "that Java, when it evaluates an expression containing more than one operation, it performs each operation one at a time. The natural question then, is which operation Java performs first."

"That's right," Jack said. "If there's an expression that contains more than one operation, how does it decide which operation to execute first?"

"I would think," Rose said, "that Java would perform the operations left to right in the expression. That's how I would do it."

"That's probably what most people would think Rose," I said, "but that's not the way Java does it. Java follows a set of rules, known as the Order of Operations, which governs the order in which it performs these operations. A knowledge of the Order of Operations is crucial if you want your program to execute the way you intend."

I then displayed this code on the classroom projector and before running it, I asked everyone in the class to perform the calculation mentally themselves, and tell me the number they thought would be displayed in the console:

```
class Example3_24 {
  public static void main(String[] args) {
    System.out.println(3 + 6 + 9 / 3);
  }
}
```

I asked for, and received, a number of different responses. A couple of students suggested the number 12 would be displayed, a few said 6, and a number of students said that the answer would depend on exactly when the division operation was performed. Not wishing to keep them in suspense any longer, I compiled the program and then executed it. The following screenshot was displayed on the classroom projector:

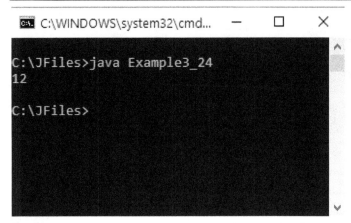

"It looks as though Java performed the division first," Dave said.

"You're right, Dave," I said. "Java evaluated the expression and broke it into three separate operations:"

1. 3 + 6
2. + 9
3. / 3

"Following the rules for the Order of Operations, Java actually performed the *third* operation, division, first," I said. "The Order of Operations is determined by the following rules:"

1. Operations in parentheses () are performed first

2. Multiplication or division operations are performed, from left to right in the expression

3. Addition or subtraction operations are performed next, from left to right in the expression

"What does all that mean?" Rhonda asked.

"Here's what happens," I said, "When Java examines an expression, it first looks to see if there are any operations within parentheses. If it finds parentheses, it performs every operation within the parentheses first. Once all of the operations within parentheses are executed, Java then looks for any operations involving multiplication or division and performs them. If it finds more than one, it performs them from left to right.

"Finally, Java looks for operations involving addition or subtraction and performs them. Once again, it performs each one in turn starting at the left side of the expression and working its way to the right."

"Can you relate the Order of Operations to the code example you showed us?" Kathy asked.

"Sure," I said. "Java first looked for parentheses in the expression. You've probably noticed that whenever we code a **println()** method, there's a pair of parentheses around the expression that we want to display in the console. Since the entire expression appeared within parentheses, it had no impact on the evaluation of the expression. Java then looked for an exponentiation operator, but it found none. Next, it looked for multiplication or division operators. It found just the single division operator, which it performed first."

"So it performed the operation of 9 divided by 3 first," Valerie said. "No wonder the answer didn't agree with mine."

"After the division operation," I continued, "Java looked for any addition or subtraction operators. It found two of them and performed these operations left to right: it added 3 plus 6 first, then added that result, 9, to 3. I can show you how this all took place step by step. Here are the results of the intermediate operations." I displayed this on the classroom projector:

1. Step 1 : 3 + 6 + 9 / 3
2. Step 2 : 3 + 6 + 3
3. Step 3 : 9 + 3
4. Step 4 : 12

I gave everyone a chance to take all of this in. "I hope this example shows you not only how Java evaluates an expression containing mathematical operators, but how important it is to compose the expressions you code carefully. For instance," I said, "suppose we had intended to calculate the average of three numbers—3, 6, and 9—with this piece of code. We know that to calculate an average, we would add 3 plus 6 plus 9 and then divide by 3.

However, if we were to wager our jobs on getting the answer we wanted using this Java code, we wouldn't have one very long!"

"You're right about that," Rose said, "but how could we code the expression to correctly compute the average of 3, 6, and 9?"

"One word," Jack suggested. "Parentheses."

"That's right," I said, agreeing with Jack, as I modified the code and displayed it on the classroom projector:

```
class Example3_25 {
  public static void main(String[] args) {
    System.out.println((3 + 6 + 9) / 3);
  }
}
```

Now when I compiled and executed the program, the following screenshot appeared on the classroom projector:

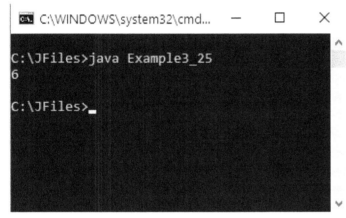

```
C:\JFiles>java Example3_25
6

C:\JFiles>
```

"That's better," I said, "This time, because we sandwiched the addition operations within a set of parentheses, Java performed both addition operations prior to the division--exactly what we wanted to happen. Step by step, it looks like this:"

1. **Step 1 :** (3 + 6 + 9) / 3
2. **Step 2 :** (9 + 9) /3
3. **Step 3 :** 18 / 3
4. **Step 4 :** 6

"Please excuse my dear Aunt Sally," I heard Linda mutter silently.

"What was that Linda?" Rhonda asked. "Please excuse what?"

"**P**lease **E**xcuse **M**y **D**ear **A**unt **S**ally," Linda repeated. "I learned that in ninth grade Math class as a way to remember the Order of Operations. **P**arentheses-**E**xponentiation-**M**ultiplication-**D**ivision-**A**ddition-**S**ubtraction."

> Note: Unlike some other programming languages, Java DOES NOT HAVE an Exponentiaton Operator. Exponentiation can be achieved, however, using the POW function. Check out my Java Language Reference guide available on Lulu.com

"I had forgotten all about that Linda," I said, "That expression does summarize the Order of Operations perfectly."

"Except for one thing," Dave pointed out, "you didn't mention where the Modulus operator falls in the Order of Operations. I just did an experiment, and it appears to have precedence equal to the Multiplication and Division."

"That's right Dave," I said.

"Perhaps," Linda said, "we should modify our easy-to-remember phrase to read: **P**lease **E**xcuse **M**y **M**other's **D**ear **A**unt **S**ally---**P**arentheses-**E**xponentiation-**M**odulus-**M**ultiplication-**D**ivision-**A**ddition-**S**ubtraction."

"Sounds great to me Linda," Rhonda said, "I don't think I'll be able to forget it now!"

Comparison Operators

"I was talking to a programmer friend of mine," Ward said, "and she mentioned something called Comparison operators. Will we be covering those as well?"

"Yes, we will," I replied. "Just as arithmetic or mathematical operators perform an operation based on operands to the left and right of an operator and return a result, Comparison operators compare two expressions to the left and right of a comparison operator and return a result. In the case of a comparison operator, however, the result isn't a number---it's either a value of True or False. Here are the six Java comparison operators:"

Symbol	Explanation
==	Equal to
!=	Not equal to
<	Less than
<=	Less than or equal to
>	Greater than
>=	Greater than or equal to

"We'll only be discussing the most common comparison operator today: the equal to (==) operator," I said.

"Is that symbol correct?" Barbara asked. "Should that be two equal signs? Isn't the equal sign also used to assign a value to a variable?"

"You're right," I said. "The equal sign is used to assign a value to a variable in Java--however, two equal signs are used for the comparison operator. We haven't yet learned about If statements---we'll do that next week--but in Java, we can use this code to determine if the value of the variable *number1* is equal to the number 22…"

```
class Example3_26 {
  public static void main(String[] args) {
    int number1 = 22;
    if (number1 == 22)
      System.out.println("number1 is equal to 22");
  }
}
```

"Notice that the assignment statement uses one equal sign…"

```
int number1 = 22;
```

"…but within the If statement, we use the double equal sign (==) to compare the value of *number1* to the literal 22…"

"So the result of the If statement expression will either be True or False depending upon the current value of *number1*?" Dave said.

"That's exactly right Dave," I replied. "If the current value of *number1* is 22, the result of this comparison will be True. As you'll see next week, when an If statement expression evaluates to True, the imperative statement following it---in this case a statement to display a message in the Java Console Window---is executed."

I then compiled and executed the program, and the following screenshot was displayed on the classroom projector:

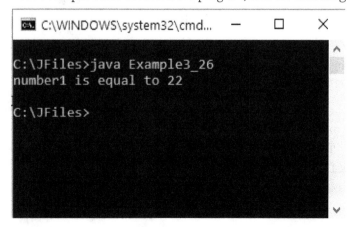

"By the way," I continued, "this code could also be written this way with the single imperative statement sandwiched between a pair of curly braces."

```java
class Example3_26 {
  public static void main(String[] args) {
    int number1 = 22;
    if (number1 == 22)  {
      System.out.println("number1 is equal to 22");
    }
  }
}
```

"As you'll learn next week, when there is more than one imperative statement to be executed, curly braces are required to sandwich the multiple imperative statements. Curly braces are not required with a single imperative statement, but sandwiching the single imperative statement like this is the preferred method of Java purists, who feel that most likely in the future, that single imperative statement will be expanded to multiple imperative statements by modifications to the program. Either method will compile cleanly."

I pause before continuing.

"Let's modify the program slightly," I said, "so that you can actually see the result of the comparison operation..."

```java
class Example3_27 {
  public static void main(String[] args) {
    int number1 = 22;
    System.out.println(number1 == 22);
  }
}
```

I compiled and executed the program, and the following screenshot appeared on the classroom projector:

"That's cool," Kate said. "We really did display the result of the comparison operation, didn't we?"

"Yes we did Kate," I replied, "likewise, if the value of *number1* is NOT equal to 22, the result of the comparison operation would be False. Like this..." I modified the code slightly....

```java
class Example3_28 {
  public static void main(String[] args) {
    int number1 = 99;
    System.out.println(number1 == 22);
  }
}
```

I compiled and executed the program again, and the following screenshot was displayed on the classroom projector:

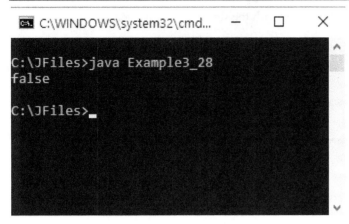

Logical Operators

"So far," I said, "we've examined Arithmetic operators and Comparison operators. Now it's time to look at a set of operators that sometimes cause beginner's hearts to skip a beat---Logical operators."

"Are those the And, Or and Not operators?" Blaine asked.

"That's right Blaine," I said. "In this Java class, we'll be discussing three Logical operators: And, Or and Not. Just like Comparison operators, Logical operators return a True or False value as the result of performing an operation on two operands. I must warn you that Logical operations can be confusing for the beginner, primarily because of the necessity to understand the 'truth' or 'falseness' of their expressions. Let's take a look at these operators individually."

The And Operator (&)

"An And operation," I said, "returns a True value if the expressions on *both* sides of the And operator evaluate to True."

"Can you give us a real-world example to make this easier to understand?" Ward asked.

"I think so, Ward" I said, as I thought a moment. "On Wednesday morning, your best friend Melissa telephones you and invites you to lunch on Friday. You'd love to go, but you have two problems that prevent you from saying 'yes' right away. First, you and your boss have not been on the best of terms lately, and you don't want to chance taking an extra long lunch on Friday--something which invariably happens when you go to lunch with Melissa. The only way you can envision going to lunch with your friend is if your boss happens to be out of the office on Friday."

"And the second problem," Barbara asked. "You said there were two problems."

"The second problem," I said, "is that you're short of cash and it's your turn to pick up the tab for lunch. Luckily though, Friday happens to be payday and cash won't be a problem---provided the direct deposit of your paycheck goes through early Friday morning, something that is 50-50 at best. You decide to call your friend on Friday at 11 AM to let her know for sure."

I could see that some of the students were wondering what my heart-felt example had to do with the And operator. I explained that we can express our dilemma in the form of two expressions joined with the And operator in this way.

"You can go to lunch with your friend Melissa if your boss is out of the office on Friday AND if the Direct Deposit of your paycheck gets into your bank account by 11 AM on Friday morning." I said.

"In other words, both expressions, the left-hand expression 'Boss out of office?' and the right-hand expression 'Money in Account?' must both be true for the AND operator to return a value of True.

Boss out of office AND Money in Account

"So what happens?" Rhonda asked.

"On Friday morning," I said, "you arrive at the office. You're saddened to hear that your boss has called in to say she has the flu and won't be in at all that day."

"So the left hand expression, Boss out of the office, is True," Dave said.

"That's right Dave," I said. "We're half way there. Our left hand expression evaluates to True. Now we have to wait on the Direct Deposit. The morning drags by as lunch time gets closer and closer. For the moment though, the AND operation is returning a False value, since the right-hand expression, Money in bank, is still returning a False value. Remember, the AND operation is True only if both the left-hand expression and right-hand expressions are True. Right now, only the left-hand expression, Boss out of Office, is True. Unfortunately, the last time you checked your balance, you find that your Direct Deposit still hasn't been made to your account, and $1.38 won't buy you and your friend Melissa much of a lunch."

"I wish we could see this graphically," Peter said.

"Actually Peter," I said, "we can express this dilemma in the form of something called a Truth Table---here it is."

Expression 1	And	Expression 2	Statement
True	And	True	True
True	And	False	False
False	And	True	False
False	And	False	False

"A Truth Table," I said, "shows you the four possible outcomes for the And operation. As you can see, there's only *one* way for an AND operation to return a True value, and that's if *both* Expression 1 (the left hand side) and Expression 2 (the right hand side) are True. On the other hand, there are *three* ways for the AND operation to return a value of False."

"I don't like those odds," Kate said laughing. "I don't think lunch looks too promising!"

"Can you re-write the True Table in terms of the boss and the money?" Rhonda said. "I think that might help me visualize this."

I took a moment to work up this revised table and then displayed it on the classroom projector. The current situation is highlighted in bold:

Boss Out?	And	Money in Bank?	Go to Lunch
True	And	True	True
True	**And**	**False**	**False**
False	And	True	False
False	And	False	False

"That's better," Steve said. "This is beginning to make some sense to me now."

"Let's continue on with the story," I said. "As of 10:30, with no cash in the bank, lunch is a remote possibility. Just as you're about to call Melissa and tell her 'no', one last check of your bank balance shows that the Direct Deposit has made it, which means the right hand expression, Expression 2, is now True. Since both the left-hand and right-hand expressions evaluate to True, the entire AND operation is True, and you and Melissa can now go off to lunch."

Boss Out?	And	Money in Bank?	Go to Lunch?
True	**And**	**True**	**True**
True	And	False	False
False	And	True	False
False	And	False	False

"What is the And Operator in Java," Kate asked. "Is it the word 'And'?"

"Thanks Kate," I said, "I almost forgot---the Java 'And' Operator is the Ampersand (&)."

"Can you give us an example of the use of the AND operation in Java?" Dave asked.

I thought for a moment, then came up with this example...

```
class Example3_29 {
  public static void main(String[] args) {
    String name = "Smith";
    int number = 99;
    if (name == "Smith" & number == 22)
      System.out.println("Both sides of the AND expression are True");
```

```
    }
}
```

"Once again," I said, "let's use an If statement to evaluate the Truth or Falseness of the Logical expression we've coded, where we check to see if the value of the name variable is 'Smith' AND the value of the number variable is 22. If the expression evaluates to True, then we display an appropriate message in the console"

I then compiled and executed the program, and the following screenshot was displayed on the classroom projector:

"Nothing happened," Rhonda said.

"You're right Rhonda," I said, "in that no message was displayed. In this expression, the left-hand side of the expression is True, since ***name*** is equal to Smith---but the right-hand side expression is False, because the value of ***number*** is 99, not 22. Therefore, the And Operation returns a value of False (consult the Truth Table to see this for yourself."

I then changed the code to assign the value 22 to the variable number...

```
class Example3_30 {
  public static void main(String[] args) {
    String name = "Smith";
    int number = 22;
    if (name == "Smith" & number == 22)
      System.out.println("Both sides of the AND expression are True");
  }
}
```

I recompiled the program and executed it. When I ran the program, the following screenshot appeared on the classroom projector:

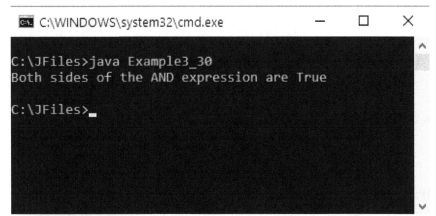

Don't Forget: If typing these examples and exercises isn't something you want to do, feel free to follow this link to find and download the completed solutions for all of the examples and exercises in the book. Just click on the Java book, then follow the link entitled exercises ☺

http://www.johnsmiley.com/main/books.htm

"Now the And operation returns a True value," I said, "because both the left hand and right-hand expressions are True---True And True equals True."

The Or Operator (|)

"I think if you're comfortable with the And operation," I said, "you won't have too much trouble with the Or operation. An Or operation, just like the And operation, evaluates expressions to the left and right of the Or operator, returning a value of True or False. The differences are the rules for determining if the expression is True or False."

I displayed this Truth Table representing the Or operation on the projector:

Expression 1	Or	Expression 2	Statement
True	Or	True	True
True	Or	False	True
False	Or	True	True
False	Or	False	False

"Notice," I said, "that with the Or operation, as was the case with the And Operation, we have four possibilities. In the case of the Or operator, however, three out of four results are True. In fact, with the Or operation, there is only one combination that returns a False value, and that's if both the left-hand and right-hand expressions are False."

"Can you give us another real world example to illustrate the Or operation?" Linda asked, "although I think it will be pretty hard for you to top that last one."

I thought for a moment. "OK," I said, "let's try this one. It's Friday morning. While dressing for work, you receive a phone call from the host of an early morning radio show that is running a contest. He tells you that if the month of your birthday ends in 'r' OR the last digit of your Social Security Number is 4, you'll be the lucky winner of $10,000!"

"Sounds great to me!" Ward said.

"Let me get this straight," Rhonda said. "All you need to do to win the $10,000 is to have one of those conditions be True--is that right?"

"That's right Rhonda," I said. "According to the rules of the contest, you'll win the $10,000 if either the left-hand expression is True---month of your birthday ends in the letter 'r'--or the right-hand expression is True---last digit of your Social Security Number ends in 4. Unlike our lunch date dilemma, where we needed both expressions to be True to go to lunch with our friend, with an Or operation only one side of the expression needs to be True. How do you like your odds now Kate?"

"I love them," she answered. "If that call were placed to me, I'd win the prize."

Kate wasn't alone---a quick poll of the class revealed that 4 out of the 18 students would win using the Or Operation. And guess what--if the contest had called for the AND operation, none of the students in the class would have won the cash!

I then displayed this truth table to reflect the radio contest. The three outcomes where the Or operation returns a True value are highlighted in BOLD...

Birthday Month ends in 'r'	Or	Last Digit of Social Security is '4'?	Win $10,000?
True	Or	True	True
True	Or	False	True
False	Or	True	True
False	Or	False	False

I then took the previous code example and modified it by changing the And operator to an Or; in Java, the Or operator is the pipe character (|):

```java
class Example3_31 {
  public static void main(String[] args) {
    String name = "Smith";
    int number = 99;
    if (name == "Smith" | number == 22)
      System.out.println("One or both sides of the OR expression are True");
```

```
  }
}
```

NOTE: The OR Operator is typed using this character | which is the character appearing on the same key as the backslash (\)--Beginners frequently mistake it for the exclamation point

I compiled and executed the program, and the following screenshot appeared on the classroom projector:

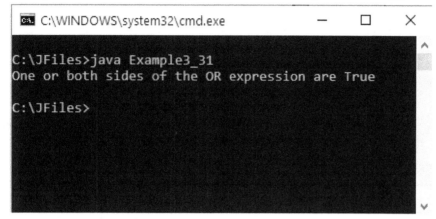

"Because one side of the expression is True--the left-hand side," I said, "True is returned from the Or Operation. If we were to change the value of Name from Smith to Smiley, both the left-hand and right-hand expressions would be false and the Or Operation would return a False value…"

I did exactly that, changing the code to look like this …

```
class Example3_32 {
  public static void main(String[] args) {
    String name = "Smiley";
    int number = 99;
    if (name == "Smith" | number == 22)
      System.out.println("One or both sides of the OR expression are True");
  }
}
```

I compiled and executed the program, and the following screenshot appeared on the classroom projector:

```
C:\WINDOWS\system32\cmd.exe                    —    □    ×

C:\JFiles>java Example3_32

C:\JFiles>_
```

"Nothing is displayed in the Console because the OR expression evaluates to False," I said. "The only way that an Or Operation can return a False value is if both the left-hand and right-hand expressions evaluate to False. That's the case here---number, with a value of 99, is NOT 22, and name, with a value of Smiley, is definitely NOT Smith."

"I just entered some code on my own and received an error message when I tried to compile it," Kathy said.

I took a quick walk to her PC, and saw that she had written the following code:

```
class Example3_33 {
  public static void main(String[] args) {
```

```
    String name = "Smiley";
    int number = 99;
    if (number == 22 | 99 )
      System.out.println("One or both sides of the OR expression are True");
  }
}
```

I took Kathy's code and compiled it on my PC, and the following error message was displayed on the classroom projector:

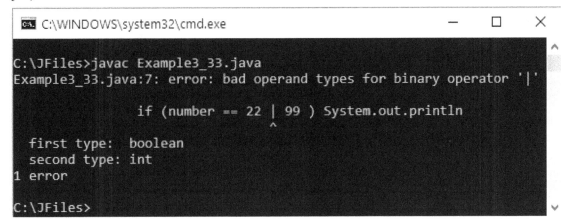

"What did I do wrong?" she asked.

"I know what you intended to do," I said, "but you confused Java. Your code was very English like, which is very tempting to do in Java, but you see, you don't really have two expressions on either side of the Or operator. Your left-hand expression is 'number == 22', and your right-hand expression is just the number 99. Remember, both your left-hand and right-hand expressions must be able to be evaluated to a True or False value. Your right hand expression can't be evaluated to a True or False value, so Java generated this error message."

"So how could I rewrite this?" she asked.

"Like this," I said, "by repeating the variable name number in the right side expression."

I displayed the correct code on the classroom projector…

```
class Example3_34 {
  public static void main(String[] args) {
    String name = "Smiley";
    int number = 99;
    if (number == 22 | number == 99 )
      System.out.println("One or both sides of the OR expression are True");
  }
}
```

I then recompiled the program and executed. The following screen shot was displayed on the classroom projector…

```
C:\WINDOWS\system32\cmd.exe                    —    □    ×

C:\JFiles>java Example3_34
One or both sides of the OR expression are True

C:\JFiles>_
```

"See the difference," I said, "Java recognized that the right side expression of our Or statement evaluated to True."

"Wow, that was simple," Kathy said. "Why didn't I think of that?"

"You did what a lot of beginners do, Kathy," I answered. "You wrote the code the way you would ask the question in conversation. Unfortunately, as English like as Java may appear to be, there are still some statements that can confuse it."

The Not Operator (!)

"We have one more logical operator to discuss today," I continued, "and it's the Not operator. As opposed to the other logical operators, which operate on two expressions, the Not operator is called a unary operator because it operates on just a single expression. The operator itself is the exclamation point (!)."

"What does the Not operator do?" Steve asked.

"The Not operator is used as a negation," I replied. "It evaluates an expression, takes the True or False result, and then returns the opposite value. So if an expression evaluates to True, the Not operator returns False. If the expression evaluates to False, the Not operator returns True."

"Why in the world would you want to do something like that?" Rhonda asked.

"The Not operator can simplify some types of program code," I said, "and make it easier to read and understand. Let me show you…"

I then displayed this code on the classroom projector.

```java
class Example3_35 {
  public static void main(String[] args) {
    int number = 13;
    System.out.println(number == 13);
  }
}
```

"Can anyone tell me what will happen when we run this code?" I asked. Dave suggested that the word True would be output in the console. .

"That's right," I said. "Since the value of number is 13, Java will evaluate the expression number = 13 as True."

I then compiled the program and executed it. As Dave had predicted, the word True appeared in the console.

```
C:\WINDOWS\system32\cmd.exe                      —    □    ✕

C:\JFiles>java Example3_35
true

C:\JFiles>_
```

"Exactly as Dave predicted," I said. I then changed the code to look like this (notice the exclamation point in the line of code)

```java
class Example3_36 {
  public static void main(String[] args) {
    int number = 13;
    System.out.println(!(number == 13));
  }
}
```

"Now what will happen?" I asked. Dave answered that he thought the word *False* would appear in the console.

"Can you tell us why?" I replied.

"Because," he said, "the expression number == 13 will evaluate to True. Executing the Not operator on a True value gives us a False value."

"Excellent Dave," I said, "Bill Gates himself couldn't have stated it better." I then compiled the program with the change and executed it. Dave was right; the word False was output in the console.

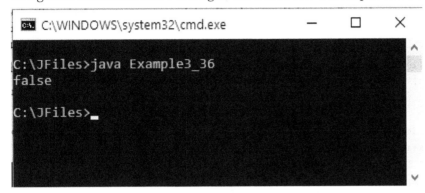

Dave was right; the word false was displayed in our Java Console Window.

"Without the Not operator, to determine if a variable's value isn't a particular number would require some very hard to read and understand code, like this…"

```
System.println(number < 13 ! (number > 13))
```

"Is that all there is to the Not operator then?" Barbara asked.

"Basically, yes," I said. I paused before suggesting that we end the class by completing an exercise.

"In this exercise," I said, "you'll have a chance to continue working with the Grades Calculation Project that you created last week. We don't have a lot of changes to make to it, but we will enhance it with some variable and constant declarations."

I then distributed this exercise for the class to complete.

Exercise 3-1 Add Variables and Constants to the Grades Calculation Program

In this exercise you'll find and load up the Grade's program you wrote last week--and then modify it to include variable and constant declarations. For the sake of demonstration, you'll calculate the grade for an English student who has received a midterm grade of 70, a final examination grade of 80, a research grade of 90, and a presentation grade of 100 for the four individual component pieces.

1. Use the editor of your choice (if you are using Windows, use Notepad) and locate and load up the Grades.java source file you created last week. It should be located in the\JFiles\Grades folder.
2. Modify the code so that it looks like this...

```java
class Grades {
  public static void main(String[] args) {
    final double MIDTERM_PERCENTAGE = .25;
    final double FINALEXAM_PERCENTAGE = .25;
    final double RESEARCH_PERCENTAGE = .30;
    final double PRESENTATION_PERCENTAGE = .20;
    int midterm = 100;
    int finalExamGrade = 100;
    int research = 100;
    int presentation = 100;
    double finalNumericGrade = 0;

    finalNumericGrade =
      (midterm * MIDTERM_PERCENTAGE) +
      (finalExamGrade * FINALEXAM_PERCENTAGE) +
      (research * RESEARCH_PERCENTAGE) +
      (presentation * PRESENTATION_PERCENTAGE);
```

```
    System.out.println("Midterm grade is : " + midterm);
    System.out.println("Final Exam grade is : " + finalExamGrade);
    System.out.println("Research grade is : " + research);
    System.out.println("Presentation grade is: " + presentation);

    System.out.println("\nThe final grade is: " + finalNumericGrade);
  }
}
```

3. Save your source file as **'Grades.java'** in the \JFiles\Grades folder (select File-Save As from Notepad's Menu Bar). Be sure to save your source file with the file name extension 'java'.

4. Compile your source file into a Bytecode file. (If you have forgotten how to compile your Java source file into a Bytecode file, consult Exercise 2-2 from last week.)

5. Execute your Bytecode file. (If you have forgotten how to execute your Java program, consult Exercise 2-3 from last week.) You should see output similar to this screenshot:

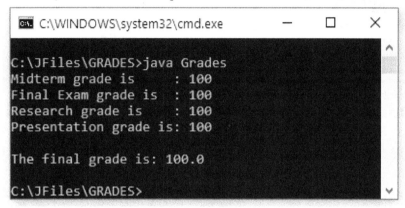

Discussion

Java is a sensitive language and, as such, I didn't expect everything to go smoothly with this exercise. All in all, the exercise went well, although some students, particularly those who didn't follow the exercise precisely, had a number of problems. For instance, it took Rhonda four or five compilations of her source file before she wound up with a compiled Bytecode file. In fact, the first time she compiled her source file, she just went right ahead and executed her Bytecode file. Because she still had the old one from last week, the program ran, but it produced the results from the previous week. Most of her problems stemmed from not spelling her variable names the same way she declared them.

"I admit," Rhonda said, smiling, "I should have paid more attention to the syntax of the variable names. I guess I'm just not used to the case sensitivity of Java."

Ward entirely missed the fact that the constants were declared as double data types. When he compiled his program, he received a somewhat nonuser-friendly message flagging his first assignment statement saying that Java had found a double when it was looking for a float.

A number of students just forgot to end statement with a semicolon, something you need to do in Java.

After about ten minutes, all of the class had finally compiled their programs, and it was time to discuss what they had done.

"As you are beginning to realize by now," I said, "the main or startup class of a Java program must have a **main()** method."

```
public static void main(String[] args) {
```

"Java convention suggests that constant names be capitalized, and if there is more than one word in the constant name, that they be separated by an underscore. That's why we named these constants like this."

```
final double MIDTERM_PERCENTAGE = .25;
final double FINALEXAM_PERCENTAGE = .25;
final double RESEARCH_PERCENTAGE = .30;
final double PRESENTATION_PERCENTAGE = .20;
```

"Notice that we needed to initialize the constants," I said. "I should tell you that as our project evolves, much of the code you see in this class will be moved to one or more support classes. In fact, this code will be placed in a class called EnglishStudent—but more on that in a few weeks."

"I was a little confused," Blaine said, "about your variable naming conventions. I think I would have begun the variable names with a capital letter."

"By convention," I said, "variable names begin with a lowercase letter. If a variable name consists of more than one word, as some of ours do, the words are joined together and each word after the first begins with an uppercase letter. That's why we named these variables like this,"

```
int midterm = 100;
int finalExamGrade = 100;
int research = 100;
int presentation = 100;
double finalNumericGrade = 0;
```

I had thought that this next section of code would give the class problems, but it hadn't, although Mary did have a question:

```
finalNumericGrade =
  (midterm * MIDTERM_PERCENTAGE) +
  (finalExamGrade * FINALEXAM_PERCENTAGE) +
  (research * RESEARCH_PERCENTAGE) +
  (presentation * PRESENTATION_PERCENTAGE);
```

"I understand what you were doing in this next section of code," she said. "You're multiplying the component grade pieces by the applicable constant values—but why didn't each line of code end with a semicolon?"

"Because those five lines of code are really just a single Java statement," I answered. "Because a Java statement can span more than one line—in this case, five—we only needed the semicolon at the very end."

"Did we really need those parentheses?" Dave asked. "Based on the Order of Operations, wouldn't the multiplication operations have been performed before the additions?"

"That's right, Dave," I said. "We could have written the code like this, and the answer would still be correct."

```
finalNumericGrade =
  midterm * MIDTERM_PERCENTAGE +
  finalExamGrade * FINALEXAM_PERCENTAGE +
  research * RESEARCH_PERCENTAGE +
  presentation * PRESENTATION_PERCENTAGE;
```

"But I'm a big believer in readability. I think the parentheses make the code easier for someone else to read and leave no doubt about our intentions."

"I understood everything that was going on in this next section," Kate said, "except for the \n on the final **println()** statement—what's going on with that?"

Kate was referring to the last line of the following:

```
System.out.println("Midterm grade is : " + midterm);
System.out.println("Final Exam grade is : " + finalExamGrade);
System.out.println("Research grade is : " + research);
System.out.println("Presentation grade is: " + presentation);
System.out.println("\nThe final grade is: " + finalNumericGrade);
```

"That \n stands for the newline character," I said, "and it tells Java to print a blank line prior to displaying the output in the console."

"So that's where that blank line came from," Linda said. "I was wondering about that. Is formatting like this something that we'll concern ourselves with a great deal?"

"Only in the beginning of our course," I said. "Remember, ultimately, we'll be developing a graphical user interface (GUI). Toward the latter part of the class, we won't be using the console at all."

"Next week," I said, "we'll learn how to make our program a lot more intelligent through the use of selection structures."

I then dismissed class for the day—it had been a long, but very valuable one.

"Next week," I said, "we'll learn how to make our program a lot more intelligent through the use of Selection Structures."

Summary

This was quite an exhaustive look at the use of data in Java. In this chapter, you learned about the importance of variables in Java. You learned when, where, and how to use variables and about the different Java variable types that you can declare. In addition, you discovered how we can use a variety of operations to manipulate the data contained in those variables.

Variables are defined in memory to hold data or information. Each variable has a scope that determines what other parts of your program can see the variable and a lifetime that determines when the variable dies. Some variables live for as long as your program runs; others live only for as long as a method executes. We discussed the need to declare and initialize variables.

Java data types can be categorized in four broad ways:
- **Boolean**. True or False values only.
- **Numeric**. Numbers only, which can be integer and floating-point data types.
- **Char**. A single character.
- **String**. A set of characters, treated as text. Strings can hold characters representing numbers, but these are not numbers that you can perform arithmetic on.

A constant is like a fixed variable and is declared using the Final keyword. Constants should be named in all capital letters so they stand out in your code. Once a value is assigned to a constant, its value cannot be changed.

Finally, we took a look at arithmetic, comparison, and logical operators. Operators act on expressions and return a result. An example of a mathematical operator is the plus sign. You learned that multiple operators are treated in a defined order called the Order of Operations: operations in parentheses are performed first, followed by exponentiation, multiplication and division, and finally, addition and subtraction.

An example of a comparison operator is the double equal sign. An example of a logical operator is the And operator, represented by the ampersand (&).

You should now be familiar, if not totally comfortable, with the ways we can manipulate data in Java programs. In the next chapter, you'll see how selection structures permit your program to make decisions.

Chapter 4---Selection Structures

In programming, one of the most important capabilities your program must possess is the ability to adapt to conditions that are encountered while the program is running. In this chapter, we'll continue to follow my Java class as we examine Selection Structures, programming constructs that enable your program to adapt to those runtime conditions. Specifically, we'll learn about the If statement and the Switch statement. Along the way, we'll also get our first taste of writing a program that accepts input, and also writes to an output window.

Selection Structures

I arrived in the classroom a little later than usual, and found a little bit of a commotion.

"What's wrong?" I asked, noting that there was a group of students surrounding Rose and Jack.

"As you know," Jack said, "Rose and I are both engineers by trade and we work for the same company. For the last few months, we've been working on our company's biggest account---overseeing the construction of a new cruise ship in the United Kingdom. Construction is way ahead of schedule, and yesterday our supervisor told us that we're being called away to participate in the sea trials. So you see, this will probably be our last class!"

"I'm disappointed," Rose said, "because we had both hoped to finish the coding for the Grades Calculation Project before we left for the sea trials---but there's no way we'll be near to that point today."

I explained to both Rose and Jack that we would all be sorry not to have them present all the way through the project, but we hoped they would be able to return in time to see the final version of the Grades Calculation Project implemented in the English, Math and Science departments.

"But as far as the Grades Calculation Project," I said. "I have a surprise for you. By the end of today's class, we'll have coded a working prototype of the Grades Calculation Project---it's not quite what we'll be delivering to Frank Olley in a few weeks, but I think you'll be pleased with it---and pretty amazed at just how full featured it is."

As the obvious shock of my last statement subsided, I began our fourth class by telling everyone that during the next two weeks, we would be learning about the three types of programming 'structures' that form the building blocks of all computer programs.

"Structure?" Ward said. "That sounds like a house or a building."

"The building analogy is a good one Ward," I said. "We've already learned how the first step in developing a program is to develop a "blueprint" in the form of a Requirements Statement. Many years ago computer scientists discovered that any program can be written using a combination of three coding structures—much like a house can be constructed using a series of standard components. These three structures—the Sequence Structure, the Selection Structure and the Loop Structure---will form the basis of our discussion over the next few weeks."

"Will we be writing any code ourselves today?" Rhonda asked. "I know we wrote a bit of code last week--but I'm really getting anxious to get going."

"You'll have a chance to write a lot of code today," I answered. "Whenever possible, I try to have the exercises that we complete here in class ultimately lead to the completion of the Grades Calculation Project. However, from time to time we'll complete some exercises just for practice, and so that we don't confuse that work with the Grades Completion Project, if you want to save your practice exercises, you should save those in the Practice folder you created earlier in the class. Let's take a look at the Java Sequence Structure now."

The Sequence Structure---Falling Rock

"As you'll see later on," I said, "both the Selection and Loop Structures require a special syntax to implement---but that's not the case with the Sequence Structure. Any code that we write is automatically part of a Sequence Structure. I like to analogize a Sequence Structure to the behavior of an falling rock."

"Falling Rock? What do you mean by that?" Steve said, obviously amused.

"Have you seen signs warning you of falling rock on the highway?" I said. "If you've ever seen rock fall, you know that once it gets rolling there's no stopping it. The same is true of Java program code. For instance, let's look at the code we wrote last week that displays the final grade of an English student to the Java Console..."

```
class Grades {
    public static void main(String[] args) {
```

```
    final double MIDTERM_PERCENTAGE = .25;
    final double FINALEXAM_PERCENTAGE = .25;
    final double RESEARCH_PERCENTAGE = .30;
    final double PRESENTATION_PERCENTAGE = .20;
    int midterm = 100;
    int finalExamGrade = 100;
    int research = 100;
    int presentation = 100;
    double finalNumericGrade = 0;

    finalNumericGrade =
      (midterm * MIDTERM_PERCENTAGE) +
      (finalExamGrade * FINALEXAM_PERCENTAGE) +
      (research * RESEARCH_PERCENTAGE) +
      (presentation * PRESENTATION_PERCENTAGE);

    System.out.println("Midterm grade is : " + midterm);
    System.out.println("Final Exam grade is : " + finalExamGrade);
    System.out.println("Research grade is : " + research);
    System.out.println("Presentation grade is: " + presentation);
    System.out.println("\nThe final grade is: " + finalNumericGrade);
  }
}
```

"…this code is a perfect example of the Sequence structure. Last week, we observed that the first line of code in the **main()** method executes, followed by the second line of code, then the third and so forth, in *sequence*."

"Oh, I see where the term Sequence Structure comes from now," Valerie said. "You mean each line of code is executed, one after the other. But I guess I have to ask, what else could happen? Isn't every line of code evaluated by Java?"

"Every line of code is evaluated by Java," I said, "but not every line of code is necessarily executed once--some lines of code can be 'skipped' based on conditions found when the program is running. In other cases, lines of code may be executed more than once. That's where the Java Selection and Loop Structures come into play. The Selection structure gives 'intelligence' to our program, in the form of decision-making capabilities, something the falling rock behavior of a Sequence Structure simply can't do. The Selection Structure allows us to SELECTIVELY execute lines of code based on conditions our program finds at run-time. Next week, we'll examine the Loop Structure that allows us to execute a line or lines of code REPETITIVELY."

I paused a moment before adding: "In order to illustrate the alternatives to the falling rock behavior of a Sequence Structure, I'd like you to complete a series of exercises based on a fictitious collection of seven restaurants in New York City. Pretend, for a few moments, that you have been hired by the owners of these seven restaurants to write a program to display their ads on a giant display screen in Times Square---in our case we're going to use the Java console as our giant display screen.."

"I don't mean to rush things," Valerie said, "but I'm getting a little bored with the Java console. Are we ever going to write any windows code?"

"Your timing is perfect, Valerie," I answered. "At the end of today's class, we'll do exactly that by writing some code that displays a window for both input and output. But for now, our first exercise of the day will illustrate, I hope, the falling rock behavior of Java code."

I then distributed this exercise for the class to complete.

Exercise 4-1 Eat at Joe's – The Sequence Structure---Falling Rock behavior

In this exercise, you'll write a Java program that displays information to the Java console about the days of operation of seven restaurants in New York City. Pretend that the Java Console is actually a giant display screen in New York City's Times Square.

1. Create a folder on your hard drive called \JFiles\Practice. This will be the home of the Java programs we create here in class that are not part of the Grades Calculation Project.
2. Use the editor of your choice (if you are using Windows, use Notepad) and enter the following code. Be extremely careful of the capitalization: Java is very picky.

```
class Practice4_1 {
  public static void main(String[] args) {
    System.out.println("Eat at Joe's");
    System.out.println("Eat at Tom's");
    System.out.println("Eat at Kevin's");
    System.out.println("Eat at Rich's");
    System.out.println("Eat at Rose's");
    System.out.println("Eat at Ken's");
    System.out.println("Eat at Melissa's");
  }
}
```

3. Save your source file as Practice4_1 in the \JFiles\Practice folder (select File | Save As from Notepad's menu bar). Be sure to save your source file with the filename extension .java.

4. Compile your source file into a Bytecode file.

5. Execute your Bytecode file. You should see output similar to this screenshot.

Discussion

Aside from a couple of student's continued anxiety with writing code and compiling it into a Bytecode file, this exercise went very smoothly. Because I warned them in the instructions, my students were very careful with their capitalization— something that had tripped them up in the previous week's exercise. I gave everyone a chance to complete the exercise and then began to explain what we had done with this small program.

"This program seemed pretty straightforward," Rhonda said. "What were you trying to illustrate with it?"

"The Sequence structure," I answered. "The code that makes up the **main()** method of this class represents something known as a programming Sequence structure. As I mentioned a little earlier, all that means is that the second line of code executes after the first line of code, the third after the second, and so on."

"Falling rock behavior," Ward chimed in.

"Exactly right, Ward," I said. "Does everyone remember how the **println()** method of the System object works?"

"No problem," Valerie said. "The **println()** method displays output to the Java console—although you promised us we'll be writing output to a window later on today, isn't that right?"

"That's right, Valerie," I said.

There were no other questions about the exercise, so I continued.

"Having written this program for the owners of the seven restaurants," I said, "suppose that the owner of Joe's restaurant goes into semiretirement and decides to open his restaurant only on Sundays. Tom, proprietor of Tom's restaurant, hearing the news about Joe, thinks semiretirement is a great idea and decides to open his restaurant only on Mondays. Kevin follows suit and opens only on Tuesdays. Soon the rest of the owners hear about this, figure that one day of work a week is a great idea, and the next thing we know, Rich is open only on Wednesdays, Rose only on Thursdays, Ken only on Fridays, and Melissa only on Saturdays. Hoping to save advertising costs in Times Square, each owner contacts us and informs us they want to advertise on our giant display screen only on the days that their restaurant is actually open. How can we handle this with our program?"

I gave everyone a moment or two to think about the problem.

"I suppose," Peter said, "we could write separate Java programs for different days of the week. Although if you tell me there isn't a better way than that, I may need to drop out of the class!"

"Peter is right," I said to the class, "we could write separate Java programs for each day of the week, and he's also right that there is a better way. We can make our program smart enough to know what the date is, and based on that, the day of the week. Armed with that knowledge, we can then use the Java Selection structure to decide which restaurant advertisement to display on our giant display screen."

The Java Selection Structure---the If Statement

"Selection structures," I continued, "can alter the default (falling rock) behavior of Java code, but they are a little more complicated to write. Selection Structures require that the programmer specify one or more conditions to be evaluated---or tested---by the program, along with a statement or statements to be executed if the condition is determined to be True, and optionally, other statements to be executed if the condition is determined to be False. In the next exercise, you'll implement one of the two Java Selection Structures--the If statement--and the condition that you'll ask Java to evaluate is the current day of the week. Based on Java's determination of the day of the week, decisions as to which restaurant advertising to display in the Console will be made. As you'll see, coding Selection Structures requires a little more 'up front' thought than merely coding a plain sequence structure."

I then distributed this exercise for the class to complete.

Exercise 4-2 The If Statement (or which restaurant is open today?)

In this exercise, we'll modify the code from Exercise 4-1 to determine the current date, the day of the week, and to use an If statement to determine which restaurant to advertise in the Java Console.

1. Use Notepad (if you are using Windows) and enter the following code.

```java
import java.util.*;
class Practice4_2 {
  public static void main(String[] args) {
    Calendar cal = Calendar.getInstance();
    Date now = new Date();
    cal.setTime(now);
    int dayofweek = cal.get(Calendar.DAY_OF_WEEK);
    if (dayofweek == Calendar.SUNDAY)
      System.out.println("Eat at Joe's");
    if (dayofweek == Calendar.MONDAY)
      System.out.println("Eat at Tom's");
    if (dayofweek == Calendar.TUESDAY)
      System.out.println("Eat at Kevin's");
    if (dayofweek == Calendar.WEDNESDAY)
      System.out.println("Eat at Rich's");
    if (dayofweek == Calendar.THURSDAY)
      System.out.println("Eat at Rose's");
    if (dayofweek == Calendar.FRIDAY)
      System.out.println("Eat at Ken's");
    if (dayofweek == Calendar.SATURDAY)
      System.out.println("Eat at Melissa's");
  }
}
```

2. Save your source file as Practice4_2 in the \JFiles\Practice folder (select File | Save As from Notepad's menu bar). Be sure to save your source file with the filename extension .java.

3. Compile your source file into a Bytecode file.

4. Execute your Bytecode file. You should see one restaurant advertisement displayed in the Java console (which one it is will depend upon the day of the week on which you run the program) similar to this screenshot:

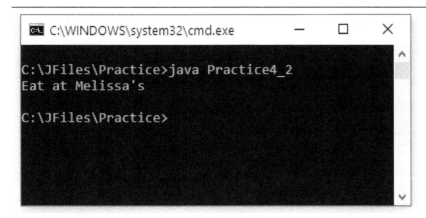

Discussion

Note: The computer week goes from Sunday (day 0) to Saturday (day 6)

I gave my students about ten minutes to complete the exercise. They seemed mesmerized with the ability of their program to behave intelligently. Although no one had any trouble completing the exercise, there were still a number of puzzled looks in the classroom.

"This is really cool," Steve said. "I had no idea you could do something like this with a programming language, although I must confess I don't think I understand half of the code we just wrote, starting with that first line of code. What exactly are we importing?"

What exactly are we importing?"

"I was wondering that myself," Kathy said. "What's the function of an Import statement?"

"An Import statement," I said, "allows you to use objects in your program that are not part of the default object set. As you discovered while coding this program, we needed to determine both the date and the day of the week corresponding to the current date. In order to do that, we needed to use a Java object called the Calendar object. As we learned in prior weeks, Java objects are defined by a class. What I haven't told you is that Java classes are bundled into packages. So far, during the course, all of the Java objects that we've needed to work with—for instance, the System object and the String object—have automatically been found by our programs because they can be found in a default package called java.lang. Some classes, however, such as the Calendar class we use in this program, are found in special packages that are not automatically searched when we compile and execute our programs. For that reason, we need to specifically include a reference to these classes in our program. We do that by including an Import statement for their package. The Calendar class is found in a package called java.util, and this Import statement tells Java to search through every class in the java.util package for any objects that it can't find in the default package."

```
import java.util.*;
```

"There's also another option of the Import statement," I said, "in which we specify the specific class we wish to reference, like this:"

```
import java.util.calendar;
```

"In general, it's best to be as specific as possible, although using the asterisk does not make your program any less efficient. However, if you know you need a specific class, just include that one via the Import statement."

"How would we know that?" Rose asked. "Are there many packages that are not the default?"

"There are quite a few packages," I said. "In this class, you'll be learning about the major types of packages, so that will help you out there. Another good source of information is the Java documentation that comes with the Java Developer's Kit, which can let you know about the many types of packages, along with the powerful functionality that they provide."

I waited a moment before continuing with my discussion of the code.

"I think you are all comfortable with the next two statements," I said. "The first declares the name of the class, and the second declares the **main()** method…"

```
class Practice4_2 {
    public static void main(String[] args)        {
```

"I suspect these next two variable declarations may have thrown some of you for a loop," I said.

```
Calendar cal = Calendar.getInstance();
Date now = new Date();
```

"They sure did," Rhonda said. "We didn't cover these data types last week."

"These aren't primitive data types, like Int or Float," I said. "Calendar and Date are both objects. These statements declare variables of type Calendar and Date."

"What does that mean?" Lou asked.

"Well," I replied, "when we declare a variable of type Int, we name and set aside some storage in the computer's memory to hold data that is an integer. When we declare a variable of type Calendar, we name and set aside some store in the computer's memory to hold data that is a Calendar object."

"Where's the variable name here?" Blaine asked. "I think I'm missing something somewhere."

"This statement," I said, "declares a Calendar variable called cal and then invokes the **getInstance()** method of the Calendar object that actually creates the Calendar object. Once the Calendar object is created using the **getInstance()** method, thereafter we refer to the Calendar object by using the variable name cal:"

```
Calendar cal = Calendar.getInstance();
```

"That makes sense," Jack said. "I think it's just a matter of getting used to a variable referring to something other than a number or a character."

"It does take some getting used to," I said. "But remember, Java is very much object-oriented. You'll be dealing with object variables like this quite often."

I waited for questions before continuing.

"In a similar way," I said, "this statement declares a Date variable called now and then uses the new keyword to tell Java to create an instance of a Date object:"

```
Date now = new Date();
```

"In the declaration of the variable cal, we used the **getInstance()** method to create the Calendar object. Here the Date object is created using the new keyword; once it's created, we refer to the Date object by using the object variable name now."

"I think I'm OK with the variable declarations," Steve said, "but can you tell me what's happening with that next statement? What's now?"

"Now is our Date object," I said. "This statement executes the **setTime()** method of the Calendar object, using the current date and time which is contained in the Date object **now**:"

```
cal.setTime(now);
```

"So what happens after that statement executes," Ward asked. "Where does Java get the current date and time?"

"Executing the **setTime()** method," I answered, "initializes the Calendar object with the current date and time which is maintained by our Date object now. Once the date and time is stored in the Calendar object, we can use some of the Calendar object's methods and attributes to our advantage. Here we are executing the **get()** method of the Calendar object and passing to it as an argument the constant DAY_OF_WEEK:"

```
int dayofweek = cal.get(Calendar.DAY_OF_WEEK);
```

"DAY_OF_WEEK, when passed to the **get()** method of the Calendar object, tells Java to determine the current date and time of the Calendar object and to return an Integer value between 1 and 7 that equates to the day of the week, where Sunday is 1, Monday is 2, through Saturday, which is 7. That return value is then assigned to the Integer variable *dayofweek*. Since today is a Saturday, executing this method assigns the value 7 to the variable *dayofweek*."

I waited to see if anyone was confused—I wouldn't blame them if they were. A discussion of objects is a topic that, in other courses, I would ordinarily postpone until much later in the course, but in Java, it just can't be helped.

"It seems to me," Dave said, "that working with these built-in Java objects can save the programmer a lot of effort and time. In other programming languages I've used, I've spent a bunch of time writing code to do what just this single line of Java code just did."

"That's the idea of object-oriented programming," I said. "There are a bunch of Java objects available to use to make our programming lives easier."

"Getting back to the code," Rhonda interrupted, "now that the variable dayofweek has a number in it, what do we do with it?"

"That's where the next few lines of code come in," I said. "This line of code introduces us to our first Java Selection structure: the If Statement, which determines if the dayofweek variable equates to Sunday:"

```
if (dayofweek == Calendar.SUNDAY)
```

"A Java If statement evaluates an expression to determine if it is True or False. In this case, the expression is 'dayofweek == Calendar.SUNDAY'."

"Didn't you say that constants are written in all caps?" Joe asked. "And didn't you say that dayofweek would be equal to the number 1 if the current date equated to Sunday?"

"That's right, Joe," I said. "In this case, SUNDAY is a built-in constant belonging to the Calendar object, and it has a value of 1. Using built-in constants like this is a lot easier than using hard-to-remember numbers, plus the code is a lot more readable. We could have written the code like this:"

```
if (dayofweek == 1)
```

"But I think you'll agree that it's not nearly as easy to read and understand."

"The expression that is evaluated as part of the If statement, does it have to be within parentheses?" Chuck asked.

"Good question, Chuck," I said. "The answer is yes, the expression must be enclosed within parentheses, and it must be an expression that can evaluate to a True or False result."

"What happens if the expression evaluates to True?" Kate asked.

"If the expression evaluates to True," I said, "then any imperative statements following it are executed."

"What's an imperative statement?" Rhonda asked.

"Simply speaking," I said, "an imperative statement is a command. In this case, we coded just a single imperative statement to be executed if the day of week happens to be a Sunday:"

```
System.out.println("Eat at Joe's");
```

"If you want to execute more than one imperative statement if the expression is true, you need to place each one within a block. In Java, a block is code that is placed within curly braces, like this:"

```
if (dayofweek == Calendar.SUNDAY) {
  System.out.println("Imperative Statement #1");
  System.out.println("Imperative Statement #2");
  System.out.println("Imperative Statement #3");
}
```

Note: A block is a group of statements between curly braces { }. As noted last week, a block is only required in an If statement if there are multiple imperative statements to execute. With a single imperative statement, the curly braces are not required.

"Provided you understand how our first If statement works, the remainder of the If statements are pretty straightforward. All we're doing is evaluating the value of the variable dayofweek against the other built-in Calendar constants which represent the other six days of the week. Since we've covered all of our bases here, one of these should evaluate to True, depending upon the current day of the week:"

```
if (dayofweek == Calendar.MONDAY)
  System.out.println("Eat at Tom's");
if (dayofweek == Calendar.TUESDAY)
  System.out.println("Eat at Kevin's");
if (dayofweek == Calendar.WEDNESDAY)
  System.out.println("Eat at Rich's");
if (dayofweek == Calendar.THURSDAY)
  System.out.println("Eat at Rose's");
if (dayofweek == Calendar.FRIDAY)
  System.out.println("Eat at Ken's");
```

"Since our class meets on Saturdays, it's this expression that will evaluate to True, resulting in the advertisement for Melissa's restaurant being displayed in the Java Console:"

```
if (dayofweek == Calendar.SATURDAY)
  System.out.println("Eat at Melissa's");
```

"What happens if the expression should evaluate to False?" Valerie asked. "Didn't you say earlier we could specify a statement or statements to execute if the expression is False?"

"Optionally, you can do that, yes," I answered, "using an Else clause of the If statement. In this case we opted to have the next If statement executed instead."

"So if the If statement evaluates to False," Dave asked, "the Imperative statement or statements are skipped, and execution of the program picks up with the next line of code following them?"

"That's excellent, Dave," I said. "I couldn't have said it better myself."

"I feel pretty good about If statements," Lou said. "Is that all there is to them?"

"We still have some more to learn about them, Lou," I replied. "There's still the Else clause to consider, plus there's another Selection structure called the Switch statement we need to learn about. However, I thought this portion of the class would be a great time to give you an introduction to the world of windows."

An Introduction to Windows

"Do you mean Microsoft Windows?" Kate asked.

"No," I answered. "I mean the generic type of windows that can be produced in a variety of operating systems. Remember, the great thing about Java is that its compiler and interpreter is available for almost every operating system there is. Because of that, we can produce programs that run on a PC running Microsoft Windows or the many flavors of Unix and Linux and that run on the Macintosh, too."

"So when you say 'windows,'" Dave asked, "you're referring to windows with a lowercase w?"

"Exactly right, Dave," I said. "Later on in the course, we'll learn how to write an entire program that is windows-based, but I thought I would take a few moments to show you how easy it is to display a window in Java. Let's take the program we wrote during the first week of class, the IloveJava class, and see if we can display its message in a window instead of to the Java Console."

Windows Out

I could sense that the class was getting a bit excited as I continued. "Here's the code from that first program," I said, as I displayed it on the classroom projector:

```java
class ILoveJava {
  public static void main(String[] args) {
    System.out.println("I love Java!");
  }
}
```

"When we run this program, the phrase 'I Love Java' is displayed in the Java Console. Nowadays, I think it's safe to say that most users expect to see their output in a window or a message box of some kind, so let's convert this program to do exactly that."

I then displayed this code on the classroom projector:

```java
import javax.swing.JOptionPane;
class Example4_1 {
  public static void main(String[] args) {
    JOptionPane.showMessageDialog (null, "I Love Java!");
  }
}
```

I saved the program as Example4_1.java, compiled it, and ran it for the class. The following screenshot was displayed on the classroom projector:

"I love this," Ward said. "Finally, output to something other than the Console."

"That Import statement at the top of the code window," Mary said, "is that what enabled us to create this window?"

"That's part of it, Mary," I said. "There's a great deal of functionality available in Java, if you know where to find it. All of the windows functionality that we'll discuss in this course is available in a package called javax.swing—which is a relatively new package. The Swing objects, their methods and attributes, allow us to add windows functionality in the programs we write."

"Relatively new package?" Dave asked. "Java's been out for a while—didn't early versions of Java permit you to create windows programs?"

"Yes, they did," I answered, "but to do so you had to use the older Abstract Windowing Toolkit, or AWT for short. AWT has some drawbacks, and in this course, we'll be dealing exclusively with the newer Swing package. Swing is a much more powerful package of objects. Its only drawback is that creating applets—Java classes that run in a Web browser—is more complicated to implement. But we'll get into that toward the end of the course."

"Can we take a look at the code now?" Peter asked.

"Sure thing, Peter," I said. "As Mary sensed, this line of code was extremely important— importing the javax.swing package. In this case, specifically the import of the JOptionPane class of the javax.swing package:"

```
import javax.swing.JOptionPane;
```

"That Import statement is a little different than the Import statement we used in our Grades class last week," Valerie said. "What's the difference?"

"It's a subtle one, Valerie," I said. "In the case of the Grades class, our Import statement looks like this:"

```
import java.util.*;
```

"There, the asterisk in the Import statement tells Java that we may be using every class in the java.util package. In the case of this program, we're telling Java to import a specific class called JOptionPane from the javax.swing package."

"Is there an advantage to using one Import statement over the other?" Dave asked. "Why didn't we just use an Import statement to include every class in the javax.swing package?"

"Efficiency-wise," I said, "there's no difference whether you reference a specific class in the Import statement or use an asterisk to reference each one. However, for readability's sake, it's probably a good idea to be specific as you can be in the Import statement. For instance, if you know you'll be using only a specific class from the package, as we did here, some programmers would choose to name that specific class in the Import statement. Other programmers wouldn't bother and instead would opt to include each class by using an asterisk. I'll leave the final decision up to you."

"So JoptionPane in this case is a specific class found in the javax.swing package?" Linda asked. "That's right," I said. "JOptionPane is a class whose **showMessageDialog()** method results in the display of a specific type of Java window called a message box:"

```
JOptionPane.showMessageDialog (null, "I Love Java!");
```

"What are those values in the parentheses?" Mary asked.

"Those values are called arguments," I said. "An argument is a value that is passed to an object's method that provides additional information about its operation. The number and type of arguments are said to make up the method's signature. You may not have realized it, but we passed a single argument to the **println()** method in the previous version of this program—the argument was the message we wanted to display in the Java Console. In this case, we're passing two arguments to the **showMessageDialog()** method of the JOptionPane class."

Note: A method's signature is the number and type of arguments that it expects.

"What are the arguments used for, again?" Blaine asked.

"Arguments are used to qualify or affect the behavior of a method," I said. "Earlier today, we learned how using Selection structures can alter the falling rock behavior of a Java program. In the same way, when a method accepts arguments, and virtually all of them do, the arguments can be used to alter or affect the behavior of the method. In the case of the **showMessageDialog()** method, the first argument is used to specify the frame, or window, in which the message will be displayed, and the second argument is used to specify the message itself."

"What is **null**?" Chuck asked.

"Null tells Java to display the message in a default frame," I said. "Since in this program we have no other windows defined, null tells Java to create one for us."

"I'm a little confused," Dave said. "I just brought up Java Help on my PC, and I see three different **showMessageDialog()** methods listed—one with two arguments, one with four arguments, and one with five. What's going on?"

Dave was right: there are three methods of the JOptionPane object called **showMessageDialog()**.

"Good question, Dave," I said. "When we create objects of our own later on in the course, you'll learn that it's possible to define more than one method with the same name but different code."

"If two methods have the same name," Kate asked, "how does Java know which method to execute if a program invokes the method?"

"Java knows the number and type of arguments in its signature," I said. "As Dave discovered, there are actually three different **showMessageDialog()** methods of the JOptionPane object. When we executed the method here in our code, we passed two arguments to it, and that told Java to execute the version of the method that calls for two arguments. If we had passed the **showMessageDialog()** four arguments, then Java would have executed the version of the method that calls for four arguments. This process is called method overloading. It's when methods have the same name but can be differentiated by the number and type of arguments they accept."

> Note: Method overloading occurs when more than one method has the same name but can be differentiated by the number and type of arguments it accepts.

"Wow," Ward said, "that explains what Dave discovered. But why would you want to do something like that—why not give the methods different names? Isn't it confusing to have more than one method with the same name?"

"It can be confusing at first," I said, "but you'll get used to it, and you will probably grow to appreciate the fact that you don't need to remember a bunch of different names to execute a method that essentially does the same thing as the others. All you'll need to do is pass it the correct number and type of arguments to do the job."

"Will we be creating overloaded methods of our own in the Grade Calculation Project?" Dave asked.

"We certainly could," I answered. "We'll be writing code to calculate the final grade of an English, Math, or Science student, and we'll probably place that code within a **Calculate()** method. The English student's grade is comprised of four component grades: midterm, final, research paper, and a presentation grade. The Math student's grade is comprised of two component grades: midterm and final. And the Science student's grade is comprised of three component grades: midterm, final, and research grade."

"I think I see what you are getting at," Dave said. "We could create three different methods all called **Calculate()** and based on the number of arguments passed—the signature—Java can determine which of the three methods to execute."

"You've got it, Dave!" I said, excitedly, although I recognized that most of the other students in the class would need a few more weeks for this concept of overloading for it to really sink in.

"Don't concern yourself with method overloading too much right now," I said. "We'll discuss the concept in more detail later on when we create objects and methods of our own. For now, I just wanted to give you a heads up on the concept since Dave discovered it with the **showMessageDialog()**."

Oops, There's Problem

"I was wondering if anyone else noticed," Linda said, "that after clicking the OK button in the message box, the program never ended. The DOS window— if that's what I should call it—stays open."

Linda was right: there was a problem.

"She's right," Steve said. "I hadn't noticed that before, but when I typed in your example code and compiled and then executed it, the message box was displayed. But after I clicked the OK button, my DOS window remained open. Even worse, I can't type the word 'Exit' at the DOS prompt to close it."

"Both of you are right," I said. "The previous version of the program in which we displayed the phrase 'I Love Java!' to the Java Console came to a graceful end, but this program didn't behave nearly as well. It turns out that whenever you write a program that displays a graphical user interface as this one does, you need to explicitly terminate the program yourself."

"I'm not sure what you mean," Blaine said. "We never had to do that before. How do we do it?"

"You're right," I said. "For a program that displays no windows, the falling rock behavior of the Java program will end the program on its own. Here, however, we need to execute the **exit()** method of the System object to end the program. Here's the modified code that will enable the program to end gracefully."

I then displayed this modified code on the classroom projector:

```
import javax.swing.JOptionPane;
class Example4_2 {
  public static void main(String[] args) {
    JOptionPane.showMessageDialog (null, "I Love Java!");
    System.exit (0);
  }
}
```

I saved the program as Example4_2.java, compiled it, and ran it for the class. As with the previous version of the program, a message box was displayed on the classroom projector. However, this time when I clicked the OK button, the program ended gracefully.

"That's better," I said. "All we needed to do was execute the **exit()** method of the System object."

System.exit (0);

"I presume that zero is an argument to the **exit()** method," Mary said. "What's that all about?"

"Zero," I said, "is an argument that tells the **exit()** method that the program has ended normally. This is pretty much a universal convention used when closing an application. This could be used when another program, such as a Windows batch file or a Unix shell script, executes our Java program and has access to a return value from the **exit()** method. In this case, it doesn't really matter what argument we pass to the **exit()** method, but again, by convention, zero is used to indicate a successful termination of a program."

I could sense that my students were really excited about our first foray into the world of windows programming so I decided to give them a chance to work with a program of their own. I then distributed this exercise for the class to complete.

I then distributed this exercise for the class to complete.

Exercise 4-3 The Restaurant Program---a Windows Version

In this exercise, we'll modify the code from Exercise 4-2 to display the restaurant advertisements in a Java message box instead of the Java Console.
1. Use Notepad (if you are using Windows) and enter the following code.

```
import java.util.*;
import javax.swing.JOptionPane;
class Practice4_3 {
  public static void main(String[] args) {
    Calendar cal = Calendar.getInstance();
    Date now = new Date();
    cal.setTime(now);
    int dayofweek = cal.get(Calendar.DAY_OF_WEEK);
    if (dayofweek == Calendar.SUNDAY)
      JOptionPane.showMessageDialog(null, "Eat at Joe's");
    if (dayofweek == Calendar.MONDAY)
      JOptionPane.showMessageDialog(null, "Eat at Tom's");
    if (dayofweek == Calendar.TUESDAY)
```

```
      JOptionPane.showMessageDialog(null, "Eat at Kevin's");
   if (dayofweek == Calendar.WEDNESDAY)
      JOptionPane.showMessageDialog(null, "Eat at Rich's");
   if (dayofweek == Calendar.THURSDAY)
      JOptionPane.showMessageDialog(null, "Eat at Rose's");
   if (dayofweek == Calendar.FRIDAY)
      JOptionPane.showMessageDialog(null, "Eat at Ken's");
   if (dayofweek == Calendar.SATURDAY)
      JOptionPane.showMessageDialog(null, "Eat at Melissa's");
   System.exit (0);
   }
}
```

2. Save your source file as Practice4_3 in the \JFiles\Practice folder (select File | Save As from Notepad's menu bar). Be sure to save your source file with the filename extension .java.

3. Compile your source file into a Bytecode file.

4. Execute your Bytecode file. You should see one restaurant advertisement displayed in the Java console (which one it is will depend upon the day of the week on which you run the program) similar to this screenshot:

Discussion

As I mentioned, everyone in the class seemed genuinely excited to get going with a windows program. Despite their excitement, no one had any major problems completing the exercise although, as always, there were the occasional typos. As we have seen by now, Java code can be a bit wordy and tedious to type, and you always have to watch out for the proper capitalization of the class-object names.

"All we've done with this program," I said, "is output the display of the restaurant advertisements in a message box instead of the Java Console. Does anyone have any questions?"

Rhonda made a comment that as our programs grew larger, she was having trouble discerning the end points of the **main()** method and the class itself.

"That's a good point, Rhonda," I pointed out. "Some Java programmers use comments to delineate the end points of their methods and class definitions. Like this:"

```
   JOptionPane.showMessageDialog(null, "Eat at Melissa's"); System.exit (0);
   }             // end of method main()
}             // end of class Practice4_3
```

"You may want to consider doing the same thing, particularly as your programs grow in size."

"I see what you mean," Rhonda said, "I think that will help me."

No one had any questions about the exercise and, because of the great progress we were making, I decided to cover the topic of accepting input into our program from the user before our first break.

Windows In

"Up to this point," I said, "we have not yet written a program that accepts data from outside of the program while it's running. In the programming world, this is a common need, and there are many ways to accomplish this. For instance, a program can open and read data from a file on the user's PC or network; it can also open and read data from a database, which is a more sophisticated form of a data file. It can also accept data directly from the user."

"Do you mean our program can ask the user a question and do something with their answer?" Rhonda asked.

"Yes, Rhonda, " I said, "that's exactly what I'm getting at. In the next few minutes, I'll demonstrate two ways to accomplish this. One way is to use an Input Console window, which is similar to the Java Console we used earlier to display output. The other way is to use a Java input box, which is very similar to the Java message box."

I thought for a moment and then wrote and displayed this program on the classroom projector:

```
import java.io.*;
class Example4_3 {
  public static void main (String[] args) throws IOException {
    BufferedReader stdin = new BufferedReader (new InputStreamReader(System.in));
    String response;
    System.out.println ("What is your favorite programming language?");
    response = stdin.readLine();
    System.out.println("You have great taste. " + response+"isa great language");
  }
}
```

I saved the program as Example4_3.java, compiled it, and ran it for the class. The following screenshot was displayed on the classroom projector:

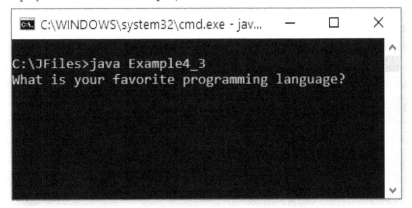

"It's not obvious," I said, "but the program is prompting us to name our favorite programming language. At this point, all we need to do is type our answer and press the ENTER key." I did so, and the following screenshot was displayed on the classroom projector:

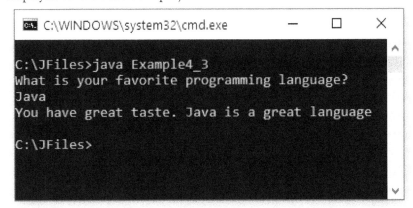

"Let me explain what's going on here," I said. "As we did with our last few programs, we begin the program by importing a package. This one's a new one called the java.io package, which gives us access to a number of objects that permit us to work with input and output within our program."

import java.io.*;

"Let me guess," Rhonda said, "is stdin an object?"

"Not quite, Rhonda," I answered, "but you're close. With this line of code we are declaring an object variable called stdin of type BufferedReader."

BufferedReader stdin = new BufferedReader (new InputStreamReader(System.in));

"The BufferedReader class, which is contained in the java.io package, allows us to create an object which accepts data via the Java Console. I know this line of code is a bit complicated, but what we are doing is telling Java to create a stream—think of it as a connection or a pipeline— from the Console to the object variable stdin. Once that stream is established, whatever the user types into the Console window until they hit the ENTER key will be directed to the variable *stdin*."

I paused to see if everyone was still with me. They were.

"Once the variable *stdin* is declared to refer to an instance of a BufferedReader object, we then declare a variable called response, which will actually hold the contents of the user's response:"

```
String response;
```

"If we want the user to give us an answer, we mustn't forget to ask the question, and we use the now-familiar **println()** method to do that:"

```
System.out.println ("What is your favorite programming language?");
```

"This line of code executes the **readLine()** method of the BufferedReader object. The **readLine()** method tells Java to read from the Console whatever the user types in until they hit the ENTER key."

```
response = stdin.readLine();
```

"Finally, since we have the user's answer in the response variable, we can use it to confirm the user's great taste in a programming language, using the plus (+) operator to concatenate the value of the response variable to the string 'You have great taste.'"

```
System.out.println ("You have great taste. " + response + " is a great language");
```

"I'm amazed that I actually understand what's going on here," Rose said, "but can you explain the difference in the declaration of the **main()** method line? There's something new there."

"Thanks for reminding me, Rose," I said. "I almost forgot about that. The **main()** method line does have something new you haven't seen before: it's called the 'throws' keyword."

```
public static void main (String[] args) throws IOException {
```

"Later in the course, we'll learn about Java exceptions," I said, "but it's way too early to get into exceptions too deeply here. In brief, an exception is an error that occurs as a result of Java code being executed. In our program, the **readLine()** method of the BufferedReader object can potentially trigger an error, and the developers of the **readLine()** method defined the **readLine()** method with the clause 'throws IOException'."

"What does that mean?" Lou asked.

"A method defined with the throws IOException clause," I said, "means that some kind of input-output error might occur when it is executed. In Java, if a method, such as the **readLine()** method being executed within the **main()** method is defined with the Throws keyword, you also need to include the 'throws' keyword in the **main()** method declaration as well."

"What should we do if an exception does occur as a result of executing the **readLine()** method?" Dave asked.

"In this case, we don't need to do anything," I answered. "The **readLine()** method has been written with code to handle any IOExceptions that may occur when it's executed. We'll see later in the course that we can define actions for our program to take in the event that an exception does occur—but more on that later."

"What happens if we don't include the Throws keyword in the **main()** method declaration?" Linda asked.

"If we fail to include the Throws keyword here," I said, "the program simply won't compile. We would see this error message from the compiler, which is telling us that a method we are executing within the **main()** method is defined with the Throws clause:"

Everyone seemed content with that explanation—at least, for the time being.

"I love what this program does," Jack said, "but I'm anxious to see how this program will work with a Java input box. Will you be showing us that?"

"Sure thing, Jack," I answered. "Here's the same program written using a Java input box." I then displayed this version of the program on the classroom projector:

```
import javax.swing.JOptionPane;
class Example4_4 {
  public static void main (String[] args) {
    String response;
    response = JOptionPane.showInputDialog
      ("What is your favorite programming language?");
    System.out.println
      ("You have great taste. " + response + " is a great language");
    System.exit (0);
  }
}
```

I then saved the program as Example4_4.java, compiled it, and ran it for the class. The following screenshot was displayed on the classroom projector:

"Just like the previous version of the program," I said, "this program is asking us to name our favorite programming language, but this time the question is posed in a more user-friendly window with OK and Cancel buttons. Most importantly, there's an area into which we can type a response. Let's provide it with an answer."

After entering Java as my favorite language and clicking the OK button, we received the same message as before complimenting us on our good taste.

"This version of the program" I said, "isn't much different from the previous version. Instead of using the BufferedReader object found in the java.io package to accept input from the user, we used the JoptionPane object, found in the javax.swing package to display an input box by executing its **showInputDialog()** method:"

```
response = JOptionPane.showInputDialog
  ("What is your favorite programming language?");
```

"**showInputDialog()** is similar to the **showMessageDialog()** method we executed to display a message box. The **showInputDialog()** method we used here has a flavor that requires just a single argument: the prompt to display to the user. By default, the showInputDialog() method displays an area, technically called a TextField, into which the user can make an entry, along with two buttons, an OK button and a Cancel button."

I told my students that I'd like to give them a chance to experiment just a bit with both the Java input box and the Java message box, and so I distributed this exercise for them to complete.

Exercise 4-4 Experimenting with the Java showInputDialog() Method

In this exercise, we'll write code to display a Java input box and to display the entry the user makes into a Java message box. We'll discover several limitations of the input box, namely, whatever value we enter into the TextField portion of the input box will be displayed in the Java message box, and if we enter noting into the TextField or immediately click the Cancel button, we'll receive some unsatisfactory results.

1. Use Notepad (if you are using Windows) and enter the following code.

```java
import javax.swing.JOptionPane;
class Practice4_4 {
public static void main (String[] args) {
  String response;
  response = JOptionPane.showInputDialog
    ("What is your first name?");
  JOptionPane.showMessageDialog
    (null, "It's nice to meet you, " + response);
  System.exit (0);
  }
}
```

2. Save your source file as Practice4_4 in the \JFiles\Practice folder (select File | Save As from Notepad's menu bar). Be sure to save your source file with the filename extension .java.
3. Compile your source file into a Bytecode file.
4. Execute your program. Enter your name in the input box and click the OK button. Your name should then be displayed in a message box.
5. Execute your program again, and this immediately click the OK button of the input box. What does Java display in the message box?
6. Execute your program once more, enter your name into the TextField of the input box, but then click then Cancel button. What does Java display in the message box?

Discussion

No one had any problems completing the exercise—by now they were getting pretty good with coding a simple Java program and having a great time doing it. I ran the program myself and entered my name, and a message box reading, "It's nice to meet you, John" was displayed on the classroom projector:

"Did everyone have a chance to observe?" I asked. "What happens when you made no entry into the input box or when you make an entry into the input box but then click the Cancel button?"

I ran the program, entered nothing into the input box, and clicked the OK button. The following screenshot was displayed on the classroom projector:

"Java is confused," I said, "so it's displaying what it believes to be my name: an empty string. If we run the program again but this time enter my name and then click the Cancel button, we'll get a slightly different result." I did exactly that and the following screenshot was displayed on the classroom projector:

"Null?" Rhonda asked.

"That's right," I said. "When we enter a value into the input box and then click the OK button, the value entered into the input box is then assigned to the variable response. When we click the Cancel button, however, the value assigned to the variable response is the special Java value null. In programming, null has a special significance: it literally means nothing. The developers of the Java **showInputDialog()** method decided to return a null value if the user clicks the Cancel button. This is simply a signal to the program using the **showInputDialog()** method that the user has clicked the Cancel button. By the way, as you can see from the difference in the display of the message box, null is not the same as an empty string."

"What can we do about this?" Linda asked

The If…Else Statement

"If we want to ensure that the user enters something into the input box," I said, "then this code has a few deficiencies. The code is just blindly executing the **showMessageDialog()** method, regardless of what value is stored in the response variable."

"I guess the question is," Kate said, "what do we want to do if the user enters nothing into the input box and then clicks the OK button or just clicks the Cancel button?"

"I would think if the user clicks the Cancel button," Dave said, "their intent is pretty clear: they don't wish to enter their name, and we should probably just end the program. But clicking the OK button without entering any value in the input box sounds like a mistake on their part, and I would think we should ask them again."

"I think you're right on the mark, Dave," I said. "Ending the program if the user clicks the Cancel button is no big deal. We can use an If statement to do that. Your last suggestion for what to do when they make no entry and click the OK button—asking them the question once again—is a bit more complicated and is something we'll learn how to do next week when we discuss the Java Loop structure. Today, we'll see that we can use an If statement to determine if the user has clicked the Cancel button and to then display a warning message to them. In fact, having to do so will give us a chance to work with the Else clause of the If statement I mentioned a little earlier."

"The Else clause?" Mary asked.

"That's right, Mary," I said. "With the If statements we've seen so far, we've specified only the imperative statements to execute if the expression evaluates to True. Using the Else clause, we can specify one or more imperative statements to execute if the expression evaluates to False. Before we tackle the issue of checking for an empty input box or to see if they have clicked the Cancel button, let me show you a program that uses a simple If…Else statement."

I then displayed this program on the classroom projector:

```
import javax.swing.JOptionPane;
class Example4_5 {
  public static void main (String[] args) {
    String response;
    response = JOptionPane.showInputDialog
      ("What is your favorite programming language?");
    if (response.equals("Java"))
      JOptionPane.showMessageDialog
        (null, "You have great taste. Java is a great language");
    else
```

```
    JOptionPane.showMessageDialog
        (null, "it's not as good as Java but " +
        response + " is also a great language");
    System.exit (0);
    }
}
```

I saved the program as Example4_5.java, compiled it, and ran it for the class. The program asked me what my favorite programming language was. I answered Java and was congratulated on my good taste.

"As you can see, we used an If Statement to determine if the user entered 'Java'," I said. "Since the If Statement found what it was looking for—Java—it executed this imperative statement:"

```
if (response.equals("Java"))
    JOptionPane.showMessageDialog
        (null, "You have great taste. Java is a great language");
```

"I have a question," Dave said. "Why is it that we didn't use the double equal sign to check for the equality here?"

"That's because the variable response is defined as a String," I answered, "You may remember that in Java Strings are not primitive data types, they are objects. As a result, whenever you need to check the value of a String variable the way we did here, you need to use the **equals()** method of the String object, not the == operator."

I could see some confusion in my students' faces, so I added that we would be devoting some time to discussing the String object later on in the course.

"I see we used the Else clause here," Kate said. "Do I understand that the statement following the word Else will be executed if the user enters anything other than 'Java' into the input box?"

"That's right, Kate," I answered. "If the evaluation of this expression results in a False condition, "then the statement or statements following the word 'Else' are executed:"

```
Else
    JOptionPane.showMessageDialog
        (null, "it's not as good as Java but " +
        response +
        " is also a great language");
```

"By the way, note that if the user enters the word 'Java' in any other fashion than with a capital J and the lowercase letters a-v-a, our program will discern that as a false condition also. We'll see how we can improve upon that later on in the course. For now, let's run this program again and answer the question with another language."

I did exactly that, this time providing an answer of C++ as my language of choice. When I did, the following screenshot was displayed:

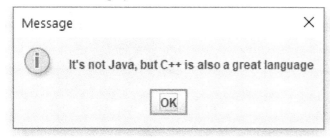

"The display of this message box was handled by the Else clause of the If statement," I said. "I should also mention that it's possible to code an If statement as the imperative statement that follows the Else clause."

"Wow, that sounds confusing," Rhonda said. "Why would we want to do that?"

"That allows us to handle situations where we have multiple conditions to test for," I answered. "For instance, if we wanted to display unique messages for a variety of answers that the user might provide to us."

No one had any questions about the If statement or the Else clause, so I suggested that we turn our attention to using an If statement to handle the problems from Exercise 4-4 that arose from the user entering nothing into the input box and then clicking the OK Button or from clicking the Cancel button.

Exercise 4-5 Using an If statement to check for an Empty Input Box

In this exercise, we'll modify the code from Exercise 4-4 so that if the user makes no entry in the input box or clicks the Cancel button an appropriate message will be displayed.

1. Use Notepad (if you are using Windows) and enter the following code.

```java
import javax.swing.JOptionPane;
class Practice4_5 {
  public static void main (String[] args) {
    String response;
    response = JOptionPane.showInputDialog
      ("What is your first name?");
    if (response == null)
      JOptionPane.showMessageDialog
        (null, "You clicked on the Cancel button");
    else
    if (response.equals(""))
      JOptionPane.showMessageDialog
        (null, "You must make an entry in the InputBox");
    else
      JOptionPane.showMessageDialog
        (null, "It's nice to meet you, " + response);
    System.exit (0);
  }
}
```

2. Save your source file as Practice4_5 in the \JFiles\Practice folder (select File | Save As from Notepad's menu bar). Be sure to save your source file with the filename extension .java.
3. Compile your source file into a Bytecode file.
4. Execute your program. When prompted, type your name into the input box and click the OK button. Your name should then be displayed in the message box.
5. Execute your program again, and this time immediately click the OK button of the input box. What does Java display in the message box?
6. Execute your program once more, enter your name into the input box, but then click the Cancel button. What does Java display in the message box?

Discussion

"Because of the If statements we've added to our code," I said, "this program now exhibits quite a bit of intelligence. If the user clicks the Cancel button, our program detects that by checking the value of the variable response against the keyword 'null' and displays a message box to the user.

```java
if (response == null)
  JOptionPane.showMessageDialog
    (null, "You clicked on the Cancel button");
```

I ran the program, immediately clicked the Cancel button and the following screenshot was displayed:

"Likewise," I continue, "if the user clicks the OK button without making an entry in the input box, we can use this code to determine if the value of the variable response is equal to the empty string."

```
if (response.equals(""))
    JOptionPane.showMessageDialog
        (null, "You forgot to make an entry in the InputBox");
```

I ran the program again, immediately clicked the OK button and the following screenshot was displayed:

"I'm OK with the way we checked for an empty string by using the **equals()** method with an empty set of quotation marks," Dave said, "but I notice that we didn't use the **equals()** method of the String object to determine if the value of the variable response was equal to null. Why is that?"

"Null is a special case," I said. "This syntax is necessary because we need to determine if the String object referred to by the response object variable is null, which will be the condition of the variable if the user clicks the Cancel button."

```
if (response == null)
```

"That's different from the condition of the response variable if the user clicks the OK button, in which case an empty string (sometimes called a null string) is assigned to the value of the variable. We check for an empty string by using the **equals()** method."

```
if (response.equals(""))
```

"The bottom line here is that whenever a method, such as **showInputDialog()**, might return a null like this, you should first check to see if the object variable is null using this syntax."

"I'm still not absolutely sure about the If statement syntax," Joe said. "Can you show us another example?"

After thinking for a few moments, I said, "To make this all a little more understandable for everyone, let me use pseudo code to illustrate an Else statement intended to display the number of years until an employee is eligible for retirement."

I saw some puzzled looks.

"I think I mentioned pseudo code earlier in the course," I said. "Pseudo code is a way that programmers use to express complex problems. Instead of coding the problem in a particular language, pseudo code lets us concentrate on expressing the problem in an English-like way. Then, when we have it worked out to our satisfaction, we can translate the pseudo code into whatever language we happen to be working in. Remember, what you see here isn't Java code, so don't try to type it into a code window!"

I then displayed this pseudo code on the classroom projector:

> **NOTE: Pseudo code is a way of expressing a complex problem in an English-like way, prior to coding it up in an actual programming language.**

There is an employee working for a company. According to the rules of the company:

If the employee's age is 62 or greater
  he/she must be retired
Else If the employee's age is 61
  he/she has 1 year until retirement
Else If the employee's age is 60
  he/she has 2 years until retirement
Else If the employee's age is 59
  he/she has 3 years until retirement
Else
  he/she has a really long time to go

I then suggested that we try implementing this Pseudo code in Java, but I warned everyone that our code would be a bit unwieldy.

"Using a series of Else If statements can be pretty cumbersome," I said. "After we write the code for this exercise, in Exercise 4-7 we'll look at an alternative Selection Structure called the Switch Statement which many times can be used to streamline If…Else statements.."

Exercise 4-6 The If…Else…If Statement

In this exercise, we'll create a program to determine how long an employee has until he or she can retire.
1. Use Notepad and enter the following code.

```java
import javax.swing.JOptionPane;
class Practice4_6 {
  public static void main (String[] args) {
    String response;
    response=JOptionPane.showInputDialog("What is your age?");
    if (response==null)
      JOptionPane.showMessageDialog(null, "You clicked on the Cancel button");
    else
    if (response.equals(""))
      JOptionPane.showMessageDialog
        (null, "You must make an entry in the InputBox");
    else
    if (Integer.parseInt(response) > 61)
      JOptionPane.showMessageDialog
        (null, response+"-You must be retired");
    else
    if (Integer.parseInt(response)==61)
      JOptionPane.showMessageDialog
        (null, response+"-You have 1 year until retirement");
    else
    if (Integer.parseInt(response)==60)
      JOptionPane.showMessageDialog
        (null, response+"-You have 2 years until retirement");
    else
    if (Integer.parseInt(response)==59)
      JOptionPane.showMessageDialog
        (null, response+"-You have 3 years until retirement");
    else
      JOptionPane.showMessageDialog
        (null, response+"-You have a long time until retirement");
    System.exit (0);
  }
}
```

2. Save your source file as Practice4_6 in the \JFiles\Practice folder (select File | Save As from Notepad's menu bar). Be sure to save your source file with the filename extension .java.
3. Compile your source file into a Bytecode file.
4. Execute your program multiple times, entering 62, 61, 60, 59, and 40 into the input box, and click the OK Button

after each entry. Observe the various messages that are displayed.

5. Execute the program one more time, this time clicking the OK Button without making an entry into the input box. You should receive a warning message from your program.

Discussion

There was probably more code in this exercise than in any of the others we had done so far, and several of my students became confused and lost their places. Fifteen minutes later, though, I was happy to see that everyone in the class had successfully completed the exercise.

"I don't think we've ever written that much code," Rhonda said.

"I think you're right, Rhonda," I replied. "We haven't written this much code before. When you write code that tests for a variety of conditions like we did here, your code can really balloon, but sometimes that's something that just can't be helped. The code you've written for this exercise, though lengthy, is still pretty manageable. Suppose we had a requirement to display a different message for every age between 1 and 100?"

"That would really balloon the code," Mary said. "Will the Switch statement you alluded to help cut down on the number of lines of code we have to write to test for multiple conditions?"

"It can," I said, "but before we discuss the Switch statement, I'd like to explain this code first which, by my count, contains a total of six Else statements."

I displayed the first line of code from the **main()** method on the classroom projector:

```
String response;
```

"You've seen this code before," I said. "What we're doing here is declaring a variable to hold the value of the user's response that they will type into the input box. Remember, the value that the user enters is returned to our program as a String, which is why we must declare the variable response as a string. This statement then uses the **showInputDialog()** method to prompt the user to tell us their age and then assigns the user's answer to the response variable."

```
response = JOptionPane.showInputDialog("What is your age?");
```

"These next few lines of code check to see if the user has clicked the Cancel button," I said.

"In a real-world program, at this point we would end the program but for now, while we're still getting comfortable with Java, we'll display a message instead:"

```
if (response == null)
   JOptionPane.showMessageDialog (null, "You clicked on the Cancel button");
```

"This section of code checks to see if the user has clicked the OK button without first entering a value into the input box. If they have, we warn them that they need to make an entry."

```
else
if (response.equals(""))
   JOptionPane.showMessageDialog
      (null, "You must make an entry in the InputBox");
```

"I noticed," Rhonda said, "that in both of these cases, as soon as the message is displayed to the user, the program ends. At least in the case where the user clicks the OK button without making an entry, shouldn't they be given the opportunity to type something into the input box without having to run the program all over again?"

"You're right, Rhonda," I said. "There is a way to do that—and that's something we'll learn how to do next week when we take up the topic of Java Loop structures."

"What's going on with this next line of code?" Ward asked. "What is **Integer.parseInt**?"

"Good question, Ward," I said. "**parseInt()** is a method of the Integer object, not to be confused with the Integer data type."

Ward (and the other students) seemed thoroughly confused.

"Do you remember what I said earlier about the variable response being a String variable?" I continued. "Our code needs to work with the user's response as a number, so that we can perform numeric comparison operations against them. To do that, we first need to convert the String value in the response variable to an Integer data type, and we do that by executing the **parseInt()** method of the Integer object. Once that conversion is performed, we can determine if the value the user has entered is greater than 61 using the greater than Comparison operator:"

```
else if (Integer.parseInt(response) > 61)
```

NOTE: There are corresponding parseShort, parseByte, and parseLong methods as well.

"We learned last week that Comparison operations return a True or a False value, and in this case, if the number entered into the input box is greater than 61, a True value is returned from this operation. We then display the user's age, concatenated with the string 'You must be retired' in a message box."

```
JOptionPane.showMessageDialog(null, response+"-You must be retired");
```

"What would have happened if we didn't convert the String value in response to an Integer?" Kate asked. "Our program would bomb," I answered. "Java is very picky. If we code an arithmetic operation, it will only perform them against numeric data types."

"What if the user's age is not greater than 61?" Kate asked. "This is where I became confused."

"If the user's age is not greater than 61," I said, "the Comparison operation returns a False value. Then, because of the Else statement, our code executes the imperative statement following the word Else. Of course, it turns out that the imperative statement is another If statement that is then evaluated by Java."

"Can we go back to that line of code where we display the message?" Chuck asked. "Why do we have a plus operator there?"

I explained that this line of code uses the concatenation operator, the plus sign (+) to join the string 'You must be retired' with the value of the response variable.

```
JOptionPane.showMessageDialog(null, response+"-You must be retired");
```

"Therefore, if the number 73 is entered into the input box, the Message Dialog box displays the following message: '73 - You must be retired.'"

"That's clever," Steve said. "So we're actually using the value of the variable response in the message, not a numeric literal."

"That's right, Steve," I said. "Using the value the user has entered in the message by using the value of the variable response gives us a much more flexible and descriptive message. In this way, no matter what age the user enters into the input box, that age is displayed in the message box."

I waited to see if there were any questions before continuing.

"In a similar way," I said, "we can use this code to determine if the value the user has entered into the input box is exactly equal to 61."

```
else
if (Integer.parseInt(response) == 61)
   JOptionPane.showMessageDialog
   (null, response + " - You have 1 year until retirement");
```

"If it is, we then execute the imperative statement to display an appropriate message. If the entry in the input box is not equal to 61, we execute the imperative statement of the Else clause, itself another If statement, to determine if the user's age is 60."

```
else
if (Integer.parseInt(response) == 60)
   JOptionPane.showMessageDialog
   (null, response+"-You have 2 years until retirement");
```

"I'm OK with this," Linda said. "This is basically the same code we used to determine if the user's age is 61. If it is, we display a slightly different message."

"That's right," I agreed, "and this code works in the same way, checking to see if the user's age is 59:"

```
else
if (Integer.parseInt(response) == 59)
   JOptionPane.showMessageDialog
   (null, response+"-You have 3 years until retirement");
```

"Now can you imagine," I said, "if we needed to write individual lines of code for every age from 59 on down to 1. Fortunately, we can take care of all of those possibilities with this single Else statement:"

```
else
JOptionPane.showMessageDialog
  (null, response + " - You have a long time until retirement");
```

"By using the Else statement here," I said, "we tell Java that all of the remaining ages fit into one category and to display a generic message indicating that the user has a long time until retirement."

I asked if there were any questions. "We didn't discuss the line of code outside of the If…Else structure, although I'm pretty sure I know what it does," Rhonda said. "Good point," I replied. "This line of code is executed regardless of the age that the user enters into the input box—as you saw earlier, the **exit()** method of the System object ends the program:"

```
System.exit (0);
```

I waited to see if there were any other questions. To my surprise, everyone in the class seemed pretty comfortable with the If statement. Now it was time to discuss another Selection structure—the Switch statement.

The Switch Statement

"The more alternatives we have in an If…Else…If statement," I said, "the harder the program is to write, read and modify, and the more likely it is that we'll make a mistake when we code it. I'd like to introduce you to another Java Selection Structure called the Switch statement. Here's the code for a program that asks the user to enter a number, between 1 and 3, into an input box."

I displayed this code on the classroom projector:

```java
import javax.swing.JOptionPane;
class Example4_6 {
  public static void main (String[] args) {
    String response;
    response = JOptionPane.showInputDialog("Pick a number between 1 and 3");
    if (response == null) {
      JOptionPane.showMessageDialog(null, "You clicked on the Cancel button");
      System.exit (0);
    }
    else
      if (response.equals("")) {
        JOptionPane.showMessageDialog
          (null, "You must make an entry in the InputBox");
        System.exit (0);`
      }
    switch (Integer.parseInt(response)) {          //Switch begins
      case 1:
        JOptionPane.showMessageDialog(null, "You entered the number 1");
        break;
      case 2:
        JOptionPane.showMessageDialog(null, "You entered the number 2");
        break;
      case 3:
        JOptionPane.showMessageDialog(null, "You entered the number 3");
        break;
      default:
        JOptionPane.showMessageDialog
          (null, "Oops, you entered a number not in the range 1 to 3");
    }                                              // Switch ends
    System.exit (0);
  }
}
```

"Let me explain what I've done here," I said. "As has become our custom in any program that presents an input box to the user, the first thing we do is declare our response variable as a String, and the next thing we do is to prompt the user to enter a number between 1 and 3:"

```
String response;
response = JOptionPane.showInputDialog("Pick a number between 1 and 3");
```

"As we did in the previous exercise, we test the response variable for a null value to determine if the user has clicked the Cancel button:"

```
if (response == null)
```

"This time, instead of merely displaying a message to the user, we specify two imperative statements to be executed if the condition evaluates as True. One imperative statement will display a message box; the other will end the program by executing the **exit()** method of the System object. We sandwich both of these imperative statements within curly braces:"

```
{
  JOptionPane.showMessageDialog(null, "You clicked on the Cancel button");
  System.exit (0);
}
```

"Why is it?" Dave asked, "that we went the extra yard this time by ending the program in addition to displaying the message to the user—that's new, isn't it?"

"We need to end the program at that point because of the falling rock behavior of our code," I said. "If all we did was display a message to the user, our code would continue executing, and within the Switch statement we would wind up evaluating the value of the response variable using the **parseInt()** method. In this case, since the value of the response variable does not contain an integer, our program would bomb."

I waited a moment before continuing.

"We then follow the test for the click of the Cancel button by checking to see if the user clicked the OK button but failed to make an entry into the input box:"

```
else
if (response.equals(""))
```

"If the user has clicked the OK button, but made no entry in the Input box, the value of response will be equal to ""—and we execute two imperative statements: a message to the user and the **exit()** method of the System object:"

```
{
  JOptionPane.showMessageDialog
    (null, "You must make an entry in the InputBox");
    System.exit (0);
}
```

"With these two tests out of the way, we now know that the user entered something into the textbox. We're expecting a number between 1 and 3, but of course, users don't always do what we expect them to. I should also tell you at this point that if the user enters something other than a number into the input box—the letter a, for instance—this code will bomb. There are ways to check for a nonnumeric entry in the input box, but at this point in the course, it's a little beyond us. For now, let's concentrate on understanding the Switch statement which we execute with this line of code:"

```
switch (Integer.parseInt(response))    {        //Switch begins
```

"The Switch statement," I said, "begins with the word 'switch.' The entirety of the Switch statement is enclosed within a pair of curly braces, which I've marked with comments in this example. The word 'switch' is followed by what is called a test expression. The test expression can be a variable, but in actuality it can be anything that evaluates to a Byte, Short, Int, or Char data type."

"So that's why we were able to use the **parseInt()** method within the test expression here," Dave said, "because it returns an Integer data type."

"That's right Dave," I answered. "According to the rules for the Switch statement, the test expression must return only a primitive data type—Byte, Char, Short, or Int. Now, here comes the tricky part. The result of the test expression is then evaluated, in turn, by each one of the successive Case statements. If the result of the test expression matches the first Case statement, then the imperative statement or statements following that Case statement are executed. If the result does not match, then the next Case statement is matched to the test expression result. Once again, if the test expression matches the Case statement, the imperative statement or statements following that Case statement are executed. If the result does not match, then each successive Case statement is tested. You can code an optional Default case, which if present, is executed if NONE of the Case statements match the test expression. Here's our first Case statement looking to see if the test expression evaluates to the number 1. Notice, by the way, the spelling of the word 'case': it's lowercase. If you spell it any other way, your program won't compile at all. Notice also that the line containing the Case statement ends with a colon:"

```
case 1:
```

"Once again, if the Case statement finds that the test expression is equal to 1, then the two imperative statements following the Case statement are executed. In this example, what that means is that we display a message to user and then execute the Break statement."

"What does the Break statement do?" Lou asked.

"The Break statement," I said, "tells Java to skip the remaining Case statements and to resume execution with the next line of code following the end of the Switch statement."

"You mean after the ending curly brace?" Rose asked.

"That's right, Rose," I replied. "In this code, we execute the Break statement after a Case statement matches the test expression because of a peculiarity with the Switch statement in Java. In Java, when a Case statement matches the test expression, all of the remaining imperative statements in each one of the Case statements is executed, regardless of whether the individual Case statements match the test expression. In most cases, you don't want that code to execute, and the only way to prevent it is to execute the Break statement:"

```
JOptionPane.showMessageDialog(null, "You entered the number 1");
break;
```

> **NOTE: Within a Case statement, there's no need to 'sandwich' multiple statements within curly braces**

"Now at this point, it's just a matter of evaluating the remainder of the Case statements:"

```
case 2:
   JOptionPane.showMessageDialog(null, "You entered the number 2");
   break;
case 3:
   JOptionPane.showMessageDialog(null, "You entered the number 3");
   break;
```

"The default case," I said, "as I mentioned, is executed if none of the other Case statements matches the test expression."

```
default:
JOptionPane.showMessageDialog
   (null, "Oops, you entered a number not in the range 1 to 3");
```

"…this curly brace marks the end of the Switch statement…"

```
}                 // Switch ends
```

"…and finally, outside of the Switch statement, we execute the **exit()** method of the System object…"

```
System.exit (0);
```

"What do you mean outside of the Switch statement?" Rhonda asked.

"In theory," I said, "code within the Switch statement—everything within the starting and ending curly braces—is part of a big Selection structure and therefore executes only under certain conditions. If there's some code that you want to execute every time the code runs, regardless of program conditions, place it outside of the Switch statement—that is, following the ending curly brace of the Switch statement."

"So that means is that the **exit()** method of the System object is executed regardless," Kate said.

"That's right, Kate," I said.

"The Switch statement seems pretty powerful," Barbara said. "Are there any limitations to it, other than the fact that the test expression must evaluate to a primitive data type? That means we can't use a test expression that evaluates to a String—is that right?"

"That's right, Barbara," I said. "We couldn't code a test expression that returned a String object, which means we can't use a test expression to handle the user's input in an input box. There are also restrictions as to the formulation of the Case statements. Case statements in Java, unlike some other languages, must be an equality. For instance, you CAN'T specify a Case statement that looks like this:"

```
"Case > 5            // NOT A VALID SYNTAX
```

or

```
Case 1 to 5          // NOT A VALID SYNTAX
```

There were no questions. I thought it would be a good idea to let everyone take a turn at coding their own Switch statement before taking a break, so I handed out this exercise for the class to complete.

Exercise 4-7 The Switch Statement/Structure

In this exercise, you'll work with the program from Exercise 4-6, modifying it to use a Switch statement instead of a series of If…Else statements.

1. Use Notepad (if you using Windows) and enter the following code.

```java
import javax.swing.JOptionPane;
class Practice4_7 {
  public static void main (String[] args) {
    String response;
    response = JOptionPane.showInputDialog("What is your age?");
    if (response == null) {
      JOptionPane.showMessageDialog
        (null, "You clicked on the Cancel button");
      System.exit (0);
    }
    else
    if (response.equals("")) {
      JOptionPane.showMessageDialog
        (null, "You must make an entry in the InputBox");
      System.exit (0);
    }
    if (Integer.parseInt(response) > 61) {
      JOptionPane.showMessageDialog
        (null, response +"-You must be retired");
      System.exit (0);
    }
    switch (Integer.parseInt(response)) {
      case 61:
        JOptionPane.showMessageDialog
          (null, response +"-You must be retired");
        break;
      case 60:
        JOptionPane.showMessageDialog
          (null, response +"-You have 1 year until retirement");
        break;
      case 59:
        JOptionPane.showMessageDialog
          (null, response +"-You have 2 years until retirement");
        break;
      default:
        JOptionPane.showMessageDialog
          (null, response +"-You have a long time until retirement");
    }
```

```
    System.exit (0);
  }
}
```

2. Save your source file as Practice4_7 in the \JFiles\Practice folder (select File | Save As from Notepad's menu bar). Be sure to save your source file with the filename extension .java.

3. Compile your source file into a Bytecode file.

4. Execute your program multiple times, entering 62, 61, 60, 59, and 40 into the input box, and click the OK button after each entry. Observe the various messages that are displayed.

Discussion

No one seemed to have any problems completing the exercise, although there were some students who spelled 'case' in non-lowercase letters.

"Don't forget about the spelling of the word 'case'," I said, "and also be sure you include a Break statement in each one of the Case statements. Remember, the Break statement prevents all of the code in the Switch structure from being executed."

"I can vouch for that," Rhonda said. "I forgot to include it and all of the code in the other Case statements really did execute—seeing is believing!"

"I really enjoyed this exercise, and I'm glad we took the time to do it," Ward said. "This exercise really helped solidify the concept of the Switch statement in my mind. It's just a shame that we couldn't have expressed every condition we were looking for in the form of a Case statement. I guess there was no way out of having one or two If statements."

"That's right, Ward," I said. "Because we are restricted to expressing our Case statements in terms of an equality, we needed to check for an age greater than 61 using an If statement:"

```
if (Integer.parseInt(response) > 61) {
  JOptionPane.showMessageDialog
    (null, response+"-You must be retired");
  System.exit (0);
}
```

"Did we forget to check for an age less than 59?" Rhonda asked.

"We didn't forget. We did it by using the default Case statement," I said.

```
    default:
      JOptionPane.showMessageDialog
        (null, response + " - You have a long time until retirement");
    }
  System.exit (0);
  }
}
```

"How so?" Rhonda asked. "Since we had already checked for ages greater than 61 and for ages exactly equal to 61, 60, and 59, if we got to the point of executing the code in the default Case statement it would mean that the age entered into the input box was less than 59."

"I see," Rhonda said. "I was a little confused because we didn't explicitly code what we were looking for, but I see the default Case statement is aptly named."

"We could have coded another If statement to be a little more explicit," I said.

```
if (Integer.parseInt(response) < 59) {
  JOptionPane.showMessageDialog
    (null, response + " - You have a long time until retirement");
  System.exit (0);
}
```

"However, I really wanted to give everyone a chance to work with the default Case statement."

The classroom was pretty quiet—everyone seemed to be OK with the Switch statement. I asked if there were any questions. There were none, so I told them to take a well-earned break.

"When we return from break," I said, "we'll use the Selection structures we learned today to enhance the Grade Calculation Project. I think you'll be very pleased with what we're about to do with the project."

Continuing with the Grades Calculation Project

"We now know enough about Java," I said, resuming after a 15-minute break, "to add some intelligence to our Grade Calculation Project that we began working on last week. Last week we added code to the project to calculate the grade for a mythical English student whose midterm, final examination, research, and presentation grades were all perfect scores of 100. We displayed the student's perfect final grade of 100 in the Java Console window."

"We hard-coded the component grade pieces in the program code itself," Blaine said.

"That's right, Blaine," I said. "Last week we didn't have the Java skills to allow our program to accept input from a user, so we had no choice but to hard-code the component grade scores. After what we've learned today about the **showInputDialog()** method and Java Selection structures, we'll be able to ask the user what type of student they wish to calculate and to conditionally accept the component grade scores from the user based on that student type."

"Wow, do you mean we'll be able to calculate the grade for an actual student today?" Ward asked. "That's right," I replied. "That's exciting," Rhonda said. "But if I'm not mistaken, based on what you're saying we'll be doing with the project today, won't we be done with it?"

"That's an interesting point you raise, Rhonda," I said. "And strictly speaking, you're correct. By the end of today's class, we will have a working Java program that basically fulfills the Requirements Statement we developed several weeks ago. What will we be doing for the remainder of the class, you may be wondering? We'll spend it learning even more about Java and enhancing the Grade Calculation project with our new knowledge."

I then distributed this exercise for the class to complete.

Exercise 4-8 Enhance the Grades Calculation Project

In this exercise, you'll modify the Grades Calculation Project you last worked on last week in Exercise 3-1 by giving it the ability to accept input from the user, and to calculate grades (both numeric and letter grades) for an English, Math or Science Student.

1. Using Notepad (if you are using Windows), locate and open the Grades.java source file you worked on last week. (It should be in the \JFiles\Grades folder.)
2. Modify the code so that it looks like this...

```java
import javax.swing.JOptionPane;
class Grades {
  public static void main(String[] args) {
    final double ENGLISH_MIDTERM_PERCENTAGE = .25;
    final double ENGLISH_FINALEXAM_PERCENTAGE = .25;
    final double ENGLISH_RESEARCH_PERCENTAGE = .30;
    final double ENGLISH_PRESENTATION_PERCENTAGE = .20;
    final double MATH_MIDTERM_PERCENTAGE = .50;
    final double MATH_FINALEXAM_PERCENTAGE = .50;
    final double SCIENCE_MIDTERM_PERCENTAGE = .40;
    final double SCIENCE_FINALEXAM_PERCENTAGE = .40;
    final double SCIENCE_RESEARCH_PERCENTAGE = .20;
    int midterm = 0;
    int finalExamGrade = 0;
    int research = 0;
    int presentation = 0;
    double finalNumericGrade = 0;
    String finalLetterGrade = "";
    String response;
    // What type of student are we calculating?
    response = JOptionPane.showInputDialog
      ("Enter student type (1=English, 2=Math, 3=Science)");
    if (response == null) {
      JOptionPane.showMessageDialog
```

```java
      (null, "You clicked on the Cancel button");
    System.exit (0);
}
else
if (response.equals("")) {
  JOptionPane.showMessageDialog
    (null, "You must make an entry in the InputBox");
  System.exit (0);
}
else
  if (Integer.parseInt(response)<1 | Integer.parseInt(response) > 3) {
    JOptionPane.showMessageDialog
      (null, response+"- is not a valid student type");
    System.exit (0);
}
// Student type is valid, now let's calculate the grade
switch(Integer.parseInt(response)) {
  // Case 1 is an English Student
  case 1:
    midterm = Integer.parseInt(JOptionPane.showInputDialog
      ("Enter the Midterm Grade"));
    finalExamGrade = Integer.parseInt(JOptionPane.showInputDialog
      ("Enter the Final Examination Grade"));
    research = Integer.parseInt(JOptionPane.showInputDialog
      ("Enter the Research Grade"));
    presentation = Integer.parseInt(JOptionPane.showInputDialog
      ("Enter the Presentation Grade"));
    finalNumericGrade =
      (midterm * ENGLISH_MIDTERM_PERCENTAGE) +
      (finalExamGrade * ENGLISH_FINALEXAM_PERCENTAGE) +
      (research * ENGLISH_RESEARCH_PERCENTAGE) +
      (presentation * ENGLISH_PRESENTATION_PERCENTAGE);
    if (finalNumericGrade >= 93)
      finalLetterGrade = "A";
    else
    if ((finalNumericGrade >= 85) & (finalNumericGrade < 93))
      finalLetterGrade = "B";
    else
    if ((finalNumericGrade >= 78) & (finalNumericGrade < 85))
      finalLetterGrade = "C";
    else
    if ((finalNumericGrade >= 70) & (finalNumericGrade < 78))
      finalLetterGrade = "D";
    else
    if (finalNumericGrade < 70)
      finalLetterGrade = "F";
    JOptionPane.showMessageDialog
      (null, "*** ENGLISH STUDENT ***\n\n" +
      "Midterm grade is: " + midterm + "\n" +
      "Final Exam is: " + finalExamGrade + "\n" +
      "Research grade is: " + research + "\n" +
      "Presentation grade is: " + presentation + "\n\n" +
      "Final Numeric Grade is: " + finalNumericGrade + "\n" +
      "Final Letter Grade is: " + finalLetterGrade);
    break;
```

```java
// Case 2 is a Math Student
case 2:
  midterm = Integer.parseInt(JOptionPane.showInputDialog
    ("Enter the Midterm Grade"));
  finalExamGrade = Integer.parseInt(JOptionPane.showInputDialog
    ("Enter the Final Examination Grade"));
  finalNumericGrade =
    (midterm * MATH_MIDTERM_PERCENTAGE) +
    (finalExamGrade * MATH_FINALEXAM_PERCENTAGE);
  if (finalNumericGrade >= 90)
    finalLetterGrade = "A";
  else
  if ((finalNumericGrade >= 83) & (finalNumericGrade < 90))
    finalLetterGrade = "B";
  else
  if ((finalNumericGrade >= 76) & (finalNumericGrade < 83))
    finalLetterGrade = "C";
  else
  if ((finalNumericGrade >= 65) & (finalNumericGrade < 76))
    finalLetterGrade = "D";
  else
  if (finalNumericGrade < 65)
    finalLetterGrade = "F";
  JOptionPane.showMessageDialog
    (null,"*** MATH STUDENT ***\n\n" +
    "Midterm grade is: " + midterm + "\n" +
    "Final Exam is: " + finalExamGrade + "\n\n" +
    "Final Numeric Grade is: " + finalNumericGrade + "\n" +
    "Final Letter Grade is: " + finalLetterGrade);
  break;

// Case 3 is a Science Student
case 3:
  midterm = Integer.parseInt(JOptionPane.showInputDialog
    ("Enter the Midterm Grade"));
  finalExamGrade = Integer.parseInt(JOptionPane.showInputDialog
    ("Enter the Final Examination Grade"));
  research = Integer.parseInt(JOptionPane.showInputDialog
    ("Enter the Research Grade"));
  finalNumericGrade =
    (midterm * SCIENCE_MIDTERM_PERCENTAGE) +
    (finalExamGrade * SCIENCE_FINALEXAM_PERCENTAGE) +
    (research * SCIENCE_RESEARCH_PERCENTAGE);
  if (finalNumericGrade >= 90)
    finalLetterGrade = "A";
  else
  if ((finalNumericGrade >= 80) & (finalNumericGrade < 90))
    finalLetterGrade = "B";
  else
  if ((finalNumericGrade >= 70) & (finalNumericGrade < 80))
    finalLetterGrade = "C";
  else
  if ((finalNumericGrade >= 60) & (finalNumericGrade < 70))
    finalLetterGrade = "D";
  else
  if (finalNumericGrade < 60)
    finalLetterGrade = "F";
  JOptionPane.showMessageDialog
```

```
         (null,"*** SCIENCE STUDENT **\n\n" +
         "Midterm grade is: " + midterm + "\n" +
         "Final Exam is: " + finalExamGrade + "\n" +
         "Research grade is: " + research + "\n\n" +
         "Final Numeric Grade is: " + finalNumericGrade + "\n" +
         "Final Letter Grade is: " + finalLetterGrade);
     break;
   default:
     JOptionPane.showMessageDialog
        (null, response+ " - is not a valid student type");
     System.exit (0);
    }
  System.exit (0);
  }
}
```

3. Save your source file as Grades.java in the \JFiles\Grades folder (select File | Save As from Notepad's menu bar). Be sure to save your source file with the filename extension .java.

4. Compile your source file into a Bytecode file (if you have forgotten how to do this, consult Exercise 3-4 from last week).

5. Execute your program and test it thoroughly. See what happens if you click the Cancel button. See what happens if you click the OK button without entering a Student Type into the input box.

6. Indicate that you wish to calculate the grade for an English student. Enter 70 for the midterm, 80 for the final examination, 90 for the research grade, and 100 for the presentation. A final numeric grade of 84.5 should be displayed with a letter grade of C.

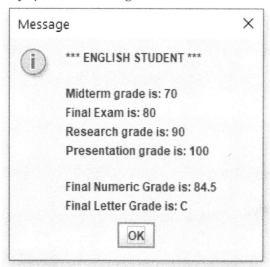

7. Indicate that you wish to calculate the grade for a math student. Enter 70 for the midterm and 80 for the final examination. A final numeric grade of 75 should be displayed with a letter grade of D.

8. Indicate that you wish to calculate the grade for a science student. Enter 70 for the midterm, 80 for the final examination, and 90 for the research grade. A final numeric grade of 78 should be displayed with a letter grade of C.

Discussion

"This exercise was a lot of fun," Rhonda said, "but although I was able to complete it, I must confess I'm not absolutely sure about everything that's going on here."

"I suspect you're not the only who feels that way, Rhonda," I said. "There's a bunch of code in this exercise and I think one or two things that the class has not seen before. Because the program needs to use the JOptionPane object from the javax.swing package, we need to include this Import statement:"

```
import javax.swing.JOptionPane;
```

"As you all know by now, this line of code defines the class, giving it the name Grades:"

```
class Grades {
```

"In addition, every startup class needs to have a **main()** method:"

```
public static void main(String[] args) {
```

"Some of these constants appeared in the previous version of the program, and some are new to this version. Last week, we were only concerned with calculating the grade for an English student. In this version of the program, we're calculating math and science students also, so we need to declare and initialize constants for those student types also. Constants, by convention, are named in uppercase, and we assign to this group of constants values equating to the relative percentage of the component grade for each one of the three student types we'll be calculating. Constants make your code more readable, and if we need to change the percentage of any one of the component grade pieces, all we need to do is change the value of the constant in the assignment statement:"

```
final double ENGLISH_MIDTERM_PERCENTAGE = .25;
final double ENGLISH_FINALEXAM_PERCENTAGE = .25;
final double ENGLISH_RESEARCH_PERCENTAGE = .30;
final double ENGLISH_PRESENTATION_PERCENTAGE = .20;
final double MATH_MIDTERM_PERCENTAGE = .50;
final double MATH_FINALEXAM_PERCENTAGE = .50;
final double SCIENCE_MIDTERM_PERCENTAGE = .40;
final double SCIENCE_FINALEXAM_PERCENTAGE = .40;
final double SCIENCE_RESEARCH_PERCENTAGE = .20;
```

"I think you explained this last week," Mary said, "but can you explain why these constants are declared as Doubles and not as Float data types?

"Both Float and Double data types permit the constant to have a fractional part," I said, "but the Double data type is considered to be more accurate for numbers less than one. In fact, if we were to change the data types of these constants from Double to Float, the program wouldn't even compile—Java recognizes the problems with the accuracy."

I paused a moment before continuing. "We declared these same variables in previous version of the program," I said, "but this time we're initializing their values to 0:"

```
int midterm = 0;
int finalExamGrade = 0;
int research = 0;
int presentation = 0;
double finalNumericGrade = 0;
```

"finalLetterGrade is a new String variable for this version of the program. We'll use it to hold the student's calculated letter grade. Notice how we initialize it to an empty string:"

```
String finalLetterGrade = "";
```

"Response should be a familiar variable to you now. We'll use it to store any responses we get from the user via the **showInputDialog()** method:"

```
String response;
```

"This line of code is just a comment. As our programs get larger, using comments is a good idea:"

```
// What type of student are we calculating?
```

"At this point, with all of our constants and variables declared, it's time to ask the user what type of student they will be calculating a grade for. This is a crucial piece of information for our program, and quite honestly, we're making things a little easier on ourselves by prompting the user to give us a number equating to the student type—1 for an English student, 2 for a math student, and 3 for a science student:"

```
response = JOptionPane.showInputDialog
   ("Enter student type (1=English, 2=Math, 3=Science)");
```

"I was wondering why you did that," Peter said.

"We could have asked the user to type in the actual student type as a string," I said, "but that can be tricky."

"How so?" Kate asked.

"There are two problems," I answered. "First, you really want to avoid having the user type in anything into your program. Keystrokes lead to typing errors, and typing errors cause program problems. Later on in the class you'll see that we'll avoid this whenever possible by having the user interact with graphical user interface components like check boxes, radio buttons, and so on. If the user must type, and sometimes it's unavoidable, then reduce their typing to a minimum, which is what we're doing here by having them enter a single number—1, 2 or 3—instead of actually typing out English, math or science."

"You said there are two problems," Blaine said. "What's the second?"

"A second problem would be this," I said. "Even if the user managed to type in English, Math or Science properly, capitalization is an issue as well. For instance, some users might spell their entry in all uppercase, some in lowercase, and some in a combination of both."

"I hadn't thought of that," Linda commented.

"Did you know there are 128 different ways to spell the word 'science' if you count the various combinations of upper- and lowercase letters?" I asked. "In theory then, we would need 128 different If statements for each student type—that's why we're prompting for a number instead of a String. Although I must tell you that when we learn a little bit more about the String object, we'll find there's an easy way around this. For now, though, it's best if we prompt the user for the number 1, 2, or 3."

No one had any major objections to my rationale, so I continued. "These next few lines of code we've dealt with all day long. Here, we're checking to see if the user has clicked the Cancel button. If they have, we display a message and end the program by executing the **exit()** method of the System object:"

```
if (response == null) {
  JOptionPane.showMessageDialog
    (null, "You clicked on the Cancel button");
  System.exit (0);
}
```

"Next, we check to see if the user has clicked the OK button without entering anything into the input box. Most likely this is a mistake, and if they have, we display a message to the user and end the program by executing the **exit()** method of the System object:"

```
else
if (response.equals("")) {
  JOptionPane.showMessageDialog
    (null, "You must make an entry in the InputBox");
  System.exit (0);
}
```

"It really would be great," Ward said, "if instead of just ending the program here we could redisplay the input box."

"I totally agree, Ward," I said, "and that's something we'll be able to do after next week's class when we learn about the Java Loop structure. For now though, we just gracefully end the program in either of these two cases. At this point in the program, if the Cancel button hasn't been clicked, and if the input box has something in it, we know that the user has made an entry into the input box. Now it's time to determine what's in it. As I mentioned earlier, if the user makes an entry into the input box that is not an integer, the program will bomb. It will be a few weeks before we learn how to handle that problem. For now, let's assume that the user has entered a valid integer into the input box. We need to determine if it's outside the range of valid numbers we're looking for. In other words, if it's less than 1 or greater than 3, it's not 1, 2, or 3. Last week, we learned about the Java OR (|) Operator and, coupled with an If statement, this line of code allows us to determine if the number entered is outside the range of numbers we're looking for:"

```
else
if (Integer.parseInt(response) < 1 | Integer.parseInt(response) > 3) {
  JOptionPane.showMessageDialog
    (null, response + " - is not a valid student type");
  System.exit (0);
}
```

"If the number entered into the input box is either less than 1 or greater than 3 (the < operator means less than, and the > operator means greater than), we display a message to the user indicating that they have entered an invalid student type, and we end the program."

"Now we're in business!" Kathy said. "If the number entered isn't less than 1, and it's also not greater than 3, then it must be 1, 2, or 3."

"You hit the nail right on the head, Kathy," I said. "We now know that the number in the input box is either a 1, 2, or 3, and that allows us to use a Switch statement to deal with each one of those cases, each of which equate to a different student type:"

```
switch(Integer.parseInt(response)) {
```

"Case 1 is the English student. Within the Case statement, we use multiple **showInputDialog()** methods of the JOptionPane object to prompt the user for the four component pieces that comprise the English student's final grade—midterm, final exam, research, and presentation grades. Notice how we use the return value of the **showInputDialog()** method as an argument to the **parseInt()** method of the Integer object:"

```
case 1:
  midterm = Integer.parseInt(JOptionPane.showInputDialog
    ("Enter the Midterm Grade"));
  finalExamGrade = Integer.parseInt(JOptionPane.showInputDialog
    ("Enter the Final Examination Grade"));
  research = Integer.parseInt(JOptionPane.showInputDialog
    ("Enter the Research Grade"));
  presentation = Integer.parseInt(JOptionPane.showInputDialog
    ("Enter the Presentation Grade"));
```

"I see that now," Bob said, "but initially I had absolutely no idea what was going on. I knew what the **parseInt()** method did in the other programs we worked with today, but you're saying that we can use the return value of one method as an input argument to another?"

"That's exactly right, Bob," I answered. "If we had wanted to, we could have done this with two lines of code, assigning the return value of the **showInputDialog()** method to a response variable and then using the value of that variable as an argument to the **parseInt()** method like this:"

```
response = JOptionPane.showInputDialog
  ("Enter the Midterm Grade");
midterm = Integer.parseInt(response)
```

"Which coding style is considered to be more acceptable?" Dave asked. "The single-line style or the two-line style?"

"Either one is fine, as far as I'm concerned," I answered. "When you are first learning how to program, you should write code that makes sense to you and that you'll be able to read later and understand later on, but you should probably get used to the single-line style. In the real world of programming, the rule of thumb is never use two lines of code when one will do."

I waited to see if there were any questions before continuing. "This next sequence of code calculates the final numeric grade for an English student," I said. "Here we multiply the value entered by the user for each component piece of the grade by the appropriate constant and then sum them to arrive at the final grade:"

```
finalNumericGrade =
  (midterm * ENGLISH_MIDTERM_PERCENTAGE) +
  (finalExamGrade * ENGLISH_FINALEXAM_PERCENTAGE) +
  (research * ENGLISH_RESEARCH_PERCENTAGE) +
  (presentation * ENGLISH_PRESENTATION_PERCENTAGE);
```

"Once we have the final numeric grade calculated, we use a series of If...Else statements to calculate the final letter grade. This code is pretty tedious, but relatively straightforward:" in the entire Switch statement. The only way to stop that behavior is to execute the Break statement, which then skips execution of the program to the next line of code following the end of the Switch structure:"

```
if (finalNumericGrade >= 93)
  finalLetterGrade = "A";
else
```

```
if ((finalNumericGrade >= 85) & (finalNumericGrade < 93))
  finalLetterGrade = "B";
else
  if ((finalNumericGrade >= 78) & (finalNumericGrade < 85))
finalLetterGrade = "C";
  else
if ((finalNumericGrade >= 70) & (finalNumericGrade < 78))
  finalLetterGrade = "D";
else
if (finalNumericGrade < 70)
  finalLetterGrade = "F";
```

"Now that we have the final numeric grade and the final letter grade calculated, it's time to display the results in a message box. This also is pretty straightforward. First, we display the type of student for whom we have calculated a grade:"

```
JOptionPane.showMessageDialog
  (null, "*** ENGLISH STUDENT ***\n\n" +
```

"I'm not sure I've seen that \n syntax before," Rhonda said. "What are those backslash and n characters for?"

"Backslash (\) n is called an escape sequence," I answered. "When Java sees this combination of characters, it knows it's receiving some special formatting instructions. Instead of displaying that combination of characters in the message box, Java takes whatever characters follow this escape sequence and places them on a new line in the message box. That's why all lines of code, despite the fact that they are concatenated to the ones above them, don't run together on a single line in the message box, they appear on separate lines:"

```
"Midterm grade is: " + midterm + "\n" +
"Final Exam is: " + finalExamGrade + "\n" +
"Research grade is: " + research + "\n" +
"Presentation grade is: " + presentation + "\n\n" +
"Final Numeric Grade is: " + finalNumericGrade + "\n" +
"Final Letter Grade is: " + finalLetterGrade);
```

"I see," Rhonda said, "so that's how that happened."

"Notice how at this point the last line of code in this Case statement we execute is the Break statement," I said, "because we don't want the code in each of the other Case statements to execute. Remember, in Java, when a Case statement matches the test expression, not only do the imperative statements for that Case statement execute, so do the statements for every Case statement

```
break;
```

"Here's the Case statement for the math student," I continued. "It's similar to the English student, the obvious difference being that math students do not have a research or presentation grade component, and of course, their component percentages are different:"

```
// Case 2 is a Math Student
case 2:
  midterm = Integer.parseInt(JOptionPane.showInputDialog
    ("Enter the Midterm Grade"));
  finalExamGrade = Integer.parseInt(JOptionPane.showInputDialog
    ("Enter the Final Examination Grade"));
  finalNumericGrade =
    (midterm * MATH_MIDTERM_PERCENTAGE) +
    (finalExamGrade * MATH_FINALEXAM_PERCENTAGE);
  if (finalNumericGrade >= 90)
    finalLetterGrade = "A";
  else
  if ((finalNumericGrade >= 83) & (finalNumericGrade < 90))
    finalLetterGrade = "B";
  else
  if ((finalNumericGrade >= 76) & (finalNumericGrade < 83))
```

```
      finalLetterGrade = "C";
    else
    if ((finalNumericGrade >= 65) & (finalNumericGrade < 76))
      finalLetterGrade = "D";
    else
    if (finalNumericGrade < 65)
      finalLetterGrade = "F";
      JOptionPane.showMessageDialog
        (null,"*** MATH STUDENT ***\n\n" +
        "Midterm grade is: " + midterm + "\n" +
        "Final Exam is: " + finalExamGrade + "\n\n" +
        "Final Numeric Grade is: " + finalNumericGrade + "\n" +
        "Final Letter Grade is: " + finalLetterGrade);
      break;
```

"Here's the Case statement for the Science Student…"

```
// Case 3 is a Science Student
case 3:
  midterm = Integer.parseInt(JOptionPane.showInputDialog
    ("Enter the Midterm Grade"));
  finalExamGrade = Integer.parseInt(JOptionPane.showInputDialog
    ("Enter the Final Examination Grade"));
  research = Integer.parseInt(JOptionPane.showInputDialog
    ("Enter the Research Grade"));
  finalNumericGrade =
    (midterm * SCIENCE_MIDTERM_PERCENTAGE) +
    (finalExamGrade * SCIENCE_FINALEXAM_PERCENTAGE) +
    (research * SCIENCE_RESEARCH_PERCENTAGE);
  if (finalNumericGrade >= 90)
    finalLetterGrade = "A";
  else
  if ((finalNumericGrade >= 80) & (finalNumericGrade < 90))
    finalLetterGrade = "B";
  else
  if ((finalNumericGrade >= 70) & (finalNumericGrade < 80))
    finalLetterGrade = "C";
  else
  if ((finalNumericGrade >= 60) & (finalNumericGrade < 70))
    finalLetterGrade = "D";
  else
  if (finalNumericGrade < 60)
    finalLetterGrade = "F";
  JOptionPane.showMessageDialog
    (null,"*** SCIENCE STUDENT ***\n\n" +
      "Midterm grade is: " + midterm + "\n" +
      "Final Exam is: " + finalExamGrade + "\n" +
      "Research grade is: " + research + "\n\n" +
      "Final Numeric Grade is: " + finalNumericGrade + "\n" +
      "Final Letter Grade is: " + finalLetterGrade);
  break;
```

"Finally, here's the code for the default case. In theory, this code should probably never execute, but it's a good idea to include it anyway:"

```
default:
  JOptionPane.showMessageDialog
    (null, response + " - is not a valid student type");
  System.exit (0);
```

"This curly brace marks the end of the Switch statement:"

```
}
```

"And this code, which ends the program, is outside of the Switch structure and is executed when any of the break statements is executed:"

```
System.exit (0); } }
```

"Great," Ward said. "This is starting to be a lot of fun."

"I just realized," Dave said, "that we don't have any validation for the component grade values that the user enters. Is that a problem?"

"In theory, we would have the same problem with the input of those values as we do with the input of the Student type—that is, if the user enters a noninteger value into the input box, the program will bomb. But again, this is something we'll take care of in a few weeks when we develop our graphical user interface."

Dave and the rest of the class seemed content to wait until then to resolve the issue. I waited for questions, but there were none. I had expected my students to be pretty worn out at this point, but instead they were playfully experimenting with a program they seemed genuinely proud of. I dismissed class for the day, telling everyone that next week we would learn about the Java Loop structures.

Summary

In this chapter, we examined Selection structures and how they are used to vary the way a program behaves based on conditions found at runtime. We saw that there are several types of Selection structures: two varieties of the If statement and the Switch statement.

Remember the falling rock? You've seen how you can use Selection structures to change this behavior, starting with the plain If statement. If a condition evaluates to True, then the imperative statement or statements following the If statement are executed. The If statement can be expanded to include alternative instructions for a False condition as well, using the Else keyword, and even further with a set of Else...If keywords.

After a number of else's, your code will begin to look cumbersome. At this point, it's more elegant to use the Switch statement, although it does have some limitations.

We've also come to a significant point in our project: the working prototype of the Grade Calculation Project. This is a very important stage in the development process, because all the key working parts of the program are now in place. From this point on, we'll be adding functionality and code to turn our prototype into a professional-level program Java program.

Chapter 5---Loops

In this chapter, we'll discuss the various types of Loop Structures available in Java. As you'll see, Loop processing can give your programs tremendous power.

Why Loops?

"Last week I mentioned the term 'loops' quite often," I said, as I began our fifth class. "In today's class, we'll examine in some detail the Loop structures available in Java."

I continued by explaining that a loop allows the programmer to repeatedly execute sections of code without having to type those lines of code over and over again in the source code.

"The ability to have parts of your program repeatedly execute," I said, "can give it enormous power to do many types of operations that would otherwise be impossible."

"Can you give us an example?" Mary asked.

"Sure, Mary," I said. "For instance, a common programming problem is one in which you need to read records from an external disk file into your program. Time permitting, we may even do that in this class. Reading a single record from a disk file isn't difficult. The trick to reading records from an external disk file (or a database) is that you do not know ahead of time how many records the program will need to read."

"What do you mean?" Peter asked.

"For instance," I replied, "a file may contain ten records, or it may contain five billion. The point is, when you write your program source file, you don't know how many times to execute the line of code that in Java is used to read a record from a file. This is where the Loop structure comes in handy: with just a few lines of code, it's possible to write code to read every record in a file, regardless of whether there are ten or five billion."

"Are there different types of loops in Java?" Dave asked. "I know there are in other languages such as C or Visual Basic."

"Yes, there are, Dave," I said. "Java has several different types of Loop structures, and we'll examine all of them today. One type of loop, called the For loop, executes a section of code, called the body of the loop, a definite number of times, and for that reason I call the For loop a definite type of loop. Other Java Loop structures are less definite in nature, which means that the number of times the body of the loop is executed is less definite. These types of loops, and how many times their loop bodies are executed, are dependent upon the evaluation of a test condition at runtime. Let's go back to that example of reading an external disk file again. If we need to read all of the records from the disk file into our program, we do not know ahead of time how many records are in that file—the file could even be empty! This type of programming problem requires the use of an indefinite type of loop, of which there are two in Java: the While loop and the Do-While loop."

I suggested that we begin our examination of Java loops with the For loop.

The For Loop

I displayed the syntax for the For Loop on my classroom projector…

For (initialization; termination; increment)
statement or statements with statements appearing in a block

"This syntax," I said, "is the 'official' syntax for the For Loop, but I think for the time being, you may prefer this translation, which I think is a little easier for beginners to deal with…"

For (start at this value; keep looping as long as this expression is true; increment or decrement the value)
statement or statements with statements appearing in a block

"I always say a picture is worth a thousand words. Here's the way the code for a Java For Loop would look like in a program designed to display the numbers from 1 to 10 in the Java Console Window," I said, as I displayed this code on the classroom projector.

```
class Example5_1 {
  public static void main(String[] args) {
    for (int counter = 1;counter< 11;counter++)
```

```
    System.out.println (counter);
  }
}
```

"The For Loop," I continued, "begins with the keyword *for*, in lower case, followed by <u>three</u> arguments that appear in parentheses. A semicolon separates each argument. I think you're pretty familiar with arguments by now—arguments affect or determine the behavior of a Java statement or method. In the case of the For Loop, these three arguments---initialization, termination and increment---determine the duration of the loop as you'll see in a just a few moments. In our example program, our first argument…"

```
for (int counter = 1;counter< 11;counter++)
```

"…declare the variable 'counter' as an Integer Data Type and then assigns a value of 1 to it."

"I'm a little confused by that first argument," Rhonda said. "Is there anything magical about it? Or is it just an ordinary variable declaration?"

"It's really just an ordinary variable declaration," I said. "What makes it seem out of the ordinary is that the variable is declared and initialized as part of the For statement. This variable---sometimes called the Loop Control Variable---is just an ordinary variable. You can name the Loop Control variable anything you want. Typically, Java programmers don't bother to name their Loop Control variables with very meaningful names, preferring instead to name them with single letter names such as i, j or k. Myself, I prefer to give my Loop Control variables a more meaningful name, and so I've named ours 'counter."

"So both the declaration and assignment of the Loop Control variable are done as part of that first argument?" Ward asked.

"That's right Ward," I replied. "Now on to the second argument, called the termination argument, which is actually a test expression, much like the one we saw last week with the If statement. In a For Loop, as long as the test expression evaluates and returns a True, the body of the loop, that is the statement or statements following the 'For' line are executed…."

```
for (int counter = 1;counter< 11;counter++)
```

"…In this case, we're telling Java to continue to execute the statements within the body of the loop for as long as the value of the Loop Control variable--counter—is less than 11. It's important to understand that in a For Loop, the body of the loop will NOT be executed, not even once, until the test expression is first evaluated. So long as the test expression returns a True value, the body of the loop is executed. If the test expression evaluates to a False value, the next statement following the body of the loop is executed."

"Let me make sure I follow," Barbara said. "The value of counter was initialized to 1--and we're telling Java to execute the body of the loop as long as *counter* is less than 11."

"That's right Barbara," I answered.

"So what's to keep that from happening forever," she replied. "If counter starts out as 1, and the loop will execute as long as counter is less than 11, something needs to make the value of counter 11 or greater in order for the loop to stop--is that right?"

"That's excellent Barbara," I said, "that's exactly right. If we don't do anything to increment the value of counter, it will remain 1, and this loop will execute forever."

"Is that where the term 'Endless Loop' comes from," Valerie said. "I've heard some of the programmers at work use that term."

"That's right Valerie," I said, "that's exactly what that means—an 'Endless Loop' is a loop that continues to execute, usually because the programmer forgets to take steps to ensure that it will eventually stop."

"How will this loop ever stop then?" Rhonda asked.

"That's where the third argument--the increment argument---comes into play," I said.

```
for (int counter = 1;counter< 11;counter++)
```

"The third argument, the increment argument" I continued, "tells Java what to do to the Loop Control variable---which usually means we add 1 to it--but as you'll see later, we can add to or subtract from it anything we wish. In our example program, we use the Java Increment Operator (++) to add 1 to the value of counter each time the test expression is evaluated."

"Based on what you're telling us then," Peter asked, "does that mean this loop will execute 10 times?"

"Excellent Peter, that's exactly what it means!" I said.

I then compiled and executed the example program, and the following screenshot was displayed on the classroom projector::

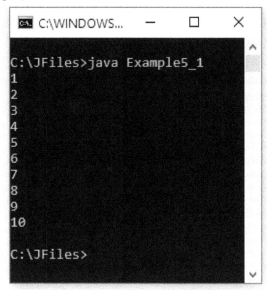

"Hey, that's pretty amazing," Kate said, "considering the fact that we displayed 10 numbers in the Console Window with so little code."

"See what I mean about the power of loops," I said. "They can give a program enormous power."

"I'm still a little confused about what's happening here," Rhonda said, "I wish we could see this in slow motion."

"Maybe this will help," I said, as I displayed this table on the classroom projector.

step	Value of counter	*counter* <11	Body of Loop Executed?	Number displayed in Java	New Value of counter afer counter++
1	1	True	Yes	1	2
2	2	True	Yes	2	3
3	3	True	Yes	3	4
4	4	True	Yes	4	5
5	5	True	Yes	5	6
6	6	True	Yes	6	7
7	7	True	Yes	7	8
8	8	True	Yes	8	9
9	9	True	Yes	9	10
10	10	True	Yes	10	11
11	11	False	No		

"Step 1 shows you the value for the counter variable as the loop begins to execute," I said. "When the For line is executed for the first time, counter is declared and initialized to 1. After that, the test expression is evaluated for the first time. Since the value of counter is less than 11 (1 < 11), the body of the loop is executed, resulting in the number 1 being displayed in the Java Console Window. Next, and it's important to understand the sequence, the value of counter is incremented using the Java Increment operator (++)."

"So the incrementation of counter actually takes place after the body of the loop is executed?" Dave asked.

"That's right Dave," I replied. "That fools everyone the first time they see it. Now, in Step 2, the current value of counter---which is 2--is compared to 11. 2 is less than 11, which results in the test expression returning a True value, and so the body of the loop is executed. Therefore, the value 2 is displayed in the Java Console. *Counter* is incremented by 1, giving it a new value of 3. Some beginners mistakenly believe that counter is initialized to 1 all over again--but as you can see, that only happens the first time the loop is executed."

"Just to make sure I understand what you've saying, the value of counter is incremented after the body of the loop is executed?" Linda asked.

"That's right," I said, "I know that takes some time getting used to---the test expression is evaluated, if it returns a True value, then the body of the loop is executed, followed by the increment or decrement of the Loop Control variable."

"I think I understand everything that's going on," Blaine said, "but what about when you get to Steps 10 and 11 of the table--that's when the loop ends, right?"

"In Step 10," I replied, "the value of the variable counter is 10. Since 10 is less than 11, the test expression once again evaluates to True, therefore the body of the loop--the display of the current value of the variable counter in the Console Window---is executed. Then the value of counter is incremented by 1, giving it a value of 11."

"Doesn't the loop just 'end' at this point?" Joe asked.

"Not quite Joe," I answered. "Even though the value of counter has been incremented to 11, the test expression must formally be evaluated once more. At that point, the test expression returns a value of False, since 11 is NOT less than 11--it's equal to it. Once the test expression returns a False value, the loop is exited, meaning the line of code following the For statement or statements is executed. By the way, if you need to execute more than one statement as part of the body of the loop, you need to use a block, like this."

```java
class Example5_2 {
  public static void main(String[] args) {
    for (int counter = 1;counter< 11;counter++) {
      System.out.println ("statement1");
      System.out.println ("statement2");
    }                           // end of for statement
  }                             // end of main function
}                               // end of class
```

"My personal preference," I added, "is to use the block style--even if I'm only executing a single line of code within the body of the loop."

Variations on the For Loop Theme

I pointed out that our For Loop was a pretty 'vanilla' version of what the For Loop can do.

"What do you mean by vanilla?" Bob asked.

"By vanilla," I said, "I mean that in this example we specified all three arguments for the For Loop. Believe it or not, all three arguments are NOT required, and not including them can produce some behavior that interesting to say the least. Not providing all three arguments is not something I would recommend, but Java does permit you to omit any one of the three arguments--or all three if you want to. For instance, you can code a For Loop that looks like this…"

I then displayed this code on the classroom projector.

```java
for ( ; ; )
```

"What will this do?" Rhonda asked.

"This For statement would result in an endless loop," I said.

"An endless loop" Ward said. "Why would you want to do this?"

"Most likely you wouldn't," I said. "but there are occasions in the programming world where you would want to create an endless loop---and then use the Break statement to 'break out' of it. The point is, with all three arguments of the For statement being optional, it's really easy to do something like this--either because you think it's a good idea or because you accidentally code it that way. The example I showed you earlier is the prototypical example of the For Loop--but there are many other ways to code a For Loop. Some programmers, for instance, choose to increment their Loop Control variable within the body of the loop itself--leaving the third argument---the increment argument--empty like this…"

```java
for (int counter = 1;counter< 11;)
```

"…again, this isn't something I would recommend, but you may see some programmers do this. Still other programmers choose to leave the first argument--the initialization argument---empty like this…"

for (;counter< 11;counter++)

"...this is something you can do provided you initialize the Loop Control variable elsewhere in your program."

"Again, I presume that's something you don't recommend?" Bob asked.

"That's right Bob," I agreed, "I recommend coding all three arguments in the For Loop unless you can think of a very persuasive reason for not doing so--and in the beginning stages of your Java programming career, I don't think you'll think of any."

"Assuming we do code all three arguments for the For Loop," Dave said, "are there any other variations possible with the For Loop."

"That's a great question Dave," I answered. "It's possible to vary all three arguments in such a way as to produce some very interesting results. For instance, if instead of incrementing your Loop Control variable you decrement it, the value of the Loop Control variable will decrease---and you can actually make your loop go 'backward'. And speaking of the Loop Control variable--it doesn't have to start out as 1--- it can be any value, in fact, it doesn't even have to be a positive number."

I explained that it's possible to simulate real-world situations more accurately if you get a little creative with the argument of a For Loop.

"Last week we examined some mythical restaurants in New York City," I said. "Today, let's deal with a mythical Manhattan hotel you own in which the floors of the hotel are numbered from 2 to 20. Let's further pretend that the hotel has three elevators. Elevator #1 stops at all the floors of the hotel, Elevator #2 stops only at the even numbered floors and Elevator #3 stops only at the odd numbered floors. Now suppose that we want to write a Java program that displays, in the Java Console window, the floor numbers at which Elevator #1 stops. Here's an exercise to do exactly that using the Java For Loop."

Exercise 5-1 Your first For Loop

In this exercise, you'll code a For Loop to display the floors at which Elevator #1 stops.

1. Use Notepad (if you are using Windows) and enter the following code.

```java
class Practice5_1 {
  public static void main(String[] args) {
    System.out.println("Elevator #1 stops at these floors...");
    for (int counter = 2;counter< 21;counter++)
      System.out.println (counter);
  }
}
```

2. Save your source file as Practice5_1 in the \JFiles\Practice folder (select File | Save As from Notepad's menu bar). Be sure to save your source file with the filename extension .java.
3. Compile your source file into a Bytecode file.
4. Execute your program. You should see the following output in the Java console window:

```
C:\WINDOWS\system32\cmd.exe                    —    □    ✕

C:\JFiles\Practice>java Practice5_1
Elevator #1 stops at these floors...
2
3
4
5
6
7
8
9
10
11
12
13
14
15
16
17
18
19
20
C:\JFiles\Practice>
```

Discussion

Only one person had trouble completing the exercise---they accidentally included this line of code

System.out.println("Elevator #1 stops at these floors...");

inside of the body of the For loop. As a result, 'Elevator #1 stops at these floors..." was displayed 19 times.

"Heading like this," I said, "need to be displayed only once--therefore, they should appear 'outside' the body of the loop."

"Where's the first floor of the hotel?" Kathy asked. "Why did the display start with the number 2?"

"Remember, the floors are numbered from 2 to 20," Mary said. "that's why the Loop Control variable was initialized to 2."

"That's right Kathy," I replied. "This was a good exercise to get your feet wet with the For Loop. Now let's get to work on a more challenging problem, Elevator #2---that's the elevator that stops only at the even numbered floors of the hotel. Do you have any ideas on how we should code a For Loop to display only the even numbered floors of the hotel?"

After a minute or two, Dave suggested that we code a For Loop, initializing our Loop Control variable to 2, using a test condition in which we compare the value of the variable to less than 21, and most importantly, that we increment the value of the Loop Control variable by 2---instead of 1.

"Excellent idea Dave," I said, as I distributed this exercise for the class to complete.

Exercise 5-2 Modifying the For Loop to Handle Even numbered Floors

In this exercise, you'll code a For Loop to display the even numbered floors of the hotel at which Elevator #2 stops.

1. Use Notepad (if you are using Windows) and enter the following code.

```
class Practice5_2 {
  public static void main(String[] args) {
    System.out.println("Elevator #2 stops at these floors...");
    for (int counter = 2;counter< 21;counter=counter+2)
      System.out.println (counter);
```

```
        }
}
```

2. Save your source file as Practice5_2 in the \JFiles\Practice folder (select File | Save As from Notepad's menu bar). Be sure to save your source file with the filename extension .java.

3. Compile your source file into a Bytecode file.

4. Execute your program. You should see the following output in the Java console window:

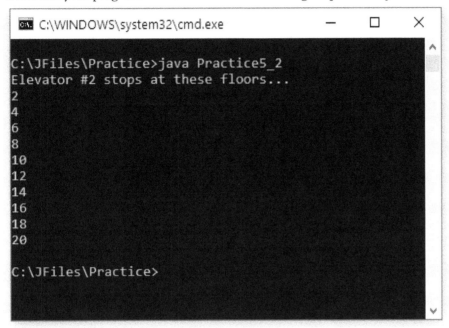

Discussion

"That was very clever, Dave," Rhonda said, obviously impressed. "I don't think I would have thought of incrementing the Loop Control variable by 2."

"Solving programming problems like this requires some imagination," I told Rhonda. "The more programs you write, the easier it will be to envision little 'tricks' like this to solve these types of problems."

"I noticed," Linda said, "that we incremented the value of our Loop Control variable 'counter' by taking the value of *counter* and adding 2 to it. It sure would be great if there was an increment operator to add 2 to a variable the way the (++) operator adds 1?"

"Actually Linda, there is," I replied. "Instead of using this code to increment the value of the counter variable by 2…"

```
counter=counter+2
```

"…we can use this code instead, which is a variation of the increment operator (++) we learn about a few weeks ago. The Addition Assignment (+=) Operator is used to increment the value of a variable by the number which follows it--in this case, +=2 adds 2 to a variable…"

```
counter+=2
```

"Cool," Chuck said. "Can you increment the variable by any number that way---and is there a way to subtract numbers as well?"

"You're right on both counts Chuck," I said, "This syntax can be used to add 3 to the variable counter.."

```
counter+=3
```

"…and this syntax will subtract 3 from the variable counter…"

```
counter-=3
```

"I've been thinking about Elevator #3," Lou said, "the one that stops only at odd numbered floors in the hotel? I know what you said about using your imagination to solve this problem--but so far, I haven't been able to get it to work. How should we code that loop?"

Linda suggested that a For Loop with a Loop Control variable initialized to 3, a test condition in which we compare the value of the variable to less than 21, and once again, incrementing the value of the Loop Control variable by 2 would be the way to go.

```
for (counter = 3;counter< 21;counter+=2)
```

"Of course," Lou lamented, "that was my mistake--I kept initializing the value of the Loop Control variable to 2 instead of 3."

"Shouldn't the initial value of the Loop Control variable be 1?" Rhonda asked.

"Don't forget Rhonda," I said, "the hotel has no first floor--the first odd numbered floor is 3---initializing the Loop Control variable to 3 takes care of that.."

I then distributed this exercise for the class to complete.

Exercise 5-3 Modifying the For Loop to Handle Odd Floors

In this exercise, you'll code a For Loop to display the odd numbered floors at which Elevator #3 stops.

1. Use Notepad (if you are using Windows) and enter the following code.

```
class Practice5_3 {
  public static void main(String[] args) {
    System.out.println("Elevator #3 stops at these floors...");
    for (int counter = 3;counter< 21;counter+=2)
      System.out.println (counter);
  }
}
```

2. Save your source file as Practice5_3 in the \JFiles\Practice folder (select File | Save As from Notepad's menu bar). Be sure to save your source file with the filename extension .java.
3. Compile your source file into a Bytecode file.
4. Execute your program. You should see the following output in the Java console window:

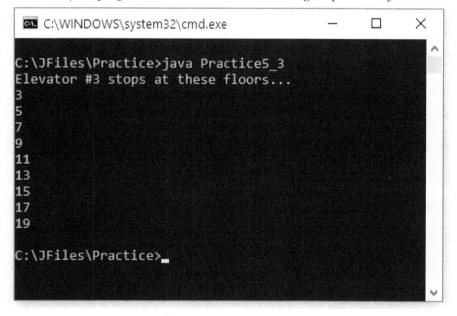

Discussion

By this point, no one seemed to be having any problems with our 'elevator' exercises.

"This is great fun," Joe said. "I didn't know you could do this kind of thing in a program. I can't wait to apply Java loops to something practical."

"You'll get a chance to work with loop in the Grades Calculation project," I said. "But we still have some more work to do before we get to that point."

I continued by saying that all three of the For Loop's arguments (initialization, termination, and increment) could be expressed not only as numerical literals (that is numbers), as we had in the previous exercises, but also as variables. I then distributed this exercise to demonstrate my point.

Exercise 5-4 Modifying the For Loop to Work with Constants

In this exercise, you'll code a For Loop to display the floors at which Elevator #1 stops--but instead of using numeric literals for the Initialization, Termination and Increment arguments, you'll use a combination of variables.

1. Use Notepad (if you are using Windows) and enter the following code.

```java
class Practice5_4 {
  public static void main(String[] args) {
    final int TOP_FLOOR = 20;
    System.out.println("Elevator #1 stops at these floors...");
    for (int bottom_floor = 2;bottom_floor < TOP_FLOOR+1;bottom_floor++)
      System.out.println (bottom_floor);
  }
}
```

2. Save your source file as Practice5_4 in the \JFiles\Practice folder (select File | Save As from Notepad's menu bar). Be sure to save your source file with the filename extension .java.
3. Compile your source file into a Bytecode file.
4. Execute your program. You should see the following output in the Java console window:

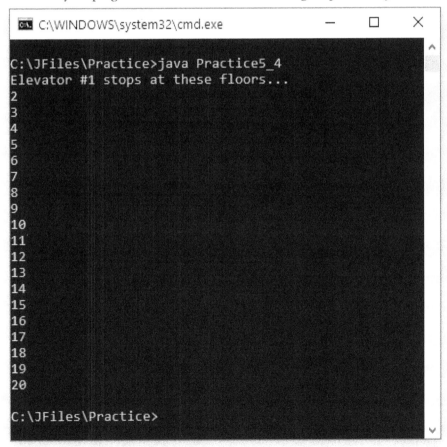

Discussion

"Does everyone see what we're doing here?" I asked.

"It looks like we've done two new things here," Linda said. "First, we used a more meaningful name for the Loop Control variable--*floor*--and we also declared a variable called TOP_FLOOR to use as part of the test expression in the termination argument of the For Loop."

"That's an excellent analysis Linda," I said. "Using a variable like this doesn't impact the behavior of the loop--but it does make your code a lot more readable."

I waited to see if there were any questions.

"Now let's suppose." I said, "that as an added challenge, we want to display the floors of our hotel backwards?"

"Wow, is that possible?" Steve asked.

"It can be done with a For Loop," I said, "but I have to warn you, we will have to be careful."

I then distributed this exercise for the class to complete.

Exercise 5-5 Displaying the Floors Backwards--but there's a problem

In this exercise, you'll code a For Loop to display the floors of the hotel--backwards. But beware---this code has a bug in it and won't behave properly.

1. Use Notepad (if you are using Windows) and enter the following code.

```java
class Practice5_5 {
  public static void main(String[] args) {
    System.out.println("Floors in the hotel, listed backwards are...");
    for (int counter = 20;counter >20;counter--)
      System.out.println (counter);
  }
}
```

2. Save your source file as Practice5_5 in the \JFiles\Practice folder (select File | Save As from Notepad's menu bar). Be sure to save your source file with the filename extension .java.
3. Compile your source file into a Bytecode file.
4. Execute your program. You should see the following output in the Java console window:

Discussion

"*Nothing* happened," Rhonda said. "No floor numbers were displayed--did the loop execute?"

Rhonda was correct. Nothing--except for the heading---was displayed in the Console Window.

"Can anyone tell me what happened?" I asked.

No one had an immediate solution to what had, or hadn't, happened---but then Barbara spoke up.

"I think I know what the problem is," she said. "I know we intended to have the loop go 'backwards', but in the termination argument---the test expression immediately evaluates to False--that's why the body of the loop never executes."

"What's that Barbara?" Rhonda asked.

"Take a look at the initial value of our Loop Control variable," Barbara continued. "It starts at 20, because that's the top floor of our hotel and since we want to display the floors backward, that's where we want to start. But then the test expression asks whether the value of the counter variable is greater than 20. This is where the problem lies. As long as the test expression returns a True value, the body of the loop will execute---but the value of counter is 20, and obviously 20 is not greater than 20. Therefore, the test expression immediately evaluates to False, and the loop terminates."

"Excellent Barbara," I said. "That's exactly what happened. What we have here is a problem in the way I--and beginner programmers---sometimes code their loops."

"I would have thought," Ward said, "that Java would have executed the body of the loop at least once."

"Not with a For Loop Ward," I answered. "although we'll see in just a few moments that there are some types of Java loops where that is the case---that is, the body of the loop is executed at least once. With a For Loop, the test expression is always evaluated prior to the body of the loop executing."

"So how can we make this loop count backwards?" Rhonda asked. "What do we need to change?"

"We need to correct our test expression," I said, "to make the loop count backwards."

I then distributed this exercise for the class to complete.

Exercise 5-6 Displaying the Floors Backwards Correctly

In this exercise, you'll correct the code from Exercise 5-5, so that the floors of our hotel are correctly displayed backwards.

1. Use Notepad (if you are using Windows) and enter the following code.

```
class Practice5_6 {
  public static void main(String[] args) {
    System.out.println("Floors in the hotel, listed backwards are...");
    for (int counter = 20;counter >1;counter--)
      System.out.println (counter);
  }
}
```

2. Save your source file as Practice5_6 in the \JFiles\Practice folder (select File | Save As from Notepad's menu bar). Be sure to save your source file with the filename extension .java.
3. Compile your source file into a Bytecode file.
4. Execute your program. You should see the following output in the Java console window:

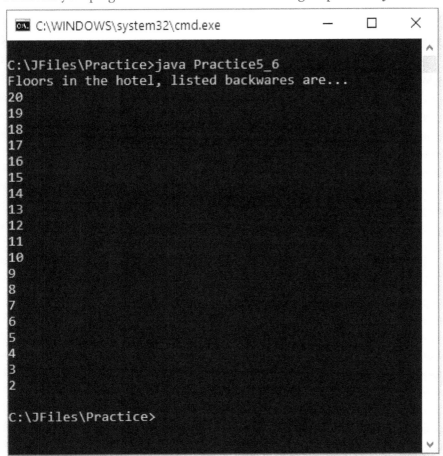

Discussion

"That's better," Mary said. "Now the floors are displayed backwards."

"To make the loop count 'backwards'," I said, "you need to specify a test expression that evaluates the value of the Loop Control variable against the lower limit of the loop. That's what we did here."

There were no more questions, and so I suggested we take a break.

"When we return from break," I said, "we'll examine the indefinite kinds of Java loops I've mentioned--the While Loop family."

While Loops

Resuming after break, I began a discussion of what I call the Java indefinite loops, the family of While Loops.

"Compared to the For Loop," I said, "beginners to Java find the While Loop a bit confusing at first, perhaps because there are actually two variations of it--the While Loop and the Do-While Loop. But you'll see that the only real difference in the behavior of the two variations is that, like the For Loop, the body of the While Loop is NOT guaranteed to execute even once, but with the Do-While Loop, the body of the loop is executed AT LEAST ONCE. We'll examine both types of While Loops during the last half of today's class."

"What are the differences between the While Loop and the For Loop," Steve asked, "and what are the similarities?"

"Just like the For Loop," I said, "the While Loop structure permits the programmer to repetitively execute a section of code. But as you'll see, when a While Loop ends is not nearly as 'definite' as it is for the For Loop."

"How so?" Mary asked.

"With the For Loop," I continued, "you saw that we designate a definite end point in the way in which we specify our termination argument. With a While Loop, there is no built-in Loop Control variable as there is with the For Loop--instead you need to specify an expression in the While statement that is very much like the test expression specified in the For Loop. What makes the While loop a bit trickier is that the expression is not written to test the Loop Control variable---instead the test expression is written to evaluate something else. Unfortunately, when first learning, quite a few beginners mis-code the test expression in a While Loop, resulting in something we mentioned earlier---an endless or infinite loop."

"What kinds of test conditions can you specify as the expression in the While Loop?" Ward asked.

"You can specify any condition that evaluates to a True or False value," I said, "just like the test expression we saw in the first For Loop we coded today."

"Can we see an example of the While Loop," Mary said.

The While Loop

"Sure thing Mary," I said, "let's take a look at the While Loop first, that's the type of While Loop in which the test expression is evaluated prior to the body of the loop executing even once."
I then displayed the syntax for the While Loop on the classroom projector:

```
while (expression) {
   statement or statements
```

"You're right," Joe said, "this does look a little confusing to me."

"Let's take it a step at a time," I said. "and I'm sure you'll be OK with this. The While Loop begins with the word 'while', followed by a test expression, which as I indicated earlier, is much like the test expression in an If statement. Unlike the For Loop, there isn't an initialization of a Loop Control variable at the top of the loop structure--just this single test expression. There's also no termination argument. As long as the test expression evaluates to True, the body of the loop will be executed. Therefore, it's up to the programmer to ensure that eventually the test expression evaluates to False--and that needs to be done using code within the loop itself--something we'll see in just a few moments. As was the case with the For Loop, the test expression is evaluated before the body of the loop is executed---this means that the body of the While loop is not guaranteed to execute even one time--if the text expression immediately evaluates to False, the loop structure is exited. As you'll see in a few moments, there's a variation of this loop in which the body of the loop is always executed at least once."

"Wouldn't you want every loop you code to execute at least once?" Rhonda asked.

"Not necessarily," I answered. "For instance, suppose you are using a loop to read records from a disk file, and you include the instructions to read the records within the body of the loop. If the file is empty---which can happen---you wouldn't want to execute the body of the loop even once--if you did, you would attempt to read a record from an empty file, which would generate an error."

"OK," Rhonda answered, "that makes sense to me."

At this point, there were no other questions, and I suggested that we complete an exercise to give everyone a chance to work with the While Loop---once again displaying the floors of our hotel.

Exercise 5-7 Use the While Loop to display the floors of our hotel

In this exercise, you'll code a While Loop to display the floors of our hotel in the Java Console Window.

1. Use Notepad (if you are using Windows) and enter the following code.

```
class Practice5_7 {
  public static void main(String[] args) {
    int counter = 2;
    System.out.println ("The floors in the hotel are...");
    while (counter < 21) {
      System.out.println (counter);
      counter++;
    }
  }
}
```

2. Save your source file as Practice5_7 in the \JFiles\Practice folder (select File | Save As from Notepad's menu bar). Be sure to save your source file with the filename extension .java.
3. Compile your source file into a Bytecode file.
4 Execute your program. You should see the following output in the Java console window:

Discussion

"As you can see," I said, "we've successfully displayed the floors of our hotel, this time using a While loop to do the job instead of a For loop. I think once you get used to the format, you'll find that working with the While loop, specifically, coding the test expression, is somewhat intuitive. Remember, though, we need to do a little more work with the While loop than with the For loop. For instance, since there is no initialization argument, we needed to take care of that ourselves, before the Loop structure is encountered, with this line of code:"

int counter = 2;

"Then comes the While loop and it's test expression in which we tell Java to execute the body of the loop while the value of counter is less than 21 and to display the value of counter in the Java Console window:"

```
while (counter < 21) { System.out.println (counter);
```

"As I mentioned earlier, because the While loop does not have an increment argument of its own, it's imperative that we take care of incrementing the variable we are using to determine the duration of the loop. We do that with this code:"

```
counter++;
```

"The variable counter," Blaine said, "reminds me of the Loop Control variable from the For loop."

"You're right about that, Blaine," I said. "With the While loop, there is no formal Loop Control variable as there is in a For loop. In effect, we have to create our own."

"How important is it to increment the value of counter inside the loop?" Kathy asked.

"Vitally important," I said. "Beginners typically make two kinds of mistakes with the While loop. Either they initialize the value of a variable they're using in their test expression inside the body of loop, or they increment the value of that variable outside the loop."

"What's wrong with that?" Rhonda asked.

"In our case, if we were to initialize the value of counter within the body of the loop," I said, "each time the body of the loop is executed, the value of counter is reset to 2. That's not good, in that the value of counter never gets to the point where the loop can terminate. Alternatively, if we were to increment the value of counter outside the body of the loop, the value of counter would always be 2. As a result, the test expression (counter < 21) is always True, and the loop never terminates. In both cases, we wind up with an endless loop."

"Why didn't the number 21 display in the Java Console window?" Joe asked. "Why did it stop at 20?"

"Because," I said, "our expression told Java to execute the body of the loop while counter is less than 21. As soon as counter is equal to 21, the test expression returns a False value, and the loop immediately terminates."

"You said earlier that While loops are more of an indefinite nature of loops," Linda said, "but this loop seems pretty definite to me. Can you give us a better example of that?"

"I sure can," I said. "How about a loop that runs until the user tells it to stop?"

I then distributed this exercise for the class to complete.

Exercise 5-8 An Indefinite Version of the While Loop

In this exercise, you'll create a While Loop structure that displays numbers in the Java console window. However, the numbers will only be displayed for as long as the user chooses to continue to display them. A few words of warning here: in order to cut down on the number of lines of code we need to write, in this exercise we are not checking to see if the user clicks the Cancel button in the input box. For a reminder on that technique, check your notes from Week 4.

1. Use Notepad (if you are using Windows) and enter the following code.

```java
import javax.swing.JOptionPane;
class Practice5_8 {
  public static void main (String[] args) {
    int counter = 1;
    String response;
    response = JOptionPane.showInputDialog("Should I start counting?");
    response = response.toUpperCase();
    while (response.equals ("YES")) {
      System.out.println("counter is " + counter);
      counter++;
      response = JOptionPane.showInputDialog("Should I continue?");
      response = response.toUpperCase();
    }
    JOptionPane.showMessageDialog(null, "Thanks for counting with me!");
    System.exit (0);
```

```
  }
}
```

2. Save your source file as Practice5_8 in the \JFiles\Practice folder (select File | Save As from Notepad's menu bar). Be sure to save your source file with the filename extension .java.

3. Compile your source file into a Bytecode file.

4. Execute your program. The program will ask you if you wish to start counting. Type **Yes** into the Input box.

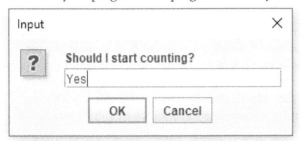

5. Now click the OK button. The number 1 should appear in the Java Console window.

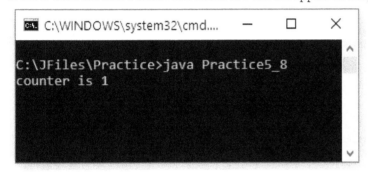

6. After the number 1 is displayed in the Java console window, the program will then ask you if you wish to continue counting. Type **Yes** once again and click the OK button.

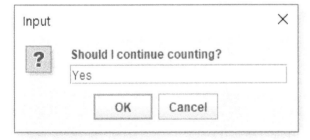

7. The number 2 will then be displayed in the Java console window, and once again you'll be asked if you wish to continue counting. Numbers will continue to be displayed in the Java console window for as long as you type **Yes**.

8. Type **No** in answer to the prompt to continue counting. A thank you message will be displayed in a Java message box, and the program will end.

Discussion

There was a fair amount of confusion and problems with this exercise, and it took us about 15 minutes to get through it. The exercise was tedious to type. In addition, not everyone in the class was as attentive to the case of the word 'YES' as they needed to be, probably because of our use of the **toUpperCase()** method. Despite the use of the **toUpperCase()** method, the word 'YES' still needed to be typed in uppercase.

"This code is a good example of the indefinite capabilities of the While loop," I explained. "How long this loop executes is entirely up to the user and is determined at runtime, not when the program is being coded. When we wrote this program, we had no idea how many numbers the user would want displayed in the Java Console window. The While loop gives us a way for the loop to run indefinitely, but still with a way to end it. That's the beauty of the While loop. In this case, as soon as the test expression evaluates to False, the loop ends."

I continued by saying that, as we had done in Exercise 5-7, the first thing we did here was to declare the variables we would use in the program.

"Remember," I said, "I can't emphasize this enough: with a While loop there is no built-in Loop Control variable, so in order for the loop to eventually end, we need to declare a variable of our own which will then be used in a test expression to see if the loop should be terminated. In our previous exercise, we used the value of counter to determine if the loop should end. This program is a bit different in that we will let the user's response to the question determine when the loop ends. That's the function of the variable response here, a variable whose value will be determined by the user. The variable counter, as it was in Exercise 5-7, is the number we will display in the Java Console window, and we initialize it to 1:"

```
int counter = 1;
String response;
```

"Now it's time," I said, "to use the **showInputDialog()** method of the JoptionPane class to display a message to the user, asking them if they wish to start counting. The user's response will then be stored in the variable response:"

```
response = JOptionPane.showInputDialog("Should I start counting?");
```

"This next line of code is very significant:"

```
response = response.toUpperCase();
```

"I was going to ask you about that," Linda said. "What is the **toUpperCase()** method? And how do I know it's a method?"

"The **toUpperCase()** method is in the standard Java language class," I said, "and it's designed to take a string value and convert it to all uppercase characters. The tip-off that it's a method is the pair of parentheses following the name. In this case, the value of the response variable—that is, the user's answer—is replaced by that same answer in all uppercase characters. For instance, the string j-o-h-n would be converted to J-O-H-N."

"Why are we doing this?" Kate asked.

"In short," I said, "because we want to make the intent of our test expression manageable. In this way, no matter how the user spells the word 'YES'—all lowercase, all uppercase, or something in between, ultimately their response is converted to the word 'YES' in all uppercase letters, and that will make determining if they answered 'YES' or something else much easier."

"I guess I'm missing something here," Chuck said, "but how can converting the user's response to uppercase make the comparison easier?"

"Did you realize," I answered, "that the user can type the word 'YES' into the input box in eight different ways?"

"What do you mean, eight different ways?" asked Barbara.

"Each letter of the word 'YES" can be entered by the user in either upper or lowercase," I explained. "And while it's nice to believe that the user would enter 'YES' in all caps if we asked them to, in reality, some users mix and match case as they're entering values into an input box or a text field. Let's take a moment to come up with all the possible combinations of the word 'YES,' and you'll see that there are eight different ways of writing it."

YES	yES
YEs	yEs
YeS	yeS
Yes	yes

"Now if we converting the user's response to all upper case characters," I said, "that means we only need to perform the comparison in our text expression to the word 'YES' in all capital letters. The alternative would be to write code using a series of Or operations that would look like this..."

```
while (
  response.equals ("YES") | response.equals ("YEs") |
  response.equals ("YeS") | response.equals ("Yes") |
  response.equals ("yES") | response.equals ("yEs") |
  response.equals ("yeS") | response.equals ("yes"))
{
```

"I see what you mean now," Ward said. "That makes sense, and even more sense if the user entered a word with 13 characters."

"That's right Ward," I said. "A word with 13 letters can be entered 8,192 different ways by the user--that's a comparison I wouldn't want to make using the Or Operator. Let's get back to that first line of the While loop, in which we tell Java to execute the body of the loop provided the variable response is equal to the upper case value 'YES'..."

```
while (response.euqals ("YES") {
```

"Oh, so that's the benefit of having converted the user's response to upper case," Rhonda said. "The light bulb just went on!"

"Is this the type of loop in which the body is NOT necessarily executed once?" Blaine asked.

"That's right Blaine," I said. "Because the test expression in a While Loop is evaluated 'at the top' of the loop structure, the body of the loop will be executed only if the test expression evaluates to True--something that can only happen if the user answers 'Yes' to the question 'Should I start counting?' Provided the user answers 'YES' (or any of the eight varieties of 'YES', this next line of code will display the value of the counter variable in the Java Console Window..."

```
System.out.println("counter is " + counter);
```

"And then this line of code will increment the value of counter:"

```
counter++;
```

"Incrementing the value of counter is important, but it's not as important as it was in Exercise 5-7, since it's no longer the value of counter that determines if and when the loop ends. The responsibility for ending the loop is the response the user gives us to the question, 'Should I continue?', which is stored in the response variable. That's the key to the loop eventually ending. Notice how we must uppercase the user's response to this question also:"

```
response = JOptionPane.showInputDialog("Should I continue?");
response = response.toUpperCase();
```

"So the loop will continue until the user answers 'No'?" Ward asked.

"Not exactly, Ward," I said. "The loop will continue as long as the user enters 'Yes' or any of its eight variations into the input box. That means the loop will end if the user enters anything else into the input box, or until they click the Cancel button, something which I mentioned earlier we are not checking for in this exercise. So, if the user enters anything other than 'Yes' into the input box, the loop will end, and we then display this message to the user thanking them for counting with us and end the program."

```
JOptionPane.showMessageDialog(null, "Thanks for counting with me!");
System.exit (0);
```

Prior to moving on, I repeated that my earlier assertion that one of the biggest mistakes beginners make with the While loop is to forget to include code within the body of the loop that enables the loop to end.

"Because the test condition we set up is to compare the value of the response variable to 'YES'," I said, "if we forget to give the user the opportunity to change the value of that variable, we'll wind up with an endless loop condition."

Do-While Loop

No one had any questions about the While loop, so it was time to move onto a discussion of the Do-While loop. I displayed the syntax for the Do-While loop on the classroom projector:

```
do {
  statement(s)
} while (expression);
```

"This variation of the While loop is called the Do-While loop," I said, "because the first line of the Loop structure begins with the single word 'Do,' and the last line of the loop contains the While statement. Everything else in between is considered the body of the loop."

"How is this Do-While loop different from the While loop we just worked with?" Mary asked.

"Unlike the While loop and the For loop," I answered, "in which the body of the loop is not guaranteed to execute even once, with the Do-While loop, the body of the loop will execute at least one time."

"Is it the location of the word 'While' that causes that behavior?" Linda asked. "I notice that the test expression is located after the body of the loop."

"Great observation, Linda," I said. "In the While loop structure we examined, because the word 'While' appeared as the first line of the Loop structure, the test expression was evaluated prior to the body of the loop executing. With the Do-While loop, because the test expression appears as the last line of the Loop structure, the body of the loop is guaranteed to execute at least once, even if the test expression is always false."

No one had any other questions, so I suggested that we complete an exercise in which we implemented the functionality from Exercise 5-8 using a Do-While loop instead.

Exercise 5-9 The Do-While Loop

In this exercise, you'll create a Do-While loop structure that displays numbers in the Java Console Window. However, the numbers will only be displayed for as long as the user chooses to continue to display them. A few words of warning here---in order to cut down on the number of lines of code we need to write, in this exercise we are <u>not</u> checking to see if the user clicks the Cancel button in the Input Box.

1. Use Notepad (if you are using Windows) and enter the following code.

```java
import javax.swing.JOptionPane;
class Practice5_9 {
  public static void main (String[] args) {
    int counter = 1;
    String response;
    response = JOptionPane.showInputDialog("Should I start counting?");
    do {
      System.out.println("counter is " + counter);
      counter++;
      response = JOptionPane.showInputDialog("Should I continue counting?");
      response = response.toUpperCase();
    } while (response.equals ("YES"));
    System.out.println(response);
    JOptionPane.showMessageDialog(null, "Thanks for counting with me!");
    System.exit (0);
  }
}
```

2. Save your source file as Practice5_9 in the \Jfiles\Practice folder (select File | Save As from Notepad's menu bar). Be sure to save your source file with the file name extension java.
3. Compile your source file into a Bytecode file.
4. Execute your program. The program will ask you if you wish to start counting. Enter Yes into the input box and click the OK button. As was the case with Exercise 5-8, the number 1 should appear in the Java Console window.
5. After the number 1 is displayed in the Java Console window, the program will then ask you if you wish to continue counting. Answer Yes once again and click the OK button. The number 2 will then be displayed in the Java Console window, followed by the same question. Numbers will continue to be displayed in the Java Console window for as long as you answer Yes.
6. Answer No. A goodbye message will be displayed and the program will end.

Discussion

No one had any major problems completing the exercise.

"It looks like this program is behaving the same way as the program from Exercise 5-8," Rhonda said.

"You're right, Rhonda," I said. "We've proven that we can implement the same functionality using a Do-While loop as we did when we coded the program using a While loop."

"So what's the difference?" Joe asked.

"The difference in the behavior," I said, "won't become apparent unless the user answers 'No' to the first question asked of them, 'Do you want to start counting?' If the user answers 'No' to this question in the Exercise 5-8 version of the program, the body of the loop will never execute. That's not the case with the Exercise 5-9 version of the program. Because the test expression is at the bottom of the Do-While structure, the body of the loop will always execute at least once. Let me show you what I mean."

I then ran the code from Exercise 5-8, and answered 'No' to the question asking me if I wanted to start counting. The program immediately ended without displaying any numbers in the Java Console window.

"That's what I would expect," Ward said.

"Now let's see what happens," I said, "when we run the code from Exercise 5-9."

I then ran the code from Exercise 5-9, and answered 'No' to the question asking me if I wanted to start counting. Despite my answer of 'No,' the program displayed the number 1 in the Java Console window:

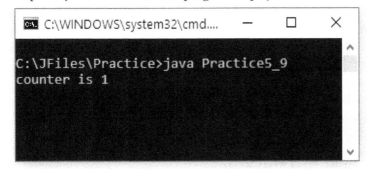

"I see the difference now," Rhonda said. "The program ignored our answer."

"It's not so much that the program ignored our answer," I answered, "but that it didn't check our answer until the body of the loop had executed once. In Exercise 5-8, the answer was evaluated at the beginning of the loop. Since the test condition evaluated immediately to False, the body of the loop was never executed. In Exercise 5-9, the test condition was evaluated after the body of the loop had already executed and displayed the number 1 in the Java Console Window."

I asked if there were any questions about the While family of loops. There were none, and so I asked everyone to take a break.

"When we return from break," I said, "we'll be working on a modification to the Grades Calculation project to include loop processing."

Adding a Loop to the Grades Calculation Project

When my students returned from break, a couple of them immediately asked what we would be doing with the Grade Calculation Project that involved a loop.

"Right now," I said, "as the project stands, it properly calculates the grade for an English, math or science Student, but it only performs one calculation before ending."

"That's right," Blaine said. "One grade calculation, and the program ends. By using loop processing, will we be able to make the program perform multiple calculations before ending?"

"You hit the nail right on the head, Blaine" I said.

"How will we do that?" Chuck asked.

"What we'll do," I said, "is sandwich the code that performs the grade calculation within a Loop structure so that we can calculate the grades for many students instead of just one. Can anyone suggest the kind of loop we should use to do that?"

"I suppose we could use a For loop," Rhonda suggested, "but from what we've learned today, a For loop is the best choice when we know for certain the number of times we want the body of the loop to execute. That wouldn't be the case here since it's each time the program runs, there's likely to be a different number of grades to be calculated. I guess for that reason, the While loop is the way to go."

"Great thinking, Rhonda," I said, "and I agree, a While loop makes sense to use. Now another question: should we use the While loop or the Do-While variety? "

"I would vote for the While loop," Valerie answered. "I think we should evaluate the test expression we code at the top of the Loop structure, not at the end of it."

"I agree, Valerie," I said. "Although it's not likely that the user will run the program and then have no grades at all to calculate, it is possible. I think it's safer to ask the user if he or she has grades to calculate, and if so, execute the body of the loop to calculate grades."

I saw some confusion in the eyes of my students, but I knew this would be cleared up when they started to code the modifications to the Grade Calculation Project. I then distributed this exercise for the class to complete.

Exercise 5-10 Add a loop to the Grades Calculation Project

In this exercise, you'll modify the Grades Calculation Project you worked on last week in Exercise 4-8 by giving it the ability to calculate more than one student's grade before ending.
1. Using Notepad (if you are using Windows) locate and open the Grades.java source file you worked on last week. (It should be in the \JFiles\Grades folder)
2. Modify your code so that it looks like this.

```java
import javax.swing.JOptionPane;
class Grades {
  public static void main(String[] args) {
    final double ENGLISH_MIDTERM_PERCENTAGE = .25;
    final double ENGLISH_FINALEXAM_PERCENTAGE = .25;
    final double ENGLISH_RESEARCH_PERCENTAGE = .30;
    final double ENGLISH_PRESENTATION_PERCENTAGE = .20;
    final double MATH_MIDTERM_PERCENTAGE = .50;
    final double MATH_FINALEXAM_PERCENTAGE = .50;
    final double SCIENCE_MIDTERM_PERCENTAGE = .40;
    final double SCIENCE_FINALEXAM_PERCENTAGE = .40;
    final double SCIENCE_RESEARCH_PERCENTAGE = .20;
    int midterm = 0;
    int finalExamGrade = 0;
    int research = 0;
    int presentation = 0;
    double finalNumericGrade = 0;
    String finalLetterGrade = "";
    String response;
    String moreGradesToCalculate;

    moreGradesToCalculate = JOptionPane.showInputDialog
      ("Do you want to calculate a grade?");
    moreGradesToCalculate = moreGradesToCalculate.toUpperCase();
    while (moreGradesToCalculate.equals ("YES")) {
      // What type of student are we calculating?
    response = JOptionPane.showInputDialog
      ("Enter student type (1=English, 2=Math, 3=Science)");
    if (response == null) {
      JOptionPane.showMessageDialog(null, "You clicked on the Cancel button");
    System.exit (0);
    }
    else
    if (response.equals("")) {
      JOptionPane.showMessageDialog
        (null, "You must make an entry in the input box");
      System.exit (0);
```

```
  }
  else
  if (Integer.parseInt(response)<1| Integer.parseInt(response) > 3) {
    JOptionPane.showMessageDialog
      (null, response+"- is not a valid student type");
    System.exit (0);
  }
}
// Student type is valid, now let's calculate the grade
switch(Integer.parseInt(response)) {
  // Case 1 is an English Student
  case 1:
    midterm = Integer.parseInt(JOptionPane.showInputDialog
      ("Enter the Midterm Grade"));
    finalExamGrade = Integer.parseInt(JOptionPane.showInputDialog
      ("Enter the Final Examination Grade"));
    research = Integer.parseInt(JOptionPane.showInputDialog
      ("Enter the Research Grade"));
    presentation = Integer.parseInt(JOptionPane.showInputDialog
      ("Enter the Presentation Grade"));
    finalNumericGrade =
      (midterm * ENGLISH_MIDTERM_PERCENTAGE) +
      (finalExamGrade * ENGLISH_FINALEXAM_PERCENTAGE) +
      (research * ENGLISH_RESEARCH_PERCENTAGE) +
      (presentation * ENGLISH_PRESENTATION_PERCENTAGE);
    if (finalNumericGrade >= 93)
      finalLetterGrade = "A";
    else
    if ((finalNumericGrade >= 85) & (finalNumericGrade < 93))
      finalLetterGrade = "B";
    else
    if ((finalNumericGrade >= 78) & (finalNumericGrade < 85))
      finalLetterGrade = "C";
    else
    if ((finalNumericGrade >= 70) & (finalNumericGrade < 78))
      finalLetterGrade = "D";
    else
    if (finalNumericGrade < 70)
      finalLetterGrade = "F";
    JOptionPane.showMessageDialog
      (null, "*** ENGLISH STUDENT ***\n\n" +
      "Midterm grade is: " + midterm + "\n" +
      "Final Exam is: " + finalExamGrade + "\n" +
      "Research grade is: " + research + "\n" +
      "Presentation grade is: " + presentation + "\n\n" +
      "Final Numeric Grade is: " + finalNumericGrade + "\n" +
      "Final Letter Grade is: " + finalLetterGrade);
    break;
  // Case 2 is a Math Student
  case 2:
    midterm = Integer.parseInt(JOptionPane.showInputDialog
      ("Enter the Midterm Grade"));
    finalExamGrade = Integer.parseInt(JOptionPane.showInputDialog
      ("Enter the Final Examination Grade"));
    finalNumericGrade =
      (midterm * MATH_MIDTERM_PERCENTAGE) +
      (finalExamGrade * MATH_FINALEXAM_PERCENTAGE);
    if (finalNumericGrade >= 90)
```

```java
      finalLetterGrade = "A";
    else
    if ((finalNumericGrade >= 83) & (finalNumericGrade < 90))
      finalLetterGrade = "B";
    else
    if ((finalNumericGrade >= 76) & (finalNumericGrade < 83))
      finalLetterGrade = "C";
    else
    if ((finalNumericGrade >= 65) & (finalNumericGrade < 76))
      finalLetterGrade = "D";
    else
    if (finalNumericGrade < 65)
      finalLetterGrade = "F";
    JOptionPane.showMessageDialog
      (null,"*** MATH STUDENT ***\n\n" +
      "Midterm grade is: " + midterm + "\n" +
      "Final Exam is: " + finalExamGrade + "\n\n" +
      "Final Numeric Grade is: " + finalNumericGrade + "\n" +
      "Final Letter Grade is: " + finalLetterGrade);
    break;
    // Case 3 is a Science Student
case 3:
midterm = Integer.parseInt(JOptionPane.showInputDialog
  ("Enter the Midterm Grade"));
finalExamGrade = Integer.parseInt(JOptionPane.showInputDialog
  ("Enter the Final Examination Grade"));
research = Integer.parseInt(JOptionPane.showInputDialog
  ("Enter the Research Grade"));
finalNumericGrade =
  (midterm * SCIENCE_MIDTERM_PERCENTAGE) +
  (finalExamGrade * SCIENCE_FINALEXAM_PERCENTAGE) +
  (research * SCIENCE_RESEARCH_PERCENTAGE);
if (finalNumericGrade >= 90)
  finalLetterGrade = "A";
else
if ((finalNumericGrade >= 80) & (finalNumericGrade < 90))
  finalLetterGrade = "B";
else
if ((finalNumericGrade >= 70) & (finalNumericGrade < 80))
  finalLetterGrade = "C";
else
if ((finalNumericGrade >= 60) & (finalNumericGrade < 70))
  finalLetterGrade = "D";
else
if (finalNumericGrade < 60)
  finalLetterGrade = "F";
JOptionPane.showMessageDialog
  (null,"*** SCIENCE STUDENT ***\n\n" +
  "Midterm grade is: " + midterm + "\n" +
  "Final Exam is: " + finalExamGrade + "\n" +
  "Research grade is: " + research + "\n\n" +
  "Final Numeric Grade is: " + finalNumericGrade + "\n" +
  "Final Letter Grade is: " + finalLetterGrade);
break;
default:
  JOptionPane.showMessageDialog
    (null, response + " - is not a valid student type");
```

```
            System.exit (0);
         }
      moreGradesToCalculate = JOptionPane.showInputDialog
         ("Do you have another grade to calculate?");
      moreGradesToCalculate = moreGradesToCalculate.toUpperCase();
      }
      JOptionPane.showMessageDialog
         (null, "Thanks for using the Grades Calculation program!");
      System.exit (0);
   }
}
```

3. Save your source file as Grades.java in the \JFiles\Grades folder (select File |Save As from Notepad's menu bar). Be sure to save your source file with the filename extension Java.

4. Compile your source file into a Bytecode file.

5. Execute your program and test it thoroughly. We need to verify that the looping behavior of the program is working correctly. After you start up your program, it should ask you if you have a grade to calculate.

6. Answer **Yes** and calculate the grade for an English student. Enter **70** for the midterm, **80** for the final examination, **90** for the research grade, and **100** for the presentation. A final numeric grade of **84.5** should be displayed with a letter grade of **C**.

7. After the message box is displayed with the calculated grade, the program should ask you if you have more grades to calculate.

8. Answer **Yes** and calculate the grade for a Math student. Enter **70** for the midterm and **80** for the final examination. A final numeric grade of **75** should be displayed with a letter grade of **D**.

9. After the message box is displayed with the calculated grade, the program should ask you if you have more grades to calculate.

10. Answer **Yes** and calculate the grade for a s Science student. Enter **70** for the midterm, **80** for the final examination, and **90** for the research grade. A final numeric grade of **78** should be displayed with a letter grade of **C**. After the message box is displayed with the calculated grade, the program should ask you if you have more grades to calculate.

11. Answer **No**. You should be thanked for using the program, and the program should end.

Discussion

Making the modifications to the code in the Grades class required careful attention to detail, but in the end, everyone was able to complete the exercise without a great deal of trouble.

"I have to say I'm really impressed with the practical use for this loop," Ward said.

"Me too," Rhonda said. "In a way, this program kind of reminds me of an Automated Teller Machine that, once you are done withdrawing your money, asks you if you have any more transactions to complete before giving you your card back."

"Can you go over the code?" Mary asked. "I think I understand what's going on here, but I want to be absolutely sure."

"I'd be glad to do that, Mary," I said. "We made just a few enhancements to the code from last week's version of the Grade Calculation program, the major one being to sandwich in a While loop, the code that actually does the calculations. Prior to that, we needed to declare a variable to store the value of the user's answer to the question we are going to pose—does he or she have a grade to calculate. Because we already had a variable in the program called response that we use to accept the individual grade component values from the user, we declared a new variable called moreGradesToCalculatel for this purpose:"

```
String moreGradesToCalculate;
```

"Having declared that variable to hold the user's response to our question, it's now time ask the question:"

```
moreGradesToCalculate = JOptionPane.showInputDialog
   ("Do you want to calculate a grade?");
```

"Again, we uppercase the user's response and store it right back in the moreGradesToCalculate variable:"

```
moreGradesToCalculate = moreGradesToCalculate.toUpperCase();
```

"Now here's the critical line of code," I said. "It's where we set up the While Loop structure, using the user's response in the test expression:"

```
while (moreGradesToCalculate.equals ("YES")) {
```

"If the user has answered 'Yes' to the question that they have a grade to calculate, the value of moreGradesToCalculate is 'Yes,' and we execute the body of the loop—the code that we wrote last week to calculate the student's final numeric and letter grades."

"So really, not all that much has changed with this code," Joe said.

"That's right, Joe," I said. "The really difficult code used to calculate the grade was written last week. All we've done by placing it in the body of the loop is give our program the ability to calculate more than one student. We do that by asking the user this question:"

```
moreGradesToCalculate = JOptionPane.showInputDialog
   ("Do you have another grade to calculate?");
moreGradesToCalculate = moreGradesToCalculate.toUpperCase();
}
```

"If the user answers anything other than 'Yes' or its many varieties," I said, "our test expression will evaluate to False, and the loop will terminate, followed by this code which thanks the user for using our program and gracefully ends the program:"

```
JOptionPane.showMessageDialog
   (null, "Thanks for using the Grade Calculation program!");
System.exit (0);
```

"If the user answers 'Yes,' the body of the loop will execute once more, permitting a second student's grade to be calculated."

Ward expressed some concern over the growing length and complexity of the code in the Grade Calculation Project.

"The code just keeps growing and growing," he said. "I realize there isn't much we can do about its length. However, it's getting so complex that I'm having a harder and harder time following it."

"I agree," Rhonda said, "but as I said last week, aren't we just about done with this project? I think we've fulfilled all of the requirements for the project, haven't we?"

"I think we have, Rhonda," I replied. "From a functional point of view, there really isn't much that we'll be adding to the project. In the remainder of the course, we will streamline and fine-tune the program and take advantage of the some of the object-oriented characteristics of the Java programming language. I think in doing so we'll be addressing Ward's concerns about the growing complexity of the code, although you'll see the overall number of lines of code in the project won't decrease. Object-oriented programs have a way of simplifying the complex nature of code. And we'll start doing that next week when we create some functions and methods of our own, which should make our program a little easier to follow."

It had been a long class. I could see that everyone was feeling proud of the product they were producing week by week. I could also see that they were pretty worn out; it had been an intense session. I dismissed class for the day.

Summary

In this chapter, we discussed how loop processing can make our programming lives a lot easier, and make our programs extremely powerful. There are several types of loop statements.

Here's a reminder of some of the different loop structures we discussed:

- **For Loops**: these loops execute a definite number of times. The number of times that the loop runs is determined by the Start, End and Step parameters set in the 'For' line of the Loop Control.

- **While Loops**: these loops execute an indefinite number of times, determined by a test condition. The While loop continues to run while a specified condition is True. In a While loop, the test expression is evaluated prior to the body of the loop executing even one time--therefore, in a While Loop, there is the possibility that the code in the body of the loop will not execute even one time.

- **Do-While Loops**: Like the While loop, the Do-While loop executes an indefinite number of times, determined by a test condition. The Do-While loop continues to run while the test expression evaluates to True. In a Do-While loop, the test expression is evaluated after the body of the loop executes--therefore, in a Do-While loop, the body of the loop is always executed at least one time.

We have also modified the Grades Calculation project so that it calculates more than one student's grade.

In the next chapter, we'll take a closer look at creating classes that simulate real-world objects.

Chapter 6---Creating Your Own Methods

In this chapter, we'll discuss how to make our programs more readable and efficient by creating our own methods. As we'll see during the course of the chapter, methods are pieces of code that perform a single task, and promote a concept called modularity.

Modular programs are easier to maintain and understand

"Starting today," I said, as I began our sixth class, "and continuing for the next three weeks or so, we'll be examining ways in which we can use some of Java's object-oriented features to make programs that are more readable, more efficient, and easier to maintain. Even more importantly, you'll discover object-oriented programming languages like Java promote the concept of something called "software reuse," which means that a piece of code, once written, should not be tossed away or rewritten for another program, but incorporated into classes for use in another program. In other words, the same piece of code can be used in multiple programs. We'll look at that in more detail next week when you see how you can create classes of your own. In today's class, we take the first step along the path of software reuse when you learn how to write methods of your own. We've already used Java methods throughout the class—for instance, the **println()** method of the System object and the **parseInt()** method of the Integer object. Today we'll learn how to create methods of our own that reside in the same class as the code that will execute the method. Next week we'll learn how to create methods that reside in separate classes and which can then be executed or called from other classes."

"If I'm correct," Dave said, "I believe that every program that we've written in this class has had just one method—the **main()** method. Isn't that right?"

"That's right, Dave," I answered, "and you have probably noticed that as our programs have gotten more complex, the number of lines of code in the **main()** method has grown and grown."

"Is that bad?" Kate asked. "I mean, is there a limit to the number of lines of code that can go into the **main()** method?"

"There's no limit to the number of lines of code that can be placed in the **main()** method, or in any method for that matter," I said. "However, the more lines of code in a method, the more difficult the program is to follow, understand, and maintain."

"What do you mean by maintain?" Rhonda asked. "Is that like automobile maintenance?"

"Maintaining a program," I answered, "means changing or modifying the program. Programs need to be maintained for a number of different reasons. Some programs need to be modified because of a change in the business environment for which the program is written. Other programs need to be modified due to new governmental regulations. Other programs need to be modified because of requests from users. Regardless of the reason, you can be almost certain that any program you write will eventually need to be modified—if not by you, then by someone else. And even if all you need to change is a single line of code, if that line of code happens to appear in a **main()** method with hundreds or thousands of other lines of code, you're going to have a heck of a time finding that line of code unless the program was written in a modular fashion."

"Modular?" Lou asked.

"We'll see a little later on, Lou," I said, "that modular programs are programs that are written in distinct, logical units."

"Do programs need to be changed all that often that we need to worry about this?" Blaine asked.

"Most programs that are written for commercial purposes will at one time or other need to be changed." I answered. "In fact, it's been estimated that the programming staff in a large corporation may spend up to 85 percent of its time modifying the code in already existing programs."

"That's incredible," Chuck said. "So making programs easier to read and maintain is important."

"Absolutely," I said. "In fact, it's pretty likely that the program we're writing for Frank Olley will need to be changed at some point. If the English, Math, or Science Departments change the formula for the way a student's final grade is calculated, we'll need to change the Grade Calculation program."

"I see why programs need to be changed," Valerie said, "but how can creating methods of our own in addition to the **main()** method make that process easier?"

"So far," I answered, "in all of the code you've written for this class, I've pretty much told you exactly what line or lines of code to write and where you needed to place them. In the real world, however, this won't be the case. You're more likely to be asked by a supervisor or project leader to make a functional change to a program. In other words, you'll be told what change to make in terms like 'change the federal tax withholding rate from 18 percent to 22 percent.' It will be up to you to find the appropriate Java class file, locate the line or lines of code in the class that performs that calculation, decide upon the necessary changes and then apply them. From experience, I can tell you if all of the code in your program is located within the **main()** method of a single Java class, finding and making changes to that code can be pretty tough."

"And this is where having more than one method in a class will come in handy?" Rhonda asked. "I'm afraid I just don't see why."

"I think I can help," Dave said. "I work in a department that gets a tremendous amount of mail. We have a super-efficient secretary, Millie, who by the time I sit down in my cubicle each morning, has separated everyone's mail and placed it on the individual's desk. On those days when Millie isn't in, the place is chaos. Anyone who is expecting an important piece of correspondence sifts through a huge pile of mail. Eventually they find the piece they're looking for, but it's a painstaking job, and sometimes they accidentally pull out a piece of mail belonging to someone else."

"So that huge pile of mail, Dave," Rhonda said, "is like one big **main()** method?"

"That's right," Dave replied. "Millie, by sorting and distributing the mail each morning, produces logical 'modules' of mail. It makes the whole process much easier."

"That's a great analogy, Dave, thanks," I said. "In terms of modular programming, that means that when we write code, we should place code that performs a single function into a method of its own. For instance, if we write a program to calculate payroll, all of the code to calculate the <u>Federal</u> withholding tax should be placed in a method of its own. Similarly, the code to calculate the <u>State</u> withholding tax should be placed in a method of its own. This process has traditionally been described as modular programming, although the concepts and techniques have been enhanced quite a bit by modern object-oriented programming languages such as Java."

What is a method?

"So in theory," Bob said, "a method is code that performs a single function?"

"That's right, Bob," I said. "Last week, all of the code that we wrote for the Grade Calculation Project went into the **main()** method of the Grades class. By the end of today's class, we'll have taken that code, and redistributed much of it into separate functions. For instance, all of the code that performs the calculation for the final grade of an English student will be placed in a method of its own called **calculateEnglishStudent()**. In a similar way, the code to perform the calculation for the final grade of a math student will be placed in a method of its own called **calculateMathStudent()**, and the code to perform the calculation for the final grade of a science student will be placed in a method of its own called calculateScienceStudent."

"I see what you're getting at now," Ward said. "If the code to calculate the final grade for a math student is in a method of its own, I would think finding it and making the correct changes to it would be much easier."

"Right on the mark, Ward," I said. "Not only is code that is broken down and placed in methods easier to find and modify, but when it's also bundled in the form of an object, it can be easily reused in other applications."

"How's that?" Peter asked.

"The **println()** method of the System object is a perfect example of that," I said. "It's probably no exaggeration to say that millions of Java programs use the code in the **println()** method of the System object, yet the code in the **println()** was written just once."

I gave everyone a chance to take in what I was saying.

"Are there any rules or guidelines for writing methods?" Steve asked. "Do you write them from scratch right away, or do you place all of your code in the **main()** method and then at some point move the code out of there into separate methods?"

"With a little experience, Steve," I said, "you'll find yourself writing methods of your own write from the very start of your program. It seems strange to you now because for the last five weeks we've dealt with just the single **main()** method, but the more programs you write, the more natural placing code in your own methods will become. Just remember: place code that performs a single function into a method of its own. Needless to say, we haven't done that yet with the Grade Calculation Project, but that's because we needed to concentrate on learning the fundamentals of the Java language and how to create a working program before we could worry about making our program more readable, efficient, and easy to modify. For the remainder of today's class we'll worry about all of that, and in next week's class and the one after that, we'll learn how the methods we create today can be placed in classes of their own that can then be incorporated into programs written by other programmers."

"Just like the **println()** method of the System object?" Kate asked.

"You hit the nail on the head, Kate," I said. "Programmers who write good code and are insightful enough to place that code in classes are rewarded by having their code used by hundreds of other programmers—not only by programmers in their own companies but by programmers all over the world. We'll learn more about how to create code and place it in those types of classes next week."

"I can imagine that's quite an ego trip," Ward said, "having your code used like that—but it's also quite an incentive for me to learn this language."

"I have just one question," Mary said. "If we take all of the code out of our **main()** method and place it in those other methods you mentioned, what will be left in the **main()** method?"

"We won't take all of the code out of the **main()** method," I answered. "The **main()** method in a startup class is required, and it will contain the code that 'calls' or requests the execution of the code contained in those other methods. The code in the **main()** method frequently resembles the outline of a book, with each call to a method appearing as a chapter heading."

Creating your own Methods...

"This all sounds very exciting," Rhonda said. "So how do we create methods of our own, and what do we name them?"

"You can name your methods virtually anything you want, Rhonda," I said, "but be sure to pick a meaningful name. As far as how to create them, like the **main()** method we've worked with since the start of the course, methods of your own must be defined within the class itself—that means within the class braces. By convention, they should follow the **main()** method, and although it's not required, it's a good idea to separate any custom methods you write from the **main()** method with a blank line. Let's examine a now-familiar Java program containing just a single **main()** method and then modify it to include a custom method of our own."

I then displayed this code on the classroom projector.

```
public class Example6_1 {
  public static void main(String[] args) {
    System.out.println ("I love Java");
  }
}
```

"Look familiar?" I asked, "This is the first Java program we wrote in the course. As you know, it displays the message 'I love Java' in the Java Console Window. Let's see how we can take the code to display that message out of the **main()** method and place it in a method of its own which we'll call **displayMessage()** .."

I then modified the code to look like this…

```
public class Example6_2 {
  public static void main(String[] args) {
    displayMessage();  // Call to Custom Method
  }

  public static void displayMessage()  {        // Custom Method
    System.out.println ("I love Java");
  }
}
```

I compiled it and executed it. The message "I love Java!" was displayed in the Java console window.

"This program behaves in the same manner as the previous version did," I said, "but in this version of the program, the Java instruction to display the message 'I love Java!' is no longer being executed directly from the **main()**

method. Instead, the instruction is executed from a method called **displayMessage()**, and this is the code that tells Java to execute the code in the **displayMessage()** method:"

```
displayMessage();               // Call to Custom Method
```

"Notice," I continued, "that the code to call or execute the **displayMessage()** method references the name of the method precisely because method names, like variable names, are case sensitive. Notice also that the **displayMessage()** method follows the **main()** method, but it is still located within the body of the class. Beginner Java programmers sometimes make the mistake of coding their custom methods outside the closing brace of the class definition, and that will cause an error when you compile the class. Let's take a closer look at the first line of the **displayMessage()** method."

Method Header

"I notice that the first line of the **displayMessage()** method is quite different from the **main()** method," Kathy said. "I think at some point in the class you promised to explain that first line of the **main()** method in more detail—is now the time?"

"You're right, Kathy," I said. "The first line of both methods, which is sometimes called the method header, the method definition, or the method signature, are different. And you're also right that now is a great time to discuss what that first line means in some detail."

```
public static void main(String[] args)
```

"That looks so complicated to me!" Rhonda said, looking at the **main()** method header on the classroom projector in a bewildered manner.

"Let's see if this will help," I said, as I displayed this graphic on the classroom projector. "This is a schematic of the **main()** method header."

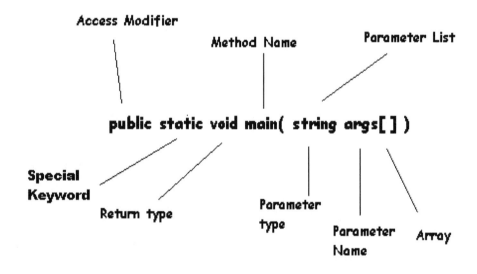

"For comparison purposes," I said, "here's the header for the **displayMessage()** method we just created:"

```
public static void displayMessage() {
```

"And, just to confuse the issue even further, we could have written the header to look like this:"

```
void displayMessage() {
```

"If both of these are method headers," Linda asked, "why do they appear to be so different? Is the **main()** method somehow special?"

"The only 'special' quality to the **main()** method," I said, "is that its code is automatically executed when the startup class is executed from the command-line prompt. What makes it appear different from the **displayMessage()** header is the fact that the **main()** method uses some of the optional keywords permitted in a method declaration. Refer to the chart on the classroom projector as we take a closer look at the declaration for the **main()** method. From left to right:"

- An Access Specifer, in this case public, followed by

- The keyword Static (more on that later), followed by

- The return type of the method, in this case <u>void</u>, followed by

- The name of the method, followed by

- A pair of parentheses within which any parameters to the method are specified with both a type and name

"What's a parameter?" Bob asked.

"A parameter is a piece of information," I said, "which in some way provides additional information to the method about how it should behave. A method that is defined with one or more parameters is seeking qualifying information from the code that calls it, and any code that executes that method is required to supply that qualifying information. Parameters are specified in the method header within parentheses. If the parentheses are empty, as is the case with the **displayMessage()** method, that means the method is defined without parameters, so the code calling the method need not worry about supplying it with qualifying information. By the way, you will also hear the term 'arguments' used interchangeably with parameters. Technically, methods are defined with parameters, and the qualifying information itself is passed to the header as an argument. There's a subtle difference."

"Is the word 'args' in the **main()** method header the name of the parameter?" Dave asked.

public static void main(String[] args)

"That's right, Dave," I said. "Parameters are given unique names in the method header, and <u>args</u> is the name of the String parameter that the **main()** method is expecting. Actually, the pair of square brackets following the word args designates something known as an array. An array is a data structure that we'll discuss later on in the course."

Access Specifers Error! Bookmark not defined.

"What's an Access Specifer?" Chuck asked.

"Access Specifers," I answered, "tell Java how *visible* your method should be to other programs (or classes) using your class."

"Other programs can use our class?" Valerie asked.

> NOTE: A client program is a program that creates an object from a special kind of class called an Instantiable class. We'll create those next week.

"That's right, Valerie," I said. "Remember, with Java you will spend quite a bit of time creating those 'reusable' components I spoke of earlier—those are classes from which 'objects' will be created by something known as a client program. It won't be until next week that you learn how to create one of these classes and see how a client program creates an object from one of these classes, so you'll have to wait until then to see exactly how it happens. However, one thing you must do when you design your class is to decide which, if any, of the methods you've written within your class, should be visible, and therefore executable, by client programs that create objects from it. It is the <u>Access Specifer</u> that tells Java the type of access to give to the client program, and in Java, there are four Access Specifers you can use for this purpose: Public, Protected, Private, and Package."

> NOTE: Access specifers should be typed in lowercase letters in your code

Public Access Specifer

"The first Access Specifer we'll discuss today is Public," I said. "Any method defined with the Public Access Specifer can be seen and executed by code both within the same class and in a client program."

"You're implying," Dave said, "that without the Public Access Specifer, some methods of the classes we'll create won't be able to be seen by a client program? Is that right?"

"That's right, Dave," I said. "For instance, a method defined with the Private Access Specifer, which we'll discuss next, cannot be seen or executed by a client program."

"It would seem pretty silly to me," Dave replied, "to write code that can't be executed by a client program using your class. After all, isn't that why you said we will create classes, to provide a way for other programs to use the code we've written in methods, like the **println()** method of the System object?"

"You make a good point, Dave," I said, "and I agree. Most times, but not all, you want the client program using objects created from your class to be able to see and execute the methods you've defined in your class, and your example of the **println()** method of the System object is a good one. Methods such as this are called Public methods, which means that they can be seen and executed by code both inside and outside the class—those client programs I've been talking about."

"How do you designate a method for Public access?" Mary asked.

"Simply," I said, "by preceding the name of the method with the keyword Public, which is the Public Access Specifer. Take note that both our **main()** and **displayMessage()** methods were defined with the Public Access Specifer."

> NOTE: The main() method of any class must be defined as Public; otherwise, the program can't be run from a command-line prompt.

Private Access Specifer

"At the opposite end of the spectrum from Public access is Private," I said. "Private access means that the method can only be seen and executed by other code within the class. Private access is the access to specify when you don't want your method to be executable by a client program using an object created from your class."

"Why would you want to do that?" Ward asked.

"You may write a method," I answered, "which is just too dangerous to allow someone using an object created from your class to use. For instance, suppose you create a method called **deleteTable()** that contains code to delete one of your company's production Oracle database tables. Is this a method that you want to define with Public access, and therefore allow any client program to execute directly? Or is it a method better executed by other code within your class only when several preliminary checks and tests have been performed?"

"I see what you mean," Ward said.

"It's not only the methods we create ourselves that have Private access," I said. "I bet there are some methods of the System object defined with Private access that we can't get at directly but which are perhaps executed when we execute another method."

"Will we be coding any Private methods in the Grade Calculation Project?" Peter asked.

"Yes, we will," I said. "There will be one method which will only be executed from code within the class itself. In fact, the client program using the object created from the class won't even know the method exists."

No one seemed to have any problems with either the Public or Private Access Specifers, so it was time to move on.

Protected Access Specifer

"The next level of access," I said, "is Protected access. Protected access is very much like Private access. However, with Protected Access code in same class, code in subclasses of the class and code from classes in the same package can access the method. In Private access, only code within the same class can access the method, not subclasses."

> NOTE: You'll learn what subclasses are in two weeks when we talk about Inheritance.

"What's a package?" Rhonda asked.

"Packages are groups of related classes," I said. "In Java, you can designate a class as belonging to a package, kind of like placing multiple word processing documents into a single folder."

"How do you create a package?" Dave asked. "We haven't done that yet, have we?"

"No, we haven't created any packages," I answered. "Package creation is a program distribution issue, and we really don't get into it in this introductory level class, but I can tell you that creating a package is pretty easy. All you need to do is use the Package keyword at the top of your class file before you code any import statements, like this:"

```
package Smiley;              // Add this class to the Smiley package
public class Example6_2      {
   public static void main(String[] args)
```

"Ordinarily, in any commercial application you write, you would place classes pertaining to a particular project in a specially named folder and designate them to be part of the same package."

Package Access Specifer

"The last of the four Access Specifers is called Package," I said.

"And, unlike the other three Access Specifers in which the access keyword is specifically coded, Package access is the default—what you get if you don't specify any Access Specifer. In other words, if we code our **displayMessage()** method like this, we will get Package access:"

```
static void displayMessage()
```

"Package access is like Protected access, in that code from the same class and code from other classes in the package can execute the method. The difference is that code in subclasses cannot see and execute the method, unless they happen to be part of the same package."

Access Specifers Are NOT Class Specifiers

"It looks to me as though the class header itself in Example6_2 has an Access Specifer," Kate said. "Is that what the word 'Public' means there?"

I displayed the line of code declaring the Example6_2 Class on the classroom projector:

```
public class Example6_2    {
```

"That's a good point, Kate," I answered. "Classes are declared with something that appears to be an Access Specifer but which is officially termed a specifier. Specifiers are similar to Access Specifers, and we'll talk more about class specifiers next week when we examine creating Instantiable classes."

"I've heard some of the Java programmers at work use the term 'member.'" Mary said. "What is a member?"

"A member is either a method or a variable," I said. "You hear the term member used to refer to the group as a whole."

"Is the word 'static' an Access Specifer?" Blaine asked.

"That's a good question, Blaine," I replied. "Static is a keyword, not an Access Specifer, and it can be applied to both methods and variables. Using the Static keyword has no effect on the extent to which a method—or a variable for that matter—can be seen from code outside the class."

"So what does it mean?" Rhonda asked.

"In order to explain what Static means," I said, "I need to tell you that when a client program creates an object from a class that you define, more than one object can be created from that same class. Ordinarily, each object has its own copy of the variables and methods defined within the class, but not when the Static keyword is used. In that case, each object shares just one copy of the method or variable with other objects created from that same class."

I could see some confusion in the faces of my students.

"If this explanation doesn't make a lot of sense to you now," I said, "I think it will make a bit more sense next week when we start to create objects from classes we define. Remember, up until now, we've created a single startup class with a single method called **main()** that automatically executes upon start up. The programs we'll create in next week's class will create objects from other classes, and we'll learn more about Static members then."

"Does the **main()** method have to be declared using the Static keyword?" Lou asked.

"Yes it does, Lou," I said. "You'll find that if you fail to include the Static keyword in front of the **main()** method name, your program will compile, but if you try to execute the program, you'll receive an error message. Again, we'll learn more about the Static keyword next week."

"I know we've covered this before," Valerie said, "but does every program need to have a **main()** method?"

"I was about to ask that myself," Rhonda said. "Now that we have a method of our own—**displayMessage()** in Example6_2—is it really necessary to have a **main()** method also?"

"Yes it is, Rhonda." I said. "**main()** is a method that must be included in every startup class."

"And the startup class is the class we execute from the command line?" Joe asked.

"That's right, Joe," I said. "Only the startup class is required to have a **main()** method. Next week we'll create classes which have no **main()** method, but they won't be startup classes—they'll be classes from which we'll create objects."

"I noticed that both the **main()** and **displayMessage()** methods are declared with the Static keyword," Dave said. "I know you said that the **main()** method must be declared with the Static keyword, but why is **displayMessage()** declared with the Static keyword also?"

"This is a bit of a tough concept to digest," I said, "but a method, in this case **displayMessage()**, that is called from a Static method in the same class, in this case **main()**, must also be declared as Static. Ordinarily, using the Static keyword isn't required, as the methods we'll ordinarily call from **main()** will be methods located in other classes. But in today's class, the methods we define will need to be declared with the Static keyword because they're in the same class as **main()**."

The Return Type

"In the **main()** method definition, what is 'void'?" Chuck asked. "That's a strange-sounding word."

"In Java," I said, "methods perform some sort of processing, and many then return a value of some kind to the program that calls them. The return value can be used to notify the calling program as to the success or failure of the operation, or something along those lines. Ordinarily, the return type is a Java data type, such as Int or Double. The return type can also be an object. When the method, by design, returns no value, Java needs to know this, and the return type of void is designated."

NOTE: The return type void indicates that the method does not return a value.

"So both the **main()** and **displayMessage()** methods perform some kind of processing but don't return a value to the code that calls them, is that right?" Dave asked.

"That's exactly right, Dave," I said.

"I'm a bit confused," Rhonda said.

"Sometimes," I said, "I analogize methods to favors that you ask a friend to do for you. Perhaps you ask your friend to feed your fish while you're away on vacation, and because you tend to be a worrier, you request a 'return value' in the form of a phone call or an e-mail from your friend to confirm that she actually remembered to feed the fish. On the other hand, your friend may be the type of person who never forgets to do anything, in which case, your mind is at ease, and no 'return value' is necessary."

"So sometimes," Kate said, "methods return a value, and sometimes they do not?"

"That's right, Kate," I said, "and it's entirely up to the designer of the method to decide. In the case of the **displayMessage()** method we just wrote, did we return a value?"

Kate checked for a minute and then said, "No."

"That's right, we didn't return a value from the **displayMessage()** method," I said, "but we could have. In the case of **displayMessage()**, I didn't think it was really necessary."

"So the return type will be the same Java data types we've already learned about?" Mary asked. "Like Int, Single, and Double?"

"To name a few," I said. "The return data type can also be an object such as a String, or even an object of your own design, the kind we'll create next week."

"I'm trying to recall if we've executed methods that return a value?" Lou asked.

"I think we have, Lou," Linda said. "When we executed the **parseInt()** method last week, it returned a value which we then assigned to a variable."

"That's right, I forgot about that," Lou said.

"Can we see how to write a method of our own that returns a value?" Barbara asked.

"Sure thing, Barbara," I said. "We can modify the **displayMessage()** method we wrote in Example6_2 to return a value, in this case, a Boolean data type."

```
public class Example6_3 {
  public static void main(String[] args) {
    boolean messageDisplayed;
    messageDisplayed = displayMessage();
    System.out.println ("The value of messageDisplayed is " + messageDisplayed);
  }
```

```
public static boolean displayMessage() {
    System.out.println ("I love Java");
    return true;
  }
}
```

I then compiled the program and executed it. The following screenshot was displayed on the classroom projector:

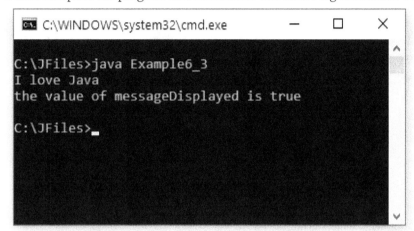

"To return a value from a method," I said, "we need to do two things. First, we need to tell Java that the method will return a value. We do that by changing the method's return type from void, which again, means that the method returns nothing, to our desired return type. In this case, we wanted to display a Boolean value—either True or False—so we declared the return type as Boolean:"

public static boolean displayMessage() {

> NOTE: Be sure to spell 'boolean' in lowercase letters in your Java code

"You said we need to do two things," Chuck said. "What's the second?"

"Having told Java that the method returns a value by declaring so in the method declaration," I said, "we next have to return the value, and we do that somewhere within the body of the method— usually the last statement—by executing a return statement. Java is pretty smart about this: if we forget to execute the return statement, the program simply won't compile. Here's the statement that returns the Boolean return value we committed to returning when we declared the method:"

return true;

> CAUTION: Be sure to spell 'true' in lowercase letters in your Java code. Spelling it 'True' will generate a compiler error.

"As you can see, all we need to do is execute the return statement, followed by an appropriate value for the declared data type of the return value. In this case, since we committed to returning a bool data type, we need to return the Java value true or false."

"What does the program that calls the method do with the return value?" Kate asked.

"The code calling the **displayMessage()** method," I said, "can do one of three things with it. It can store the return value in a variable; it can use the return value in an expression, for instance, as an argument to the **println()** method of the System object; or interestingly enough, it can choose to ignore the return value simply by executing the method and not doing anything at all with the return value. In this example code, we declared a Boolean variable called messageDisplayed into which we stored the return value from the method call. Remember, since we declared the **displayMessage()** method with a return type of Boolean, the variable we declare to store the return value must be declared as a Boolean data type also …"

boolean messageDisplayed;

"Having declared the messageDisplayed variable, we now execute the **displayMessage()** method, but notice how we place the call of the method to the right of the assignment operator (=). In this way, after the **displayMessage()** method executes, its return value is immediately stored in the variable messageDisplayed:"

messageDisplayed = displayMessage();

"Finally, we display the return value stored in the messageDisplayed variable to the Java Console by using the **println()** method of the System object:"

```
System.out.println ("The value of messageDisplayed is " + messageDisplayed);
```

"I should mention here," I said, "that instead of storing the return value of **displayMessage()** in a variable the way we did here, we could have used the return value directly as an argument to the **println()** method of the System object, like this:"

```
public class Example6_4 {
  public static void main(String[] args) {
    System.out.println ("The value of messageDisplayed is " + displayMessage());
  }

  public static boolean displayMessage() {
    System.out.println ("I love Java");
    return true;
  }
}
```

"This version of the code is a bit trickier to follow, but many Java programmers love the compact nature of this style of code—just something to watch out for."

"I'm surprised," Rhonda said. "I actually understand what's going on here."

"Can a method return more than one value?" Chuck asked.

"Excellent question, Chuck," I replied. "The answer is no. A method is limited to returning just a single return value. However, it is possible to return an array. An array is a data structure that is actually a collection of variables. So there is a way around the limitation of returning just a single return value."

Method Parameters and Arguments

We were making some pretty good progress in examining the method header. "What's next in the method header?" I asked.

"After the word void in the **main()** method," Steve said, "comes the name of the method—no problem there. But then comes the part that confuses me: the part in the parentheses."

I displayed the **main()** method header on the classroom projector:

```
public static void main(String[] args) {
```

"Let me assure you, Steve," I said, "that the part within parentheses confuses everyone at first. That's the parameter list. With the **main()** method, the parameter list consists of a String array called args. With the **displayMessage()** method, there are no parameters defined, and that's why there's just an empty set of parentheses:"

```
public static boolean displayMessage()
```

"What are parameters, anyway?" Linda asked. "Are they the same as arguments, such as the ones we've been passing to some of the methods we've executed like **println()**?"

"You're right, Linda," I said. "Arguments are the actual values that we pass to a method. Many programmers use the terms arguments and parameters interchangeably, and really, only a computer scientist would argue with you. In theory, parameters are the names that appear in a method header, and arguments are the actual values that are passed to the method by the code that calls it. For each parameter in the method's header, there must be an argument passed to it."

"So parameters appear in the method header, and arguments are the actual values passed to the method when it is called?" Dave asked.

"Perfect, Dave," I said. "I—"

"I know," Rhonda said laughing. "You couldn't have said it any better yourself!"

"Can we modify the **displayMessage()** method to include a parameter?" Linda asked.

"I don't see why not," I answered. "Let's do this: let's modify the **displayMessage()** method to allow the programmer to pass an argument specifying his favorite programming language." I thought for a moment, and then displayed this code on the classroom projector:

```java
public class Example6_5 {
  public static void main(String[] args) {
    displayMessage("Java");
    displayMessage("Visual Basic");
    displayMessage("C#");
  }

  public static void displayMessage(String language) {
    System.out.println ("I love " + language);
  }
}
```

I compiled the program and then executed it. The following screenshot was displayed on the classroom projector:

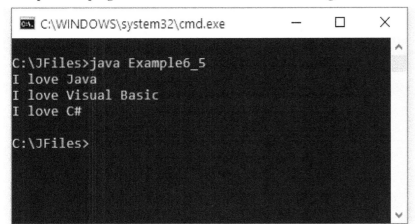

"Let's take a look at the new header for the **displayMessage()** method," I said. "I decided to remove the return value from the method header—it doesn't really add anything to the program. Here's the original method header:"

```java
public static void displayMessage()
```

"And here's the new method header declared with a parameter:"

```java
public static void displayMessage(String language)
```

"Within the parentheses," I continued, "we are telling Java that the **displayMessage()** method will accept a single parameter called *language* and that the parameter will be a String data type."

I could see some confusion in the eyes of my students, but I knew that would be cleared up momentarily.

"Let's see the code to call the **displayMessage()** method." I said. "Calling a method that requires a parameter is easy, provided you know the method's signature."

"Signature?" Joe asked.

"The method's signature is the number and type of arguments required," I said. "Here we know that we need to pass **displayMessage()** just a single String argument, and we do that—actually executing it three times—with this code:"

```java
displayMessage("Java");
displayMessage("Visual Basic");
displayMessage("C#");
```

"I'm a little confused as to what the **displayMessage()** method does with the argument once it receives it from the calling code," Barbara said. "Can you clear that up?"

"I'll try, Barbara," I answered. "Let's look at the code from the body of the Example6_4 program, in which the program was hard coded to display Java as its favorite language:"

```java
System.out.println ("I love Java");
```

"Here's the modified code, which uses the parameter Language as an argument to the **println()** method of the System object:"

```
System.out.println ("I love " + language);
```

"Is *language* a variable?" Lou asked. "And if so, why isn't it declared within the body of the method?"

"Parameters are a lot like variables," I said, "but they don't need to be declared within the body of the method since they are declared within the method header."

"That makes sense," Barbara said. "I have another question. Is it possible to create a method that accepts more than one argument, and if so, how does Java know which parameter is which when the code that calls the method passes the arguments?"

"Another good question," I said. "Yes, it is common to design a method that accepts more than one argument. In Java, arguments are passed positionally. That means that if the method's header specifies two parameters, Java assumes that the first argument passed to the method is the first parameter, the second argument passed to the method is the second parameter, and so on. Let me show you exactly what I mean by modifying the code we just wrote to accept two parameters."

I then modified the code from Example6_5 to look like this, and displayed it on the classroom projector:

Don't Forget: If typing these examples and exercises isn't something you want to do, feel free to follow this link to find and download the completed solutions for all of the examples and exercises in the book. Just click on the Java book, then follow the link entitled exercises ☺

http://www.johnsmiley.com/main/books.htm

```java
public class Example6_6 {
    public static void main(String[] args {
        displayMessage("Java", "a bunch");
        displayMessage("Visual Basic", "lots");
        displayMessage("C#", "a little bit");
    }

    public static void displayMessage(String language, String howMuch) {
        System.out.println ("I love " + language + " " + howMuch);
    }
}
```

"Notice the difference in the method header for **displayMessage()**," I said. "It's now defined with two String parameters: *language* and *howMuch*. Both of these parameters are used in the body of the method as arguments to the **println()** method of the System object:"

```java
public static void displayMessage(String language, String howMuch) {
    System.out.println ("I love " + language + " " + howMuch);
}
```

"Also, as you would expect, if the method header now specifies two String parameters, the call to the method must specify two String arguments, which appear after the method name within parentheses, separated by a comma. Notice that because these are String arguments, they are enclosed within quotation marks:"

```java
displayMessage("Java", "a bunch");
displayMessage("Visual Basic", "lots");
displayMessage("C#", "a little bit");
```

I then compiled and executed the modified program, and the following screenshot appeared on the classroom projector:

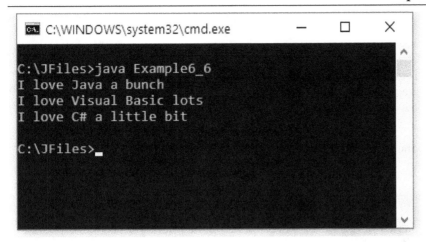

"Now the calling program can not only designate a favorite language, but also an assessment as to how much the user likes it," I said.

"I can see," Ward said, "that two parameters make this method even more flexible. This stuff is pretty neat."

"You're right, Ward," I said. "The more parameters a method accepts, the more flexible it can be. Of course, the more parameters a method accepts, the more complex the code in the method needs to be to handle the multiple arguments that it will receive. Later on today, we'll create methods for the Grade Calculation Project that will accept several parameters and you'll see what I mean."

"Suppose we had forgotten to supply the method call with two arguments?" Lou asked. "What would have happened? Would the program bomb when we ran it?"

"That depends on whether the method is in the same class as the code calling it," I said. "If it is, the Java compiler will flag the method call as an error when we try to compile the program. However, if we are calling the method from another class, then the program will bomb at runtime with a runtime error. That's why when you change a method definition the way we just did here, you have to be very careful, especially in a corporate or commercial environment."

"What do you mean?" Valerie asked.

"If you change the method's signature," I said, "which is the number, type, or even order of the parameters, programs that have already been written to call your method may bomb with runtime errors. Even worse, they could execute with incorrect results."

"Do changes to a method's signature happen a lot in the real world?" Blaine asked.

"Methods do change in the real world," I said, "and it's vitally important not to change a method's signature when they do. When you do that, in programming talk, you have 'broken' the client's code. However, sometimes changing a method like this just can't be helped. A method that you designed and coded last year may, in some cases, require more information from the calling program in order to do its job."

"How can you implement a change like that without changing the method's signature?" Bob asked.

"You can't," I said. "But fortunately, in Java, it's possible to have more than one method with the same name but with different signatures. This is called 'method overloading,' and it enables existing programs that call the method with its old signature to run fine and at the same time permits new programs to be written calling the method with its new signature. But let's put that off for a little bit. Right now, I'd like to discuss an alternative way to passing arguments to a method."

"What do you mean?" Rhonda asked.

"So far," I replied, "we've passed String literals to the **displayMessage()** method we've designed."

"What else can we pass?" Chuck asked.

"We can pass a variable," I said. "Let me show you."

I then displayed this code on the classroom projector:

```
public class Example6_7 {
  public static void main(String[] args) {
    String favorite = "Java";
```

```
    String intensity = "enormously";
    displayMessage(favorite, intensity);
  }

  public static void displayMessage(String language, String howMuch) {
    System.out.println ("I love " + language + " " + howMuch);
  }
}
```

I compiled and executed the program, and the following screenshot was displayed on the classroom projector:

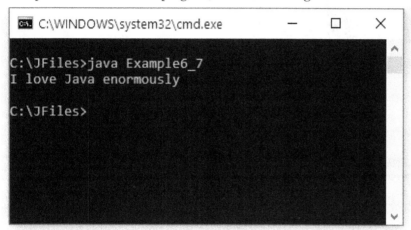

"This version of the program," I said, "displays just a single message in the Java Console window, but aside from that, behaves in the same manner as the other version did. However, we've changed the code by first declaring two String variables called favorite and intensity and assigning them values:"

```
String favorite = "Java";
String intensity = "enormously";
```

"And then we passed them as arguments to the **displayMessage()** method:"

```
displayMessage(favorite, intensity);
```

"Doing this has no impact on the execution of the method—the method doesn't really care whether a String literal is passed to it as an argument or a variable is passed."

In Java, by Default, Arguments are passed by Value

"Suppose," Linda said, "that for some reason, within the body of the method, we change the value of the passed argument. Does that have any effect on the value of the variable in the code that called it?"

"I'm not sure I know what Linda is asking," Rhonda said.

"Let me try to explain, Rhonda" I said. "In some programming languages, when a change is made to the value of a parameter that is passed to it via a variable, the value of the variable itself back in the code that called it is also changed."

I gave everyone a moment to think about that.

"Is that good?" Joe asked.

"Some programmers find this a convenient way of arriving at a programming solution," I said. "In those other languages, variables passed as arguments can either be passed by value or by reference. 'By value' simply means that the actual value of the variable is passed to the method as an argument, and in that case, changing the parameter within the body of the method has no impact on the variable in the calling code. When those other languages pass a variable as an argument to a method by reference, it isn't the actual value of the variable that is passed to the method, but the computer's memory address of the variable. That means that when the method changes the value of the parameter, it directly updates the value of the variable back in the calling code."

"But Java's not like that?" Mary said.

"That's right, Mary," I said. "In Java, variables are passed by value only. That means that although a variable is passed as an argument to a method, there's no way that changing the value of the parameter within the body of the method can impact the value of the variable in the code that calls the method."

"Can we see an example of this?" Mary asked.

"Sure thing Mary," I answered. "When we reference the variable name as an argument when we call the method, we aren't giving the method direct access to the variable itself—we are just passing it the value. That means that nothing the method does to the argument can impact the value of the variable in the code that calls it. Let me show you what I mean."

I then displayed this code on the classroom projector:

```
public class Example6_8 {
  public static void main(String[] args) {
    String favorite = "Java";
    String intensity = "enormously";
    displayMessage(favorite, intensity);
    System.out.println ("The value of favorite in main() is " + favorite);
  }

  public static void displayMessage(String favorite, String intensity) {
    System.out.println ("The value of favorite in displayMessage() is " + favorite);
    favorite = "VB";
    System.out.println ("The value of favorite in displayMessage() is now " + favorite);
  }
}
```

I compiled and executed the program, and the following screenshot was displayed on the classroom projector:

```
C:\WINDOWS\system32\cmd.exe                    —    □    ×

C:\JFiles>java Example6_8
The value of favorite in displayMessage() is Java
The value of favorite in displayMessage() is now VB
The value of favorite in main() is Java

C:\JFiles>
```

"Let me explain what's going on here," I said. "As we did in Example6_7, within the **main()** method, we declared two variables called *favorite* and *intensity* and initialized both of them with values:"

```
string favorite = "Java";
string intensity = "enormously";
```

"We then passed the variables as arguments to the **displayMessage()** method:"

```
displayMessage(favorite, intensity);
```

"We didn't need to do this to prove that Java passes variables by value" I said, "but notice that we've changed the names of the parameters within the method's header. We're still accepting two String parameters, but in this version of the program we've named them with the same names as the variables in the **main()** method:"

```
public static void displayMessage(String favorite, String intensity)
```

"Can we do that?" Ward asked. "Shouldn't the names of the parameters be different from the variables in the **main()** method?"

"They don't have to be," I said, "I know that in Example6_6, the parameter names were different from the names of the variables in the **main()** method, but there's no rule that they have to be. The variables declared in the **main()**

method are local to the main() method, and the parameters week. Local variables are variables declared within a method. A variable declared within a method in the **displayMessage()** method are local to the method—Java considers each of these variables to be different animals. We prove that by executing this line of code within the **displayMessage()** method that displays, in the Java Console, the original value of the argument passed to it as the favorite parameter, which is Java:"

```
System.out.println ("The value of favorite in displayMessage() is " + favorite);
```

"With this line of code, we change the value of the favorite parameter to 'VB':"

```
favorite = "VB";
```

"You might be inclined to believe that we have also changed the value of the favorite variable in the **main()** method, but you'll see in a moment we haven't. First, we prove that the value of the favorite parameter has indeed been changed by executing this line of code:"

```
System.out.println ("The value of favorite in displayMessage() is now " + favorite);
```

"This displays, in the Java Console, the altered value of the favorite parameter, which is now 'VB'. The **displayMessage()** method ends, and this line of code is then executed from the body of the **main()** method, proving that the value of the favorite variable in the **main()** method has not changed."

```
System.out.println ("The value of favorite in main() is " + favorite);
```

"We've proven," I concluded, "that changing the value of the favorite parameter within the displayMessage() method has had no impact on the value of the favorite variable in the **main()**method."

"I think I understand what's going on here," Linda said. "Even though the variables in the **main()** method and the parameters in the **displayMessage()** method have the same names, they're really separate things, aren't they?"

"That's right, Linda," I said. "Both the variables and the parameters are declared 'local' to each method in which they appear."

Variable Scope

"You've used the term 'local' several times this morning," Blaine said. "Can you tell us exactly what it means?"

"Local is a term that refers to the scope of a variable," I said. "A variable's scope describes what other parts of your program can 'see' the variable. In Java, there are three types of variables: Instance, Class, and Local variables. We'll discuss both Instance variables and Class variables next week. Local variables are variables declared within a method. A variable declared within a method can be seen or accessed only by code within that same method."

"So a local variable is one declared within a method?" Kate asked.

"That's basically correct, Kate," I said. "Technically, a local variable is one declared within a block, that is, within a pair of curly braces. That means that if you declare a variable within the curly braces of an If statement, the variable can only be seen by the code within the If statement."

"I think at work I've seen some variables declared just above the **main()** method," Linda said. "They don't appear to belong to any method."

"Those are either Instance or Class variables," I said. "A variable declared in a class, but are not part of any method, are either Instance or Class variables. We'll talk more about those next week."

Variable Lifetime

"I've heard some programmers at work refer to the lifetime of a variable," Valerie said. "Is lifetime the same as scope?"

"No, but they are related," I replied. "Scope affects what parts of your program can see the variable. Lifetime, on the other hand, affects how long your variable lives. A variable declared as a local variable within a method has local scope and can only be seen by other code within the method. It's also 'born' when its declaration statement within the method is executed and 'dies' after the last line of code in the method is executed. Next week, we'll see that the lifetime for Instance and Class variables are different. In the case of an Instance variable, it exists for as long an object that is created from its class exists. Class variables may live even longer: as long as *any* object created from its class exists. More on that next week."

We had been working for quite some time, so I suggested we all take a break before completing our first hands-on exercises of the day.

Using methods to fine tune your code

Fifteen minutes later, when we returned from break, I resumed class by reminding my students that the main benefit to creating methods of our own—custom methods, as I call them—is that it promotes program modularity.

"Remember," I said, "modularity means that, as much as possible, you should create methods in your programs that perform one function and one function only. In the long run, this makes your programs easier to read, understand, and modify in the future. Creating custom methods and placing them in Instantiable classes allows our code to be easily used by other programmers. That's something we'll do next week. Today, I have a pretty extensive first exercise for you to complete. There's a lot of code to it, and as you write it, you'll find that all of it is being placed within the **main()** method of the class. As you complete the exercise, try to think of ways that you could use custom methods to make the program modular, because that's exactly what we'll be doing in the next exercise."

I then distributed the exercise for the class to complete.

Exercise 6-1---The Smiley National Bank program with All of the Code in the main() Method

In this exercise, you'll write a program that allows the user of the program to display their bank balance or make deposits and withdrawals from their account.

1. Use Notepad (if you are using Windows) and enter the following code.

```java
import javax.swing.JOptionPane;

class Practice6_1 {
  public static void main (String[] args) {
    double balance = 0;
    double newBalance = 0;
    double adjustment = 0;
    String response;
    String moreBankingBusiness;
    moreBankingBusiness = JOptionPane.showInputDialog
     ("Do you want to do some banking?");
    moreBankingBusiness = moreBankingBusiness.toUpperCase();
    while (moreBankingBusiness.equals ("YES")) {
      response = JOptionPane.showInputDialog
        ("What would you like to do? (1=Deposit, 2=Withdraw, 3=Get Balance)");
      if (response == null) {
        JOptionPane.showMessageDialog
          (null,"You clicked on the Cancel button");
        System.exit (0);
      }
      else
      if (response.equals("")) {
        JOptionPane.showMessageDialog
          (null,"You must make an entry in the InputBox");
        System.exit (0);
      }
      else
      if (Integer.parseInt(response) <1 | Integer.parseInt(response) > 3) {
        JOptionPane.showMessageDialog
          (null, response + " - is not a valid banking function");
        System.exit (0);
      }

      //1 is a Deposit
      if (Integer.parseInt(response) == 1) {
        adjustment = Double.parseDouble
          (JOptionPane.showInputDialog("Enter the Deposit Amount"));
        newBalance = balance + adjustment;
```

```
   JOptionPane.showMessageDialog
     (null, "*** SMILEY NATIONAL BANK ***\n\n" +
   "Old Balance is: " + balance + "\n" +
   "Adjustment is: +" + adjustment + "\n" +
   "New Balance is: " + newBalance + "\n");
}

//2 is a Withdrawal
if (Integer.parseInt(response) == 2) {
   adjustment = Double.parseDouble
     (JOptionPane.showInputDialog("Enter the Withdrawal Amount"));
   newBalance = balance -adjustment;
   JOptionPane.showMessageDialog
     (null, "*** SMILEY NATIONAL BANK ***\n\n" +
   "Old Balance is: " + balance + "\n" +
   "Adjustment is: -" + adjustment + "\n" +
   "New Balance is: " + newBalance + "\n");
}


// 3 is a Balance Inquiry
if (Integer.parseInt(response) == 3) {
   JOptionPane.showMessageDialog
     (null, "*** SMILEY NATIONAL BANK ***\n\n" +
   "Your Current Balance is: " + balance );
}

   balance = newBalance;
   moreBankingBusiness = JOptionPane.showInputDialog
     ("Do you have more banking business?");
   moreBankingBusiness = moreBankingBusiness.toUpperCase();
}                                          //end of while
JOptionPane.showMessageDialog(null, "Thanks for banking with us!");
System.exit (0);
}                                          //end of main
}
}                                          //end of class
```

2. Save your source file as Practice6_1 in the \JFiles\Practice folder (select File | Save As from Notepad's menu bar). Be sure to save your source file with the filename extension .java.

3. Compile your source file into a Bytecode file.

4. Execute your program. The program will ask you if you wish to do some banking. Type **Yes** in the Input Box.

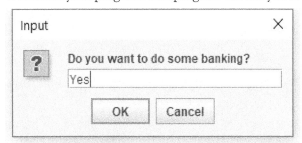

5. Click the OK button. The program will then ask you what you wish to: make a deposit, make a withdrawal, or get a balance. Type **1** in the Input Box to indicate you wish to make a deposit.

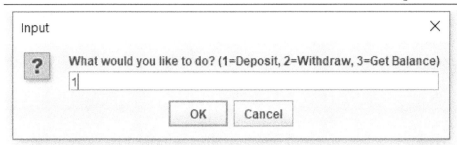

6. Click the OK button. The program will then ask you how much you wish to deposit into your account. Type **50** in the Input Box to indicate your deposit amount.

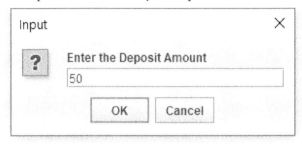

7. Click the OK button. The program will display a confirmation message, indicating your deposit amount and your old and new balance.

8. Click the OK button. The program will then ask if you have more banking business. Type **Yes**.

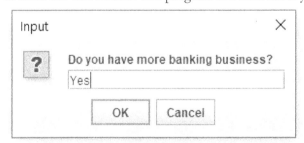

9. Click the OK button. The program will then ask you what you wish to do: make a deposit, make a withdrawal, or get a balance. Type **2** in the Input Box to indicate you wish to make a withdrawal.

10. Click the OK button. The program will then ask you how much you wish to withdraw. Enter **20** in the Input Box to indicate your withdrawal amount.

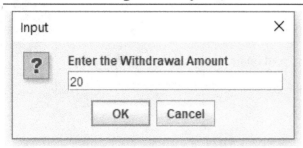

11. Click the OK button. The program will display a confirmation message, indicating your transaction (withdrawals are designated with a negative transaction amount) and your old and new balances.

12. Click the OK button. The program will then ask if you have more banking business. Type **Yes.**

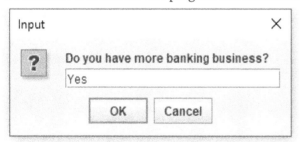

13. Click the OK button. The program will then ask you what you wish to do: make a deposit, make a withdrawal, or get a balance. Type 3 in the Input Box to indicate you wish to display the current balance.

14. Click the OK button. The program will then display the current balance of your account.

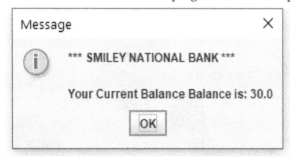

15. Click the OK button. The program will then ask if you have more banking business. Type **No.**

16. Click the OK button. The program will then display a message thanking you for using it. Click the OK button again, and the program will end.

Discussion

Although this program was very tedious to type, everyone was pretty much comfortable with the code in it. There really wasn't anything new in the program, and in about 15 minutes, all of my students had successfully coded the exercise.

"This program," I said, "is one we'll be working with in quite a few exercises and is a good example of the type of program you may be asked to develop in the future. It's also a good example of the type of program that can be enhanced significantly by writing custom methods. As you undoubtedly noticed while you keyed in the program, there's a lot of code, and all of it is in the **main()** method of the class. As I mentioned earlier, that makes reading and understanding the code difficult, and it toughens the task of making modifications to this program if they are ever required."

"I agree with that," Kate said. "I made a mistake or two while coding it, and the task of finding the mistake was certainly compounded by the length of the code and the fact that it's all in one place. Will we be able to break the **main()** method into modules?"

"I think so, Kate," I said. "If we examine the code in the **main()** method, we'll find that we're performing three distinct functions: making a deposit, making a withdrawal, and displaying a balance. Those three functions, according to what you've learned today about modularity, should be in three separate custom methods, and that's what we'll be doing in the next exercise. Before we start with that, do you have any questions about anything in this code?"

"I think just about everything in this program is something we've done before," Steve said, "but I was a little confused about the two variables, oldBalance and balance. Did we need to have these two variables because we chose to display both the old balance and the new balance whenever the user made a transaction?"

"That's exactly the case, Steve," I answered. "It isn't until after we display a confirmation of the user's transaction that we actually calculate a new balance.

For that reason, we need to keep both the old balance and the new balance in memory to display both in the message box. The old balance is no problem—it's stored in the balance variable. To calculate the new balance, we perform one of two lines of code, depending upon the transaction type. If a deposit was made, we perform this calculation:"

newBalance = balance + adjustment;

"And if the user makes a withdrawal we perform this calculation:"

newBalance = balance - adjustment;

"Regardless of the type of transaction, though, just before asking the user if she has more banking business, we must set the value of the balance variable equal to the value of the newBalance variable:"

```
balance = newBalance;
moreBankingBusiness = JOptionPane.showInputDialog
  ("Do you have more banking business?");
```

"Makes sense to me," Steve answered. "Thanks for the explanation."

I waited to see if there were more questions before continuing.

"OK," I said, "let's take a shot at modifying this program to use three custom methods: one for a deposit, one for a withdrawal, and one to display a balance. There will still be some code in the **main()** method—we're not moving it all into custom methods—but the **main()** method will appear more condensed this time around, with calls to the three methods. When all is said and done, the new version of the program should behave identically to the one we just wrote, but you should find the program easier to read and much easier to modify, which we'll be doing next week when we move the code in the three methods you are about to create and place them into Instantiable classes."

No one had any questions about what we were about to do, so I handed out this exercise for my class to complete.

Exercise 6-2--The Smiley National Bank Program with Three Custom Methods

In this exercise, you'll modify the program you wrote in Exercise 6-1, taking much of the code in the **main()** method and placing it in one of three custom methods you'll create.

1. Use Notepad (if you are using Windows) and enter the following code.

```java
import javax.swing.JOptionPane;
class Practice6_2 {
  static double balance = 0;
  static double newBalance = 0;
  static double adjustment = 0;

  public static void main (String[] args) {
    String response;
    String moreBankingBusiness;
    moreBankingBusiness = JOptionPane.showInputDialog
      ("Do you want to do some banking?");
    moreBankingBusiness = moreBankingBusiness.toUpperCase();
    while (moreBankingBusiness.equals ("YES")) {
      response = JOptionPane.showInputDialog
        ("What would you like to do? (1=Deposit, 2=Withdraw, 3=Get Balance)");
      if (response == null) {
        JOptionPane.showMessageDialog
          (null, "You clicked on the Cancel button");
        System.exit (0);
      }
      else
      if (response.equals("")) {
        JOptionPane.showMessageDialog
          (null, "You must make an entry in the InputBox");
        System.exit (0);
      }
      else
      if (Integer.parseInt(response) <1 | Integer.parseInt(response) > 3) {
        JOptionPane.showMessageDialog
          (null, response + " – is not a valid banking function");
        System.exit (0);
      }
      if (Integer.parseInt(response) == 1) {
        makeDeposit();
      }
      if (Integer.parseInt(response) == 2) {
        makeWithdrawal();
      }
```

```
    if (Integer.parseInt(response) == 3) {
      getBalance();
    }
    moreBankingBusiness = JOptionPane.showInputDialog
      ("Do you have more banking business?");
    moreBankingBusiness = moreBankingBusiness.toUpperCase();
  }                              // end of while
  JOptionPane.showMessageDialog(null, "Thanks for banking with us!");
  System.exit (0);
}                              // end of main

private static void makeDeposit() {
  adjustment = Double.parseDouble
  (JOptionPane.showInputDialog("Enter the Deposit Amount"));
  newBalance = balance + adjustment;
  JOptionPane.showMessageDialog
    (null, "*** SMILEY NATIONAL BANK ***\n\n" +
    "Old Balance is: " + balance + "\n" +
    "Adjustment is: +" + adjustment + "\n" +
    "New Balance is: " + newBalance + "\n");
  balance = newBalance;
}

private static void makeWithdrawal() {
  adjustment = Double.parseDouble
  (JOptionPane.showInputDialog("Enter the Withdrawal Amount"));
  newBalance = balance - adjustment;
  JOptionPane.showMessageDialog
    (null, "*** SMILEY NATIONAL BANK ***\n\n" +
    "Old Balance is: " + balance + "\n" +
    "Adjustment is: -" + adjustment + "\n" +
    "New Balance is: " + newBalance + "\n");
  balance = newBalance;
}

private static void getBalance() {
  JOptionPane.showMessageDialog
  (null, "*** SMILEY NATIONAL BANK ***\n\n" +
  "Your Current Balance is: " + balance );
}
}                              // end of class
```

2. Save your source file as Practice6_1 in the \JFiles\Practice folder (select File | Save As from Notepad's menu bar). Be sure to save your source file with the filename extension .java.

3. Compile your source file into a Bytecode file.

4. Execute your program. The program will ask you if you wish to do some banking. Type **Yes** in the Input Box.

5. Click the OK button. The program will then ask you what you wish to: make a deposit, make a withdrawal, or get a balance. Type **1** in the Input Box to indicate you wish to make a deposit.

6. Click the OK button. The program will then ask you how much you wish to deposit into your account. Type **50** in the Input Box to indicate your deposit amount.

7. Click the OK button. The program will display a confirmation message, indicating your deposit amount and your old and new balance.

8. Click the OK button. The program will then ask if you have more banking business. Type **Yes**.

9. Click the OK button. The program will then ask you what you wish to do: make a deposit, make a withdrawal, or get a balance. Type **2** in the Input Box to indicate you wish to make a withdrawal.

10. Click the OK button. The program will then ask you how much you wish to withdraw. Enter **20** in the Input Box to indicate your withdrawal amount.

11. Click the OK button. The program will display a confirmation message, indicating your transaction (withdrawals are designated with a negative transaction amount) and your old and new balances.

12. Click the OK button. The program will then ask if you have more banking business. Type **Yes.**

13. Click the OK button. The program will then ask you what you wish to do: make a deposit, make a withdrawal, or get a balance. Type 3 in the Input Box to indicate you wish to display the current balance.

14. Click the OK button. The program will then display the current balance of your account.

15. Click the OK button. The program will then ask if you have more banking business. Type **No.**

16. Click the OK button. The program will then display a message thanking you for using it. Click the OK button again, and the program will end.

Discussion

During the completion of this exercise, the question as to the most efficient way to modify the code from the previous exercise came up. Many of my students created a new Java class, and copied and pasted the old code into the new class. Then they modified the old code for the new exercise. Copying and pasting is not without its perils, however, and this method of creating the Practice6_2 class was probably no quicker than just creating the code from scratch.

"This program should behave the same as the previous version, is that right?" Rhonda asked.

"That's right, Rhonda," I said, but I could tell from her face that something wasn't right. I paid a quick visit to her PC and discovered that even though she had properly created the three custom methods, she had failed to call them from the **main()** method of the class. Therefore, the program wasn't permitting her to do any banking business.

"The behavior of the program hasn't changed," I said, after getting Rhonda on the right track. "What we've done is take the code to make a deposit, a withdrawal, and display a balance out of the **main()** method and move it into three custom methods called **makeDeposit()**, **makeWithdrawal()**, and **displayBalance()**."

"In addition to those obvious changes," Dave said, "I did notice a few other subtle modifications in the program. Can you go over those?"

"Sure thing, Dave," I said. "I suspect you're talking about the three variables: *balance*, *newBalance*, and *adjustment*, that are declared outside of any of the four methods that we now have in the class."

"Why are they there?" Blaine asked.

"As I mentioned before our break," I said, "variables declared within a method have local scope. That means that a variable that is declared within the **makeDeposit()** method cannot be seen by code outside of it. Also, when the **makeDeposit()** method ends, the variable and its value dies. All three of these variables have values that need to be seen by code in the three custom methods. The only way to give the code in all three of those methods access to the value in a variable is to declare the variable as an Instance or Class variable, which is what happens when the variable is declared outside of a method:"

```
static double balance = 0;
static double newBalance = 0;
static double adjustment = 0;
```

"We'll learn more about Instance and Class variables next week," I said, "but for now, just realize that all three of these variables are accessible by every method in the class, and their values live for as long as our program is running. Aside from these changes and the creation of our three custom methods, I believe the program is now pretty much identical to the previous version."

No one seemed to disagree, so I continued.

Method Overloading

"In a few minutes," I said, 'we'll be modifying the Grade Calculation Project by creating custom methods. Before we do that, however, there's one more concept we need to go over, and that's method overloading. Earlier in today's class I mentioned that method overloading allows you to define multiple methods with the same name, as long as each one of the methods has a different signature."

"Signature, as I recall you saying," Linda said, "is the combination of the method name along with the number and type of parameters in the method header?"

"That's right, Linda," I said. "So long as the number and type of parameters is different in the method header, you can have any number of methods with the same name. You'd be surprised how comfortable you'll get with method overloading as you use it more and more, and we'll be creating some overloaded methods of our own."

"If I'm not mistaken," Dave said, "I think we've used some overloaded methods in this class. Isn't the **println()** method of the System object an overloaded method?"

"Dave's right," I said. "The last time I checked, there were actually ten distinct **println()** methods of the System object—each one differentiated by the uniqueness of the number of type of its parameters."

"So Java knows which of the overloaded methods to execute by examining the arguments that are passed to it?" Kate asked. "That's exactly right, Kate," I said. "Let me show you an example of an overloaded method. I think you'll find it pretty interesting." I thought for a moment, and then displayed the following code on the classroom projector:

```java
public class Example6_9 {
  public static void main(String[] args) {
    displayMessage("Java");
    displayMessage("Java", "a lot");
  }

  public static void displayMessage(String favorite) {
    System.out.println ("I love " + favorite);
  }

  public static void displayMessage(String favorite, String intensity) {
    System.out.println ("I love " + favorite + " " + intensity);
  }
}
```

I then compiled and executed the program, and the following screenshot was displayed on the classroom projector:

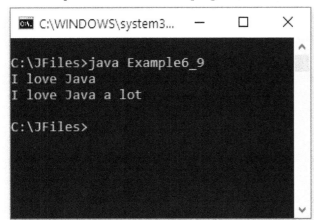

"That is impressive," Ward said. "I think I can see a lot of practical applications for method overloading at my work."

"This is a pretty simple example," I said, "but I think it illustrates the concept over method overloading quite nicely. What we've done here is define two custom methods, each one with the same name called **displayMessage()**, but with different signatures. The first method accepts a single String argument called *favorite:*"

```java
public static void displayMessage(String favorite) {
  System.out.println ("I love " + favorite);
}
```

"And the second method accepts two String arguments called favorite and intensity:"

```java
public static void displayMessage(String favorite, String intensity) {
  System.out.println ("I love " + favorite + " " + intensity);
}
```

"Java determines which one of the two methods to execute," I said, "by matching up the number of type of arguments that are supplied with the method call. This line of code tells Java to execute the **displayMessage()** function that requires just a single String parameter:"

```java
displayMessage("Java");
```

"This line of code tells Java to execute the **displayMessage()** method that requires two String parameters:"

```
displayMessage("Java", "a lot");
```

"Somehow," Rhonda said, "with the term 'overloading,' I thought this would be a lot more difficult than it turned out. This isn't bad at all. In this case, a picture was really worth a thousand words."

"Are the names of the parameters within the method header considered when Java determines which method to execute?" Dave asked. "For instance, suppose you have two identically named methods, requiring the same number and types of parameters, but the names of the parameters are different?"

"That's a good question, Dave," I said. "The names of the parameters in the header are not considered by Java, only the numbers and types of parameters. For instance, if we were to define two methods named **displayMessage()** and specify that each one accept a single String parameter, the fact that we name the String parameter in the first method Elton and the String parameter in the second method Elvis doesn't matter. When we compiled the program, Java would generate a compiler error, informing us that we attempted to define a duplicate method."

"What about the return value of the method?" Linda asked. "Is that considered to be part of the method's signature?"

"Another good question," I said, "and the answer is no. The return value is not considered to be part of the method's signature and is not used by Java when determining if the method can be overloaded."

"I'm not sure I understand what Linda means about the return value being considered part of the method's signature," Chuck said.

"In other words, Chuck," I said, "let's say you have two identically named methods, both requiring the same number and type of arguments, but one has a return value of void and the other a return value of string. Does Java consider them to be unique? The answer is no. When you compile the class in which these two methods appear, Java will tell you that you're trying to define to identical methods. The bottom line is that only the number and type of parameters affects the uniqueness of an overloaded method in Java's eyes. If you declare two methods with same signature you'll generate a compiler error."

I waited for more questions, but everyone seemed satisfied with the concept of method overloading.

"With the remaining time we have left today," I said, as I glanced at the classroom clock, "I'd like to make changes to the Grade Calculation program we wrote last week by adding several custom methods to the program. You'll also have a chance to work with an overloaded method."

I then distributed the final exercise of the day for the class to complete.

Exercise 6-3---The Grades Calculation Project with Custom Methods

In this exercise, you'll modify the Grades Calculation program by taking some of the code currently residing in the **main()** method and creating several custom methods: **whatKindOfStudent()**, **calculateEnglishGrade()**, **calculateMathGrade()**, **calculateScienceGrade()**, and three overloaded versions of **displayGrade()**.

1. Using Notepad (if you are using Windows), locate and open the Grades.java source file you worked on last week. (It should be in the \JFiles\Grades folder)
2. Modify your code so that it looks like this.

```java
import javax.swing.JOptionPane;
class Grades {
    static final double ENGLISH_MIDTERM_PERCENTAGE = .25;
    static final double ENGLISH_FINALEXAM_PERCENTAGE = .25;
    static final double ENGLISH_RESEARCH_PERCENTAGE = .30;
    static final double ENGLISH_PRESENTATION_PERCENTAGE = .20;
    static final double MATH_MIDTERM_PERCENTAGE = .50;
    static final double MATH_FINALEXAM_PERCENTAGE = .50;
    static final double SCIENCE_MIDTERM_PERCENTAGE = .40;
    static final double SCIENCE_FINALEXAM_PERCENTAGE = .40;
    static final double SCIENCE_RESEARCH_PERCENTAGE = .20;
    static int midterm = 0;
    static int finalExamGrade = 0;
    static int research = 0;
    static int presentation = 0;
```

```java
static double finalNumericGrade = 0;
static String finalLetterGrade = "";
public static void main(String[] args) {
  String moreGradesToCalculate;
  String response;
  moreGradesToCalculate = JOptionPane.showInputDialog
    ("Do you want to calculate a grade?");
  moreGradesToCalculate = moreGradesToCalculate.toUpperCase();
  while (moreGradesToCalculate.equals ("YES")) {
    response = whatKindOfStudent();
    switch(Integer.parseInt(response)) {
      case 1:
        calculateEnglishGrade();
        displayGrade (midterm, finalExamGrade, research,
                   presentation, finalNumericGrade, finalLetterGrade);
        break;
      case 2:
        calculateMathGrade();
        displayGrade (midterm, finalExamGrade, finalNumericGrade,
              finalLetterGrade);
        break;
      case 3:
        calculateScienceGrade();
        displayGrade (midterm, finalExamGrade, research,
              finalNumericGrade, finalLetterGrade);
        break;
      default:
        JOptionPane.showMessageDialog(null, response + " - is not a valid student type");
        System.exit (0);
    }                                    // end of switch
    moreGradesToCalculate = JOptionPane.showInputDialog
      ("Do you have another grade to calculate?");
    moreGradesToCalculate = moreGradesToCalculate.toUpperCase();
  }                                    // end of while
  JOptionPane.showMessageDialog
    (null, "Thanks for using the Grades Calculation program!");
  System.exit (0);
}                                    // end of main
public static String whatKindOfStudent() {
  String response;
  response = JOptionPane.showInputDialog
    ("Enter student type (1=English, 2=Math, 3=Science)");
  if (response == null) {
    JOptionPane.showMessageDialog(null, "You clicked on the Cancel button");
    System.exit (0);
  }
  else
  if (response.equals("")) {
    JOptionPane.showMessageDialog(null, "You must make an entry in the InputBox");
    System.exit (0);
  }
  else
  if (Integer.parseInt(response) < 1 | Integer.parseInt(response) > 3) {
    JOptionPane.showMessageDialog(null, response+"-is nota valid student type");
    System.exit (0);
  }
```

```java
 return response;
 }                                          // end of whatKindOfStudent method


public static void calculateEnglishGrade() {
  midterm = Integer.parseInt
    (JOptionPane.showInputDialog("Enter the Midterm Grade"));
  finalExamGrade = Integer.parseInt
    (JOptionPane.showInputDialog("Enter the Final Examination Grade"));
  research = Integer.parseInt
    (JOptionPane.showInputDialog("Enter the Research Grade"));
  presentation = Integer.parseInt
    (JOptionPane.showInputDialog("Enter the Presentation Grade"));
  finalNumericGrade =
    (midterm * ENGLISH_MIDTERM_PERCENTAGE) +
    (finalExamGrade * ENGLISH_FINALEXAM_PERCENTAGE) +
    (research * ENGLISH_RESEARCH_PERCENTAGE) +
    (presentation * ENGLISH_PRESENTATION_PERCENTAGE);
  if (finalNumericGrade >= 93)
    finalLetterGrade = "A";
  else
  if ((finalNumericGrade >= 85) & (finalNumericGrade < 93))
    finalLetterGrade = "B";
  else
  if ((finalNumericGrade >= 78) & (finalNumericGrade < 85))
    finalLetterGrade = "C";
  else
  if ((finalNumericGrade >= 70) & (finalNumericGrade < 78))
    finalLetterGrade = "D";
  else
  if (finalNumericGrade < 70)
    finalLetterGrade = "F";
 }                                          // end of calculateEnglishGrade
public static void calculateMathGrade() {
  midterm = Integer.parseInt
    (JOptionPane.showInputDialog("Enter the Midterm Grade"));
  finalExamGrade = Integer.parseInt
    (JOptionPane.showInputDialog("Enter the Final Examination Grade"));
  finalNumericGrade =
    (midterm * MATH_MIDTERM_PERCENTAGE) +
    (finalExamGrade * MATH_FINALEXAM_PERCENTAGE);
  if (finalNumericGrade >= 90)
    finalLetterGrade = "A";
  else
  if ((finalNumericGrade >= 83) & (finalNumericGrade < 90))
    finalLetterGrade = "B";
  else
  if ((finalNumericGrade >= 76) & (finalNumericGrade < 83))
    finalLetterGrade = "C";
  else
  if ((finalNumericGrade >= 65) & (finalNumericGrade < 76))
    finalLetterGrade = "D";
  else
  if (finalNumericGrade < 65)
    finalLetterGrade = "F";
 }                                          // end of calculateMathGrade method
```

```java
public static void calculateScienceGrade() {
  midterm = Integer.parseInt
    (JOptionPane.showInputDialog("Enter the Midterm Grade"));
  finalExamGrade = Integer.parseInt
    (JOptionPane.showInputDialog("Enter the Final Examination Grade"));
  research = Integer.parseInt
    (JOptionPane.showInputDialog("Enter the Research Grade"));
  finalNumericGrade =
    (midterm * SCIENCE_MIDTERM_PERCENTAGE) +
    (finalExamGrade * SCIENCE_FINALEXAM_PERCENTAGE) +
    (research * SCIENCE_RESEARCH_PERCENTAGE);
  if (finalNumericGrade >= 90)
    finalLetterGrade = "A";
  else
  if ((finalNumericGrade >= 80) & (finalNumericGrade < 90))
    finalLetterGrade = "B";
  else
  if ((finalNumericGrade >= 70) & (finalNumericGrade < 80))
    finalLetterGrade = "C";
  else
  if ((finalNumericGrade >= 60) & (finalNumericGrade < 70))
    finalLetterGrade = "D";
  else
  if (finalNumericGrade < 60)
    finalLetterGrade = "F";
}                            // end of calculateScienceGrade method

public static void displayGrade(int midterm, int finalexamGrade,
          int research, int presentation,
          double finalNumericGrade, String finalLetterGrade) {
  JOptionPane.showMessageDialog(null, "*** ENGLISH STUDENT ***\n\n" +
    "Midterm grade is: " + midterm + "\n" +
    "Final Exam is: " + finalExamGrade + "\n" +
    "Research grade is: " + research + "\n" +
    "Presentation grade is: " + presentation + "\n\n" +
    "Final Numeric Grade is: " + finalNumericGrade + "\n" +
    "Final Letter Grade is: " + finalLetterGrade);
}                            // end of displayGrade method with 6 parameters


public static void displayGrade(int midterm, int finalexamGrade,
          double finalNumericGrade, String finalLetterGrade) {
  JOptionPane.showMessageDialog(null,"*** MATH STUDENT ***\n\n" +
  "Midterm grade is: " + midterm + "\n" +
    "Final Exam is: " + finalExamGrade + "\n\n" +
    "Final Numeric Grade is: " + finalNumericGrade + "\n" +
    "Final Letter Grade is: " + finalLetterGrade);
}                            // end of displayGrade method with 4 parameters

public static void displayGrade(int midterm, int finalexamGrade,
          int research, double finalNumericGrade,
          String finalLetterGrade) {
  JOptionPane.showMessageDialog(null,"*** SCIENCE STUDENT ***\n\n" +
  "Midterm grade is: " + midterm + "\n" +
  "Final Exam is: " + finalExamGrade + "\n" +
  "Research grade is: " + research + "\n\n" +
  "Final Numeric Grade is: " + finalNumericGrade + "\n" +
  "Final Letter Grade is: " + finalLetterGrade);
```

```
}                              // end of displayGrade method with 5 parameters
}                              // end of class
```

3. Save your source file as Grades.java in the \JFiles\Grades folder (select File | Save As from Notepad's menu bar). Be sure to save your source file with the filename extension Java.

4. Compile your source file into a Bytecode file.

5. Execute your program and test it thoroughly. We need to verify that the looping behavior of the program is working correctly. After you start up your program, it should ask you if you have a grade to calculate.

6. Enter **Yes**, and then calculate the grade for an English student. Enter **70** for the midterm, **80** for the final examination, **90** for the research grade, and **100** for the presentation. A final numeric grade of **84.5** should be displayed, with a letter grade of **C**.

7. After the message box is displayed with the calculated grade, the program should ask you if you have more grades to calculate.

8. Enter **Yes**, and then calculate the grade for a math student. Enter **70** for the midterm and **80** for the final examination. A final numeric grade of **75** should be displayed, with a letter grade of **D**.

9. After the message box is displayed with the calculated grade, the program should ask you if you have more grades to calculate.

10. Enter **Yes**, and then calculate the grade for a science student. Enter **70** for the midterm, **80** for the final examination, and **90** for the research grade. A final numeric grade of **78** should be displayed, with a letter grade of **C**. After the message box is displayed with the calculated grade, the program should ask you if you have more grades to calculate.

11. Enter **No**. You should be thanked for using the program, and the program should end.

Discussion

"Wow, that was intense," Rhonda said. "My program works, and amazingly, I think I actually understand what we did here. Essentially, we've taken a bunch of code out of the **main()** method and put it into one of several custom methods."

"Exactly right, Rhonda," I said. "We created several custom methods: **whatKindOfStudent()**, **calculateEnglishStudent()**, **calculateMathStudent()**, **calculateScienceStudent()**, and three overloaded methods called **displayGrade()**. As much as possible, I think the program is now pretty modular, although I'm sure one of you might be able to suggest the creation of some additional methods."

"I think the program is very modular," Kate said. "We have a method to determine the type of student for whom the user wishes to calculate a final grade, three methods for the calculation for each one of the three different student types, plus three overloaded methods for the display of the grade."

"The number of lines of code in the **main()** method has really been reduced," I said. "The first thing we did was move some of the variable declarations out of the **main()** method and convert them to Class and Instance variables so that their values could be accessible to the code in each of the custom methods we created. All that really remains in the **main()** method is a loop that asks the user if she wants to calculate a grade, and based on their response, we execute the **whatKindOfStudent()** method and assign its return value to a response variable:"

```
while (moreGradesToCalculate.equals ("YES")) {
  response = whatKindOfStudent();
```

"What does the return value of the **whatKindOfStudent()** method indicate?" Chuck asked.

"The **whatKindOfStudent()** method prompts the user for a number from 1 to 3 indicating the type of student for which they wish to calculate a grade," I said. "That number is then returned to the calling code, which assigns it to the response variable. Based on the value of the response variable, we then call one of the three custom methods we wrote to calculate the student's grade and execute the overloaded **displayGrade()** method. Java decides which one of the three overloaded methods to execute by the number and type of arguments supplied:"

```
switch(Integer.parseInt(response)) {
  case 1:
    calculateEnglishGrade();
    displayGrade (midterm, finalExamGrade, research,
        presentation, finalNumericGrade, finalLetterGrade);
  break;
```

"Each one of the three calculate methods is fairly well encapsulated," I said.

"Encapsulated?" Kathy asked.

"Encapsulated," I said, "means that everything that is needed to perform the calculations, including prompting the user for the component pieces of the grade, is included in the method. Not all programmers would write these methods like this. Some might very well include a separate method to prompt the user for the grade components, then execute one of the calculate methods, followed by the display methods."

"Why is that?" Ward asked. "Is there something wrong with the way we've done it?"

"There's a science and art to designing methods," I said. "No two people are likely to write their program in the same way, which is one of the things I love about teaching programming. The reason some programmers would choose to write a separate method to prompt the user for input is that eventually we will no longer use the showInputDialog() method of the JOptionPane object to prompt the user for the grade components. Instead, we'll build a window, complete with text boxes, radio buttons, and buttons, and that's how the user will let us know for what kind of student they wish to calculate the grade. Some programmers would argue that we've built too much dependence upon a particular input method into the Calculate methods, and that eventually we'll have to change it. That may be correct: we will have to change it, but in this classroom environment, that will be great experience."

"Something I found pretty interesting," Joe said, "is how you chose to create overloaded methods to display the grades. Why didn't you just display the grades from within the various calculate methods?"

"Calculating a grade and displaying a grade are different functions," I said. "Separating the code for each makes sense, especially if you consider the fact that the manner in which we are displaying the information for Frank Olley is completely arbitrary. He doesn't really care how the display of the information looks."

"In other words," Dave said smiling, "he may want it changed as soon as he sees it. Placing the code to display the grades in methods separate from the calculation code will make modifying the code easier."

"But why not just go with three uniquely named methods?" Ward asked. "Why did you use overloaded methods to display the grades?"

"That's simple, Ward," I said. "I wanted to give you experience working with overloaded methods. That experience will come in handy later on in the course."

It had been an extremely long and interesting, class. No one had any further questions, so I dismissed class for the day.

Summary

In this chapter, you learned about the concept of program modularity and the benefits of creating custom methods in our Java programs. We discussed details of creating our own methods, including the four types of Access Specifers, return types of methods, and how to define methods to accept one or more parameters. You also learned how overloaded methods permit you to define more than one method with the same name, provided the method headers are unique in terms of number and type of arguments supplied. We finished the chapter by modifying the Grades Calculation Project to include several custom methods, including an overloaded method.

Chapter 7---Creating Objects from Instantiable Classes

In Chapter 6, we began to learn how to introduce modularity into the programs we write by creating custom methods in our startup class module. Once defined, these methods were then called from its **main()** method. In this chapter, we take modularity several steps further by creating what Java calls Instantiable classes—that is, classes from which objects can be created by another class, sometimes called a client program. Creating objects from classes is the name of the game in object-oriented programming languages such as Java, and by the end of today's class, you'll see why. The data and the code in your classes will be easier to work with, the number of lines of code in your startup class shrinks, and overall, your programs become easier to follow, maintain, and modify. Plus, the code you place in Instantiable classes is available to hundreds, even thousands of other programmers in your company or even throughout the world. This is truly object-oriented programming.

Creating Objects from Instantiable Classes

"Early on in our course," I said, as I began our seventh class, "I mentioned to you that Java is an object-oriented programming language, in which in we work with standard packages of classes and objects that make the job of writing a program much easier. I also told you that at some point, you would be able to design classes of your own from which objects could be created. However, I warned you that it would be some time before you could do this. Well, today's the day. Up until now, we've used methods of objects created from classes provided to us in the standard Java packages—methods like the **println()** method of the System object and the **showInputDialog()** method of the JOptionPane object. In today's class, you'll learn how to design and create classes from which your other classes will be able to instantiate objects."

"Instantiate?" Rhonda asked.

"Instantiate is a term that means to create an object from a class," I said. "In Java, an Instantiable class is a model for an object, much like an architectural blueprint is a model for a house or a building. Just like from one blueprint, many 'instances' of a house can be built, from one Instantiable class, many instances of an object can be created. I know what you're probably thinking. The classes that we've created so far haven't been used like that. That's because they've been startup classes, which are classes intended to be executed from the command prompt. Instantiable classes are different. They are not intended to be run from the command prompt; in fact, they can't be. Instantiable classes are meant to enable other classes, mainly startup classes, to create objects from them. Today you'll learn how to create those Instantiable classes, and by the end of today's class, you'll have designed and coded several classes which will model real-world objects."

"This sounds exciting!" Ward said. "What kind of real-world objects can be modeled using Instantiable classes?"

"In the real world of programming," I said, "we can use Instantiable classes to model many things, such as employees, students, and inventory, to name a few. In today's class, we'll create an Instantiable class to model a bank transaction, and of course, we'll also be creating a class to model the English, math and science students here at the university."

"This process sounds to me like it may not be all that easy," Rhonda said.

Creating Classes Is an Extension of Modular Programming

"I don't want to make creating Instantiable classes sound too easy," I said, "but I think you'll find that it's just an extension of the modular programming process we learned about and practiced last week when we broke our code up into modules by creating custom methods. Creating Instantiable classes is a matter of determining what real-world objects need to be represented in your program and apportioning variables and methods to each one. In many ways, this is nearly complete with the Grade Calculation Project. I think we all realize by now that the project is modeling a real-world student. In the Grade Calculation Project, that's one object, and there may be more. The bottom line is that if you are comfortable with what we did last week concerning method creation, you'll have no trouble going through the mechanics of creating Instantiable classes. Experience will help you identify the objects you need to model in your program, along with the characteristics and behavior of that object you need to simulate."

"Do Instantiable classes look like startup classes?" Peter asked.

"Startup classes require a **main()** method so that they can be executed from a command prompt, " I said. "Instantiable classes do not contain a **main()** method, and for that reason, Instantiable classes can't be executed directly from a command prompt the way the programs we've written so far can. Instantiable classes are meant to provide their blueprint to other classes so that objects can be created from them. Instantiable classes are designed in such a way that the objects created from them simulate the characteristics and behavior of a real world object, such as an employee or a piece of inventory."

Objects Have Data that Simulate Object Characteristics

"What do you mean by characteristics of an object?" Blaine asked. "Can you give us an example of an object's characteristics"

"Yes I can, Blaine," I said. "For instance, if we create an Instantiable class designed to represent a real-world employee in a corporation, we would want to create a class capable of representing the employee's name, address, social security number, and salary, to name a few characteristics. The characteristics of the Employee object are represented and stored inside the object by the implementation of the Instance and Class variables I briefly mentioned last week."

> NOTE: Remember, a Class is a template or model for the Object that is instantiated from it, just like a house is an object created from an architectural blueprint.

Objects Have Behavior

"That makes sense to me," Linda said, "but what about an object's behavior that you mentioned? What kind of behavior can an object possess?"

"Well," I said, thinking for a moment, "an employee has certain kinds of behaviors, such as working on a particular task, attending meetings, traveling to a customer site, taking a vacation day. These kinds of behavior can be simulated in an object by the implementation of a class method, the kind that we wrote last week."

"I see," Kate said, "but wouldn't the code for that be pretty complex? I'd hate to have to write it."

"You're right, Kate," I said. "I bet that code would be pretty complex to write, but the beauty of Instantiable classes is that if you wanted to use an Employee object in one of your programs, you wouldn't have to write a bit of that code. It's the designer of the Employee class who needs to worry about the details of the code to model that behavior, and once it's written, it can be used over and over again by hundreds, even thousands of other programmers. You see, all of the really difficult code necessary to implement the behavior of the object resides within the class itself. A programmer who wants to use the Employee object, just like we've been using the Console object to execute its **println()** method, only needs to execute the object's method in order to implement the behavior."

"So the programmer who designs the class from which an object is created isn't necessarily the programmer who will later use the object in a program?" Ward asked.

"That's right, Ward," I said. "It's usually senior level programmers and designers who design the classes from which objects in a corporate environment are created. I know Java programmers who spend all of their time designing Instantiable classes just like that and never write any code that actually creates any of those objects."

"So what happens after the Instantiable class is designed?" Steve asked.

"Usually," I answered, "the class is placed in a package, advertised, and made available to other programmers in the company or corporation. And if the Instantiable class you design is really good, it may be used by other programmers all over the world, like the Java System object is."

"I think you mentioned this a minute ago, but I may have missed it," Mary said. "If characteristics of an object are implemented via Class and Instance variables, how is the behavior of an object implemented?"

"Behavior in an object is implemented via methods," I said, "just like the methods we wrote last week."

"I'm anxious to see one of these Instantiable classes," Linda said. "Can you show us one?"

"Sure thing, Linda," I said. "Let's create an Instantiable class called **Banner** designed to display the user's favorite programming language in the Java Console. The class will contain just a single attribute called *favoriteProgram*, implemented via an Instance variable, and it will possess just one kind of behavior, *display*, designed to display that single attribute. This behavior will be implemented via a method.

I then displayed this code on the classroom projector:

```
public class Banner {
String favoriteProgram;
  public void display() {
    System.out.println ("I love " + favoriteProgram);
  }
}
```

> NOTE: Class definitions that begin with the keyword Public must be stored in a file with the same name.

"Where's the **main()** method?" Rhonda asked. "I don't see it anywhere."

"Instantiable classes ARE NOT required to have a **main()** method," I said, "because they are not intended to be executed directly from a command prompt. Instantiable classes are meant to serve as blueprints for objects that are created from another class—you'll see that in a moment. Before we do that, however, let's take a closer look at the code in the Banner Instantiable class. The first line of the class looks just like the other classes we've seen so far. It begins with the Public keyword, called a class specifer, followed by the name of the class:"

```
public class Banner {
```

"The keyword Public in the class definition," I said, "is required so that objects of this class can be instantiated or created from another class. You'll see how that happens in a few moments."

"That next line of code," Valerie said, "looks like a variable declaration. Is that the Instance variable you were telling us about?"

"That's right, Valerie," I said. "An Instance variable is a variable declared within a class, but not within any method of the class. That way, the variable is visible, or scoped, to all of the methods in the class. The string Instance variable *favoriteProgram* is used to implement the one and only attribute of the Banner class:"

```
String favoriteProgram;
```

"Let me make sure I understand why this is an Instance variable," Dave said. "It's the fact that the declaration does not appear within the **display()** method, is that right? Otherwise, it appears to be an ordinary variable declaration to me."

"That's right, Dave," I said. "Instance variables are variables that are declared outside of any method. Instance variables, by convention, appear at the top of the class, just after the class name."

I waited to see if anyone had any more questions before continuing.

"Now, let's take a look at the one and only behavior of the Banner class, display, which is implemented via a method:"

```
public void display() {
    System.out.println ("I love " + favoriteProgram);
}
```

As I think you can see," I said, "this method is very much like the methods you learned to code last week. The **display()** method merely displays the value of the Instance variable favoriteProgram to the Java Console using the **println()** method of the System object. What makes this special is that it isn't code from the Banner class itself that will execute the **display()** method but code from another class that will first create an instance of the Banner object, which will then execute this method."

"When you say an object is created from the Banner class," Dave said, "does that mean that each object gets its own copy of each of the Instance variables and methods to work with?"

"That's right, Dave," I said. "Later on in today's class, you'll see that it's possible to create in a program more than one object from the same class. When that happens, each object has separate copies of each of the Instance variables and methods defined in the class. In this way, there's no danger of one object stepping on the foot of the other."

"Are we going to execute this class?" Rhonda asked. "I can't wait to see how this works."

"Since it has no **main()** method, we can't directly execute this Banner class from the command prompt," I said. "Remember, Instantiable classes are intended to have objects built from their blueprint. These objects are created in other classes. Let me show you."

Creating objects from your classes

"To create an instance of a Banner object from our Banner class," I said, "we must first create a startup class. This startup class will look like the others that we've coded in the course so far. What you'll find strange, I'm sure, is the code necessary to create or instantiate the Banner object. Take a look:"

I then displayed this code on the classroom projector.

```java
public class Example7_1 {
  public static void main(String[] args) {
    Banner x = new Banner();
    x.favoriteProgram = "Java";
     x.display();
  }
}
```

I could see a lot of confusion on the faces of many of my students.

"Let's break this code down line by line," I said. "As you can see, this startup class begins like the others we've seen, with a class definition:"

```java
public class Example7_1          {
```

"The class definition is then followed by the **main()** method, which is required of every class that will be executed from a command prompt:"

```java
public static void main(String[] args) {
```

"What's going on with that next line of code?" Kathy asked. "I don't recall you discussing a Banner data type a few weeks back."

"This line of code looks like a variable declaration, doesn't it?" I said.

```java
Banner x = new Banner();
```

"In fact, it is. However, instead of seeing the familiar Java data types of Int or String, what we see instead is a variable declaration that begins with the class name Banner."

"Can you do that?" Ward asked.

"Yes, we can," I said. "When you declare a variable of type Int, Java allocates space in the computer's memory for an Integer data type. When you declare a variable of type Banner, Java allocates space in the computer's memory for the Banner object's Instance variables and for its method definitions."

"That's right," Dave said excitedly, "you did say that each object gets a copy of the class's Instance variables and methods. So that's how it's done."

"That's right, Dave," I said. "This syntax looks very confusing at first, but that's what's going on: we're telling Java to allocate enough room in the PC's memory for a Banner object."

"What's x?" Lou asked.

"X is just the name of the variable," I said. "Hereafter, the instance of the Banner object we're about to create will be referred to by this name. But let's not forget the rest of the line: we also need to follow the variable name x with an equal sign, followed by the keyword New, followed by the name of the Banner class once again, followed by an empty pair of parentheses."

"What's the significance of the empty set of parentheses?" Linda asked.

"We'll see a little later on," I said, "that the new keyword tells Java to execute something known as the Constructor method of the Banner class. Constructors are just methods which help set up or initialize an object created from its class. In this case, the empty set of parentheses tells Java to execute the specific Constructor method that requires no arguments. As it turns out, we didn't code a Constructor method in the Banner class—so Java automatically executes something known as the default Constructor method, and all that means is that the Banner object is created."

"Will we learn how to create Constructor methods in this course?" Steve asked.

"Yes we will, Steve," I said. "We'll spend quite a bit of time in today's class learning how to create Constructor methods."

I gave everyone a further chance to study the line of code that declares and then creates an instance of a Banner object. It had been my experience that this single line of code is sometimes the most confusing single concept for beginning Java programmers.

"You're right, this syntax is pretty confusing," Kate said. "I'm just so used to seeing a data type specified for a variable declaration. Seeing a class name that we've defined ourselves specified as the type declaration is strange."

"I agree, Kate," I said. "It is strange at first, but believe me, once you get used to it, declaring variables to refer to instances of your own classes will become second nature to you. As I think I've mentioned before, that's the name of the game in Java, and Java programmers are forever defining classes with attributes and behavior and then instantiating objects from these classes in their programs."

Changing an Object's Attributes

"Can you go over how to change an object's attribute?" Mary asked. "It seemed like you used an assignment statement, but I was a little confused by the syntax."

"Good question, Mary," I said. "Once you've declared an instance of your class's object, you can easily set—by that I mean change—one of its attributes just by changing the value of the Instance variable that implements that attribute. Remember, behind the scenes, the attributes or characteristics of an object are really just Instance variables defined in the object's class. Changing the attributes of an object is easy, but we can't just assign a value to the Instance variable. We need to assign a value to the Instance variable associated with this particular object. Because of that, we need to use a special notation called object dot notation."

"Object dot notation?" Rhonda asked. "This is getting more complicated."

"It's not bad at all, Rhonda," I replied. "Object dot notation is just a way of telling Java the name of the object whose Instance variable we wish to update. With object dot notation, we first specify the name of the variable that we used to declare an instance of our object, followed by a 'dot,' or a period, followed by the name of the Instance variable that implements the attribute. After that, we're basically working with an ordinary Java assignment statement, in that we use the equal sign assignment operator, followed by the value we wish to assign to the Instance variable."

```java
x.favoriteProgram = "Java";
```

"So what we've done here is change the value of the Instance variable favoriteProgram inside the Banner class?" Steve asked.

"That's close, Steve," I said. "But more specifically, we've changed the value of the Instance variable favoriteProgram within a particular instance of the Banner object referenced by the variable x. Remember, each object has its own copy of every Instance variable and method in the memory. It's a subtle distinction, I know, but the distinction will become important later on today when we learn that we can create another type of variable within a class called a Class variable. A Class variable is a variable that is shared by every instance of an object instantiated from that class."

"I assume we can retrieve the value of an object's attribute using the same object dot notation?" Ward asked.

"That's right, Ward," I said. "We could display the value of the favoriteProgram attribute using this syntax:"

```java
System.out.println(x.favoriteProgram);
```

"I see," Linda said. "Really, except for the name of the object variable and the dot, this syntax is just like working with a variable."

"That's a good way of thinking about it," I said.

Everyone seemed to understand how to change and view the value of an object's attribute.

Calling an Object's Methods

"Calling the method for an object that we've declared," I said, "should be familiar to you: it's the same way that we execute methods of the standard Java objects, such as System and JOptionPane. Once again, we use object dot notation, specifying the name of our object variable, followed by a dot, followed by the name of the method we wish to execute:"

```java
x.display();
```

"What's the purpose of the empty set of parentheses following the method name?" Mary asked.

"Any arguments required by the method appear within the parentheses," I said. "We defined the **display()** method of the Banner class to require no parameters. The empty set of parentheses are required even when no arguments are required."

"I'm anxious to see a Banner class in action," Rhonda said. "What do we need to do?"

"First, we need to compile the Banner class," I said. "If we compile Example7_1 first, the Java compiler will find a reference to a class called Banner in the program, will look for a compiled Banner Bytecode file, and if it doesn't find it, will generate a compiler error for Example7_1."

"Where exactly does Java look for the compiled Banner Bytecode file?" Dave asked. "In the same folder as the Example7_1 class?"

"That's a good question, Dave," I said. "The Java compiler will look for any Instantiable classes which are referenced in Example7_1 in the same folder in which Example7_1 is located. If the compiler doesn't find the other class there, it looks to see if there's a Package statement coded in the class. I showed you how to include a Package statement in your code last week, I believe. For those of you who may have forgotten, the Package statement is a way of managing classes that are related to one another. When you include the Package statement in your class, you make that class a member of that package. Most importantly, you tell Java to look in that package for any class references that it can't locate. We won't be specifically discussing Package creation on this class. Just remember that in an application with a large number of classes, the Package statement can be used to manage those classes very effectively."

"I don't want to get off on a tangent," Ward said, "but when is it appropriate to create packages?"

"Package creation," I said, "makes sense in an environment where the project you are working on is very large, and contains many classes. Packages are like folders in a directory—they can really help you to manage large projects, and they're something to bear in mind when you get your first professional Java programming job."

I then compiled the Banner class, followed by the Example7_1 class with no problem.

> Note: If Banner.java is in the same folder as Example7_1.java, when you compile Example7_1.java, it will find and compile the Banner.java program into a Bytecode file.

"Remember," I said, "we can't execute the Banner class from the command prompt—it has no **main()** method. We need to execute Example7-1 from the command prompt."

I did just that, and the following screenshot was displayed on the classroom projector:

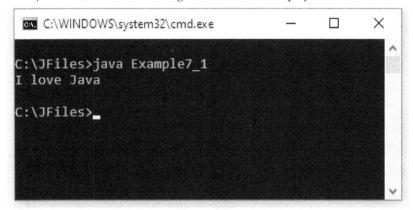

"Does everyone realize what's happened here?" I asked. "The code in Example7_1 created an instance of a Banner object from the Banner class, set the value of its *favoriteProgram* attribute, and executed its **display()** method."

"One class executing code in another," Kate said. "Pretty cool."

"I don't want to be a downer about all of this," Rhonda said, "but couldn't we have just executed all of this code from a single startup class? What has all this extra code really bought us? Quite honestly, I think it's just complicated things."

"That's usually the first reaction that beginners have," I said. "You're right in that we could have placed all of the code we executed in a single class, and as you know, we could place it all within the **main()** method of a single class. But many years of experience has shown that modular programming—and in Java, that means creating objects—

leads to better programs. I think as the day progresses you'll begin to understand that placing code in classes whose objects are then instantiated within other classes actually uncomplicates programs."

Creating multiple objects from your classes

"You told us that it's possible to create more than one instance of the same object in the startup class," Bob said. "How would we do that? For example, suppose I was creating an instance of that Employee object you were describing earlier, and I wanted to instantiate an object for every employee in a particular department?"

"Yes, it is possible, and quite common," I said. "You just need to declare more than one object variable, like this:"

I then displayed the following code on the classroom projector:

```
public class Example7_2 {
  public static void main(String[] args) {
    Banner x = new Banner();
    Banner y = new Banner();
    x.favoriteProgram = "Java";
    x.display();
    y.favoriteProgram = "C#";
    y.display();
  }
}
```

I compiled and executed the program. The following screenshot was displayed on the classroom projector:

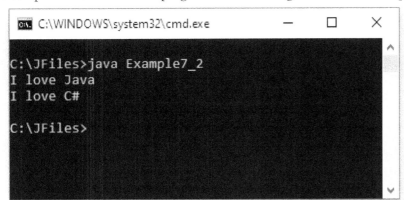

"What we've done here," I said, "is to declare two instances of the Banner object…"

```
Banner x = new Banner();
Banner y = new Banner();
```

"How is it possible to have two object instances of the same class in a program?" Blaine asked.

"It's no problem," I said, "because as I mentioned earlier, each instance of an object is maintained separately in the computer's memory. Keeping the object and its attributes in separate locations of memory keeps one object from being confused with another. When we modify the attribute value of an object, Java knows exactly which object to act upon by the object variable name we use:"

```
x.favoriteProgram = "Java";
x.display();
y.favoriteProgram = "C#";
y.display();
```

"That's pretty amazing," Rhonda said. "Is there a limit to the number of objects you can instantiate?"

"The only limit," I said, "is the available memory in your computer because that's where the objects are maintained. In some large commercial applications, it's not unusual to have thousands of objects in memory at one time."

Class Constructors

"I think working with Instantiable classes like this to create objects is great," Ward said, "and I really can't wait to start working with them back at my office. Is there anything else we need to know about creating Instantiable classes?"

"There are some more features of Instantiable classes that I want to discuss with you that can give your programs tremendous power," I said. "For instance, we can write code that is automatically executed each time an instance of our object is created."

"Kind of like a startup macro in Microsoft Word," Valerie added.

"Constructor methods are very similar," I said. "Code that you want to be executed when an instance of an object is created from a class you place inside a special method called a Constructor method. Constructor methods are named with the same name as the class."

"What kind of code goes into a Constructor method?" Joe asked.

"Any kind of code that in some way initializes our object," I said.

"Initializes?" Rhonda asked.

"That's right, Rhonda," I said. "For instance, if the class is used to gain access to records in a database, the Constructor method is an ideal location to place code that finds and opens the database. Other types of initialization code are to set attributes of the object—Instance variables—to default values, if that's appropriate. For instance, if your class has a *currentDate* Instance variable, you could place code in its Constructor method to interrogate the system date on the user's PC, and set the value of the *currentDate* Instance variable accordingly."

"I see," Kate said. "That makes sense."

"Speaking of Instance variables," I said, "take a look at this code."

I then displayed this code on the classroom projector:

```java
public class Example7_3 {
  public static void main(String[] args) {
    Banner x = new Banner();
    x.display();
  }
}
```

I compiled and executed the program. The following screenshot was displayed on the classroom projector:

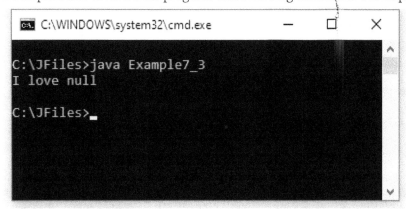

"What happened?" Blaine asked. "What's up with that message? What's null?"

"Null is a value that indicates that a variable has no value," I said. "What happened here is that we created an instance of a Banner object, but prior to assigning a value to the Instance variable favoriteProgram, we immediately executed the Banner object's **display()** method. We displayed in the Java Console the value of the *favoriteProgram* Instance variable: null."

"I hadn't noticed that we hadn't initialized the value of *favoriteProgram*," Dave said. "I thought that in Java you **must** initialize your variables."

"That's only the case with local variables," I said. "Java doesn't require us to initialize Instance variables. As a result, accidents like this can easily happen. The bottom line is that it's a good idea to initialize all of our Instance variables, either at the time we declare them, or as part of the class's Constructor method."

"Can you show us how to code a Constructor method?" Ward asked. "Is it complicated?"

"Creating a Constructor method is very easy, Ward," I said. "The class Constructor method is just an ordinary method with the same name as the class. For instance, the Constructor method for the Banner class would look like this:"

```
public Banner(){
   System.out.println ("Banner's Constructor");
}
```

NOTE: A Constructor is a method of the class, having the same name as the class, which is automatically executed when an object of the class is created.

"That is easy," Linda said, pausing a moment before adding. "I notice you didn't specify a return type for the method. Isn't a return type always required?"

"That's a good point, Linda," I answered. "Return types for methods are required *except* in the case of a Constructor method. In fact, Constructor methods **may not** return a value of any kind, not even the void return type—that's why no return type is permitted here."

"I'm going to have to remember that," Rhonda said. "That's the type of thing I'm likely to forget, but I guess the compiler will warn me."

"Unfortunately, Rhonda," I said, "if you code a Constructor method and specify a return type by accident, Java will still compile your class, but the Constructor method won't automatically execute when an object of the class is created. Essentially, the method you intended to be a Constructor will become just an ordinary method of the class."

NOTE: A Constructor method <u>may not</u> specify a return type of any kind, not even void.

"I bet that can have you scratching your head for hours," Kate said. "Can we see the Constructor method in action?"

"Sure thing, Kate," I said. "Let's modify the Banner class to include a Constructor method. All we'll do is display a message in the Java Console that tells us the Constructor method has been executed."

I then modified the Banner class to look like this, and displayed its code on the classroom projector:

```
public class Banner {
   String favoriteProgram;
   public Banner() {
      System.out.println ("Banner's Constructor");
   }

   public void display() {
      System.out.println ("I love " + favoriteProgram);
   }
}
```

"Does everyone see the Constructor method?" I asked. "It's the method called **Banner():**"

```
public Banner() {
   System.out.println ("Banner's Constructor");
}
```

"Notice that the name of the Constructor method is identical to the class name, and also notice that no return value is specified for the method."

"So when an object of this class is created," Steve asked, "the code in the Constructor method will automatically be executed?"

"That's right, Steve," I said.

I then compiled the modified version of the Banner class.

"Here's some simple code that will illustrate the behavior of the Constructor method," I said. "All we're doing here is creating an instance of the Banner object, nothing else:"

```
public class Example7_4 {
   public static void main(String[] args) {
      Banner x = new Banner();
```

```
  }
}
```

I compiled and executed the program. The following screenshot was displayed on the classroom projector:

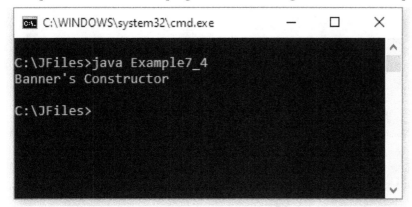

"As you can see," I said, "when we executed this line of code in Example7_4, the Banner object was created, and its Constructor method was automatically executed:"

```
Banner x = new Banner();
```

"That resulted in the message we see in the Java console."

"What did you say earlier about using a Constructor to initialize Instance variables?" Rhonda asked.

"Constructors are also an ideal place to initialize any Instance variables in your class with default or startup values," I said. "Let me show you."

I displayed this modified code on the classroom projector:

```
public class Banner {
  String favoriteProgram;
  public Banner() {
    System.out.println ("Banner's Constructor");
    favoriteProgram = "Java";
  }
  public void display() {
    System.out.println ("I love " + favoriteProgram);
  }
}
```

I then compiled the modified version of the Banner class.

"Do you remember when we executed Example7_3 a few minutes ago?" I asked.

"I do," Kate said, "because we didn't set the *favoriteProgram* attribute prior to executing the Banner object's **display()** method; we displayed the message 'I love null' in the Java Console window."

"Right on the mark, Kate," I said. "Having changed the Banner class to initialize the value of *favoriteProgram* in its Constructor method, let's re-execute Example7_3, and see what happens."

I re-executed Example7_3, and the following screenshot was displayed on the classroom projector:

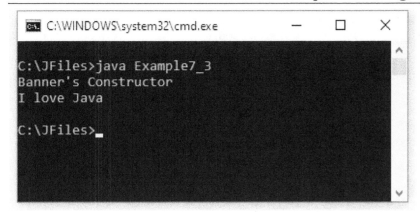

"That's better, isn't it?" I asked. "Now if the user forgets to tell us, via an assignment statement, what their favorite program is, we'll just display the default value of the favoriteProgram Instance variable."

Class Contracts

"I'm a little confused," Rhonda said. "We changed the Banner class to include a Constructor method and recompiled it. Didn't we need to recompile Example7_3 also?"

"No, we didn't," I said. "When we declare and create an instance of the Banner object from within Example7_3, Java looks for the Banner Bytecode file and builds the Banner object based on the current definition of the class. Even though the Banner class was changed and recompiled, there's no need to recompile Example7_3."

"Is that true in all cases?" Dave asked. "For instance, suppose we changed the name of the **display()** method in the Banner class?"

"You're right, Dave," I said. "In the word of object-oriented programming," I said, "there is a presumed 'contract' between the designer of the object and the many users of the object, and there's also a hard and fast rule: ***don't break the contract***. What that means is that a class should not be modified in such a way as to cause programs already using objects from that class to bomb."

"What could cause programs using the class to bomb?" Bob asked.

"A number of things," I said. "One reason would be the case that Dave just cited," I said. "A program that is written to execute a method of a class will bomb if the method name is changed or removed altogether. Also, if the method's signature—the number and type of arguments—is changed, the program will bomb."

"Obviously, adding a Constructor method to the class had no detrimental impact on Example7_3," Ward said.

"That's right, Ward," I said, "and that's a big benefit to modularizing code into objects like this. A minor change like this to the code in another class has no impact on the program using it."

"I understand," Peter said, "that if we change the name of a method, or change the signature of a method in a class, the program using its object will bomb. And I see that adding a new method to the class is not a problem. Suppose we change some of the code in an existing method? Is that a problem?"

"That's the beauty of object-oriented programming," I said. "By hiding the details of exactly how a method does its work and simply having the client program execute it, in theory, a change to the method has no impact on the client program. For instance, when we add objects to the Grade Calculation Project later on today, the code for the calculation of an English student will reside in the **calculate()** method of an EnglishStudent object. If Frank Olley should request a change in the way the final grade for an English student is calculated, all we need to do is change the code in the method, and any client program using the method won't have a problem."

"How often are the signatures of methods changed in the commercial world?" Valerie asked.

"They're usually not," I said. "If something requires a change to the method signature, it's better to create an—"

"Overloaded method," Kate yelled out. "Now I understand."

"You took the words right out of my mouth, Kate," I said. "That's one good reason to create an overloaded method. By maintaining a method with the old signature and creating a method with the new signature, you ensure that older programs will still run, while new programs can take advantage of the functionality in the new method."

"I know in the previous version of the Banner class, we didn't code a Constructor method," Chuck said. "I assume that means the Constructor method is not required. Is that correct?"

"That's right, Chuck," I answered. "Constructor methods are not required in a class, but as you'll learn as you progress in your Java career, coding a Constructor method is frequently a good idea. In fact, it's even possible to code more than one Constructor method for a class."

"You mean an overloaded Constructor?" Dave asked.

Overloaded Constructors

"Exactly right, Dave," I said. "When your class has two or more Constructor methods with the same name but with a different method signature then you have overloaded Constructors."

"I didn't realize you could pass arguments to a Constructor method," Kate said.

"Yes you can, Kate," I said. "I'll show you an example of a Constructor method requiring arguments in a minute."

"Why would you want to create more than one Constructor method?" Rhonda asked.

"Since Constructor methods are automatically executed when an object of your class is created," I said, "coding overloaded Constructor methods gives the user of your program more flexibility in the way they create objects from your class. For example, you might code a Constructor method with no arguments. This Constructor, when executed, would create a no frills object from your class, initializing Instance variables to default values. But you might also want to code a Constructor method that does much more, such as permitting the creator of an object of your class to specify values for one or more Instance variables at the time the object is created."

I could see some confusion in the classroom, so I suggested that we modify the Banner class to provide two Constructor methods.

"The first Constructor method," I said, "will have no arguments required and will initialize the value of the *favoriteProgram* Instance variable to Java. The second Constructor method will require a single argument, and it will initialize the value of the *favoriteProgram* Instance variable to whatever value is passed to the method."

I displayed the modified code for the Banner class on the classroom projector:

```java
public class Banner {
  String favoriteProgram;
  public Banner() {
    System.out.println ("Banner's Constructor");
    favoriteProgram = "Java";
  }

  public Banner(String param1 ) {
    System.out.println ("Banner's overloaded Constructor");
    favoriteProgram = param1;
  }

  public void display() {
    System.out.println ("I love " + favoriteProgram);
  }
}
```

I then compiled the modified version of the Banner class.

"Do you see that we now have two Constructor methods?" I asked. "Both are named Banner. The first requires no arguments, but the second requires a single argument called *param1:*"

```java
public Banner(String param1 ) {
  System.out.println ("Banner's overloaded Constructor");
  favoriteProgram = param1;
}
```

"I was pretty comfortable with creating overloaded methods last week," Steve said, "and I see what you're doing here in the class to create the overloaded Constructor methods. But how do you call an overloaded Constructor using the new keyword?"

"Let me show you," I said, as I displayed this program on the classroom projector:

```java
public class Example7_5 {
  public static void main(String[] args) {
```

```
    Banner x = new Banner();            // Call Constructor
    x.display();
    Banner y = new Banner("Visual Basic");      // Call Overloaded Constructor
    y.display();
  }
}
```

I compiled and executed the program. The following screenshot was displayed on the classroom projector:

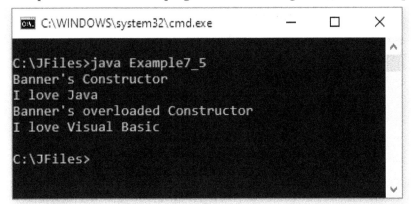

"This syntax," I said, "creates an instance of the Banner object, and because there's nothing within the parentheses, Java automatically executes the Constructor method requiring no arguments:"

Banner x = new Banner();

"When that Constructor method is executed, the value of the *favoriteProgram* Instance variable is set to Java, which is why when we executed this code, 'I love Java' was displayed in the Java console window:"

x.display();

"This syntax creates an instance of the Banner object, and because there's a single string argument contained within the parentheses, Java automatically executes the Constructor method requiring a single string argument:"

Banner y = new Banner("Visual Basic");

"When that Constructor method is executed, the value of the *favoriteProgram* Instance variable is set to the value of the passed argument, which is Visual Basic. That's why, when we executed this code, 'I love Visual Basic' was displayed in the Java Console window:"

y.display();

"This is really neat," Ward said. "I would imagine you could come up with quite a few different Constructor methods."

"That's right, Ward," I said. "Programmers frequently have more than one. The important thing to remember is that Constructor methods are an ideal place for code to initialize the state of your object at the time of its creation."

Class Variables

"I mentioned earlier," I said, "that each object and its attributes or Instance variables are maintained in separate locations in the computer's memory. This protects the data in one object from being confused with the data of another object. There's another type of variable you can declare in a class called a **Class variable** that allows you to share its value with every instance of an object created from that class."

"I was just about to ask if such a thing was possible," Dave said. "I've worked with other languages where I could do that, and it can be a pretty beneficial feature."

"When you say share," Kate asked, "you mean that every object created from the same class can see the value of the variable and update it as well?"

> NOTE: Class Variables 'share' their data with every instance of the object created from the class

That's right, Kate," I said. "As Dave said, this can be a very beneficial feature. Class variables are a great way for objects of the same class to share data."

"Is that important?" Mary asked. "Is that something that's commonly required?"

"It can be," I said. "For instance, have you ever worked with an accounting program? One part of an accounting program typically is used to generate invoices to your customers, and it's customary to assign a unique invoice number to each invoice. If you write the accounting program using Java, each invoice can be an object, and you could create a Class variable called *nextInvoiceNumber*, which would enable each object to access the next available invoice number when the invoice object is created."

"I see what you mean," Valerie said. "That makes sense. By storing the value of the next invoice number in a Class variable, each instance of the object can get at the value, plus increment the value by one after they use it."

"Excellent, Valerie," I said. "The alternative is to force your **main()** method or startup class to keep track of the next invoice number, and that's contrary to the good practice of encapsulation that we are trying to develop."

"Can we add a Class variable to the Banner class to see how it works?" Steve asked.

"Sure, Steve," I said. "Remember in Example7_2, we created two Banner objects, both of which were alive at the same time. Suppose we want each object to be able to know how many Banner objects are currently alive? A Class variable is an ideal way to do that."

"How exactly would we do that?" Peter asked.

"We can declare an Integer Class variable in the Banner class," I said, "and then, within its Constructor method, increment the value of that Class variable by 1. Since the Constructor method is automatically executed each time an object of the class is created, the value of the Class variable should always reflect the number of Banner objects that are currently in existence."

I then modified the Banner class to look like this, and displayed it on the classroom projector:

```java
public class Banner {
  String favoriteProgram;
  static int numberOfBannerObjects;
  public Banner() {
    System.out.println ("Banner's Constructor");
    numberOfBannerObjects++;
    favoriteProgram = "Java";
  }

  public Banner(String param1 ) {
    System.out.println ("Banner's Constructor");
    numberOfBannerObjects++;
    favoriteProgram = param1;
  }
  public void howMany() {
    System.out.println ("The number of Banner objects is " +
      numberOfBannerObjects);
  }
  public void display() {
    System.out.println ("I love " + favoriteProgram);
  }
}
```

I then compiled the new Banner class.

"Let's take a look at the new code in the Banner class," I said. "We added a Class variable called *numberOfBannerObjects*, added a line of code in each of the two Constructor methods, and created a new method called **howMany()**. Let's take a look at the declaration of the Class variable first. A Class variable is like an Instance variable in that it is declared outside any methods in the class. What differentiates a Class variable from an Instance variable is that it is declared with the *Static* keyword:"

```java
static int numberOfBannerObjects;
```

"Static means that *numberOfBannerObjects* is a Class variable and not an Instance variable?" Blaine asked.

"That's right, Blaine," I said. I waited a moment before continuing.

"We also needed to modify both Constructor methods to increment the value of the *numberOfBannerObjects* Class variable by using the Increment (++) operator. Here's the code for the first Constructor method:"

```java
public Banner() {
  System.out.println ("Banner's Constructor");
  numberOfBannerObjects++;
  favoriteProgram = "Java";
}
```

"And here's the code for the second:"

```java
public Banner(String param1 ) {
  System.out.println ("Banner's Constructor");
  numberOfBannerObjects++;
  favoriteProgram = param1;
}
```

"Finally, here's the code for the new method called **howMany()**. This method will be used by client programs to display the number of Banner objects that are currently 'alive':"

```java
public void howMany() {
  System.out.println ("The number of Banner objects is " +
    numberOfBannerObjects);
}
```

"Now let's write the code to see the effect of the Class variable in action." I said. "What we'll do is create two Banner objects and then execute the **howMany()** method of each one." I then displayed this code on the classroom projector:

```java
public class Example7_6 {
  public static void main(String[] args) {
    Banner x = new Banner();
    x.favoriteProgram = "Java";
    x.display();
    x.howMany();

    Banner y = new Banner("C#");
    y.display();
    y.howMany();
  }
}
```

I compiled and executed the program. The following screenshot was displayed on the classroom projector:

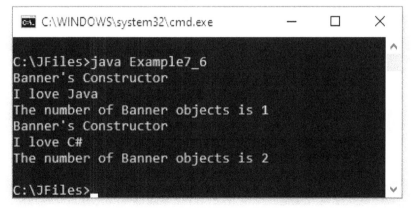

"Do you see what happened here?" I asked. "After we create the first instance of the Banner object using this syntax, the value of the Class variable *numberOfBannerObjects* is incremented by 1 (giving us 1—remember, Integer variables, when **uninitialized**, are automatically set to 0) when the no-arguments Constructor method is executed:"

```java
Banner x = new Banner();
```

"Executing the **howMany()** method displays the value of that Class variable (1) on the Java Console:"

x.howMany();

"This syntax is then used to create a second instance of the Banner object:"

Banner y = new Banner("C#");

"This results in the value of the Class variable **numberOfBannerObjects** being incremented by 1 (giving us 2) when the single argument version of the Constructor method is executed. Executing the **howMany()** method displays the value of the Class variable (2) on the Java Console:"

y.howMany();

"From this example," Dave said, "I can see that both of our Banner objects can see the value of the Class variable **numberOfBannerObjects**, but can both of them modify its value?"

"Good question, Dave," I said, "and the answer is yes. Each object can modify the value of the Class variable as well. Take a look at this."

I then modified the code from Example7_6 to look like this:

```java
public class Example7_7 {
  public static void main(String[] args) {
    Banner x = new Banner();
    x.howMany();
    Banner y = new Banner();
    y.howMany();
    y.numberOfBannerObjects = 0;
    x.howMany();
    y.howMany();
  }
}
```

I compiled and executed the program. The following screenshot was displayed on the classroom projector:

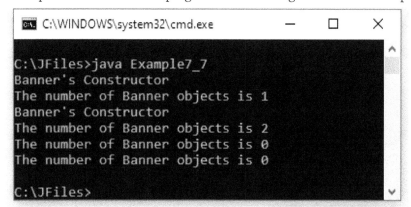

```
C:\JFiles>java Example7_7
Banner's Constructor
The number of Banner objects is 1
Banner's Constructor
The number of Banner objects is 2
The number of Banner objects is 0
The number of Banner objects is 0

C:\JFiles>
```

"I know this code is a bit confusing," I said, "but it does illustrate the ability of an object to modify the value of a Class variable. As we did in Example7-6, here we've also created two Banner objects. The first Banner object is created by this code:"

Banner x = new Banner();

"As a result, the no-arguments version of the Constructor method is executed, incrementing the value of the Class variable **numberOfBannerObjects** from 0 to 1. Executing the **howMany()** method of the first Object results in the message 'The number of Banner objects is 1' being displayed on the Java Console:"

x.howMany();

"The second Banner object is then created by this code:"

Banner y = new Banner();

"Once again, the no-arguments version of the Constructor method is executed, incrementing the value of the Class variable *numberOfBannerObjects* from 1 to 2. Executing the **howMany()** method of the second object results in the message 'The number of Banner objects is 2' being displayed on the Java console:"

```
y.howMany();
```

"With this line of code, we gain direct access to the Class variable *numberOfBannerObjects* and update it to 0 using an assignment statement with the first object."

```
y.numberOfBannerObjects = 0;
```

"Has the value of the Class variable really been updated? Yes, it has, and we can prove that by executing the **howMany()** method of the second Banner object, resulting in the message, 'The number of Banner objects is 0' being displayed on the Java Console:"

```
x.howMany();
```

"By the way, notice how we used the first object to update the Class variable and the second object to display its value. It doesn't matter which object we use to access or modify a class variable, since each object is working with the same Class variable. Not surprisingly, we get the same results in the Java Console when we execute the **howMany()** method of the second Banner object:"

```
y.howMany();
```

"I'm convinced there really is just the single Class variable called *numberOfBannerObjects* shared among all the objects created from the class," Rhonda said. "I think I'm really beginning to understand this. But isn't there a potential problem here?"

"How so, Rhonda?" I asked.

"Well," she continued, "the Class variable *numberOfBannerObjects* was intended to keep track of the number of Banner objects in existence, and one of our objects was able to subvert that by resetting the value to 0. If other objects are dependent upon the value of *numberOfBannerObjects*, being able to change the value the way we did here seems more than a little dangerous to me."

"You raise some good points, Rhonda," I said "Actually, this topic is one that we'll cover next week when we discuss ways to protect the data—variables—in our classes from intentional and unintentional updates."

"Is there any way to validate the types of updates that an object can make to Instance and Class variables?" Dave asked.

"The answer is yes," I said, "and again, next week, we'll spend the entire class examining ways to protect the data within our objects. For example, you'll learn there are techniques we can use to prevent an object from directly updating an Instance or Class variable by forcing all updates to be performed through special validation methods—but more on that next week."

Destroying an Object---the Java Garbage Collector

"I've got to say that I feel pretty confident about working with objects," Ward said. "Now that you've shown us how to create classes of our own and create objects from them, is there anything special we need to know to destroy them? What happens to the objects we create in our program? Do they just go away when the program that creates them ends?"

"There's no need in Java to explicitly destroy an object when you are done working with it," I said. "There are some object-oriented programming languages in which the objects you create must be explicitly destroyed. Failing to do so can result in the object, its data, and the code in its methods remaining in memory, thereby consuming valuable memory resources and creating a phenomenon called 'memory leak.' But Java is not like that. Java performs automatic garbage collection."

"What was that?" Rhonda said with a start. "Did you say garbage collection?"

"That's right, Rhonda," I said. "Behind the scenes in the Java runtime environment is a program called the Java garbage collector. It keeps track of objects, and when it detects that an object is no longer being used by a program because the program has ended the garbage collector takes care of destroying the object for us. In the process, it frees the computer's memory of the resources that were allocated for the object."

"I understand there's nothing we need to do when we're done with an object," Linda said, "but suppose we would like to have code execute when the client program using our object is done with it. Is there a way to do that?"

Class Finalizers

"Java does permit us to code something called a **finalize()** method," I said. "The **finalize()** method is guaranteed to be executed just before the Java garbage collector does its job of destroying an object."

"The **finalize()** method sounds similar to the Constructor method," Kate said, "except that instead of executing when the object is born, it's executed just before it dies. How do we create one?"

> NOTE: The finalize() method has been deprecated in JDK versions 9 and above. I'm including this discussion here because the method does exist, and I discussed it in previous versions of my Java book. The Java community suggests that you NOT include it in your code.

"There are some pretty strict rules for creating the **finalize()** method," I said. "In all, there are four of them. It must be named <u>finalize</u>, it must be declared with the Protected keyword, it returns a void data type, and it may accept no arguments. Its header should look like this:

```
protected void finalize()
```

"What kind of code would we place in the **finalize()** method?" Bob asked.

"Any kind of code that needs to be executed when the object dies," I said. "For instance, you might want to store the object's data in a database or file of some kind when the client program is done with it. Placing code in the object's **finalize()** method is one way to ensure that the data is saved prior to the object dying, when the values of its Instance variables would be lost. Let's modify the Banner class we've been using this morning to see the **finalize()** method in action."

I then displayed the modified code for the Banner class on the classroom projector:

```java
public class Banner {
  String favoriteProgram;
  static int numberOfBannerObjects;
  public Banner() {
    System.out.println ("Banner's Constructor");
    numberOfBannerObjects++;
    favoriteProgram = "Java";
  }

  public Banner(String param1 ) {
    System.out.println ("Banner's overloaded Constructor");
    numberOfBannerObjects++;
    favoriteProgram = param1;
  }

  protected void finalize() {
    System.out.println ("Banner's finalize");
  }

  public void howMany() {
    System.out.println ("The number of Banner objects is " +
      numberOfBannerObjects);
  }

  public void display() {
    System.out.println ("I love " + favoriteProgram);
  }
}
```

"Here's the code for the **finalize()** method," I said. "Nothing fancy here—we're just writing a message to the Java Console to let us know that the object is about to be destroyed by the Java Garbage Collector:"

```java
protected void finalize() {
  System.out.println ("Banner's finalize");
}
```

I compiled the Banner class, but there was a warning message from the compiler.

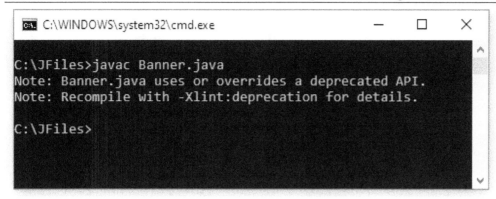

"What happened?" Kate asked. "What is a deprecated API?"

"The Java compiler," I answered, "is warning us.that the **finalize()** method we are calling in the Banner Class has been deprecated. That means that the Java community no longer considers this a method that we should be using and has deprecated it. A deprecated method is essentially one that has been retired."

"It appears that the Banner program has compiled successfully," Dave pointed out.

"That's right Dave," I said, "the compiler is merely giving us a warning that something in our Banner source code has been deprecated. However, as you point out, the class has compiled successfully and we can use it in our program."

> NOTE: I'm including the finalize() method here in our discussion because students in prior sessions of this course have been introduced to it. However, having said that, I recommend that you not use it yourself."

"How do we know exactly what in our program has been deprecated?" Mary asked.

"As the warning suggests Mary," I answered, "if we recompile our source code with the –Xlint argument, we'll get a little more detail about the warning."

I then recompiled the Banner class with the –Xlint argument.

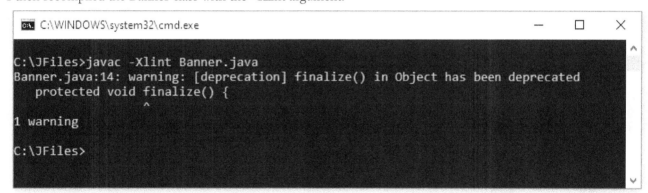

"That's better," I said, "the compiler is telling us that the **finalize()** method has been deprecated. If you Google finalize+deprecated you'll be presented with a bunch of reasons the Java community has determined it's not a great idea to rely on it in your programs. However, as we've seen, the source code will compile into a class file."

I paused to see if I had lost anyone.

"Now let's write some code to see the **finalize()** method in action," I said. "I need to warn you that I'm going to force the execution of the garbage collector by executing the **gc()** method of the System object. As I mentioned, the Java garbage collector runs on its own in the Java runtime environment—the problem with that is we might have to wait several minutes before it detects that our Banner object is no longer being used and destroys it. (a major reason that the **finalize()** method has been deprecated by the way.) For that reason, we'll assign a null value to the Banner object and then force the garbage collector to destroy our object—this will give us a chance to see the **finalize()** method execute."

I then displayed this code on the classroom projector:

```
public class Example7_8 {
  public static void main(String[] args) {
```

```
    Banner x = new Banner();
    x.favoriteProgram = "Java";
    Banner y = new Banner("C#");
    x=null;          //Tell garbage collector we're done with object
    y=null;          //Tell garbage collector we're done with object
    System.gc();     //Force execution of the Garbage Collector
  }
}
```

I compiled and executed it. The following screenshot was displayed on the classroom projector:

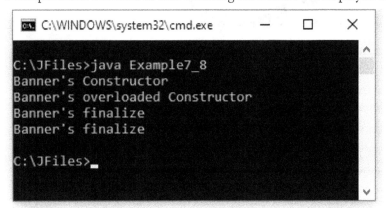

"Does everyone see what happened here?" I asked. "We created two Banner objects, triggering their Constructor methods. Then when the Java garbage collector was about to destroy them, the **finalize()** method of the object was triggered."

"We wouldn't ordinarily have to do anything to make the garbage collector run, is that right?" Kathy asked.

"That's right, Kathy," I said. "Only for purposes of demonstration did we have to set our objects to null:"

```
x=null;                    //Tell garbage collector we're done with object
y=null;                    //Tell garbage collector we're done with object
```

"And then we had to execute the gc() method of the System object:"

```
System.gc();               //Force execution of the Garbage Collector
```

"This is all great stuff," Rhonda said, "but I'd be lying if I didn't say that I would feel a lot more confident about creating my own classes and objects if I had a chance to work with them a little bit. Will we have time to do that today?"

"Absolutely," I said. "I have a series of exercises for you to complete that will give you plenty of practice in creating classes and objects. We'll start by taking the Smiley National Bank program we created last week and modifying it to use objects. Then, toward the end of today's class, you'll modify the Grade Calculation Project to use objects also."

We had been working a long time without a break, and so I asked everyone to take a 15-minute break. When my students returned, I distributed this exercise for them to complete.

Exercise 7-1 Create the BankTransaction Instantiable Class for the Smiley National Bank

In this exercise, you'll take the code you wrote last week in Practice6_2, and include it in a BankTransaction class. This class will then be used by a client program you'll write in Exercise 7-2 to instantiate BankTransaction objects which will handle the details of making Deposits, Withdrawals, and displaying Bank Balances.

1. Use Notepad (if you are using Windows) and enter the following code.

```java
import javax.swing.JOptionPane;

public class BankTransaction {
  double adjustment;
  double newBalance;
  static double balance;                           // Class Variable
  public BankTransaction() {
```

```
    System.out.println ("BankTransaction's Constructor");
}
public void makeDeposit() {
    adjustment = Double.parseDouble(JOptionPane.showInputDialog
      ("Enter the Deposit Amount"));
    newBalance = balance + adjustment;
    JOptionPane.showMessageDialog
      (null, "*** SMILEY NATIONAL BANK ***\n\n" +
      "Old Balance is: " + balance + "\n" +
      "Adjustment is: +" + adjustment + "\n" +
      "New Balance is: " + newBalance + "\n");
    balance = newBalance;
}                                          // end of makeDeposit method
public void makeWithdrawal() {
    adjustment = Double.parseDouble(JOptionPane.showInputDialog
      ("Enter the Withdrawal Amount"));
    newBalance = balance - adjustment;
    JOptionPane.showMessageDialog
      (null, "*** SMILEY NATIONAL BANK ***\n\n" +
      "Old Balance is: " + balance + "\n" +
      "Adjustment is: -" + adjustment + "\n" +
      "New Balance is: " + newBalance + "\n");
    balance = newBalance;
}                                          // end of makeWithDrawal method
public void getBalance() {
    JOptionPane.showMessageDialog
      (null, "*** SMILEY NATIONAL BANK ***\n\n" +
      "Your Current Balance is: " + balance );
}                                          // end of getBalance method
}                                          // end of Bank Transaction class
```

2. Save your source file as '**BankTransaction.java**' in the \JFiles\Practice folder (select File-Save As from Notepad's Menu Bar). Be sure to save your source file with the file name extension 'java'.

3. Compile your source file into a Bytecode file

4. Because this is not a startup class, we cannot execute it directly from a command prompt,. In order to test it, we'll need to write code in a startup class to instantiate objects from it. We'll do that in Exercise 7-2.

Discussion

Creating the BankTransaction Instantiable class took us about 15 minutes to complete. Much to my surprise, most of the students seemed comfortable completing the exercise---I think they were beginning to enjoy working with objects.

"Somehow I thought this would be more confusing," Rhonda said, "but I think I've surprised myself by more or less understanding what's going on here. Not only that, but I'm beginning to get the sense that the changes we've made to the Smiley National Bank application are doing exactly what you said they would do. They'll make the program easier to read, follow, and modify in the future. If I'm correct, what we've done in this exercise is take a bunch of code out of Practice6_2 and include it in an Instantiable object called BankTransaction. Is that right?"

"That's right, Rhonda," I said. "We've taken some, but not all, of the code we had in written in Practice6_2 and included it in a BankTransaction class, from which we will create objects in a client program. The BankTransaction class contains three variables. Two of the variables, *adjustment* and *newBalance*, are Instance variables, which means that each object created from the class has a separate copy of them. One variable, however, *balance*, was designated with the **Static** keyword, and that means it's a Class variable."

"I got it! A Class variable can be seen by every object of that class," Ward said, "plus, it exists for as long as any object of that class is alive."

"That's excellent, Ward," I said.

"Why is the *balance* declared as a Class variable?" Peter asked.

"We have elected to have the BankTransaction object take on the responsibility of tracking the value of the account balance," I said. "The alternative would have to be declare and track the balance from within the startup class, but that would have been less encapsulated. If another object needs to access the current balance, we can add a method to the BankTransaction class to retrieve that value. We'll discuss that kind of method next week. Ultimately, designating *balance* as a Class variable will enable our client program to keep a running total of the bank account balance as it is updated by various objects."

"I notice," Mary said, " that our three variables, *balance*, *newBalance*, and *adjustment*, aren't defined as Public like the variables were in the examples you worked up earlier. What's the difference here?"

"How many methods are there in the BankTransaction class?" Chuck asked.

"The BankTransaction class has three methods," I said. "**makeDeposit()**, **makeWithdrawal()**, and **getBalance()**. The code in each of these methods hasn't changed from that found in the methods in Practice6_2. All we've done is **move** the methods from a Startup class to an Instantiable class called BankTransaction. Plus, in order to illustrate the lifetime of our BankTransaction object, we've written code for a Constructor and Destructor method."

"You're right," Valerie said, "I was a little amazed at that myself. It seems that the work we did last week creating custom methods for this application enabled us to create the BankTransaction class pretty easily."

I waited a moment to see if there were any questions. No one had any, so I distributed this exercise to create the client program in which we would instantiate objects from the BankTransaction class we just created.

Exercise 7-2---The Smiley National Bank Client Program Using BankTransaction objects

In this exercise, you'll create a client program to instantiate objects from the BankTransaction class you created in Exercise 7-1.

1. Use Notepad (if you are using Windows) and enter the following code.

```java
import javax.swing.JOptionPane;
class Practice7_1 {
  public static void main (String[] args) {
    String response;
    String moreBankingBusiness;
    moreBankingBusiness = JOptionPane.showInputDialog
      ("Do you want to do some banking?");
    moreBankingBusiness = moreBankingBusiness.toUpperCase();
    while (moreBankingBusiness.equals ("YES")) {
      response = JOptionPane.showInputDialog
        ("What would you like to do? (1=Deposit, 2=Withdraw, 3=Get Balance)");
      if (response == null) {
        JOptionPane.showMessageDialog
          (null, "You clicked on the Cancel button");
        System.exit (0);
      }
      else
      if (response.equals("")) {
        JOptionPane.showMessageDialog
          (null, "You must make an entry in the InputBox");
        System.exit (0);
      }
      else
      if (Integer.parseInt(response) < 1 | Integer.parseInt(response) > 3) {
        JOptionPane.showMessageDialog
          (null, response + " - is not a valid banking function");
        System.exit (0);
      }
      if (Integer.parseInt(response) == 1) {
        BankTransaction transaction = new BankTransaction();
        transaction.makeDeposit();
```

```
      }
      if (Integer.parseInt(response) == 2) {
        BankTransaction transaction = new BankTransaction();
        transaction.makeWithdrawal();
      }
      if (Integer.parseInt(response) == 3) {
        BankTransaction transaction = new BankTransaction();
        transaction.getBalance();
      }
      moreBankingBusiness = JOptionPane.showInputDialog
        ("Do you have more banking business?");
      moreBankingBusiness = moreBankingBusiness.toUpperCase();
    }                                              // end of while
    JOptionPane.showMessageDialog(null, "Thanks for banking with us!");
    System.exit (0);
  }                                                // end of main
}                                                  // end of class
```

2. Save your source file as Practice7_1 in the \JFiles\Practice folder (select File | Save As from Notepad's menu bar). Be sure to save your source file with the file name extension java.

3. Compile your source file into a Bytecode file.

4. Execute your program. The program will ask you if you wish to do some banking. Type **Yes** in the Input Box.

5. Click the OK button. The program will then ask you what you wish to do: make a deposit, make a withdrawal, or get a balance. Type **1** in the input box to indicate you wish to make a deposit.

6. Click the OK button. The program will then ask you how much you wish to deposit into your account. Enter **50** into the input box to indicate your deposit amount.

7. Click the OK button. The program will display a confirmation message, indicating your deposit amount and your old and new balance.

8. Click the OK button. The program will then ask if you have more banking business. Enter **Yes**.

9. Click the OK button. The program will then ask you what you wish to do: make a deposit, make a withdrawal, or get a balance. Type **2** in the input box to indicate you wish to make a withdrawal.

10. Click the OK button. The program will then ask you how much you wish to withdraw. Enter **20** in the input box to indicate your withdrawal amount.

11. Click the OK button. The program will display a confirmation message, indicating your transaction (withdrawals are designated with a negative transaction amount) and your old and new balances.

12. Click the OK button. The program will then ask if you have more banking business. Type **Yes**.

13. Click the OK button. The program will then ask you what you wish to do: make a deposit, make a withdrawal, or get a balance. Type **3** in the input box to indicate you wish to display the current balance.

14. Click the OK button. The program will then display the current balance of your account.

15. Click the OK button. The program will then ask if you have more banking business. Type **No**.

16. Click the OK button. The program will then display a message thanking you for using it. Click the OK button again, and the program will end.

17. In the Java Console window, observe messages indicating that three BankTransaction objects have been created.

Discussion

"This program behaves in an identical manner to the code in Practice6_2," I said. "The difference is in the way the code is implemented, with this version using a client program to create instances of the BankTransaction object we created in Exercise 7-1. In this version of the program, it's the BankTransaction object that does the majority of the work. This client program creates objects, and based on the type of banking business the user wishes to do, executes one of the three methods of the BankTransaction class:"

```
if (Integer.parseInt(response) == 1) {
  BankTransaction transaction = new BankTransaction();
  transaction.makeDeposit();
}
if (Integer.parseInt(response) == 2) {
  BankTransaction transaction = new BankTransaction();
  transaction.makeWithdrawal();
```

```
}
if (Integer.parseInt(response) == 3) {
    BankTransaction transaction = new BankTransaction();
    transaction.getBalance();
}
```

"We've really taken the notion of modular programming to its extreme by creating classes and objects, haven't we?" Dave commented.

"That's right, Dave," I said. "By encapsulating the code for making deposits and withdrawals and displaying balances within the BankTransaction object, all the client program using our object needs to know is how to instantiate the object and what methods to execute. It's pretty easy, isn't it?"

"Will we be modifying the Grades Calculation Project to use objects today?" Joe asked.

"That's our next step, Joe," I said. "Right now, the Grades Calculation Project contains a single Startup class called Grades. Grades contains eight methods: **main()**, **whatKindOfStudent()**, **calculateEnglishGrade()**, **calculateMathGrade()**, **calculateScienceGrade()**, and three overloaded methods called **displayGrade()** to handle each of the three different types of student grade calculations. Any suggestions as to how we can turn this code into an Instantiable class?"

"I guess we could create a single class called Student," Mary said, "containing the same eight methods that we created last week. That's essentially what we just did with the banking program."

"That's a possibility," I agreed.

"From what I've been reading about object-oriented programming," Dave said, "I think we need at least three classes, one for each of the three different types of students."

"Wow Dave, you must have a lot of time on your hands," Rhonda said smiling, turning to Dave, but addressing her question to me. "Is that right?"

"Dave's definitely on the right track," I said. "Object design will start to go more smoothly for you when we discuss a concept called Inheritance in two weeks, but right now, it makes the most sense to create a separate class for each type of student."

Getting back to Mary's suggestion, I said. "Mary, I'd have no objection if you created a single class called Student. You wouldn't really be wrong, but I think you'll see that creating three student classes is the better approach of the two."

"Sounds great," Rhonda said. "I'm ready to start!"

"Before we begin," I said, "I'd also like to suggest that we create one other class called DisplayGrade. We currently have three overloaded methods called DisplayGrade, and I think that tells us that displaying grades is a distinct function in this program. Creating an object to handle the display of the grades will make things even easier on us."

"If the EnglishStudent, MathStudent, and ScienceStudent objects do the work of prompting the user for information and calculating a grade," Dave said, "and the DisplayGrade object takes care of displaying the student's grade, I think we have ourselves a very modular program."

"Yes, we do," I agreed.

"Is there more than one way to design the classes in this project?" Blaine asked. "I hadn't thought of a DisplayGrade class at all."

"That's a good point, Blaine," I said. "I want to emphasize that while there are some agreed upon rules for the construction of objects, believe me, if we asked five programmers to review the requirements for this project and asked them to design classes based on them, I bet we would come up with five different object models. As I frequently say, in the world of programming, there are many ways to paint a picture, and there's rarely a single correct solution to a problem."

"Can we get going on this?" Rhonda repeated impatiently. "This sounds like great fun to me, and I'm anxious to get started."

I then distributed this exercise for the class to complete.

Exercise 7-3---Create the EnglishStudent Instantiable Class

In this exercise, you'll create the EnglishStudent class for the Grades Calculation project. This class will allow a client program to create an object that will prompt the user for information necessary to calculate the final grade for an English student.

1. Use Notepad (if you are using Windows) and enter the following code.

```java
import javax.swing.JOptionPane;

class EnglishStudent {
  final double ENGLISH_MIDTERM_PERCENTAGE = .25;
  final double ENGLISH_FINALEXAM_PERCENTAGE = .25;
  final double ENGLISH_RESEARCH_PERCENTAGE = .30;
  final double ENGLISH_PRESENTATION_PERCENTAGE = .20;
  int midterm = 0;
  int finalExamGrade = 0;
  int research = 0;
  int presentation = 0;
  double finalNumericGrade = 0;
  String finalLetterGrade = "";

  public EnglishStudent() {
    System.out.println ("EnglishStudent's Constructor");
  }

  public void calculate() {
    midterm = Integer.parseInt(JOptionPane.showInputDialog
      ("Enter the Midterm Grade"));
    finalExamGrade = Integer.parseInt(JOptionPane.showInputDialog
      ("Enter the Final Examination Grade"));
    research = Integer.parseInt(JOptionPane.showInputDialog
      ("Enter the Research Grade"));
    presentation = Integer.parseInt(JOptionPane.showInputDialog
      ("Enter the Presentation Grade"));
    finalNumericGrade =
      (midterm * ENGLISH_MIDTERM_PERCENTAGE) +
      (finalExamGrade * ENGLISH_FINALEXAM_PERCENTAGE) +
      (research * ENGLISH_RESEARCH_PERCENTAGE) +
      (presentation * ENGLISH_PRESENTATION_PERCENTAGE);
    if (finalNumericGrade >= 93)
      finalLetterGrade = "A";
    else
    if ((finalNumericGrade >= 85) & (finalNumericGrade < 93))
      finalLetterGrade = "B";
    else
    if ((finalNumericGrade >= 78) & (finalNumericGrade < 85))
      finalLetterGrade = "C";
    else
    if ((finalNumericGrade >= 70) & (finalNumericGrade < 78))
      finalLetterGrade = "D";
    else
    if (finalNumericGrade < 70)
      finalLetterGrade = "F";
  }
}
```

2. Save your source file as '**EnglishStudent.java**' in the \JFiles\Grades folder (select File-Save As from Notepad's Menu Bar). Be sure to save your source file with the file name extension 'java'.

3. Compile your source file into a Bytecode file. Remember, an Instantiable class cannot be run directly from the command prompt. You'll be creating an EnglishStudent object from this class via the startup Grades class, which you'll modify in Exercise 7-7.

Discussion

No one had any trouble creating the EnglishStudent class, although I did notice a student or two try to execute the class from the command prompt, something you can't do because the EnglishStudent class is an Instantiable class.

"I noticed that you changed the name of the method **calculateEnglishGrade()** to **calculate()**," Dave said. "Is there a reason for that?"

"There's an object-oriented programming term called '**polymorphism**.'" I said, "which means it's OK, even preferable, to have identically named methods in different classes, provided the methods perform the same function. Because each one of our student classes has a method to perform a calculation, I thought it made sense to give each one of them the same name. Therefore, we'll have a **calculate()** method in each one of the three student classes."

"I noticed that we have a Constructor method in the class," Linda said. "Is that really necessary?"

"You're right, Linda," I said. "We coded a Constructor method, although as you can see it doesn't do very much:"

```
public EnglishStudent() {
    System.out.println ("EnglishStudent's Constructor");
}
```

"Whenever I'm developing a new application, I like to code Constructor methods that write a message out to the Java Console. That way, when I run the program, I can see if and when my objects are being created. This can sometimes help you understand how your program is behaving. At any rate, it can't hurt, provided we remember to remove the code from the Constructor methods prior to delivering the final version of the program to Frank Olley."

There were no other questions, so we moved onto creating the MathStudent class.

Exercise 7-4 Create the MathStudent Instantiable Class

In this exercise, you'll create the MathStudent class for the Grades Calculation project. This class will allow a client program to create an object which will prompt the user for information necessary to calculate the final grade for a Math student.

1. Use Notepad (if you are using Windows) and enter the following code.

```
import javax.swing.JOptionPane;
class MathStudent {
    final double MATH_MIDTERM_PERCENTAGE = .50;
    final double MATH_FINALEXAM_PERCENTAGE = .50;
    int midterm = 0;
    int finalExamGrade = 0;
    double finalNumericGrade = 0;
    String finalLetterGrade = "";

    public MathStudent() {
        System.out.println ("MathStudent's Constructor");
    }
    public void calculate() {
        midterm = Integer.parseInt(JOptionPane.showInputDialog
            ("Enter the Midterm Grade"));
        finalExamGrade = Integer.parseInt(JOptionPane.showInputDialog
            ("Enter the Final Examination Grade"));
        finalNumericGrade =
            (midterm * MATH_MIDTERM_PERCENTAGE) +
            (finalExamGrade * MATH_FINALEXAM_PERCENTAGE);
        if (finalNumericGrade >= 90)
            finalLetterGrade = "A";
        else
        if ((finalNumericGrade >= 83) & (finalNumericGrade < 90))
            finalLetterGrade = "B";
        else
        if ((finalNumericGrade >= 76) & (finalNumericGrade < 83))
```

```
      finalLetterGrade = "C";
    else
    if ((finalNumericGrade >= 65) & (finalNumericGrade < 76))
      finalLetterGrade = "D";
    else
    if (finalNumericGrade < 65)
      finalLetterGrade = "F";
  }
}
```

2. Save your source file as '**MathStudent.java**' in the \JFiles\Grades folder (select File-Save As from Notepad's Menu Bar). Be sure to save your source file with the file name extension java'.

3. Compile your source file into a Bytecode file.

4. You won't be able to test your MathStudent class for a while. Remember, an Instantiable class cannot be run directly from the command prompt. You'll be creating a MathStudent object from this class via the startup Grades class, which you'll modify in Exercise 7-7.

Discussion

Again, there were no major problems in completing the exercise, and to my surprise, absolutely no questions. We then moved onto the next exercise—the creation of the ScienceStudent class.

Exercise 7-5 Create the ScienceStudent Instantiable Class

In this exercise, you'll create the ScienceStudent class for the Grades Calculation project. This class will allow a client program to create an object that will prompt the user for information necessary to calculate the final grade for a Science student.

1. Use Notepad (if you are using Windows) and enter the following code.

```
import javax.swing.JOptionPane;

class ScienceStudent {
  final double SCIENCE_MIDTERM_PERCENTAGE = .40;
  final double SCIENCE_FINALEXAM_PERCENTAGE = .40;
  final double SCIENCE_RESEARCH_PERCENTAGE = .20;
  int midterm = 0;
  int finalExamGrade = 0;
  int research = 0;
  double finalNumericGrade = 0;
  String finalLetterGrade = "";

  public ScienceStudent() {
    System.out.println ("ScienceStudent's Constructor");
  }

  public void calculate() {
    midterm = Integer.parseInt(JOptionPane.showInputDialog
      ("Enter the Midterm Grade"));
    finalExamGrade = Integer.parseInt(JOptionPane.showInputDialog
      ("Enter the Final Examination Grade"));
    research = Integer.parseInt(JOptionPane.showInputDialog
      ("Enter the Research Grade"));
    finalNumericGrade =
      (midterm * SCIENCE_MIDTERM_PERCENTAGE) +
      (finalExamGrade * SCIENCE_FINALEXAM_PERCENTAGE) +
      (research * SCIENCE_RESEARCH_PERCENTAGE);
    if (finalNumericGrade >= 90)
      finalLetterGrade = "A";
    else
    if ((finalNumericGrade >= 80) & (finalNumericGrade < 90))
      finalLetterGrade = "B";
    else
```

```
    if ((finalNumericGrade >= 70) & (finalNumericGrade < 80))
      finalLetterGrade = "C";
    else
    if ((finalNumericGrade >= 60) & (finalNumericGrade < 70))
      finalLetterGrade = "D";
    else
    if (finalNumericGrade < 60)
      finalLetterGrade = "F";
  }
}
```

2. Save your source file as '**ScienceStudent.java**' in the \JFiles\Grades folder (select File-Save As from Notepad's Menu Bar). Be sure to save your source file with the file name extension 'java'.

3. Compile your source file into a Bytecode file.

4. You won't be able to test your MathStudent class for a while. Remember, an Instantiable class cannot be run directly from the command prompt. You'll be creating a MathStudent object from this class via the startup Grades class, which you'll modify in Exercise 7-7.

Discussion

"These three classes have been very similar," I said. "with just minor differences in the way the final grade is calculated. This is something that will come into play when we discuss inheritance in two weeks."

"Is it time to modify Grades.java?" Steve asked?

"Not quite yet Steve," I said. "We still need to create a DisplayGrade Instantiable class."

There were no other questions, and so I distributed this exercise for the class to complete.

Exercise 7-6 Create the DisplayGrade Instantiable Class

In this exercise, you'll create the DisplayGrade class for the Grades Calculation Project. This class will allow a client program to create an object that will display the final grade for an English, Math or Science student. This class has three overloaded Constructor methods to code, so be careful.

1. Use Notepad and enter the following code.

```
import javax.swing.JOptionPane;

class DisplayGrade {
  public DisplayGrade(int midterm, int finalExamGrade,
            int research, int presentation,
            double finalNumericGrade, String finalLetterGrade) {
    JOptionPane.showMessageDialog
      (null, "*** ENGLISH STUDENT ***\n\n" +
      "Midterm grade is: " + midterm + "\n" +
      "Final Exam is: " + finalExamGrade + "\n" +
      "Research grade is: " + research + "\n" +
      "Presentation grade is: " + presentation + "\n\n" +
      "Final Numeric Grade is: " + finalNumericGrade + "\n" +
      "Final Letter Grade is: " + finalLetterGrade);
  }                             // end of displayGrade method with 6 parameters

  public DisplayGrade(int midterm, int finalExamGrade,
            double finalNumericGrade, String finalLetterGrade) {
    JOptionPane.showMessageDialog
      (null,"*** MATH STUDENT ***\n\n" +
      "Midterm grade is: " + midterm + "\n" +
      "Final Exam is: " + finalExamGrade + "\n\n" +
      "Final Numeric Grade is: " + finalNumericGrade + "\n" +
      "Final Letter Grade is: " + finalLetterGrade);
  }                             // end of displayGrade method with 4 parameters

  public DisplayGrade(int midterm, int finalExamGrade,
            int research, double finalNumericGrade,
```

```
                     String finalLetterGrade) {
JOptionPane.showMessageDialog
  (null,"*** SCIENCE STUDENT ***\n\n" +
  "Midterm grade is: " + midterm + "\n" +
  "Final Exam is: " + finalExamGrade + "\n" +
  "Research grade is: " + research + "\n\n" +
  "Final Numeric Grade is: " + finalNumericGrade + "\n" +
  "Final Letter Grade is: " + finalLetterGrade);
}                             // end of displayGrade method with 5 parameters
}                             // end of DisplayGrade class
```

2. Save your source file as DisplayGrade.java in the \JFiles\Grades folder (select File | Save As from Notepad's menu bar). Be sure to save your source file with the file name extension java.

3. Compile your source file into a Bytecode file.

4. You won't be able to test your DisplayGrade class for a while. Remember, an Instantiable class cannot be run directly from the command prompt. You'll be creating a DisplayGrade object from this class via the startup Grades class, which you'll modify in Exercise 7-7.

Discussion

No one seemed to have any problems completing the exercise, but I could sense some confusion.

"Does everyone understand what's going on here?" I asked. "We've created a class that has three overloaded Constructor methods."

"Constructor methods have the same name as the class, is that right?" Rhonda asked. "And they are automatically executed when an object from the class is created?"

"That's excellent, Rhonda," I said. "Constructor methods are guaranteed to execute when an object of the class is created. Furthermore, you can create more than one Constructor method with the same name. These are called Overloaded Constructor methods, and Java decides which one of them to execute based on the number and type of arguments passed to the Constructor when the object is created. I'll give you a preview of the code change we're about to make in the Grades class. This is the code that will instantiate a DisplayGrade object and pass the Constructor method six arguments to display the final grade for an English Student:"

```
DisplayGrade x = new DisplayGrade (midterm, finalExamGrade,
                          research, presentation,
                          finalNumericGrade, finalLetterGrade);
```

No one had any other questions, so we moved onto the final exercise of the day: modifying the Grades class to create objects from the Instantiable classes we had just created.

Exercise 7-7 Modify the Grades Calculation Program to Use Instantiable objects

In this exercise, you'll modify the Grade class from last week to create objects from the Instantiable Classes you just created.

1. Using Notepad (if you using Windows), locate and open the **Grades.java** source file you worked on last week. (It should be in the \JFiles\Grades folder)

2. Modify your code so that it looks like this.

import javax.swing.JOptionPane;

```
class Grades {
  public static void main(String[] args) {
    String moreGradesToCalculate;
    String response;
    moreGradesToCalculate = JOptionPane.showInputDialog
      ("Do you want to calculate a grade?");
    moreGradesToCalculate = moreGradesToCalculate.toUpperCase();
    while (moreGradesToCalculate.equals ("YES")) {
      response = whatKindOfStudent();
      switch(Integer.parseInt(response)) {
        case 1:
          EnglishStudent eStudent = new EnglishStudent();
```

```
            eStudent.calculate();
            DisplayGrade x = new DisplayGrade (eStudent.midterm,
                    eStudent.finalExamGrade,
                    eStudent.research,
                    eStudent.presentation,
                    eStudent.finalNumericGrade,
                    eStudent.finalLetterGrade);
          break;
        case 2:
          MathStudent mStudent = new MathStudent();
          mStudent.calculate();
          DisplayGrade y = new DisplayGrade (mStudent.midterm,
                    mStudent.finalExamGrade,
                    mStudent.finalNumericGrade,
                    mStudent.finalLetterGrade);
          break;
        case 3:
          ScienceStudent sStudent = new ScienceStudent();
          sStudent.calculate();
          DisplayGrade z = new DisplayGrade (sStudent.midterm,
                    sStudent.finalExamGrade,
                    sStudent.research,
                    sStudent.finalNumericGrade,
                    sStudent.finalLetterGrade);
          break;
        default:
          JOptionPane.showMessageDialog
            (null, response + " - is not a valid student type");
          System.exit (0);
      }
      moreGradesToCalculate = JOptionPane.showInputDialog
        ("Do you have another grade to calculate?");
      moreGradesToCalculate = moreGradesToCalculate.toUpperCase();
    }
    JOptionPane.showMessageDialog
      (null, "Thanks for using the Grades Calculation program!");
    System.exit (0);
  }                                                  // end of main

  public static String whatKindOfStudent() {
    String response;
    response = JOptionPane.showInputDialog
      ("Enter student type (1=English, 2=Math, 3=Science)");
    if (response == null) {
      JOptionPane.showMessageDialog
        (null, "You clicked on the Cancel button");
       System.exit (0);
    }
    else
    if (response.equals("")) {
      JOptionPane.showMessageDialog
        (null, "You must make an entry in the InputBox");
      System.exit (0);
    }
    else
    if (Integer.parseInt(response) < 1 | Integer.parseInt(response) > 3) {
      JOptionPane.showMessageDialog
```

```
            (null, response + " - is not a valid student type");
      System.exit (0);
   }
   return response;
}                                            // end of whatKindOfStudent method
}
```

3. Save your source file as Grades.java in the \JFiles\Grades folder (select File | Save As from Notepad's menu bar). Be sure to save your source file with the file name extension java.

4. Compile your source file into a Bytecode file.

5. Execute your program and test it thoroughly. After you start up your program, it should ask you if you have a grade to calculate.

6. Enter **Yes**, and then calculate the grade for an English student. Enter **70** for the midterm, **80** for the final examination, **90** for the research grade, and **100** for the presentation. A final numeric grade of 84.5 should be displayed, with a letter grade of **C**.

7. After the message box is displayed with the calculated grade, the program should ask you if you have more grades to calculate.

8. Enter **Yes**, and then calculate the grade for a Math student. Enter **70** for the midterm and **80** for the final examination. A final numeric grade of **75** should be displayed, with a letter grade of **D**.

9. After the message box is displayed with the calculated grade, the program should ask you if you have more grades to calculate.

10. Enter **Yes**, and then calculate the grade for a Science student. Enter **70** for the midterm, **80** for the final examination, and **90** for the research grade. A final numeric grade of **78** should be displayed, with a letter grade of **C**. After the message box is displayed with the calculated grade, the program should ask you if you have more grades to calculate.

11. Enter **No**. You should be thanked for using the program, and then the program should end.

Discussion

Changing the Grades Class to use Instantiable objects was pretty tedious, and it took most of my students about 15 minutes to complete the exercise. Despite that, there were no major problems (one or two students had trouble with the compiler string necessary to compile the application), and I think most everyone understood what was going on.

"In the final analysis," Ward said, "we took a bunch of the code from the Grades class and placed it in the EnglishStudent, MathStudent, ScienceStudent, and DisplayGrade classes. Is that right?"

"That's right, Ward," I said. "Notice that the amount of code in the Grades class itself has been drastically reduced because so much of it was moved into one of four other classes. Most importantly, the code is easier to read, understand, and maintain, although the overall code is larger when you consider all of the classes that comprise it."

"How so?" Rhonda asked. "I mean, how is it easier to maintain?"

"Let me ask you this question," I said. "If Frank Olley walked into our classroom right now, and told you that the calculation of the final grade for an English student needs to be changed, could you tell me what class we would need to change?"

"That's easy," Dave said. "That code is in the EnglishStudent class. In fact, it's in the **calculate()** method of the EnglishStudent class."

"I couldn't have said it better myself, Dave," I said. "And finding the code that needs to be modified is half the battle in code modification."

"Can you review the code that instantiates the various student objects?" Barbara said after a moment.

"Sure thing, Barbara," I said. "Here it is:"

```
case 1:
   EnglishStudent eStudent = new EnglishStudent();
   eStudent.calculate();
   DisplayGrade x = new DisplayGrade (eStudent.midterm,
            eStudent.finalExamGrade,
            eStudent.research,
            eStudent.presentation,
            eStudent.finalNumericGrade,
```

```
                eStudent.finalLetterGrade);
  break;
case 2:
  MathStudent mStudent = new MathStudent();
  mStudent.calculate();
  DisplayGrade y = new DisplayGrade (mStudent.midterm,
            mStudent.finalExamGrade,
            mStudent.finalNumericGrade,
            mStudent.finalLetterGrade);
  break;
case 3:
  ScienceStudent sStudent = new ScienceStudent();
  sStudent.calculate();
  DisplayGrade z = new DisplayGrade (sStudent.midterm,
            sStudent.finalExamGrade,
            sStudent.research,
            sStudent.finalNumericGrade,
            sStudent.finalLetterGrade);
  break;
```

"All of the code necessary to instantiate the EnglishStudent, MathStudent, or ScienceStudent objects is contained within this Switch structure. The test condition for the Switch structure is the user's response of 1, 2, or 3 in an Input Box. If the user's response is 1, we declare an instance of the EnglishStudent object, using the object variable eStudent."

```
EnglishStudent eStudent = new EnglishStudent();
```

"We then execute the **calculate()** method of the EnglishStudent object using this code:"

```
eStudent. calculate();
```

"This is followed by an instantiation of the DisplayGrade object. Depending upon the number and type of arguments supplied, one of the three Constructor methods we created is executed:"

```
DisplayGrade x = new DisplayGrade (eStudent.midterm,
                    eStudent.finalExamGrade,
                    eStudent.research, eStudent.presentation,
                    eStudent.finalNumericGrade,
                    eStudent.finalLetterGrade);
```

"I probably should have asked this earlier," Linda said, "but why didn't we place the code for the grade calculation in a Constructor method of the EnglishStudent class like we did with the DisplayGrade class, instead of creating a separate method called **calculate()**?"

"That's a good question, Linda," I said. "We certainly could have done that. It's another case of there being more than one way to paint a picture. In theory, Constructor methods should be used to initialize the state or data variables of an object. I stretched the intended purpose of the Constructor methods for the DisplayGrade object just a bit, in part because I wanted to give you all a chance to work with one."

I waited to see if anyone had any questions, but there were none. "This class has been a very productive one," I said, "in that you learned how to code classes and create objects from them, which gives us access to the object's data and behavior. Next week, you'll learn that sometimes in our haste to give a client program access to an object's data, we permit too much access, which can have some pretty nasty effects on the data integrity of our objects. You'll learn how to correct that problem next week."

With that, I dismissed the class for the day.

Summary

In this chapter, we learned how we can create Instantiable classes—that is, classes from which objects can be created. These objects can have attributes, which are implemented via Instance and Class variables within the class, and behavior, which is implemented via class methods. Instantiable classes cannot be executed via a command prompt; their objects must be created from within another class, typically a startup class possessing a main() method.

Instantiable objects are created using the New keyword. Instantiable objects are destroyed by the Java garbage collector when no program is using them any longer, so there is no need to explicitly destroy a Java object as there is in other programming languages.

Instantiable classes have two special types of methods. The first, the Constructor method, has the same name as the class, and its code is guaranteed to execute when an object of the class is first created. Constructor methods may be overloaded, that is, you may have more than one Constructor method with the same name, provided each one has a different signature—the number and type of arguments.

The second special method is called a **finalize()** method, and its code is guaranteed to execute when the Java garbage collector is about to destroy the object. **finalize()** methods must be named finalize and should be declared with the Protected keyword, and return a void return value. However, as I pointed out earlier, the **finalize()** method is now deprecated and its usage is NOT recommended.

Chapter 8---Controlling Access To The Data In Your Object

In Chapter 7, we learned how to create Instantiable classes, which are classes from which other objects can be created. These objects are just like the standard Java objects, such as *System* and *JOptionPane*, that we've been working with all along. Instantiable objects possess characteristics or attributes, which are created via Instance and class variables. An Instantiable object's attributes can be read or updated by the Java class (program) that creates the object. Instantiable objects also possess certain types of behavior, which are created via methods. An Instantiable object's methods can be executed by the Java class (program) that creates it. In this chapter, we'll learn that while it's great that the Java class that creates an Instantiable object can access and update the object's Instance and class variables, it's not always desirable for these variables to be directly updateable by the client program. The same can be said of client programs that execute the object's methods. There may be cases where some methods of the Instantiable class need to be hidden from the client program. We'll learn that there are ways to deal with these potential problems.

Controlling Access to your Object's data

"Last week," I said, as I began our eighth class, "we learned how to create Instantiable classes, which are classes from which objects can be created. We learned how we can design an Instantiable class to model a real-world object, complete with characteristics or attributes and behaviors. When an object is created from an Instantiable class, the Java class creating the object can read and update the object's attributes and trigger its behavior by executing its methods. In today's class, we'll continue studying Instantiable class creation which we began last week."

"I wouldn't have thought there was a lot more to cover with Instantiable classes," Mary said. "I thought we were pretty much done with this topic last week."

"In terms of Instantiable classes," I said, "what we've done so far has been fine, but in today's class, we'll learn that the Instantiable classes we created last week, while fully functional, may have some potential data problems."

"Data problems?" Rhonda asked. "That sounds serious. Do you mean that there are problems with the classes we created last week?"

"There's no need to be alarmed, Rhonda," I said. "In terms of the mechanics of creating Instantiable classes, everything we did last week was just fine. But in our excitement about learning how to use a Java class to model an object, its attributes and its behavior, we didn't consider, in the least, whether the data in the object needs to be protected, and if so, how to protect it."

"Protecting the data?" Peter asked. "I'm afraid I don't understand. From whom do we need to protect data?"

"That's a great question, Peter," I said. "It may be difficult for you to fathom right now, but the Java programs you will later write, particularly if you are writing programs to run in a commercial environment, have potential for exposing data that is sensitive."

"Such as?" Ward asked.

"In a Customer object, sensitive data would be customer account numbers and Social Security numbers," I said. "In an Employee object, sensitive data would be employee salary information or employee performance appraisals. These are examples of data that, if the designer of the Instantiable class is not careful, can wind up in the hands of the wrong person. It seems that nearly every week there's a story in the newspaper about sensitive data finding its way into the wrong hands. This is something we need to consider when we design our Instantiable classes."

"How do we do that?" Blaine asked. "Can you give us an example?"

"Sure thing, Blaine," I said. "Every class we've created so far in the course has been created as a public class, with public methods and default access specifers for each of its Instance and class variables."

"What's an access specifer?" Kathy asked.

"An access specifer is the keyword that precedes the data type of our Instance or class variables," I said. "Let's take a look at the code that we wrote last week to implement the attributes of the EnglishStudent class:"

```
final double ENGLISH_MIDTERM_PERCENTAGE = .25;
final double ENGLISH_FINALEXAM_PERCENTAGE = .25;
final double ENGLISH_RESEARCH_PERCENTAGE = .30;
```

```
final double ENGLISH_PRESENTATION_PERCENTAGE = .20;
int midterm = 0;
int finalExamGrade = 0;
int research = 0;
int presentation = 0;
double finalNumericGrade = 0;
String finalLetterGrade = "";
```

"There is *no* keyword in front of these Constants and Instance variables," Rhonda said.

"That's my point exactly, Rhonda," I said. "When we created the EnglishStudent class last week, we omitted the Access Specifer. When you don't include an Access Specifer to an Instance or class variable, the variable is set up with what is known as default access."

"What does default access mean?" Steve wondered.

"Default access," I said, "means that other classes within the same package or folder can directly access the variables in the class."

"What do you mean by 'directly access'?" Valerie asked.

"When I say directly access," I replied, "I mean that a class can create an instance of the EnglishStudent object, and using object dot notation, directly update the value of an Instance or a class variable. Like this:"

```
public class Example8_1 {
  public static void main(String[] args) {
    EnglishStudent x = new EnglishStudent();
    x.midterm = 99;
  }
}
```

"Is that a problem?" Steve asked. "Don't we want the program that creates our object to be able to work directly with the object's attributes and methods?"

"In some cases," I said, "but perhaps not all. Updating the midterm attribute of the EnglishStudent may be fine, but suppose one of the programmers using the EnglishStudent class discovers he or she can directly update the *finalNumericGrade* attribute, like this:"

```
public class Example8_2 {
  public static void main(String[] args) {
    EnglishStudent x = new EnglishStudent();
    x.finalNumericGrade = 99;
  }
}
```

I could see Steve (and the other students) pondering this.

"Now we're starting to get into dangerous territory," I said. "Allowing a program to create an object and then update the component pieces of the English student's final grade is fine, but by design, only the **calculate()** method of the EnglishStudent object should determine the final numeric grade. To allow a programmer to **directly** update the *finalNumericGrade* or *finalLetterGrade* attributes of the EnglishStudent object is to invite problems."

"Like what?" Rhonda asked.

"The only way a final grade should be calculated," I said, "is via the code that the designer of the object wrote. By permitting the user of the object to directly update the finalNumericGrade or finalLetterGrade attributes, we've allowed him or her to bypass the correct calculation. This can lead to results that are incorrect at best and fraudulent at worst."

"In other words," Dave said, "an unscrupulous programmer could update the final grade for a student by bypassing the code in the **calculate()** method of the EnglishStudent object?"

"That's right, Dave," I said, "and it has happened. As I said before, fraudulent activity is the worst case scenario. But even if the programmer doesn't intend to do something dishonest, allowing the programmer to directly update an attribute that can only properly be updated by complex code is a big mistake. Remember, one of the great things about objects is that they allow the developer of the object to shield the complexities of a task from the programmer who needs to use the object. In the real world of programming, programmers work with objects like this all the time, and the objects are many times more complex than that of an English student at a university. Programmers are developing object-oriented programs today to monitor switches in a nuclear power plant or hydrogen level values on the Space shuttle just before launch. Can you imagine what the dire effects might be if the designer of one of these objects accidentally permitted the programmer using the object to directly update one of these object's attributes?"

"I get the point," Valerie said. "Certain attributes of an object shouldn't be updateable by the programmer using the object."

"That's right, Valerie," I said, "and some attributes are best not seen as well. My point is that whether or not to allow access to an object's attributes and methods is something to which the designer of the class needs to give careful thought before distributing the class for use by other programmers."

I waited a moment before continuing.

"I'm not sure that there is a consensus among class designers," I said, "but I think it's safe to say that some attributes, but not all, can be directly accessible by the program creating the object, and therefore should be designated with the Public Access Specifer. Other attributes can be visible to the program creating the object but should not be directly updateable by it. Other attributes should be invisible to certain users of the program creating the object, and still others should be totally invisible to the program creating the object—accessible only by code within methods of the object itself. These attributes should be designated with the Private Access Specifer."

"Can you give us an example of each one of these categories?" Kate asked. "I'm afraid I'm still not getting it."

"Let's imagine," I said, "that a programmer at XYZ University designs a Student class to model the university's real-world student, and that the Student class has this list of attributes:"

```
class Student {
   String studentID;
   String name;
   String address;
   int age;
   String SSN;
   double GPA;
```

"SSN is the student's Social Security number, and GPA is the student's grade point average. Let's further suppose that the designer of the Student class coded a Constructor method so that when a Student object is created, the value of the studentID attribute is used to locate student information in a database record and to assign values to the rest of the Student class attributes. Finally, let's suppose that another programmer at the University finds the Student class and decides to use it in a program she is writing, which is designed to permit a work-study student to update student address and age information."

"I see some potential problems with this Student class right away!" Dave said. "Because there's no Access Specifer for the Instance attributes, each one of them has default access, which, according to what you told us earlier, means that if the client program is located in the same folder as the Student class, there's nothing stopping that program from creating a Student object that then exposes private information about the student, such as Social Security number and grade point average."

"I agree," Steve added. "I think that the client program using the Student object should have full access—by that I mean read and update—to just two attributes, the address and age attributes. Furthermore, I would suggest read-only access to the studentID and name attributes. We don't want either of those attributes being changed by accident. Finally, I would suggest that both SSN and GPA should be totally invisible to the user of the Student object, at least in this particular case."

"I agree with both Dave and Steve," Rhonda said. "But how can we do all of that in Java, hide some attributes and make others invisible? Is that what you were talking about earlier when you were discussing Access Specifers?"

"That's part of it, Rhonda," I said. "By specifying a private Access Specifer, we can prevent the client program from being able to access the attribute at all, and in a moment, you'll see that we can also use special methods to selectively restrict what the client program using our object can do with the data inside of it. Let's create a Student class with the attributes I just listed, and create a method called **display()** to display its data."

"Will we be accessing data in a database today?" Rhonda asked excitedly.

"No, Rhonda," I said, "working with data from a database within Java is beyond the scope of this introductory course. Instead of looking up the student's information in a database record, we'll simulate its lookup by assigning a set of default values to the object's attributes via its Constructor method."

I displayed the code for the Student class on the classroom projector:

```java
import javax.swing.JOptionPane;
class Student {
  String studentID;
  String name;
  String address;
  int age;
  String SSN;
  double GPA;

  public Student() {                    // Constructor Method
    studentID = "123";
    name = "Mary Smith";
    address = "22 Twain Drive";
    age = 22;
    SSN = "111-22-3333";
    GPA = 2.00;
  }

  public void display() {
    JOptionPane.showMessageDialog
      (null,"*** STUDENT RECORD ***\n\n" +
      "Student ID: " + studentID + "\n" +
      "Name: " + name + "\n" +
      "Address: " + address + "\n" +
      "Age: " + age + "\n" +
      "SSN: " + SSN + "\n" +
      "GPA: " + GPA);
  }

}
```

I then compiled the code.

"Here's the Student class," I said. "As you can see, the Student class contains the six attributes we discussed. Notice that all six Instance variables lack an explicit Access Specifer. This means they have what is known as default access. Not specifying an Access Specifer is a decidedly bad idea because your code will be difficult to read and your intentions will not be understood by the programmer whose job it may be to modify your code at some future date. Notice also that the Student class has two methods: the Constructor method, called **Student()**, is given the same name as the class. In it, we placed code to assign a set of default values to each one of the six attributes of the class so that we can experiment a bit with Student objects created from the class. As I mentioned earlier, ordinarily we would obtain this information from a data source such as a database, but that's beyond the scope of this introductory course, so we'll just 'pretend' to do so via the Constructor method. The second method is the **display()** method, which displays the values of the attributes in a Java message box. Now let's create a client program and write the code necessary to instantiate a Student object from this class."

I displayed this code on the classroom projector:

```java
public class Example8_3 {
  public static void main(String[] args) {
    Student x = new Student();
    x.display();
  }
}
```

I then compiled the code and executed the program. The following screenshot was displayed on the classroom projector:

"Can anyone tell me what this code did?" I asked.

"What we've done here," Chuck said, "is to create a Student object, initialize the values of all six attributes via its Constructor method, and then display those values in a message box via the Object's **display()** method."

"That's excellent, Chuck," I said. "Any other comments?"

"Right now," Dave said, "the data in this class is very much unprotected. The user of the Student object is seeing every Student attribute."

"Absolutely right, Dave," I said, "We had previously agreed that we didn't want a client program to have access to the student's Social Security number or grade point average, and both of these are now prominently displayed in the message box. Worse yet, the user of this Student object can directly update both of those attributes, something we also said we didn't want to happen. Let's change the grade point average for Mary Smith."

I displayed this modified code on the classroom projector:

```
public class Example8_4 {
  public static void main(String[] args) {
    Student x = new Student();
    x.GPA = 4.0;
    x.display();
    System.exit (0);
  }
}
```

I then compiled the code and executed the program. The following screenshot was displayed on the classroom projector:

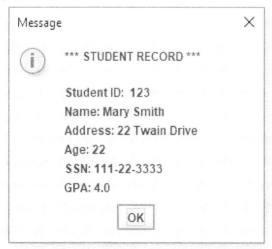

"Wow," Kate said. "We've really done that Mary Smith a favor: her grade point average went from 2.0 to 4.0. I see what you mean by allowing the client program full access to the GPA attribute of the Student class."

"I totally forgot we could update these attributes directly using object dot notation," Ward said, "but as you indicated, without an Access Specifer, the Instance variables in the class are set up for default access."

"What's default access, again?" Rhonda asked.

"Default access means that any class in the same package as the Student class, or any class located in the same folder as the Student class, can see and update the Instance or Class variable," I said. "That's why it's always a good idea to be explicit about your Access Specifers. For instance, here's the same class with public access specified:"

```java
import javax.swing.JOptionPane;
class Student {
  public String studentID;
  public String name;
  public String address;
  public int age;
  public String SSN;
  public double GPA;

  public Student() {                    // Constructor Method
    studentID = "123";
    name = "Mary Smith";
    address = "22 Twain Drive";
    age = 22;
    SSN = "111-22-3333";
    GPA = 2.00;
  }
  public void display() {
    JOptionPane.showMessageDialog
      (null,"*** STUDENT RECORD ***\n\n" +
      "Student ID: " + studentID + "\n" +
      "Name: " + name + "\n" +
      "Address: " + address + "\n" +
      "Age: " + age + "\n" +
      "SSN: " + SSN + "\n" +
      "GPA: " + GPA);
  }
}
```

"Changing the Access Specifer from default to public," I said, "has no obvious impact on the client program that creates objects from it, since both the Student class and the Example8_4 class are in the same folder. However, with default access, if the Student class and the Example8-4 class were in different folders, Example8_4 wouldn't compile successfully. Even if we gave directions to the Java compiler as to where to find the Student class, default access would prevent a client class from another package or folder from begin able to even see the Instance variables of the Student class."

NOTE : Access Specifers are typed in lowercase (for example, public and private).

"Besides public access," Mary asked, "what are the other Access Specifers again?"

"We've seen **default** access," I said, "which is what you get if you don't explicitly code an Access Specifer, plus, there's **public**, which is what we just used here. Public gives full access to the variable by code in any other client class, regardless of whether they both belong to the same package or are located in the same folder. There's also **private** and **protected**. Protected access applies only when inheritance is a factor. Inheritance is something we'll be discussing next week."

"What about private access?" Steve asked. "Did you skip that?"

"Private access," I said, "means that the Instance variable can be used only by code located within the same class as the Instance variable."

I gave everyone a chance to ponder that statement for a moment.

"In the case of the Student class," I said, "that means that if the Instance variable GPA is defined with a private Access Specifer, only code in the methods of the Student class itself will be able to access the Instance variable."

"That seems pretty worthless, doesn't it?" Mary said. "What's the use of having an attribute if it can't be seen or updated from outside the Instantiable class?"

"We'll see in a moment," I said, "how the private Access Specifer is the perfect way to protect data within our object. What we do is make the Instance variables private but provide public methods to access and modify them. Right now, I'd like to show you what happens if we define our Instance variables with the private Access Specifer."

I then modified the code in the Student class to look like this:

```
import javax.swing.JOptionPane;
class Student {
  private String studentID;
  private String name;
  private String address;
  private int age;
  private String SSN;
  private double GPA;

  public Student() {                 // Constructor Method
    studentID = "123";
    name = "Mary Smith";
    address = "22 Twain Drive";
    age = 22;
    SSN = "111-22-3333";
    GPA = 2.00;
  }

  public void display() {
    JOptionPane.showMessageDialog
      (null,"*** STUDENT RECORD ***\n\n" +
      "Student ID: " + studentID + "\n" +
      "Name: " + name + "\n" +
      "Address: " + address + "\n" +
      "Age: " + age + "\n" +
      "SSN: " + SSN + "\n" +
      "GPA: " + GPA);
  }
}
```

"By specifying an Access Specifer of private for the Instance variables of the Student class," I said, "we're now preventing the code from the Example8_4 class from being able to **directly** access the values of these Instance variables. Look at what happens when we try to recompile the code from Example8_4."

I first recompiled the Student class with no problem, and then recompiled Example8_4. The following screenshot was displayed:

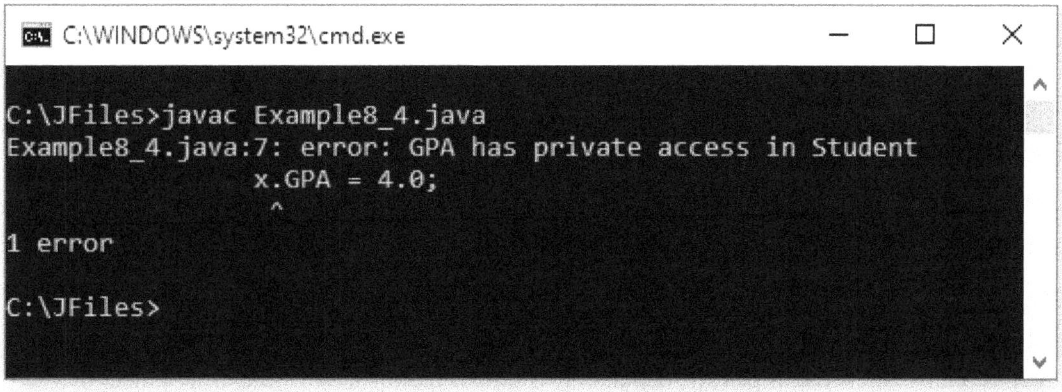

"What happened?" I heard Rhonda say.

"The Java compiler has recognized that the code in Example8_4 is trying to access the private Instance variables in the Student class and has flagged those lines of code as errors," I said. "With the private Access Specifer, access to these Instance variables from code outside the class is no longer possible."

"I see that private access means we can't update the value of the Instance variable," Rhonda said. "Does it also mean we can't see the value as well?"

"That's right, Rhonda," I said. "We can neither see nor update them directly. However, and this is where the 'trick' comes in, we can indirectly see and update them, provided that a public method of the Student class is written to do that. Remember, private access allows methods within the same class to get at the private Instance variables. We can modify the code in Example8_4 to look like this:"

```
public class Example8_5 {
  public static void main(String[] args) {
    Student x = new Student();
    x.display();
    System.exit (0);
  }
}
```

"This code will compile and run just fine, with the public **display()** method of the Student class taking care of allowing our program to **see** the values of the Student object's attributes."

I then compiled the program and executed it. The following screenshot was displayed on the classroom projector:

"I see what you mean now," Mary said. "Even though the Instance variables are declared as private, the public **display()** method allows us to see the values of the Student class's Instance variables."

"That's right, Mary," I said.

"But suppose," Mary continued, "we want to be able to **update** the Instance variables as well as **see** them?"

"Then we need to write a public method to permit the update as well," I said. "The point is that instead of allowing a client program to directly view or update an Instance variable, we write a public method that permits either one. You'll see the benefits of doing so in just a few minutes."

Instance Variables: Public or Private?

"Should all of our Instance variables be declared as private?" Linda asked.

"That's a good question, Linda," I said. "In the Java world, it's considered best to create private Instance variables, and many programmers follow this guideline, declaring all of their Instance variables as private and writing public methods to provide access to the Instance variables and their values. On the other hand, you will find programmers who declare all of their Instance variables as public. You'll also find programmers who pick and choose, declaring some Instance variables as public and some as private, depending upon the particular attribute of an object the Instance variable represents."

"What's your recommendation?" Steve asked.

"My recommendation," I said, "is that you declare your Instance variables as private and write public methods to access them. You'll find the same recommendation in the official Java documentation, although it does hedge a bit and say that it's OK to declare public Instance variables at times. The bottom line is that the Java language allows you to create public Instance variables—if you choose to do so, that's up to you. However, it may be something that a prospective employer frowns upon, since public Instance variables can cause data integrity problems, the type we just saw with the Student class example."

"I'm still having problems with this concept of private Instance variables and public methods," Chuck said. "In the Student class we just wrote, is the **display()** method the type of public method you are talking about?"

"Good question, Chuck," I said. "More typically, the public methods I'm referring to are specially named methods called **Get** and **Set** methods. Get methods are public methods that permit a client program to get or retrieve the value of a private Instance variable. Set methods are public methods that permit a client program to set or update the value of a private Instance variable."

"So we should code a pair of Get and Set public methods for each Instance variable?" Linda asked.

"If you declare your Instance variables as private," I said, "you will need a Get and Set public method for each one. Without them, there's no way that the client program can access the object's attribute represented by that Instance variable. As you'll see in a minute, you can place code in the Get method to determine if the client program requesting the value of the private Instance variable really should have it, and you can place code in the Set method to determine if the client program attempting to update the value of the private Instance variable should be able to do so."

"That would come in very handy with the SSN and GPA attributes of the Student class," Mary said.

"Absolutely," I said. "The Set method is a great place to place code to verify if the client program has the authority to update the private Instance variable. Code in the Set method can also be used to perform validation on the proposed update before the Instance variable is actually changed and the object is set to an Invalid state."

"Validation code?" Rhonda asked. "Invalid state? What do you mean?"

"The 'state' of an object is the values of the data that represent the object," I said. "An object must always maintain its data in a valid state. In Example8_4, we saw how a client program can inappropriately change the value of the GPA Instance variable. Still, the value of GPA was set to a value that is consistent with a grade point average. With a public Instance variable, it's easy for a client program to make a mistake and cause the object's state to become invalid, like this:"

```
public class Example8_6 {
  public static void main(String[] args) {
    Student x = new Student();
    x.age = -6;                    // OOPS! Negative Age?
  }
}
```

Using Set and Get Statements

"Does anyone see a problem here?" I asked. "I do," Rhonda called out. "You've assigned a negative number to the Student object's age attribute. I'm sure you didn't mean to do that."

"Is that what you mean by invalid state?" Ward asked.

"You're both absolutely right," I said. "I didn't intend to do that, but if the age Instance variable is declared with public Access, there's absolutely no way to prevent this. And now the Student object does have an Invalid state: one of its attributes makes no sense. The Student's age cannot be negative."

"A Set method could prevent this from happening?" Lou asked.

"That's right, Lou," I said. "Using a Set method, also called a Mutator method, we can alert the user if the update they've attempted to make to a private Instance variable is invalid. By the way, Get methods, which permit the retrieval of the value of a private Instance variable, are also called Access methods. Take a look at this code."

I then modified the code in the Student class to look like this…

```
import javax.swing.JOptionPane;
class Student {
  private String studentID;
```

```java
private String name;
private String address;
private int age;
private String SSN;
private double GPA;

public Student() {          // Constructor Method
  studentID = "123";
  name = "Mary Smith";
  address = "22 Twain Drive";
  age = 22;
  SSN = "111-22-3333";
  GPA = 2.00;
}

public void setAddress(String temp) {
  address = temp;
}

public String getAddress() {
  return address;
}

public void setAge(int temp) {
  if (temp < 1) {
    JOptionPane.showMessageDialog
      (null, "Invalid Age " + temp + " Program Terminating");
    System.exit (0);
  }
  else
    age = temp;
}

public int getAge() {
  return age;
}

public void display() {
  JOptionPane.showMessageDialog
    (null,"*** STUDENT RECORD ***\n\n" +
    "Student ID: " + studentID + "\n" +
    "Name: " + name + "\n" +
    "Address: " + address + "\n" +
    "Age: " + age);
}
}
```

"What we've done here," I said, "is declare a Get and Set method for two of our Instance variables: address and age."

"Are those the Accessor and Mutator methods you mentioned?" Valerie asked.

"That's right Valerie," I answered. "Get methods are also called Accessor methods and permit the client program to retrieve the value of a private Instance variable. Set methods are also called Mutator methods and permit the client program to update the value of a private Instance variable."

"Why didn't we create Accessor and Mutator methods for each one of the private Instance variables?" Kate asked. "Didn't you say that was your recommendation?"

"Not quite, Kate," I replied. "My recommendation is to create private Instance variables for every attribute of the object but to create Accessor and Mutator methods only where necessary. We are not interested in providing our client program with direct access to the Student object's other four attributes, and by providing no Accessor or Mutator methods for those Instance variables, there's no way the our client program can view them or update them."

"Except through the public **display()** method," Dave said, "and I notice that you've modified that method, and it no longer displays the SSN or GPA Instance variables."

"That's right, Dave," I said. "Does everyone see the benefits of declaring our Instance variables as private?"

"I think I do," Linda said, "but isn't providing Accessor and Mutator methods the same as making the instance variable public in the first place?"

"That's the argument that some programmers make," I said, "but that's only true if no validation is being performed in the Accessor or Mutator methods. You have to remember that when a direct retrieval or update is made to a public Instance variable by a client program, there's nothing that the object can do to stop it. Accessor and Mutator methods, on the other hand, are much smarter. For instance, code in an Accessor method can determine the identity of the user of the client program and make a decision as to whether the user can see the data. Code in a Mutator method can validate the proposed update before it occurs."

"I'm convinced," Linda said. "Can we take a closer look at the Accessor and Mutator methods before we test this code?"

"Sure thing, Linda," I said. "Let's take a look at the Mutator methods first. Remember, we created Mutator methods only for the age and address private Instance variables."

"That means that the other four private Instance variables can't be updated?" Linda asked.

"That's right," I said. "If we declare an Instance variable as private, without a Mutator method or some other public method that updates it, the Instance variable is shut off from the client program."

"So it's up to the designer of the object to decide if an Accessor or Mutator method will be written for each private Instance variable?" Joe asked.

"Exactly," I answered. "If no access to the private Instance variable is required, then neither an Accessor nor Mutator method will be written. If the private Instance variable's value can be seen but not updated, only an Accessor method will be written."

Mutator Methods

"Where's the Mutator method for the address attribute?" Blaine asked. "Is that the **setAddress()** method?"

"That's right, Blaine," I said, as I displayed it on the classroom projector. "Mutator methods by convention begin with the prefix 'set'."

```
public void setAddress(String temp) {
   address = temp;
}
```

"Is there anything special about a Mutator method?" Barbara asked. "SetAddress looks like an ordinary method to me."

"Barbara's right," I said. "Mutator methods are just ordinary methods with code that permits the user of the object to update the value of a private Instance variable. This is accomplished by the client program passing the proposed updated value of the private Instance variable as an argument to the Mutator method. Notice that **setAddress()** is declared to accept a single String argument called **temp**. This argument, when passed to the method, is then assigned to the private Instance variable called *address*."

"So that's how it works," Rhonda said. "The address Instance variable is declared private, but even so, code within the class itself has full access to it."

"You have the idea now, Rhonda," I said. "Notice that there was no validation code in the **setAddress()** method. However, the Mutator method for the age attribute is a bit more complicated:"

```
public void setAge(int temp) {
   if (temp < 1) {
      JOptionPane.showMessageDialog
         (null, "Invalid Age " + temp + " Program Terminating");
      System.exit (0);
   }
   else
```

```
    age = temp;
}
```

"As was the case with the **setAddress()** Mutator method, **setAge()** also accepts a single argument, although this one is an integer, since the passed argument must match the data type of the private Instance variable. **SetAge()** contains validation code, using an If statement, to handle the negative number that we 'accidentally' assigned to the age attribute in Example 8_4. If the value of the passed argument is less than one, we display a message to the user and execute the **exit()** method of the System object; otherwise, we assign the value of the passed argument to the private Instance variable called age."

"What's the impact of executing the **exit()** method of the System object within the Mutator method?" Dave asked. "Will it end the program or just destroy the Student object?"

"Executing the **exit()** method of the System object ends the entire program," I said.

"Is there a more elegant way of handling the error than that?" Linda asked.

"Yes, there is," I said. "We could have defined the Mutator method to return a value to the client program."

"So Mutator methods can return a value?" Bob asked.

"Mutator methods can return a value just like any other method," I said. "In the case of **setAge()**, we could have chosen to return a value to the client program indicating the success or failure of the update. Traditionally, a return value of 0 indicates __success__, and some other value, such as –1, indicates __failure__."

Everyone seemed anxious to see the Mutator method of the Student class in action. But first, we needed to quickly examine the Accessor methods.

Accessor Methods

"Let's take a look at the two Accessor methods we created, **getAddress()** and **getAge()**. As you can see, by convention, Accessor methods are named beginning with the prefix 'get.' Accessor methods return the value of the private Instance variable as a return value to the client program that calls them. Here's the **getAddress()** Accessor method:"

```
public String getAddress() {
    return address;
}
```

"…and here's the **getAge()** Accessor method…"

```
public int getAge() {
    return age;
}
```

"We had no reason to do so," I continued, "but it's within the Accessor method that we can write code to determine if the client program should have access to the value of the private Instance variable. One way to do so would be to require the client program to supply, as an argument, a password."

I waited to see if there were any questions, but there were none.

"I'm anxious to see how the Mutator and Accessor methods work," Rhonda said.

"Rhonda's right," I said. "It's time to test the Accessor and Mutator methods of the Student class. Let's see if we can assign a negative value to the age attribute of the Student object."

Don't Forget: If typing these examples and exercises isn't something you want to do, feel free to follow this link to find and download the completed solutions for all of the examples and exercises in the book. Just click on the Java book, then follow the link entitled exercises ☺

http://www.johnsmiley.com/main/books.htm

I then displayed this code on the classroom projector…

```
public class Example8_7 {
    public static void main(String[] args) {
        Student x = new Student();
        x.setAddress("222 Elm Street");
        x.setAge(-6);
```

```
      x.display();
      System.exit (0);
    }
}
```

"Here's code that creates an instance of a Student object," I said, "and then uses the Mutator methods **setAddress()** and **setAge()** to update the private Instance variables of address and age. Notice how we're passing values for both via arguments to the respective Mutators."

"I was about to say," Kate said, "that there is no assignment statement in the code. I forgot that we no longer assign a value directly to an Instance variable and that instead we pass a value as an argument to the Mutator method."

"Does everyone notice that I've made the mistake that I made earlier," I asked, "by '**accidentally**' passing a negative number as an argument to the **setAge()** Mutator method? Let's see if the Mutator catches it."

I compiled the latest version of the Student class and Example8_7, and then executed Example8_7. The following screenshot was displayed:

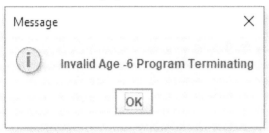

"Looks like the Mutator worked," I heard Steve say. I clicked the OK button and the program ended.

"The **setAge()** Mutator detected a value less than 1," I said, "and displayed the message box. When I clicked the OK button, the program ended. Now, let's see how the program behaves if we pass it a good value for the age attribute."

I displayed this code on the classroom projector:

```
public class Example8_8 {
  public static void main(String[] args) {
    Student x = new Student();
    x.setAddress("222 Elm Street");
    x.setAge(46);
    x.display();
    System.exit (0);
  }
}
```

I then compiled the program and executed it. The following screenshot was displayed on the classroom projector.

"Does everyone see how the two Mutator methods have allowed us to update the private Instance variables address and age?" I asked.

"I'm fine with that," Linda said, "but we haven't used the Accessor methods, have we? We used the public **display()** method of the Student object to display the values for the address and age Instance variables. Can we see their Accessor methods in action?"

"That's a good point, Linda," I said. "Let's do that."

I then displayed this code on the classroom projector.

```
public class Example8_9 {
  public static void main(String[] args) {
    Student x = new Student();
    x.setAddress("222 Elm Street");
    x.setAge(46);
    System.out.println("The value of age is: " + x.getAge());
    System.out.println("The value of address is: " + x.getAddress());
    System.exit (0);
  }
}
```

"Where are the Accessor methods for age?" Rhonda asked. "I'm not seeing them."

"They're in these two lines of code," I said. "You may have missed them because their return values are being used as an argument to the **println()** method of the System object."

```
System.out.println("The value of age is: " + x.getAge());
System.out.println("The value of address is: " + x.getAddress());
```

I compiled the program and executed it. The following screenshot was displayed on the classroom projector:

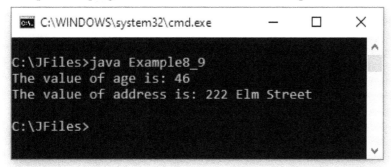

"I see," Rhonda said.

We had been working for some time, and so I suggested we take a break prior to examining the Grades Calculation project for data integrity issues. While my class was out of the room, I placed a quick phone call to coordinate a visit with a special guest.

Let's Analyze the Grades Calculation Project for Data Integrity

Fifteen minutes later I resumed class by explaining that it was now time to examine the Grade Calculation Project for data integrity concerns, the type that we had been studying all morning.

"Does anyone see any data integrity problems with the Grade Calculation Project?" I asked. "Don't forget, you'll need to examine all of the classes in the project."

I gave everyone a few minutes to find and load up their own versions of the Grade Calculation Project on their PCs.

"The first thing that strikes me as being suspect, at least based on what we learned this morning," Dave said, "is that the Instance variables in the EnglishStudent, MathStudent, and ScienceStudent classes are defined with the default Access Specifer. That means that a client program can, in theory, directly access those Instance variables—and also modify them."

"Absolutely right," I replied. "That's definitely something that we'll need to correct."

"Does that mean that we'll need to write Accessor and Mutator methods for each of the Instance variables?" Joe asked.

"You're right, Joe," I replied. "We'll need to write both Accessor and Mutator methods for each one."

"I think," Linda said, "that the Mutator methods will be a great place to put the validation code we'll need for the midterm, final exam, research, and presentation Instance variables. Just like the negative number that we assigned to the age attribute a few minutes ago, each one of the Instance variables of the various Student classes in the Grades calculation project can have invalid numbers assigned to them by the user. Isn't the Mutator method the place for that code?"

"Absolutely, Linda," I said. "At this point, the user can specify a negative number for a student's midterm, and our program will calculate a final grade anyway. We'll definitely need to correct that. One more thing: I'd suggest coding the Mutator methods with an Access Specifer of private. This will ensure that only code within the class can update the Instance variables."

"Can we do that?" Ward asked, "I mean, code a method with an Access Specifer, just like our Instance variables?"

"Yes, we can," I said. "It works the same way."

"Will anything we do in the next few minutes require a change to the Grades class itself?"

Kate asked. "I notice that the Grades class directly references the Instance variables in each one of the student objects when it creates a DisplayGrade object."

"You hit the nail on the head, Kate," I said. "The Grades class will also need to be changed for exactly that reason."

We then spent the next few minutes agreeing on what everyone believed would be the final versions of the various Student classes (they didn't realize they would change it again after we learned about Inheritance the following week). We agreed that for every Student class we would do the following:

- Modify all of the Instance variables to have private Access Specifers.

- Create an Accessor and Mutator method for the midterm, final exam, research, and presentation Instance variables. We agreed to incorporate validation code in the Mutator, with valid grades ranging from 0 to 100. Since these Mutator methods were being executed only by code within the Student classes themselves, we agreed to specify an Access Specifer of private for the methods.

We further agreed that there was no need to code a Mutator for either the finalNumericGrade or the finalLetterGrade Instance variables. I further suggested that I thought it would be a good idea to code an Accessor method for the finalNumericGrade and finalLetterGrade Instance variables. I envisioned that we would need both of these when we developed our graphical user interface a few weeks from now.

"I just thought of something," Rhonda said. "What about the DisplayGrade class? Are any changes required of it?"

Rhonda's question was a good one, but after a quick analysis of the DisplayGrade class, we saw that it contained no Instance variables of any kind. Therefore, no changes were required of it. I then distributed this exercise for the class to complete.

Exercise 8-1 Modify the EnglishStudent Class

In this exercise, you'll modify the EnglishStudent class you created last week.
1. Using Notepad (if you are using Windows) locate and open the EnglishStudent.java source file you worked on last week. (It should be in the \JFiles\Grades folder)
2. Modify your code so that it looks like this.

```
import javax.swing.JOptionPane;

class EnglishStudent {
  private final double ENGLISH_MIDTERM_PERCENTAGE = .25;
  private final double ENGLISH_FINALEXAM_PERCENTAGE = .25;
  private final double ENGLISH_RESEARCH_PERCENTAGE = .30;
  private final double ENGLISH_PRESENTATION_PERCENTAGE = .20;
  private int midterm = 0;
  private int finalExamGrade = 0;
  private int research = 0;
  private int presentation = 0;
  private double finalNumericGrade = 0;
  private String finalLetterGrade = "";
```

```
public EnglishStudent() {
  System.out.println ("EnglishStudent's Constructor");
}
private void setMidterm(int temp) {
  if (temp<0| temp > 100) {
    JOptionPane.showMessageDialog(null,
      "Invalid Midterm Grade (" + temp + ") " +
        "Program Terminating");
    System.exit (0);
  }
  else
    midterm = temp;
}
public int getMidterm() {
  return midterm;
}
private void setFinalExamGrade(int temp) {
  if (temp<0| temp > 100) {
    JOptionPane.showMessageDialog(null,
      "Invalid Final Exam Grade (" + temp + ") " +
        "Program Terminating");
    System.exit (0);
  }
  else
    finalExamGrade = temp;
}
public int getFinalExamGrade() {

  return finalExamGrade;

}
private void setResearch(int temp) {
  if (temp<0| temp > 100) {
    JOptionPane.showMessageDialog(null,
      "Invalid Research Grade (" + temp + ") " +
        "Program Terminating");
    System.exit (0);
  }
  else
    research = temp;
}
public int getResearch() {
  return research;
}
private void setPresentation(int temp) {
  if (temp<0| temp > 100) {
    JOptionPane.showMessageDialog(null,
      "Invalid Presentation Grade (" + temp + ") " +
        "Program Terminating");
    System.exit (0);
  }
  else
    presentation = temp;
}
```

```
public int getPresentation() {
    return presentation;
}
public double getFinalNumericGrade() {
    return finalNumericGrade;
}
public String getFinalLetterGrade() {
    return finalLetterGrade;
}
public void calculate() {
    midterm = Integer.parseInt(JOptionPane.showInputDialog
        ("Enter the Midterm Grade"));
    finalExamGrade = Integer.parseInt(JOptionPane.showInputDialog
        ("Enter the Final Examination Grade"));
    research = Integer.parseInt(JOptionPane.showInputDialog
        ("Enter the Research Grade"));
    presentation = Integer.parseInt(JOptionPane.showInputDialog
        ("Enter the Presentation Grade"));
    finalNumericGrade =
        (midterm * ENGLISH_MIDTERM_PERCENTAGE) +
        (finalExamGrade * ENGLISH_FINALEXAM_PERCENTAGE) +
        (research * ENGLISH_RESEARCH_PERCENTAGE) +
        (presentation * ENGLISH_PRESENTATION_PERCENTAGE);
    if (finalNumericGrade >= 93)
        finalLetterGrade = "A";
    else
    if ((finalNumericGrade >= 85) & (finalNumericGrade < 93))
        finalLetterGrade = "B";
    else
    if ((finalNumericGrade >= 78) & (finalNumericGrade < 85))
        finalLetterGrade = "C";
    else
    if ((finalNumericGrade >= 70) & (finalNumericGrade < 78))
        finalLetterGrade = "D";
    else
    if (finalNumericGrade < 70)
        finalLetterGrade = "F";
    }
}
```

3. Save your source file as '**EnglishStudent.java**' in the \JFiles\Grades folder (select File-Save As from Notepad's Menu Bar). Be sure to save your source file with the file name extension 'java'.

4. Compile your source file into a Bytecode file.

5. You won't be testing your EnglishStudent class until we have completed the work on the other classes in the project.

Discussion

"Let's take a look at what we've done in the EnglishStudent class," I said. "We made three major types of changes. First, we changed the Access Specifer of each one of the Instance variables from the default value to private. Here's the Access Specifer for the midterm Instance variable:"

```
private int midterm = 0;
```

"Second," I continued, "we created Mutator methods for each one of the Instance variables. As Linda pointed out earlier, the Mutator method is a great place to put validation code for our Instance variables. Here's the Mutator method for the midterm Instance variable:"

```
private void setMidterm(int temp) {
  if (temp < 0 | temp > 100) {
    JOptionPane.showMessageDialog(null,
      "Invalid Midterm Grade (" + temp + ") " +
    "Program Terminating");
    System.exit (0);
  }
  else
    midterm = temp;
}
```

"Notice that within the Mutator method," I said, "we are accepting input from the user and validating it to ensure that it's a value between 1 and 100. If it is, we assign the value to the Private Instance Variable midterm."

I waited for questions, but everyone seemed fine.

"Finally," I said, "we created Accessor methods for each one of the Instance variables. In comparison to the Mutator method, these are quite simple. Here's the Accessor method for the midterm Instance variable:"

```
public int getMidterm() {
  return midterm;
}
```

"We won't be able to see the Accessor or Mutator methods in action until we modify the Grades class," I said. There were no questions about the modifications we had made to the EnglishStudent class, so we moved onto the next exercise.

Exercise 8-2 Modify the MathStudent Class

In this exercise, you'll modify the MathStudent class you created last week.
1. Using Notepad (if you are using Windows), locate and open the MathStudent.java source file you worked on last week. (It should be in the \JFiles\Grades folder.)
2. Modify your code so that it looks like this:

```
import javax.swing.JOptionPane;
class MathStudent {
  private final double MATH_MIDTERM_PERCENTAGE = .50;
  private final double MATH_FINALEXAM_PERCENTAGE = .50;
  private int midterm = 0;
  private int finalExamGrade = 0;
  private double finalNumericGrade = 0;
  private String finalLetterGrade = "";

  public MathStudent() {
    System.out.println ("MathStudent's Constructor");
  }

  private void setMidterm(int temp) {
    if (temp < 0 | temp > 100) {
      JOptionPane.showMessageDialog
        (null, "Invalid Midterm Grade (" + temp + ") " +
          "Program Terminating");
      System.exit (0);
    }
    else
      midterm = temp;
  }

  public int getMidterm() {
    return midterm;
  }

  private void setFinalExamGrade(int temp) {
    if (temp < 0 | temp > 100) {
```

```
      JOptionPane.showMessageDialog
        (null, "Invalid Final Exam Grade (" + temp + ") " +
          "Program Terminating");
      System.exit (0);
    }
    else
      finalExamGrade = temp;
  }

  public int getFinalExamGrade() {
    return finalExamGrade;
  }

  public double getFinalNumericGrade() {
    return finalNumericGrade;
  }

  public String getFinalLetterGrade() {
    return finalLetterGrade;
  }

  public void calculate() {
    midterm = Integer.parseInt(JOptionPane.showInputDialog
      ("Enter the Midterm Grade"));
    finalExamGrade = Integer.parseInt(JOptionPane.showInputDialog
      ("Enter the Final Examination Grade"));
    finalNumericGrade =
      (midterm * MATH_MIDTERM_PERCENTAGE) +
      (finalExamGrade * MATH_FINALEXAM_PERCENTAGE);
    if (finalNumericGrade >= 90)
      finalLetterGrade = "A";
    else
    if ((finalNumericGrade >= 83) & (finalNumericGrade < 90))
      finalLetterGrade = "B";
    else
    if ((finalNumericGrade >= 76) & (finalNumericGrade < 83))
      finalLetterGrade = "C";
    else
    if ((finalNumericGrade >= 65) & (finalNumericGrade < 76))
      finalLetterGrade = "D";
    else
    if (finalNumericGrade < 65)
      finalLetterGrade = "F";
  }
}
```

3. Save your source file as **MathStudent.java** in the \JFiles\Grades folder (select File | Save As from Notepad's menu bar). Be sure to save your source file with the filename extension .java.

4. Compile your source file into a Bytecode file.

5. You won't be testing your MathStudent class until we have completed the work on the other classes in the project.

Discussion

Again, there were no major problems completing the exercise—the changes we made to the MathStudent class were nearly identical to those we made in the EnglishStudent class. Rhonda did attempt to create properties for the presentation and research Instance variables that the Math student does not possess, but she quickly realized her mistake. We then moved onto updating the ScienceStudent class.

Exercise 8-3 Modify the ScienceStudent Class

In this exercise, you'll modify the ScienceStudent class you created last week.

1. Using Notepad (if you are using Windows), locate and open the ScienceStudent.java source file you worked on last week. (It should be in the \JFiles\Grades folder.)

2. Modify your code so that it looks like this:

```java
import javax.swing.JOptionPane;
class ScienceStudent {
  private final double SCIENCE_MIDTERM_PERCENTAGE = .40;
  private final double SCIENCE_FINALEXAM_PERCENTAGE = .40;
  private final double SCIENCE_RESEARCH_PERCENTAGE = .20;
  private int midterm = 0;
  private int finalExamGrade = 0;
  private int research = 0;
  private double finalNumericGrade = 0;
  private String finalLetterGrade = "";

  public ScienceStudent() {
    System.out.println ("ScienceStudent's Constructor");
  }
  private void setMidterm(int temp) {
    if (temp<0 | temp > 100) {
      JOptionPane.showMessageDialog
        (null, "Invalid Midterm Grade (" + temp + ") " +
          "Program Terminating");
      System.exit (0);
    }
    else
      midterm = temp;
  }
  public int getMidterm() {
    return midterm;
  }
  private void setFinalExamGrade(int temp) {
    if (temp<0 | temp > 100) {
      JOptionPane.showMessageDialog
        (null, "Invalid Final Exam Grade (" + temp + ") " +
          "Program Terminating");
      System.exit (0);
    }
    else
      finalExamGrade = temp;
  }
  public int getFinalExamGrade() {
    return finalExamGrade;
  }
  private void setResearch(int temp) {
    if (temp<0 | temp > 100) {
      JOptionPane.showMessageDialog
        (null, "Invalid Research Grade (" + temp + ") " +
      "Program Terminating");
      System.exit (0);
    }
    else
      research = temp;
  }
```

```
  public int getResearch() {
    return research;
  }

  public double getFinalNumericGrade() {
    return finalNumericGrade;
  }

  public String getFinalLetterGrade() {
    return finalLetterGrade;
  }

  public void calculate() {
    midterm = Integer.parseInt(JOptionPane.showInputDialog
      ("Enter the Midterm Grade"));
    finalExamGrade = Integer.parseInt(JOptionPane.showInputDialog
      ("Enter the Final Examination Grade"));
    research = Integer.parseInt(JOptionPane.showInputDialog
      ("Enter the Research Grade"));
    finalNumericGrade =
      (midterm * SCIENCE_MIDTERM_PERCENTAGE) +
      (finalExamGrade * SCIENCE_FINALEXAM_PERCENTAGE) +
      (research * SCIENCE_RESEARCH_PERCENTAGE);
    if (finalNumericGrade >= 90)
      finalLetterGrade = "A";
    else
    if ((finalNumericGrade >= 80) & (finalNumericGrade < 90))
      finalLetterGrade = "B";
    else
    if ((finalNumericGrade >= 70) & (finalNumericGrade < 80))
      finalLetterGrade = "C";
    else
    if ((finalNumericGrade >= 60) & (finalNumericGrade < 70))
      finalLetterGrade = "D";
    else
    if (finalNumericGrade < 60)
      finalLetterGrade = "F";
  }
}
```

3. Save your source file as **ScienceStudent.java** in the \JFiles\Grades folder (select File | Save As from Notepad's menu bar). Be sure to save your source file with the filename extension .java.

4. Compile your source file into a Bytecode file.

5. You won't be testing your Science class until we have completed the work on the Grades class.

Discussion

No one had any problems at all making the changes to the ScienceStudent class. Almost immediately, Linda had a question.

"I know you told us that we would need to make changes to the Grades class in order to see the impact of the changes we just made," she said. "But for the heck of it, I just ran the Grades class, and everything worked fine. Why is that? The Grades class directly references the now private Instance variables of the various student classes, yet it seems that Java is permitting the Grades class full access."

"I did the same thing," Ward said, "but then I compiled the Grades class and received a bunch of compiler messages indicating I was trying to refer to a private Instance variable. What's going on?"

"Until we recompile the Grades class," I said, "when we run the Grades program, we still have full access to the now private Instance variables of the various student classes. When we attempt to recompile the Grades class, that's when the Java compiler checks to ensure that the Grades class can access the Instance variables of the student classes."

"That's right," Dave said, "you mentioned that earlier when we were working with Example8_4. Didn't you say that if we execute the program with the Java –verify command line option we force Java to make this check at runtime?"

"Exactly right, Dave," I said. "The –verify option will cause Java to verify the Access Specifers of referenced Instance variables at runtime."

I noticed several students nodding their heads in recognition of this concept.

"What kinds of changes will we need to make to the Grades class?" Mary asked.

"All we really need to do," I said, "is to find any code that directly references an Instance variable of the student classes and modify the code to use an Accessor or Mutator method instead."

I then distributed this exercise for the class to complete.

Exercise 8-4 Modify the Grades Class to Reference Properties Instead of Instance Variables

In this exercise, you'll modify the Grades class you created last week

1. Using Notepad (if you are using Windows), locate and open the Grades.java source file you worked on last week. (It should be in the \JFiles\Grades folder.)
2. Modify your code so that it looks like this.

```java
import javax.swing.JOptionPane;

class Grades {
  public static void main(String[] args) {
    String moreGradesToCalculate;
    String response;
    moreGradesToCalculate=JOptionPane.showInputDialog
      ("Do you want to calculate a grade?");
    moreGradesToCalculate=moreGradesToCalculate.toUpperCase();
    while (moreGradesToCalculate.equals ("YES")) {
      response=whatKindOfStudent();
      switch(Integer.parseInt(response)) {
      case 1:
        EnglishStudent eStudent=new EnglishStudent();
        eStudent.calculate();
        DisplayGrade x=new DisplayGrade (eStudent.getMidterm(),
            eStudent.getFinalExamGrade(),
            eStudent.getResearch(),
            eStudent.getPresentation(),
            eStudent.getFinalNumericGrade(),
            eStudent.getFinalLetterGrade());
        break;
      case 2:
        MathStudent mStudent=new MathStudent();
        mStudent.calculate();
        DisplayGrade y=new DisplayGrade (mStudent.getMidterm(),
            mStudent.getFinalExamGrade(),
            mStudent.getFinalNumericGrade(),
            mStudent.getFinalLetterGrade());
        break;
      case 3:
        ScienceStudent sStudent=new ScienceStudent();
        sStudent.calculate();
        DisplayGrade z=new DisplayGrade (sStudent.getMidterm(),
            sStudent.getFinalExamGrade(),
            sStudent.getResearch(),
            sStudent.getFinalNumericGrade(),
            sStudent.getFinalLetterGrade());
        break;
      default:
```

```
        JOptionPane.showMessageDialog
          (null, response + " - is not a valid student type");
        System.exit (0);
      }                                            // end of switch
      moreGradesToCalculate=JOptionPane.showInputDialog
        ("Do you have another grade to calculate?");
      moreGradesToCalculate=moreGradesToCalculate.toUpperCase();
    }                                            // end of while
    JOptionPane.showMessageDialog
      (null, "Thanks for using the Grades Calculation program!");
    System.exit (0);
  }                                              // end of main method
  public static String whatKindOfStudent() {
    String response;
    response=JOptionPane.showInputDialog
      ("Enter student type (1=English, 2=Math, 3=Science)");
    if (response==null) {
      JOptionPane.showMessageDialog
      (null, "You clicked on the Cancel button");
      System.exit (0);
    }
    else
    if (response.equals("")) {
      JOptionPane.showMessageDialog
        (null, "You must make an entry in the InputBox");
      System.exit (0);
    }
    else
    if (Integer.parseInt(response)<1 | Integer.parseInt(response) > 3) {
      JOptionPane.showMessageDialog
        (null, response + " - is not a valid student type");
      System.exit (0);
    }
    return response;
  }                                              // end of whatKindOfStudent method
}                                                // end of class
```

3. Save your source file as ScicenceStudent.java in the \JFiles\Grades folder (select File | Save As from Notepad's menu bar). Be sure to save your source file with the file name extension java.

4. Compile your source file into a Bytecode file.

5. Execute the Grades class and test it thoroughly. After you start up your program, it should ask you if you have a grade to calculate.

6. Enter **Yes**, and calculate the grade for an English student. Enter **70** for the midterm, **80** for the final examination, **90** for the research grade, and **100** for the presentation. A final numeric grade of **84.5** should be displayed, with a letter grade of **C**.

7. After the message box is displayed with the calculated grade, the program should ask you if you have more grades to calculate.

8. Enter **Yes**, and then calculate the grade for a math student. Enter **70** for the midterm and **80** for the final examination. A final numeric grade of **75** should be displayed with a letter grade of **D**.

9. After the message box is displayed with the calculated grade, the program should ask you if you have more grades to calculate.

10. Enter **Yes**, and then calculate the grade for a science student. Enter **70** for the midterm, **80** for the final examination, and **90** for the research grade. A final numeric grade of **78** should be displayed, with a letter grade of **C**. After the message box is displayed with the calculated grade, the program should ask you if you have more grades to calculate.

11. Enter **No**. You should be thanked for using the program, and the program should end.

Discussion

I gave everyone in the class a chance to make their changes to the Grades class and to experiment with their own versions of the Grades program. "Did everyone notice the changes we made to the program?" I asked.

"I did," Blaine said. "We modified the sections of code that created instances of the DisplayGrade student. Previously, we directly referenced Instance variables of each of the student classes in the Constructor method of the DisplayGrade class. Now we're executing the various Accessor methods of the student classes instead."

"Excellent, Blaine," I said. "Here's the modified code that is executed to display the grade for an English student:"

```
DisplayGrade x = new DisplayGrade (eStudent.getMidterm(),
    eStudent.getFinalExamGrade(),
    eStudent.getResearch(),
    eStudent.getPresentation(),
    eStudent.getFinalNumericGrade(),
    eStudent.getFinalLetterGrade());
```

"In a similar way," I continued, "we execute the Accessor methods for the math and science students as well."

I waited to see if anyone had any questions, but there were none.

A surprise visit from Frank Olley

Just then, I heard a voice call from outside my classroom door. Unknown to the students in the class, Frank Olley had been outside and had just witnessed the execution of the Grade Calculation Project from the hallway. I had phoned Frank during the break to confirm some aspects of the validation of the component grades (I wanted to be sure that valid grades ranged from 0 to 100), and when I found out he was on campus, I invited him down for a demo.

"I've got to tell you," Frank said, "I'm most impressed with the progress you've made with the program in such a short time. In fact, I love it so much, I'd like you to install it on my PC today— but John tells me you still have some work to do on it."

I could see that the students in the class were just about to burst with pride.

Frank then spent some time admiring the work of the individual students. About ten minutes later, I dismissed class for the day.

Summary

This chapter dealt with a topic that is extremely important in the world of Java: protecting the data in your objects from accidental or willful manipulation that can cause the state of your objects to become invalid.

We learned that the primary way to protect your data is to declare your Instance variables with a private Access Specifer, which allows only code within the class itself to view or update the variable. Having done that, if you wish client programs (those creating instances of your object) to be able to see or update these Instance variables, you need to write Accessor and Mutator methods.

Accessor methods enable a client program to see the values of your Instance variables. Mutator methods enable a client program to update the values of your Instance variables.

Chapter 9---Inheritance and Interfaces

In the last two chapters, we've learned how to create Instantiable classes that permit client programs (other classes) to create objects from them. In that regard, we've seen that a Java programmer does more than just write code, a Java programmer is also a class architect, designing classes that can be used by other programmers. This is an illustration of the software reusability of Java—one class and the object it represents can be used in thousands of other programs.

In this chapter, we'll take software reusability one step further by learning how a Java programmer can design a class which can then be used as the basis for other new classes, once again illustrating how an object-oriented programming language can help avoid reinventing the wheel. This feature of object-oriented programming languages is called inheritance, and it can be an enormous time saver when creating classes in the programs we write.

Inheritance

"Today's topic is inheritance," I said, as I began our ninth class. "In object-oriented programming languages, inheritance means that a new class can be coded or derived based on an already existing class. The new class is called a subclass, and the already existing class is called a Superclass. Deriving one class from an already existing class can be an enormous time saver for programmers, especially if the Superclass already has features such as instance variables and methods that the subclass can use."

"Sounds complicated," Rhonda said.

"Inheritance isn't unique to object-oriented programming," I said. "I have a friend who is a structural engineer who designs bathroom shower doors. I didn't know this until it came up in conversation, but there are many different styles and types of bathroom shower doors and, as in the fashion industry, each year hundreds of new styles are introduced. My friend is constantly designing new shower doors and, much to my surprise, I learned recently that structural engineers use something similar to class inheritance in their own work."

"How does an engineer implement the type of inheritance that you're talking about with Java?" Barbara asked. "Does an engineer work with classes?"

"Not quite," I said, "but an engineer does work with blueprints. Blueprints, as I think I mentioned in our first class meeting, are to an architect or an engineer what classes are to a Java programmer. A blueprint is the model for something that is built, just like a class is a blueprint for an object. Ultimately, both blueprints and classes are nothing more than designs. My friend the structural engineer turns her completed blueprints over to a manufacturing facility that produces the actual shower doors. As Java programmers, we turn our classes over to other programmers who then create objects from them."

"I'm OK with your analogy about blueprints and classes," Kate said, "but where does this notion of inheritance come into play with your friend the structural engineer?"

"I'm getting to that," I said, smiling. "Just last week I was talking to my friend the engineer, and I commented how frustrating it must be to have to design a shower door from scratch every year to produce a new door with a different style or with slightly different features. That's when she told me that she doesn't design every shower door from scratch. The blueprints for her previous years' designs are stored on the hard drive of her personal computer, and she can derive the design for a new shower door based on a previous model."

"In other words," Dave said, "she's not reinventing the wheel."

"That's right, Dave," I said. "The basic features of last year's door very likely will be identical to the basic features of this year's door, with some stylistic differences. Perhaps it may be the color of the chrome on the door that is different or the style of the glass or even the location of the door handles. However, the shape and thickness of the supporting steel structure may be identical, the dimensions of the door, as well as the size and location of the class may be identical—my point is that there are a lot more similarities than there are differences."

"I see where you're coming from," Steve said. "By starting her design of a new shower door with the blueprints from a previous one, she saves herself a whole bunch of work. But I don't quite see how this will work in Java. Are you saying that if one class is similar to another, we can copy and paste the code from that first class into Notepad as a starting point for the new class?"

"That's not quite it, Steve," I said, "although we could certainly do that—copy and paste, I mean. But copying and pasting doesn't quite give us the software reusability that I'm talking about. Instead of copying and pasting code from one class to another, we can tell Java that the class we're coding is derived from another class—that is, the new class should be considered to have variables and methods found in another class—without having to explicitly code those variables and methods in the class itself. We can then add attributes and methods to the subclass to provide it with its own unique features."

"So are you saying," Valerie asked, "that if an existing class already has most of the functionality you need in your new class, you can derive or 'inherit' variables and methods from that existing class and then add some functionality of its own to it?"

"That's exactly right, Valerie," I said. "Technically, the existing class is called the Superclass, and the derived class is called the subclass. Think of the Superclass as a parent to the child subclass. At the risk of oversimplifying this, all that's really required is that the subclass use the keyword Extends followed by the name of the Superclass to derive the functionality (variables and methods) from the Superclass. But you'll see that in just a few minutes."

"From the way you're describing it," Dave said, "I bet that inheritance would have made the work of creating the three Student classes in the Grades Calculation Project a little easier."

"How so?" Rhonda said, directing her attention to Dave.

"Well," Dave said, "if you think about it, all three Student classes—EnglishStudent, MathStudent, and ScienceStudent—have a lot in common. In fact, some of their code is even duplicated. I would think that being able to derive one class from another would have come in very handy there, wouldn't it have?"

"Dave's absolutely right about the Student classes," I said. "In fact, we'll be modifying these classes later on in today's class to incorporate the concepts of inheritance that we'll learn today."

"I wish we had learned about inheritance last week," Chuck said. "Coding those classes has been a real pain in the neck for me. Why did we wait until now to discuss inheritance?"

"We first needed to learn how to create classes and protect their data before we could start to learn about inheritance," I said.

"Inheritance sounds like something I can really use back at work," Ward said. "It seems I'm forever reinventing the wheel there. Personally, I can't wait to get started. Can you show us an example of inheritance in Java?"

Before Inheritance Came Along...

"Sure thing, Ward," I said. "Let me demonstrate inheritance by first creating an ordinary Java class and then deriving other classes from it."

I thought for a moment before continuing. "Let's pretend that after completing this Introductory Java course, you're hired by a small consulting firm as a Java programmer. In your first week on the job, you are asked to write what appears to be a simple program to calculate the payroll for a relatively large plumbing company in the area. Having learned about the benefits of the Systems Development Life Cycle in this class, you then spend a fair amount of time working with the client in determining the requirements for the payroll system. Sometime in the Analysis phase of the SDLC, it becomes obvious to you that you should create a Java class called Employee to model the company's employees. You decide that the Employee class will have the following attributes, implemented as instance variables:"

- empID
- name
- hourlyRate
- hoursWorked
- grossPay

"You also decide to implement a **display()** method to output the employee's gross pay to the Java Console (to keep things simple for our demonstration, that's all we'll calculate). Within the **display()** method, you include a calculation of grossPay equal to the multiplication of *hourlyRate* by **hoursWorked**."

"Sounds simple enough," Rhonda said, smiling. "I bet I could code that up in no time." I was tempted to take Rhonda up on her offer, but since I had already coded up the Employee class myself, I displayed the code for the Employee class on the classroom projector:

```java
import javax.swing.JOptionPane;

class Employee {
  private String empID;
  private String name;
  private double hourlyRate;
  private int hoursWorked;
  private double grossPay;

  public Employee()  {                    // Constructor Method
    System.out.println("Employee's Constructor");
  }

  public void setEmpID(String temp) {
    empID = temp;
  }

  public String getEmpID() {
    return empID;
  }

  public void setName(String temp) {
    name = temp;
  }

  public String getName()  {
    return name;
  }

  public void setHourlyRate(double temp) {
    hourlyRate = temp;
  }

  public double getHourlyRate() {
    return hourlyRate;
  }

  public void setHoursWorked(int temp)  {
    hoursWorked = temp;
  }

  public int getHoursWorked() {
    return hoursWorked;
  }

  public double getGrossPay() {
    grossPay = hourlyRate * hoursWorked;
    return grossPay;
  }

  public void display() {
    JOptionPane.showMessageDialog
      (null,"*** EMPLOYEE RECORD ***\n\n" +
      "Employee ID: " + empID + "\n" +
      "Name: " + name + "\n" +
      "Hourly Rate: $ " + hourlyRate + "\n" +
      "Hours Worked: " + hoursWorked + "\n" +
      "Gross Pay: $ " + getGrossPay());
  }
}
```

"I don't think there's anything in this Employee class that we haven't seen before," I said. "We have the five attributes of the Employee class, each implemented as private instance variables. Also, based on what we learned last week, we've created Accessor and Mutator methods for four of the attributes—empID, name, hourlyRate, and hoursWorked. We don't want any client programs using our object to be able to directly update the grossPay attribute, so we have created an Accessor method **getGrossPay()** but no Mutator method. Notice that the **getGrossPay()** method does the work of calculating the employee's gross pay. Finally, we also have the public **void()** method, which outputs the Employee's information to the Java Console. To keep things simple, we have no validation in this class—obviously, in something other than a demo like this, we would have plenty of that."

"I noticed that we created a Constructor method," Kate said. "Is that really necessary here? Isn't this class going to be used as a Superclass for other classes? Is a Constructor required?"

"Good question, Kate," I said. "A Constructor isn't required, but I thought it would be a good idea to code one here. We'll be able to see when the Constructor of the Superclass is executed. I think you'll find that pretty fascinating when you see it in action."

"I'm a little confused with a line of code in the **display()** method," Rhonda said. "What's going on with that line of code to display the gross pay?"

"This can be a little confusing," I said. "Here we're using the return value of the Access method **getGrossPay()** as an argument to the **showMessageDialog()** method of the JOptionPane object."

```
"Gross Pay: $ " + getGrossPay());
```

"OK," Rhonda answered. "I think I do remember you doing that before."

I waited to see if there were any more questions before continuing. There were none.

"Remember," I said, "all we've done so far is create a simple class—we haven't done any inheritance yet. Now let's write code in a client program that will create an instance of an Employee object and calculate the gross pay for that employee." I then displayed this code on the classroom projector:

```
public class Example9_1 {
  public static void main(String[] args) {
    Employee x = new Employee();
    x.setEmpID("086");
    x.setName("John Smith");
    x.setHourlyRate(12.50);
    x.setHoursWorked(40);
    x.display();
    System.exit(0);
  }
}
```

"Nothing too fancy here," I said. "All we're doing is creating an instance of an Employee object:"

```
Employee x = new Employee();
```

"We then use its Mutator methods to assign values to its attributes (instance variables). Notice that we indicate that the hourly rate for this employee is $12.50 per hour and that his total number of hours worked is 40:"

```
x.setEmpID("086");
x.setName("John Smith");
x.setHourlyRate(12.50);
x.setHoursWorked(40);
```

"We then execute its **display()** method:"

```
x.display();
```

I then compiled both the Student class and Example9_1 class and executed Example9_1. The following screenshot was displayed on the classroom projector:

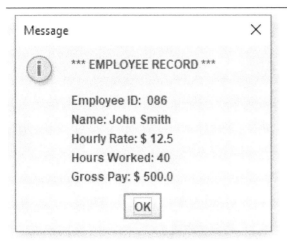

"Nothing surprising here," I said. "We created an instance of the Employee object, updated the empID, name, hourlyRate, and hoursWorked attributes via the Mutator methods of the class, then executed the **display()** method of the class to display this window, complete with the calculated gross pay of $500. Take note that a message was also displayed in the Java Console window to let us know that the Constructor method of the Employee class was executed."

"How did the grossPay attribute of the Employee class get updated?" Rhonda asked.

"That was done as part of the **display()** method," I said. "The **display()** method concatenated the return value of the **getGrossPay()** Accessor method of the Employee class to the string "Gross Pay:":"

```
"Gross Pay: $ " + getGrossPay());
```

"It was in the **getGrossPay()** Access method where the grossPay attribute was updated when the actual calculation was performed:"

```
public double getGrossPay() {
  grossPay = hourlyRate * hoursWorked;
  return grossPay;
}
```

"OK, that makes sense," Rhonda said.

"I understand what we just did," Chuck said, "but how does this relate to inheritance?"

Creating Classes from Other Classes Using Inheritance

"It doesn't, yet," I said. "That will be our next step. Before I show you how to implement inheritance in your program, I need to clue you in a little bit about real-world programming, but I don't think you'll be at all surprised about what I have to tell you. In the real world of Java programming, there are two ways that inheritance comes into play. First, you meticulously plan it. That is, right from the start you design a class, known as a Superclass, possessing some basic functionality—attributes and methods—from which you will derive other classes. For a number of reasons, this structured approach to building Superclasses and subclasses, like the structured approach of the Systems Development Life Cycle, is ideal."

"I can see why this structured approach is the way to go," Kate said. "An organized approach is always best. But what's the other way in which inheritance comes about? You said there were two."

"The second approach is what I call the evolutionary approach to inheritance," I replied. "What happens is that one day you have the need to create a class to model a real-world object, and you realize that you already have a class that is very close to what you need, but it's not quite right. I should tell you that real-world Java classes may have hundreds of attributes and methods— so you see, the last thing you want to do is to start from scratch by creating a new class."

"So, in this case," Steve said, "you would borrow the functionality of the existing class by deriving the new class from it?"

"Exactly, Steve," I said. "If you or another programmer already have a class that is close enough in functionality to the class you need to create, you can save yourself a bunch of work by deriving the new class from it. This process isn't nearly as efficient as planning a Superclass and later deriving classes from it, but in the real world that's not always possible."

"I'm not sure I'm fully understanding this." Blaine said.

"Let's try it this way, Blaine," I said. "Suppose that two months after we create the Employee class we just coded, the plumbing company asks us to modify the program to calculate payroll for biweekly salaried employees as well as hourly ones."

"I sense a problem here," Ward said. "The calculation for an hourly employee is nothing like that of a salaried employee."

"That's right, Ward," I agreed. "Salaried employees draw a straight salary, regardless of the number of hours they work. The hoursWorked and hourlyRate attributes of the Employee class have no meaning for a Salaried employee."

"Will we be able to use the Employee class for the salaried employee calculation?" Rhonda asked. "Or will we need to create a Salaried class to do the job?"

"Without inheritance, Rhonda," I said, "that's exactly what we would need to do: create a new class entirely from scratch. But using inheritance, we can borrow the functionality of the Employee class. It's not a perfect fit—remember, the existing Employee class contains two attributes, hourlyRate and hoursWorked, that don't make any sense for a salaried employee. However, the remaining three attributes, empID, name, and grossPay are fine for the salaried employee."

"We will also need to add a new attribute to the Subclass to represent the salaried employee's annual salary," Dave said. "The calculation of the gross pay for a salaried employee is different from that of an hourly employee, which means that the getGrossPay Mutator method of the subclass will have to be different. Since he or she is paid every other week, the salaried employee's pay will be equal to the annual salary divided by 26."

"That was an excellent analysis, Dave," I said. "It really illustrates why inheritance can be useful in our programming. The Employee class probably has 20 to 30 lines of code, and a new Salaried class would probably have a similar number of lines of code, much of it duplicating that found in the Employee class. Why bother writing that code from scratch—and therefore reinventing the wheel—if we already have a class that is very close to what we need? For that reason, we'll create a subclass called SalariedEmployee and base it on the Employee class."

"I'd like to get back to something Dave mentioned," Barbara said. "When he said that the getGrossPay method in the subclass will need to be different from the one in the Superclass. Are you saying that we can have a method in the subclass with the same name as one in the Superclass?"

"That's right, Barbara," I said. "In that regard, it's very similar to an overloaded method in which two identically named methods appear in the same class. In this case, we have identically named methods, one appearing in the Superclass, one in the subclass. The method in the subclass overloads the identically named method in the Superclass. If a client program creates an object from the subclass, the code in that method will be executed. However, if a client program uses the Superclass in its program, the code in the method of the Superclass will be executed."

The Superclass (Parent Class)

"Will the Employee class become a Superclass then?" Mary asked. "What will we need to change in the Employee class?"

"That's an excellent question, Mary," I said. "The beauty of Inheritance is that nothing needs to be done to a class in order for it to be used as a Superclass. The only thing that makes a class a Superclass is the fact that other classes—Subclasses—choose to be derived from it."

The Subclass (Child Class)

"How does Java know that a Subclass wishes to be derived from a Superclass?" Chuck asked.

"That's done using the Extends keyword," I said, "followed by the name of the class that is to be used as the Superclass. In Java, you can derive from just one Superclass, so there should be just the name of a single class following the Extends keyword. Let me show how we do this by creating the SalariedEmployee subclass now, using the Employee class as a Superclass."

I then displayed this code on the classroom projector:

```
import javax.swing.JOptionPane;

class SalariedEmployee extends Employee {
    protected double annualSalary;
    public void setAnnualSalary(double temp) {
```

```
    annualSalary = temp;
  }
  public double getAnnualSalary() {
    return annualSalary;
  }
  public double getGrossPay() {
    grossPay = annualSalary / 26;
    return grossPay;
  }
  public void display() {
    JOptionPane.showMessageDialog
      (null,"*** EMPLOYEE RECORD ***\n\n" +
      "Employee ID: " + empID + "\n" +
      "Name: " + name + "\n" +
      "Annual Salary: $ " + annualSalary + "\n" +
      "Gross Pay: $ " + getGrossPay());
  }
}
```

"Aren't we missing some attributes?" Rhonda said. "I don't see empID or name—yet we're referring to them in the **display()** method."

"That's the point, Rhonda," I said. "By deriving SalariedEmployee from the already existing Employee class, we don't need to define them here in this class. The Extends keyword tells Java to use the Employee class as the starting point for SalariedEmployee."

```
class SalariedEmployee extends Employee {
```

"Every variable and method that Employee has is automatically made a part of the SalariedEmployee subclass—in other words, the subclass derives the instance variables and methods of its Superclass. That means that, without any coding, the SalariedEmployee subclass automatically possesses the 5 instance variables of the Employee class and its 11 methods."

"So, are you saying that all we need to code in the subclass are any new instance variables and methods?" Dave asked.

"That's basically correct, Dave," I said, "but let's take it a step further. When it comes to deriving a subclass from a Superclass, there are three things your subclass can choose to do with the existing instance variables and methods of the Superclass parent:"

- **Accept** the instance variable or method as is because it fits the needs of the subclass. For example, the instance variable empID and its Accessor method getEmpID of the Superclass Employee are also necessary in the subclass SalariedEmployee. Accepting an instance variable or method requires absolutely no action on the part of the programmer—these are automatically included when you extend the Superclass.

- **Ignore** the instance variable or method derived from the Superclass because it is not required in the subclass. Ignoring the instance variable or method requires no extra effort on the part of the programmer. For example, in the subclass SalariedEmployee, we have no need for either the instance variable hourlyRate or its Accessor method getHourlyRate. We ignore it by not using it in anywhere in the subclass or client programs using the subclass.

- **Add** new instance variables or methods to the subclass. Instance variables and methods are added to give the subclass the unique behavior that differentiates it from the Superclass. In the case of SalariedEmployee, we added one new instance variable: annualSalary, which is required by the subclass since it needs an annual salary to properly calculate a biweekly gross pay for a salaried employee.

- **Override** the derived instance variables or methods in the subclass, in effect changing the definition of the instance variable or method. For instance, both the Superclass Employee and the subclass SalariedEmployee need to possess a **getGrossPay()** and **display()** method, but the code for these methods in the two classes needs to be different. To override an instance variable or method, just place the definition in the subclass, and the derived instance variable or method of the Superclass will be overridden.

"So, in short," Kate said, "we can accept, ignore, add or override instance variables or methods derived from the Superclass."

"That's perfect, Kate," I said. "Here's a table detailing the actions we took with the instance variables and methods of the Employee Superclass in the derived SalariedEmployee subclass."

Employee Superclass	SalariedEmployee Subclass Action
empID	Accepted
name	Accepted
hourlyRate	Ignored
hoursWorked	Ignored
	annualSalary added to Subclass
Employee()	Accepted
setEmpID()	Accepted
getEmpID()	Accepted
setName()	Accepted
getName()	Accepted
setHourlyRate()	Ignored
getHourlyRate()	Ignored
setHoursWorked()	Ignored
getHoursWorked()	Ignored
getGrossPay()	Overridden
display()	Overridden
	setAnnualSalary() added to subclass
	getAnnualSalary() added to subclass

"As you can see," I said, "in the subclass SalariedEmployee, we accepted two instance variables (empID and name) and five methods (Employee, setEmpID, getEmpID, setName, getName) of the Superclass Employee. We ignored two instance variables (hourlyRate and hoursWorked) and four methods (setHourlyRate, getHourlyRate, setHoursWorked, getHoursWorked) of the Superclass Employee—all of these pertained to an hourly employee, and we had no need for these in our subclass. It's important to note that even though we are ignoring these instance variables and methods in our subclass, they're still part of the subclass and a client program could still use them. Finally, we overrode two methods—**getGrossPay()** and **display()**—by writing new code, unique to the subclass SalariedEmployee."

"I see we also added one instance variable (annualSalary) and two Methods (**setAnnualSalary()** and **getAnnualSalary()**) to the subclass that don't exist in the Superclass," Mary said.

"That's right, Mary," I answered. "annualSalary is an instance variable we need to store the employee's annual salary, and **setAnnualSalary()** and **getAnnualSalary()** are its Mutator and Accessor methods. We also use annualSalary in the **getGrossPay()** and **display()** methods we overrode."

"Do we compile a subclass the same way we compile any other class?" Blaine asked after a few seconds of silence.

"That's right, Blaine," I said. "We compile a subclass the same way we compile any other class, by using the java compiler. Of course, the Superclass must have been compiled first, otherwise the Java compiler won't be able to extend it into the subclass."

I then compiled the SalariedEmployee subclass, but with less than satisfactory results. The following screenshot was displayed:

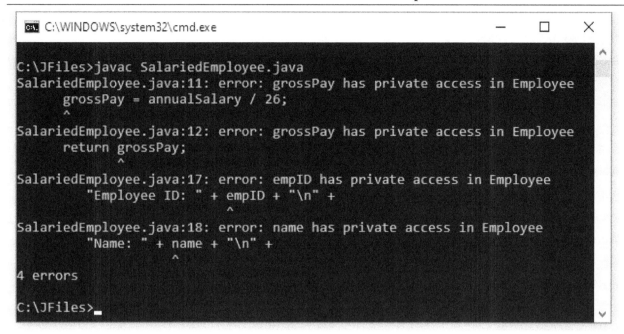

NOTE: Depending upon the version of the Java compiler you are running, you might see a more explicit message about trying to access a private access variable in a Superclass

"Uh-oh," I heard Rhonda say. "What happened? The SalariedEmployee subclass didn't compile. Did we forget to compile the Employee class?"

"No, that's not the problem. We did that a few minutes ago," I said. I had to take a close look at the error messages for a few moments before I realized the problem myself.

"Oh, I see what happened," I said. "The problem is that we defined the instance variables in the Employee class with Private access."

"Last week we learned that only code in the same class can access instance variables defined with the Private Access Specifer," Blaine said. "So that's the problem?"

"That's right, Blaine," I said. "We can't derive private instance variables from a Superclass."

"Does this mean we can't create a subclass from a Superclass unless the instance variables are declared as public?" Barbara asked. "From what we learned last week, won't that impact the data integrity of the Employee class? How would the designer of the Superclass feel about that?"

"You're right, Barbara," I agreed. "Changing the instance variables from private to public would fix this problem, but it's something that the original designer would not be in favor of us doing just so we can derive a subclass from it. Fortunately, we don't need to do that to fix this problem. Does anyone remember last week that when I was discussing Access Specifers, I mentioned in addition to the Private, Public, and Package Access Specifers, there's a fourth Access Specifer, one that I told you wouldn't mean much to us until we learned about inheritance?"

"I do," Dave quickly volunteered. "I think it's the Protected Access Specifer, isn't it?"

"Dave's absolutely right," I said. "Protected access comes into play only when we are dealing with a class used as a Superclass. Protected access is just like Private access—except that instance variables and methods defined with Protected access can be derived and used in a subclass with no problem."

"So all we need to do is go back and change the Access Specifers in the Employee Superclass from Private to Protected, and our SalariedEmployee subclass will compile OK?" Peter asked.

"Absolutely," I said. I then made these changes to the Employee class, changing every Private instance variable in Employee from Private to Protected, and displayed the modified code on the classroom projector:

```
import javax.swing.JOptionPane;

class Employee {
  protected String empID;
  protected String name;
  protected double hourlyRate;
```

```java
  protected int hoursWorked;
  protected double grossPay;

  public Employee() {                          // Constructor Method
    System.out.println("Employee's Constructor");
  }

  public void setEmpID(String temp) {
   empID = temp;
  }

  public String getEmpID() {
    return empID;
  }

  public void setName(String temp) {
    name = temp;
  }

  public String getName() {
    return name;
  }

  public void setHourlyRate(double temp) {
    hourlyRate = temp;
  }

  public double gethourlyRate() {
    return hourlyRate;
  }

  public void setHoursWorked(int temp) {
    hoursWorked = temp;
  }

  public int getHoursWorked() {
    return hoursWorked;
  }

  public double getGrossPay() {
    grossPay = hourlyRate * hoursWorked;
    return grossPay;
  }

  public void display() {
    JOptionPane.showMessageDialog
      (null,"*** EMPLOYEE RECORD ***\n\n" +
      "Employee ID: " + empID + "\n" +
      "Name: " + name + "\n" +
      "Hourly Rate: $ " + hourlyRate + "\n" +
      "Hours Worked: " + hoursWorked + "\n" +
      "Gross Pay: $ " + getGrossPay());
  }
}
```

I then recompiled the Employee class, followed by the SalariedEmployee class. This time SalariedEmployee compiled with no errors.

"That's better," I said. "Now that we have changed the instance variables in the Employee class from Private to Protected access, the subclass SalariedEmployee can derive those instance variables with no problem. Now let's write some code to use the SalariedEmployee subclass in a client program."

I then displayed this code on the classroom projector:

```java
public class Example9_2 {
  public static void main(String[] args) {
```

```
    SalariedEmployee x = new SalariedEmployee();
    x.setEmpID("337");
    x.setName("Mary Jones");
    x.setAnnualSalary(52000);
    x.display();
    System.exit(0);
  }
}
```

I then compiled Example9_2 and executed it. The following screenshot was displayed on the classroom projector:

"I'm still not quite sure what's going on here," Rhonda said. "Can you explain it to us?"

"Sure thing, Rhonda," I said. "What we've done is create an instance of a SalariedEmployee object using the SalariedEmployee subclass:"

```
SalariedEmployee x = new SalariedEmployee();
```

"We then executed the setEmpID and setName Mutator methods of the empID and name instance variables:"

```
x.setEmpID("337");
x.setName("Mary Jones");
```

"Take note that both of those methods don't explicitly appear in the SalariedEmployee subclass but are actually methods of the Employee Superclass. We never defined them ourselves in the SalariedEmployee subclass."

"I just realized that myself," Chuck said. "I don't think I really understood this whole concept of inheritance until just now, but now I see exactly how much time and effort deriving one class from another class can save us."

"Exactly, Chuck," I said, waiting for more questions and comments. "Now, with this line of code, we execute one of the two 'new' methods in the SalariedEmployee class, setAnnualSalary:"

```
x.setAnnualSalary(52000);
```

"This is followed by the execution of the overridden **display()** method:"

```
x.display();
```

"So this code is executing the **display()** method of the subclass SalariedEmployee, not the **display()** method of the Superclass Employee?" Linda asked.

"That's right, Linda," I said, "because we created an instance of the SalariedEmployee class, it's the **display()** method of SalariedEmployee that we're executing here."

"Very impressive," Ward said. "I can see a lot of practical applications for inheritance back at my job. I think this can save me a lot of work."

"I have a question," Dave said. "I just ran this code myself, and I noticed a message in the Java Console indicating that the Constructor method of the Superclass Employee had been run. I know we didn't code a Constructor method for the SalariedEmployee subclass, so I'm presuming that without a Constructor method in the subclass, the Constructor method for the Superclass executes. Is that correct?"

"Good observation, Dave," I said. "And you're right, the Constructor method for the Employee Superclass was executed when an instance of the SalariedEmployee subclass was created. A subclass automatically inherits the Constructor method of its Superclass."

"Suppose we code a Constructor method in the subclass?" Kathy asked. "What happens then? Do they both execute?"

"Let's see," I said.

I then modified the code for the SalariedEmployee subclass by adding a Constructor method of its own. In other words, now both the Employee Superclass and the subclass SalariedEmployee had Constructor methods of their own:

```java
import javax.swing.JOptionPane;
class SalariedEmployee extends Employee {
  protected double annualSalary;
  public SalariedEmployee() {            // Constructor Method
    System.out.println("SalariedEmployee's Constructor");
  }

  public void setAnnualSalary(double temp) {
    annualSalary = temp;
  }

  public double getAnnualSalary() {
    return annualSalary;
  }

  public double getGrossPay() {
    grossPay = annualSalary / 26;
    return grossPay;
  }

  public void display() {
    JOptionPane.showMessageDialog
      (null,"*** EMPLOYEE RECORD ***\n\n" +
      "Employee ID: " + empID + "\n" +
      "Name: " + name + "\n" +
      "Annual Salary: $ " + annualSalary + "\n" +
      "Gross Pay: $ " + getGrossPay());
  }
}
```

"Any guesses as to what will happen when I re-execute Example9_2?" I asked, after recompiling the SalariedEmployee class. "How many Constructor methods will execute? And which ones?" My students seemed evenly divided—half of the class felt that both Constructors would execute. The other half felt that only the Constructor for SalariedEmployee would execute. I then re-executed Example9_2. The following was displayed on the classroom projector.

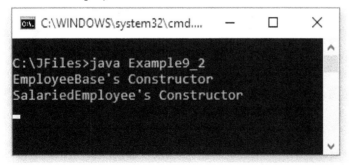

"There's our answer," I said. "Both Constructors were executed. With the Superclass and the subclass each having its own Constructor methods, both Constructors were executed. This is something to bear in mind when you derive a subclass from a Superclass—you need to be aware that any code contained within the Constructor method of the Superclass will be executed, and it will be executed prior to code in the Constructor method of the subclass being executed. In general, since Constructor methods are used to perform initialization of instance variables, you'll find that Superclass Constructor methods are performing initialization of the instance variables of the Superclass. If you code a Constructor method for your subclass, you should use it to perform initialization of the instance variables unique to the

Planning Your Object Hierarchy in Advance

I paused for a few moments before continuing.

"Not all Superclasses and subclasses are built using the scenario we've just seen here," I said.

"What do you mean?" Kate asked. "Is this what you were getting at earlier when you were talking about the structured approach versus the evolutionary approach?"

"Exactly, Kate," I said. "In the case of the Employee and SalariedEmployee classes, we started out with a class, Employee, that was originally intended to stand on its own. At the time we designed the Employee class, we didn't envision that any classes would be derived from it— although as we saw, when it became evident a little later that we would need a class very similar to the Employee class, it made sense to derive the SalariedEmployee class from it."

"It doesn't always happen this way?" Bob asked.

"Not always," I said. "Using a structured approach, we can design a class hierarchy right from the very start."

"I'm not sure I understand what you mean by a class hierarchy." Kate said.

"A class hierarchy is a planned collection of classes," I said, "with some of them designed to be Superclasses, and some of them designed to be subclasses. The key point here is that there is a plan to the creation of the classes. Usually all of them are created roughly at the same time, early in the process of the design of the program for which they are being written. As an example, it's likely that an experienced Java programmer, when interviewing the clients at the plumbing company, would have anticipated that sometime in the future, the need would arise for their program to calculate the gross pay for a salaried employee as well as the gross pay for an hourly employee. Having recognized this need ahead of time, he or she most likely would have designed an Employee Superclass. A Superclass is a class designed in advance to have subclasses derived from it. Let me illustrate what I mean by a Superclass by showing you how different our scenario would have been if, instead of creating an Employee class designed to calculate the gross pay for an hourly employee, we coded a Superclass called EmployeeBase and then derived two subclasses—HourlyEmployee and SalariedEmployee from it."

I then displayed this code for the EmployeeSuperclass on the classroom projector:

```java
import javax.swing.JOptionPane;
abstract class EmployeeBase {
  protected String empID;
  protected String name;
  protected double grossPay;

  public EmployeeBase() {                    // Constructor Method
    System.out.println("EmployeeBase's Constructor");
  }
  public void setEmpID(String temp) {
    empID = temp;
  }
  public String getEmpID() {
    return empID;
  }
  public void setName(String temp) {
    name = temp;
  }
  public String getName() {
    return name;
  }
  public abstract double getGrossPay();

  public abstract void display();
```

}

I compiled the class with no problem

Abstract Methods and Classes

"The Superclass EmployeeBase," I said, "implements the instance variables, empID, name, and grossPay, that are common to any type of employee, whether hourly or salaried. In addition, the corresponding Access and Mutator methods for empID and name are included."

"What's up with the **getGrossPay()** and **display()** methods?" Kate asked. "Why are they defined with the keyword Abstract?"

"That's also true for the name of the class," Steve said. "It's also prefixed with the keyword Abstract. What's going on?"

"Plus," Barbara added, "neither one of those methods have any code in them, and I notice that their curly braces are missing. I don't remember discussing the Abstract keyword before. Have we?"

"Abstract methods are nothing more than method signatures without code," I said. "Abstract methods are characteristic of Superclasses, particularly those at a high level in the class hierarchy such as this."

"What's the purpose of an Abstract method?" Kate asked. "Why would the designer of a Superclass use one?"

"The designer of the class," I continued, "may decide that it makes perfect sense to include a **display()** method in the EmployeeBase Superclass but isn't exactly sure how subclasses inheriting from the Superclass will choose to implement the details of the **display()** method. As we saw with our previous example of hourly and salaried employees, the display for each type is slightly different."

"Does the presence of an Abstract method in the Superclass force the designer of a subclass derived from it to provide the detailed code?" Dave asked.

"Yes, Dave, that's exactly what it means," I replied. "When you derive a subclass from a Superclass containing Abstract methods, you are forced to provide actual implementations of the Abstract methods in the subclass. Of course, how you choose to do that is entirely up to you."

"Are you saying," Linda asked, "that if a subclass that is derived from the EmployeeSuperclass does not contain its own method called **display()**, the subclass won't compile?"

"Exactly right, Linda," I said. "Any subclass derived from the EmployeeBase Superclass must implement both the **getGrossPay()** and **display()** methods."

"This is all pretty interesting," Rhonda said. "In some ways, an Abstract method reminds me of when I worked as a secretary in a law firm. If a client came in to have a will drawn up, one of the staff attorneys would take some notes, hand them to me, and I would then incorporate their notes into boilerplate sections in a will template we had created in WordPerfect."

"Boilerplate sections?" Mary asked, looking at Rhonda.

"Boilerplate is standard legal language," Rhonda answered, "and much of a standard will is standard legal jargon. In the templates with which I would work, there were many boilerplate section headers that had nothing in them—in essence, they were just there to serve as reminders to us to ensure that we didn't forget to include the necessary verbiage to make the will valid."

"Kind of like an Abstract method!" I said. "Rhonda, that's a brilliant analogy. That's exactly the idea behind Abstract methods in a Superclass. Abstract methods ensure that the designer's vision for the Superclass, and the subclasses to be derived from it, are adhered to. Through the use of Abstract methods in a Superclass, the designer knows that each and every subclass derived from the Superclass will implement that method, even though the implementation details are up to the programmer who codes the subclass."

"Is that why the class name is also designated with the keyword Abstract?" Steve wondered.

"Not exactly," I answered. "Any class that contains an Abstract method must also be designated as an Abstract class," I said. "One consequence of the class being designated as Abstract is that no objects can be directly instantiated from it."

"That means we can't create an EmployeeBase object?" Blaine asked.

"Right on the mark, Blaine," I said. "A class containing Abstract methods is automatically an Abstract class, and that means it's really nothing more than the boilerplate for subclasses to be derived from it. There are also some Abstract classes that contain only Abstract methods—these classes can then be implemented as something called an interface, something we'll discuss later on. What I'd like to do now is show you how we can derive a subclass called HourlyEmployee from the EmployeeBase Abstract class we just coded."

I then displayed this code on the classroom projector:

```java
import javax.swing.JOptionPane;
class HourlyEmployee extends EmployeeBase {
  protected double hourlyRate;
  protected int hoursWorked;
  public HourlyEmployee() {          // Constructor Method
    System.out.println("HourlyEmployee's Constructor");
  }

  public void setHourlyRate(double temp) {
    hourlyRate = temp;
  }

  public double gethourlyRate() {
    return hourlyRate;
  }

  public void setHoursWorked(int temp) {
    hoursWorked = temp;
  }

  public int getHoursWorked() {
    return hoursWorked;
  }

  public double getGrossPay() {
    grossPay = hourlyRate * hoursWorked;
    return grossPay;
  }

  public void display() {
    JOptionPane.showMessageDialog
      (null,"*** EMPLOYEE RECORD ***\n\n" +
      "Employee ID: " + empID + "\n" +
      "Name: " + name + "\n" +
      "Hourly Rate: $ " + hourlyRate + "\n" +
      "Hours Worked: " + hoursWorked + "\n" +
      "Gross Pay: $ " + getGrossPay());
  }
}
```

"Notice," I said, "how the HourlyEmployee subclass has implemented two instance variables unique to an hourly employee: hourlyRate and hoursWorked. In addition, Accessor and Mutator methods for each have also been coded. Finally, did you notice that the HourlyEmployee subclass supplied code for the **getGrossPay()** and **display()** methods that were defined as Abstract methods in the EmployeeBase Superclass? If we failed to do that in a subclass derived from the EmployeeBase Superclass, we would have generated a compiler error when we compiled the subclass."

"Can we see the compiler error that would generate?" Kate asked.

"Sure thing, Kate," I said. I then temporarily deleted the implementation of the **getGrossPay()** and **display()** methods from HourlyEmployee and compiled it. The following screenshot was displayed on the classroom projector:

```
HourlyEmployee.java:2: error: HourlyEmployee is not abstract and does not
override abstract method display() in EmployeeBase
class HourlyEmployee extends EmployeeBase {
^
1 error

C:\JFiles>_
```

"Do you see what happened?" I asked. "The compiler is telling us that we failed to define a **display()** method. At a minimum, we need to include a **display()** method, even if we define it as abstract method with no code."

I then reinserted the **display()** and **getGrossPay()** methods into the HourlyEmployee subclass and recompiled it with no problem.

"Now," I said, "before we write code to use the HourlyEmployee class in a client program, let's modify the subclass SalariedEmployee that we created earlier so that it's derived from EmployeeBase instead of Employee. Remember, SalariedEmployee currently possesses some of the instance variables and methods that we decided to place in the EmployeeBase Superclass. We no longer need them in SalariedEmployee. We can derive them from EmployeeBase instead, like this."

I then displayed this code on the classroom projector:

```
import javax.swing.JOptionPane;
class SalariedEmployee extends EmployeeBase {
  protected double annualSalary;

  public SalariedEmployee()  {            // Constructor Method
    System.out.println("SalariedEmployee's Constructor");
  }
  public void setAnnualSalary(double temp) {
    annualSalary = temp;
  }
  public double getAnnualSalary() {
    return annualSalary;
  }
  public double getGrossPay() {
    grossPay = annualSalary / 26;
    return grossPay;
  }
  public void display() {
    JOptionPane.showMessageDialog
      (null,"*** EMPLOYEE RECORD ***\n\n" +
      "Employee ID: " + empID + "\n" +
      "Name: " + name + "\n" +
      "Annual Salary: $ " + annualSalary + "\n" +
      "Gross Pay: $ " + getGrossPay());
  }
}
```

"Notice," I said, "that this version of the SalariedEmployee subclass has implemented one instance variable unique to a Salaried employee, annualSalary. In addition, Accessor and Mutator methods for the annualSalary attribute have also been coded. Finally, the SalariedEmployee subclass implements code for the **getGrossPay()** and **display()** methods that were defined in the EmployeeBase Superclass as abstract methods."

"Overall, then," Dave said, "it looks like the EmployeeBase Superclass has three instance variables and seven methods, two of which are Abstract. The HourlyEmployee subclass has two instance variables and seven methods, two of which are overriding Abstract methods in the EmployeeBase Superclass. SalariedEmployee has one instance variable and five methods, two of which are overriding Abstract methods in the EmployeeBase Superclass."

"Excellent analysis," I said. "Using inheritance and giving some thought to the Base Superclass can result in less code in the subclasses derived from it."

"Is there a way to keep a subclass from overriding a method in the Superclass?" Dave asked.

"Suppose the designer of the Superclass writes a method, and he or she never wants the code in the method to be different from what they've written? Is there a way to stop that?"

"Good question, and the answer is yes," I replied. "Sometimes designers of a Superclass want to do exactly that. All you need to do is to declare the method in the Superclass with the Final keyword.

For instance, this code would prevent the Mutator method called **getName()** from being overridden by any of the subclasses derived from the Superclass:"

```
final String getName() {
  return name;
}
```

"I'm starting to get a feel for the class hierarchy you're talking about," Linda said. "Now I see that if the need arose to create a new type of employee class—a member of the board of directors, for instance, who receives a one-time stipend payment each year—we can create a subclass called EmployeeBoardOfDirectors, and derive it from the EmployeeBase class, adding just the instance variables necessary to describe that kind of employee and add code to implement the Abstract **getGrossPay()** and **display()** methods."

"Excellently stated, Linda," I said. I paused a moment before continuing. "Now, let's write a client program that creates an instance of each one of these subclass objects, HourlyEmployee and SalariedEmployee. You'll see that creating an instance of a subclass object is no different from creating an instance of an ordinary object."

I displayed this code on the classroom projector:

```java
public class Example9_3 {
  public static void main(String[] args) {
    HourlyEmployee x = new HourlyEmployee();
    x.setEmpID("086");
    x.setName("John Smith");
    x.setHourlyRate(12.50);
    x.setHoursWorked(40);
    x.display();

    SalariedEmployee y = new SalariedEmployee();
    y.setEmpID("337");
    y.setName("Mary Jones");
    y.setAnnualSalary(52000);
    y.display();
    System.exit(0);
  }
}
```

I compiled it and ran the program. The following screenshot was displayed on the classroom projector:

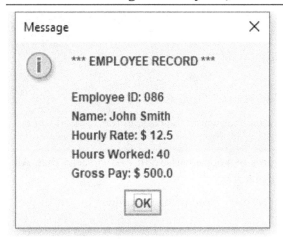

It was followed by this one:

"As you can see," I said, "our client program has created an instance of both the HourlyEmployee and SalariedEmployee objects. It set some properties and displayed the calculated Gross pay for each type of object."

Interfaces Are Not Inheritance

"I'm finding this whole topic of Inheritance very interesting," Ward said. "A few minutes ago you mentioned something called an Interface. How is an Interface different from a Superclass?"

"In Java, an Interface is a way to define a contract," I said. "Java defines an Interface as a named collection of method definitions and, possibly, constants."

> NOTE: An Interface is a contract between the Superclass and its Subclasses and is a way of enforcing Corporate or Company standards.

"Does that mean an interface has no instance variables?" Mary asked.

"That's right, Mary," I said, "an interface has no instance variables, and its methods are just like the Abstract methods we created in the EmployeeBase class—method definitions with no code."

"So how does an interface differ from an Abstract class?" Valerie asked, obviously pondering the difference. "I'm afraid I don't see the difference."

"An Abstract class, although it doesn't need to, can still implement methods containing code," I said, "whereas an interface may not. Do you remember that in the EmployeeBase class, we had implementation code for the Accessor and Mutator methods of its instance variables?"

"What are the advantages to creating an interface over an Abstract class?" Steve asked.

"The main feature of an interface that makes it attractive to many advanced Java programmers," I replied, "is the fact that you can implement more than one interface in the same class. This allows you to implement a variation of a feature that some object-oriented programs called multiple inheritance."

"Can you give us an example of that?" Lou asked.

"Sure thing, Lou," I said. "In theory, you could create one interface called Employee to describe an employee and another interface called Pilot to describe people who can fly an aircraft. If you then wanted to create a class to represent the employees in the company who can fly an airplane, you could implement both interfaces in the same class. However, you must be careful to realize that an interface has no actual code, only method signatures."

"Can't you do the same thing by creating a class that is derived from two Superclasses?" Steve asked.

"A class can only derive from a single Superclass," I said. "In Java, you can't use the keyword Extends with more than one Superclass."

"I guess I didn't realize that," Steve said, checking his notes.

"I appreciate your example of the Employee and Pilot interfaces," Blaine said. "But what's the purpose of an interface? Isn't this just a form of inheritance?'

"Interfaces do not enable you to implement code inheritance," I said, "Since there's no code at all in any of the methods of an interface, there's no way that a class implementing an interface can take advantage of any code that's already been written. Ultimately, to the programmer using it, an interface serves as a guide to what methods he or she needs to implement in the class that implements the interface. But those methods will be written from scratch—there's no code reusability."

"I guess," Linda said "I'm just having trouble envisioning why anyone would write an interface if it doesn't save someone down the line time and effort in writing code."

"The reason is standards," I said. "In a large corporate setting, the newly hired Java programmer might be told that all classes written to access the company's Oracle database must implement the Security interface, and as such, implement code for three methods: **determineUserId()**, **obtainPassword()**, and **writeAuditRecord()**. The programmer using the interface would be forced to write code to implement the methods."

"Why not just make those required methods part of a Superclass and tell your junior programmers to derive their classes from them?" Dave asked.

"That's always a possibility," I said. "One reason not to go in that direction would be that the individual implementation of these three methods is unique according to the individual Oracle database and tables being accessed—in which case, only the programmer writing code to access them would know the exact implementation details. Insisting that every class written in the company to access an Oracle database has these three methods ensures that the programmer doesn't forget to write code to perform these functions."

"So an interface is a way to enforce standards?" Bob asked.

"That's right, Bob," I said. "And you'll see in the coming weeks that we'll be implementing interfaces in our code as we start to develop the graphical user interface (GUI) for the Grade Calculation Project."

"Can you show us how to create an interface," Valerie asked, after a moment, "and how to implement one in a class?"

"I'd be glad to show you," I answered. Thinking for a moment, I said, "Let's create the Security interface I talked about earlier. Remember, an interface has no actual code, just method signatures."

I then displayed this code on the classroom projector:

```
interface Security {
   String programmerName = "John Smiley";
   void determineUserID();
   void obtainPassword();
   void writeAuditRecord();
}
```

I saved the Interface as Security.java and compiled it as I would any other class.

"As you can see," I said, "an interface definition is similar to a class definition, but notice there is no word 'class' in it. Instead, we begin an interface with the word 'interface' in lowercase, followed by the name of the interface. This is then followed by either constants or method definitions—notice that the method definitions have no curly braces—they're just the Method definitions followed by a semicolon."

"I did notice that," Ward said, "and at first I thought something was wrong—but that's the idea, right? Method definitions, followed immediately by a semicolon?"

"That's right, Ward," I said.

"Is programmerName a constant?" Mary asked. "How come it doesn't have the keyword Public in front of it?"

"Good question, Mary," I said. "As I mentioned earlier, interfaces have no variables, so programmerName is a constant. By default, constants within an interface are defined both as Public and Final. Stylistically, most programmers omit the Public and Final keywords, although you can include both of them if you wish."

"Along the same lines," Dave said, "I notice that we didn't use the keyword Abstract for the methods."

"That's right, Dave," I said. "Method definitions in an interface are implicitly Abstract—there's no reason to code the keyword. In fact, the Java documentation explicitly recommends against doing so."

"Now that we have an interface, what can we do with it?" Kate asked. "Incorporate it within a class?"

"Exactly, Kate," I said. "Let's test the Security interface within the HourlyEmployee class we created a while ago. I can't emphasize enough that an interface is designed to enforce standards or rules. If we use the Security interface within the HourlyEmployee class, what will that force us to do?"

"It will force us to implement the **determineUserID()**, **obtainPassword()**, and **writeAuditRecord()** methods declared in the Security interface," Dave said. "However, exactly what we do within those methods will be entirely up to us."

"That's excellent, Dave," I replied. "Using the Security interface will also allow us to access the value of the programmerName constant declared in the Security interface."

"But what code will we write in those three methods?" Valerie asked. "From what you've told us, we can't just inherit code in those methods, since there is none specified in the interface. That means we'll actually need to write the code for those methods?"

"Exactly right, Valerie," I said. "In a Superclass, the code in its methods may be specified and a subclass can gain access to the code in those methods by using the keyword extends, but an interface is much different. When we implement an interface in a class, we are committed to implementing the methods, but how we do that is entirely up to the programmer using the interface. For our test purposes, we'll implement the interface's three methods by simply displaying the name of each one of the methods to the Java Console."

"Do we use the keyword Extends to incorporate an interface in a class?" Barbara asked.

"No, Barbara, to incorporate an interface in a class we use the keyword Implements," I answered.

I then displayed this code for the modified HourlyEmployee class on the classroom projector:

```java
import javax.swing.JOptionPane;
class HourlyEmployee extends EmployeeBase implements Security {
  protected double hourlyRate;
  protected int hoursWorked;
  public HourlyEmployee() {                // Constructor Method
    System.out.println("HourlyEmployee's Constructor");
  }
  public void setHourlyRate(double temp) {
    hourlyRate = temp;
  }
  public double gethourlyRate() {
    return hourlyRate;
  }
  public void setHoursWorked(int temp) {
    hoursWorked = temp;
  }
  public int getHoursWorked() {
    return hoursWorked;
  }
  public double getGrossPay() {
    grossPay = hourlyRate * hoursWorked;
    return grossPay;
  }
```

```
public void display() {
  JOptionPane.showMessageDialog
    (null,"*** EMPLOYEE RECORD ***\n\n" +
    "Employee ID: " + empID + "\n" +
    "Name: " + name + "\n" +
    "Hourly Rate: $ " + hourlyRate + "\n" +
    "Hours Worked: " + hoursWorked + "\n" +
    "Gross Pay: $ " + getGrossPay());
}

public void determineUserID() {        //Security Interface methods
  System.out.println
    ("Security Interface determineUserID method");
}

public void obtainPassword() {         //Security Interface methods
  System.out.println
    ("Security Interface obtainPassword method");
}

public void writeAuditRecord() {       //Security Interface methods
  System.out.println
    ("Security Interface writeAuditRecord method");
}
}
```

"This code is very interesting," I said, "because it illustrates how we can inherit the code from a Superclass in a subclass using the Extends keyword and at the same time implement one or more interfaces using the Implements keyword:"

```
class HourlyEmployee extends EmployeeBase implements Security {
```

"So it is possible to implement more than interface in a class?" Blaine asked.

"Yes, it is," I said. "You can implement more than one interface in a class by specifying the Implements keyword and listing each interface separated by commas. But remember, you can only inherit from one Superclass. You can't extend more than one Superclass in a subclass.

"What happens when we execute the code in the HourlyEmployee class now?" Rhonda asked.

"We can't execute the code in the HourlyEmployee class directly," I said, "since HourlyEmployee doesn't have a **main()** method. We can, however, take the code we wrote in Example9_3 and modify it to create an instance of an hourlyEmployee object—and through it, execute the implemented Security interface."

I then displayed this code on the classroom projector:

```
public class Example9_4 {
  public static void main(String[] args) {
    HourlyEmployee x = new HourlyEmployee();
    x.setEmpID("086");
    x.setName("John Smith");
    x.setHourlyRate(12.50);
    x.setHoursWorked(40);
    x.display();
    x.determineUserID();              //Security Interface method
    x.obtainPassword();               //Security Interface method
    x.writeAuditRecord();             //Security Interface method
    System.out.println(x.programmerName); //Security Interface constant

    SalariedEmployee y = new SalariedEmployee();
    y.setEmpID("337");
    y.setName("Mary Jones");
    y.setAnnualSalary(52000);
    y.display();
```

```
    System.exit(0);
  }
}
```

I compiled this class, along with the modified HourlyEmployee class, and executed Example9_4. As was the case with Example9_3, we saw two message boxes displayed indicating the gross pay for both an hourly and salaried employee. In addition, the following messages were displayed in the Java Console:

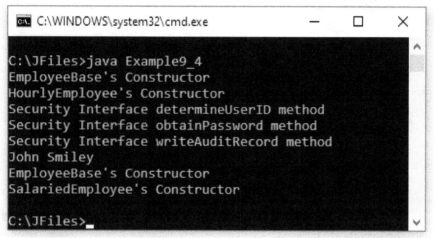

"As you can see," I said, "when we created an instance of the HourlyEmployee object, both the EmployeeBase and HourlyEmployee Constructor methods were executed. This makes sense since HourlyEmployee extends EmployeeBase:"

```
HourlyEmployee x = new HourlyEmployee();
```

"Since HourlyEmployee also implements the Security interface, we can then execute the **determineUserID()**, **obtainPassword()**, and **writeAuditRecord()** methods of the HourlyEmployee class within Example9_4:"

```
x.determineUserID();        //Security Interface method
x.obtainPassword();         //Security Interface method
x.writeAuditRecord();       //Security Interface method
```

"Finally, this line of code displays the value of the programmerName constant defined within the Security interface itself:"

```
System.out.println(x.programmerName);       //Security Interface constant
```

"Interfaces are frequently used by Java programmers as a great place to define and store constant values. In fact, many program teams do exactly that: create an interface called Constants that contains the constant values used within the company."

I waited to see if there were any questions on what we had covered in the first half of the class. Much to my surprise, it seemed that everyone in the class was OK with the complex topics of inheritance and interfaces. I suggested that we take a break before continuing on with the modification of the Grade Calculation Project to incorporate inheritance.

Creating a Superclass and Subclasses in the Grades Calculation Project

Fifteen minutes later we resumed class by explaining that it was now time to examine the Grade Calculation Project to see if we had a candidate for a Superclass.

"Normally," I said, "we would do this kind of analysis prior to this point, but since we're learning Java while writing the Grade Calculation Project, it can't really be helped."

"Will we be creating an interface for the Grade Calculation Project?" Lou asked.

"No, we won't," I answered. "An interface for a project this size doesn't make sense. Interfaces are useful in large corporate or departmental settings where the types of rules and standards we discussed a few minutes ago need to be enforced. For the Grade Calculation Project, we can do without an interface. What about Superclasses and subclasses, though?"

"I think one obvious Superclass would be a Student class," Dave said. "Right now, the EnglishStudent, MathStudent and ScienceStudent classes have a lot of duplicated code. If we create a Student Superclass, we'll be able to cut down significantly on the size of those three classes."

"Dave's right," I said. "The instance variables midterm, finalExamGrade, finalNumericGrade, and finalLetterGrade are used in all three of those classes—plus the research and presentation instance variables are used in the EnglishStudent class, and research is used in the ScienceStudent class."

"We also have duplication of the Mutator and Access methods for each of those instance variables," Linda said. "These are all candidates for inclusion in a Superclass."

"Each one of the three student classes also have a **calculate()** method," Mary said, "although the code details are different in each one. Might the **calculate()** method be a good candidate for an Abstract method in a Student Superclass?"

"That would be a great idea, Mary" I said. "That way, any class that inherits from the Superclass would be required to implement its own version of the **calculate()** method." I then distributed this exercise for the class to complete.

Don't Forget: If typing these examples and exercises isn't something you want to do, feel free to follow this link to find and download the completed solutions for all of the examples and exercises in the book. Just click on the Java book, then follow the link entitled exercises ☺

http://www.johnsmiley.com/main/books.htm

Exercise 9-1 Create the Student Superclass Class for the Grades Calculation Project

In this exercise, you'll create the Student Superclass for the Grades Calculation Project.

1. Use Notepad (if you are using Windows) and enter the following code.

```java
import javax.swing.JOptionPane;

abstract class Student {
  protected int midterm = 0;
  protected int finalExamGrade = 0;
  protected int research = 0;
  protected int presentation = 0;
  protected double finalNumericGrade = 0;
  protected String finalLetterGrade = "";

  protected void setMidterm(int temp) {
    if (temp < 0 | temp > 100) {
      JOptionPane.showMessageDialog(null,
        "Invalid Midterm Grade (" + temp + ") " +
        "Program Terminating");
      System.exit (0);
    }
    else
      midterm = temp;
  }

  protected int getMidterm() {
    return midterm;
  }

  protected void setFinalExamGrade(int temp) {
    if (temp < 0 | temp > 100) {
      JOptionPane.showMessageDialog(null,
        "Invalid Final Exam Grade (" + temp + ") " +
        "Program Terminating");
      System.exit (0);
    }
    else
      finalExamGrade = temp;
  }
```

```
  protected int getFinalExamGrade() {
    return finalExamGrade;
  }
  protected void setResearch(int temp) {
    if (temp < 0 | temp > 100) {
      JOptionPane.showMessageDialog(null,
        "Invalid Research Grade (" + temp + ") " +
        "Program Terminating");
      System.exit (0);
    }
    else
      research = temp;
  }
  protected int getResearch() {
    return research;
  }
  protected void setPresentation(int temp) {
    if (temp < 0 | temp > 100) {
      JOptionPane.showMessageDialog(null,
        "Invalid Presentation Grade (" + temp + ") " +
        "Program Terminating");
      System.exit (0);
    }
    else
      presentation = temp;
  }
  protected int getPresentation() {
    return presentation;
  }
  protected double getFinalNumericGrade() {
    return finalNumericGrade;
  }
  protected String getFinalLetterGrade() {
    return finalLetterGrade;
  }
  abstract void calculate();
}
```

2. Save your source file as Student.java in the \JFiles\Grades folder (select File | Save As from Notepad's menu bar). Be sure to save your source file with the filename extension .java.

3. Compile your source file into a Bytecode file.

4. You won't be testing your Student class until we have completed the work on the other classes in the project.

Discussion

No one had any problems completing the exercise.

"All we've really done then," Rhonda said, "is to take the Instance Variables common to all three classes, EnglishStudent, MathStudent, and ScienceStudent and incorporate them into the Student class—is that right?"

"That's basically correct, Rhonda," I said, "but remember, research and presentation are not common to all three classes."

"That's right," Peter said, obviously troubled. "Research and presentation don't appear in the MathStudent class, and the presentation instance variable doesn't appear in the ScienceStudent class. Is it OK to place these in the Student Superclass anyway?"

"It's not a problem, Peter," I said. "We could have chosen to declare only the two common instance variables in the Student Superclass, but we really should design the Student Superclass not only for the existing three student types that currently exist, but for those that may be required in the future as well."

"Other student types?" Mary asked. "Such as?"

"Well," I suggested, "there's always the possibility that other departments in the university—such as the Business Department or the Computer Science Department—after hearing about the fine work we've done for Frank Olley, may ask us to modify the Grade Calculation program for their use as well. These departments, I suspect, may compute their final grades based on combinations of midterm, finalExamGrade, research, and presentation components, so that's why we should include all of these in the Student Superclass."

There were no more questions, so I distributed the next exercise for the class to complete.

Exercise 9-2 Modify the EnglishStudent Class to Inherit from the Student Superclass

In this exercise, you'll modify the EnglishStudent class to inherit from the Student Superclass.

1. Using Notepad (if you are using Windows), locate and open the EnglishStudent.java source file you worked on last week (It should be in the \JFiles\Grades folder).
2. Modify your code so that it looks like this.

```java
import javax.swing.JOptionPane;
class EnglishStudent extends Student {
  private final double ENGLISH_MIDTERM_PERCENTAGE = .25;
  private final double ENGLISH_FINALEXAM_PERCENTAGE = .25;
  private final double ENGLISH_RESEARCH_PERCENTAGE = .30;
  private final double ENGLISH_PRESENTATION_PERCENTAGE = .20;

  public EnglishStudent() {
    System.out.println ("EnglishStudent's Constructor");
  }

  public void calculate() {
    midterm = Integer.parseInt(JOptionPane.showInputDialog
      ("Enter the Midterm Grade"));
    finalExamGrade = Integer.parseInt(JOptionPane.showInputDialog
      ("Enter the Final Examination Grade"));
    research = Integer.parseInt(JOptionPane.showInputDialog
      ("Enter the Research Grade"));
    presentation = Integer.parseInt(JOptionPane.showInputDialog
      ("Enter the Presentation Grade"));
    finalNumericGrade =
      (midterm * ENGLISH_MIDTERM_PERCENTAGE) +
      (finalExamGrade * ENGLISH_FINALEXAM_PERCENTAGE) +
      (research * ENGLISH_RESEARCH_PERCENTAGE) +
      (presentation * ENGLISH_PRESENTATION_PERCENTAGE);
    if (finalNumericGrade >= 93)
      finalLetterGrade = "A";
    else
    if ((finalNumericGrade >= 85) & (finalNumericGrade < 93))
      finalLetterGrade = "B";
    else
    if ((finalNumericGrade >= 78) & (finalNumericGrade < 85))
      finalLetterGrade = "C";
    else
    if ((finalNumericGrade >= 70) & (finalNumericGrade < 78))
      finalLetterGrade = "D";
    else
    if (finalNumericGrade < 70)
      finalLetterGrade = "F";
```

```
  }
}
```

3. Save your source file as EnglishStudent.java in the \JFiles\Grades folder (select File | Save As from Notepad's menu bar). Be sure to save your source file with the filename extension .java.

4. Compile your source file into a Bytecode file.

5. You won't be testing your EnglishStudent class until we have completed the work on the other classes in the project.

Discussion

"So EnglishStudent is now a subclass, is that right?" Joe asked.

"That's right, Joe," I said. "It's this line of code using the Extends keyword that tells Java that the EnglishStudent class is deriving the instance variables and methods of the Student class:"

```
class EnglishStudent extends Student {
```

"In addition to inheriting from the Student Superclass," I continued, "we removed from the EnglishStudent class the instance variables and methods that are now contained in the Student Superclass. The EnglishStudent class contains constants necessary for its unique **calculate()** method to function properly:"

```
private final double ENGLISH_MIDTERM_PERCENTAGE = .25;
private final double ENGLISH_FINALEXAM_PERCENTAGE = .25;
private final double ENGLISH_RESEARCH_PERCENTAGE = .30;
private final double ENGLISH_PRESENTATION_PERCENTAGE = .20;
```

"It also contains its own Constructor method, **EnglishStudent()**, which will simply display a message to the Java console:

```
public EnglishStudent() {
  System.out.println ("EnglishStudent's Constructor");
}
```

"And it contains its own unique **calculate()** method, which overrides the Abstract **calculate()** method in the Student Superclass:"

```
public void calculate() {
  midterm = Integer.parseInt (JOptionPane.showInputDialog
    ("Enter the Midterm Grade"));
  finalExamGrade = Integer.parseInt (JOptionPane.showInputDialog
    ("Enter the Final Examination Grade"));
  research = Integer.parseInt(JOptionPane.showInputDialog
    ("Enter the Research Grade"));
  presentation = Integer.parseInt(JOptionPane.showInputDialog
    ("Enter the Presentation Grade"));
  finalNumericGrade =
    (midterm * ENGLISH_MIDTERM_PERCENTAGE) +
    (finalExamGrade * ENGLISH_FINALEXAM_PERCENTAGE) +
    (research * ENGLISH_RESEARCH_PERCENTAGE) +
    (presentation * ENGLISH_PRESENTATION_PERCENTAGE);
  if (finalNumericGrade >= 93)
    finalLetterGrade = "A";
  else
  if ((finalNumericGrade >= 85) & (finalNumericGrade < 93))
    finalLetterGrade = "B";
  else
  if ((finalNumericGrade >= 78) & (finalNumericGrade < 85))
    finalLetterGrade = "C";
  else
  if ((finalNumericGrade >= 70) & (finalNumericGrade < 78))
    finalLetterGrade = "D";
  else
  if (finalNumericGrade < 70)
```

```
    finalLetterGrade = "F";
  }
}
```

"So none of the code in the EnglishStudent has really changed, has it?" Linda asked. "We've really just removed code from it."

"That's right, Linda," I replied. "Because we're deriving instance variables and methods from the Student Superclass, we've been able to reduce the amount of code in the EnglishStudent class. The code that remains is just the code we wrote last week."

"Where are the variables that are in the EnglishStudent's **calculate()** method located?" Rhonda asked. "Are those the instance variables found in the Student class?"

"That's exactly right, Rhonda," I said. "EnglishStudent derives these instance variables from Student, so the **calculate()** method can refer to them as if they were declared in EnglishStudent."

There were no more questions, and I distributed the next exercise for the class to complete.

Exercise 9-3 Modify the MathStudent Class to Inherit from the Student Superclass

In this exercise, you'll modify the MathStudent class to inherit from the Student Superclass.

1. Using Notepad (if you are using Windows), locate and open the MathStudent.java source file you worked on last week (It should be in the \JFiles\Grades folder).
2. Modify your code so that it looks like this.

```java
import javax.swing.JOptionPane;

class MathStudent extends Student {
  private final double MATH_MIDTERM_PERCENTAGE = .50;
  private final double MATH_FINALEXAM_PERCENTAGE = .50;

  public MathStudent() {
    System.out.println ("MathStudent's Constructor");
  }

  public void calculate() {
    midterm = Integer.parseInt(JOptionPane.showInputDialog
      ("Enter the Midterm Grade"));
    finalExamGrade = Integer.parseInt(JOptionPane.showInputDialog
      ("Enter the Final Examination Grade"));
    finalNumericGrade =
      (midterm * MATH_MIDTERM_PERCENTAGE) +
    (finalExamGrade * MATH_FINALEXAM_PERCENTAGE);
    if (finalNumericGrade >= 90)
      finalLetterGrade = "A";
    else
    if ((finalNumericGrade >= 83) & (finalNumericGrade < 90))
      finalLetterGrade = "B";
    else
    if ((finalNumericGrade >= 76) & (finalNumericGrade < 83))
      finalLetterGrade = "C";
    else
    if ((finalNumericGrade >= 65) & (finalNumericGrade < 76))
      finalLetterGrade = "D";
    else
    if (finalNumericGrade < 65)
      finalLetterGrade = "F";
  }
}
```

3. Save your source file as MathStudent.java in the \JFiles\Grades folder (select File | Save As from Notepad's menu bar). Be sure to save your source file with the filename extension .java.
4. Compile your source file into a Bytecode file.
5. You won't be testing your MathStudent class until we have completed the work on the other classes in the project.

Discussion

Hardly anyone had any problems completing their work on the MathStudent class. Modifying it was just a matter of removing some code, the same process we had followed for the EnglishStudent class. We then moved onto the next exercise.

Exercise 9-4 Modify the ScienceStudent Class to Inherit from the Student Superclass

In this exercise, you'll modify the ScienceStudent class to inherit from the Student Superclass.

1. Using Notepad (if you are usingWindows), locate and open the ScienceStudent.java source file you worked on last week (It should be in the \JFiles\Grades folder).

2. Modify your code so that it looks like this.

```java
import javax.swing.JOptionPane;
class ScienceStudent extends Student {
  private final double SCIENCE_MIDTERM_PERCENTAGE = .40;
  private final double SCIENCE_FINALEXAM_PERCENTAGE = .40;
  private final double SCIENCE_RESEARCH_PERCENTAGE = .20;

  public ScienceStudent() {
    System.out.println ("ScienceStudent's Constructor");
  }

  public void calculate() {
    midterm = Integer.parseInt(JOptionPane.showInputDialog
      ("Enter the Midterm Grade"));
    finalExamGrade = Integer.parseInt(JOptionPane.showInputDialog
      ("Enter the Final Examination Grade"));
    research = Integer.parseInt(JOptionPane.showInputDialog
      ("Enter the Research Grade"));
    finalNumericGrade =
      (midterm * SCIENCE_MIDTERM_PERCENTAGE) +
      (finalExamGrade * SCIENCE_FINALEXAM_PERCENTAGE) +
      (research * SCIENCE_RESEARCH_PERCENTAGE);
    if (finalNumericGrade >= 90)
      finalLetterGrade = "A";
    else
    if ((finalNumericGrade >= 80) & (finalNumericGrade < 90))
      finalLetterGrade = "B";
    else
    if ((finalNumericGrade >= 70) & (finalNumericGrade < 80))
      finalLetterGrade = "C";
    else
    if ((finalNumericGrade >= 60) & (finalNumericGrade < 70))
      finalLetterGrade = "D";
    else
    if (finalNumericGrade < 60)
      finalLetterGrade = "F";
  }
}
```

3. Save your source file as ScienceStudent.java in the \JFiles\Grades folder (select File | Save As from Notepad's menu bar). Be sure to save your source file with the filename extension .java.

4. Compile your source file into a Bytecode file.

5. We can now test the work we've done with the four classes (Student, EnglishStudent, MathStudent and ScienceStudent) by executing the Grades class and testing it thoroughly. After you start up your program, it should ask you if you have a grade to calculate.

6. Enter **Yes**, and calculate the grade for an English student. Enter **70** for the midterm, **80** for the final examination, **90** for the research grade, and **100** for the presentation. A final numeric grade of 84.5 should be displayed, with a letter grade of **C**.

7. After the message box is displayed with the calculated grade, the program should ask you if you have more grades

to calculate.

8. Enter **Yes**, and calculate the grade for a Math student. Enter **70** for the midterm and **80** for the final examination. A final numeric grade of **75** should be displayed, with a letter grade of **D**.

9. After the message box is displayed with the calculated grade, the program should ask you if you have more grades to calculate.

10. Enter **Yes**, and calculate the grade for a Science student. Enter **70** for the midterm, **80** for the final examination, and **90** for the research grade. A final numeric grade of **78** should be displayed, with a letter grade of **C**. After the message box is displayed with the calculated grade, the program should ask you if you have more grades to calculate.

11. Enter **No**. You should be thanked for using the program, and the program should end.

12. Observe the creation of the various student objects during the running of your program.

Discussion

"Everything works the same as it did prior to creating the Superclass and converting EnglishStudent, MathStudent, and ScienceStudent to Subclasses," I said. "Ultimately, we've made the size of our Subclasses smaller, which is always a good thing, and the class hierarchy we've created through the creation of the Student Superclass will make future modifications to this project much easier."

No one had any questions, and everyone seemed quite pleased with the work they had done today.

I then dismissed class for the day.

Summary

In this chapter, we covered two basic topics: inheritance and interfaces.

Inheritance is the process whereby one class (called a subclass) can derive the instance variables and methods of a parent class (called the Superclass). Deriving properties and behaviors of another class can save the programmer of the subclass a lot of coding. More importantly, creating class hierarchies, in which a Superclass (a Superclass is the top of the hierarchy) has instance variables and methods that are common to classes that will be derived from it, offers the utmost in software reusability.

We also learned about interfaces. Inheritance and interfaces are not the same. Inheritance permits a subclass to derive the code in a parent class. A class which incorporates the interface of another class agrees to use the Abstract method definitions of the interface. Interfaces don't define the details of their methods—that is, there is no code in an interface method, only the method header. A class that implements an interface is responsible for writing that code.

Chapter 10---Arrays

In this chapter, you'll learn about one of the most fundamental data structures in the world of programming: arrays. Arrays are collections of variables, each having the same name but a unique index. Arrays permit a programmer to easily solve certain types of problems that would otherwise be extremely tedious to code.

Why Arrays

I began our tenth class by telling my students that the entirety of that day's class would be devoted to the topic of arrays.

"Are arrays similar to regular variables?" Dave asked.

"Yes, they are, Dave," I said. "You've learned that a variable is a single piece of data given a name and stored in the computer's memory. An array is a collection of variables—I sometimes call arrays a family of variables—of the same data type, such as int or string, stored in the computer's memory. Each member of the collection has the same name but possesses a unique number called a subscript, which is used to identify it. Individual members of an array are called elements of the array."

> NOTE: You sometimes see the terms Subscript and Index used interchangeably.

"In the world of programming," I continued, "certain kinds of programming problems can more easily be solved using arrays. In fact, it's probably safe to say that there are certain types of programming problems that could not be solved without the use of arrays."

"What kinds of problems?" Chuck asked, his curiosity obviously aroused.

"In general, Chuck," I said, "problems where there is a requirement to manipulate large amounts of data and where the data isn't really unique but there are huge volumes of it."

"Could you give us an example of something like that?" Kate asked.

I thought for a moment and then said, "Let's suppose, Kate, that you are a weather meteorologist and, armed with the knowledge of Java that you have picked up in this class, you decide to write a Java program to keep track of 365 days worth of daily high temperature readings."

"That sounds interesting," Ward said. "That's an awful lot of data—at least more than we're used to."

"Furthermore," I continued, "let's presume that Kate would also like to calculate the yearly average for her temperature readings. From what we've learned so far in the class, we know that we could declare and store these temperature readings in 365 separate variables called highTemperature1 through highTemperature365."

"I agree, that would do the trick," Dave said, "but who really wants to code 365 variable declaration statements, plus the 365 assignment statements to store the value of the variable? Plus, the calculation for the yearly average would require that we sum each and every one of those variables—what a tedious exercise that would be! Is this where an array can help us?"

"That's exactly the case, Dave," I answered. "Let's think about this for a moment. Each one of the 365 recorded high temperature readings really represents the same thing: a temperature reading. What's different about each one? Only the day that the temperature is recorded. You'll see in a few minutes that an array is a much better choice than an ordinary variable in which to store those 365 temperature readings. In fact, you'll be surprised to learn that an array declaration to store 365 high temperature readings is just a single line of code."

"Amazing," I heard Valerie say.

"Not only does an array eliminate the need to declare 365 separate variables," I continued, "but once the values for the year's temperature readings are stored in the array, it's a simple process to use a For loop to access each individual element of the array and then retrieve the value, add it to an accumulator variable, and then calculate an average temperature. Believe it or not, we can do that in about five lines of code."

"I can't wait to see this in action," Steve said.

"Let me give you another example," I said. "On Wednesday evenings, I teach a Database Administration class here at the University. Last Wednesday, I gave a quiz to each one of the six students in the class. What would you say if I asked you to write a Java program to calculate the overall class average for that quiz? Based on what you've learned in the first nine weeks of the course and excluding what we've discussed so far about arrays, do you have any idea as to how we could calculate the class average?"

"I guess," Rhonda suggested, "that one way would be to borrow the functionality that we are currently using with the Grade Calculation program."

"How's that, Rhonda?" I asked.

"Well, we could prompt the user of the program to enter quiz grades for each one of the six students," she replied. "Since you told us to discount today's discussion of arrays, the best I can suggest is to declare six variables, one to represent the quiz grades for each one of the students, and to assign the user's input to one of those variables. Once the user has entered all six student grades, we can then sum the values of the variables and divide by six to calculate an overall class average."

"Based on what we've learned in the first nine weeks of class Rhonda, that's an excellent approach," I said. "However, once you learn more about arrays, I bet you'll come to the conclusion that this method, as effective as it is, is what I term the 'brute force method.'"

I gave everyone a chance to ponder that statement. "Now, suppose I told you that my Database Management class doesn't have just six students; it really has 150 students. Would that change your approach to solving the problem?"

"I would think we need to find a better approach to solving the problem than this," Rhonda replied. "I really don't want to have to declare 150 variables! There must be a better way."

"Absolutely, Rhonda," I said, "and we'll see shortly that the 'better approach' you sense must exist is to use an array instead of individual variables. But before we start to discuss arrays in detail, I think it's a good idea if we code up the solution to the problem using the 'brute force' method. That will allow us to see how tedious programming would be without arrays."

I then distributed this exercise for the class to complete.

Don't Forget: If typing these examples and exercises isn't something you want to do, feel free to follow this link to find and download the completed solutions for all of the examples and exercises in the book. Just click on the Java book, then follow the link entitled exercises ☺

http://www.johnsmiley.com/main/books.htm

Exercise 10-1 Brute Force---Life without Arrays

In this exercise, you'll write a program that prompts the user for six quiz grades, then calculates and displays the grades plus the overall class average to the Java console.

1. Use Notepad (if you are using Windows) and enter the following code.

```java
import javax.swing.JOptionPane;

class Practice10_1 {
  public static void main (String[] args) {
    int grade1 = 0;
    int grade2 = 0;
    int grade3 = 0;
    int grade4 = 0;
    int grade5 = 0;
    int grade6 = 0;
    int accumulator = 0;
    int counter = 6;
    double average = 0;

    grade1 = Integer.parseInt(JOptionPane.showInputDialog
      ("What is the first grade?"));
    grade2 = Integer.parseInt(JOptionPane.showInputDialog
      ("What is the second grade?"));
    grade3 = Integer.parseInt(JOptionPane.showInputDialog
      ("What is the third grade?"));
    grade4 = Integer.parseInt(JOptionPane.showInputDialog
      ("What is the fourth grade?"));
```

```
    grade5 = Integer.parseInt(JOptionPane.showInputDialog
        ("What is the fifth grade?"));
    grade6 = Integer.parseInt(JOptionPane.showInputDialog
        ("What is the sixth grade?"));

    accumulator = grade1 + grade2 + grade3 +
                    grade4 + grade5 + grade6;
    average = accumulator / counter;
    System.out.println(grade1);
    System.out.println(grade2);
    System.out.println(grade3);
    System.out.println(grade4);
    System.out.println(grade5);
    System.out.println(grade6);
    System.out.println();
    System.out.println("The class average is " + average);
    System.exit(0);
  }
}
```

2. Save your source file as **'Practice10_1.java'** in the \JFiles\Practice folder (select File-Save As from Notepad's Menu Bar). Be sure to save your source file with the file name extension 'java'.

3. Compile your source file into a Bytecode file.

4. Execute your program. The program will prompt you for six grades. Enter **82** for the first grade, **90** for the second, **64** for the third, **80** for the fourth, **95** for the fifth, and **75** for the sixth.

5. The program will then display the grades, plus the calculated overall class average, which is **81**.

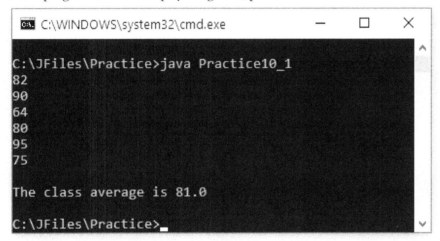

Discussion

Everyone agreed that the code in this exercise did what every good program must do: it worked. Beyond that, it had been an extremely tedious exercise to code.

"Brute force is right," Peter said. "What a boring program to write! I can't wait to see how an array can improve upon this."

"We'll see that in a minute, Peter," I said, "but first, let's take a look at the code. Much of it will be pretty familiar to you, as we're using the same technique we use in the Grades Calculation Project. As usual, the first thing we do is to declare the variables that we will need to use in our program. We have six local variables in the **main()** method:"

```
int grade1 = 0;
int grade2 = 0;
int grade3 = 0;
int grade4 = 0;
int grade5 = 0;
int grade6 = 0;
```

"Notice that we've declared an Integer variable for each one of the six quiz grades," I continued, "and we've initialized each one of them to 0. In addition, I've introduced two special types of variables in this code. The first variable, appropriately named *accumulator*, is called an Accumulator. It's really just an ordinary variable that is used to sum values. In this case, we'll use *accumulator* to sum the values of the six grade variables:"

```
int accumulator = 0;
```

"The second special type of variable, which we've named *counter*, is called a Counter and, like the Accumulator variable, a Counter variable is just an ordinary variable that is used to count something—in this case, we're using it to count the number of students in the class. We could get fancier than this, but for now, since we will eventually divide the value of *counter* into *accumulator* to arrive at a class average, we immediately assign the number 6 to the Counter variable:"

```
int counter = 6;
```

"We also declare a Double variable type called *average*, into which we will store the class average:"

```
double average = 0;
```

"Double, that's a data type with a fractional part, isn't it?" Blaine asked.

"That's right, Blaine," I answered. "Because we want to calculate the class average as precisely as possible, we need to declare a variable that can handle fractions."

I went on to explain that in the next section of code, we used the **showInputDialog()** method of the JOptionPane object to prompt the user for each of the six quiz grades for the class.

"Notice that the return value of the user's response is assigned to a unique variable," I said. "This is where a problem arises: if all of a sudden we have 150 students in the class, not the 6 that we have here, this code can really balloon in size:"

```
grade1 = Integer.parseInt(JOptionPane.showInputDialog
   ("What is the first grade?"));
grade2 = Integer.parseInt(JOptionPane.showInputDialog
   ("What is the second grade?"));
grade3 = Integer.parseInt(JOptionPane.showInputDialog
   ("What is the third grade?"));
grade4 = Integer.parseInt(JOptionPane.showInputDialog
   ("What is the fourth grade?"));
grade5 = Integer.parseInt(JOptionPane.showInputDialog
   ("What is the fifth grade?"));
grade6 = Integer.parseInt(JOptionPane.showInputDialog
   ("What is the sixth grade?"));
```

"Here's the code that assigns a value to the Accumulator variable. As we progress through today's class, the code we use with the Accumulator variable will become a little more elegant. For now, we just assign it the values of each one of the six grade variables:"

```
accumulator = grade1 + grade2 + grade3 +
              grade4 + grade5 + grade6;
```

"This line of code is probably the most important one in the program," I continued, "in that it assigns the class average to the Average variable. Notice that we take the value of the Accumulator variable and divide by the value of the Counter variable:"

```
average = accumulator / counter;
```

"Is there anything magical about the names of those two variables, the Accumulator and Counter variables?" Joe asked.

"Not at all, Joe," I answered. "We can name them anything we want."

I paused before continuing.

"This next section of code displays the values of the individual grades," I said. "This is another problematic section of code if the number of students in the class increases, because we would need to add additional lines of code:"

```
System.out.println(grade1);
System.out.println(grade2);
System.out.println(grade3);
System.out.println(grade4);
System.out.println(grade5);
System.out.println(grade6);
```

"Finally," I said, "this line of code displays a blank line in the Java console:"

```
System.out.println();
```

"The blank line is followed by the display of the class average:"

```
System.out.println("The class average is " + average);
```

I checked the classroom for signs of confusion, but no one seemed to be having any trouble understanding what we had just done.

"I think you're all pretty comfortable with this code," I said. "There's really nothing in this code that we haven't seen before."

I then made this suggestion.

"Now I'd like you all to modify this code to calculate the class average for a class with 500 students," I said.

"I hope you're kidding," Joe said smiling.

"Well, I am...but suppose we really needed to calculate the average for a class with 500 students. Could we do it?" I asked.

Everyone agreed that modifying the code to calculate the class average for 500 students would be a real nightmare.

"We would need 500 prompts to the user and 500 variables in which to store their responses," Kate said. "Plus, we would need multiple lines of code to sum the values of the 500 variables and assign them to the Accumulator variable."

What's an Array?

"All of your points are excellent ones, Kate," I said. "Examining the brute force method gives us a chance to see the types of problems that can be more easily solved using array processing."

"Is an array a separate data type, like an Integer or a Single?" Peter asked.

"Many beginners make the mistake of thinking of an array as a separate data type," I said, "but arrays are just a special implementation of one of the other Java data types. In Java, you can have Integer arrays, Double arrays, String arrays and as we'll see later, even Object arrays."

"I'm still a little confused as to exactly what an array is," Rhonda said. "Do you have any analogies up your sleeve that might make this a little clearer?"

"In the past when I've taught arrays," I said, "many of my students have found my analogy of an array to a hotel to be pretty useful."

"A hotel?" Rhonda asked.

"That's right, Rhonda," I said. "Just about everyone at one time or other has stayed in a hotel or motel. As you know, a variable is just a storage location in your computer's memory. Getting back to the hotel analogy, think of an ordinary variable as a storage location consisting of just a single floor. An array, on the other hand, is a storage location having more than just one floor, with each floor having its own unique floor number."

"Just like a hotel," Joe said. "I see what you mean."

"I'm not much of an artist," I said, "but here's a graphic depiction of what I mean."

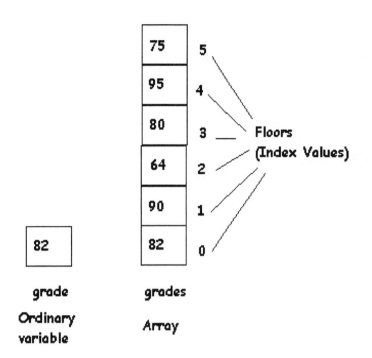

"This drawing is an attempt to illustrate the difference between an ordinary variable and an array," I said. "On the left side of the drawing, we have an ordinary Integer variable called grade with an assigned value of 82. On the right side of the drawing, we have an array of Integer variables called grades, the array containing six elements and each element having its own value. As you can see, the ordinary variable grade can hold only one value at a time. The Integer array, however, can hold all six quiz grades at one time."

"What are those numbers to the right of the grades in the array?" Barbara asked.

"In keeping with our hotel analogy," I said, "those are the floor numbers of the hotel or, in computer terms, the array subscript or index values. A subscript uniquely identifies the element within the array. Each element has a subscript, and subscripts cannot be duplicated. This ensures that once a value is entered into an element of the array, you'll later be able to retrieve that value by using its subscript."

"Why does the first element of the array begin with zero?" Ward asked. "Why doesn't it begin with one?"

"Let me guess, that's the basement!" Rhonda said, obviously joking.

"In a way, Rhonda, you're right," I replied. "In the computer world, many things begin with the number zero instead of one, and array element numbers are one of them. In Java, the first element of an array begins with the number zero—it's just something that you'll need to get used to."

Declaring and Initializing an Array

"How do you declare an array?" Steve asked. "Is declaring an array different from declaring an ordinary variable?"

"Declaring an array isn't much different from declaring an ordinary variable," I continued. "Java knows you are declaring an array if you follow the name of a variable with a pair of square brackets, like this:"

```
int grades[];
```

"Does everyone see the empty pair of square brackets?" I asked. "What we've done here is to tell Java that we are declaring an Integer array called grades. Just like with an ordinary variable declaration, an array declaration must begin with a data type, in this case, int for Integer."

"And it's the square brackets that follow the variable name—I mean the array name—that tells Java that?" Chuck asked.

"That's right, Chuck," I said. "Java knows we are declaring an array because of the square brackets. By the way, I should mention that you will sometimes see the square brackets following the data type instead of the array name, like this:"

```
int[] grades;
```

"That looks a bit strange to me," Ward said. "Is there a preferred method to declaring the array?"

"Both methods declare the array," I said, "and Java recognizes both. Personally, like you, I prefer to specify the square brackets after the array name."

"Isn't something missing in the array declaration?" Dave asked. "Don't we need to tell Java the number of elements in the grades array? How does Java know if grades contains 6 elements or 150?"

"Good question, Dave," I said, "and you're right—in essence, all we've done is to announce to Java that we have an array called grades, but we haven't told Java how many elements it contains. Until we do that—technically called initializing the array—this array declaration isn't going to be very useful to us. At this point, we can't even store a single value in the array."

"So what do we have to do?" Rhonda asked. "How do we initialize an array?"

"In Java, there are actually several ways to initialize an array," I said. "One way is to include the data values for the array as part of its declaration, in which case Java infers the size of the array from the data values in the declaration. We'll take a look at that method in a few minutes. The other way is to use the New keyword."

"Is that the same keyword we use when we create instances of objects?" Lou asked.

"That's right, Lou," I said. "Behind the scenes in Java, arrays are really objects, so once we have declared an array, we can initialize the array by using the New keyword. The initial value for each element is dependent upon its data type; for instance, Integer elements are initialized to zero. When you use the New keyword, you must also specify the size of the array, like this, which creates an array called grades with six elements:"

```
int[] grades;
grades = new int[6];
```

"In practice," I continued, "most Java programmers combine the array declaration and initialization with a single line of code like this:"

```
int grades[] = new int[6];
```

"Here we are telling Java with a single statement that we are declaring an Integer array called grades and that it will have a total of six elements or floors."

"I want to be certain I'm clear about this," Kate said. "Is the number six the number of elements in the array or the top floor of the hotel?"

"That's a key distinction, Kate" I said. "In Java, the number within square brackets represents the total number of elements in the array, which is not the same as the top floor. This array has six elements, with its subscripts numbered from 0 through 5."

Adding data to the Elements of an Array

"How do we assign a value to an individual element of an array?" Steve asked. "And once we have values in the array elements, how can we retrieve the value from one of those elements?"

"Working with array elements isn't much different from working with an ordinary variable," I said. "The difference is that we need to reference the element number within the array by using its subscript within square brackets. For example, if we had an array called grades, this code would be used to assign the value of 64 to element number 2:"

```
grades[2] = 82;
```

"By the way," I cautioned, "the array element with a subscript equal to 2 is actually the third element in the array. Remember, element numbers start with zero, not one. Therefore, the first element in the array has a subscript of 0, the second element has a subscript of 1, and so forth."

"Are array values referred to in the same way?" Steve asked. "Using the subscript number within square brackets?"

"That's right, Steve," I replied. "Again, as was the case with the assignment statement, just reference the subscript of the array element within square brackets. For instance, you can use this syntax to display the value of element number 0 of the grades array in the Java console:"

```
System.out.println(grades[0]);
```

"This isn't too bad at all," Kathy said. "I must confess, when I first heard the name 'array,' I thought it would be a lot more complicated than this."

"I've been experimenting with an array of my own," Rhonda said. "I'm getting an error message when I try to assign a value to one of my array elements, and I don't know why. I declared the array with ten elements, but when I tried to assign a value to the tenth element, I received a runtime error."

I took a walk to Rhonda's PC and quickly saw the problem.

"I see what the problem is, Rhonda," I said. "You did declare your array with ten elements using this code, which was great:"

```
int rhonda[] = new int{10};
```

"But when you tried to assign a value to the tenth element, you used the number 10 within square brackets:"

```
rhonda[10] = 22;
```

"The array element with subscript 10 is actually the eleventh element of the array and, since you told Java, via the declaration statement, that it would have only 10 elements, you received an error message. Remember, an array declared with 10 elements has its first element numbered 0, and its last element numbered 9. Subscript 10 does not exist."

"That is confusing, isn't it?" Peter said, as Rhonda nodded her head knowingly.

"I agree, Peter," I said. "The fact that elements of an array are numbered starting with zero can be confusing. Just remember that the last element number in the array—the top floor of our hotel—is always one less than its size. So if an array is declared with 10 elements, the last element number is 9."

"Can we use other than a numeric literal to refer to the array's subscript?" Dave asked.

"You can use any expression within the square brackets, as long as the expression evaluates to a valid subscript." I answered.

"I'm not sure I'm following this," Chuck said.

"For instance," I explained, "if you have a variable called counter containing an Integer value, and that value represents a valid subscript in the grades array, this is a valid assignment statement that uses the value of the variable not an actual number to represent the subscript:"

```
grades[counter] = 80;
```

"The ability to do this," I said, "will come in very handy in the exercise we're about to complete, as it will enable us to use loop processing to quickly access all of the elements of an array."

I waited for questions, but there were none. I think everyone, for the moment anyway, felt pretty comfortable declaring and working with arrays.

"I have an exercise for you to complete that will give you a chance to use an array to perform the same average calculation we did in the last exercise using the brute force method—but I think you'll enjoy it a whole lot more."

I then distributed this exercise for the class to complete.

Exercise 10-2 Our First Look at Arrays

In this exercise, you'll create your first Array.
1. Use Notepad (if you are using Windows) and enter the following code.

```
class Practice10_2 {
  public static void main (String[] args) {
    int grades[] = new int[6];
    int accumulator = 0;
    int counter = 6;
    double average = 0;

    grades[0] = 82;
    grades[1] = 90;
    grades[2] = 64;
    grades[3] = 80;
```

```
    grades[4] = 95;
    grades[5] = 75;

    accumulator = grades[0] + grades[1] + grades[2] +
                grades[3] + grades[4] + grades[5];
    average = accumulator / counter;
    System.out.println(grades[0]);
    System.out.println(grades[1]);
    System.out.println(grades[2]);
    System.out.println(grades[3]);
    System.out.println(grades[4]);
    System.out.println(grades[5]);
    System.out.println();

    System.out.println("The class average is " + average);
  }
}
```

2. Save your source file as Practice10_2 in the \JFiles\Practice folder (select File | Save As from Notepad's menu bar). Be sure to save your source file with the filename extension .java.

3. Compile your source file into a Bytecode file.

4. Execute the program. The program will then display each of the six grades, plus the calculated overall class average, which is **81**.

Discussion

Except for a student or two who confused the parentheses with square brackets, no one had any trouble completing this exercise.

"As you can see," I said, "the results of this program are identical to those in Exercise 10-1: the display of six grades, plus the calculated overall class average. Of course, this version uses an array. Let's take a closer look at the code now. It's this line of code that declares a six-element array called grades. And as you know by now, that means the first element in the array has a subscript of 0 and the last element has a subscript of 5. By the way, I didn't mention this before, but it's a good idea to name arrays using the plural form of a noun—that enables programmers reading your code to recognize immediately that the variable is actually an array:"

```
int grades[] = new int[6];
```

"Using an array here, we reduced the number of lines of code necessary to declare the variables to store our six grades from six to one. As was the case with Exercise 10-1, these next three lines of code declare our Accumulator variable, our Counter variable, and our Average variable. Once again, we initialize the value of our Counter variable to 6, although shortly you'll see there's a more elegant way to keep track of the number of grades to use in our average calculation. For now, we initialize it to 6:"

```
int accumulator = 0;
int counter = 6;
double average = 0;
```

"You probably remember that the previous version of this program assigned values to variables named grade1 through grade6; this version does the same, but this time we assign values to individual elements of the grades array. In the next exercise, we'll learn that there's a more compact method for assigning values to array elements:"

```
grades[0] = 82;
grades[1] = 90;
grades[2] = 64;
grades[3] = 80;
grades[4] = 95;
grades[5] = 75;
```

"As in Exercise 10-1, we then sum the values of all six grades and assign the result to the Accumulator variable. This time we refer to the individual elements of the grades array:"

```
accumulator = grades[0] + grades[1] + grades[2] +
            grades[3] + grades[4] + grades[5];
```

"And with this line of code we calculate the overall class average:"

```
average = accumulator / counter;
```

"This next section of code is similar to Exercise 10-1—it displays the values of the individual grades to the Java console referring to the individual elements in the grades array to do so:"

```
System.out.println(grades[0]);
System.out.println(grades[1]);
System.out.println(grades[2]);
System.out.println(grades[3]);
System.out.println(grades[4]);
System.out.println(grades[5]);
System.out.println();
```

"Finally, this line of code displays the calculated class average in the Java console:"

```
System.out.println("The class average is " + average);
```

The wonders of Array processing

"So far," Ward said, "I can see that array processing reduces the number of variables we need to declare in our program, but quite honestly, I don't see what the big deal is all about. Everything we did in this exercise was very similar to what we did in Exercise 10-1, but instead of referencing individual variable names, we referenced element of an array. There was still quite a bit of tedious typing referring to individual elements of the array."

"I agree with Ward," Lou said. "Surely there's got to be an easier way to assign values to an array? And once we have the values in the array, what then? Suppose you have an array with 365 elements like the daily high temperature readings you mentioned earlier. Would we need to code up 365 separate assignment statements?"

"Glad you asked that, Lou," I said. "There is a shorter form of assigning values to an array, and its one to which I alluded earlier when I said there's a method to declare and initialize an array just by assigning values to it. Check out this code:"

```
int grades[] = {82,90,64,80,95,75};
```

"Notice that the values for the array elements are contained within the curly braces," I said. "Now, with a single line of code, we have both declared an array called grades and initialized it with values. How does Java know how large to size the array? The six values within the curly braces tell Java that the grades array should have six elements."

"This is an improvement," Ward persisted, "but I still say big deal. I see that this method will reduce the number of lines of code required to assign values to the elements of an array. But what else can arrays do for me? Why is it that the programmers at work always tell me they couldn't live without them? If I still need to refer to each and every element within the array individually, I still have quite a bit of work ahead of me."

"Arrays allow you to use loop processing to quickly refer to each element in the array," I said, "and that can be a big time saver. This exercise, I believe, will illustrate why the programmers at your work love arrays so much."

I then handed out this exercise for the class to complete.

Exercise 10-3 The wonders of Array processing

In this exercise, you'll modify the code from exercise 10-2, using a Java For Loop to quickly and easily access the elements of an Array.

1. Use Notepad (if you using Windows) and enter the following code.

```java
class Practice10_3 {
  public static void main (String[] args) {
    int grades[] = { 82, 90, 64, 80, 95, 75};
    int accumulator = 0;
    int counter = 0;
    double average = 0;

    for (int row = 0; row < grades.length; row++) {
      System.out.println(grades[row]);
      accumulator = accumulator + grades[row];
      counter++;
    }
```

```
        System.out.println();
        average = accumulator / counter;
        System.out.println("The class average is " + average);
    }
}
```

2. Save your source file as Practice10_3 in the \JFiles\Practice folder (select File | Save As from Notepad's menu bar). Be sure to save your source file with the filename extension .java.

3. Compile your source file into a Bytecode file.

4. Execute the program. The program will then display each of the six grades, plus the calculated overall class average, which is 81.

Discussion

"OK, I'm beginning to see the light," Ward said. "This version of the program is certainly a lot more streamlined than the other code, and I'm happy to see we never directly referred to an individual element of the array."

"I'm not quite sure I understand what's happening," Rhonda said. "Can you explain the code to us?"

"Sure thing, Rhonda," I said. "This time, instead of declaring and initializing the grades array using the new statement, we declare and initialize the array in a single statement by assigning values to each one of the six elements of the grades array:"

```
int grades[] = { 82, 90, 64, 80, 95, 75};
```

"As before, we declare variables for accumulator, counter, and average. But notice that this time, the Counter variable is assigned a value of 0, not 6. We'll be arriving at a value for the Counter variable a little later on in the code, and it will make our program much more flexible in being able to deal with different numbers of quiz grades to calculate:"

```
int accumulator = 0;
int counter = 0;
double average = 0;
```

"At this point in our program," I continued, "the grades array now has six elements, with values assigned to each. In the previous version of this program, we then used the **println()** method of the System object to display the values for each element of the array, using six separate executions of the **println()** method. The problem with that version—and it's one that bothered the heck out of Ward—is that if the number of students in the class increases, we'll have to change the number of elements in the array and write another line of code to display that student's grade. That's why this next section of code is so powerful: it uses a Java For loop to access every element in the grades array, displaying its value in the Java console, adding its value to the Accumulator variable, and incrementing the value of the Counter variable by one:"

```
for (int row = 0; row < grades.length; row++) {
    System.out.println(grades[row]);
    accumulator = accumulator + grades[row];
    counter++;
}
```

"The wonderful thing about this code is that it works without modification, regardless of the number of elements in the array."

"Are you saying," Linda said, "that if we changed the declaration of the grades array to have 250 student grades, this code wouldn't need to be changed?"

"That's exactly right, Linda," I said.

"I'm a little confused," Rhonda said. "How are we specifying the subscript for the array elements?"

"Do you remember a little earlier I said that we could refer to an array's subscript using a variable?" I said. "That's what we're doing here by using the row variable, which is the Loop Control variable for the For loop. As you can see, row is initialized to zero, which is the value for the first element of the array. We then increment row by one each time the For loop executes. The For loop continues to execute while the value of the row variable is less than the Length attribute of the grades array:"

```
for (int row = 0; row < grades.length; row++) {
```

"Length attribute?" Linda asked. "What's that?"

"Do you remember a few minutes ago I mentioned that in Java, arrays are actually objects?" I asked. "As a byproduct of that, each array that we declare has a Length attribute, which tells us exactly how many elements are in the array. By specifying that the For loop should continue to execute while the value of the row Loop Control variable is less than the **length** attribute of the array, we ensure that we access each and every element of the array."

"Powerful," Ward said.

"I'm afraid I still don't see how we specify the subscript for the individual array elements," Rhonda said. "Is it because we are using the Loop Control variable row within the curly braces?"

"That's exactly right, Rhonda," I said. "The Loop Control variable is used, within curly braces, to specify the subscript of the array element we wish to display in the Java console. Each time the body of the For loop is executed, an incrementing value of row is used as the subscript for the array element:"

```
System.out.println();
```

"After we have displayed the value of the array element in the Java console, we then add it to the current value of the variable accumulator," I continued. "In this way, the Accumulator variable maintains a running total of the value of the array elements we have displayed in the Java console."

```
accumulator = accumulator + grades[row];
```

"To make things easier to understand," I said, "visualize that the first time the body of the For loop is executed, the value of the row variable is zero. That means that this statement is interpreted by Java like this:"

```
accumulator = accumulator + grades[0]
```

"This statement in turn is then interpreted by Java like this:"

```
accumulator = 0 + 82
```

"The second time through the loop," I continued, "the value of row in incremented, making it 1, and the statement is then interpreted by Java like this:"

```
accumulator = accumulator + grades[1]
```

"Or like this:"

```
accumulator = 82 + 90
```

I explained that this process is repeated until all the For loop terminates and all the elements of the array had been processed.

"We can't forget the role of the Counter variable in the process," I said. "It's this line of code that increments the value of the Counter variable, each time the For loop is executed. When the For loop terminates, the value of the Counter variable is equal to the number of elements in the array:"

```
counter++;
```

"Finally, this section of code is identical to the previous versions, displaying a blank line in the Java console, calculating the average, and displaying it in the Java console as well. The big difference here is that the value of the Counter variable is assigned within the For loop, not at the time the Counter variable is declared:"

```
System.out.println();
average = accumulator / counter;
System.out.println("The class average is " + average);
```

Using an Array for Averaging

"I would really love to see arrays used with the code we wrote in Exercise 10-1," Mary said. "Is it possible to use arrays there, even when the user is being prompted for grades to calculate?"

"Yes, it is possible," I said. I hadn't really considered having the class do this, but it sounded like a great idea, and so, after a few minutes of thought, I distributed this exercise for the class to complete.

Exercise 10-4 Using Arrays with Interactive Processing

In this exercise, you'll modify the program you wrote in Exercise 10-1, using Arrays to make the process of calculating the average of six grades much easier.

1. Use Notepad (if you are using Windows) and enter the following code.

```java
import javax.swing.JOptionPane;
class Practice10_4 {
  public static void main (String[] args) {
    int grades[] = new int[6];
    int accumulator = 0;
    int counter = 0;
    double average = 0;

    String moreGradesToCalculate;
    moreGradesToCalculate = JOptionPane.showInputDialog
      ("Do you want to enter a grade?");
    moreGradesToCalculate = moreGradesToCalculate.toUpperCase();
    while (moreGradesToCalculate.equals ("YES")) {
      grades[counter] = Integer.parseInt
        (JOptionPane.showInputDialog("What is the grade?"));
      moreGradesToCalculate = JOptionPane.showInputDialog
        ("Do you have another grade to calculate?");
      moreGradesToCalculate = moreGradesToCalculate.toUpperCase();
      counter++;
    }

    for (int row = 0; row < grades.length; row++) {
      System.out.println(grades[row]);
      accumulator = accumulator + grades[row];
    }

    System.out.println();
    average = accumulator / counter;
    System.out.println("The class average is " + average);
    System.exit (0);
  }
}
```

2. Save your source file as Practice10_4.java in the \JFiles\Practice folder (select File | Save As from Notepad's menu bar). Be sure to save your source file with the filename extension .java.

3. Compile your source file into a Bytecode file.

4. Execute your program. The program will ask if you if you have grades to enter. Enter **Yes**.

5. The program will then prompt you for a grade. Enter **82**.

6. The program will then ask if you have more grades to enter. Enter **Yes**.

7. The program will then prompt you for a grade. Enter **90**, and continue entering grades in this manner (**64** for the third grade, **80** for the fourth, **95** for the fifth, and **75** for the sixth).

8. After entering the sixth grade, the program will ask if you have more grades to enter. Enter **No**. The program will then display the calculated average, which is **81**.

Discussion

"As you can see," I said, "the changes between this version of the program and the one from Exercise 10-1 are pretty dramatic. Using arrays to process a series of grades like this is a great deal easier than using six variables."

"I see that," Steve said, "and I can also see that we married the methodologies from Exercise 10-1 and Exercise 10-3 to write a program that allows the user to load values into the elements of the array themselves, instead of the program doing so within code."

"That's right, Steve," I said. "Much of the code in this program is found in Exercise 10-1. The main difference is that the user's input of a quiz grade is assigned to an element of an array instead of to a dedicated variable. Before I forget, I should mention that this program has some potential problems in that it only works if the user enters exactly six quiz grades, but we'll see how we can fix that later. Let's take a look at the code now. As we did in

Exercise 10-3, the first thing we did was declare an Integer array called grades containing six elements, plus variables for the Accumulator, Counter, and Average variables:"

```
int grades[] = new int[6];
int accumulator = 0;
int counter = 0;
double average = 0;
```

"You should recognize the String variable moreGradesToCalculate," I said, "from the Grades Calculation Project as a variable we use in a While loop test expression to determine if we should continue processing the loop to prompt the user for more grades."

```
String moreGradesToCalculate;
```

"This section of code asks the user if they have a grade to enter, takes their response and, using the **toUpperCase()** method, converts it to uppercase:"

```
moreGradesToCalculate = JOptionPane.showInputDialog
   ("Do you want to enter a grade?");
moreGradesToCalculate = moreGradesToCalculate.toUpperCase();
```

"This section of code establishes a While loop, in which the user is prompted for a grade, then asked if they have any others to input:"

```
while (moreGradesToCalculate.equals ("YES")) {
```

"This line of code is crucial, in that it uses the value of the Counter variable to establish the subscript number as the user's value for a grade is then added as an element to the array:"

```
grades[counter] = Integer.parseInt
   (JOptionPane.showInputDialog("What is the grade?"));
```

"Now it's time to ask the user if they have more grades to enter. Once again, their response is converted to uppercase, then stored in the *moreGradesToCalculate* variable:"

```
moreGradesToCalculate = JOptionPane.showInputDialog
   ("Do you have another grade to calculate?");
moreGradesToCalculate = moreGradesToCalculate.toUpperCase();
```

"This line of code is also crucial: it's here that we increment the value of the Counter variable so that if the user does have another grade to input, we load that value into the next element in the grades array. We'll also use the value of the Counter variable later to calculate the class average:"

```
counter++;
```

"The While loop continues to execute until the user indicates they have no more grades to input. At that point, we have an array loaded with grade values, and it's time to read the values in the grades array and calculate an average, just as we did in Exercise 10-3. In fact, this code is identical to that in Exercise 10-3, in which we use a For loop to move through the elements of the grades array and to calculate an average:"

```
for (int row = 0; row < grades.length; row++) {
   System.out.println(grades[row]);
   accumulator = accumulator + grades[row];
}

System.out.println();
average = accumulator / counter;
System.out.println("The class average is " + average);
System.exit (0);
```

A Problem with our Array

"I just noticed a slight problem," Rhonda said. "When I ran the program and entered only one quiz grade, the program gave me the correct average, but it also displayed a bunch of zeros as if it thought I had entered six grades."

"That's right, Rhonda," I said. "That's what I was alluding to earlier when I said this version of the program only works if the user enters exactly six grades.

I then ran the program myself and, instead of entering six grades, I entered the first grade, 82, and told the program that I had no more grades to enter. The following screenshot was displayed on the classroom projector:

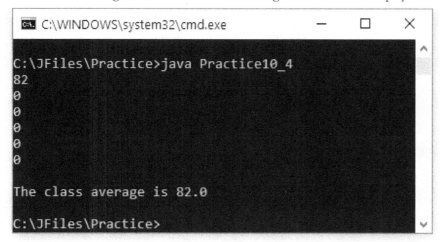

"That's exactly what happened to me," Rhonda said. "The average is correct, but what are all those zeros?"

"Those are the empty array elements," I said. "This version of the program works OK, in that it calculates the correct class average regardless of the number of grades entered. However, as you can see, it displays the values for each and every array element, including those which were initialized to zero but never assigned a grade value. Remember, we initialized the grades array to six elements, and since we only loaded one element to the grades array, it's this code, using the length attribute of the array, that poses the problem:"

```
for (int row = 0; row < grades.length; row++) {
  System.out.println(grades[row]);
  accumulator = accumulator + grades[row];
}
```

"What's wrong with the code?" Blaine asked.

"The code presumes that the array has been fully loaded," I said, "because it uses the length attribute of the grades array to determine the end point of the For loop."

"And the length attribute returns a value equal to the number of elements in the array, not the number of elements that have had values loaded to them," Dave said.

"Dave's right," Linda said. "How can we modify the For loop so that it ends based on the number of elements that actually contain grades, not just initialized zeros?"

"We can actually do that pretty easily by changing the construct of the For loop to use the value of the Counter variable to determine its end point rather than the length attributes of the array, like this:"

```
for (int row = 0; row < counter; row++)
```

"I see," Valerie said. "Counter contains a value equal to the actual number of elements with grades in the array."

"That's right, Valerie," I said. "If we compile and execute this program, our results will be much better." I did exactly that, entered a single grade, and the following screenshot was displayed on the classroom projector:

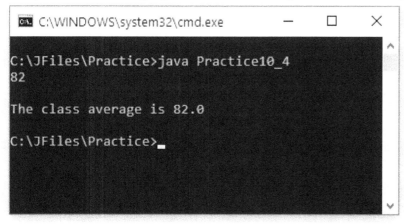

"That's better," Ward said, "but I just noticed another problem. I tried to enter a seventh grade, and the program bombed with an error."

"That will happen, Ward," I replied. "That's because we declared our array to have six elements. Trying to add a seventh element to the array will cause a runtime error." I then demonstrated for the class what happens when you try to input a seventh grade; the following screenshot was displayed on the classroom projector:

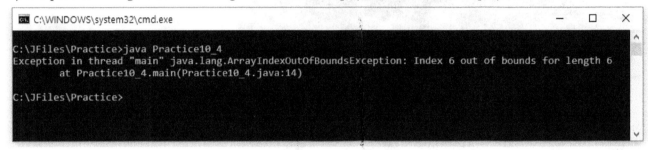

What's that error message telling us?" Rhonda asked.

"Java is telling us we have an OutOfBoundsException," I said. "That's the error we trigger when we refer to an array element that does not exist. In this case, when I entered a seventh grade, I attempted to reference element number 6 of the grades array, and we know the 'top floor' of the grades array is 5."

"Wow, this opens up a whole can of worms," Dave said. "I would think there would be times when you don't know ahead of time how many elements you need to have in your array, such as when you use an array to store values you read from a file. What should we do, declare the array with a large number?"

"You raise a good point, Dave," I said. "There will be times when, as is the case here, you can't be certain of the size of your array prior to writing the program. In that case, one approach is to declare the array with an overly large size. For instance, we could declare the grades array with 10,000 elements—that would certainly take care of our needs."

```
int grades[] = new int[10000];
```

"Isn't that a waste of the computer's memory?" Bob asked. "Isn't there a way, while the program is running, to make the array larger if it needs to be?"

"Unfortunately, no," I said. "Once you declare an array, its number of elements is set in stone; you absolutely cannot change the number of elements in it. And you're right, Bob—this can be a waste of the computer's memory. It's possible to declare an array with so many elements that it exceeds the available memory in your PC. If you do, you'll receive an error message when you run the program."

> NOTE: In previous versions of this book, I was able to demonstrate an OutOfMemoryError, but with the computer I'm using now (huge amounts of RAM) I found it impossible.

"So what's the answer?" Linda said. "Are there certain types of problems that we can't use an array to solve?"

"You'll see that in the Advanced Java course," I said, "but there are other types of objects similar to arrays—ArrayLists and vectors—that have the same power as arrays, use less resources, and give us a little more flexibility and control in managing large amounts of data. Both of these objects are beyond the scope of this introductory course, but feel free to experiment with them on your own if you wish."

Multiple Dimensioned Arrays

We were making great progress on what can be a difficult topic, so I began my discussion of multidimensional arrays.

"All of the arrays that we've seen so far have been one-dimensional arrays," I explained. "Now it's time to discuss multidimensional arrays."

"Dare I ask the difference?" said Kathy tentatively.

"They say a picture is worth a thousand words," I said. "Let's use Notepad to see the difference. In Notepad, one-dimensional arrays appear as a single column of data. Two-dimensional arrays appear as rows and columns of data, much like a worksheet. For instance," I said, as I displayed this file on the classroom projector:

I displayed this file on the classroom projector:

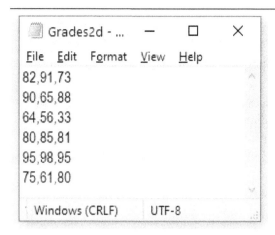

"This is a two-dimensional text file," I explained. "This file contains not only the original quiz grades we worked with in our exercises so far today, but also two other quiz grades."

"So the first column of numbers are scores from the first quiz, the second column is scores from the second quiz, and the third column is scores from the third quiz?" Ward asked.

"That's right," I replied. "Each row represents a record of three quiz scores for one student, and each column represents a different quiz."

"You mentioned the word multidimensional a minute ago," Joe said, "and you just said this is the depiction for a two-dimensional array. Does that mean you can have an array with more than two dimensions?"

"Yes you can, Joe," I answered. "Creating an array with more than two dimensions is easy in Java. Visualizing one is something else and requires a little imagination, but Java doesn't limit you to a two-dimensional array. In fact, Java allows you to declare an array with up to 255 dimensions."

"So far," Kathy said, "both types of arrays you've shown us, the one-dimensional and two-dimensional varieties, have represented some real-world object. What kind of real-world object would you represent with a three-dimensional array?"

"One classic example," I said, "is a farm. We can use a three-dimensional array to represent a farmer's crops. A farmer plants crops in fields (the first dimension), and within a field, he or she plants crops in rows (the second dimension) and columns (the third dimension). Try to imagine a farm that has ten fields, each field made up of one hundred rows and columns,. A three-dimensional array is a perfect way to represent the crop plants in a particular row and column of a field on the farm."

I gave everyone a chance to visualize this.

"Is there any limitation to how large an array can be?" Steve asked.

"In theory, no," I said, "but as we saw just a few minutes ago when we ran out of memory by declaring a huge one-dimensional array, there is a practical limitation in terms of your PC's memory. Multidimensional arrays, in particular, can use up the available memory in your computer very quickly. Each dimension that you add to an array geometrically increases the storage requirements for the array."

I sensed that my students were becoming tense with this discussion of multidimensional arrays, so I sought to comfort them a bit.

"Don't worry," I told everyone, "in the real-world of programming, most of your work will be with one- and two-dimensional arrays—just remember that everything you learn today about two-dimensional arrays can be applied to an array with three or more dimensions."

"How are two-dimensional arrays declared?" Joe asked.

"The declaration for a multidimensional array is slightly different from that of a one-dimensional array," I said. "With a multidimensional array, you need to declare a size for each dimension of the array. For instance, here's the declaration for the file we just viewed in Notepad that contains scores for three quizzes for six different students:"

```
int grades[] [] = new int[6] [3];
```

"Notice that there are two sets of square brackets," I said, "one for each dimension of the array. The two sets of square brackets tell Java that we wish to declare a two-dimensional array. For a three-dimensional array we would have three sets of square brackets. By convention, for a two-dimensional array, the declaration for the rows appears first, followed by the declaration for the columns, although there's no requirement to do it that way."

"So the number 6 refers to the number of rows in the array, and the number 3 refers to the number of columns?" Barbara asked.

"That's right," I said. "Java knows that the number of bracket pairs it sees in the declaration equates to the number of dimensions in the array. With this declaration, Java initializes a two-dimensional array, the first dimension having six elements, with the lowest subscript being 0, and the highest subscript being 5. The second dimension has three elements, with the lowest subscript being 0 and the highest being 2. Let me ask you a question: If this array were actually a worksheet, how many cells would it contain?"

"Eighteen," Dave said. "Just multiply the two size figures—six by three is eighteen."

"That's right, Dave," I said. "A two-dimensional array containing six rows and three columns contains a total of 18 elements, each element holding a quiz score. You can see why I said earlier that each dimension you add to an array increases its storage requirements geometrically."

"How do we refer to individual elements within a multidimensional array?" Peter asked. "Is it similar to referring to the elements of a one-dimensional array?"

"It is similar," I answered. "As we've seen, one-dimensional arrays are referenced by using a single subscript within square brackets. Two-dimensional array elements are referenced by using two subscripts, one for each dimension. For example, to refer to the third quiz grade for the second student, we would use this notation:"

```
grades[1] [2] = 88;
```

"The number within the first pair of square brackets," I said, "refers to the first dimension, or row, of the array, and that's the dimension that represents students. Don't forget, subscript 1 is actually the second row, or student, in the array. The number within the second set of square brackets refers to the second dimension, or column, of the array, and that's the dimension that represents quizzes. Subscript 2 is the third quiz score."

I looked for signs of confusion in the faces of my students, but happily, I didn't see any. I suggested that now would be a great time for them to get their feet wet completing an exercise with a two-dimensional array.

Exercise 10-5 A Two-Dimensional Array

In this exercise, you'll create your first two-dimensional Array.
1. Use Notepad (if you are using Windows) and enter the following code.

```java
import javax.swing.JOptionPane;
class Practice10_5 {
  public static void main (String[] args) {
    int grades[] [] = new int[6] [3];

    grades[0] [0] = 82;
    grades[0] [1] = 91;
    grades[0] [2] = 73;

    grades[1] [0] = 90;
    grades[1] [1] = 65;
    grades[1] [2] = 88;

    grades[2] [0] = 64;
    grades[2] [1] = 56;
    grades[2] [2] = 33;

    grades[3] [0] = 80;
    grades[3] [1] = 85;
    grades[3] [2] = 81;

    grades[4] [0] = 95;
    grades[4] [1] = 98;
    grades[4] [2] = 95;

    grades[5] [0] = 75;
    grades[5] [1] = 61;
    grades[5] [2] = 80;
```

```
    for (int row = 0; row < grades.length; row++) {
      for (int col = 0; col < grades[row].length; col++)
        System.out.print(grades[row] [col] + " ");
      System.out.println();
    }
  }
}
```

2. Save your source file as **Practice10_5.java** in the \JFiles\Practice folder (select File | Save As from Notepad's menu bar). Be sure to save your source file with the filename extension .java.

3. Compile your source file into a Bytecode file.

4. Execute your program. The program will display the three quiz grades for the six students in row and column format.

Discussion

I immediately ran the program myself and the following screenshot was displayed on the classroom projector:

"As you can see," I said, "what we've done is write code to load the three quiz grades for six students into a two-dimensional array and then display them in the Java console."

"This is pretty impressive," Rhonda said. "Although I must confess, I'm not real clear with how you did this."

"Don't worry, Rhonda," I said, "I'll be glad to explain it."

"That first line of code, is that the declaration for the two-dimensional array?" Peter asked.

"Yes it is, Peter," I replied. "Here we are declaring a two-dimensional array, and the numbers within the square brackets indicate the size of each dimension. Remember, by convention, in a two-dimensional array, the row is specified first, followed by the column:"

```
int grades[] [] = new int[6] [3];
```

"Once we've declared the array," I said, "this next section of code initializes each element of the array, here, one line of code at a time:"

```
grades[0] [0] = 82;
grades[0] [1] = 91;
grades[0] [2] = 73;

grades[1] [0] = 90;
grades[1] [1] = 65;
grades[1] [2] = 88;

grades[2] [0] = 64;
grades[2] [1] = 56;
grades[2] [2] = 33;

grades[3] [0] = 80;
grades[3] [1] = 85;
grades[3] [2] = 81;
```

```
grades[4] [0] = 95;
grades[4] [1] = 98;
grades[4] [2] = 95;

grades[5] [0] = 75;
grades[5] [1] = 61;
grades[5] [2] = 80;
```

"It's possible to initialize the elements of a two-dimensional array the same way we initialized the elements of the one-dimensional array in Exercise 10-3, like this:"

```
int grades[] [] = {
  { 82, 91, 73},
  { 90, 65, 88},
  { 64, 56, 33},
  { 80, 85, 81},
  { 95, 98, 95},
  { 75, 61, 80}
};
```

"Some students find this syntax confusing, so I'll leave it up to you to determine which syntax you prefer to use. Now, with our two-dimensional array loaded with values, what remains is to navigate through the 18 elements of the array and display them on the Java console. This next section of code is similar to the code you saw in Exercise 10-4, but because we are dealing with an array that has not just one dimension but two, the technique is more complex, requiring us to use something called nested For loops:"

```
for (int row = 0; row < grades.length; row++) {
   for (int col = 0; col < grades[row].length; col++)
      System.out.print(grades[row] [col] + " ");
   System.out.println();
}
```

"This is where I got totally lost when I did the exercise," Kate said. "You say this is a nested For loop? I think I've heard some programmers at work use that term. It sounds very complicated."

"Nested For loops can be intimidating, Kate," I said, "but if you just remember that a nested For loop is nothing more than a loop whose body itself contains a For loop, I think you'll be OK."

I paused a moment to give everyone in the class to take in what I had just said.

"A nested For loop is a For loop that contains another For loop in its body," I repeated. "The first For loop structure is called the outer loop, and the For loop that appears in its body is called the inner loop. If you check the code, you'll see that each For loop has its own unique Loop Control variable. I've named the Loop Control variable of the outer loop row, and the Loop Control variable of the inner loop col. This is because the outer loop is intended to process the columns in the two-dimensional array, and the inner loop is intended to process the rows. Think of these For loops almost like a mouse pointer that is directing a screen cursor to various positions within the array."

"This is confusing," Rhonda chimed in. "I keep trying to visualize what's going on with the code but..."

"I think if you take it a step at a time, you'll be fine," I said. "And that's exactly what we're going to be doing in a minute. Notice that the outer loop has a body consisting of three lines of code: another For loop, a **print()** method, and a **println()** method. The inner loop has a body consisting of just one line of code: the **print()** method."

"Isn't the **println()** method part of the body of the inner loop?" Barbara asked.

"No, it's not," I said. "The inner loop—the one that uses col as the Loop Control variable—has just one line of code in it, the **print()** method."

I paused for a moment before continuing.

"You'll see in a minute," I said, "as we step through this code, that the body of the inner loop will be executed a total of 18 times, while the body of the outer loop will be executed just six times."

"Is that because there are six rows of data in the array?" Dave asked.

"Exactly, Dave," I said.

"But there are only three columns in the array," Blaine said, "Why would the inner loop be executed 18 times? Shouldn't it be executed just three times?"

"That's a good question, Blaine," I responded. "The inner loop is executed three times, but each time the outer loop is executed, which is six times, the inner loop is once again executed three times. Six multiplied by three is 18—that's the total number of times the inner loop is executed."

"It also happens to be the number of elements in the array," Dave said.

I saw a great deal of confusion on the faces of my students.

"Don't worry if you feel a little overwhelmed by this right now," I said. "I think this will all make a lot more sense to you in a few moments. Let's get back to the body of the inner loop now. Amazingly, it consists of just this single line of code:"

```
System.out.print(grades[row] [col] + " ");
```

"This line of code will be executed a total 18 times," I explained, "which, as Dave pointed out, is the total number of elements, or quiz grades, in our two-dimensional array. Using nested For loops, the values of the two Loop Control variables, row and col, are varied to point to each element in the array and displayed in the Java console:"

```
for (int row = 0; row < grades.length; row++) {
    for (int col = 0; col < grades[row].length; col++)
```

"Again, the first loop is known as the outer loop," I continued, "and we use it to move through the rows in the array. We initialize its Loop Control variable, row, to 0, and for its termination point, we use the length attribute of the grades array, which is six. Ultimately, Java interprets this line of code to look like this:."

```
for (int row = 0; row < 6; row++) {
```

to look like this:"

"That means that the outer loop is executed six times, is that right?" Chuck asked.

"Exactly right, Chuck," I said. "Now let's take a closer look at the inner loop, which is used to process the columns in the array:"

```
for (int col = 0; col < grades[row].length; col++)
```

"I want you to notice the length attribute as we use it here. We used the length attribute in the outer loop also, and in that case, it returned a value equal to the number of rows in the array. In this case, we're asking Java to return the length attribute for a particular row of the array, and that's why we used the qualifier row here. Ultimately, Java interprets this code to look like this:"

```
for (int col = 0; col < 3; col++)
```

"And that's why the inner loop is executed three times?" Chuck asked.

"That's right, Chuck," I said.

"Maybe this will help," I said, "to give you an appreciation for the sequence of code execution." I then displayed this table on the classroom projector:

Statement	row	col	grades	Value of grades	Comment
For (int row…)	0				First execution of outer loop
For (int col…)	0	0	0,0	82	First execution of inner loop
print(grades[row] [col]	0	0	0,0	82	Displays 82 in Java Console
For (int col…) incremented by 1.	0	1	0,1	91	Second execution of inner loop. Value of col is
print(grades[row] [col]	0	1	0,1	91	Displays 91 in Java Console
For (int col…) incremented by 1.	0	2	0,2	73	Third execution of inner loop. Value of col is
print(grades[row] [col]	0	2	0,2	73	Displays 73 in the Java Console
println()	0	2	0,2	73	New line is generated in the Java Console

For (int row…) incremented by 1.	1				Second execution of outer loop. Value of row is
For (int col…)	1	0	1,0	90	First execution of inner loop
print(grades[row] [col]	1	0	1,0	90	Displays 90 in Java Console
For (int col…) incremented by 1.	1	1	1,1	65	Second execution of inner loop. Value of col is
print(grades[row] [col]	1	1	1,1	65	Displays 65 in Java Console
For (int col…) incremented by 1.	1	2	1,2	88	Third execution of inner loop. Value of col is
print(grades[row] [col]	1	2	1,2	88	Displays 88 in the Java Console
println()	1	2	1,2	88	New line is generated in the Java Console
For (int row…) incremented by 1.	2				Third execution of outer loop. Value of row is
For (int col…)	2	0	2,0	64	First execution of inner loop
print(grades[row] [col]	2	0	2,0	64	Displays 64 in Java Console
For (int col…) incremented by 1.	2	1	2,1	56	Second execution of inner loop. Value of col is
print(grades[row] [col]	2	1	2,1	56	Displays 56 in Java Console
For (int col…) incremented by 1.	2	2	2,2	33	Third execution of inner loop. Value of col is
print(grades[row] [col]	2	2	2,2	33	Displays 33 in the Java Console
println()	2	2	2,2	33	New line is generated in the Java Console
For (int row…) incremented by 1.	3				Fourth execution of outer loop. Value of row is
For (int col…)	3	0	3,0	80	First execution of inner loop
print(grades[row] [col]	3	0	3,0	80	Displays 80 in Java Console
For (int col…) incremented by 1.	3	1	3,1	85	Second execution of inner loop. Value of col is
print(grades[row] [col]	3	1	3,1	85	Displays 85 in Java Console
For (int col…) incremented by 1.	3	2	3,2	81	Third execution of inner loop. Value of col is
print(grades[row] [col]	3	2	3,2	81	Displays 81 in the Java Console
println()	3	2	3,2	81	New line is generated in the Java Console
For (int row…) incremented by 1.	4				Fifth execution of outer loop. Value of row is
For (int col…)	4	0	4,0	95	First execution of inner loop
print(grades[row] [col]	4	0	4,0	95	Displays 95 in Java Console
For (int col…) incremented by 1.	4	1	4,1	98	Second execution of inner loop. Value of col is
print(grades[row] [col]	4	1	4,1	98	Displays 98 in Java Console
For (int col…) incremented by 1.	4	2	4,2	95	Third execution of inner loop. Value of col is
print(grades[row] [col]	4	2	4,2	95	Displays 95 in the Java Console
println()	4	2	4,2	95	New line is generated in the Java Console

For (int row...) incremented by 1.	5				Sixth execution of outer loop. Value of row is
For (int col...)	5	0	5,0	75	First execution of inner loop
print(grades[row] [col]	5	0	5,0	75	Displays 55 in Java Console
For (int col...) incremented by 1.	5	1	5,1	61	Second execution of inner loop. Value of col is
print(grades[row] [col]	5	1	5,1	61	Displays 61 in Java Console
For (int col...) incremented by 1.	5	2	5,2	80	Third execution of inner loop. Value of col is
print(grades[row] [col]	5	2	5,2	80	Displays 80 in the Java Console
println()	5	2	5,2	80	New line is generated in the Java Console

We then spent the next few minutes going over the table.

"This table shows the statements that are being executed," I said, "as well as the values of the row and col Loop Control variables, the array element that is being pointed to by the value of row and col, the value of that array element, and the result of the execution of the statement."

We spent the next few minutes going over the table.

"I hope that helped," I said, as I scanned the faces of my students for signs of confusion.

"Yes, it did," Ward said. "I have just one question: why did we use the **print()** method in the body of the inner loop to print the values of the individual elements of the array and not the **println()** method?"

"The **print()** method doesn't generate a new line character," I said. "If we had used the **println()** method, we would have had a single column of values displayed in the Java console, with each value appearing on a line by itself. Instead, we executed the **print()** method, which tells Java to display a value in the Java console but not to generate a new line character. As a result, the cursor in the Java console remains on the same line. We did execute the **println()** method, but only at the end of each row, as the last statement in the body of the inner loop."

That explanation satisfied Ward and the other students, so before continuing onto the next topic of creating arrays of objects, I asked everyone to take a 15-minute break.

Creating Arrays of Objects

That explanation satisfied Ward and the other students, so before continuing onto the next topic of creating arrays of objects, I asked everyone to take a 15-minute break.

"Something that's asked of me all the time," I said, after resuming from break, "is whether it's possible to create an array of objects in Java."

"You mean like the Student objects we've been working with throughout the class?" Mary asked.

"That's right, Mary," I said, "that kind of object. The answer is yes. In fact, creating an array of objects is easy to do. Do you remember the Banner object we worked with several weeks ago? Let's create an array of Banner objects."

I displayed this code on the classroom projector:

```java
public class Example10_1 {
  public static void main(String[] args) {
    Banner x[] = new Banner[10];
    x[0] = new Banner();
    x[0].favoriteProgram = "Java";
    x[0].display();

    x[1] = new Banner();
    x[1].favoriteProgram = "Visual Basic";
    x[1].display();

    for (int row = 0; row < 2; row++) {
      System.out.println(x[row].favoriteProgram);
    }
```

```
    }
}
```

I compiled and executed the program. The following screenshot was displayed on the classroom projector:

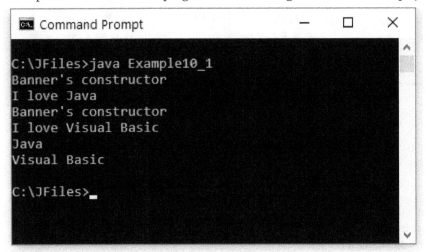

"Working with an array of objects is a little different than working with an array of Java primitive data types, such as int or string," I said. "It's really a two-step process. First, we need to declare the array of objects, and then we need to go about the business of actually creating the objects, just as we would normally. But because we're dealing with an array of objects, we need to use subscript values when we refer to the object. Let's start with the array declaration. This line of code declares a 10-element array of Banner objects called x. This is the same as an array declaration for an array of integers."

```
Banner x[] = new Banner[10];
```

"With the array declared, we can then go about creating the Banner objects themselves, but we need to tell Java where in the array this object, once created, will be referenced. In this case, it's element number 0:"

```
x[0] = new Banner();
```

"With the Banner object created and referenced as element 0 of the x array, we can now work with the object just as we normally would—we just need to remember to reference the element number any time we refer to the object. With this line of code, we set the favoriteProgram attribute of the Banner object to 'Java':"

```
x[0].favoriteProgram = "Java";
```

"And then we execute its **display()** method:"

```
x[0].display();
```

"Just to prove that we can have multiple Banner objects alive at the same time, this code creates a second Banner object, establishes it as element 1 of the x array, sets its favoriteProgram attribute to 'Visual Basic' and then executes its display() method:"

```
x[1] = new Banner();
x[1].favoriteProgram = "Visual Basic";
x[1].display();
```

"So we have two Banner objects loaded in our array?" Mary asked.

"You can think of it that way, Mary," I said. "In reality, the array contains a reference—a memory address, really—pointing to both objects. The important thing is that when we refer to an element in the array, Java can find the Banner object we intend to work with in the computer's memory, along with any attributes that belong to that particular object. That's why we can use the For loop logic we've been employing in today's class to display the favoriteProgram attribute of every Banner object referenced by our array:"

```
for (int row = 0; row < 2; row++) {
  System.out.println(x[row].favoriteProgram);
}
```

"That is really neat," Blaine said. "I'm beginning to like arrays more and more—too bad we can't include one in the Grade Calculation Project."

"I don't see why we can't," I said. "Frank Olley never requested it, but I don't think he would mind if we calculated an overall average for every student's grade entered into the program. I think an array would be a perfect way to do that."

I then distributed this exercise for the class to complete.

Exercise 10-6 Modify the Grades Calculation Project to use an Array

In this exercise, you'll modify the Grades class to include Array processing to calculate an overall class average.
1. Using Notepad (if you are using Windows) locate and open the Grades.java source file. (It should be in the \JFiles\Grades folder)
2. Modify your code so that it looks like this.

```java
import javax.swing.JOptionPane;
class Grades {
  public static void main(String[] args) {
    String moreGradesToCalculate;
    String response;
    double grades[] = new double[1000];
    double accumulator = 0;
    int counter = 0;
    double average = 0;

    moreGradesToCalculate = JOptionPane.showInputDialog
      ("Do you want to calculate a grade?");
    moreGradesToCalculate = moreGradesToCalculate.toUpperCase();
    while (moreGradesToCalculate.equals ("YES")) {
      response = whatKindOfStudent();
      switch(Integer.parseInt(response)) {
        case 1:
          EnglishStudent eStudent = new EnglishStudent();
          eStudent.calculate();
          grades[counter] = eStudent.getFinalNumericGrade();
          counter++;
          DisplayGrade x = new DisplayGrade(eStudent.getMidterm(),
              eStudent.getFinalExamGrade(),
              eStudent.getResearch(),
              eStudent.getPresentation(),
              eStudent.getFinalNumericGrade(),
              eStudent.getFinalLetterGrade());
          break;
        case 2:
          MathStudent mStudent = new MathStudent();
          mStudent.calculate();
          grades[counter] = mStudent.getFinalNumericGrade();
          counter++;
          DisplayGrade y = new DisplayGrade(mStudent.getMidterm(),
              mStudent.getFinalExamGrade(),
              mStudent.getFinalNumericGrade(),
              mStudent.getFinalLetterGrade());
          break;
        case 3:
          ScienceStudent sStudent = new ScienceStudent();
          sStudent.calculate();
          grades[counter] = sStudent.getFinalNumericGrade();
          counter++;
          DisplayGrade z = new DisplayGrade(sStudent.getMidterm(),
              sStudent.getFinalExamGrade(),
              sStudent.getResearch(),
              sStudent.getFinalNumericGrade(),
```

```
                    sStudent.getFinalLetterGrade());
            break;
        default:
          JOptionPane.showMessageDialog
            (null, response + " - is not a valid student type");
          System.exit (0);
      }                                             // end of switch
      moreGradesToCalculate = JOptionPane.showInputDialog
        ("Do you have another grade to calculate?");
      moreGradesToCalculate = moreGradesToCalculate.toUpperCase();
    }                                               // end of while

    for (int row = 0; row < counter; row++) {
      System.out.println(grades[row]);
      accumulator = accumulator + grades[row];
    }
    average = accumulator / counter;
    JOptionPane.showMessageDialog(null, "The class average is " + average);
    JOptionPane.showMessageDialog
      (null, "Thanks for using the Grades Calculation program!");
    System.exit (0);
  }                                                 // end of main

  public static String whatKindOfStudent() {
    String response;
    response = JOptionPane.showInputDialog
      ("Enter student type (1=English, 2=Math, 3=Science)");
    if (response == null) {
      JOptionPane.showMessageDialog
        (null, "You clicked on the Cancel button");
      System.exit (0);
    }
    else
    if (response.equals("")) {
      JOptionPane.showMessageDialog
        (null, "You must make an entry in the InputBox");
      System.exit (0);
    }
    else
    if (Integer.parseInt(response) < 1 | Integer.parseInt(response) > 3) {
      JOptionPane.showMessageDialog
        (null, response + " - is not a valid student type");
      System.exit (0);
    }
    return response;
  }                                     // end of whatKindOfStudent method
}  // end of class
```

3. Save your source file as Grades.java in the \JFiles\Grades folder (select File | Save As from Notepad's menu bar). Be sure to save your source file with the filename extension .java.

4. Compile your source file into a Bytecode file.

5. Execute your program and test it thoroughly. After you start up your program, it should ask you if you have a grade to calculate.

6. Answer **Yes** and calculate the grade for an English student. Enter **70** for the midterm, **80** for the final examination, **90** for the research grade, and **100** for the presentation. A final numeric grade of **84.5** should be displayed with a letter grade of **C**.

7. After the message box is displayed with the calculated grade, the program should ask you if you have more grades to calculate.

8. Answer **Yes** and calculate the grade for a Math student. Enter **70** for the midterm and **80** for the final

examination. A final numeric grade of **75** should be displayed with a letter grade of **D**.

9. After the message box is displayed with the calculated grade, the program should ask you if you have more grades to calculate.

10. Answer **Yes** and calculate the grade for a Science student. Enter **70** for the midterm, **80** for the final examination, and **90** for the research grade. A final numeric grade of **78** should be displayed with a letter grade of **C**. After the message box is displayed with the calculated grade, the program should ask you if you have more grades to calculate.

11. Answer **No**, and an overall average of **79.16** will be displayed. In addition, all three final numeric grades will be displayed in the Java Console.

Discussion

"I'm not sure that the changes we've just made to the Grades Calculation Project are something Frank Olley requires," I said, "but I think they will add greatly to your learning experience—and it didn't require all that much additional code. Our first step was to declare a grades array to store the values of the individual calculated final grades. We declared grades as an array of the Double data type having 1000 elements, which should be more than large enough to hold the grades a user will calculate in this program:"

```
double grades[] = new double[1000];
```

"We needed to modify our existing code to add the student's calculated grade as an element of the grades array. To do that, all we needed to do was to add a line of code to each of the individual case statements and to add the FinalNumericGrade Property of the various student objects to the array, using the current value of the counter variable to specify the subscript. Here's the code to do that for the EnglishStudent object:"

```
case 1:
  EnglishStudent eStudent = new EnglishStudent();
  eStudent.calculate();
  grades[counter] = eStudent.getFinalNumericGrade();
```

"Once we have the student's grade in the grades array, we need to increment the value of the Counter variable so that the next student's grade is assigned to the next available location in the array:"

```
counter++;
```

"This process of adding an element to the grades array continues for each student calculated. Finally, when the user indicates there are no more grades to calculate, it's time to move through the elements of the array, calculate the average, and display it:"

```
for (int row = 0; row < counter; row++) {
  System.out.println(grades[row]);
  accumulator = accumulator + grades[row];
}

average = accumulator / counter;
  JOptionPane.showMessageDialog(null, "The class average is " + average);
```

"Seeing the array used in the Grades Calculation Program really helped me," Rhonda said.

I waited to see if there were any questions, but there were none. I then dismissed class for the day.

Summary

In this chapter, you learned just about everything you could want to know about array processing. In particular, you learned about the various types of arrays and about array dimensions. Arrays are a frequent source of confusion for new programmers, and I hope our coverage of them will make your future work with them easier.

Specifically, you learned the following:

- Why arrays are useful in making our code easier to write and use

- How to use one-, two-, and multidimensional arrays

- How arrays can reduce the amount of hard coding we write in our projects

In the next chapter, we'll explore some of the common errors that can occur in Java programming and examine ways to make allowances for problems that might occur when our programs run.

Chapter 11---Exception Handling

In this chapter, you'll learn how to avoid some of the common mistakes that beginner Java programmers make. You'll see that in spite of your best efforts, some errors can be introduced into your program by the users themselves, and you'll spend the second half of this chapter learning how to detect and handle those errors as well.

Common Beginner Errors

I began our eleventh class by explaining that as a teacher of computer programming, it's frequently tempting to show my students examples of bad code early on in a class in an effort to show them what not to do. However, after many years of teaching, I have learned that there's a huge danger in illustrating bad code or code that contains errors too early in the class.

"For that reason," I said, "I try to wait until we've established a strong foundation in good coding techniques before discussing the types of errors you can make that can quickly ruin your programming reputation. In today's class, we'll examine the types of common errors that beginners make and then learn how to implement error handling techniques in our Java programs to handle the errors that can occur even in the best of programs."

"What kinds of errors are you talking about detecting?" Dave asked. "I assume you mean runtime errors and you're not talking about compiler errors?"

"That's a good point, Dave," I said. "There are actually three kinds of errors that we'll be discussing today. The first kind are compiler errors, and those are the errors which are detected by the Java compiler. Compiler errors prevent us from ever getting to the point where we can run our program. The second kind are runtime errors. These are the kinds of errors that the Java compiler can't detect and which unfortunately occur when we run our compiled program. Runtime errors display nasty error messages to the users of our program. The third kind of errors are the most dangerous. These are logic errors, and they are not detected by the compiler, nor, for the most part, do they cause your program to bomb or abnormally terminate at runtime. Logic errors are programming mistakes that can cause horrific results such as generating a paycheck for an employee for one million dollars instead of one thousand dollars, ordering a dosage of medicine for a patient that is incorrect, or opening a valve or an engine of the space shuttle prematurely. Logic errors can be very difficult to track down—in fact, there are programs that have run for years with subtle logic errors that went unnoticed."

Compiler Errors

"Let's start by examining the common types of compiler errors that you are likely to make," I said. "Remember, compiler errors are those errors which are detected by the Java compiler."

Java is Case Sensitive

"Probably the most common types of compiler errors," I said, "are caused by the case sensitivity of Java. In Java, just about everything is case sensitive. The names of classes, the names of methods, and the names of variables are all case sensitive. This can give programmers, especially those who have experience in other languages that are not case sensitive, a lot of trouble. Improperly referencing the name of a class, a method, or a variable in your program will generate a 'cannot resolve symbol' compiler error. Remember, any reference to a class name, the method of a class, or a variable that you declare in your program must match the case exactly. For instance, if we declare a variable called counter (in lowercase) and then attempt to increment its value like this:

Don't Forget: If typing these examples and exercises isn't something you want to do, feel free to follow this link to find and download the completed solutions for all of the examples and exercises in the book. Just click on the Java book, then follow the link entitled exercises ☺

http://www.johnsmiley.com/main/books.htm

```
public class Example11_1 {
  public static void main(String[] args) {
    int counter = 0;
    Counter++;
```

```
        }
}
```

"We'll generate a compiler error indicating that Java 'cannot resolve symbol,' like this:"

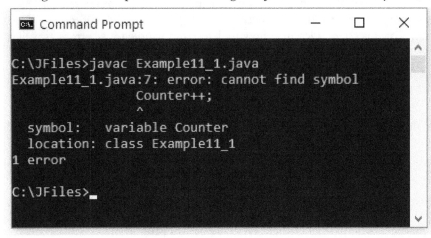

"What's a symbol?" Lou asked.

"Java keeps track of class, method, variable, and constant names in something called a symbol table," I said. "So you see, Java is just telling us that we're referencing a name that it doesn't have a record of, and that's because in this case we declared the variable counter in all lowercase but later referenced it with a capital C.

"A symbol is just a fancy name for a variable, constant, or method. Java is telling us that it doesn't know the variable Counter, and that's because we declared it as counter in all lowercase letters."

"I think I've seen this error a million times," Rhonda said, laughing.

"I would say this is probably the most common error message that a beginner will see," I said. "Until you get used to the case sensitivity of Java, this may be an error that you generate every time you compile your program. Just remember, whenever you see the unresolved symbol error, check the spelling of your class, method, or variable name."

"I sometimes get a runtime error when I'm not careful with the spelling of my class name," Peter said. "For instance, I had a lot of trouble with the ILoveJava class we created in our first week of class. I think it took me about ten minutes before I was able to execute the program."

"That's a good point, Peter," I said. "Let's take a look at the kind of runtime error we can generate if we make a mistake with the case sensitivity of our class name. For example, if we name our class IloveJava, we need to execute the program with that exact spelling: capital I and capital J. If we try to execute our class with the name iLoveJava instead—capital L and capital J—this is the runtime error that we will receive:"

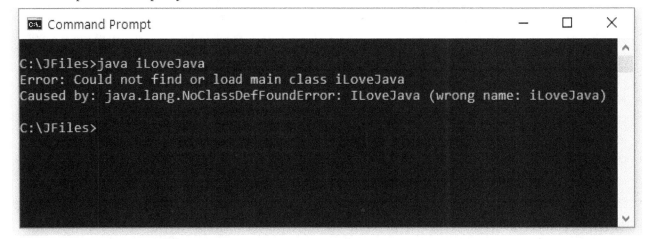

"Notice," I said, "the error message, in part anyway, indicates NoClassDefFound. That's the clue that Java tried to locate the class name you referenced, but it didn't exist."

Public Class---File name Must Be the Same

"I believe a few of you may have seen this error during the course," I said. "When you declare a class as public—and all of our classes have been public—the filename of the class must be identical to the class name in both spelling and capitalization."

"I'm not quite sure I understand what you mean," Blaine said. "Can you give us an example?"

"Sure thing, Blaine," I said. "For instance, let's create a public class called Example11_2, beginning with a capital letter **E**, we must save the class in a file named identical to the class name:"

```
public class Example11_2 {
  public static void main(String[] args) {
    int counter = 0;
    counter++;
  }
}
```

"If we save the class we've named Example11_2 in a file called example11_2 in all lowercase letters, like this:"

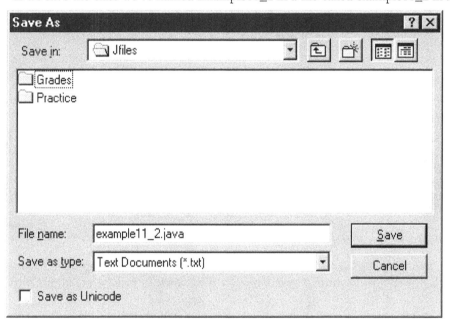

"When I try to compile the class using the Java compiler, I'll receive an error message indicating that a Public class needs to be saved in a file with the same name:"

```
C:\JFiles>javac example11_2.java
example11_2.java:3: error: class Example11_2 is public, should be declared in
 a file named Example11_2.java
public class Example11_2  {
       ^
1 error

C:\JFiles>
```

"Unlike the other error message we just saw," Steve said, "this one was pretty explicit. I think I would be able to figure that one out."

Forgetting the Semicolon at the End of a Statement

"The next error I'd like to discuss may seem pretty obvious to you," I said, "but I've seen many students ponder over this one for minutes on end without realizing what they had done."

"What's that one?" Rhonda asked. "I bet it's one I've seen!"

"Forgetting to end a statement with a semicolon," I said, "like this:"

```
public class Example11_3 {
  public static void main(String[] args) {
    int counter = 0;
    counter++
  }
}
```

"I see the problem," Lou said, "there should be a semicolon on the line of code incrementing the counter variable."

"Exactly," I agreed.

"What kind of error message will this generate?" Kate asked.

"It's a pretty explicit error message," I said, as I compiled Example11_3:

Curly Braces (and Parentheses) Must Occur in Matching Pairs

"Another common error that beginner programmers make," I said, "is dealing with curly braces in their code. In a Java class, everything following the class name must be sandwiched between curly braces. In addition, methods such as the **main()** method must also be sandwiched between curly braces. The same applies to blocks, such as If statement blocks. Here's an example of correct code. Notice that we have the same amount of left curly braces as we do right curly braces: three of each. The same applies for parentheses and square brackets: we have the same number of left and right parentheses and square brackets:"

```
public class Example11_4 {
  public static void main(String[] args) {
    int counter = 0;
    if (counter == 0) {
      System.out.println("The variable counter is equal to 0");
    }
  }
}
```

"I have to admit," Linda said, "I did find the issue of all those curly braces and parentheses confusing at first."

"I don't blame you," I said. "By the way, that's a good reason to indent your code. Another way to eliminate this error altogether is to double-check your code to ensure that you have the same number of right and left curly braces and parentheses."

"What kind of error message will you get if you make this kind of mistake?" Rhonda asked. "Is it as user friendly as some of the others we've seen this morning?"

"Let's see, Rhonda," I said. "Let's modify the code from Example11_4 by intentionally eliminating the right closing curly brace of the If statement:"

```
public class Example11_5 {
  public static void main(String[] args) {
    int counter = 0;
    if (counter == 0) {
      System.out.println("The variable counter is equal to 0");
    }
}
```

"Now let's compile the program and see what kind of error message we get," I said. I did so, and the following error message was displayed on the classroom projector:

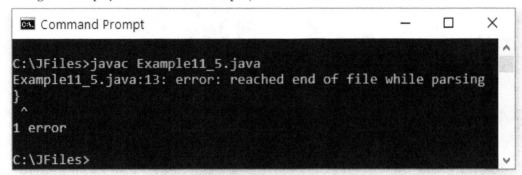

"This error message does a good job of telling us that a right curly brace is missing," I said. "Unfortunately, it does a terrible job of telling us where in our source file the missing right curly brace should be. The Java compiler leaves that up to you, and it can sometimes prove to be a difficult task. You just need to reexamine your code until you find it."

Forgetting the Left and Right Parentheses for the Condition in an If Structure

"An error that is closely related to the one we just examined," I said, "is another one I see a lot of beginners make, and it concerns the If statement. Beginners tend to forget that the test condition for an If statement must be enclosed within parentheses."

"Ah, yes," I heard Joe say.

"What's that?" Rhonda asked. "Test expression?"

"That's right, Rhonda," I said. "Let me show you an example."

"This code," I said, "uses an If statement to determine if the value of the counter variable is 0."

I then displayed this code on the classroom projector:

```
public class Example11_6 {
  public static void main(String[] args) {
    int counter = 0;
    if (counter == 0) {
      System.out.println("The variable counter is equal to 0");
    }
  }
}
```

"Notice," I said, "how the test condition *counter == 0* is enclosed within parentheses:"

```
if (counter == 0)
```

"Oh, my gosh," Rhonda said, "you're right. I totally forgot about having to do that. What kind of compiler error will that generate if we forget to do that?"

"Let me show you," I said, as I changed the code in Example11_6 to look like this:

```
public class Example11_7 {
  public static void main(String[] args) {
    int counter = 0;
    if counter == 0 {
      System.out.println("The variable counter is equal to 0");
```

```
        }
      }
    }
}
```

"Notice how the test expression is no longer enclosed within parentheses," I said. "Now, let's compile the program and see what error message it generates." I did so, and the following error message was displayed on the classroom projector:

```
Command Prompt                                    —    □    ×

C:\JFiles>javac Example11_7.java
Example11_7.java:8: error: '(' expected
                if counter == 0
                ^
Example11_7.java:8: error: ')' expected
                if counter == 0
                             ^
2 errors

C:\JFiles>_
```

"This error message is not quite as clear as some of the other compiler messages we've seen," I said. "but it does point us in the right direction by listing the line of code in error and telling us that Java is expecting a right parentheses."

Confusing the Equality Operator (==) with the Assignment Operator (=)

"This next error is one I see all the time from beginners," I said. "It occurs when beginners confuse the equality operator (==) with the assignment operator (=), usually in the test expression of an If statement. Here's the code we just examined with a properly formatted test expression checking to see if the value of the counter variable is 0:"

```java
public class Example11_8{
  public static void main(String[] args) {
    int counter = 0;
    if (counter == 0) {
      System.out.println("The variable counter is equal to 0");
    }
  }
}
```

"Notice how we check the value of counter against the numeric literal 0 by using the equality operator (==):"

```java
if (counter == 0) {
```

"It's relatively easy," I said, "especially for those you have programmed in other languages, to confuse the equality operator (==) with the assignment operator (=) and code the test expression like this instead:"

```java
if (counter = 0) {
```

"If we compile a program that includes a test expression formatted like this:"

```java
public class Example11_9{
  public static void main(String[] args) {
    int counter = 0;
    if (counter = 0) {
      System.out.println("The variable counter is equal to 0");
    }
  }
}
```

"We will get this somewhat cryptic error message:"

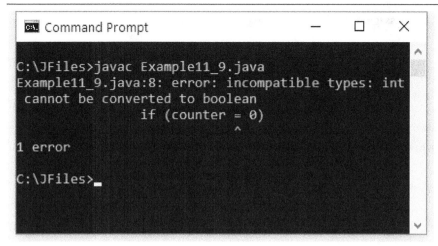

"What does that error message mean?" Rhonda asked. "'Required: boolean?'"

"Java is confused," I said, "because the test expression in an If statement must evaluate to a Boolean data type, that is, a true or false value. By using the assignment operator in the test expression, we didn't generate a Boolean result, and that's what Java is telling us."

"I understand," Blaine said. "That's something that I've been guilty of on more than one occasion."

Not Initializing a Variable Defined in a Method Before that Variable is Used in the Method Body.

"For the most part," I said, "in this class we've initialized all of the variables that we've used in our programs, and it's a good practice to get into."

"Don't we have to initialize variables?" Bob asked.

"Only local variables are required to be initialized," I said. "Instance variables, which are variables declared outside of a method, do not need to be initialized before being used. Local variables, however, which are variables declared inside the body of a method, must be initialized before they can be used. Failure to do so will generate a compiler error. Here's a program in which we declare a variable called *counter* within the **main()** method. Notice that we have forgotten to initialize it:"

```java
public class Example11_10{
  public static void main(String[] args) {
    int counter;
    if (counter == 0) {
      System.out.println("The variable counter is equal to 0");
    }
  }
}
```

I then compiled the program, and the following compiler error message was displayed on the classroom projector:

```
Command Prompt                                          —    □    ✕

C:\JFiles>javac Example11_10.java
Example11_10.java:8: error: variable counter might not have been initialized
                if (counter == 0)
                    ^
1 error

C:\JFiles>_
```

"This is a pretty descriptive compiler message," I said. "It indicates that the variable 'counter' hasn't been assigned a value."

"I agree," Rhonda said. "That is an explicit message. I don't think I would have any trouble deciphering that one."

Forgetting to Specify a Return Type for a Method You Write

"It's time to turn our attention," I said, "to a series of compiler errors that are related to methods that we write in our classes. The first one we'll examine occurs when we forget to specify a return type for a method. Remember, every method except for a Constructor method requires that we specify a return type. Even a method that will not return a value requires that we specify a return type of **<u>void</u>**. Here's the proper construction of a method called **test()** that does **<u>not</u>** return a value. Notice, however, that we specify the ***void*** return type:"

```
public class Example11_11{
  public static void main(String[] args) {
    test();
  }

  public static void test() {
    System.out.println("I love Java");
  }
}
```

"Here's the same code with the omission of the **<u>void</u>** return type:"

```
public class Example11_12{
  public static void main(String[] args) {
    test();
  }

  public static test() {
    System.out.println("I love Java");
  }
}
```

"Let's see what happens when we compile this class." I did so, and the following screenshot was displayed on the classroom projector:

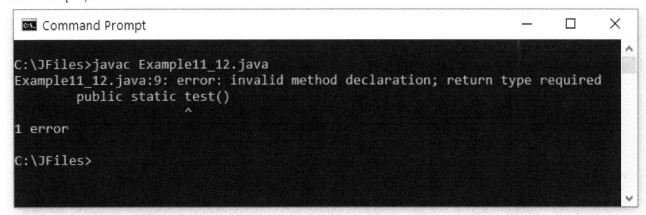

```
C:\JFiles>javac Example11_12.java
Example11_12.java:9: error: invalid method declaration; return type required
        public static test()
                      ^
1 error

C:\JFiles>
```

"Again," I said, "this is a pretty informative compiler message."

I waited to see if anyone had a question before continuing.

Forgetting to Specify the Return Value for a Method You Write

"Another error related to a method," I continued, "occurs when we declare a method with a return type, such as int or String, but forget to return a value within the method. This will generate a compiler error. Take a look at this code. Once again, we've created a method called **test()**, this time with a declaration specifying that it returns an integer return value. Notice that the last line of the method properly uses the return statement to return an integer value to the **main()** method from where it is called:"

```
public class Example11_13{
  public static void main(String[] args) {
    int returnValue = 0;
```

```
      returnValue = test();
      System.out.println("The return value of test is " + returnValue);
  }

  public static int test() {
    return 1;
  }
}
```

"However, if we forget to code a return statement, like this:"

```
public class Example11_14{
  public static void main(String[] args) {
    int returnValue = 0;
    returnValue = test();
    System.out.println("The return value of test is " + returnValue);
  }

  public static int test() {
  }
}
```

"When we compile the program, we'll receive this compile error:"

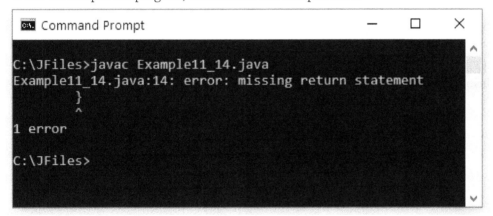

"I've got to tell you," Ward said, "I'm pretty impressed with Java's descriptive compiler messages. Many languages I've used aren't nearly this precise."

Returning the Wrong Type of Return Value for a Method You Write

"Suppose you return the wrong type of return value?" Kathy asked.

"Kathy, you must have read my mind," I said. "That's exactly the next type of compiler error I intended to cover."

"What does Kathy mean?" Rhonda asked.

"In the previous example, Rhonda," I said, "we declared our method with a return type of int and returned the integer 1 within the body of the method. Suppose, for example, instead of returning an integer, we make a mistake and return a string instead?"

```
public class Example11_15{
  public static void main(String[] args) {
    int returnValue = 0;
    returnValue = test();
    System.out.println("The return value of test is " + returnValue);
  }

  public static int test() {
    return "I love Java";
  }
}
```

"I see what you mean," Rhonda said. "Here we're returning the string 'I love Java', not an integer."

"Exactly," I replied. "If we compile this class, the following compiler error will be generated:"

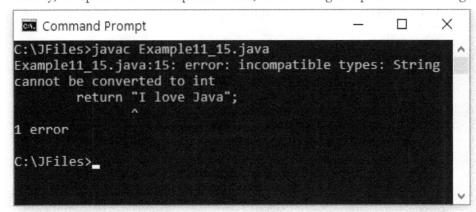

"So that's what an incompatible type means," Chuck said. "I think I've probably gotten that one myself once or twice during the class."

Returning a Value from a Method Whose Return Type is Void

"I didn't realize there were so many ways to foul up a method!" Rhonda said, laughing. "Tell me, are there any others?"

"There are at least two other ways, Rhonda," I said. "You can generate a compiler error simply by executing the return statement when you have declared your return type to be void. Let me show you:"

```java
public class Example11_16{
  public static void main(String[] args) {
    int returnValue = 0;
    returnValue = test();
    System.out.println("The return value of test is " + returnValue);
  }
  public static void test() {
    return 1;
  }
}
```

"Notice that the declaration for the **test()** method specifies a return type of *void*, " I said. "Yet, within the body of the method, we execute the return statement. Let's see what happens when we compile this class:"

```
C:\JFiles>javac Example11_16.java
Example11_16.java:8: error: incompatible types: void cannot be converted
to int
                returnValue = test();
                              ^
Example11_16.java:15: error: incompatible types: unexpected return value
        return 1;
               ^
2 errors

C:\JFiles>
```

"This compiler message," I said, "is telling us that we are returning an unexpected value. This could be clearer. Previous versions of Java stated that we cannot return a value from a method whose return type is declared as void. Unfortunately, this not a great error message."

Creating an Overloaded Method with What You Believe to Be a Different Signature

"Here's the last of the error messages pertaining to methods that we'll examine today," I said, "and it deals with overloaded methods. Does everyone remember what an overloaded method is?"

"Overloaded methods are methods that have the **same name**, but a **different signature**—that is, number and type of arguments." Dave said.

"Exactly right, Dave," I said. "Beginners tend to make two mistakes when creating overloaded methods, and both pertain to a misunderstanding of what comprises the signature. First, beginners sometimes incorrectly believe that creating two methods with identical numbers and types of arguments but different argument names differentiates the two. That's not the case. For instance, in the following code, we have two Overloaded methods called **test()**, the signature of each specifying a single Integer parameter or argument. The parameter name in the first **test()** method is called **a**; in the second **test()** method, it's called **b**."

```
public class Example11_17{
  public static void main(String[] args) {
    int returnValue = 0;
    test(22);
    test(44);
  }

  public static void test(int a) {
    System.out.println("The value of the passed argument is " + a);
  }

  public static void test(int b) {
    System.out.println("The value of the passed argument is " + b);
  }
}
```

"Do you think that Java considers both **test()** signatures to be different?" I asked.

"I'm not really sure," Valerie said. No one else wagered a guess.

"The answer," I said, "is that to Java, both method signatures are identical, and compiling this code will result in the following compiler error message:"

```
Command Prompt                              —    □    ✕

C:\JFiles>javac Example11_17.java
Example11_17.java:18: error: method test(int) is already
 defined in class Example11_17
        public static void test(int b)
                    ^

1 error

C:\JFiles>
```

"As you can see," I said, "this is another informative message. In this one, Java is telling us that the **test()** method is already defined. As far as Java's concerned, it already has a method called **test()**, having a single Integer argument. To Java, argument names mean nothing. In a similar way, some beginners also believe that creating two methods with identical signatures but with different return types will differentiate the two, but that isn't the case either. Identical method signatures with different return types will generate the same compiler error we just saw."

Runtime Errors/Logic Errors

"The types of errors that we've examined so far this morning have been compiler errors," I said. "Compiler errors, though sometimes a nuisance to correct, do little to tarnish the image of your program in the eyes of the user, since the user never sees them. Unfortunately, there are some types of errors that escape the watchful eye of the Java compiler and don't show up until runtime,   when an unsuspecting user is interacting with your program. These types of errors are called runtime errors and usually result in your program abnormally terminating or 'bombing,' as we sometimes call it. Runtime errors are serious and can sometimes result in the user of your program losing hours of work. Another series of errors that we'll examine today, called logic errors, are even more serious. Logic errors do not result in your program abnormally terminating. In fact, the program seems to be working just fine. Logic errors produce incorrect results, which if detected by the user, minimize their damage. However, many logic errors are not discovered by the user for a long period of time, in which case the damage done by them is multiplied. As you can imagine, both runtime and logic errors can drastically affect your programming career and reputation."

Referring to an Element Outside the Array Bounds

"Let's start by examining one of the more frequent runtime errors that occurs when working with arrays," I said, "and that's when we try to access an array element that is outside of the array's defined boundaries. Let's take a look at this code in which we have declared an array called grades that has six elements:"

```java
public class Example11_18{
  public static void main(String[] args) {
    int grades[] = new int[6];
    grades[0] = 82;
    grades[1] = 90;
    grades[2] = 64;
    grades[3] = 80;
    grades[4] = 95;
    grades[5] = 75;
    grades[6] = 44;
  }
}
```

"I don't see anything wrong with this code," Rhonda said. "Is there a problem with it?"

"Yes, there is," I said. "This particular error is one that beginners quite often make: they forget that the number within the square brackets of the array declaration is the **number of elements** in the array, not the **size** of the array:"

```java
int grades[] = new int[6];
```

"But since element numbers in an array begin with the number zero, the 'upper floor' of the array is always one less than its size. In other words, with a size of 6, the highest element number that we can legally reference is 5. Therefore, this line of code is referencing an element of the array that does not exist since the upper floor of the array is actually 5:"

```java
grades[6] = 44;
```

"I understand now," Rhonda said. "And you say if we compile this program, the Java compiler won't detect the problem?"

"Unfortunately not, Rhonda," I said. "The compiler isn't smart enough to alert us to the problem. It won't be until runtime that this error becomes evident."

I then compiled the program and, as I predicted, there were no error messages.

"Let's see what happens if we run the program," I said. "We'll produce the ArrayIndexOutOfBoundsException that we saw last week:"

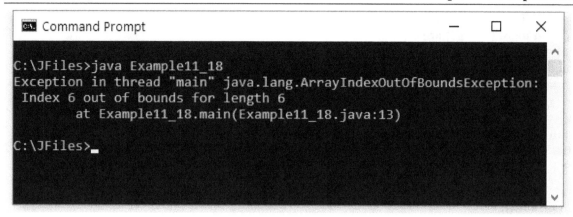

Forgetting to Call System.exit() in an Application that Displays a Graphical User Interface

"I've included this type of error in our discussion of runtime errors," I said, "although strictly speaking, forgetting to call the **exit()** method of the System object for a program that displays a graphical user interface doesn't generate a runtime error—it just creates a program that never ends. As you'll probably recall from the programs we've written earlier in the class, any time you write a program that displays a graphical user interface component, such as an input box or a message box, you need to execute the **exit()** method of the System object. Otherwise, the user of your program will find themselves with a DOS or operating system window that never closes. For instance, this code displays a Java message box:"

```
import javax.swing.JOptionPane;
class Example11_19 {
  public static void main(String[] args) {
    JOptionPane.showMessageDialog(null, "I love Java");
  }
}
```

"The code will compile fine. When we run the program, it displays the message 'I love Java' on the Java console. However, after we click OK in the message box, the program doesn't end. It just sits there, forcing us to close the DOS window ourselves. In order to allow this program to end gracefully, we need to code the **exit()** method of the System object as the last statement in the **main()** method, like this:"

```
import javax.swing.JOptionPane;
class Example11_20 {
  public static void main(String[] args) {
    JOptionPane.showMessageDialog(null, "I love Java");
    System.exit (0);
  }
}
```

"Now when we run the program, it displays the message 'I love Java', and when we click OK, the program ends gracefully."

Forgetting to Increment a Counter Variable

"Forgetting to increment a counter variable," I said, "is one of the most common errors I see."

"Counter variable?" Steve asked.

I explained that many of the programs we had written during the course, particularly those we wrote last week when dealing with arrays, depended heavily upon declaring, incrementing, and examining a counter variable somewhere within a program.

"Counter variables," I explained, "are variables that you declare to do exactly that: count something. For example, last week in Exercise 10-3, we wrote code that loaded the values of six quiz grades to an array. We then used a For loop to access each element of the array, add its value to an accumulator variable, increment a counter, and finally calculate an average. Here's the code from Exercise 10-3:"

```java
class Example11_21 {
  public static void main (String[] args) {
    int grades[] = { 82, 90, 64, 80, 95, 75};
    int accumulator = 0;
    int counter = 0;
    double average = 0;
    for (int row = 0; row < grades.length; row++) {
      System.out.println(grades[row]);
      accumulator = accumulator + grades[row];
      counter++;
    }

    System.out.println();
    average = accumulator / counter;
    System.out.println("The class average is " + average);
  }
}
```

I compiled the program, ran it, and an average of 81 was displayed on the classroom projector.

"Crucial to this program correctly calculating the class average," I said, "is knowing the number of student grades in the array. To keep track of that number, we declared a variable called *counter*, and incremented it by 1 each time we added an element to the array:"

```java
counter++;
```

"Had we forgotten to increment this counter variable, a number of problems could have resulted. Most often, we get a division by zero runtime error. Let me show you."

I then deleted the line of code that increments the counter so that the program looked like this:

```java
class Example11_22 {
  public static void main (String[] args) {
    int grades[] = { 82, 90, 64, 80, 95, 75};
    int accumulator = 0;
    int counter = 0;
    double average = 0;

    for (int row = 0; row < grades.length; row++) {
      System.out.println(grades[row]);
      accumulator = accumulator + grades[row];
    }

    System.out.println();
    average = accumulator / counter;
    System.out.println("The class average is " + average);
  }
}
```

I recompiled the program and then ran it. The following screenshot was displayed on the classroom projector:

"This is the division by zero error I said might occur," I continued. "Division by zero is a big no-no in most computer languages. Because we never incremented the counter variable, we divided the value of our accumulator variable by the initial value of the counter variable, which is zero. Division by zero is something we'll discuss later in a little more detail. For now, just remember that it's vitally important to increment the value of any counter variables you declare."

Forgetting to Add to an Accumulator

"Forgetting to add values to an accumulator," I said, "is similar to forgetting to increment a counter variable: both mistakes result in runtime errors. A counter variable is used to count the instances of something, such as the number of quizzes taken or the number of employees in a company. An accumulator variable is a little different in that it is used to hold the running total of something, such as the total scores of all of the quiz grades taken or the total value of all employee salaries in a company. In the same example we used to illustrate the problem with a counter variable, we also added the value of the quiz grade to an accumulator variable. If we had forgotten to add the grade to the accumulator variable, we would have displayed an incorrect average in the Java console, most likely zero."

"And there goes our reputation!" Rhonda said.

"That's right, Rhonda" I agreed. "It only takes a few mistakes to tarnish it."

I displayed the code from Example11_22 on the classroom projector and highlighted the line of code where we added the grade to the accumulator variable.

```
accumulator = accumulator + grades[row];
```

"Forgetting to add a value to the accumulator variable is a very common type of Java error," I explained.

"What kind of error would this generate?" Ward asked.

"The program would run," I said, "but most likely the program would display an average of zero."

I then **deleted** the line of code in which we added the value of the quiz grade to the accumulator variable and **added back** the line of code to correctly increment the counter variable so that it looked like this:

```
class Example11_23 {
  public static void main (String[] args) {
    int grades[] = { 82, 90, 64, 80, 95, 75};
    int accumulator = 0;
    int counter = 0;
    double average = 0;

    for (int row = 0; row < grades.length; row++) {
      System.out.println(grades[row]);
      counter++;
    }
```

```
    System.out.println();
    average = accumulator / counter;
    System.out.println("The class average is " + average);
  }
}
```

I then recompiled the program and ran it. The following screenshot was displayed on the classroom projector:

```
C:\JFiles>java Example11_23
82
90
64
80
95
75

The class average is 0.0

C:\JFiles>
```

"As you can see," I said, "because we forgot to increment the value of the accumulator variable, its value was equal to its initial value of zero. Therefore, when we divided it by the value of the counter variable, which in this case was 6, our result is zero. The program didn't bomb, but it did result in an incorrect answer."

"So this is a logic error," Valerie said, "since the program didn't bomb?"

"That's right, Valerie," I said, "and as you can all see, an error like this can be far worse than a runtime error, particularly if an unsuspecting user takes the result at face value."

Not providing a way for a while structure to end

"Another type of runtime error that is common for beginners," I said, "is to code a While loop and forget to provide a way for it to end. A few weeks ago, we wrote this code in Exercise 5-7 to display the floor numbers of a hotel:"

```
class Practice5_7 {
  public static void main(String[] args) {
    int counter = 2;
    System.out.println("The floors in the hotel are...");
    while (counter < 21) {
      System.out.println (counter);
      counter++;
    }
  }
}
```

"Beginners," I continued, "frequently forget that in a While loop, it's important to include somewhere within the body of the loop code that enables the loop to eventually end. Otherwise, we have what is known as an **endless loop**. In the case of this code, we told Java to continue executing the loop while the value of the counter variable is less than 21. Since we initialized the counter variable to 2, if we didn't place some code in the body of the loop to do something to cause the value of the counter variable to become 21 or greater, the loop would never end. What we did, of course, was write this line of code that increments the value of the counter variable every time the body of the loop is executed:"

```
counter++;
```

"What happens if we forget this code?" Joe asked.

"We'd create a program that would display the number 2 indefinitely—in other words, an infinite loop," I replied, as I displayed this code on the classroom projector.

```java
class Example11_24 {
  public static void main(String[] args) {
    int counter = 2;
    System.out.println("The floors in the hotel are...");
    while (counter < 21) {
      System.out.println (counter);
    }
  }
}
```

I then compiled the program and executed it, and that's exactly what happened. The number 2 continued to display on the Java console. Because the program wouldn't stop, I had to use the Windows Task Manager to terminate it.

"So that's an infinite loop," Rhonda said, "and all because we forgot one little line of code."

Forgetting to Code a Break Statement when One is Needed in a Switch Structure

"This next error isn't so much an error as it is a Java feature," I said. "But it's a feature that can trip many beginners up. When coding a Switch structure, once a Case statement evaluates to True, the code in every succeeding Case statement is also executed."

"That's why we use the Break statement, isn't it?" Dave asked.

"That's right, Dave," I said. "The Break statement is normally included as the last statement of a Case statement to tell Java to skip the remainder of the Case statements if the Case statement is found to be true. Here's a program that uses a Switch statement to evaluate the value of the variable x. Depending on the value of the variable, the program displays one of several alternative messages to the Java Console. Notice the Break statement in each of the Case statements. This program, when run, will display the message 'x is 2' in the Java Console."

```java
class Example11_25 {
  public static void main (String[] args) {
    int x = 2;
    switch (x) {
      case 1:
        System.out.println("x is 1");
        break;
      case 2:
        System.out.println("x is 2");
        break;
      case 3:
        System.out.println("x is 3");
        break;
      default:
        System.out.println("x is not 1, 2 or 3");
    }
  }
}
```

"If, however, we remove the Break statements from the program, so that it looks like this, we get a different result:"

```java
class Example11_26 {
  public static void main (String[] args) {
    int x = 2;
    switch (x) {
      case 1:
        System.out.println("x is 1");
      case 2:
        System.out.println("x is 2");
      case 3:
```

```
        System.out.println("x is 3");
    default:
        System.out.println("x is not 1, 2 or 3");
    }
  }
}
```

"When we compile and execute this version of the program, because of our failure to include a Break statement, we get multiple messages displayed in the Java console."

I compiled the program, executed it, and the following screenshot was displayed on the classroom projector:

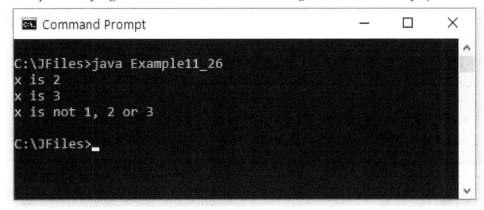

"As you can see, forgetting to code the break statements led to the execution of each one of the Case statements following the first Case statement that evaluated to True."

Division by Zero

"Let's revisit that issue of division by zero again," I said. "We saw earlier that in Java, like most programming languages, division by zero generates a runtime error. Now I'm going to explain why. What's 12 divided by 1?"

"12," Mary replied.

"Now what about 12 divided by 1/2?" I continued.

After a moment's hesitation, Dave answered, "24."

"Correct," I said.

There were some puzzled faces.

"I know I caught you math-phobics on that one," I said. "A number divided by a number smaller than one, always results in an answer larger than the original number."

"In math terms," Ward said, "I believe you mean to say that when we divide a number, called the dividend, by another number, called the divisor, smaller than one, we take the reciprocal of that number and multiply by it. In other words, 12 divided by 1/2 becomes 12 multiplied by 2, and the result is 24."

"Well said, Ward," I stated. I then displayed the following chart on the board:

Number 1 (Dividend)	Number 2 (Divisor)	Answer
12	1	12
12	1/2	24
12	1/3	36
12	1/4	48
12	1/10	120
12	1/100	1200
12	1/1000	12000

I continued by telling my students that as the divisor approaches zero, the answer becomes larger and larger. In fact, it becomes an infinite number, which is impossible to represent in a computer. "For that reason," I continued, "dividing a number by 0 in your computer program causes most programs to bomb, and Java is no exception. Let's take a look at this code:"

```
class Example11_27 {
  public static void main(String[] args) {
    System.out.println(4 /0 );
  }
}
```

I then compiled this program. The following screenshot was displayed on the classroom projector:

```
Command Prompt                                    —    □    X

C:\JFiles>java Example11_27
Exception in thread "main" java.lang.ArithmeticException: / by zero
        at Example11_27.main(Example11_27.java:5)

C:\JFiles>
```

I explained that most beginners aren't aware of the problems with division by zero and their immediate response would most likely be that they would never **intentionally** divide by zero.

"That's what I was going to say," Dave said. "However, I can imagine that this kind of error can occur in many different ways—for instance, input from a user via a Java input box."

"That's excellent, Dave," I said. "That's exactly how it could happen. The user can enter zero into an input box at runtime, and if our program divides by that value, we have a division by zero error."

"Isn't that something we could prevent with an If statement?" Barbara suggested.

"It is," I agreed. "However, division by zero and the other runtime errors we just examined can be detected and handled even more easily by using Java error handling routines. That's what we'll be examining when we return from break."

Java Error Handling

After break, I told my students that during the first part of our class, we had intentionally created errors to cause our programs to bomb. During the last half of our class, we would be examining ways of gracefully handling those errors in such a way that our programs don't stop in midstream.

"As we discussed," I said, "nothing can ruin your reputation faster than having one of your customers tell a prospective client that he or she loves your programs, but it's too bad they bomb once in a while. As you can imagine, this can be very bad for business!"

I explained that it isn't always possible to write a program that will never produce a runtime error. As we've seen, sometimes the user can introduce data via an input box that causes a runtime error. You might also write a program that reads data from a disk file, the name and location of which is specified by the user at runtime.

"Suppose," I said, "the user of your program indicates that the file is located on a diskette, but then forgets to insert the disk into the diskette drive?"

"I do that all the time," Rhonda said. "Will that cause our program to bomb?"

"It can," I said, "since our program is attempting to open a file that doesn't exist."

"That generates an error?" Ward asked. "I'm surprised. When I do that while using Microsoft Word, a warning message is displayed."

"That's exactly the point, Ward" I replied. "The programmers who wrote Microsoft Word implemented error handling in their program, intercepting the runtime error that is triggered and substituting in its place a more user-friendly message. That's the warning message you see in Word. Most importantly, though, Microsoft Word continues running instead of coming to a grinding halt, which is what we want our Java program to do. Remember, when a Java program comes to a jarring stop, it can result in the loss of hours of work on the part of the user."

"So we can do something like that in our Java program?" Barbara asked. "I mean, intercept those nasty runtime error messages we saw earlier and replace them with user-friendly messages of our own?"

"Yes, we can," I said. "As you'll see, it's actually pretty easy to intercept those nasty Java error messages and replace them with more soothing, user-friendly messages that appear as warning messages. Let's begin our look at Java error handling by completing an exercise in which we intentionally cause a division by zero error."

I then distributed this exercise to the class.

Exercise 11-1 Intentionally Generate an Error

In this exercise, you'll write a program that prompts the user for two numbers and then divides the first number by the second number. You'll then execute the program and intentionally generate a division by zero error. But don't worry: in the next exercise, you'll implement error handling to gracefully handle it.

1. Use Notepad (if you are using Windows) and enter the following code.

```java
import javax.swing.JOptionPane;

class Practice11_1 {
  public static void main(String[] args) {
    int number1;
    int number2;
    number1 = Integer.parseInt
      (JOptionPane.showInputDialog("Enter Number 1"));
    number2 = Integer.parseInt
      (JOptionPane.showInputDialog("Enter Number 2"));
    JOptionPane.showMessageDialog
      (null, number1 + " divided by " +
            number2 + " is " +
            number1/number2);
    JOptionPane.showMessageDialog(null, "Thanks for using my program");
    System.exit (0);
  }
}
```

2. Save your source file as Practice11_1 in the \Jfiles\Practice folder (select File | Save As from Notepad's menu bar). Be sure to save your source file with the filename extension Java.
3. Compile your source file into a Bytecode file.
4. Execute your program. Enter **4** for the first number and **1** for the second—the program will display a result of **4**. After you click **OK**, the program will thank you for using the program.
5. Now run the program again. Enter **4** for the first number and **0** for the second. The program will terminate with a division by zero exception:

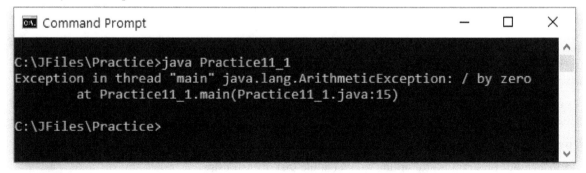

Discussion

"What we did here," I said, "was write some innocent-looking code that prompts the user for two numbers. Certainly, there's nothing in the code itself that suggests the program will have a problem. It isn't until the user enters a 0 for the second number and we divide the first number by that value that the program bombs with a runtime error. Once that happens, there's nothing we can do to close the program window short of going into the Windows Task Manager to kill the program. As you can see, a program that terminates abnormally can be pretty nasty."

"So will we be able to prevent this type of problem?" Kate asked.

"There's nothing we can do to prevent the user from entering zero for the second number, although we could write code to check for the presence of a zero before performing the division operation," I said. "However, we won't be going into those techniques today. Instead, we'll concentrate on intercepting Java exceptions so that when they do occur, the program doesn't come to a grinding halt."

Java Exceptions

"Is a Java exception the same as a Java error?" Steve asked. "I think you've used both terms in the last few minutes."

"The Java language," I said, "prefers to call its errors 'exceptions.' In fact, when a Java runtime error occurs, an Exception object is created. Once the Exception object is created, we have access to its attributes, which can provide us information about the exception."

"The Exception object is an object that we don't have to create ourselves?" Kate asked.

"That's right, Kate," I said. "When the runtime error is generated, Java automatically creates the Exception object for us."

"What can we do when a Java runtime error occurs?" Ward asked.

Ignore the Exception

"One thing we can do is to **ignore** the error," I said.

"What's that?" Ward asked.

"We can ignore the error," I said, "and just let the program bomb. This is an alternative that many Java programmers choose."

"Is it OK to ignore exceptions?" Mary asked.

"No, it's not Mary," I said. "It's foolish to ignore an exception that you suspect may occur, and you should do your best to anticipate them and react to them. As you gain experience in Java, you'll see that most of the code you write won't trigger exceptions. You'll also learn the kind of code that is likely to trigger an exception."

"Such as prompting a user to give us a number we then use in division!" Valerie asked.

"That's right, Valerie," I said. "Also, code that opens external files or databases is the kind of code that can trigger runtime exceptions. The point is, not every piece of code you write needs to be written to handle exceptions. The code that experience and testing has revealed is capable of triggering a runtime exception is the code that needs to include error handling code, and that means coding a Try-Catch-Finally block."

Handle the Exception with Try-Catch-Finally Blocks

"Try-Catch-Finally block?" Kate asked. "Is that what you just said?"

"That's right, Kate," I replied. "A Try-Catch-Finally block. The idea is to try the code in the Try block that may cause an exception and then use the Catch block to specify the code that should execute if an exception occurs."

"So that's the reason it's called a Try block?" Mary asked.

"That's the reason, Mary," I said.

"What about the Finally block?" Steve asked.

"The Finally block specifies code that is to be executed whether an exception occurs or not," I said. "Usually, this is code that performs some kind of housekeeping function such as closing files."

"Are you going to show us an example of the Try-Catch-Finally block?" Rhonda asked. "Even better," I said, "I'm going to give you a chance to work with them on your own by modifying the code from Exercise 11-1 to include exception handling."

I then distributed this exercise for the class to complete.

Exercise 11-2 Try-Catch-Finally Block

In this exercise, you'll modify the program from Exercise 11-1 to use Try-Catch-Finally blocks to deal with the Division by Zero error that resulted in Exercise 11-1.

1. Use Notepad (if you are using Windows) and enter the following code.

```java
import javax.swing.JOptionPane;
class Practice11_2 {
  public static void main(String[] args) {
    int number1;
    int number2;
    number1 = Integer.parseInt
      (JOptionPane.showInputDialog("Enter Number 1"));
    number2 = Integer.parseInt
      (JOptionPane.showInputDialog("Enter Number 2"));
    try {
      JOptionPane.showMessageDialog
        (null, number1 + " divided by " +
          number2 + " is " +
          number1/number2);
    }                                              // end of try
    catch (Exception e) {
      if (e.getMessage().equals ("/ by zero"))
        JOptionPane.showMessageDialog
          (null, "Oops, you can't divide by zero");
    }                                              // end of catch
    finally {
      JOptionPane.showMessageDialog(null, "Thanks for using my program");
      System.exit (0);
    }                                              // end of finally
  }                                                // end of main
}                                                  // end of class
```

2. Save your source file as **Practice11_2** in the \JFiles\Practice folder (select File | Save As from Notepad's menu bar). Be sure to save your source file with the filename extension .java.

3. Compile your source file into a Bytecode file.

4. Execute your program. Enter **4** for the first number and **1** for the second. The program will display a result of **4**, and after you click OK, it will thank you for using the program.

5. Now run the program again. Enter **4** for the first number and **0** for the second. This time, instead of terminating, the program will display a warning message about dividing by zero and thank you for using the program.

Discussion

I immediately ran the program, and the following screenshot was displayed on the classroom projector:

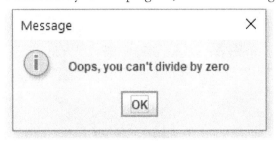

"Let me explain what we've done here," I said. "We've used a Try block to intercept the division by zero exception before it caused our program to come to an abrupt halt. The code in the Try block is the code we tell Java may cause a runtime exception:"

```java
try { JOptionPane.showMessageDialog
  (null, number1 + " divided by " +
    number2 + " is " +
    number1/number2);
}              // end of try
```

"If an exception occurs, execution of the program will jump to one or more Catch blocks. In our case, we have coded only one Catch block, and it's used to tell Java to display a much more user-friendly error message:"

```
catch (Exception e) {
  if (e.getMessage().equals ("/ by zero"))
    JOptionPane.showMessageDialog
      (null, "Oops, you can't divide by zero");
}                                    // end of catch
```

"Understandably," I said, "this syntax is confusing. What we're doing is telling the Catch block that we are expecting an Exception object to be created—that's what this line of code does:"

```
catch (Exception e) {
```

"What does the letter **e** refer to?" Bob asked.

"We're actually creating an instance of an Exception object called e," I said. "That means if an Exception object is created based on the code in the Try block, we can refer to the Exception object by the name e. The ability to do this comes in quite handy because the next thing we do is to evaluate the **getMessage** attribute of the Exception object. For a division by zero exception, the getMessage attribute—it's really the description of the Exception object—is equal to '/ by zero'. Using the **equals()** method, we can then determine if that's the exception that triggered the Catch block to be executed:"

```
if (e.getMessage().equals ("/ by zero"))
```

"If it is, we display a more user-friendly message to the user:"

```
JOptionPane.showMessageDialog
  (null, "Oops, you can't divide by zero");
```

"How do we know that a division by zero exception will have this particular getMessage attribute?" Ward asked.

"That's a good question, Ward," I said. "There are a list of exceptions in Java's online documentation, but probably the easiest thing to do is to first allow the program to bomb, then note the exception message displayed in the Java Console."

"You're right," Valerie said. "That's the text for the error message from Exercise 11-1."

"Can I presume we could also use If statements, or even a series of Case statements to check for other errors besides the division by zero exception in the Catch block?" Dave asked.

"That's right, Dave, we could," I said. "We can do what you suggest and, within a single Catch block, use selection logic to check for other types of exceptions. Or we could code additional Catch blocks, devoting each one to a particular type of exception."

"I'm afraid I don't see what you and Dave mean," Rhonda said. "Why bother checking for an error other than the division by zero?"

"It's possible," I answered, "that exceptions other than the division by zero exception could be triggered here. If we use a Switch structure, we could enumerate as many exceptions as we can think of using Case statements, and then code a Default statement to handle everything else. Or, as I just mentioned, we could code multiple Catch blocks to handle multiple exceptions."

"That makes sense," Rhonda said. "I hadn't thought about that."

"What did you mean when you said we could code multiple Catch blocks?" Blaine asked. "I'm just not getting that."

"We just wrote an error handle with a single Catch block, and it was pretty generic," I said.

```
catch (Exception e) {
```

"We could have coded the Catch block to check for a particular type of exception, such as an ArithmeticException:"

```
catch (ArithmeticException e) {
```

"That's the type of Exception the division by zero error generates, isn't it?" Valerie said. "I remember seeing that it in Exercise 11-1."

"That's right, Valerie," I said. "If we coded our Catch block specifically like this, the code in the Catch clause would only be executed if Java encountered an exception of that type."

"So the particular type of Exception object you reference in the Catch clause can be used to limit the code executed when the exception is triggered?" Dave asked.

"That's exactly right, Dave," I said. "There are a number of potential Exception objects that can be created, among them:

- IOException

- ArrayIndexOutOfBoundsException

- ClassNotFoundException

- InterruptedException

"In addition to the ArithmeticException and generic Exception objects we've already examined. Here's what our code would look like if we used multiple Catch blocks:"

```
catch (ArithmeticException e) { if (e.getMessage().equals ("/ by zero"))
   JOptionPane.showMessageDialog
     (null, "Oops, you can't divide by zero");
}                      // end of catch
catch (ArrayIndexOutOfBoundsException e) {
   JOptionPane.showMessageDialog
     (null, "Oops, there's a problem with an array");
}                      // end of catch
```

"Do we still need to check for the division by zero exception in the ArithmeticException Catch block?" Chuck asked.

"We do," I answered, "because even though we've narrowed the scope of the exception we're interested in, there are other types of ArithmeticExceptions generated besides the division by zero exception."

"Can you explain the Finally block?" Mary asked. "When does it get executed?"

"The Finally block is executed regardless of whether an exception is generated or not," I answered. "In other words, the code in the Finally block is executed both when an exception occurs and when no exception occurs. In this case, we included a message thanking the user for working with our program and executed the **exit()** method of the System object:"

```
finally {
   JOptionPane.showMessageDialog
     (null, "Thanks for using my program");
   System.exit (0);
} // end of finally
```

Can We Modify the Grades Calculation Project?

"Can we modify the Grades Calculation Project to provide for exception handling?" Kate asked.

"Yes, we can." I said. "However, at this point, I'm a little reluctant to expend much energy in doing so. The Grades Calculation Project is going to undergo some overhauling as we add a graphical user interface in the next few weeks, and placing exception handling code in the classes that make up the project at this point may be premature."

I asked if there were any other questions, but there were none. I told my students that during the evening hours I would be placing a shore-to-ship call to Rose and Jack to see how they were coming along with the ocean tests on their company's new ocean liner. I then dismissed class for the day.

Summary

This chapter was designed to show you the various types of errors that all programmers, especially beginners, can make in their programs. We covered three different types of errors here: compiler errors, runtime errors, and logic errors.

Compiler errors are errors which the Java compiler 'catches' before permitting our source code to be compiled into a Bytecode file. All that's required on our part is to figure out what's wrong and to catch them.

Runtime errors occur when our compiled Bytecode file is executed by the Java Interpreter. These errors can produce some nasty error messages and almost always cause our program to stop running. Runtime errors are the types of errors that can be more gracefully dealt with through the use of Java error handling.

The third type of error we dealt with a logic error, which, unfortunately, is the most difficult type of error to detect and can be the most dangerous, since it rarely causes our program to bomb. Logic errors can exist for years in programs without ever being detected.

You learned that Java error handling can be used to deal with runtime errors, but you can't code for every eventuality. You can insert error handlers in every class of your Java application and try to intercept every error that you can think of, but that's an extreme. You learned that you should definitely code an error handler in classes where division operations take place or when your code accesses external files or databases.

And now a word or two of advice. Everyone makes mistakes when they start programming. Never let this discourage you. When you first learn something new, it's a strange and awkward experience to become familiar with it. But it's also a new and exciting time. Never let the frustrations of learning something new thwart that excitement. As time goes by, experience will help you make fewer mistakes.

Chapter 12---Developing A Graphical User Interface

At this point in your Java journey, you've learned how to develop a working Java program that solves the problem of calculating grades for Frank Olley, Robin Aronstrom, and David Burton. The program, while fully functional, lacks a graphical user interface, known as a GUI. In this chapter, we'll create a graphical user interface for the Grades Calculation Project.

Building a Graphical User Interface

I began our next-to-last class by telling my students that my shore to ship call to Jack and Rose had gone well and that they had assured me they would return in time for next Saturday's final class. Both would be returning to the United States on the maiden voyage of the ocean liner that they had helped engineer.

"Talk about following through with the SDLC," Dave said. "They helped design the ship, now they're participating in the implementation and feedback and maintenance phases also."

"That's a good point," I said. "We'll be doing the same thing next week when we deliver the Grades Calculation Project to Frank Olley of the English Department."

I continued by explaining that although, in fact, we had already completed the Grade Calculation Project, and I'm sure Frank Olley would be pleased with what we had done so far, we would begin to develop a graphical user interface in today's class and wrap it up next week in our final class.

"Graphical user interface?" Rhonda asked. "By that do you mean a Microsoft Windows program?"

"I mean a windows program," I said, "but not a Microsoft Windows program."

"I'm afraid I don't understand," Blaine said. "What's the difference?"

"A graphical user interface," I said, "which I'll refer to as a GUI from this point forward, is a program that displays program information using frames and panels called windows, but it's not necessarily a Microsoft Windows program. Because Java programs run on a variety of different operating systems, when we run our Java program on a Macintosh PC, our program will display the look and feel of a Macintosh program. When we run our Java program on a Microsoft Windows PC, our program will display the look and feel of a Microsoft Windows program. Likewise, when we run our program on a Unix or Linux PC, our program will display the look and feel of a Unix windows program."

Designing our GUI

"I understand now," Blaine said. "Do we have any idea what our GUI will look like."

Note: A shortcut term for a Graphical User Interface is a GUI (pronounced "gooey")

"Yes, we do," I said, "we actually produced a sketch of it during the design phase of the SDLC we performed our first week of class. I've made some slight modifications to it over the course of the last few weeks. Let's take a look at it and see if it meets with your approval."

I then displayed the sketch of our GUI on the classroom projector:

"This is an illustration of our proposed GUI," I said. "The surrounding rectangle represents what Java calls a frame, and the labels, circles, and rectangles that you see within the frame represent other Java GUI elements, which we'll be discussing today. Interestingly, each one of those elements is actually a Java object that we will instantiate from a series of special Java classes designed to display GUI elements."

"When you say create an object from a class," Bob asked, "Do you mean the same way we create objects from the classes we've created ourselves, such as EnglishStudent?"

"That's right, Bob," I said. "The window that you see here is called a Java frame and will be instantiated from a Java class called JFrame. In Java, the frame acts as a container for other GUI elements, and for the Grade Calculation Project, we'll be placing four Java elements in it: Labels, Radio buttons, Buttons, and Text Fields."

Note: In Java, a frame acts as a container for other GUI elements

"What are those three round circles?" Rhonda asked.

"The three round circles," I said, "represent Java radio buttons and will be created from the JRadioButton class. Radio buttons are a GUI element that permit the user of our program to specify, via a mouse click, a True/False or a Yes/No answer."

"Why are they called radio buttons?" Joe asked.

"They're called radio buttons," I said, "because they mimic the behavior of old radios, where you pushed a button to select a channel. On a radio with five buttons, one button was always depressed or selected, but only one button, never more than one. The radio button GUI element is displayed on a Java frame with a circle and a caption or descriptive label next to it. Radio buttons can be selected when the user clicks their mouse on it. Once the radio button is selected, a small black dot is displayed within it."

Note: Only one Radio Button in a Radio Button Group can be selected at one time.

"So you're saying that of the three radio buttons that we see here on the frame, only one can be selected at one time?" Chuck asked.

"That's right, Chuck," I agreed. "When the user selects a radio button, that radio button will become selected and the radio button previously selected will become unselected. The idea here with the Grade Calculation Project is that the user will select one of the three radio buttons to select the type of student for which they wish to calculate a grade."

"What about those empty rectangles on the frame?" Mary asked. "What do they represent?"

"The empty rectangles," I said, "represent **Text Fields** and will be objects created from the JTextField class. Text Fields are much like those we've created during the course when we executed the **showInputDialog()** method of the JOptionPane class."

"What will we be using Text Fields for?" Rhonda asked.

"They'll be used by the user of our program to enter values for the midterm, final exam, research paper, and presentation grades." I said. "Once these values are entered into a text box, the idea is that the user will then click the Calculate button to trigger the calculation of the student's final grade."

"But not all student types require all four component grades," Dave said. "Will that be a problem?"

"No," I answered, "next week, when we build some 'intelligence' into our GUI, you'll see that, based on the radio button that the user selects, we'll display only those Text Fields that are required to calculate that particular type of grade."

"So if the user selects a math student," Linda said, "only the Text Fields for midterm and final exam will be displayed?"

"That's right, Linda," I said. "That will be something we program into our GUI next week when we learn about listeners."

"It appears that we have two **buttons**, one called Calculate and one called Reset," Rhonda said. "Are both of those objects?"

"Yes, they are," I said. "Both buttons are objects instantiated from the JButton class. It's important to realize that every graphical element that you see on the frame is a distinct Java object, and each one will have to be separately instantiated from a Java class. All of the GUI elements that we'll learn about in this course belong to a Java package called Swing."

"Swing?" Barbara asked. "That sounds familiar—have we discussed Swing before?"

"Yes, we have," I said. "We mentioned Swing earlier in the course. Swing is a Java package containing classes used to create GUIs. In fact, we've been using the Swing package all along in this course—the **showInputDialog()** and **showMessageDialog()** methods of the JOptionPane class are part of the Swing package."

"What about those identifying captions?" Steve asked. "I presume they're created from classes of the Java package? But which ones?"

"That's a good observation, Steve," I said, "but not all of the identifying captions you see on the frame are distinct objects. Four of the identifying captions that appear on the frame— midterm, final exam, research paper, and presentation—are Label objects, created from the JLabel class. The other captions that you see—Calculate, Reset, and the captions appearing to the right of the three radio buttons are actually attributes of the JButton and JRadioButton objects."

"What are labels used for?" Peter asked.

"Labels are used to provide instructions to the user," I said, "or to identify other objects, such as our Text Fields. For instance, the midterm label identifies the text box to be used for the input of the midterm grade."

We had discussed, more or less, all of the features of the frame. I waited a moment to see if there were any other questions.

"How and where will we be displaying the student's calculated grade?" Barbara asked. "In the current version of the Grade Calculation program, we're displaying it in a message box. Should we display the grade somewhere on the frame?"

"That's a great question, Barbara," I said. "I would like to display the student's grade on the frame itself, and using a Label object to do so is probably the best choice. Let's update the sketch to include a new GUI element."

I then updated my sketch, and displayed it on the classroom projector:

● **English Student**   **Midterm**   [70]

○ **Math Student**   **Final Exam**   [80]

○ **Science Student**   **Research Paper**   [90]

                               Presentation   [100]

[**Calculate Grade**]   **Numeric Grade: 84.5 Letter Grade: C**

[**Reset**]

"Now," I said, "the user will select a type of student, enter component grades into the appropriate text box and click on the Calculate Grade button, and the student's numeric and letter grade will appear as the caption of a label on the frame."

"Since we're on the subject of labels," Ward said, "I would suggest providing identifying labels to categorize what the radio buttons and Text Fields represent."

I wasn't quite sure what Ward meant so I asked him update my sketch. After he was done, he displayed it on the classroom projector:

Student Type   **Grades**   **ENGLISH STUDENT**

● **English Student**   **Midterm**   [70]

○ **Math Student**   **Final Exam**   [80]

○ **Science Student**   **Research Paper** [90]

                          Presentation   [100]

[**Calculate Grade**]   **Numeric Grade: 84.5 Letter Grade: C**

[**Reset**]

"Oh, I see what you mean, Ward," I said. "Yes, I think that's a better design."

Creating our GUI

"These objects that we'll be creating to form our GUI," Lou said, "will we be creating these from the Grades class we've already created?"

"That's a good question, Lou," I said. "Typically, the code for the creation of a GUI is placed in a class of its own. We'll be placing all of the code in a class called DrawGUI, which we will create, just as we've created all of the other classes in our project, by using Notepad."

"I don't mind saying that the prospect of creating a GUI seems a bit overwhelming to me," Lou said.

"Like everything else we've done in the class, Lou," I said, "I think you'll see that if we take this a step at a time, you'll be just fine. Let's start by examining the sketch for our GUI, identifying the Java GUI elements, and listing the objects and classes that will be used to create them."

I then displayed this list on the classroom projector:

Java Swing Class	GUI Element	Object Name
JButton	Calculate Button	btnCalculate
	Reset Button	btnReset
JRadioButton	English Radio Button	radEnglish
	Math Radio Button	radMath
	Science Radio Button	radScience
JLabel	STUDENT TYPES:	lblTypes
	GRADES	lblGrades
	ENGLISH, MATH OR SCIENCE	lblStudentType
	Midterm	lblMidterm
	Final Exam	lblFinalExam
	Research Paper	lblResearch
	Presentation	lblPresentation
	Numeric Grade:	lblFinalGrade
JTextField	Midterm Text Box	txtMidterm
	Final Exam Text Box	txtFinalExam
	Research Paper Text Box	txtResearch
	Presentation Text Box	txtPresentation
JFrame	The entire window	DrawGui

"Can you go over the process of creating the GUI again?" Linda asked. "You did say that the graphical user interface is built from a single class—is that right?"

"That's correct, Linda," I said. "We'll create a class called DrawGUI containing objects created from Swing classes. Then, from our startup class Grades—actually we're going to create a new startup class called GUIGrades—we'll create a single instance of the DrawGUI class, which in turn will display the GUI we've sketched. Once the GUI is displayed, it's there for the user to interact with. Next week, we'll learn how to make the GUI communicate with the startup class by writing listeners, or event handlers."

"Why is that necessary?" Mary asked.

"Listeners, or event handlers," I said, "enable our startup class to know which objects on the frame the user has interacted with. That's how we'll know if the user clicks on the Math Student radio button, what value he or she enters as the midterm grade, and when they click on the Calculate button. Without listeners, we have a displayed GUI, but nothing else. But we'll learn more about that next week when we learn how to create listeners."

Setting Up the Top-Level Component: The Frame

"So where do we start?" Linda asked. "What's our first step?"

"We start by coding the class designed to display the GUI," I said. "And the first step in that process is to create an instance of what Swing calls a top-level container. In most cases, this will be a Java frame. Once an instance of the frame has been created, we'll then place another Java swing object on it. I'd like to demonstrate this process by creating a class called GUIV1. V1 stands for version 1, as we will be creating multiple versions of this GUI class over the course of the next few minutes."

I then displayed this code on the classroom projector:

```
import java.awt.*;
import javax.swing.*;
class GUIV1 extends JFrame {
  GUIV1() {
    setSize(250,250);
    setTitle("GUIV1 Demo");
    setVisible(true);
  }
}
```

"In a minute," I said, "we'll be creating a startup class called Example12_1 that will instantiate an object from this class, resulting in the display of our first GUI. Before we do that, however, let's examine the few lines of code we have here. The first two lines of code tell Java that we'll be using classes from both the java.awt package and the Javax.Swing package:"

```
import java.awt.*;
import javax.swing.*;
```

"You mentioned that we would be using the Swing package earlier," Bob said, "but I don't recall you saying anything about an AWT package—what is that?"

"AWT," I replied, "stands for Abstract Windowing Toolkit and is an older Java Package that, prior to the development of Swing, was used to build GUI's. Some of the components that we need to build our GUI are actually part of this package—so we'll need to import this package also."

I paused before continuing.

"Do you all remember what we learned about inheritance a few weeks ago?" I asked. "This next line of code identifies our class as GUIV1, but it also tells Java that our GUIV1 class will be extending, or inheriting, from the JFrame class. It's the JFrame class that gives us access to the Swing components I just discussed."

```
class GUIV1 extends JFrame
```

"What's that next line of code?" Kathy asked. "Is that a Constructor method?"

"That's excellent Kathy," I said. "Constructor methods have the same name as the class:"

```
GUIV1()
```

"There are three lines of code in the Constructor which are used to create the frame. The first line of code executes the **setSize()** method of the JFrame object to set the dimensions of the frame to 250 by 250 pixels. The parameters are passed as width and height:"

```
setSize(250,250);
```

"This line of code executes the **setTitle()** method of the JFrame object, which displays a caption in the title bar of the displayed frame—window:"

```
setTitle("GUIV1 Demo");
```

"This line of code executes the **setVisible()** method of the JFrame object, which makes the frame visible...."

```
setVisible(true);
```

"Is that really necessary?" Steve asked.

"Believe it or not, Steve," I said, "if we didn't execute the **setVisible()** method of the JFrame object, the frame would be created, but we wouldn't be able to see it!"

"I just coded, compiled, and executed this class myself," Rhonda said, "and all I got was an error message. I expected to see the GUI displayed. What did I do wrong?"

"We need to create an instance of the GUIV1 object from a startup class," I said. I then displayed this code on the classroom projector:

```
class Example12_1 {
  public static void main(String[] args) {
    GUIV1 x = new GUIV1();
  }
}
```

"This is our startup class," I said, "and as you can see, all we have here is a single line of code within the **main()** method of Example12_1 creating an instance of a class classed GUIV1 and assigning its reference to a variable called x:"

```
GUIV1 x = new GUIV1();
```

I then compiled both GUIV1 and Example12_1 and executed Example12_1. The following screenshot was displayed:

"There's our frame," I said. "If we were to measure its dimensions, we would find it to be 250 by 250 pixels. Notice that its title bar contains the caption we specified using the **setTitle()** method of the JFrame object."

"Wow," Rhonda said, "that wasn't nearly as difficult as I thought it would be."

"That is pretty impressive," Ward said. "The Java frame looks just like a regular window."

"That's because we're executing this program in a Microsoft Windows environment," I said. "If we were executing the program on a Macintosh PC or a Unix or Linux PC, it would look slightly different, but in any case, we would have a working window."

"Working window is right," Dave said. "I've been experimenting with this window just a bit, and it seems to be fully functional. I can move and resize it, and I also notice that we didn't need to do anything to create the Minimize, Maximize, or Close buttons in the upper right-hand corner of the window. Is that the default behavior of the frame?"

"That's a great observation, Dave," I said. "Those three buttons—Minimize, Maximize, and Close—are automatically created and placed there when the frame is created. Notice also that in the upper left-hand corner of the frame we have an icon—it looks like a coffee cup—which is called a Control Menu icon. If we double-click the Control Menu icon, the window will close. If we single-click the Control Menu icon, a drop-down Control menu will appear:"

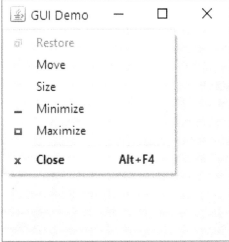

"Again, this Control menu behavior is part of the default behavior of the form. The menu items that you see here perform the same functions as the Minimize, Close, and Maximize buttons."

Adding Swing Components to the Frame

"One thing I just noticed," Dave said, "is that when I clicked on the Close button in the frame, the frame disappeared, but I was left with an open DOS or operating system window. This behavior reminds me of the problem we dealt with a few weeks back when we needed to code the **exit()** method of the System object in order to make our program terminate. Do we need to do that here?"

"Dave's right," I said. "Earlier in the course we saw that when we displayed a GUI object, such as an InputBox or a message box, our programs wouldn't end when the GUI object was closed. The solution there was to execute the **exit()** method of the System object. This problem is similar: when we display a Java frame and the user closes the frame, the startup class that created an instance of the GUI object needs to be informed of that fact. This is something we'll deal with next week when we learn about Java listeners."

"I don't know about anyone else," Rhonda said, "but I can't wait to create another GUI object. What's next? How do we place buttons, radio buttons, Text Fields, and labels on our frame? Will we be adding those soon?"

Buttons

"Yes, we will," I said. "Right now, in fact. Let's modify the code we just wrote in GUIV1 to include six buttons."

I then displayed this code on the classroom projector:

```java
import java.awt.*;
import javax.swing.*;
class GUIV2 extends JFrame {
  JButton btn1 = new JButton("Button1");
  JButton btn2 = new JButton("Button2");
  JButton btn3 = new JButton("Button3");
  JButton btn4 = new JButton("Button4");
  JButton btn5 = new JButton("Button5");
  JButton btn6 = new JButton("Button6");

  GUIV2() {
    Container c = getContentPane();
    c.setLayout ( new FlowLayout());
    c.add(btn1);
    c.add(btn2);
    c.add(btn3);
    c.add(btn4);
    c.add(btn5);
    c.add(btn6);
    setSize(250,250);
    setTitle("GUIV2 Demo");
    setVisible(true);
  }
}
```

I then modified the code in Example12_1 to create an instance of the GUIV2 class.

Don't Forget: If typing these examples and exercises isn't something you want to do, feel free to follow this link to find and download the completed solutions for all of the examples and exercises in the book. Just click on the Java book, then follow the link entitled exercises ☺

http://www.johnsmiley.com/main/books.htm

```java
class Example12_2 {
  public static void main(String[] args) {
    GUIV2 x = new GUIV2();
  }
}
```

"Before I explain the code we just wrote," I said, "I'd like to show you what it does."

I then compiled GUIV2 and Example 12_2 and executed Example12_2. The following screenshot was displayed on the classroom projector:

"As you can see," I said, "we now have the same frame we had before, but this time we have six buttons placed on it."

I used my mouse pointer to resize the window.

"See how the buttons have been rearranged?" I asked.

"Wow, how did that happen?" Linda asked. "The buttons rearranged themselves. And we didn't have to write any code to do that?"

"The rearrangement of the buttons was done for us automatically," I said, "and is a function of the Java layout manager, something we'll be discussing in just a minute or two. Let's take a closer look at the code in GUIV2 now. Once again, we start with the two import statements that give us access to classes in the AWT and Swing packages:"

```
import java.awt.*;
import javax.swing.*;
```

"As was the case with GUIV1, this line of code declares our class and tells Java that we wish to inherit from the JFrame class:"

```
class GUIV2 extends JFrame
```

"In order to create the six buttons that we displayed on the frame," I continued, "we declared and initialized six Instance variables of the JButton class, which is the Swing class used to create buttons. Notice that we have named our Instance variables beginning with the prefix btn—this makes our code a lot more readable:"

```
JButton btn1 = new JButton("Button1");
JButton btn2 = new JButton("Button2");
JButton btn3 = new JButton("Button3");
JButton btn4 = new JButton("Button4");
JButton btn5 = new JButton("Button5");
JButton btn6 = new JButton("Button6");
```

"What's the name within the parentheses?" Mary asked.

"That's the caption to be displayed in the button," I said, "and it's specified as a String argument to the JButton object's Constructor method."

"What's going on with that next line of code?" Ward asked. "That's thoroughly confusing me."

"This line of code," I said, "declares a variable called c of the Container class:"

```
Container c = getContentPane();
```

"What's a container?" Blaine asked. "Is that a data type?"

"No, it's not a data type, Blaine," I said. "The variable c is actually a variable of type Container. Do you remember earlier when I mentioned that Java frames act as a container for other GUI elements such as buttons? As it turns out, in order to place those other GUI elements on the frame, we first need to obtain a reference to the frame, and we do that by executing the **getContentPane()** method and assigning it to a Container variable, in this case, c."

> NOTE: The getContentPane() method of the JFrame object is used to obtain a reference to the frame.

"So, in essence, the variable *c* represents our frame?" Dave asked.

"That's right, Dave," I said. "Now that we have a reference to the frame, our next step is to tell Java the type of layout manager we will be using to display our GUI."

"You mentioned the layout manager a minute or so ago," Linda said. "You said it was the layout manager that dynamically rearranged the buttons on the frame when you resized the frame."

"Right you are, Linda," I aid. "When you create a GUI class, you need to specify a layout manager that you wish Java to use in drawing your GUI. The Swing package has a number of different layout managers, some of which we'll be learning about today. In this example, we used one of the simplest, the FlowLayout manager. We designated that by executing the **setLayout()** method of the Container object and specifying FlowLayout as its argument:"

```
c.setLayout ( new FlowLayout());
```

"With a reference to our frame stored in the variable c," I continued, "and with the layout manager specified, we then executed the **add()** method of the Container class to add six buttons to our frame. Notice how we specified the name of our Button object variable as the single argument to the **add()** method:"

```
c.add(btn1);
c.add(btn2);
c.add(btn3);
c.add(btn4);
c.add(btn5);
c.add(btn6);
```

"After this code is executed, we have six Button objects on our frame, and we now execute the same code we used in GUIV1 to set the size of the frame, specify a caption in its title bar, and make it visible:"

```
setSize(250,250);
setTitle("GUIV2 Demo");
setVisible(true);
```

"By the way, making the frame visible is the last line of code you should execute. If for some reason you add objects to the container after you have made the frame visible, none of your objects will be visible."

More on Layout Managers

"You said there are other layout managers?" Ward asked. "That's right, Ward," I said. "Here's a list of the more popular layout managers available in Java that we'll examine today."

Layout Manager	Description
FlowLayout	A Flow layout arranges components in a left-to-right flow, much like lines of text in a paragraph. Flow layouts are typically used to arrange buttons in a panel. By default, it will arrange buttons left to right until no more buttons fit on the same line. Each line is center.
GridLayout	The Grid Layout class is a layout manager that lays out a container's components in a rectangular grid. The container is divided into equal-sized rectangles, and one component is placed in each rectangle.

BorderLayout	A Border Layout lays out a container, arranging and resizing its components to fit in five regions: north, south, east, west, and center. Each region is identified by a corresponding constant: NORTH, SOUTH, EAST, WEST and CENTER.:

"We've already seen the FlowLayout manager," I said. "Using the FlowLayout manager, objects are automatically placed on the frame in a newspaper like format. There's no real control as to where your objects will be placed using the FlowLayout manager. Using the GridLayout manager, objects are placed on the frame in equal-sized rectangles. The GridLayout manager gives you a little more control over the placement of your objects. Using the last layout manager we'll examine today, the BorderLayout, objects are arranged on a frame according to regions that the programmer can specify. Again, there's more control over the placement of these objects than there is with FormLayout, but it's not an exact science."

"I'm not sure I'm thrilled with that prospect," Ward said. "Isn't there a way to place objects more precisely?"

"Yes, there is Ward," I said, "and that's to use a Null layout manager, something we'll examine in a few moments. For now, let's take the GUI we just developed using the FlowLayout manager, and use the GridLayout manager instead."

I then displayed this modified code on the classroom projector:

```
import java.awt.*;
import javax.swing.*;
class GUIV3 extends JFrame {
  JButton btn1 = new JButton("Button1");
  JButton btn2 = new JButton("Button2");
  JButton btn3 = new JButton("Button3");
  JButton btn4 = new JButton("Button4");
  JButton btn5 = new JButton("Button5");
  JButton btn6 = new JButton("Button6");

  GUIV3(){
    Container c = getContentPane();
    c.setLayout ( new GridLayout(2,3));
    c.add(btn1);
    c.add(btn2);
    c.add(btn3);
    c.add(btn4);
    c.add(btn5);
    c.add(btn6);
    setSize(250,250);
    setTitle("GUIV3 Demo");
    setVisible(true);
  }
}
```

And then I then modified the code in Example12_2 to create an instance of the GUIV3 class:

```
class Example12_3 {
  public static void main(String[] args) {
    GUIV3 x = new GUIV3();
  }
}
```

"Let's see how the choice of the GridLayout manager has affected the display of our six buttons," I said. I then compiled GUIV3 and Example12_3 and executed Example12_3. The following screenshot was displayed on the classroom project:

"As you can see," I said, "changing just one line of code designating our layout manager to be the GridLayout has resulted in an arrangement of buttons that is quite different from the arrangement we had when we used the FlowLayout manager. With GridLayout, there's no empty space on our frame, as there was with the FlowLayout. GridLayout placed equally sized rectangles on the frame and placed a button in each rectangle."

"I'm having trouble understanding how the frame knew how to layout the grid," Rhonda said. "Why are there three rectangles across and two down? Did the layout manager do that on its own?"

"That's a function of this line of code, Rhonda," I said.

```
c.setLayout ( new GridLayout(2,3));
```

"When we set the layout manager equal to GridLayout," I said, "we passed an argument to the **GridLayout()** Constructor method specifying the number of rows, 2, and the number of columns, 3, of the grid. If we had failed to do so, each object would have been placed in a single row."

"I see what you mean when you said that GridLayout gives us more control over our layout than FlowLayout," Dave said. "Still, I can see if you have a number of GUI objects that you wish to place on a frame, using the GridLayout manager might be frustrating."

"I think you'll find, Dave," I said, "that designing a GUI using the various layout managers— with the exception of the Null layout manager—is a lot like designing a web page. With HTML, it can also be a challenge to know exactly where your GUI objects will appear in a browser window."

I waited for more questions before continuing.

"One of the more interesting layout managers," I said, "is the BorderLayout. With the BorderLayout manager, objects are designated to be placed in five regions of the frame: north, south, east, west, or center. Let's see how designating our layout manager as BorderLayout affects our GUI."

I then displayed this code on the classroom projector:

```java
import java.awt.*;
import javax.swing.*;
class GUIV4 extends JFrame {
 JButton btn1 = new JButton("Button1");
 JButton btn2 = new JButton("Button2");
 JButton btn3 = new JButton("Button3");
 JButton btn4 = new JButton("Button4");
 JButton btn5 = new JButton("Button5");
 JButton btn6 = new JButton("Button6");

 GUIV4() {
   Container c = getContentPane();
   c.setLayout ( new BorderLayout());
   c.add("North",btn1);
   c.add("West",btn2);
   c.add("Center",btn3);
```

```
      c.add("Center",btn4);
      c.add("South",btn5);
      c.add("East",btn6);
      setSize(250,250);
      setTitle("GUIV4 Demo");
      setVisible(true);
   }
}
```

And then I then modified the code in Example12_3 to create an instance of the GUIV4 class:

```
class Example12_4 {
  public static void main(String[] args) {
    GUIV42 x = new GUIV4();
  }
}
```

"Let's execute Example12_4 now," I said. After compiling both GUIV4 and Example2_4, the following screenshot was displayed on the classroom projector:

"Again, just by changing our layout manager, we have a different arrangement of our buttons than we've seen so far," I said. "Notice how the buttons are arranged in regions of the frame. Here's the code that set the layout manager to BorderLayout:"

```
c.setLayout ( new BorderLayout());
```

"With the BorderLayout manager, we also need to specify the region of the frame in which the button should appear, and we did that when executing the **add()** method of the Container object:"

```
c.add("North",btn1);
c.add("West",btn2);
c.add("Center",btn3);
c.add("Center",btn4);
c.add("South",btn5);
c.add("East",btn6);
```

"Aren't we missing a button somewhere?" Kate asked.

"Kate's right," Blaine said. "We have six buttons that we specified in our code, but only five appear on the frame."

"You're both correct," I said. "When you use the BorderLayout manager, you may have only one object in each region—if you add more than one object, as we did here to the Center region, you will only see the last object that was added. That's why only btn4 appears in the Center region, despite the fact that we also added btn3 to it."

"More and more," Ward said, "this inability to precisely locate objects is starting to bother me. This seems to be a rather convoluted method for implementing the layout of a GUI."

"You can choose not to use a layout manager of any kind," I said, "by setting the layout manager to a Null value. Doing so implements what is known as **absolute positioning**, and it gives you the ability to specify an exact location for your object on the frame. Let me show you."

I then displayed this code on the classroom projector:

```java
import java.awt.*;
import javax.swing.*;
class GUIV5 extends JFrame {
  JButton btn1 = new JButton("Button1");
  JButton btn2 = new JButton("Button2");
  JButton btn3 = new JButton("Button3");
  JButton btn4 = new JButton("Button4");
  JButton btn5 = new JButton("Button5");
  JButton btn6 = new JButton("Button6");

  GUIV5() {
    Container c = getContentPane();
    c.setLayout ( null );
    c.add(btn1);
    c.add(btn2);
    c.add(btn3);
    c.add(btn4);
    c.add(btn5);
    c.add(btn6);

    //Absolute Positioning—x, y, width, height attributes
    btn1.setBounds ( 30, 10, 80, 40 );
    btn2.setBounds ( 130, 10, 80, 40 );
    btn3.setBounds ( 30, 70, 80, 40 );
    btn4.setBounds ( 130, 70, 80, 40 );
    btn5.setBounds ( 30, 130, 80, 40 );
    btn6.setBounds ( 130, 130, 80, 40 );

    setSize(250,250);
    setTitle("GUIV5 Demo");
    setVisible(true);
  }
}
```

I then modified the code in Example12_4 to create an instance of the GUIV5 class:

```java
class Example12_5 {
  public static void main(String[] args) {
    GUIV5 x = new GUIV5();
  }
}
```

"Let's execute Example12_5 now," I said, "and see what impact absolute positioning has on our frame." After compiling both GUIV5 and Example2_5, the following screenshot was displayed on the classroom projector:

"This should make you happy, Ward," I said. "Using absolute positioning, we can place objects on our frame in the exact location we choose. All we need to do is set the layout manager to Null:"

```
c.setLayout ( null );
```

"Then, after executing the **add()** method of the Container object to add the buttons to the frame, execute the **setBounds()** method of the button objects, designating values for their x and y coordinates, plus the width and height of the buttons:"

```
btn1.setBounds ( 30, 10, 80, 40 );
btn2.setBounds ( 130, 10, 80, 40 );
btn3.setBounds ( 30, 70, 80, 40 );
btn4.setBounds ( 130, 70, 80, 40 );
btn5.setBounds ( 30, 130, 80, 40 );
btn6.setBounds ( 130, 130, 80, 40 );
```

"When you say the x coordinate, I presume you mean the horizontal location within the frame?" Dave asked.

"That's right, Dave," I agreed. "And by y coordinate, I mean the vertical location within the frame object."

"I would think that using absolute positioning would be the preferred method for designating the location of objects on a frame."

Linda said. "Why bother using the other layout managers?"

"Absolute positioning does have the advantage of allowing you to pinpoint the location of your objects on a frame," I said. "On the other hand, it does have a significant drawback. Let me show you." I then used my mouse to resize the GUIV5 frame, with the following result:

"Do you see the problem?" I asked.

"The buttons didn't adjust the way they did when we used the other layout managers," Rhonda said. "Is that the drawback you were talking about?"

"That's right, Rhonda," I agreed. "Not only do layout managers handle rearranging objects on the frame when the frame is resized by the user, but they also take into account and adjust for subtle differences in hardware and operating systems that can impact the way your GUI appears on various PCs. Using a layout manager, your GUI can look just as good on a 21-inch monitor running on a Microsoft Windows PC as it does running on a 14-inch monitor running on a Linux PC—the same thing can't necessarily be said if you go with absolute positioning. The bottom line is that using one of the layout managers we discussed today does make pinpoint placement of objects on your frame a difficult task. On the other hand, they do ensure that your programs have a high degree or portability on a variety of PCs. Ultimately, the choice is up to you and will probably vary according to your own particular situation."

"Based on the sketch of the GUI we came up with earlier for the Grade Calculation Project," Valerie said, "I don't see how we can use the layout managers we learned about today to achieve that look and feel. Are there other layout managers that can help us get there?"

"There are other layout managers," I said, "but they're not going to be helpful either. Some Java programmers use a combination of layout managers to produce a GUI, sometimes even nesting layouts within one another. That requires quite a bit of practice and is a bit beyond the introductory scope of our class. Because of the need for pinpoint placement of our objects on the frame, I'm going to suggest that we use absolute positioning for the Grade Calculation Project."

"What about the way the frame behaves when the user resizes it?" Kate asked. "Won't that be a problem?"

"We can prevent the user from resizing the frame," I said, ."by executing the **setResizable()** method of the JFrame class and passing it an argument of false."

I then added this line of code to the GUIV5 class:

```
setResizable(false);
```

I recompiled it and executed Example12_5 again. I then tried to resize the frame but was unable to do so.

"That's better," Valerie said.

We had been working for some time, so I suggested we take a quick break before completing our discussion of the remainder of the Swing components we would be using in the Grade Calculation Project.

Labels

Ten minutes later, we resumed class, beginning with a discussion of the Label object.

"It's the Label class of the Swing Package," I said, "that allows us to display descriptive captions on our GUI. Let's create a GUI that has one button and two labels."

I then displayed this code on the classroom projector:

```
import java.awt.*;
import javax.swing.*;
class GUIV6 extends JFrame {
  JButton btn1 = new JButton("Button1");
  JLabel lbl1 = new JLabel("Label1",JLabel.LEFT);
  JLabel lbl2 = new JLabel("Label2",JLabel.LEFT);

  GUIV6() {
    Container c = getContentPane();
    c.setLayout ( null );
    c.add(btn1);
    c.add(lbl1);
    c.add(lbl2);

    btn1.setBounds ( 30, 10, 80, 40 );
    lbl1.setBounds ( 30, 70, 80, 20 );
    lbl2.setBounds ( 30, 110, 80, 20 );

    setSize(250,250);
    setTitle("GUIV6 Demo");
    setVisible(true);
    setResizable(false);
  }
}
```

I then modified the code in Example12_5 to create an instance of the GUIV6 class:

```
class Example12_6 {
  public static void main(String[] args) {
    GUIV6 x = new GUIV6();
  }
}
```

"Now let's see what our GUI looks like when we execute Example12_6," I said. After compiling both GUIV6 and Example12_6, the following screenshot was displayed:

"As you can see," I said, "we now have a GUI with one button and two labels. Notice that the Label objects have captions that appear in a light shade of blue. Also notice that both labels are left justified, that is, aligned on their left margins."

"Can we take a look at the code that placed the labels on the frame?" Rhonda asked.

"Sure thing, Rhonda," I said. "As was the case when we added buttons to our frame, the first step to adding labels to our frame is to create an instance of the appropriate Swing object. In this case, that's an object of the JLabel class."

```
JLabel lbl1 = new JLabel("Label1",JLabel.LEFT);
JLabel lbl2 = new JLabel("Label2",JLabel.LEFT);
```

"Notice how we named the Instance variable referencing the JLabel object with the prefix lbl—again, this makes the code in our class more readable. The JLabel Constructor requires no arguments, but we supplied two arguments anyway: the first argument is the caption for the Label object. The second argument specifies its alignment, and in this case we supplied a Java constant called JLabel.Left, which specifies left justification. By the way, notice that the word 'LEFT' is spelled in all capital letters."

I paused to see if anyone had any questions before continuing.

"With the variable for our labels declared," I said, "our next step is to do what we did with the button objects: execute the **add()** method to add the Label objects to the container object, the frame."

```
c.add(lbl1); c.add(lbl2);
```

"With both Labels now added to the frame, and because we've set our layout manager to Null, we needed to specify the x and y coordinate locations, plus the height and width of the Label objects, which we did using the **setBounds()** method of the JLabel class."

```
lbl1.setBounds ( 30, 70, 80, 20 );
lbl2.setBounds ( 30, 110, 80, 20 );
```

"You probably have the impression that adding Label objects to your frame is very similar to adding button objects to it," I said, "and you'll find that this is pretty much true for all of the objects you can add to a frame. Once you understand the process, adding one object to the frame is pretty much the same as adding any other: declare an instance of the appropriate Swing class, use its **add()** method to add the object to the container object, and if necessary, execute the **setBounds()** method to specify the coordinates and dimensions of the object. Now let's see how we can add two Text Fields to our frame, right next to the two Label objects we just created."

Text Fields

"It's the TextField class of the Swing Package," I said, "that allows us to add a TextField on our frame. Text Fields permit the user to interact with our program by entering text into a text input area. Let's modify the code from GUIV6 to add two Text Fields to the form."

I then displayed this code on the classroom projector:

```
import java.awt.*;
import javax.swing.*;
class GUIV7 extends JFrame {
  JButton btn1 = new JButton("Button1");
  JLabel lbl1 = new JLabel("Label1",JLabel.LEFT);
  JLabel lbl2 = new JLabel("Label2",JLabel.LEFT);
  JTextField txt1 = new JTextField();
  JTextField txt2 = new JTextField();

  GUIV7() {
    Container c = getContentPane();
    c.setLayout ( null );

    c.add(btn1);
    c.add(lbl1);
    c.add(lbl2);
    c.add(txt1);
    c.add(txt2);
    btn1.setBounds ( 30, 10, 80, 40 );
    lbl1.setBounds ( 30, 70, 80, 20 );
    lbl2.setBounds ( 30, 110, 80, 20 );
```

```
    txt1.setBounds ( 130, 70, 80, 20 );
    txt2.setBounds ( 130, 110, 80, 20 );

    setSize(250,250);
    setTitle("GUIV7 Demo");
    setVisible(true);
    setResizable(false);
  }
}
```

I then modified the code in Example12_6 to create an instance of the GUIV7 class:

```
class Example12_7 {
  public static void main(String[] args) {
    GUIV7 x = new GUIV7();
  }
}
```

"Now, let's see what our GUI looks like when we execute Example12_7," I said. After compiling both GUIV7 and Example12_7, the following screenshot was displayed:

"Do you see the Text Fields?" I asked, as I entered text into them. By now I think my students were getting comfortable with the process of adding objects to a frame.

"As was the case with the other objects we've added to our frame," I said, "our first step here was to declare an instance of the appropriate Swing class—in this case JTextField. To create two Text Fields, we declared two instances of the JTextField class, txt1 and txt2:"

```
JTextField txt1 = new JTextField();
JTextField txt2 = new JTextField();
```

"After that, we added both text box objects by executing the **add()** method of the container object:"

```
c.add(txt1);
c.add(txt2);
```

"Finally, because we are using absolute positioning, we executed the **setBounds()** method of both TextField objects:"

```
txt1.setBounds ( 130, 70, 80, 20 );
txt2.setBounds ( 130, 110, 80, 20 );
```

No one had any problems understanding what we had done with the TextField object. Now it was time to move onto the radio button object.

Radio Buttons

"The last Swing object that we'll be discussing today is the RadioButton object," I said. "The radio button is the most complicated of the GUI objects we'll learn about today."

"Why is that?" Rhonda asked.

"Because of the unique nature of the RadioButton object," I said, "in addition to the steps we followed to place the other objects on the frame, we need to execute a few additional lines of code. Do you remember earlier today I mentioned that only one radio button can be selected at one time? I'm afraid I simplified things just a bit. In actuality, more than one radio button object can be selected at a given time, provided they both are not a member of the same radio button group."

"A radio button group?" Mary asked. "What's that? I'm afraid I don't understand."

"A radio button group is a logical grouping of radio buttons," I said. "For instance, suppose we need to create a GUI in which we ask the user two distinct questions, each of which requires a Yes/No answer. Radio buttons are ideal to represent the Yes/No answers for each question, but if we have two questions, that means that two of the four radio buttons will need to be selected by the user to represent the two answers. This is where a radio button group comes into play. We can tell our frame that a pair of the Yes/No radio buttons belong to a group, and the other pair belong to another."

"So that would permit one button in each radio button group to be selected?" Dave asked.

"Exactly, Dave," I said.

"Can you illustrate this for us?" Kate asked.

"Sure thing, Kate," I said. I then took a moment to create and display this illustration on the classroom projector:

"Ordinarily," I said, "with four radio buttons on a frame, only one of the radio buttons can be selected at one time. However, if we tell Java that the two left-most radio buttons belong to Radio Button Group #1 and the two right most radio buttons belong to Radio Button Group #2, it's possible for the user to select a radio button from each one of the groups."

Everyone seemed content with this explanation, although I suspected they really wanted to see it in action.

"Let's add four radio buttons and two radio button groups to a GUI," I said, "and associate two of the radio buttons with one group, and two with the other."

I then displayed this code on the classroom projector:

```
import java.awt.*;
import javax.swing.*;
class GUIV8 extends JFrame {
  JLabel lblMarried = new JLabel("Are you married?",JLabel.LEFT);
  JLabel lblGolf = new JLabel("Do you play golf?",JLabel.LEFT);
  JRadioButton radMarriedYes = new JRadioButton("Yes?",true);
  JRadioButton radMarriedNo = new  JRadioButton("No?",false);
  JRadioButton radGolfYes = new JRadioButton("Yes?",false);
  JRadioButton radGolfNo = new JRadioButton("No?",true);

  ButtonGroup radioGroup1 = new ButtonGroup();
  ButtonGroup radioGroup2 = new ButtonGroup();
```

```
GUIV8() {
  Container c = getContentPane();
  c.setLayout ( null );

  c.add(lblMarried);
  c.add(lblGolf);
  c.add(radMarriedYes);
  c.add(radMarriedNo);
  c.add(radGolfYes);
  c.add(radGolfNo);

  radioGroup1.add ( radMarriedYes );
  radioGroup1.add ( radMarriedNo );
  radioGroup2.add ( radGolfYes );
  radioGroup2.add ( radGolfNo );

  lblMarried.setBounds ( 30, 20, 140, 20 );
  radMarriedYes.setBounds ( 30, 50, 50, 20 );
  radMarriedNo.setBounds ( 30, 80, 50, 20 );
  lblGolf.setBounds ( 150, 20, 140, 20 );
  radGolfYes.setBounds ( 150, 50, 50, 20 );
  radGolfNo.setBounds ( 150, 80, 50, 20 );

  setSize(300,200);
  setTitle("GUIV8 Demo");
  setVisible(true);
  setResizable(false);
  }
}
```

I then modified the code in Example12_7 to create an instance of the GUIV8 class:

```
class Example12_8 {
  public static void main(String[] args) {
    GUIV8 x = new GUIV8();
  }
}
```

"Now, let's see what our frame looks like when we execute Example12_8," I said. After compiling both GUIV8 and Example12_8, the following screenshot was displayed:

"Do you see how we have two radio buttons selected simultaneously," I said, "one from each group?" I then demonstrated how it was possible to select just one of the radio buttons on the left, and just one of the radio buttons on the right side of the frame, but not two from Radio Button Group 1 or two from Radio Button Group 2 simultaneously.

"Let's take a look at the code in GUIV8 now," I said. "We needed to polish this GUI quite a bit, so we added two labels to it. Here are the two declarations of the JLabel class:"

```
JLabel lblMarried = new JLabel("Are you married?",JLabel.LEFT);
JLabel lblGolf = new JLabel("Do you play golf?",JLabel.LEFT);
```

"Here are the declarations to create four instances of our RadioButton objects—notice that radio buttons are created from the Swing JRadioButton class. We provided the JRadioButton Constructor with a caption for the button and a Boolean argument specifying whether the button should be initially displayed as selected—a Boolean value of true—or not selected—a Boolean value of false:"

```
JRadioButton radMarriedYes = new JRadioButton("Yes?",true);
JRadioButton radMarriedNo = new JRadioButton("No?",false);
JRadioButton radGolfYes = new JRadioButton("Yes?",false);
JRadioButton radGolfNo = new JRadioButton("No?",true);
```

"In order to associate a radio button with a radio button group, we must first create the two radio button groups to be placed on our frame. Radio button groups are created as instances of the ButtonGroup class:"

```
ButtonGroup radioGroup1 = new ButtonGroup();
ButtonGroup radioGroup2 = new ButtonGroup();
```

"As usual, we get a reference to the container frame:"

```
GUIV8() {
  Container c = getContentPane();
```

"We set the layout manager to null:"

```
c.setLayout ( null );
```

"We add our labels to the Container object:"

```
c.add(lblMarried);
c.add(lblGolf);
```

And in a similar way, add the four RadioButton objects to the container object as well:"

```
c.add(radMarriedYes);
c.add(radMarriedNo);
c.add(radGolfYes);
c.add(radGolfNo);
```

"We now need to associate our four radio buttons to the two radio button groups. We do that by executing the **add()** method of the ButtonGroup object, specifying as its single argument the name of the radio button object:"

```
radioGroup1.add ( radMarriedYes );
radioGroup1.add ( radMarriedNo );
radioGroup2.add ( radGolfYes );
radioGroup2.add ( radGolfNo );
```

"The remainder of the code we've seen before: multiple executions of the **setBounds()** method for the Label and RadioButton objects:"

```
lblMarried.setBounds ( 30, 20, 140, 20 );
radMarriedYes.setBounds ( 30, 50, 50, 20 );
radMarriedNo.setBounds ( 30, 80, 50, 20 );
lblGolf.setBounds ( 150, 20, 140, 20 );
radGolfYes.setBounds ( 150, 50, 50, 20 );
radGolfNo.setBounds ( 150, 80, 50, 20 );
```

"It's followed by code to set the size of our frame, set its caption, make it visible, and prevent the user from resizing it:"

```
setSize(300,200);
setTitle("GUIV8 Demo");
setVisible(true);
setResizable(false);
```

I waited to see if there were any questions. I could see that many of my students had been following along with my series of demonstrations, and at this moment, were happily executing various versions of their frames. No one seemed to have any questions, so it was time to move onto implementing our design for the Grade Calculation GUI.

Create the GUI for the Grades Calculation Project

"It's time," I said, "to turn our attention to implementing the design of the GUI we created earlier in the class. With our design in place, coding the actual GUI can be loads of fun." I then distributed this exercise for the class to complete.

Exercise 12-1 Create the DrawGUI Class for the Grades Calculation Project

In this exercise, you'll create the DrawGUI class for the Grades Calculation Project. This class will be used to display the graphical user interface for the Grades Calculation Project.

1. Use Notepad (if you are usingWindows) and enter the following code to create the DrawGUI class:.

```
import java.awt.*;
import javax.swing.*;
class DrawGUI extends JFrame {
  JButton btnCalculate = new  JButton("Calculate Grade");
  JButton btnReset = new JButton("Reset");
  JRadioButton radEnglish = new JRadioButton("English Student", true);
  JRadioButton radMath = new JRadioButton("Math Student", false);
  JRadioButton radScience = new JRadioButton("Science Student", false);

  JLabel lblMidterm = new JLabel("Midterm",JLabel.CENTER);
  JLabel lblFinalExam = new JLabel("Final Exam",JLabel.CENTER);
  JLabel lblResearch = new JLabel("Research Paper",JLabel.CENTER);
  JLabel lblPresentation = new JLabel("Presentation",JLabel.CENTER);
  JLabel lblTypes = new JLabel("Student Types",JLabel.CENTER);
  JLabel lblGrades = new JLabel("Grades",JLabel.CENTER);
  JLabel lblStudentType = new JLabel("ENGLISH STUDENT",JLabel.CENTER);
  JLabel lblFinalGrade = new JLabel("",JLabel.CENTER);

  JTextField txtMidterm = new JTextField();
  JTextField txtFinalExam = new JTextField();
  JTextField txtResearch = new JTextField();
  JTextField txtPresentation = new JTextField();

  ButtonGroup radioGroup = new ButtonGroup();

  DrawGUI() {
    Container c = getContentPane();
    c.setLayout ( null );

    c.add(txtMidterm);
    c.add(txtFinalExam);
    c.add(txtResearch);
    c.add(txtPresentation);

    c.add(lblTypes);
    c.add(lblMidterm);
    c.add(lblFinalExam);
    c.add(lblResearch);
    c.add(lblPresentation);
    c.add(lblStudentType);
    c.add(lblGrades);
    c.add(lblFinalGrade);

    c.add(btnCalculate);
    c.add(btnReset);
```

```
      c.add(radEnglish);
      c.add(radMath);
      c.add(radScience);

      radioGroup.add (radEnglish);
      radioGroup.add (radMath);
      radioGroup.add (radScience);

      radEnglish.setBounds ( 1, 50, 150, 40 );
      radMath.setBounds ( 1, 100, 150, 40 );
      radScience.setBounds ( 1, 150, 150, 40 );

      lblTypes.setBounds ( 0, 0, 200, 40 );
      lblGrades.setBounds ( 150, 0, 100, 40 );
      lblStudentType.setBounds (250,0,200,40);
      lblMidterm.setBounds ( 150, 50, 100, 40 );
      lblFinalExam.setBounds ( 150, 100, 100, 40 );
      lblResearch.setBounds ( 150, 150, 100, 40 );
      lblPresentation.setBounds ( 150, 200, 100, 40 );
      lblFinalGrade.setBounds(225, 250, 250, 40);

      txtMidterm.setBounds ( 300, 50, 50, 40 );
      txtFinalExam.setBounds ( 300, 100, 50, 40 );
      txtResearch.setBounds ( 300, 150, 50, 40 );
      txtPresentation.setBounds ( 300, 200, 50, 40 );

      btnCalculate.setBounds ( 50, 250, 160, 40 );
      btnReset.setBounds ( 50, 300, 160, 40 );

      setSize(500,450);
      setTitle("Grade Calculator");
      setVisible(true);
      setResizable(false);
   }
}
```

2. Save your source file as **DrawGUI.java** in the \JFiles\Grades folder (select File | Save As from Notepad's menu bar). Be sure to save your source file with the file name extension .java.

3. Compile your source file into a Bytecode file.

4. Until we create the GradesGUI class in the next exercise, we won't be able to test this program.

Discussion

No one in the class had a great deal of trouble completing the exercise— although the exercise was pretty long and tedious, everything in it was something we had discussed earlier in the class. Still, I decided it would be a good idea to go over the code line by line.

"Let's take a look at the code now," I said. "As we've seen during today's class, we begin the process of creating our GUI by creating a class—this one we called DrawGUI. We begin with two import statements, which we now know provides our class access to the Swing classes we need to create the frame and the objects on our frame:"

```
import java.awt.*;
import javax.swing.*;
```

"This line of code identifies our class, DrawGUI, and tells Java that we will be inheriting Instance variables and methods from the JFrame class of the Swing package:"

```
class DrawGUI extends JFrame {
```

"These next two lines of code create two instances of button objects from the JButton class, objects that eventually will be used to calculate the student's grade, and to reset the GUI to its initial state."

```
JButton btnCalculate = new JButton("Calculate Grade");
JButton btnReset = new JButton("Reset");
```

"What does that mean?" Rhonda asked.

"When the Reset button is clicked on by the user," I said, "we'll clear all entries in the Text Fields, and also the displayed final grade in the Label on the frame."

I paused before continuing. "Notice," I said, "just like we did in our demonstration programs, we name our variables in such a way that the first three characters of the variable name describe the type of GUI object we're dealing with. Here's the code that creates three radio buttons objects from the JRadioButton class:"

```
JRadioButton radEnglish = new JRadioButton("English Student", true);
JRadioButton radMath = new JRadioButton("Math Student", false);
JRadioButton radScience = new JRadioButton("Science Student", false);
```

"Here's the code to create eight Label objects from the JLabel class, each one left-justified:"

```
JLabel lblMidterm = new JLabel("Midterm",JLabel.LEFT);
JLabel lblFinalExam = new JLabel("Final Exam",JLabel.LEFT);
JLabel lblResearch = new JLabel("Research Paper",JLabel.LEFT);
JLabel lblPresentation = new JLabel("Presentation",JLabel.LEFT);
JLabel lblTypes = new JLabel("Student Types",JLabel.LEFT);
JLabel lblGrades = new JLabel("Grades",JLabel.LEFT);
JLabel lblStudentType = new JLabel("ENGLISH STUDENT",JLabel.LEFT);
JLabel lblFinalGrade = new JLabel("",JLabel.LEFT);
```

"Why is the caption argument for the lblFinalGrade label empty?" Ward asked.

"The lblFinalGrade object will be used to display the student's final numeric and letter grade," I said. "When the frame is initially displayed, there's no grade to display—therefore, we just set the caption of the Label object to an empty string."

"Here's the code to declare our four TextField objects," I said.

```
JTextField txtMidterm = new JTextField();
JTextField txtFinalExam = new JTextField();
JTextField txtResearch = new JTextField();
JTextField txtPresentation = new JTextField();
```

"Here's the code to declare the ButtonGroup object we learned about just a few minutes ago:"

```
ButtonGroup radioGroup = new ButtonGroup();
```

"Here's the Constructor for the DrawGUI class," I continued, "which is automatically executed when an instance of the DrawGUI class is created..."

```
DrawGUI() {
```

"Within the Constructor, we obtain a reference to the container, the frame, by executing the **getContentPane()** method of the JFrame class:"

```
Container c = getContentPane();
```

"This code tells Java that we will not be using a layout manager by passing a null value to the **setLayout()** method:"

```
c.setLayout ( null );
```

"These next few lines of code execute the **add()** method of the Container object to add four Text Fields to our frame:"

```
c.add(txtMidterm);
c.add(txtFinalExam);
c.add(txtResearch);
c.add(txtPresentation);
```

"These lines of code execute the **add()** method of the Container object to add eight Labels to our frame:"

```
c.add(lblTypes);
c.add(lblMidterm);
c.add(lblFinalExam);
c.add(lblResearch);
c.add(lblPresentation);
c.add(lblStudentType);
```

```
c.add(lblGrades);
c.add(lblFinalGrade);
```

"These two lines of code execute the **add()** method of the Container object to add two buttons to our frame:"

```
c.add(btnCalculate);
c.add(btnReset);
```

"These three lines of code execute the **add()** method of the Container object to add three radio buttons to our frame:"

```
c.add(radEnglish);
c.add(radMath);
c.add(radScience);
```

"These three lines of code associate our three radio button objects with a single radio button group:"

```
radioGroup.add (radEnglish);
radioGroup.add (radMath);
radioGroup.add (radScience);
```

"These lines of code designate the coordinates, x and, and height and width attributes of the various objects on our frame:"

```
radEnglish.setBounds ( 1, 50, 150, 40 );
radMath.setBounds ( 1, 100, 150, 40 );
radScience.setBounds ( 1, 150, 150, 40 );

lblTypes.setBounds ( 0, 0, 200, 40 );
lblGrades.setBounds ( 150, 0, 100, 40 );
lblStudentType.setBounds (250,0,200,40);
lblMidterm.setBounds ( 150, 50, 100, 40 );
lblFinalExam.setBounds ( 150, 100, 100, 40 );
lblResearch.setBounds ( 150, 150, 100, 40 );
lblPresentation.setBounds ( 150, 200, 100, 40 );
lblFinalGrade.setBounds(225, 250, 250, 40);

txtMidterm.setBounds ( 300, 50, 50, 40 );
txtFinalExam.setBounds ( 300, 100, 50, 40 );
txtResearch.setBounds ( 300, 150, 50, 40 );
txtPresentation.setBounds ( 300, 200, 50, 40 );

btnCalculate.setBounds ( 50, 250, 160, 40 );
btnReset.setBounds ( 50, 300, 160, 40 );
```

"Finally, this section of code sets the size of the frame to 500 by 450 pixels, sets the title of our frame, makes the frame visible, and tells Java to make the frame not resizable:"

```
setSize(500,450);
setTitle("Grade Calculator");
setVisible(true);
setResizable(false);
```

I asked if anyone had any questions. No one did. It seemed like everyone was anxious to finish the next exercise: creating a new startup class called GradesGUI in which they would create an instance of the DrawGUI class to display the GUI for the Grade Calculation Project.

Exercise 12-2 Create the GradesGUI Class for the Grades Calculation Project

In this exercise, you'll create the GradesGUI class for the Grades Calculation Project.

1. Use Notepad (if you are using Windows) and enter the following code to create the DrawGUI class:.

```
import javax.swing.*;
import java.awt.*;
import java.awt.event.*;
```

```
class GradesGUI {
  public static void main(String[] args) {
    DrawGUI x = new DrawGUI();
  }
}
```

2. Save your source file as **DrawGUI.java** in the \JFiles\Grades folder (select File | Save As from Notepad's menu bar). Be sure to save your source file with the filename extension .java.

3. Compile your source file into a Bytecode file.

4. Execute the program. You should see the Grades Calculation GUI and you will be able to interact with it—to a degree. For instance, you'll be able to click on the Radio Buttons, and make entries in the Text Fields. And you'll also be able to close the Frame. But it won't be until next week that we can use it to calculate grades.

Discussion

"The GUI we designed in the DrawGUI class," I said, "is displayed simply by creating an instance of its class using this single line of code:"

DrawGUI x = new DrawGUI();

I then executed the program myself, and the following screenshot was displayed.

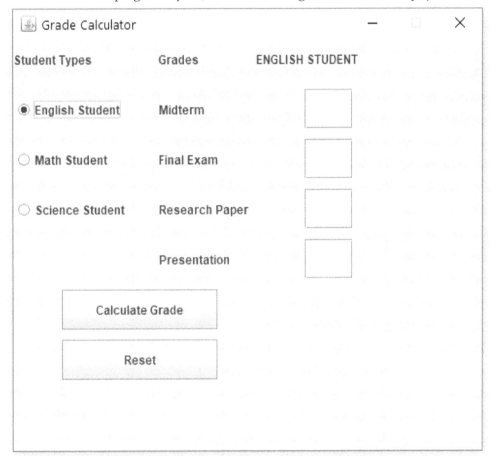

"Wow, that is really something," Ward said. "I'm really impressed with this. A real working GUI."

"It is impressive, Ward," I said. "But at this point, what we have is an attractive graphical user interface with very little functionality. In other words, the GUI looks good, but it doesn't do much of anything. You'll notice that if you click the Radio Buttons, each one displays a certain amount of default behavior in that each RadioButton is selected, and the others unselected. You can enter text into the Text Fields and click each one of the two buttons. All of these actions produce behavior of some kind, but right now, none of this behavior is contributing toward calculating the student's grade. That's what we'll work on next week."

> Note: If you close the GUI using the Close button on the Frame, you'll notice that your DOS or operating system window remains open. You'll need to use your Windows Task Manager to terminate your Java program. This is to be expected, and we'll correct this in the next chapter.

No one had any questions about what we had done. It had been a long and fulfilling class. I dismissed class for the day.

Summary

In this chapter, you learned how to create a Java graphical user interface. You saw that developing a GUI is a matter of starting with an instance of a top-level container, in our case, the JFrame, which is a class available in the Javax.Swing package.

With the JFrame created, you then add other Swing objects to the frame—objects like buttons, radio buttons, labels and Text Fields.

These objects, when placed on a frame, exhibit default behavior when a class containing them is created. Despite their default behavior, these objects do little else—it won't be until our final week of class that we learn to initiate some kind of programmed behavior that will occur when the user interacts with the object.

Chapter 13---Event Handling In Java

In this, our final chapter, we'll take the graphical user interface for the Grades Calculation Project we developed last week and create and associate listeners with the objects on our frame to give our GUI intelligence.

Java Event Handling

I began the final class of our Introduction to Java course by saying that in our final meeting together, we would complete the Grade Calculation Project by finishing up with the GUI we began last week and delivering and installing it on a PC in the English Department.

"So we'll actually be delivering the program today?" Ward asked.

"That's right, Ward," I said, "at the end of today's class. Frank Olley called me earlier in the week to find out if we were on target to complete the project today, and when I told him we were, he asked if it would be possible to deliver and install the program as part of today's class. I told him that would be fine with me. When he heard that, he was elated and told me that he would arrange to have his two work study students come in today to get acquainted with the program. This might mean that today's class goes a little bit longer than usual—I do hope you can all hang in there and help deliver and install our program in the English Department."

"I wouldn't miss it for anything," Linda said.

"Me neither," Steve said. "I think it will be exciting to see how the work study students like the program."

From the looks on the rest of my students' faces, I had a feeling that all of them felt the same way and would also be paying a visit to the English Department.

"It's a shame," Mary said suddenly, "but it doesn't look like Rose and Jack will make it to our final class. Has anyone heard from them? Are they still in Liverpool?"

"I've heard from them," I said. "I spoke with both of them on Thursday night, and at the time, they were aboard their ship somewhere in the North Atlantic. They said the weather was unusually frigid for April, and when I asked whether they would be making it back on time for today's class, they told me they had spoken to the ship's Captain who assured them they'd be arriving in New York harbor early this morning, a few hours head of schedule. I expect both of them to be here before the end of class."

"That's great news," Rhonda said. "It will be good to see them again."

"Will our delivery and installation of the Grade Calculation program on a PC in the English Department wrap up the SDLC?" Valerie asked.

"Just about," I replied. "Phase 5 of the SDLC, the Implementation Phase, will begin today with the delivery and installation of the program and conclude over the course of the next week as I and, I hope, some student volunteers train work study students in the English, Math, and Science Departments in the use of the program. Phase 6 of the SDLC, the Audit and Maintenance Phase, will also begin today, as we observe and study how well the program performs."

What's an Event?

"So what exactly do we have left to complete with the Grade Calculation Project?" Rhonda asked. "Aren't we nearly done with it?"

"Almost," I said. "Last week we created a class called DrawGUI, which takes care of displaying the graphical user interface, or GUI, for the Grade Calculation Project. As it stands right now, the GUI looks great, but it's basically an empty shell—it doesn't react to any events that the user of our program will trigger while working with it. As a result, at the moment, it's incapable of calculating the grade for a student."

"What exactly is an event?" Bob asked. "Is that something that a programmer causes to happen when he or she writes code?"

"No, Bob," I said. "An event is something that is triggered by the user of our GUI when he or she interacts with it."

"What do you mean by triggered?" Rhonda asked.

"For instance," I said, "the GUI we created last week consists of a frame, two buttons, three radio buttons, four Text Fields and several labels. When the user runs our program, the GUI will be displayed, and the user will then use their mouse to select a type of student by clicking one of the three radio buttons. Depending on the type of student the user selects, two, three, or four Text Fields will be visible. The user will then enter appropriate grades into the visible Text Fields using their keyboard, and when they are finished, the user will click the Calculate button, resulting in the display of a final numeric and letter grade in the caption of a label on the frame. At that point, if the user has more grades to calculate, they'll click the Reset button and start the process all over again; otherwise, they will click the Close button of the frame."

"Were each one of those actions you mentioned an event?" Kate asked. "In the scenario you presented, I counted three mouse clicks—one when the user clicks on a Student Type radio button, one when the user clicks on the Calculate button, and one when the user clicks on the Reset button—plus an unknown number of keystrokes when the user enters the composite student grades into the visible Text Fields. Is each one of these actions an event?"

"Not quite, Kate," I said, "but you're close. Each one of those actions isn't an event, but each action triggers an event. One way to conceptualize an event is to picture an event as a ripple in a pond caused by the action of the user tossing in a stone. The action—the stone toss—isn't the event, but rather the ripple generated by the action. Furthermore, each interaction of the user with an object on the GUI generates a ripple. We'll see shortly that our program can react to these ripples, provided we write something called an event listener. As the name implies, event listeners listen for events or ripples."

"I think I understand what you are saying," Mary said. "You're saying that when the user clicks a radio button, for instance, that an event—or one of these ripples, as you called it—is generated. Do we need to program that behavior into the radio button?"

"That's a good question, Mary," I said. "Fortunately, the behavior to generate the event is built into the radio button itself. There's nothing we need to do to generate it. What we must do is create the event listener to detect the event when it occurs, and that's what we'll be learning in the next few minutes."

What's a Listener?

"I understand that a listener is code that can detect and react to events," Lou said. "Is a listener a method that we write in the class that displays the GUI?"

"All listeners," I said, "must implement an interface, the particular interface determined by the object whose events the listener is intended to react to. The code for the listener is placed in methods. Does everyone remember what an interface is?"

"An Interface is like a class with empty method definitions, is that right?" Dave asked.

"That's right, Dave," I said. "Any class containing a listener must implement a listener interface, and that means providing code for the empty method definitions that the interface defines. It's within those methods that we place the code to react to the events the listener can detect."

"Do we implement the interface in the same class we use to draw the GUI?" Dave asked.

"There are three ways to implement a listener," I said. "First, listeners can be implemented as methods in the same class as the one which displays the GUI. Secondly, listeners can be implemented in a class of their own, which is the way we'll learn to implement them today. And finally, listeners can be implemented using an inner class, which is a topic we'll cover in our Intermediate Java Class next semester."

"Is that all we need to do?" Peter asked. "Create a class that implements the appropriate listener interface and then write code for the methods?

"That's right, Peter," I said. "That, plus one more thing: once the listener class is created, we need to declare an instance of the listener within the GUI class and then associate that listener object with the GUI object whose events we wish to react to. We call that process registering the listener."

> **NOTE :** When we associate a listener with a GUI object, we are registering it.

"Is there just one listener interface that can be implemented?" Peter asked.

"No, there are several," I said.

"How do we know which interface to implement, then?" Dave asked.

"Fortunately," I said, "there aren't that many, and they're all well documented in the Java documentation. Various Swing objects support different listeners; however, each one of the Swing objects on our frame supports the same listener interface that we'll be implementing today: the ActionListener interface."

"What do you mean when you say support?" Blaine asked.

"That just means that an object is capable of having a particular listener registered to it," I said. "There are a number of different listener interfaces, and not all objects support them."

"Will we be implementing just one listener interface to react to all of the events triggered by the DrawGUI class?" Linda asked.

"For the objects on our frame, that's true," I said. "We'll implement the ActionListener interface to react to the Button and RadioButton events, although we'll use a second interface to react to the user closing the frame itself."

"Will we be creating just one Listener class to handle the events of both the Button and RadioButton objects?" Dave asked. "Or will those be separate classes?"

"It's possible," I said, "to create one Listener class to react to events triggered by our two Button and three RadioButton objects, but it does complicate the code a bit, as we need to write code to identify the object that triggered the event."

"What will we be doing then?" Kate asked. "Will we create one class to handle the RadioButton events and one class to handle the Button events?"

"We'll create one Listener class to handle the events of all three radio buttons," I said. "And we create separate Listener classes for the Calculate and Reset buttons, although this is just my personal preference."

"What about the Text Fields on the frame?" Barbara said. "Will we be creating a Listener class for those objects?"

"At this point," I said, "I don't think we're interested in reacting to any keystroke events the user may trigger, although it may be something we add to the project if we enhance it in our Java Intermediate Programming class."

Implementing a Simple Listener in Your Code

"I'm still having trouble visualizing how this works," Rhonda said.

"I think I can help with an example," I said. "Let's create a simple GUI class to display a frame with two buttons and two radio buttons. Then we'll create Listener classes to react to the events the objects trigger. Here's the class to display the GUI."

I then displayed this code on the classroom projector:

```java
import java.awt.*;
import javax.swing.*;
class GUI extends JFrame {
  JButton btn1 = new JButton("Button1");
  JButton btn2 = new JButton("Button2");
  JRadioButton radYes = new JRadioButton("Yes", true);
  JRadioButton radNo = new JRadioButton("No", false);

  ButtonGroup radioGroup1 = new ButtonGroup();

  GUI() {
    Container c = getContentPane();
    c.setLayout ( null );

    c.add(btn1);
    c.add(btn2);
    c.add(radYes);
    c.add(radNo);
    radioGroup1.add ( radYes );
    radioGroup1.add ( radNo );

    radYes.setBounds ( 30, 30, 50, 40 );
    radNo.setBounds ( 30, 80, 50, 40 );
```

```
   btn1.setBounds ( 130, 30, 200, 40 );
   btn2.setBounds ( 130, 80, 200, 40 );

   setSize(380,200);
   setTitle("GUI Demo with no Listeners");
   setVisible(true);
   setResizable(false);
 }
}
```

"There's really nothing new here," I said. "When an object of this class is created, it will display a frame with two buttons and two radio buttons. Here's the code to create an instance of the GUI class." I displayed this code on the classroom projector:

```
class Example13_1 {
  public static void main(String[] args) {
    GUI x = new GUI();
  }
}
```

I then compiled both the GUI and Example13_1 classes and executed Example13_1. The following screenshot was displayed on the classroom projector:

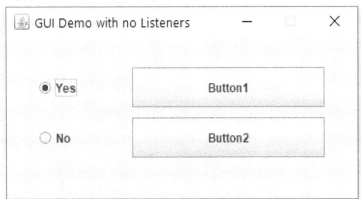

"In the next few minutes," I said, "we'll write code to handle events generated by the user of our program clicking the two RadioButton and the two Button objects. We'll learn how we can properly end our program when the user closes the frame."

The ActionListener Interface

"Let's begin by creating a class to implement a listener for the two RadioButton objects first," I said. "Let's call the class RadioButtonListener and write code that displays the caption, on the Java Console, of the radio button that the user clicks. As I mentioned briefly earlier, we'll be implementing the ActionListener interface to handle the events for every object on our frame." I then displayed this code on the classroom projector:

```
import java.awt.*;
import java.awt.event.*;
import javax.swing.*;
public class RadioButtonListener implements ActionListener{
  public void actionPerformed(ActionEvent e) {
    System.out.println(e.getActionCommand());
  }
}
```

"Wow, there's not much code in the Listener class, is there?" Valerie said.

"That's right, Valerie," I answered. "Listener classes needn't be very lengthy. Let's take a close look at the code in this one. As you can see, the first thing we do is import these three packages:"

```
import java.awt.*;
import java.awt.event.*;
import javax.swing.*;
```

"I notice that we're importing a new package," Dave said.

"That's right, Dave," I replied. "We need to import the java.awt.event package because that's where the listener interfaces are located. This next line of code is the declaration for the class itself. Notice that we are telling Java that we are implementing the ActionListener interface via the Implements keyword:"

```
public class RadioButtonListener implements ActionListener {
```

"You may remember from our discussion of interfaces," I said, "that when a class implements an interface, it must implement all of the empty methods defined in that interface."

"How many methods are defined in the ActionListener interface?" Joe asked.

"Just one," I answered, "the **actionPerformed()** method. **actionPerformed()** is a method defined in the ActionListener interface with a single argument called e, which is an ActionEvent object. The ActionEvent object is a reference to the object on the GUI that triggered the event and, as you'll see in a minute, we'll be able to use this argument to determine, within our code, which of the three RadioButton objects triggered the event."

```
public void actionPerformed(ActionEvent e) {
```

"When we implement the ActionListener interface," I said, "we are required to define our own **actionPerformed()** method—the code we place in it is entirely up to us. When the user clicks one of the three radio buttons on the frame, the **actionPerformed()** method of our listener will be executed, and it will be passed an ActionEvent object, providing the actionPerformed() method information about the object that triggered the event. The ActionEvent object itself has methods that we can use within the **actionPerformed()** method. One of these is the **getActionCommand()** method, which returns the text associated with the object that triggered this event."

"Text?" Kate asked.

"Text is the caption of the object that triggered the event," I answered.

"I can see that something like that could be useful," Barbara said.

"You're right," I agreed. "That information gives our listener intelligence as to what radio button triggered the event and allows us to fine-tune our reaction to the event based on the object that triggers it. In this version of the listener, however, we're merely displaying the caption of the radio button on the Java console, but we will get 'fancier' later on, I promise you."

```
System.out.println(e.getActionCommand());
```

"In a few minutes, we'll use an If statement to evaluate the return value of the **getActionCommand()** method to determine what object triggered the event and react accordingly."

"Does that mean the caption of the radio button that was clicked by the user will be displayed in the Java Console?" Rhonda asked.

'That's exactly right, Rhonda," I said.

"I've been following along with the creation of the GUI and the listener," Chuck said, "but when I created an instance of my GUI in a startup class and clicked the radio buttons, nothing was displayed in the Java Console. What did I do wrong?"

"Nothing. It's because we haven't registered the listener with our GUI yet," I said. "After we create the Listener class, we need to go back and modify the GUI class so that it knows to route the events it generates to the Listener object. Before we do that, we need to first compile the Listener class, and then we can modify and recompile the GUI class."

> NOTE: You must first compile your Listener class before modifying your GUI class to include a reference to it. Otherwise, you will receive a compiler error.

I then compiled the Listener class and modified the GUI class. I displayed the modified code on the classroom projector:

```
import java.awt.*;
import javax.swing.*;
```

```
class GUI extends JFrame {
  JButton btn1 = new JButton("Button1");
  JButton btn2 = new JButton("Button2");
  JRadioButton radYes = new JRadioButton("Yes", true);
  JRadioButton radNo = new JRadioButton("No", false);

  ButtonGroup radioGroup1 = new ButtonGroup();

  RadioButtonListener rbListener = new RadioButtonListener();

  GUI() {
    Container c = getContentPane();
    c.setLayout ( null );

    c.add(btn1);
    c.add(btn2);
    c.add(radYes);
    c.add(radNo);

    radioGroup1.add ( radYes );
    radioGroup1.add ( radNo );

    radYes.addActionListener(rbListener);
    radNo.addActionListener(rbListener);

    radYes.setBounds ( 30, 30, 50, 40 );
    radNo.setBounds ( 30, 80, 50, 40 );
    btn1.setBounds ( 130, 30, 200, 40 );
    btn2.setBounds ( 130, 80, 200, 40 );

    setSize(380,200);
    setTitle("GUI Demo with Radio Button Listener");
    setVisible(true);
    setResizable(false);
  }
}
```

"The process," I said, "of telling the GUI to route events to our listener only took three lines of code. First, we needed to create an instance of the RadioButtonListener object and then assign it to an instance variable which we called rbListener:"

```
RadioButtonListener rbListener = new RadioButtonListener();
```

"Next, we executed the **addActionListener()** method of our two RadioButton objects to associate or register our Listener object with both radio buttons:"

```
radYes.addActionListener(rbListener);
radNo.addActionListener(rbListener);
```

"That's it?" Ward asked.

"That's all, Ward," I answered. "Just those three lines of code told Java to route events triggered by those two radio buttons to the Listener object we coded. At this point, we need to recompile our GUI class and create an instance of it via our startup class Example13_1."

I compiled the GUI class with no problem and then executed Example13_1. The following screenshot was displayed on the classroom projector:

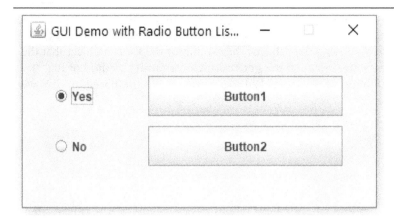

"Nothing's changed," Rhonda said.

"You're right, Rhonda," I said. "The look of our GUI, except for the title bar of the frame, hasn't changed, but let's see what happens when I click the radio button captioned No, and then click the radio button captioned Yes."

I did so, and the following screenshot was displayed on the classroom projector:

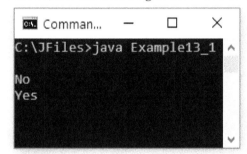

"I see," Rhonda said excitedly. "When you clicked the No radio button, the word 'No' was displayed in the Java Console, and when you clicked the Yes radio button, the word 'Yes' was displayed in the Java Console. That's really impressive."

I waited a moment before continuing. "We've just implemented our first listener to react to events on our GUI," I said, "and I think you'll agree that it wasn't all that bad."

"No, it wasn't bad at all," Kate said. "I think I understand what's going on. But what about the buttons on the frame? Do we need to create a separate Listener class for those as well, or can we use the RadioButtonListener?"

"Since both the RadioButton and Button objects both support the ActionListener," I said, "we could use the RadioButtonListener class to react to events triggered by both objects. However, it's my personal preference to create distinct Listener classes for the various types of objects on a frame. Sometimes I even create separate classes for objects of the same type, and that's something we'll do later on today when we create separate listeners for the Calculate and Reset buttons of the Grade Calculation Project. For now, let's create a listener for the Button objects called ButtonListener."

I then displayed this code on the classroom projector:

```java
import java.awt.*;
import java.awt.event.*;
import javax.swing.*;
public class ButtonListener implements ActionListener {
  public void actionPerformed(ActionEvent e) {
    if (e.getActionCommand().equals ("Button1") ) {
      System.out.println("Button1 has been clicked");
  }
    if (e.getActionCommand().equals ("Button2") ) {
      System.out.println("Button2 has been clicked");
    }
  }
}
```

"As you can see," I said, "this listener is similar to the RadioButtonListener class we created earlier. Both listeners implement the ActionListener interface and, because of that, are required to implement the **actionPerformed()** method as well. In this listener, however, instead of displaying the value of the caption of the Button object that the user clicks, we use an If statement to interrogate the return value of the **getActionCommand()** method of the ActionEvent object. This returns the caption of the button the user clicked to generate the event. Based on that, we display a custom message to the Java Console instead:"

```java
public void actionPerformed(ActionEvent e) {
  if (e.getActionCommand().equals ("Button1") ) {
    System.out.println("Button1 has been clicked");
  }
  if (e.getActionCommand().equals ("Button2") ) {
    System.out.println("Button2 has been clicked");
  }
}
```

"As before, we now need to register this class as the listener for our two Button objects within the GUI class," I said, as I compiled the ButtonListener class. I then displayed the code for the modified GUI on the classroom projector:

```java
import java.awt.*;
import javax.swing.*;
class GUI extends JFrame {
  JButton btn1 = new JButton("Button1");
  JButton btn2 = new JButton("Button2");
  JRadioButton radYes = new JRadioButton("Yes", true);
  JRadioButton radNo = new JRadioButton("No", false);

  ButtonGroup radioGroup1 = new ButtonGroup();

  RadioButtonListener rbListener = new RadioButtonListener();
  ButtonListener btnListener = new ButtonListener();

  GUI() {
    Container c = getContentPane();
    c.setLayout ( null );

    c.add(btn1);
    c.add(btn2);
    c.add(radYes);
    c.add(radNo);
    radioGroup1.add (radYes);
    radioGroup1.add (radNo);

    radYes.addActionListener(rbListener);
    radNo.addActionListener(rbListener);
    btn1.addActionListener(btnListener);
    btn2.addActionListener(btnListener);

    radYes.setBounds ( 30, 30, 50, 40 );
    radNo.setBounds ( 30, 80, 50, 40 );
    btn1.setBounds ( 130, 30, 200, 40 );
    btn2.setBounds ( 130, 80, 200, 40 );

    setSize(380,200);
    setTitle("GUI Demo with Radio Button and Button Listeners");
    setVisible(true);
    setResizable(false);
  }
}
```

"As was the case when we registered our radio button listeners," I said, "we need to add only three lines of code to the GUI class to register the button listeners. This line creates an instance of a ButtonListener object and then assigns it to an instance variable called btnListener:"

```
ButtonListener btnListener = new ButtonListener();
```

"We then execute the **addActionListener()** method of the two Button objects to associate or register the listener with both buttons:"

```
btn1.addActionListener(btnListener);
btn2.addActionListener(btnListener);
```

"We now need to recompile our GUI class and create an instance of it via our startup class, Example13_1," I said.

I compiled the GUI class with no problem, and then executed Example13_1.Once again, our GUI was displayed on the classroom projector. I first clicked the button captioned Button1, then Button2, then I clicked on the radio button captioned No and the radio button captioned Yes. The following screenshot was displayed on the classroom projector:

I could see a number of students coding up their own versions of GUI and listeners, and they were obviously fascinated with this newfound ability.

Passing Your Listener a Reference to Your GUI Object

"Is there anyway to manipulate the object that triggers an event from its listener?" Dave asked.

"What do you mean, Dave?" Linda asked.

"For instance," he said, "could you change the caption of a button when the user clicks it?"

"Interesting that you should ask that question, Dave," I said. "I was about to ask the class the same thing."

"Is there ever a need to do such as thing?" Mary asked.

"Yes, there is," I said. "Later on, we'll be wanting to do something just like that when we make some of the four Text Fields on the Grade Calculation GUI invisible, depending upon the radio button that the user clicks."

"Is that a problem?" Kate asked. "Can't we refer to or update an object on our frame from within the Listener class?"

"We can," I said, "but not directly. The **setText()** method of a button can be executed to change the caption of a Button object. Let me show you what happens if we try to change the caption of Button2 on our GUI when Button1 is clicked by executing the **setText()** method within the **actionPerformed()** method of the Button listener."

I then modified the code in the ButtonListener class to look like this:

```
import java.awt.*;
import java.awt.event.*;
import javax.swing.*;
public class ButtonListener implements ActionListener {
  public void actionPerformed(ActionEvent e) {
    if (e.getActionCommand().equals ("Button1") ) {
      System.out.println("Button1 has been clicked");
      btn2.setText("I love Java");
    }
    if (e.getActionCommand().equals ("Button2") ) {
      System.out.println("Button2 has been clicked");
    }
```

```
    }
}
```

"Here's the code that seemingly would change the change the caption of Button 2 to 'I love Java' when Button1 is clicked."

```
btn2.setText("I love Java");
```

"That seems reasonable to me," I heard Joe say.

"However," I continued, "there's a problem when we compile the listener."

I then compiled ButtonListener. The following screenshot was displayed on the classroom projector:

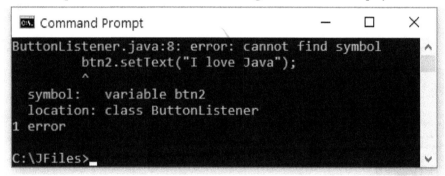

"What's wrong?" Rhonda asked. "What does this error message mean?"

"The compiler is telling us it doesn't know what btn2 is," I said.

"btn2 is the name of the instance variable representing the Button object in our GUI," Dave said. "Is this problem one of scope? Can't the code in the ButtonListener class 'see' the instance variable btn2 in the GUI class?"

"That's exactly the problem, Dave," I said. "The objects, such as RadioButton, Text Fields, and Buttons on our GUI, can't automatically be seen by our Listener object."

"So what do we do now?" Bob asked. "Being able to update objects on our GUI from our listener is an important part of the features of the Grade Calculation Project."

"No need to worry," I said. "It can be done. We just need to pass our listener a reference to our GUI object, which will give our listener access to all of the objects contained on it."

"How do we do that?" Valerie asked.

"We'll need to create a Constructor method in the Listener class that accepts an object or our GUI class as an argument," I said. "Let me show you."

I then modified the code in the ButtonListener class to look like this:

```
import java.awt.*;
import java.awt.event.*;
import javax.swing.*;
public class ButtonListener implements ActionListener {
  GUI x;

  ButtonListener (GUI a) {
    x = a;
  }

  public void actionPerformed(ActionEvent e) {
    if (e.getActionCommand().equals ("Button1") ) {
      System.out.println("Button1 has been clicked");
      x.btn2.setText("I love Java");
    }
    if (e.getActionCommand().equals ("Button2") ) {
      System.out.println("Button2 has been clicked");
    }
  }
}
```

"As you can see, not a great deal has changed here," I said. "We declared a new instance variable called x, added a Constructor method called ButtonListener, and added a line of code to change the caption of Button2."

"I'm afraid I'm a little confused about the Constructor method here," Kate said. "When does the code in the Constructor method execute? And why didn't we have a Constructor method in the ButtonListener class before?"

"Constructor methods are never required in a class," I said. "By default, each class has a default Constructor—in other words, without a custom Constructor method, Java just creates the object for us. It isn't until we need to get a bit fancier that we need to create a custom Constructor. In this case, we've created a Constructor method that tells Java to expect a GUI object as an argument when we register the listener:"

ButtonListener (GUI a)

"So that's what we're telling Java within the parentheses?" Kate asked. "To expect an argument called 'a' of the GUI class?"

"Excellent, Kate, you're exactly right," I replied. "Again, the idea with this version of our ButtonListener class is that when Button1 is clicked, the listener will detect that event and then change the caption of Button2 so that it reads 'I love Java.' In order for the listener to be able to modify the attribute of an object on our GUI, the GUI needs to pass a reference to itself to the listener—something that sounds tricky, but which you'll see in a minute is amazingly easy. Let's first take a look at the instance variable x: we declare it as an instance of the GUI class. Why we do that we'll see in a minute:"

```
public class ButtonListener implements ActionListener {
   GUI x;
```

"Here's the Constructor method. Notice that it accepts a single argument called 'a' that is actually an object of our GUI class:"

ButtonListener (GUI a)

"The Constructor itself contains just a single line of code, and with it, we assign the passed reference to our GUI to the instance variable x:"

```
x = a;
```

"Why are we doing this?" Joe asked. "Doesn't the argument 'a' give us full access to the GUI and the objects on it?"

"Unfortunately," I said, "arguments are local to the method in which they are declared, and in this case, 'a' and the GUI object to which it points can't be seen outside of the Constructor method. What that means is if we were to try to refer to the argument 'a' within the **actionPerformed()** method, we'd get a compiler error. By assigning the reference to our GUI object contained in the argument 'a' to the instance variable x, we give the reference to our GUI an object-wide scope, which allows us to execute this code in the **actionPerformed()** method:"

```
public void actionPerformed(ActionEvent e) {
  if (e.getActionCommand().equals ("Button1") ) {
    System.out.println("Button1 has been clicked");
    x.btn2.setText("I love Java");
  }
```

"If the caption of the button triggering this event is Button1, we execute this code to change the Caption of the btn2 object on our GUI to 'I love Java':"

```
x.btn2.setText("I love Java");
```

"By the way," I said, "notice that we prefix the reference to the btn2 object on our GUI with the name of the instance variable that points to the GUI itself."

"That's pretty neat," Barbara said. "So in this way, we can work with all the objects on our GUI?"

"That's right, Barbara," I said, as I compiled the listener.

"Since we now have a Constructor method that requires an argument, does that mean we have to change the GUI class?" Peter asked.

"Right you are, Peter," I said. "We'll need to pass the ButtonListener a reference to the GUI itself."

I then modified the GUI class, and displayed it on the classroom projector:

```java
import java.awt.*;
import javax.swing.*;
class GUI extends JFrame {
  JButton btn1 = new JButton("Button1");
  JButton btn2 = new JButton("Button2");
  JRadioButton radYes = new JRadioButton("Yes", true);
  JRadioButton radNo = new JRadioButton("No", false);
  ButtonGroup radioGroup1 = new ButtonGroup();

  RadioButtonListener rbListener = new RadioButtonListener();
  ButtonListener btnListener = new ButtonListener(this);

  GUI() {
    Container c = getContentPane();
    c.setLayout (null);
    c.add(btn1);
    c.add(btn2);
    c.add(radYes);
    c.add(radNo);
    radioGroup1.add ( radYes );
    radioGroup1.add ( radNo );
    radYes.addActionListener(rbListener);
    radNo.addActionListener(rbListener);
    btn1.addActionListener(btnListener);
    btn2.addActionListener(btnListener);

    radYes.setBounds ( 30, 30, 50, 40 );
    radNo.setBounds ( 30, 80, 50, 40 );
    btn1.setBounds ( 130, 30, 200, 40 );
    btn2.setBounds ( 130, 80, 200, 40 );
    setSize(380,200);
    setTitle("GUI Demo with Button Listener passed a reference to the Frame");
    setVisible(true);
    setResizable(false);
  }
}
```

"Here's the crucial line of code in the GUI class," I said. "It's the declaration of an instance of the ButtonListener class, this time specifying a single argument using the special keyword **this**:"

ButtonListener btnListener = new ButtonListener(this);

"This?" Rhonda asked.

"You use the keyword **this**," I said, "when an object needs to pass a reference to itself."

I compiled the GUI class with no problem and then executed Example13_1. Once again, our GUI was displayed on the classroom projector. When I clicked the button captioned Button1, the caption for Button2 changed to 'I Love Java':"

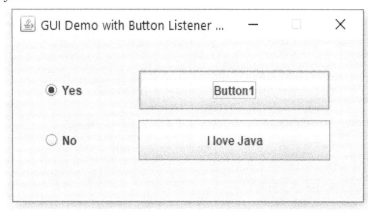

"Wow, the caption of the button changed!" Rhonda said.

"Aren't listeners great?" I asked. "The code in the ButtonListener object was triggered when we clicked Button1, and it used an If statement to determine if the event was triggered by Button1. It was, so it changed the caption of Button2 by executing the **setText()** method of the btn2 object:"

```
if (e.getActionCommand().equals ("Button1") ) {
  System.out.println("Button1 has been clicked");
  x.btn2.setText("I love Java");
}
```

"Extremely powerful," Ward said. "I can see a lot of application for code like this back at work. Is it time to modify the Grade Calculation Project now? I can't wait to see what we do with it!"

Using the WindowListener Interface to Close Your Frame

"We have just one more thing to cover before we turn our attention to the Grade Calculation Project," I said. "Do you remember the problem our GUI has when we close our frame and our program continues to run? To gracefully end our program, we need to implement a listener called the WindowListener and register it to our frame."

"How do we implement the WindowListener?" Lou asked.

"We implement the WindowListener," I said, "the same way we've implemented our other listeners today: by creating a class, extending the appropriate interface—in this case the WindowListener interface—and then implementing the methods of the WindowListener interface."

"You said methods, not method," Ward said. "Does the WindowListener define more than one method?"

"That's right, Ward," I answered. "The WindowListener interface is a bit more cumbersome to implement because it defines seven methods. However, we're really only interested in one method, the **windowClosing()** method, which is the method that is called when our frame is closed by the user."

"Even though we're only interested in using the **windowClosing()** method," Dave said, "aren't we still required to implement the other six methods?"

"You're right, Dave," I said, "although we can just code them as empty methods—by that I mean just the definitions. Let me show you by creating a FrameListener class for our GUI."

I then displayed the code for the FrameListener class on the classroom projector:

```
import java.awt.*;
import java.awt.event.*;
import javax.swing.*;
public class FrameListener implements WindowListener {
  public void windowOpened(WindowEvent e) {}

  public void windowClosing(WindowEvent e) {
    System.exit(0);
  }

  public void windowClosed(WindowEvent e) {}

  public void windowIconified(WindowEvent e) {}

  public void windowDeiconified(WindowEvent e) {}

  public void windowActivated(WindowEvent e) {}

  public void windowDeactivated(WindowEvent e) {}
}
```

"Why do we have those empty methods?" Rhonda asked.

"Those are the seven methods defined in the WindowListener interface," I said. "Any class that implements the WindowListener interface is required to account for all seven methods. When the user closes a frame, the **windowClosing()** method is triggered, so that's the only method for which we need to write code. However, we still need to code the other six methods, even if they have no actual code in them, just an empty set of curly braces."

"OK, that makes sense," Rhonda said.

"Let's take a look at the code in the **windowClosing()** method," I continued, "which takes place before the frame closes. It's in this method that we place the code to end our program using the **exit()** method of the System object:"

```
public void windowClosing(WindowEvent e) {
  System.exit(0);
}
```

"That's it?" Lou asked. "Couldn't we have just coded that statement in the GUI class itself?"

"If we had," I said, "the program would have immediately ended. The only time we want to execute the **exit()** method of the System object is when the frame closes, and the only way to ensure that happens is to place this code in a listener executed when the closing of the frame triggers it."

"OK, that makes sense," Lou said. "What now?"

"Now," I said, "we need to do what we've done with the other listeners we've created today: modify the GUI class to declare an instance of the Listener class and then register it to the object whose events we wish to listen for—in this case, the frame. Here's the modified GUI class:"

```
import java.awt.*;
import javax.swing.*;
class GUI extends JFrame {
  JButton btn1 = new JButton("Button1");
  JButton btn2 = new JButton("Button2");
  JRadioButton radYes = new JRadioButton("Yes", true);
  JRadioButton radNo = new JRadioButton("No", false);
  ButtonGroup radioGroup1 = new ButtonGroup();
  RadioButtonListener rbListener = new RadioButtonListener();
  ButtonListener btnListener = new ButtonListener(this);
  FrameListener fListener = new FrameListener();

  GUI() {
    Container c = getContentPane();
    c.setLayout ( null );
    c.add(btn1);
    c.add(btn2);
    c.add(radYes);
    c.add(radNo);
    radioGroup1.add ( radYes );
    radioGroup1.add ( radNo );
    radYes.addActionListener(rbListener);
    radNo.addActionListener(rbListener);
    btn1.addActionListener(btnListener);
    btn2.addActionListener(btnListener);
    this.addWindowListener(fListener);
    radYes.setBounds ( 30, 30, 50, 40 );
    radNo.setBounds ( 30, 80, 50, 40 );
    btn1.setBounds ( 130, 30, 200, 40 );
    btn2.setBounds ( 130, 80, 200, 40 );
    setSize(380,200);
    setTitle("GUI Demo that ends when Frame is closed");
    setVisible(true);
    setResizable(false);
  }
}
```

"Let's take a look at the code we added to the GUI," I said. "This line of code creates an instance of our FrameListener object:"

```
FrameListener fListener = new FrameListener();
```

"And this code registers the listener with our frame:"

`this.addWindowListener(fListener);`

"I noticed that you used the keyword This again," Kathy said. "Why didn't we use the name of our frame?"

"Because our frame has no explicit name," I said. "Our GUI object itself is the frame—and remember, the way to refer to our GUI in code is to use the keyword This."

"I'm afraid I still don't understand," Kate said. "I'm still having trouble conceptually with the This keyword. Could you expand on it a little?"

"The keyword This," I said, "refers to the current instance of an object. When you are writing code, and you need to refer to the instance of an object that a client program will create from your class, you have no way of knowing what the client program will name the object—it could be x, y, or the programmer's name for all we know. Using This tells Java that you want to gain a reference to that object, no matter what it winds up being called."

"That's better," Kate said, "I think what's really confusing me is that when you created an instance of the ButtonListener object, you passed a reference to This, but with the FrameListener object, you didn't. What is that?"

"That's because," I replied, "the ButtonListener object is designed to update objects on the GUI, such as Label and TextField objects. That's why when the ButtonListener object is created, we pass it a reference to the Frame using the This keyword. The FrameListener doesn't need to do work with any objects on the GUI, and therefore doesn't need a reference to the Frame. As a result, we don't need to use the This keyword. Is that better Kate?"

"Yes, I think it is," she answered. "Any Listener object that needs to reference objects on the frame must be passed a reference to that frame, and that's done using the This keyword."

"That's excellent, Kate," I said. "In our Intermediate Java class, you'll learn that using something called Inner Classes, we can include the Listener classes within the same class file as our GUI, and therefore give our Listener class direct access to the objects on the GUI without having to pass them a reference, but more on that in the Intermediate class."

I then compiled both the FrameListener and GUI classes—in that order—and executed Example13_1. The following screenshot was displayed on the classroom projector:

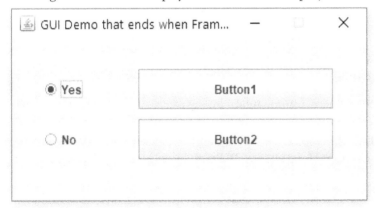

"Let's see what happens when we click the Close button of the frame," I said.

I did so, and the frame closed. This time, the program also ended normally.

"Mission accomplished," Linda said. "That seems to take care of all of our loose ends. Is it time to update the Grade Calculation Project now?

Using the WindowAdapter Class to Close Your Frame

"Almost," I said. "I know everyone is anxious to wrap up the Grade Calculation Project, but there's just one more thing I want to show you, as it's likely you'll encounter it as you get further into your Java programming career."

"What's that?" Ward asked.

"Well," I said, "we just saw that when we implemented the WindowListener interface, we needed to implement all seven methods of the interface, even though we were really only interested in the **windowClosing()** method."

"Is there a way to avoid having to do that?" Peter asked.

"Yes, there is," I answered. "The Java language has what are known as Adapter classes, These are classes which implement the Listener interface, with each method of the interface implemented as empty methods. What that means is that instead of extending the Listener interface, we can inherit or implement the corresponding Listener Adapter class. This saves us from having to define each one of the methods—we simply override the empty method we wish to use."

"So you're saying that for each interface we've studied today," Valerie said, "there's a corresponding Adapter class?"

"That's right, Valerie," I said. "For example, the corresponding Adapter class for the WindowListener interface is the WindowAdapter class. Extending it in our class means that instead of having to code seven methods, we only need to override the empty **windowClosing()** method defined in the WindowAdpater class. Here's what our FrameListener class would look like if we extend the WindowAdapter class instead of implementing the WindowListener interface:"

```
import java.awt.*;
import java.awt.event.*;
import javax.swing.*;
public class FrameListener extends WindowAdapter {
  public void windowClosing(WindowEvent e) {
    System.exit(0);
  }
}
```

"As you can see," I said, "the number of lines of code in FrameListener has been reduced because we extended the WindowAdapter class instead of implementing the WindowListener interface. Notice, however, that the **windowClosing()** method is identical in both cases."

"Does the GUI class have to change?" Steve asked.

"Not at all, Steve," I said. "Implementing the interface or extending the class is no different."

I waited to see if there were any questions. There were none, so I asked everyone to take a 15-minute break.

"After break," I said, "we'll make those modifications to the Grade Calculation Project you've all been waiting for."

Implementing Listeners in the Grades Calculation Project

Fifteen minutes later I was about to begin discussing the Grade Calculation Project modifications we were about to make when I noticed two people approach our classroom door. It was Rose and Jack, back from their long journey.

"Rose and Jack," I said. "Welcome back. It's great to see you! I was getting a little worried that you might not make it back in time for our final class."

"Professor Smiley has been keeping us apprised of the development with the Grade Calculation Project," Rose explained to the class. "And of course, we took our laptops along with us. We're right on pace—well, just about on pace—to complete the course and the project with all of you. I don't think we've missed a beat."

"I'm glad that you both were able to be with us today," I said. "Your attendance will help put a nice close to the project we all started together so many weeks ago. Let's start making those changes to the Grade Calculation Project now. The first thing we need to do is modify each one of the Student classes."

"Why is that?" Rhonda asked. "I thought they were working perfectly fine."

"We'll be using the Student classes in interaction with our GUI to calculate the student's grade," I said, "and as part of that, we'll need to execute the **calculate()** method of each one of those classes. But there's a problem."

I saw quite a few puzzled looks on the faces of my students.

"Right now," I said, "when we execute the **calculate()** methods of the student classes, the code in each displays input boxes for the input of the student grade components and then displays the result in a message box."

"We don't need to do that," Kate said. "Our GUI takes care of the input of the component grades via our four Text Fields, and it takes care of the display of the final letter and numeric grade via the caption of a Label object."

"Absolutely right, Kate," I said. "The **calculate()** methods of those classes simply won't work with our GUI. We need a **calculate()** method that can use the values the user enters into the Text Fields."

"Does that mean we need to modify the way the **calculate()** methods work in those classes?" Kate asked.

"If we do that," Ward chimed in, "we won't be able to use the non-GUI version of the project we've written."

"Ward's right," I said, "if we modify the way the existing **calculate()** methods work, the version of the Grade Calculation Project that doesn't use the GUI will no longer work. But don't forget, we can overload the **calculate()** methods in those classes, and that will enable us to have one **calculate()** method that works with the non-GUI version of our program and another **calculate()** method that works with the GUI."

"Overload means to create another **calculate()** method with a different signature, is that right?" Valerie asked.

"Absolutely correct, Valerie," I said. "For each one of the Student classes, we'll create a second **calculate()** method, this one accepting arguments that are passed to it via the TextField objects of the GUI."

I waited to see if there were any questions before distributing this exercise for the class to complete.

Exercise 13-1 Modify the EnglishStudent Class

In this exercise, you'll modify the EnglishStudent class to include an overloaded **calculate()** method. Because the English student final grade calculation is made up of four component grades, the overloaded **calculate()** method for the EnglishStudent class requires four arguments.

1. Using Notepad (if you are using Windows) locate and open the EnglishStudent.java source file you worked on previously. (It should be in the \JFiles\Grades folder)
2. Modify your code so that it looks like this.

```java
import javax.swing.JOptionPane;
class EnglishStudent extends Student {
  private final double ENGLISH_MIDTERM_PERCENTAGE = .25;
  private final double ENGLISH_FINALEXAM_PERCENTAGE = .25;
  private final double ENGLISH_RESEARCH_PERCENTAGE = .30;
  private final double ENGLISH_PRESENTATION_PERCENTAGE = .20;

  public EnglishStudent() {
    System.out.println ("EnglishStudent's Constructor");
  }

  public void calculate(int midterm, int finalExamGrade,
              int research, int presentation) {
    finalNumericGrade =
      (midterm * ENGLISH_MIDTERM_PERCENTAGE) +
      (finalExamGrade * ENGLISH_FINALEXAM_PERCENTAGE) +
      (research * ENGLISH_RESEARCH_PERCENTAGE) +
      (presentation * ENGLISH_PRESENTATION_PERCENTAGE);
    if (finalNumericGrade >= 93)
      finalLetterGrade = "A";
    else
    if ((finalNumericGrade >= 85) & (finalNumericGrade < 93))
      finalLetterGrade = "B";
    else
    if ((finalNumericGrade >= 78) & (finalNumericGrade < 85))
      finalLetterGrade = "C";
    else
    if ((finalNumericGrade >= 70) & (finalNumericGrade < 78))
      finalLetterGrade = "D";
    else
    if (finalNumericGrade < 70)
      finalLetterGrade = "F";
  }
  public void calculate() {
    midterm = Integer.parseInt(JOptionPane.showInputDialog
      ("Enter the Midterm Grade"));
    finalExamGrade = Integer.parseInt(JOptionPane.showInputDialog
      ("Enter the Final Examination Grade"));
```

```
    research = Integer.parseInt(JOptionPane.showInputDialog
      ("Enter the Research Grade"));
    presentation = Integer.parseInt(JOptionPane.showInputDialog
      ("Enter the Presentation Grade"));
    finalNumericGrade =
      (midterm * ENGLISH_MIDTERM_PERCENTAGE) +
      (finalExamGrade * ENGLISH_FINALEXAM_PERCENTAGE) +
      (research * ENGLISH_RESEARCH_PERCENTAGE) +
      (presentation * ENGLISH_PRESENTATION_PERCENTAGE);
    if (finalNumericGrade >= 93)
      finalLetterGrade = "A";
    else
    if ((finalNumericGrade >= 85) & (finalNumericGrade < 93))
      finalLetterGrade = "B";
    else
    if ((finalNumericGrade >= 78) & (finalNumericGrade < 85))
      finalLetterGrade = "C";
    else
    if ((finalNumericGrade >= 70) & (finalNumericGrade < 78))
      finalLetterGrade = "D";
    else
    if (finalNumericGrade < 70)
      finalLetterGrade = "F";
  }
}
```

3. Save your source file as EnglishStudent.java in the \JFiles\Grades folder (select File | Save As from Notepad's menu bar). Be sure to save your source file with the filename extension .java.

4. Compile your source file into a Bytecode file.

5. You won't be testing your EnglishStudent class until you have completed work on the other classes in the project.

Discussion

"It looks like all we've done is add another **calculate()** method to the EnglishStudent class," Rhonda said.

"That's right, Rhonda," I said. "Having two identically named methods in a class means that we have overloaded methods. That's perfectly fine, provided the methods have different signatures—that is, the number and types of arguments. The **calculate()** method we wrote a few weeks ago in the EnglishStudent class requires no arguments:"

```
public void calculate()
```

"Its code prompts the user for the component grade pieces by executing the **showInputDialog()** method of the JOptionPane object. The **calculate()** method that we just added to the EnglishStudent class requires four arguments:"

```
public void calculate(int midterm, int finalExamGrade,
            int research, int presentation) {
```

"Each one represents one of the component grade pieces necessary to calculate an English Student's grade. Those component pieces will be passed to the **calculate()** method by the DrawGUI class, which obtains them from the four TextField objects on the GUI."

"And the fact that we now have two **calculate()** methods means that our non-GUI version of the program can still work," Dave said, "since it executes the calculate() method but passes it no arguments?"

"Exactly, Dave," I said. "By adding an overridden **calculate()** method to the EnglishStudent class, we've ensured that any client programs dependent on the old **calculate()** method will still work."

I waited to see if there were more questions—there were none. I then distributed this exercise for the class to complete.

Exercise 13-2 Modify the MathStudent Class

In this exercise, you'll modify the MathStudent class to include an overloaded **calculate()** method. Because the Math student final grade calculation is made up of two component grades, the overloaded **calculate()** method for the MathStudent class requires only two arguments.

1. Using Notepad (if you are using Windows) locate and open the MathStudent.java source file you worked on previously (It should be in the \JFiles\Grades folder)

2. Modify your code so that it looks like this.

```java
import javax.swing.JOptionPane;
class MathStudent extends Student {
  private final double MATH_MIDTERM_PERCENTAGE = .50;
  private final double MATH_FINALEXAM_PERCENTAGE = .50;
  public MathStudent() {
    System.out.println ("MathStudent's Constructor");
  }

  public void calculate(int midterm, int finalExamGrade) {
    finalNumericGrade =
      (midterm * MATH_MIDTERM_PERCENTAGE) +
      (finalExamGrade * MATH_FINALEXAM_PERCENTAGE);
    if (finalNumericGrade >= 90)
      finalLetterGrade = "A";
    else
    if ((finalNumericGrade >= 83) & (finalNumericGrade < 90))
      finalLetterGrade = "B";
    else
    if ((finalNumericGrade >= 76) & (finalNumericGrade < 83))
      finalLetterGrade = "C";
    else
    if ((finalNumericGrade >= 65) & (finalNumericGrade < 76))
      finalLetterGrade = "D";
    else
    if (finalNumericGrade < 65)
      finalLetterGrade = "F";
  }

  public void calculate() {
    midterm = Integer.parseInt(JOptionPane.showInputDialog
      ("Enter the Midterm Grade"));
    finalExamGrade = Integer.parseInt(JOptionPane.showInputDialog
      ("Enter the Final Examination Grade"));
    finalNumericGrade =
      (midterm * MATH_MIDTERM_PERCENTAGE) +
      (finalExamGrade * MATH_FINALEXAM_PERCENTAGE);
    if (finalNumericGrade >= 90)
      finalLetterGrade = "A";
    else
    if ((finalNumericGrade >= 83) & (finalNumericGrade < 90))
      finalLetterGrade = "B";
    else
    if ((finalNumericGrade >= 76) & (finalNumericGrade < 83))
      finalLetterGrade = "C";
    else
    if ((finalNumericGrade >= 65) & (finalNumericGrade < 76))
      finalLetterGrade = "D";
    else
    if (finalNumericGrade < 65)
      finalLetterGrade = "F";
  }
}
```

3. Save your source file as MathStudent.java in the \JFiles\Grades folder (select File | Save As from Notepad's menu bar). Be sure to save your source file with the filename extension .java.

4. Compile your source file into a Bytecode file.

5. You won't be testing your MathStudent class until you have completed the work on the other classes in the project.

Discussion

No one had any major problems completing the exercise, although several students did incorrectly code four arguments for the calculate() method instead of two. Fortunately, I discovered this as I strode around the classroom.

"As was the case in the EnglishStudent class," I said, "what we've done here is to add a second **calculate()** method to the MathStudent class. Notice that the number of arguments for the new **calculate()** method of this class is only two:"

```
public void calculate(int midterm, int finalExamGrade)
```

"Why is that?" Rhonda asked. "Because," I replied, "the calculation for the math student requires just two grade components, the midterm and final exam grades. The English student calculation requires all four components. As we'll see shortly, the **calculate()** method for the ScienceStudent class will require three arguments."

There were no more questions, so I distributed this exercise to the class to complete.

Exercise 13-3 Modify the ScienceStudent Class

In this exercise, you'll modify the ScienceStudent class to include an overloaded **calculate()** method. Because the Science student final grade calculation is made up of three component grades, the overloaded **calculate()** method for the ScienceStudent class requires three arguments.

1. Using Notepad (if you are using Windows) locate and open the ScienceStudent.java source file you worked on previously (It should be in the \JFiles\Grades folder)

2. Modify your code so that it looks like this.

```java
import javax.swing.JOptionPane;
class ScienceStudent extends Student {
    private final double SCIENCE_MIDTERM_PERCENTAGE = .40;
    private final double SCIENCE_FINALEXAM_PERCENTAGE = .40;
    private final double SCIENCE_RESEARCH_PERCENTAGE = .20;

    public ScienceStudent() {
        System.out.println ("ScienceStudent's Constructor");
    }

    public void calculate(int midterm, int finalExamGrade,
                   int research) {
        finalNumericGrade =
            (midterm * SCIENCE_MIDTERM_PERCENTAGE) +
            (finalExamGrade * SCIENCE_FINALEXAM_PERCENTAGE) +
            (research * SCIENCE_RESEARCH_PERCENTAGE);
        if (finalNumericGrade >= 90)
            finalLetterGrade = "A";
        else
        if ((finalNumericGrade >= 80) & (finalNumericGrade < 90))
            finalLetterGrade = "B";
        else
        if ((finalNumericGrade >= 70) & (finalNumericGrade < 80))
            finalLetterGrade = "C";
        else
        if ((finalNumericGrade >= 60) & (finalNumericGrade < 70))
            finalLetterGrade = "D";
        else
        if (finalNumericGrade < 60)
            finalLetterGrade = "F";
    }
```

```
  public void calculate() {
    midterm = Integer.parseInt(JOptionPane.showInputDialog
      ("Enter the Midterm Grade"));
    finalExamGrade = Integer.parseInt(JOptionPane.showInputDialog
      ("Enter the Final Examination Grade"));
    research = Integer.parseInt(JOptionPane.showInputDialog
      ("Enter the Research Grade"));
    finalNumericGrade =
      (midterm * SCIENCE_MIDTERM_PERCENTAGE) +
      (finalExamGrade * SCIENCE_FINALEXAM_PERCENTAGE) +
      (research * SCIENCE_RESEARCH_PERCENTAGE);
    if (finalNumericGrade >= 90)
      finalLetterGrade = "A";
    else
    if ((finalNumericGrade >= 80) & (finalNumericGrade < 90))
      finalLetterGrade = "B";
    else
    if ((finalNumericGrade >= 70) & (finalNumericGrade < 80))
      finalLetterGrade = "C";
    else
    if ((finalNumericGrade >= 60) & (finalNumericGrade < 70))
      finalLetterGrade = "D";
    else
    if (finalNumericGrade < 60)
      finalLetterGrade = "F";
  }
}
```

3. Save your source file as ScienceStudent.java in the \JFiles\Grades folder (select File | Save As from Notepad's menu bar). Be sure to save your source file with the filename extension .java.

4. Compile your source file into a Bytecode file.

5. You won't be testing your ScienceStudent class until you have completed the work on the other classes in the project.

Discussion

Again, no one had any major problems completing this exercise. Everyone properly coded the three arguments for the **calculate()** method of the ScienceStudent class.

"What's our next step?" Rose asked. "Well," I said, "with the modifications to all three Student classes completed, it's time to turn our attention to creating the four Listener classes we'll be creating for our GUI."

"Four Listener classes?" Jack asked. "That's right, Jack," I said. "We'll be creating a listener for all three radio buttons, one listener for our Calculate button, one listener for our Reset button, and one listener for our frame."

"That should be a piece of cake, if they're similar to the ones you showed us this morning," Kate said.

"They will be," I answered. "We start with the listener for our three radio buttons, and we'll call it the RadioButtonListener class. Its main feature will be to determine which one of the three radio buttons representing a student type has been clicked and to then hide or display the appropriate TextField objects for that student type. The listener will also display, as a caption in a Label object, the student type. You'll see that we'll use this as a signal to our Calculate button listener as to the type of Student object to create."

I then distributed this exercise for the class to complete.

Exercise 13-4 Create a Listener for Our Radio Buttons

In this exercise, you'll code the RadioButton Listener class for the Grades Calculation Project.

1. Using Notepad, enter the following code.

```
import java.awt.*;
import java.awt.event.*;
import javax.swing.*;
```

```java
public class RadioButtonListener implements ActionListener {
  DrawGUI x;

  RadioButtonListener(DrawGUI a) {
    x = a;
  }
  public void actionPerformed(ActionEvent e) {
    if (e.getActionCommand().equals("English Student") ) {
      x.txtMidterm.setVisible(true);
      x.txtFinalExam.setVisible(true);
      x.txtResearch.setVisible(true);
      x.txtPresentation.setVisible(true);
      x.lblStudentType.setText("ENGLISH STUDENT");
    }
    if (e.getActionCommand().equals ("Math Student") ) {
      x.txtMidterm.setVisible(true);
      x.txtFinalExam.setVisible(true);
      x.txtResearch.setVisible(false);
      x.txtPresentation.setVisible(false);
      x.lblStudentType.setText("MATH STUDENT");
    }
    if (e.getActionCommand().equals("Science Student") ) {
      x.txtMidterm.setVisible(true);
      x.txtFinalExam.setVisible(true);
      x.txtResearch.setVisible(true);
      x.txtPresentation.setVisible(false);
      x.lblStudentType.setText("SCIENCE STUDENT");
    }
  }
}
```

2. Save your source file as RadioButtonListener.java in the \JFiles\Grades folder (select File | Save As from Notepad's menu bar). Be sure to save your source file with the file name extension java.

3. Compile your source file into a Bytecode file.

4. You won't be testing the RadioButtonListener class until you have completed the work on the other classes in the project.

Discussion

No one seemed to have any problems completing the exercise.

"Let's take a look at the code in our RadioButtonListener class," I said. "This code is very similar to the RadioButtonListener class we examined earlier today. As was the case then, we've created a dedicated class for the listener, implementing the ActionListener interface:"

```java
public class RadioButtonListener implements ActionListener {
```

"Because this listener will make modifications to the caption of a Label object on our GUI, we know that the GUI will be passing our listener a reference to itself when it creates the RadioButtonListener object. For that reason, we need to declare an instance variable called x of the DrawGUI class:"

```java
DrawGUI x;
```

"The Constructor method for the RadioButtonListener class is defined to accept a single DrawGUI object argument called 'a', and once a reference to the DrawGUI object is passed to the Constructor method, we assign that reference to the variable x:"

```java
RadioButtonListener(DrawGUI a) {
  x = a;
}
```

"And the reason for that, again?" Rose asked.

"It's a matter of scope," I said. "Because the argument 'a' is declared within the Constructor method, code within the **actionPerformed()** method won't be able to access the argument or the DrawGUI object it points to. By assigning the reference of the DrawGUI object 'a' to the DrawGUI object x, which has object-wide scope, the code in the **actionPerformed()** method will be able to access the DrawGUI object—the frame and all of the other objects on it."

"That's right," Rose said. "That makes sense."

"The ActionListener interface," I continued, "requires that we implement just one method, the **actionPerformed()** method, and we do that here, using a series of If statements to determine which of the three Student Type radio buttons triggered the event. Depending upon the type of student selected, we execute the **setVisible()** method of the TextField objects on our GUI to make the appropriate Text Fields either visible or invisible. Finally, as the last statement of our If block, we assign a caption to the lblStudentType Label object on our GUI. This caption will be used in the Calculate Button listener to determine which Student object to instantiate for the proper calculation of the student's grade. Here's the section of code to determine if the radio button that was clicked was the one with the caption English Student:"

```
public void actionPerformed(ActionEvent e) {
  if (e.getActionCommand().equals ("English Student") ) {
    x.txtMidterm.setVisible(true);
    x.txtFinalExam.setVisible(true);
    x.txtResearch.setVisible(true);
    x.txtPresentation.setVisible(true);
    x.lblStudentType.setText("ENGLISH STUDENT");
  }
}
```

"This process is repeated, checking for the other two student types."

"Wow, I can't wait to see that code execute," Rhonda said. "Making Text Fields visible and invisible—it sounds like magic."

"Unfortunately," I said, "we won't be able to test the RadioButtonListener until we're done with the rest of our exercises."

No one had any questions, so it was time to move onto coding the CalculateButtonListener class.

"The CalculateButtonListener," I said, "is probably the most complex of the listeners we'll write today. There will be no need to determine which of the two buttons have been clicked, as the listener will only be executed when the Calculate button is clicked. However, we will need to determine the caption for the lblStudentType Label object, and depending upon its value, instantiate either an EnglishStudent, MathStudent or ScienceStudent class, execute the **calculate()** method, and pass it values from the Text Fields of our GUI. Once that's done, the listener will display the student's final numeric and letter grades on the GUI."

I then distributed this exercise for the class to complete.

Exercise 13-5 Create a Listener for Our Calculate Button

In this exercise, you'll create the CalculateButtonListener class for the Grades Calculation Project.
1. Using Notepad (if you are using Windows) enter the following code.

```
import java.awt.*;
import java.awt.event.*;
import javax.swing.*;
public class CalculateButtonListener implements ActionListener {
  DrawGUI x;

  CalculateButtonListener(DrawGUI a) {
    x = a;
  }

  public void actionPerformed(ActionEvent e) {
    if (x.lblStudentType.getText() == "ENGLISH STUDENT") {
      EnglishStudent eStudent = new EnglishStudent();
      eStudent.calculate(Integer.parseInt(x.txtMidterm.getText()),
```

```
                    Integer.parseInt(x.txtFinalExam.getText()),
                    Integer.parseInt(x.txtResearch.getText()),
                    Integer.parseInt(x.txtPresentation.getText()));
        x.lblFinalGrade.setText("Numeric Grade: " +
            eStudent.getFinalNumericGrade() +
            " Letter Grade: " +
            eStudent.getFinalLetterGrade());
    }
    if (x.lblStudentType.getText() == "MATH STUDENT") {
      MathStudent mStudent = new MathStudent();
      mStudent.calculate(Integer.parseInt(x.txtMidterm.getText()),
                Integer.parseInt(x.txtFinalExam.getText()));
      x.lblFinalGrade.setText("Numeric Grade: " +
          mStudent.getFinalNumericGrade() +
          " Letter Grade: " +
          mStudent.getFinalLetterGrade());
    }
    if (x.lblStudentType.getText() == "SCIENCE STUDENT") {
      ScienceStudent sStudent =new ScienceStudent();
      sStudent.calculate(Integer.parseInt(x.txtMidterm.getText()),
                Integer.parseInt(x.txtFinalExam.getText()),
                Integer.parseInt(x.txtResearch.getText()));
      x.lblFinalGrade.setText("Numeric Grade: " +
                  sStudent.getFinalNumericGrade() +
                  " Letter Grade: " +
                  sStudent.getFinalLetterGrade());
    }
  }
}
```

2. Save your source file as CalculateButtonListener.java in the \JFiles\Grades folder (select File | Save As from Notepad's menu bar). Be sure to save your source file with the file name extension java.

3. Compile your source file into a Bytecode file.

4. You won't be testing the CalculateButtonListener class until you have completed the work on the other classes in the project.

Discussion

Again, no one seemed to have any problem completing the exercise.

"Let's take a look at the code in our CalculateButtonListener class," I said. "This code is very similar to the ButtonListener class we saw earlier today. As was the case then, we've created a dedicated class for the listener, implementing the ActionListener interface:"

```
public class CalculateButtonListener implements ActionListener {
```

"Because this listener will make modifications to the caption of a Label object on our GUI, we know that the GUI will be passing our listener a reference to itself when it creates the CalculateButtonListener object. For that reason, we need to declare an instance variable called x of the DrawGUI class:"

```
DrawGUI x;
```

"The Constructor method for the CalculateButtonListener class is defined to accept a single DrawGUI object argument called 'a', and once a reference to the DrawGUI object is passed to the Constructor method, we assign that reference to the variable x:"

```
CalculateButtonListener(DrawGUI a) {
  x = a; }
```

"The ActionListener interface requires that we implement just one method, the **actionPerformed()** method, and we do that here. Unlike the RadioButtonListener, which we'll register to handle events from all three of our RadioButton objects, the CalculateButtonListener will be registered to handle the events of only one Button object—the Calculate button—so we don't need code to determine which button has been selected. However, we do need to know which one of the three radio buttons on our GUI is selected at the time the user clicks the Calculate button, and we use an If statement to do that."

"Is that the purpose of setting the caption in the lblStudentType Label object in the RadioButtonListener?" Jack asked.

"That's right, Jack," I answered. "We wrote code in the RadioButtonListener class to set the caption of the lblStudentType Label object when one of the three radio button objects was clicked—we use an If statement here to determine the Caption of that Label object to determine the type of Student object we should instantiate."

"Instead of using the caption of a Label object," Dave asked, "why didn't we just check the GUI to see which of the three RadioButton objects is selected?"

"We could do that as well," I said, "but using the **getText()** method is a bit simpler than determining which of the three radio buttons is selected. By the way, here's the code to determine if the lblStudentType Label object is equal to 'ENGLISH STUDENT':"

```
public void actionPerformed(ActionEvent e) {
  if (x.lblStudentType.getText() == "ENGLISH STUDENT") {
```

"If it is, we create an instance of an EnglishStudent object:"

```
EnglishStudent eStudent = new EnglishStudent();
```

"Then we execute the new calculate() method of the EnglishStudent object, passing it four arguments, which are the component grades found in the TextField objects of our GUI. Notice that we execute the **parseInt()** method to convert the string value in the Text Fields to an integer, which is the data type that the **calculate()** method is expecting:"

```
eStudent.calculate(Integer.parseInt(x.txtMidterm.getText()),
        Integer.parseInt(x.txtFinalExam.getText()),
        Integer.parseInt(x.txtResearch.getText()),
        Integer.parseInt(x.txtPresentation.getText()));
```

"The **calculate()** method then updates the finalNumericGrade and finalLetterGrade attributes of the EnglishStudent object, which are then displayed as the caption of the lblFinalGrade Label object of our GUI:"

```
x.lblFinalGrade.setText("Numeric Grade: " +
  eStudent.getFinalNumericGrade() +
  "     Letter Grade: " +
  eStudent.getFinalLetterGrade());
}
```

"We also have If statements to determine if the caption of the lblStudentType Label object is equal to 'MATH STUDENT' or 'SCIENCE STUDENT' and appropriate code to instantiate both the MathStudent and ScienceStudent objects."

"Wow, I can't wait to see how this works," Ward said. "This is getting really exciting."

"We'll be able to see this in action in a few minutes," I said, "but first we need to create three more Listener classes."

"What's next?" Linda asked.

"The ResetButtonListener," I said. "Using this listener, we'll reset our GUI to the way it looks when our frame is first displayed by making all four TextField objects visible, clearing their contents, selecting the English Student radio button, clearing the caption for the lblFinalGrade Label object, and displaying 'ENGLISH STUDENT' as the caption of the lblStudentType Label object."

I then distributed this exercise for the class to complete.

Exercise 13-6 Create a Listener for Our Reset Button

In this exercise, you'll create the ResetButtonListener class for the Grades Calculation Project.
1. Using Notepad (if you are using Windows) enter the following code.

```
import java.awt.*;
import java.awt.event.*;
import javax.swing.*;
public class ResetButtonListener implements ActionListener {
```

```
  DrawGUI x;
  ResetButtonListener(DrawGUI a) {
    x = a;
  }
  public void actionPerformed(ActionEvent e) {
    x.radEnglish.doClick();
    x.txtMidterm.setVisible(true);
    x.txtFinalExam.setVisible(true);
    x.txtResearch.setVisible(true);
    x.txtPresentation.setVisible(true);
    x.txtMidterm.setText("");
    x.txtFinalExam.setText("");
    x.txtResearch.setText("");
    x.txtPresentation.setText("");
    x.lblFinalGrade.setText("");
    x.lblStudentType.setText("ENGLISH STUDENT");
  }
}
```

2. Save your source file as ResetButtonListener.java in the \JFiles\Grades folder (select File | Save As from Notepad's menu bar). Be sure to save your source file with the file name extension java.

3. Compile your source file into a Bytecode file.

4. You won't be testing the ResetButtonListener class until you have completed the work on the other classes in the project.

Discussion

"Let's take a look at the code in our ResetButtonListener," I said. "As was the case with all of our listeners we have coded today, we've created a dedicated class for the listener, implementing the ActionListener interface:"

```
public class ResetButtonListener implements ActionListener {
```

"Because this listener will make many modifications to the objects on our GUI, we know that the GUI will be passing our listener a reference to itself when it creates the ResetButtonListener object. For that reason, we need to declare an instance variable called x of the DrawGUI class:"

```
DrawGUI x;
```

"The Constructor method for the ResetButtonListener class is defined to accept a single object argument called 'a', and once a reference to the DrawGUI object is passed to the Constructor method, we assign that reference to the variable x:"

```
ResetButtonListener(DrawGUI a) { x = a; }
```

"The ActionListener interface requires that we implement just one method, the actionPerformed() method, and we do that here. Unlike the other listeners we've created today, the ResetButtonListener has absolutely no selection structures—the code in **actionPerformed()** will be registered to handle the events of only the Reset button, and when clicked, we execute this code to select the English Student radio button by executing the **doClick()** method of the JRadioButton class. The **doClick()** method simulates the action of a user clicking on a radio button:"

```
public void actionPerformed(ActionEvent e) {
  x.radEnglish.doClick();
```

"Depending upon the current state of our GUI when the Reset button is clicked, some of the Text Fields on the GUI may be invisible, so we execute the **setVisible()** method of each one of our Text Fields, passing a value of true as an argument to make them visible:"

```
x.txtMidterm.setVisible(true);
x.txtFinalExam.setVisible(true);
x.txtResearch.setVisible(true);
x.txtPresentation.setVisible(true);
```

"We execute the **setText()** method, passing it an argument of an empty string to clear all four Text Fields and the lblFinalGrade Label object. Notice also that we set the caption of the lblStudentType Label object to 'ENGLISH STUDENT', making the frame appear the same way it does when it we first start our program:"

```
x.txtMidterm.setText("");
x.txtFinalExam.setText("");
x.txtResearch.setText("");
x.txtPresentation.setText("");
x.lblFinalGrade.setText("");
x.lblStudentType.setText("ENGLISH STUDENT");
```

"This is really interesting code," Jack said. "I find the ability of our listener to work with objects on the GUI really awesome. I know I'll have a lot of application for this."

No one had any questions, so it was time to move onto coding our last listener, the FrameListener.

"The FrameListener," I said, "will enable our program to gracefully end when the use closes the frame. The class you are about to create is identical to the code I demonstrated earlier, so you should have an easy time with this exercise."

I then distributed this exercise for the class to complete.

Exercise 13-7 Create a Listener for Our Frame

In this exercise, you'll create the FrameListener class for the Grades Calculation Project.
1. Using Notepad (if you are using Windows) enter the following code.

```
import java.awt.*;
import java.awt.event.*;
import javax.swing.*;
public class FrameListener extends WindowAdapter {
  public void windowClosing(WindowEvent e) {
    System.exit(0);
  }
}
```

2. Save your source file as FrameListener.java in the \JFiles\Grades folder (select File | Save As from Notepad's menu bar). Be sure to save your source file with the file name extension java.
3. Compile your source file into a Bytecode file.
4. You won't be testing the FrameListener class until you have completed the work on the other classes in the project.

Discussion

No one had any problems with this exercise—the code was identical to that which I had demonstrated earlier, and many of the students had already created it.

"That's it for our Listener classes," I said.

"Are we done now?" Rhonda asked.

"Not quite yet, Rhonda," I said. "We have just one more exercise to complete, and that's to modify our DrawGUI class."

"What changes do we have to make to the DrawGUI class?" Lou asked. "We need to declare instances of all four listeners," I said, "and then register them to their appropriate GUI objects. After that, we'll be ready to fully test the GUI for the Grade Calculation Project!"

I then distributed this exercise for the class to complete.

Exercise 13-8 Modify the DrawGUI Class for the Grades Calculation Project

In this exercise, you'll modify the DrawGUI class to include Listeners.
1. Using Notepad (if you are using Windows) locate and open the DrawGUI .java source file you created last week. (It should be in the \Jfiles\Grades folder.)
2. Modify your code so that it looks like this:

```java
import java.awt.*;
import javax.swing.*;
class DrawGUI extends JFrame {
  JButton btnCalculate = new JButton("Calculate Grade");
  JButton btnReset = new JButton("Reset");
  JRadioButton radEnglish = new JRadioButton("English Student", true);
  JRadioButton radMath = new JRadioButton("Math Student", false);
  JRadioButton radScience = new JRadioButton("Science Student", false);
  JLabel lblMidterm = new JLabel("Midterm",JLabel.CENTER);
  JLabel lblFinalExam = new JLabel("Final Exam",JLabel.CENTER);
  JLabel lblResearch = new JLabel("Research Paper",JLabel.CENTER);
  JLabel lblPresentation = new JLabel("Presentation",JLabel.CENTER);
  JLabel lblTypes = new JLabel("Student Types",JLabel.CENTER);
  JLabel lblGrades = new JLabel("Grades",JLabel.CENTER);
  JLabel lblStudentType = new JLabel("ENGLISH STUDENT",JLabel.CENTER);
  JLabel lblFinalGrade = new JLabel("",JLabel.CENTER);
  JTextField txtMidterm = new JTextField();
  JTextField txtFinalExam = new JTextField();
  JTextField txtResearch = new JTextField();
  JTextField txtPresentation = new JTextField();
  ButtonGroup radioGroup = new ButtonGroup();

  RadioButtonListener rbListener = new RadioButtonListener(this);
  CalculateButtonListener cbListener = new CalculateButtonListener(this);
  ResetButtonListener resetListener = new ResetButtonListener(this);
  FrameListener fListener = new FrameListener();

  DrawGUI() {
    Container c = getContentPane();
    c.setLayout ( null );
    c.add(txtMidterm);
    c.add(txtFinalExam);
    c.add(txtResearch);
    c.add(txtPresentation);
    c.add(lblTypes);
    c.add(lblMidterm);
    c.add(lblFinalExam);
    c.add(lblResearch);
    c.add(lblPresentation);
    c.add(lblStudentType);
    c.add(lblGrades);
    c.add(lblFinalGrade);
    c.add(btnCalculate);
    c.add(btnReset);
    c.add(radEnglish);
    c.add(radMath);
    c.add(radScience);
    radioGroup.add ( radEnglish );
    radioGroup.add ( radMath );
    radioGroup.add ( radScience );

    radEnglish.addActionListener(rbListener);
    radMath.addActionListener(rbListener);
    radScience.addActionListener(rbListener);
    radEnglish.addActionListener(rbListener);
    btnCalculate.addActionListener(cbListener);
    btnReset.addActionListener(resetListener);
    this.addWindowListener(fListener);
```

```
        radEnglish.setBounds ( 1, 50, 150, 40 );
        radMath.setBounds ( 1, 100, 150, 40 );
        radScience.setBounds ( 1, 150, 150, 40 );
        lblTypes.setBounds ( 0, 0, 200, 40 );
        lblGrades.setBounds ( 150, 0, 100, 40 );
        lblStudentType.setBounds (250,0,200,40);
        lblMidterm.setBounds ( 150, 50, 100, 40 );
        lblFinalExam.setBounds ( 150, 100, 100, 40 );
        lblResearch.setBounds ( 150, 150, 100, 40 );
        lblPresentation.setBounds ( 150, 200, 100, 40 );
        lblFinalGrade.setBounds(225, 250, 250, 40);
        txtMidterm.setBounds ( 300, 50, 50, 40 );
        txtFinalExam.setBounds ( 300, 100, 50, 40 );
        txtResearch.setBounds ( 300, 150, 50, 40 );
        txtPresentation.setBounds ( 300, 200, 50, 40 );
        btnCalculate.setBounds ( 50, 250, 160, 40 );
        btnReset.setBounds ( 50, 300, 160, 40 );

        setSize(500,450);
        setTitle("Grade Calculator");
        setVisible(true);
        setResizable(false);
    }
}
```

3. Save your source file as DrawGUI in the \JFiles\Grades folder (select File | Save As from Notepad's menu bar). Be sure to save your source file with the file name extension java.

4. Compile your source file into a Bytecode file.

5. We can now test the GradesGUI class we wrote last week—there's no need to make any changes to it.

6. Execute GradesGUI; your frame should appear. Notice that the English Student radio button is already selected for you and that the words 'ENGLISH STUDENT' appear as the caption for the lblStudentType Label object (the label is located in the upper-right-hand portion of the frame).

7. It's time to calculate the grade for an English Student. When the frame is first displayed, the English Student radio button is already selected, so you don't need to select it. Enter **70** into the Midterm TextField, **80** into the Final Exam TextField, **90** into the Research Paper TextField, and **100** into the Presentation TextField. Click the Calculate button. A final numeric grade of **84.5** should be displayed, with a letter grade of **C**, as the caption for the lblFinalGrade Label object:

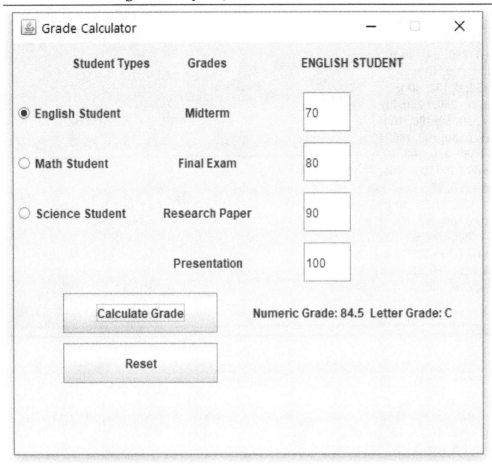

8. Click the Reset button; the frame should appear the way it was first displayed.

9. Click the Math Student radio button. The Research Paper and Presentation Text Fields should disappear, and the words 'MATH STUDENT' should appear in the lblStudentType Label object:

10. Enter **70** into the Midterm TextField and **80** into the Final Exam TextField. Click the Calculate button. A final numeric grade of **75** should be displayed, with a letter grade of **D** as the caption for the lblFinalGrade Label object:

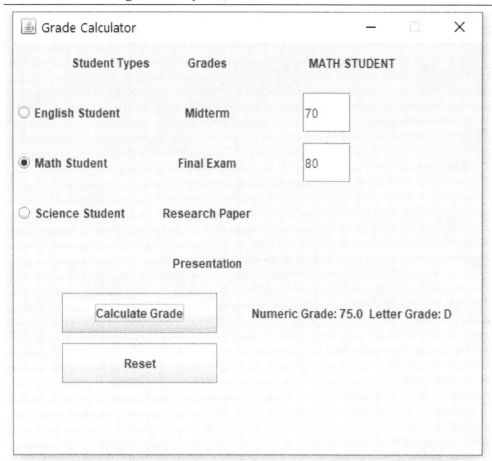

11. Click the Reset button; the frame should appear the way it did when it was first displayed.

12. Click the Science Student radio button. The Presentation TextField should disappear, and the words 'SCIENCE STUDENT' should appear as the caption for the lblStudentType Label object:

13. Enter **70** into the Midterm TextField, **80** into the Final Exam TextField, and **90** into the Research TextField. A final numeric grade of **78** should be displayed, with a letter grade of **C** as the caption for the lblFinalGrade Label object:

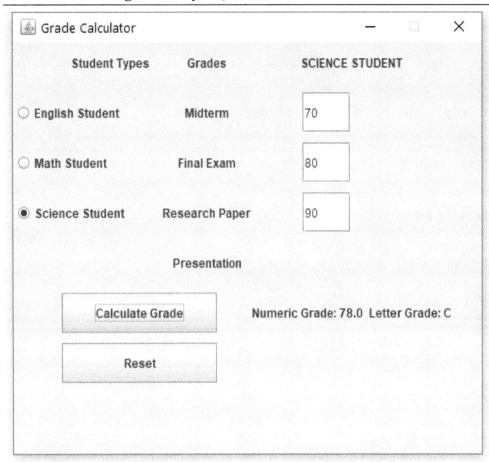

14. Click the Close button on the frame, and your program should end gracefully.

Discussion

"Wow, I'm nearly speechless, and you know how hard that is," Rhonda said. "Those listeners really work great!"

"Yes, they do," I agreed.

I could tell that Rhonda wasn't the only one who was impressed.

"Let's take a look at the code that produced this magic," I said. "In actuality, we didn't need to do all that much to achieve it. All we really did was register an instance of our Listener classes with the objects on our GUI. Our first step was to create instance variables for each of our four Listener classes:"

```
RadioButtonListener rbListener = new RadioButtonListener(this);
CalculateButtonListener cbListener = new CalculateButtonListener(this);
ResetButtonListener resetListener = new ResetButtonListener(this);
FrameListener fListener = new FrameListener();
```

"With that done, we registered each listener with the appropriate object on our GUI. The three radio buttons were registered with the instance variable for our RadioButtonListener class:"

```
radEnglish.addActionListener(rbListener);
radMath.addActionListener(rbListener);
radScience.addActionListener(rbListener);
```

"The Calculate button was registered with the instance variable for our CalculateButtonListener class:"

```
btnCalculate.addActionListener(cbListener);
```

"The Reset button was registered with the instance variable for our ResetButtonListener class:"

```
btnReset.addActionListener(resetListener);
```

"And, finally, the frame itself was registered with the instance variable for our FrameListener class using the This keyword:"

```
this.addWindowListener(fListener);
```

"Once our listeners are registered to the objects on our GUI," I said, "it's up to the Listener classes to do their work."

"And that they did," Ward said. "So we're done?"

Testing the Program

"That's right, Ward," I said. "We're now done with the Grade Calculation Project."

"When do we deliver it?" Mary asked. "And what version do we deliver?" Linda asked. "Will you be installing your version of the project?"

"When I spoke to Frank Olley earlier in the week," I said, "I explained to him that, excluding my version of the program, we had 18 different versions of the program and that, since this was a student project, I'd rather have him use one of yours, not mine."

I could see some excitement building among the students in the class.

"I invited Frank to visit us today to select the winning project," I said, "but in Frank's mind, you're all winners, and I have to agree. It's going to be hard to select one project to install in the English Department."

"So what are we going to do?" Ward asked.

"Frank had a good suggestion," I said. "He suggested that before we show up in his department at the end of today's class, we all pick one version of the program as the one we wish to install in the English Department. So I would like everyone to take a few moments to test their own version of the program to verify that it's working properly, then come up to the front of the classroom and pick up a voting ballot that I've prepared. Take the ballot, walk around the classroom, observe everyone's project, and then record your vote for what you consider the best project you see. The project that receives the most votes will be the one that we install in the English Department. Again, I'm removing my project from consideration, so please don't vote for mine! This is your project, and one of you deserves to have the place of honor in Frank Olley's English Department."

"Can you give us some guidelines on testing our programs?" Linda asked, after a moment or two.

"That's a good question," I said. "Obviously, at a minimum, the program must work—that is, it needs to properly calculate the grade for each one of the three types of students. You should also make sure that the version of the graphical user interface you designed is attractive and easy to use."

"I would think that most of the bugs have been discovered by now," Valerie commented.

"I'm not sure we can say that with 100 percent certainty," I said. "There's always the possibility that something has slipped through our fingers. But I would say that I'm fairly confident that our programs are bug free. Obviously, the more complicated the programs we write, the less certain of that you can feel and the more thorough your testing needs to be."

"Is it possible to test each and every combination of grades and student types?" Rhonda asked.

"Good point, Rhonda," I said. "There are quite a few possible combinations of different student types and grades, and testing every one of them would be next to impossible. We've been testing our programs all along with a scenario for each type of student, and we should take this testing one step further. For instance, test scenarios where each component grade is zero, where one or more component grades, but not all, are zero, where all component grades are 100 percent, where some are 100 percent. Above all, make sure you calculate the grades manually first so that you know what the correct answer should be."

"In other words," Dave said, "test the extreme limits of each component."

"That's right, Dave," I said. "We saw a few weeks ago how the introduction of a zero into a program can produce errors. Try to break your program now, before you give it to the user to work with."

"I did something similar to what you suggested," Chuck said, "except that I used Excel to develop a worksheet of possible scenarios with the correct answers, and then ran my program to test them and verify the correct answer."

"That's a great idea, Chuck," I said.

I gave the class 15 minutes to test their projects one last time and then asked them to review and evaluate their fellow students' projects and vote for the project they thought was best. As I collected their ballots and tallied the results, I asked everyone to give me a diskette with a copy of their project on it.

"Class is officially dismissed for today," I said. "I hope to see you all in the English Department in a few minutes!"

388 Learn To Program With Java JDK 15.0

I called Dave aside. Dave had volunteered to coordinate the installation of Java on a PC in the English Department, along with the installation of the winning program. I handed Dave a CD-ROM containing the Java Developer's Kit, along with a diskette containing the project that had received the most votes.

"Would you mind installing these?" I asked him. "I have a few things to wrap up here."

"Not at all," Dave said, as he glanced at the student's name on the disk and smiled. "That project really was great—I guess it pays to ask a lot of questions! I'll take care of this."

Delivering and Implementing the Grades Calculation Project in the English Department

No sooner had I packed up my things and prepared to make my way out of the classroom than a former student of mine approached me with a problem. Half an hour later, I finally arrived in the English Department.

As I entered, I could hear quite a bit of excited talk and conversation taking place. I could see an incredible amount of activity taking place. The area was packed with students—my students, plus two students whom I recognized as work-study students—plus Frank Olley, David Burton, and Robin Aronstrom.

Frank Olley caught sight of me.

"John, this program is absolutely great," he said excitedly. "I can't believe what a great job your students did with this. David, Robin, and I really love it, and so do the two people who really count, the work-study students who will be using it."

Amidst the hullabaloo, I glanced toward the middle of the open space in the English Department and noticed a small table with a computer sitting on it. Seated at the table were the two work-study students, and there was Rhonda, standing in front of the computer training the two work-study students who would be using her version of the program to calculate grades for the English, Math, and Science Departments!

"Rhonda's been proudly demonstrating her program to our work-study students for the last 15 minutes," Frank explained. "She's obviously very proud of it, and they love it also. They haven't gotten up from their chairs yet. Rhonda really did a great job with it."

I wandered over to them and caught Rhonda's eye.

"I'm flabbergasted that the class voted for my version of the project," Rhonda said. "To say that this has made my week in an understatement—more like my year! I'm just so honored that someone like me, with absolutely no programming background, could actually write a program like this. I felt like I asked so many stupid questions during the course."

"Rhonda," I interrupted, "you know what I always say, the only stupid question is the question you don't ask. Your questions were always good ones, plus I know they were questions that some of the other students in the class were dying to ask. By the way, when I put this Java course together, I had someone just like you in mind: an inquisitive person, anxious to learn, but with no programming background. You did a great job."

"Really?" she said, "You know I really enjoyed the course very much. You should consider taking those notes of yours and writing a Java book."

"Maybe I'll do that someday," I told her.

I spent the next few minutes observing the two work-study students, Rita and Gil, work with the program. They had no problem whatsoever with it: Rhonda's GUI was nicely designed, and both of them really seemed to be enjoying working with it.

"Believe me," Rita said, "this is a lot better than the method we had to use before."

"You can say that again," Gil said. "Calculating these grades using a calculator was a real pain in the neck."

"From what I can see," I told the assembled class as they gathered around us, "the system works as designed. The ultimate users of the project, Rita and Gil, have been using the program for the last few minutes to calculate grades, and as you all have probably seen, they're extremely pleased with it. I want to thank Dave for installing Java and Rhonda's version of the project on this PC. By installing the software, we have begun Phase 5 of the SDLC, the Implementation Phase. Installation, fine-tuning, and training are all part of this phase."

Frank Olley came over and stood right next to me, obviously pleased with the time savings and accuracy the program would achieve. I turned to him and told him that this phase of the SDLC would last for at least the next week.

"Pairs of students have volunteered to be on site during the week to make observations and assist with any problems that might come up," I explained.

"It's comforting to know they'll be here," he said. "What are those notes that I've seen you taking?"

"Even though we're now in the midst of Phase 5 of the SDLC," I replied, "we can proceed concurrently with Phase 6, which is Feedback and Maintenance."

"Feedback and maintenance?" Frank asked.

"We want to make sure that the program is behaving according to the Requirements Statement you and I agreed upon when we agreed to write the program for you," I explained. "A big part of this phase is observing the system to see how it's being used."

"And how it's being admired," Frank Olley added.

"Positive feedback is a wonderful thing," I said smiling.

"What about program maintenance?" Frank asked.

"The maintenance phase handles any changes to the program that are necessitated by governmental regulations, changes in business rules, or changes that you decide you want to make to the program," I replied.

"After seeing the great work you've done on the project," he said, "I'm sure I'll have more work for your class."

"Sadly though," I said, "this is the end of our introductory Java course. But many, if not all of these students, will be signed up for my Intermediate Java Programming course starting in five weeks. Maybe we can work on any enhancements you have then."

Frank Olley seemed happy with that idea and left me to chat with the two work-study students. Linda, meanwhile, stopped by to see me and asked to see the notes I had taken.

"Interesting observations," Linda said. "I can see we still have some work to do."

"One thing I think we'll need to work on immediately," I said to her, "is changing the font size of the text on our frame. I can barely see what's going on from here."

"Maybe we can tackle that in the Intermediate class," she said.

"Frank," I said as I approached him, Rhonda, and the work-study students, "on behalf of the class, I want to thank you for a wonderful learning experience. I'm sure we'll be in touch."

I shouted across the room to the rest of my students, "I've got to take off now. Everyone please be mindful of your coverage schedules, and if you have any problems at all, you all know where to find me. Remember, my e-mail address is johnsmiley@johnsmiley.com. I hope to see you all in five weeks."

Summary

Congratulations! You've finished the Introduction to Programming with Java class and completed and implemented the Grade Calculation Project. I hope you felt the excitement of completing, delivering, and installing the Grade Calculation Project as much as the students in my class did because you were a big part of it.

What's next? At this point, you should feel confident enough to tackle a variety of Java programs. I hope that by following my introductory computer programming class, you've seen how real-world applications are developed. The step-by-step methodology that we followed to complete the program should be one that you follow in your own programming work.

That's not to say that all projects go as smoothly as this one did. You can expect your share of mistakes, misinterpretations, and misunderstandings along the way. Nonetheless, developing a computer program is always exciting, and if you love it as I do, it's always fun.

As I close, I jut want to give you a few words of advice.

First, remember that in programming, there's rarely a single correct solution. Ultimately, if your program meets the requirements of the person who needs to use it, you've developed the correct solution. In the beginning of your programming experience, don't waste your time trying to achieve the best solution. Move onto other projects to broaden your experience.

Second, always be your own best friend. Inevitably, while trying to work through a solution, there will be frustrating moments. Never doubt yourself, and never get down on yourself.

Finally, remember that there is always more to learn. The world of programming is an endless series of free learning seminars. All you need to do is open up a manual, read a Help file, surf the Internet, or pick up a copy of a good book, and you are well on your way. You can never know it all, let alone master it all. But always move in that direction. Good luck, and I hope to see you in another Java class some day!